encyclopedia
of sexual
behavior
and the law

encyclopedia of sexual behavior and the law

Robert L. Maddex

CQ PRESS

Vincennes University
Shake Learning Resources Center
Vincennes, In 47591-9986

A Division of Congressional Quarterly Inc.

Washington, D.C.

CQ Press

1255 22nd Street, NW, Suite 400

Washington, DC 20037

Phone: 202-729-1900; toll-free, 1-866-4CQ-PRESS
(1-866-427-7737)

Web: www.cqpress.com

Produced by Archetype Press, Inc.

Project director and editor: Diane Maddex
Designer: Robert L. Wiser
Photo researcher: Alison Maddex

♾ The paper used in this publication exceeds the requirements of the American National Standard for Information Sciences—Permanence of Paper for Printed Library Materials, ANSI Z39.48-1992.

Printed and bound in the United States of America

10   09   08   07   06   1   2   3   4   5

Library of Congress Cataloging-in-Publication Data

Maddex, Robert L.

  Encyclopedia of sexual behavior and the law / Robert L. Maddex

    p.   cm.

  Includes index.

  ISBN-13: 978-1-933116-57-0 (alk. paper)

  ISBN-10: 1-933116-57-9

  1. Sex and law—United States—Encyclopedias. I. Title.

KF9325.A68M33 2006

345.73'0253—dc22   2006024088

Encyclopedia of Sexual Behavior and the Law covers some topics that by their nature are extremely sensitive. Our approach to compiling this resource has been mindful of this fact, while also recognizing our obligation to provide readers with complete, balanced, and reliable information vital to understanding this complex subject.

—CQ PRESS

Words and phrases that appear in the text in SMALL CAPITAL LETTERS indicate other entries in the book.

CONTENTS

Preface / ix

Milestones in Sexual Behavior and the Law / xiii

a

Abortion / 1

Abstinence / 8

Adult Materials / 9

Adultery / 11

AIDS-HIV / 14

Alimony / 18

American Civil Liberties Union / 19

American Fertility Association / 22

American Medical Association / 22

Annulment / 24

Anthony, Susan B. / 25

Assisted Reproductive Technology / 27

b

Barnes v. Glen Theatre, Inc. / 33

Bestiality / 34

Bigamy / 35

Bioethics / 37

Bisexuality / 41

A Book Named "John Cleland's Memoirs of a Woman of Pleasure" v. Attorney General of the Commonwealth of Massachusetts / 43

Bradwell v. Illinois / 45

Breastfeeding / 47

Brown, Louise / 51

Bruce, Lenny / 52

Burlington Industries, Inc. v. Ellerth / 54

c

Calderone, Mary S. / 56

Censorship / 57

Child Abuse / 61

Child Online Protection Act / 63

Child Support / 65

Children / 66

Communications Decency Act / 71

Comstock, Anthony / 72

Congress / 73

Consent / 76

Contraception / 79

Craig v. Boren / 82

Crimes Against Children Unit (FBI) / 84

d

Date Rape / 86

Defense of Marriage Act / 87

Deviant Behavior / 89

Discrimination / 90

Divorce / 96

DNA / 101

Domestic Violence / 104

Douglas, William O. / 107

Drugs / 109

e

Entertainment Industry / 113
Equal Rights / 119
Ethics / 122

f

Family Planning / 126
Federal Communications Commission / 129
Federal Marriage Amendment / 130
Feminism / 132
First Amendment / 134
Flynt, Larry / 139
Frontiero v. Richardson / 141

g

Gender / 143
Genetics / 146
Ginzburg v. United States / 152
Griswold v. Connecticut / 153

h

Hate Crimes / 156
Healthy Marriage Initiative / 160
Hefner, Hugh / 161
Homosexuality / 163
Human Rights Campaign / 167
Human Trafficking / 168

i

Illegitimacy / 170
Incest / 172
Indecent Exposure / 175
Internet / 176

j

Jacobellis v. Ohio / 181
Jeffreys, Alec / 182
Judiciary / 183

k

Kameny, Franklin / 189
Kansas v. Hendricks / 191
Kinsey, Alfred / 192

l

Lawrence v. Texas / 194
Lewd Behavior / 195

m

Marriage / 197
Media / 203
Megan's Law / 205
Military / 206
Miller, Henry / 211
Miller v. California / 212
Minor v. Happersett / 214
Miscegenation / 215
Motherhood / 216
Muller v. Oregon / 221

n

NARAL Pro-Choice America / 223
National Center for Missing and Exploited
   Children / 224
National Organization for Women / 225
Ninth Amendment / 226
Nudity / 228

o

Obscenity / 234
Office on Violence Against Women / 237

p

Pandering / 239

Paternity / 240

Planned Parenthood Federation of America / 243

Planned Parenthood of Southeastern Pennsylvania
   v. Casey / 245

Polygamy / 246

Pornography / 249

Pregnancy / 251

Premarital Sex / 254

Prenuptial Agreements / 255

President / 257

Prisoners / 260

Privacy / 263

Prostitution / 266

Prurient Interest / 269

r

Rape / 271

Rape Shield Laws / 277

Religion / 279

Reproductive Rights / 283

Roth v. United States / 286

s

Same-Sex Marriage / 289

Sanger, Margaret / 293

Sex Education / 295

Sex Offenders / 299

Sex Offenses / 302

Sexual Assault / 307

Sexual Enhancement / 310

Sexual Harassment / 312

Sexual Revolution / 317

Sexuality Information and Education Council
   of the United States / 320

Sexually Oriented Businesses / 321

Sexually Transmitted Diseases / 324

Single-Sex Education / 327

Sodomy / 328

Spousal Rights and Duties / 330

State and Local Government / 334

Stem-Cell Research and Cloning / 337

Sterilization / 341

Surgeon General of the United States / 342

t

Teenagers / 344

Telephone Sex / 347

Title IX / 348

Transsexualism / 350

Transvestism / 352

u

Unborn, Rights of the / 354

Unmarried Cohabitants / 356

Unmarried Parents / 359

U.S. Department of Health and Human
   Services / 361

v

Victims' Rights / 363

Violence Against Women Act / 366

Virginia, United States v. / 369

Voyeurism / 369

w

Williams v. Morgan / 373

Williams v. North Carolina / 374

Women's Rights / 375

z

Zoning / 380

Selected Bibliography / 382

Illustration Credits / 382

Index / 383

PREFACE

Reproduction—the continuation of the human species—is of central importance to any society, as is how society deals with various aspects of sexual behavior related to reproduction. U.S. law has traditionally treated sexual behavior in a piecemeal fashion. Antisocial behavior is typically regulated under the category of criminal law; marriage, divorce, and children are regarded as part of domestic relations or family law; individual rights are considered issues of constitutional law under the Bill of Rights (1791) and the First Amendment to the U.S. Constitution (1789) in particular; and sexually transmitted diseases and sex education are addressed under health and welfare provisions and may be targeted in appropriations laws. The past century, however, has seen a dramatic change in laws relating to sexual behavior that was previously dealt with as peripheral issues of crime, family relations, health, safety, and morality.

Today much of our national public debate relates somehow to the topic of sex. Far from wanting to keep it under wraps, as the nation's Puritan heritage sometimes seems to indicate, Americans now have a seemingly insatiable appetite for information on sexual behavior. The rights of women and homosexuals, marriage and divorce, sexual activity outside marriage, maternity leave, abortion, domestic violence, child abuse by priests and others, post-punishment restrictions on violent sex offenders, sexual predators on the Internet, pornographic movies, sexual harassment, stem-cell research and cloning, HIV and AIDS victims,

not to mention brave new ways of creating babies—these are just a few of the subjects that continue to be debated almost daily in the United States. The time seems right to begin to look at sexual behavior and the law as a discrete subject of study.

The aim of *Encyclopedia of Sexual Behavior and the Law* is to bring together in one volume information about concepts, laws, court decisions, people, organizations, and events that have made a significant impact on the current state of the law. The book as a whole is intended to give a comprehensive survey of the history of how the law in the United States deals with sexual behavior and what influences that process. Entries provide an overview of 150 topics along with analysis of how each subject relates to other areas of sexual behavior and the law, all as a starting point for additional in-depth research. Perhaps the mysteries of courtship, love, motherhood, and paternity should never be reduced to a science, but the potential legal consequences of sexual behavior make it imperative that everyone have access to authoritative information on the subject.

A Word about Sex and the Law

A dictionary definition of *sex* would include a wide range of choices: a classification of organisms according to their reproductive functions; the division of members of a species into male and female; the characteristics of being male and female and their distinguishing differences; the urges or behaviors that result from an organism's sexuality; and the act of sexual intercourse and other noncoital behavior related to sexual intimacy. As an adjective, *sexual* refers to reproduction by the union of a male and a female cell, as opposed to asexual reproduction; it also refers generally to the behavioral aspects of sexuality—that is, being of one sex or the other and behaving as such.

Sex and sexuality also encompass the identification of individuals on the basis of gender, including homosexuality and other identifications beyond simply male and female. *Sex* may refer specifically to differences based on reproductive organs, while *gender* has more to do with how individuals represent themselves, as male or female, and how that representation is perceived by others. Sexual behavior thus extends to acts, attitudes, and feelings based on this process of identification. Misogyny, homophobia, prejudice, harassment, even violence are possible forms of behavior rooted in sexual identification. A person's own sexuality is the product of many factors, including heredity and environmental conditions.

Sexual behavior as discussed in this book is not limited to strict categories of male and female but includes all behavior that relates to an individual's sexuality and sexual orientation. Sexual behavior by heterosexuals and homosexuals and the varying degrees of sexuality in between these two categories, or tangential to them, are all discussed in terms of how such behavior relates to American law. Sexual behavior may be only one component of an individual's behavior affected by laws. To take one example: rape, which has a sexual component, also constitutes a physical assault on a person that, without the sexual component, would still be punishable by law. Tax laws, for another, may treat married and unmarried persons differently, and this in turn affects property rights and the accumulation of wealth.

Law is generally defined as a rule established by authority, society, or custom. Laws in the United States may be classified as proscriptive, meaning that they prohibit some act, or directive, meaning that they require some act. There are also neutral laws that simply state that some act is neither proscribed nor required. The First Amendment to the U.S. Constitution declares: "Congress shall make no law . . . abridging the freedom of speech." Article II provides that the president "shall take care that the laws be faithfully executed." And, according to the Fifth Amendment: "No person . . . shall be compelled in any criminal case to be a witness against himself." Laws related to sexual behavior may fall into these same categories. As examples, rape is prohibited, marriage requires formal recognition by the state, and privacy rights found in the Constitution permit an abortion under certain conditions.

Another way of categorizing laws related to sexual behavior is whether they are constitutional or statutory, federal or state, legislated or based on court decisions. In addition to the legal declarations of what the law is, there is always the additional element of enforcement. Just because a law is "on the books" does not mean that infractions will always be punished by law enforcement officials or the courts. A criminal law with which a prosecutor has charged a person may not be applied for various reasons— among them the possibilities that the law is unconstitutional, too vague, or even improperly enacted. Another important example of the failure of enforcement is the Supreme Court's power to refuse to hear cases on appeal.

Legal Bookends

Although regulation of sexual behavior by the U.S. legal system has a long history, the most dramatic legal change undoubtedly came with the adoption of the Nineteenth Amendment in 1920 to finally give women the right to vote. Before then, American society, law, and lawmakers were dominated by heterosexual males. Simply contemplate what the United States might look like today if the Nineteenth Amendment had been rejected.

World War II provided another impetus for major social change. Women contributed in unprecedented measure to the success of the Allied forces during the war, especially by taking jobs traditionally held by men as they went off to war. The horrors of Nazi and Japanese military atrocities during the war also spurred a movement to protect human rights internationally and in the United States, including equal rights for persons of both sexes. Women's experience in the workplace carried over as they entered the postwar workforce and institutions of higher learning in increasing numbers.

Following the war, two additional factors spurred changes in the way Americans thought about and conducted their own sexual behavior. The first was the publication by Alfred Kinsey of his studies of male and female sexual behavior in 1948 and 1953, respectively. Next a sexual revolution was launched in the 1960s and 1970s with the introduction of the Pill, which greatly facilitated the practice of contraception. The Kinsey reports demystified actual sexual behavior of individuals, while an affordable, accessible oral contraceptive allowed women to make a wider range of choices about their sexual behavior and their lives.

As for the law, in 1957 the U.S. Supreme Court, in *Roth v. United States,* for the first time began to define obscenity in terms of materials outside the protection of the First Amendment, while condoning adult materials that have some socially redeeming value as a whole. Before then, determinations of obscenity by the courts could be based on bits and pieces of a work that might offend the most vulnerable in society. After *Roth,* the Supreme Court went on to decide many cases involving issues related to sexual behavior, including contraception, pornography, abortion, nudity, and homosexuality. In fact, the sexual revolution as far as the Supreme Court is concerned can probably be found between the bookends of *Roth* and its decision in *Lawrence v. Texas* in 2003, in which the Court approved consensual homosexual sodomy by adults in the privacy of their home. The right of privacy was key to the Court's decisions in cases striking down state laws banning contraception and abortion. It is doubtful that we will see further expansion of rights in the area of sexual behavior from the Supreme Court for some time.

Today abortion rights are under attack by citizens who believe that at conception a human is created whose life should be protected by the government, despite a woman's wishes regarding how she should control her own body. Homosexual rights, particularly the right of a homosexual couple to marry and receive the same legal benefits as heterosexual couples, remain the subject of a political and legal debate that has divided citizens and states. Stem-cell research and cloning of humans or parts of humans are also high on the national agenda for discussion and heated debate, again polarizing much of America.

Encyclopedia of Sexual Behavior and the Law brings a measure of order to the debate and provides a historical and legal context for understanding key issues. Certain aspects of sexual behavior may be uncomfortable subjects for some people, and concerns exist about when children should be exposed to information about sexual behavior. Accurate information in the proper context and at the right age can nonetheless be helpful in understanding this field of social and legal interaction so basic to human life.

This book could not have been published without the significant contributions of my wife, Diane Maddex, president of Archetype Press. I am in her debt once more. My daughter, Alison Maddex, contributed her own knowledge of this topic in assisting with the illustration research. Robert L. Wiser, the book's designer, deserves sincere appreciation for another handsome design. Special thanks go to Mary Carpenter, acquisitions editor, CQ Press, for her support and thoughtful comments throughout the editorial process. I also wish to acknowledge the contributions of David Arthur, development editor, CQ Press, and Shana Wagger, the former acquisitions editor.

ROBERT L. MADDEX

MILESTONES IN SEXUAL BEHAVIOR AND THE LAW

1690
Colonial officials impose censorship on a Boston newspaper, *Publick Occurences*, by confiscating copies that contain a story about the sexual dalliances of the king of France.

1712
Massachusetts passes the first colonial laws punishing obscenity in writings and pictures.

1791
The Bill of Rights is ratified as the first ten amendments to the U.S. Constitution; the First Amendment includes protections for freedom of speech and freedom of the press as well as freedom of religion.

1798
Congress passes the Sedition Act to censor political opposition, prohibiting "publishing any false, scandalous and malicious writing."

1815
Several men are prosecuted in Philadelphia for selling drawings that contain female nudity.

1821
Two Boston booksellers are prosecuted for selling John Cleland's eighteenth-century novel *Memoirs of a Woman of Pleasure* (also known as *Fanny Hill*) because of passages that allegedly contain obscenity.

1842
U.S. customs officials are given authority under the Tariff Act to ban the importation of contraband containing obscenity.

1843
The first federal prosecution under the Tariff Act is based on snuff boxes that portray female nudity in lacquered pictures.

1848
At a women's rights convention held in Seneca Falls, New York, a resolution demanding women's right to vote is passed.

1857
Congress amends the Tariff Act to include a ban on obscene daguerreotypes (a forerunner of photographs), and the word *pornography* appears for the first time in an English medical dictionary.

1862
Congress outlaws polygamy and requires Utah to renounce the practice to enter the Union, which it did in 1890 and became a state two years later.

1865
Congress amends the Tariff Act again to keep pornographic books out of the hands of Union soldiers.

1868

The Fourteenth Amendment to the U.S. Constitution is ratified and is later used by the Supreme Court to make provisions in the Bill of Rights applicable to the states.

An English court in *Regina v. Hicklin* holds that, based on selected excerpts, obscenity is whatever tends to cause depravity and corruption in the most susceptible part of an audience; the decision formed the basis of American obscenity law until the Supreme Court's decision in *Roth v. United States* in 1957.

1871

Massachusetts declares wife beating illegal.

1873

The Comstock Act is enacted by Congress to expand the power of postal authorities to prosecute publishers and distributors of obscene, lewd, and immoral materials, including information regarding contraception and abortion.

The U.S. Supreme Court in *Bradwell v. Illinois* affirms the refusal of the Illinois supreme court to allow Myra Bradwell to be admitted to practice law in the state solely on the basis of her sex.

1875

In *Minor v. Happersett,* the Supreme Court affirms that the Constitution provides no protection for women against states that deny them the right to vote.

1876

Congress amends the Comstock Act to give more power to the U.S. Post Office to censor the mail.

1882

Leaves of Grass, Walt Whitman's book of poetry, is banned in Boston for obscenity.

1890

The U.S. postmaster general bans Leo Tolstoy's *Kreutzer Sonata* (1890) from the mail.

1895

Thomas Edison produces *Fatima's Serpentine Dance,* which is later subject to censorship when authorities require the dancer's clothed breasts and buttocks to be obscured by black bars.

1896

The first federal prosecution under the Comstock Act for obscenity is upheld by the Supreme Court in *Rosen v. United States.*

1897

A New York court in *People v. Doris* affirms a conviction for obscenity based on the movie *Orange Blossoms,* in which a wedding night is depicted in pantomime.

1908

The mayor of New York City closes all movie theaters (about 550) on the basis that they are immoral and pose a threat to public health and safety; within a short time they reopen, and the city becomes the home of the new American film industry until it is eclipsed by Hollywood in the 1920s.

1911

The first family court system is established in Buffalo, New York, removing domestic relations matters from the jurisdiction of the criminal courts.

1912

For the first time police raid an exhibit of pornographic films in Manhattan.

1913

Anthony Comstock, acting under the 1873 federal anti-obscenity law named for him, confiscates copies of the painting of a partially nude woman entitled *September Morn* (1912) by Paul Chabas, which had just won the Medal of Honor at the Paris Salon.

1914

Anthony Comstock obtains an indictment against Margaret Sanger for writing articles about contraception that Comstock considers to be obscene.

1915

The Supreme Court in *Mutual Film Corporation v. Industrial Commission of Ohio* holds, based on the movie *Birth of a Nation* (1915), that films are not protected by the First or Fourteenth Amendments.

1916

Margaret Sanger opens the first birth control clinic, the forerunner of Planned Parenthood of America, in Brooklyn, New York.

1920

A judge rules in *Halsey v. New York Society for the Suppression of Vice* that to be declared obscene a book must be judged as a whole by qualified experts and not simply evaluated on isolated passages.

The Nineteenth Amendment to the U.S. Constitution granting women the right to vote is finally ratified.

The American Civil Liberties Union is founded to defend citizens' rights against government interference.

1922

The Motion Picture Producers and Distributors of America is formed and makes William Harrison Hays the censorship czar of Hollywood.

1925

In response to demands by the New York Society for the Suppression of Vice, police raid Minsky's Burlesque show in the National Winter Garden Theater in New York City.

1926

American Mercury, a collection of magazine stories by H. L. Mencken, is banned in Boston because one story describes the experiences of a prostitute.

1927

The actress Mae West is jailed for ten days because of an obscene dance in her play entitled *Sex.*

1929

A federal judge overturns the conviction of Mary Ware Dennett, which was based on an educational pamphlet entitled *The Sex Side of Life.*

1930

To prevent government censorship, two associations of motion picture producers and distributors create the Hays Code to self-regulate decency in the movies.

1933

A federal judge reverses an obscenity conviction based on James Joyce's book *Ulysses* (1922), reasoning that the work must be considered as a whole; the following year the decision is upheld by a federal appeals court.

1934

The Communications Act creates the Federal Communications Commission to regulate indecency and obscenity in broadcasting and telephone communications, among other things.

1946

The Supreme Court rejects the U.S. Post Office's assertion of authority to deny mailing privileges to *Esquire* magazine without a judicial hearing.

The Federal Communications Commission produces a list of responsibilities for broadcasters that want to avoid censorship.

1948

Alfred Kinsey publishes *Sexual Behavior in the Human Male*, the first serious research on the subject based on questionnaires and interviews.

1952

William George Jorgensen Jr. undergoes sex-change surgery in Denmark because it was illegal in the United States, becoming Christine and in the process probably the most famous American transsexual.

1953

Alfred Kinsey publishes *Sexual Behavior in the Human Female*.

Hugh Hefner publishes the first issue of *Playboy* magazine.

1955

A U.S. Senate subcommittee holds hearings on the relation between pornography and juvenile delinquency.

1957

In its decision in *Roth v. United States*, the Supreme Court reaffirms that obscenity is beyond the protection of the First Amendment and defines it as sexually explicit material that, when taken as a whole, appeals to the prurient interest, as judged by contemporary community standards, and that is utterly without redeeming social importance.

1959

In *Kingsley Pictures v. Regents*, the Supreme Court finds that the adultery scene in the movie of D. H. Lawrence's *Lady Chatterley's Lover* is "ideological obscenity" and thus protected by the First Amendment.

1961

The National Council of Churches, composed of Protestant, Orthodox, Anglican, evangelical, and African American religious organizations, endorses birth control.

1964

The Supreme Court finds in *Jacobellis v. Ohio* that obscenity must be judged by national standards; this decision leads in *People v. Bruce* to reversal in the same year of a conviction of the stand-up comic Lenny Bruce.

The Supreme Court also ends the prosecution of Henry Miller's *Tropic of Cancer* (1934) in *Grove Press v. Gerstein*.

The inscrutable lyrics to a popular song, "Louie, Louie," are the subject of an official review for obscenity by the Federal Bureau of Investigation.

1965

In *Griswold v. Connecticut*, the Supreme Court finds a right of privacy in the Bill of Rights and declares state laws criminalizing the use of contraception by married couples to be unconstitutional.

1966

The researchers William H. Masters and Virginia E. Johnson publish a clinical study of sexual behavior, *Human Sexual Response*.

In *Ginzburg v. United States*, the Supreme Court affirms the conviction of Ralph Ginzburg for pandering nonobscene materials through the mails.

In *A Book Named "John Cleland's Memoirs of a Woman of Pleasure" v. Attorney General of the Commonwealth of Massachusetts*, the Supreme Court reverses a state court's finding that the eighteenth-century book *Fanny Hill* is obscene.

The National Organization for Women is founded to lobby on behalf of women's rights issues, including abortion, birth control, and sex education.

1967

In *Loving v. Virginia,* the Supreme Court declares state laws against interracial marriage to be unconstitutional.

1968

The movie industry promulgates the PG (parental guidance), R (restricted), and X (adults only) rating system.

In *Levy v. Louisiana,* the Supreme Court rules that states cannot deny illegitimate children the rights accorded children born to married parents.

1969

A police raid of the Stonewall Bar in Manhattan causes homosexuals, who frequent the bar, to riot; the event launches the gay rights movement.

In *Stanley v. Georgia,* the Supreme Court finds that possession of pornography for private use is protected by the U.S. Constitution.

1970

President Richard M. Nixon rejects the recommendation of the President's Commission on Pornography and Obscenity to abolish restrictions on distribution of sexually expressive materials to consenting adults.

1972

The low-budget pornographic films *Deep Throat* and *Behind the Green Door* (both 1972) are produced to be shown in public movie theaters.

Title IX of the Education Amendments of 1972 bars sex discrimination in educational institutions and activities receiving federal aid.

1973

The Supreme Court's decision in *Roe v. Wade,* finding state laws banning abortion to be unconstitutional, becomes the focal point of renewed debate over this subject for years to come.

In *Miller v. California,* the Supreme Court refines the *Roth* criteria for determining obscenity, promoting local determinations and reducing the federal courts' role to conducting "an independent review of constitutional claims when necessary."

The Supreme Court in *Frontiero v. Richardson* finds unconstitutional a federal requirement that spouses of female military officers have to prove their dependency to qualify for benefits.

Homosexuality is removed from the category of mental disorders by the American Psychiatric Association.

1976

In *Young v. American Mini Theatres, Inc.,* the Supreme Court upholds Detroit's zoning restrictions on adult entertainment businesses.

The Supreme Court in *Craig v. Boren* announces that under the Fourteenth Amendment's equal protection clause, sex discrimination cases are entitled to "intermediate scrutiny"—a higher level of review than merely the "rational basis test," which designates an ordinary level of scrutiny.

Pennsylvania becomes the first state to authorize protective orders for domestic violence victims to keep away abusive partners.

Marvin v. Marvin sets a precedent by which unmarried partners of long standing are considered eligible for "palimony."

1978

Louise Brown is born in England, becoming the world's first "test-tube" baby and launching a new era of assisted reproductive technology.

1981

The Supreme Court in *Schad v. Mt. Ephraim* limits zoning of sex-related businesses so that they are not effectively closed down.

1983

In *Bolger v. Young Drug Products,* the Supreme Court declares unconstitutional a sweeping federal ban on mailing unsolicited advertisements for contraceptives.

1985

In the wake of congressional hearings on lyrics of popular music, the Recording Industry Association of America agrees to promulgate a rating system.

1986

The attorney general of the United States establishes the National Obscenity Enforcement Unit to rein in sexually oriented businesses.

In *Renton v. Playtime Theatres,* the Supreme Court upholds the constitutionality of zoning that isolates sex-related businesses in remote areas.

In *Bowers v. Hardwick,* the Supreme Court upholds the constitutionality of a state law that criminalized homosexual sodomy in the privacy of one's home; the decision is overturned in 2003 in *Lawrence v. Texas.*

1987

DNA evidence is used for the first time in the United States in a Florida trial of an accused rapist.

1991

An Indiana law prohibiting the knowing and intentional appearance in public in the nude is upheld by the Supreme Court in *Barnes v. Glen Theatre, Inc.*

1992

The Supreme Court reverses the conviction of a man lured into violating the Child Protection Act of 1984, which made it illegal to receive sexually explicit depictions of children through the mail.

In *Planned Parenthood of Southeastern Pennsylvania v. Casey,* the Supreme Court allows state restrictions on the right of abortion, including a twenty-four-hour waiting period and parental consent for minors; it overturns a requirement that a married women notify her husband of her intent to have an abortion.

1993

U.S. Department of Defense Directive no. 1332.14 puts in place a "don't ask, don't tell" policy, which makes overt admissions of homosexuality grounds for separation from military service.

1994

The Violence Against Women Act is passed; its civil remedies are found unconstitutional by the Supreme Court in *United States v. Morrison* (2000).

U.S. Surgeon General Joycelyn Elders suggests that masturbation is one way for young people to avoid unsafe sex and is soon pressured to resign.

1995

Title 18 of the U.S. Code, section 2257, is amended to require that producers of pornographic films keep accurate records of names and ages of all performers.

The Federal Communications Commission fines the radio "shock jock" Howard Stern $2 million for indecency.

1996

The Military Honor and Decency Act forbids the sale on military bases of magazines or videos that depict nudity in a salacious way.

The Defense of Marriage Act restricts federal laws and policies regarding marriage to legal unions between one man and one woman.

The so-called Megan's Law requires all states to establish notification systems to track dangerous sex offenders.

1997

The Supreme Court upholds the constitutionality of civil commitment and confinement in mental institutions for violent sex offenders after prison sentences have been served.

Internet restrictions imposed by Congress in the Communications Decency Act of 1996 are struck down by the Supreme Court as unconstitutional under the First Amendment.

1998

In *National Endowment for the Arts v. Finley*, the Supreme Court finds that decency standards in federal funding for the NEA do not infringe First Amendment rights.

2002

The Supreme Court remands to a lower court a challenge to the Child Online Protection Act of 1998, which made it a crime to transmit indecent material to someone under eighteen years of age; two years later it agrees with the lower court that the act violates the First Amendment.

2003

Homosexual sodomy in the privacy of one's own home is held by the Supreme Court in *Lawrence v. Texas* to be protected by the U.S. Constitution.

The supreme court of Massachusetts rules in *Goodridge v. Massachusetts Department of Public Health* that it is unconstitutional to prevent gay couples from marrying in Massachusetts.

2004

Many states rush to amend their constitutions to limit marriage to heterosexual couples in an effort to head off same-sex marriage.

A "wardrobe malfunction" that exposes the performer Janet Jackson's breast at the nationally televised halftime show during the National Football League's Super Bowl draws a $550,000 fine from the Federal Communications Commission.

2005

The Food and Drug Administration, despite approval from its advisory panel, delays a decision on whether to allow the "morning-after pill" called Plan B to be made available over the counter.

2006

South Dakota essentially outlaws abortion in an effort to test *Roe v. Wade* in the Supreme Court shortly after two new justices are appointed by President George W. Bush, an outspoken opponent of abortion rights.

The Roman Catholic Church lobbies in several states against proposed legislation that would extend the time in which victims can bring lawsuits for childhood sexual abuse by priests; to date claims of 12,500 victims have cost the Church $1.5 billion.

Massachusetts restricts its unique same-sex marriage rights by limiting marriageable couples to residents of the commonwealth.

a

ABORTION

Abortion (from the Latin *abortus,* meaning to miscarry) is the termination of the development of an embryo or a fetus before the twenty-eighth week, the age at which it is viable, or theoretically able to survive outside the womb. The *New York Times* reported in 2005 that more than twenty-five million American women had had an abortion since the procedure became legal nationwide in 1973. But new data also show a decline in abortions, from approximately 1.6 million a year in 1990 to 1.3 million in 2002; among the reasons may be improved contraceptive technology, changing ideas about acceptable family size, and reduced availability of abortion services. Nearly 90 percent of abortions were performed during the first twelve weeks of PREGNANCY, with less than 1 percent occurring after twenty-four weeks.

At the heart of the heated debate over abortion in the United States are differing views about the point at which an unborn child legally becomes a person warranting the government's protection. "Pro-choice" proponents underscore a woman's right to control her own reproduction, at least before a fetus becomes viable. In contrast, "pro-life" supporters assert that the right to life should be extended to an embryo at the moment of conception and that abortion is thus the killing of a human being. The "right-to-life" position has extensive religious support; for example, the Roman Catholic Church opposes both abortion and CONTRACEPTION by artificial means. Some states have moved to declare the precise time when a child's life begins in the womb. The Missouri code, for one, was amended in 1988 to define this event: "The general assembly of this state finds that: (1) The life of each human being begins at conception; (2) Unborn children have protectable interests in life, health, and well-being; (3) The natural parents of unborn children have protectable interests in the life, health, and well-being of their unborn child."

Before *Roe v. Wade*

Because the U.S. Constitution does not expressly grant women the right to an abortion, states began banning abortion in the 1820s, and by 1900 most jurisdictions outlawed them. Some WOMEN'S RIGHTS proponents, including SUSAN B. ANTHONY, argued against abortion because it was such an unsafe medical procedure. These laws disproportionately affected poor women, who could not afford to travel to one of the few states, such as California and New York, that did not prohibit abortion or to go outside the United States to another country, such as Canada. Poor women were also often the least able to afford to provide for a child or another child. By 1965 all states had laws prohibiting abortion, typically with exceptions for RAPE or INCEST or if the fetus was deformed.

Reminiscent of the days of Prohibition (1919–33), when bootleg alcohol was available, illegal abortions were nevertheless performed. Often the conditions were unsafe and unsanitary, greatly increasing the risk of harm to women seeking abortions and sometimes resulting in their death. But abortion opponents countered that it was a woman's choice to have sex in the first place and that her decision to terminate an unwanted child, not the law, placed her in jeopardy.

The Texas law in question in the landmark case *Roe v. Wade* (1973) prohibited abortion except to save a pregnant woman's life. Norma L. McCorvey asserted that she became pregnant as the result of a gang rape and sued to obtain an abortion, using the name Jane Roe. The 7–2 decision by the U.S. Supreme Court to overrule the Texas abortion ban grounded the right of abortion on the right of PRIVACY. That right was established in *GRISWOLD V. CONNECTICUT* (1965), in which the Court decided that several provisions of the Bill of Rights (1791), the first ten amendments to the U.S. Constitution, created a right of privacy that protected the use of contraceptives by married couples. Therefore, because this right of privacy was a fundamental constitutional right and was applicable to the states under the due process clause of the Fourteenth Amendment (1868), a state would have to show that it had a compelling interest in infringing a citizen's right of privacy. The two interests asserted by the state in *Roe*—protection of the mother's health and protection of the RIGHTS OF THE UNBORN child—were found to be insufficient to permit an infringement of the constitutional right of privacy. This right, according to the decision, includes a woman's prerogative, in consultation with her doctor, to decide to have an abortion.

In determining the extent of a woman's abortion rights, the Supreme Court identified roughly three trimesters (three-month periods) in the average nine-month pregnancy. This division marked the various stages of fetal development, from least viable to most viable, and apportioned the right to abortion accordingly. In the first trimester, a pregnant woman and her doctor were free to terminate a pregnancy. In the second trimester, however, an abortion had to be reasonably related to protecting the expectant mother's health. During the last trimester, the Court found that the state's interest in safeguarding the life of a child was sufficient for it to regulate and even proscribe abortion, except where it was necessary to preserve the life or health of the mother.

After *Roe v. Wade*

Immediately after the *Roe* decision, opponents of abortion began to attack the ruling on several fronts. Some states prohibited public of abortions for poor women, a move upheld by the Supreme Court in *Maher v. Roe* (1977). Under the Hyde Amendment (1976), CONGRESS also barred any federal funding of abortions by Medicaid, except where the mother's life was in danger or in the case of rape or incest; the Court similarly upheld this ban in *Harris v. McRae* (1980). The Uniform Code of Military Justice also restricts the use of MILITARY funds and facilities for performing an abortion. A movement for a constitutional amendment banning abortion was started, and protesters began concerted efforts to harass women, doctors, and staff members entering abortion clinics; in some extreme cases, abortion clinics were attacked and doctors who performed abortions were targeted and shot.

Another avenue for abortion opponents was to find ways at the federal and state levels to limit the legalization of abortion by placing restrictions on the right, such as requiring waiting periods and securing the CONSENT of a husband, mandating parental consent for minors, and banning so-called partial-birth (late-term) abortions. In *PLANNED PARENTHOOD OF SOUTHEASTERN PENNSYLVANIA V. CASEY* (1992), the Supreme Court reviewed a Pennsylvania law requiring that women wait at least twenty-four hours after a doctor provides detailed information about the abortion procedure and alternatives, that minors obtain the consent of at least one parent, and that married women notify their husbands of their plans to have an abortion or face criminal punishment of up to a year in jail. In an unusual three-justice joint opinion, the Court struck down only the spousal notification provision. While two justices who joined in the decision argued that all the provisions should be voided, three other justices wanted *Roe* overturned.

In an earlier case, *Webster v. Reproductive Health Services* (1989), the Supreme Court had been presented with another opportunity to overturn *Roe v. Wade*. But, in an opinion approved by less than a majority, the Court balked at such an extreme step backwards. However, it upheld a Missouri law mandating that, before an abortion, a fetus be tested for viability after the twentieth week of pregnancy.

State Laws

All states have laws concerning abortion, thirty-six of them prohibiting the procedure except when necessary to protect a woman's life or health or after a specified point in a pregnancy, most often at fetal viability. Like Pennsylvania, many states have enacted restrictions on abortion, such as requiring informed consent, setting a waiting period, demanding parental notification for minors, and banning certain abortion methods. Twenty-eight mandate that women receive counseling before an abortion, from the availability of services to purported mental and physical health consequences; four states require advice that a fetus feels pain (although in 2005 the *Journal of the American Medical Association* reported evidence that a fetus is incapable of feeling pain until around the twenty-eighth week). Some states have enacted "trap" (targeted regulation of abortion providers) laws intended to harass abortion providers.

Statutory law and policy range widely. California declares that "it is the public policy of the [state] that: . . . [e]very woman has the fundamental right to choose to bear a child or to choose and to obtain an abortion, except as specifically limited by this article"; the state defines *abortion* as "any medical treatment intended to induce the termination of a pregnancy except for the purpose of producing a live birth." The Utah code, however, defines *abortion* as "the intentional termination or attempted termination of human pregnancy after implantation of a fertilized ovum, and includes any and all procedures undertaken to kill a live unborn child and includes all procedures undertaken to produce a miscarriage. 'Abortion' does not include removal of a dead unborn child." The Utah code also declares that the state "has a compelling interest in the protection of the lives of unborn children." Under Iowa law, anyone "who intentionally terminates a human pregnancy,

with the knowledge and voluntary consent of the pregnant person, after the end of the second trimester . . . , where death of the fetus results commits feticide [fetal homicide]," which is a felony.

Arkansas's constitutional provision declaring a state policy of protecting the unborn was declared unconstitutional in 1994, but a provision of the Colorado constitution, added in 1984, provides: "No public funds shall be used . . . for the performance of any induced abortion, [except that the legislature,] by specific bill, may authorize and appropriate funds to be used for those medical services necessary to prevent the death of either a pregnant woman or her unborn child . . . where every reasonable effort is made to preserve the life of each."

According to the Guttmacher Institute, thirty-nine states require that an abortion be performed by a licensed physician, and twenty mandate that patients go to a hospital after a specified point in the pregnancy. Forty-six states allow individual health care providers to refuse to perform abortions. Idaho, Kentucky, Missouri, North Dakota, and Rhode Island (enjoined) have restricted abortion coverage in private insurance plans to cases in which the woman's life is endangered; coverage is permitted only if the woman purchases it at her own expense.

Late-Term Abortions

More than thirty states have passed laws prohibiting late-term ("partial-birth") abortions, although the majority are not in effect because of legal judgments. Opponents of this procedure contend that such laws affect only a rarely used operation known as dilation and extraction (D&X). Supporters of abortion rights, however, assert that these bans are generally written in such a way as to also include a procedure known as dilation and evacuation (D&E), often used in second-trimester abortions. A procedure called dilation and curettage (D&C) is commonly used in first-trimester abortions.

In *Stenberg v. Carhart* (2000), the Supreme Court by a 5–4 vote struck down a Nebraska ban on partial-birth abortion, declaring that it lacked an exception for the preservation of the mother's health and imposed an

State Abortion Laws

| State | Physicians Only | Partial-Birth Banned | Public Funding | | Waiting Period, in Hours | Parental Involvement Required for Minors |
			Most Medically Necessary Abortions	Only for Life, Rape, and Incest		
Alabama	Yes	1		Yes	24	Consent
Alaska	Yes	1	Yes		No	1
Arizona	Yes	1	Yes		No	Consent
Arkansas	Yes	1		Yes	Day Before	Consent
California	Yes	No	Yes		No	1
Colorado	Yes	No		Yes	No	Notice
Connecticut	Yes	No	Yes		No	No
Delaware	No	No		Yes	1	Notice
Florida	Yes	1		Yes	No	Notice
Georgia	Yes	2		Yes	24	Notice
Hawaii	Yes	No	Yes		No	No
Idaho	Yes	1		Yes	24	1
Illinois	Yes	1	Yes		No	1
Indiana	Yes	3		Yes	18	Consent
Iowa	Yes	1		Yes	No	Notice
Kansas	No	2		Yes	24	Notice
Kentucky	No	1		Yes	24	Consent
Louisiana	Yes	1		Yes	24	Consent
Maine	Yes	No		Yes	No	No
Maryland	Yes	No	Yes		No	Notice
Massachusetts	Yes	No	Yes		1	Consent
Michigan	Yes	1		Yes	24	Consent
Minnesota	Yes	No	Yes		24	Notice
Mississippi	Yes	3		Yes	24	Consent
Missouri	Yes	1		Yes	24	Consent
Montana	No	3	Yes		1	1
Nebraska	Yes	1		Yes	24	Notice
Nevada	Yes	No		Yes	No	1
New Hampshire	No	No		Yes	No	1
New Jersey	Yes	1	Yes		No	1
New Mexico	No	2	Yes		No	1
New York	No	No	Yes		No	No
North Carolina	Yes	No		Yes	No	Consent
North Dakota	Yes	3		Yes	24	Consent
Ohio	Yes	Yes		Yes	24	Consent
Oklahoma	Yes	3		Yes	24	Notice
Oregon	No	No	Yes		No	No

State	Physicians Only	Partial-Birth Banned	Public Funding		Waiting Period, in Hours	Parental Involvement Required for Minors
			Most Medically Necessary Abortions	Only for Life, Rape, and Incest		
Pennsylvania	Yes	No		Yes	24	Consent
Rhode Island	Yes	1		Yes	No	Consent
South Carolina	Yes	3		Yes	1	Consent
South Dakota	Yes	3		Yes[4]	24	Notice
Tennessee	Yes	3		Yes	1	Consent
Texas	Yes	No		Yes	24	Consent
Utah	Yes	1		Yes	24	Consent and Notice
Vermont	No	No	Yes		No	No
Virginia	Yes	1		Yes	24	Consent
Washington	No	No	Yes		No	No
West Virginia	No	1	Yes		24	Notice
Wisconsin	Yes	1		Yes	24	Consent
Wyoming	Yes	No		Yes	No	Consent

1. The law is enjoined and not in effect.

2. Only in cases where the fetus is viable.

3. Unchallenged in state court, but presumably unenforceable under *Stenberg v. Carhart* (2000).

4. Life only.

Source: Guttmacher Institute, 2006

undue burden on a woman's right to choose to have an abortion. The Court majority used this opportunity to confirm that states may regulate abortion as long as they do not overly burden the right to choose an abortion. The undue burden found in the *Stenberg* case included the use of language broadening the law's scope beyond merely banning the D&X procedure; the law thus could have prevented doctors from performing the D&E procedure for fear of going to jail for violating the law.

In response to the *Stenberg* decision, Congress enacted the Partial-Birth Abortion Ban Act (2003), based on what members saw as the Supreme Court's acceptance of questionable research that was said to render null and void the factual findings and policy determinations of Congress and many state legislatures.

The act stated that congressional hearings demonstrated that a partial-birth abortion was never necessary to preserve a woman's health, imposed significant health risks on a woman, and fell outside standard medical care. This law, however, has been declared unconstitutional by several federal courts.

Nonsurgical Abortions

In addition to the use of surgical abortions, pregnancies can now be terminated with DRUGS. The controversial drug RU-486—the "abortion pill"—was developed by Roussel Uclaf and first made available in France. Until 2000 the Food and Drug Administration withheld approval of the drug, which is sold in the United States under the trade name Mifeprex (its generic name is mifepristone). The pill blocks hormones needed for a pregnancy to continue and can be taken up to forty-nine days after the beginning of a woman's last menstrual cycle. A combination of two drugs previously approved by the FDA, methotrexate and misoprostol, has also been used in the country since 1996. Drug-based medical abortions are subject to the same legal limitations as surgical abortions.

Pro-life supporters are critical of both the abortion pill and a new emergency contraceptive known as the "morning-after pill," which uses a synthetic hormone to block ovulation (the natural expulsion of the female egg from the ovary) and fertilization of the egg. Victims of SEXUAL ASSAULT and rape and other women who have had unprotected sex are often given this drug. Because the pill may interfere with the implantation of a fertilized egg in the womb, the Catholic Church and other religious groups believe that it is comparable to abortion. It now appears that rather than inhibiting an egg's implantation, postcoital contraceptives destroy the egg. Emergency contraceptive measures carry a 20 percent failure rate.

Protests Against Abortion

Protests against abortion raise issues under the FIRST AMENDMENT (1791) to the U.S. Constitution. For example, antiabortion protesters generally argue that such protests are protected by their rights of free speech and assembly. But several court rulings in the late twentieth century permitted the establishment of buffer zones around abortion clinics to keep protesters from harassing people going in and out.

Antiabortion protesters have also used the INTERNET to identify abortion doctors on a "hit list," noting those who have been killed or injured. In 2006 the Supreme Court let stand a lower federal court ruling that affirmed the assessment of damages against antiabortion protesters who had created a Web site with Wild West–style "Wanted" posters targeting abortion doctors. Damages awarded to several doctors and abortion clinics by a jury in Portland, Oregon, were reduced from $108 million to a little under $5 million. Without comment, the Supreme Court refused to accept the protesters' appeal from the federal appeals court's decision in *Planned*

Parenthood v. American Coalition of Life Activists (2002).

The Supreme Court struck a blow against one method used to protect abortion clinics when, in *Scheidler v. National Organization for Women* and *Operation Rescue v. National Organization for Women* (both 2006), it held that the Racketeer Influenced and Corrupt Organizations Act (RICO) does not create a "freestanding physical violence offense" applicable to threats and violence directed at abortion providers. RICO was enacted in 1970 to proscribe acts or threats of physical violence during what the act refers to as robbery or extortion. The law had been used to prosecute some extreme abortion protests. The opinion, written by Associate Justice Stephen G. Breyer, noted that in 1994 Congress had passed the Freedom of Access to Clinic Entrances Act, which would not have been necessary if RICO had been intended all along to cover threats or violence against abortion clinics.

The Future of Abortion Rights

The legal battles over limitations placed on abortion and other REPRODUCTIVE RIGHTS of women are far from over. In 2004 Florida added an amendment to its constitution that states: "Notwithstanding a minor's right of privacy [protected elsewhere in the state's constitution], the Legislature is authorized to require by general law for notification to a parent or guardian of a minor before the termination of the minor's pregnancy." Some judges in Alabama, Pennsylvania, and Tennessee have refused to preside over or have recused themselves from cases involving abortion.

In addition to the *Stenberg* case overruling a state ban on late-term abortions, three lower federal courts subsequently found similar state and federal partial-birth abortion laws to be unconstitutional. In 2005 the Supreme Court accepted one case, *Ayotte v. Planned Parenthood of Northern New England,* and rejected hearing another case involving a state parental notification law that had been struck down by a lower court, which held that it did not explicitly permit a physician to perform an abortion in a medical emergency without parental notification. But in 2006 the Court merely remanded *Ayotte* to the lower court so it could consider upholding parts of the law even if the lack of a medical emergency provision is found to be unconstitutional. The Court's unanimous opinion, written by Associate Justice Sandra Day O'Connor, stated at the outset, "We do not revisit our abortion precedents today."

Congress found an indirect way to restrict abortion rights through the inclusion of a "federal refusal clause" in the annual federal appropriations bill beginning in fiscal year 2005. The clause protects health care entities such as doctors, medical professionals, hospitals, and health maintenance organizations (HMOs) from charges of discrimination by federal, state, and local governments if they refuse to "provide, pay for, provide coverage of, or refer for abortions." In effect, this clause gives the green light to anyone in the health care system to restrict abortion services. Lawsuits have been filed and grassroots campaigns mounted against the provision.

It is obvious that the right of abortion is being slowly circumscribed and is in danger of being taken away altogether. In 2005 the Bush administration called on the Supreme Court to uphold restrictions on abortion rights, specifically referring to a New Hampshire law enacted in 2003 that required parental notification for pregnant girls even when their health was at risk—the law reviewed by the Court in the *Ayotte* case. The appointments of a new chief justice of the United States in 2005 and a new associate justice in 2006 have brought renewed intensity to the long-running battle over a woman's right to have an abortion. Opponents of legalized abortion saw filling vacant Court seats as an opportunity for a president who shares their views to add justices who would overrule *Roe* and thus again allow state laws banning abortion.

As part of the reinvigorated movement to overturn *Roe v. Wade,* in early 2006 South Dakota enacted a law almost totally banning abortions within that state—an obvious effort to have *Roe* reviewed by the Supreme Court, with its two new conservative members. The law notes that the state accepts the opinion "that life begins at the time of conception, a conclusion confirmed by scientific advances since the 1973 decision of *Roe v. Wade.*" It adds that "the guarantee of due process of law … applies equally to born and unborn human beings." Abortion-rights proponents immediately took action, with the president of the Oglala Sioux Indian Nation, for example, threatening to open a clinic on the sovereign Pine Ridge Reservation, open to all women in the state; she was later removed as president. Encouraged by South Dakota's bill, similar bans were considered by a dozen other state legislatures, including Alabama, Georgia, Indiana, Kentucky, Louisiana, Mississippi, Missouri, Ohio, Rhode Island, South Carolina, and Tennessee.

For the past quarter century public opinion about abortion has remained consistent or become slightly more pro-choice. In 2005 a Gallup poll found that 26 percent of Americans thought that the procedure should always be legal, 56 percent suggested that it should be legal in certain circumstances, and only 16 percent responded that it should always be illegal. Long after *Roe v. Wade* revolutionized access to abortion, Norma McCorvey (Jane Roe) became a pro-life supporter, claiming that her pregnancy had actually resulted from a failed relationship. She never had an abortion, given the three years her case took to reach the Supreme Court. In 2005 the Court denied her petition to have the 1973 decision overturned.

If the Supreme Court should overrule *Roe v. Wade,* its decision may not result in a complete return to the days of "back-alley" surgical abortions. Today a dose of the abortion pill typically costs less than $2. In 2006 abortion opponents, however, began seeking removal of FDA approval for the abortion pill based on several unexplained deaths among users.

Contacts

NARAL Pro-Choice America, 1156 15th Street, NW, Suite 700, Washington, DC 20005 (202-973-3000). www.naral.org.www.prochoiceamerica.org.

Pro-Life Action League, 6160 North Cicero Avenue, Chicago, IL 60646 (773-777-2900). www.prolifeaction.org.

See also FAMILY PLANNING; NARAL PRO-CHOICE AMERICA; RELIGION.

ABSTINENCE

Abstinence (the practice of refraining from sexual activity with a partner) is an effective way to avoid PREGNANCY and reduce SEXUALLY TRANSMITTED DISEASES. But because studies of sexual behavior have shown that a commitment to abstain is not always foolproof, especially for young people, many organizations involved in sex education believe that contraception and disease-prevention techniques should be taught alongside abstinence. Proponents of abstinence-only sex education alternatively suggest that the teaching of other methods gives adolescents a license to become sexually active; they also argue that because contraceptives such as condoms are not 100 percent effective, young people are being put at risk.

Abstinence-Education Programs

In 1981 Congress created a grant system under the Adolescent Family Life Act to counteract the "severe adverse health, social, and economic consequences" of pregnancy and childbirth by unmarried TEENAGERS. The program, administered by the U.S. DEPARTMENT OF HEALTH AND HUMAN SERVICES, survived a FIRST AMENDMENT challenge in the U.S. Supreme Court's decision in *Bowen v. Kendrick* (1988) with respect to the constitutionally mandated separation of church and state. In *Bowen* the Court applied a test of constitutionality first used in *Lemon v. Kurtzman* (1971), finding that the act's purpose was secular—to reduce problems caused by teenage sexual behavior. It also held that the law's purpose was not to endorse RELIGION, although many religious groups were receiving funds under the act for teen educational activities. Nonetheless, the justices concluded that the programs did not involve any excessive entanglement between church and state.

As part of the Welfare Reform Act, Congress in 1996 appropriated some $250 million for abstinence-only-until-marriage programs under HHS. These programs were designed to restrict information about CONTRACEPTION and prohibited educators from giving complete or totally accurate answers to student questions about the prevention of pregnancy as well as

AIDS-HIV and other sexually transmitted diseases. In 2000 a congressionally established advisory group, the Institute of Medicine, issued a report requesting that Congress "eliminate requirements that public funds be used for abstinence-only education."

Another abstinence-education program administered by the Department of Health and Human Services was created in 2001. Special Projects of Regional and National Significance–Community Based Abstinence Education, which denies funding to any sex education activity that includes programs other than abstinence-only education—regardless of the source of any other funding—would seem to be on more shaky constitutional grounds. According to the Supreme Court's decision in *Perry v. Sindermann* (1972), a government benefit cannot be used to force a citizen to give up a fundamental constitutional right such as free speech.

In March 2005 the Bush administration announced plans for the federal government to double its efforts to promote abstinence-only sex education programs. In August, however, it suspended federal funds for a group that promoted Christianity as a part of its abstinence-education program; the move came after the AMERICAN CIVIL LIBERTIES UNION filed a lawsuit against HHS, alleging that taxpayer money was being used to promote Christianity in violation of the Constitution's principle of separation of church and state. Late that year Maine joined California and Pennsylvania in opting out of federally subsidized sex eductation funding, saying that the federal requirement to teach abstinence conflicted with state law mandating that teenagers be taught a comprehensive program from self-restraint to contraception. California and Pennsylvania officials cited the ineffectiveness of abstinence-education programs for not accepting the funding.

Program Limitations

The AMERICAN MEDICAL ASSOCIATION and more than one hundred other leading public health and medical organizations support education that includes information about contraception as well as abstinence.

Statistics show that vowing to remain a virgin until MARRIAGE does not protect a person from all sexually transmitted diseases, including some conditions such as herpes and human papilloma virus (HPV) that can be transmitted merely by skin-to-skin contact. Adolescents who take a pledge of abstinence are less likely to use condoms when they fail to live up to their commitment. Many thus have unprotected sex. A 2004 study funded by the National Institute of Child Health and Human Development and the Centers for Disease Control and Prevention found that the STD rate was actually higher in communities with a larger percentage of abstinence pledgers.

When a new vaccine protecting against cervical cancer was announced in 2005, supporters of adolescent abstinence came out in opposition to mandating its use for prepubescent teenagers. Medical authorities suggested vaccination of both girls and boys to prevent transmission of strains of the sexually transmitted HPV virus, which causes this cancer in women. Opposition groups countered that universal vaccination might encourage sexual activity before marriage by sending a message that such behavior is condoned. Cervical cancer annually strikes ten thousand U.S. women, killing more than 3,700.

For gay and lesbian adolescents, state and federal governments are sending contradictory messages to them through abstinence-only sex education programs. One says that they should abstain from sexual activity until marriage, but another declares that marriage is almost exclusively limited to heterosexual couples (Massachusetts being the only exception). The real message—one emphasizing cultural values over health—may be that homosexuals should deny their sexual orientation and accept a role as a partner in a sanctioned heterosexual relationship.

Many Americans believe that abstinence, like temperance, is an attempt to impose the morality of some on others. Like the failed experiment in prohibition of alcohol during the 1920s, it may also fail because it does not take into account the inevitability of human nature. An Ohio judge ordered a man to abstain from having more than his present seven children as a condition of his sentence to five years of probation, based on his failure to pay CHILD SUPPORT. The sentence in *State v. Talty* was overruled in 2004 by the Ohio supreme court because it did not allow the ban on having more CHILDREN to be lifted if the defendant became current on his child support payments.

Today movies, television, the INTERNET, advertising, and the fashion industry are pervaded by images that pander to the expression of sexual behavior. To assume that, in the face of this onslaught of sexual imagery and promotion of sexual pleasure, adolescents and single people will be able to postpone sex until marriage is unreasonable given the empirical evidence.

See also FAMILY PLANNING; HOMOSEXUALITY; REPRODUCTIVE RIGHTS; SAME-SEX MARRIAGE.

ABUSE

See CHILD ABUSE; DOMESTIC VIOLENCE.

ADOLESCENTS

See TEENAGERS.

ADULT MATERIALS

Adult materials encompass literary, visual, and graphic reproductions of explicit sexual activities or subjects that may not legally be made available to CHILDREN or minors. Even adults, however, may be prohibited from viewing material deemed to be obscene—items so offensive that the U.S. Supreme Court has ruled that they are not protected by the FIRST AMENDMENT (1791) to the U.S. Constitution. An adult is typically defined legally as a person who has reached what is sometimes called the "age of majority"; a younger person who is not an adult for legal purposes is referred to as a minor, a child, or an infant. To view or possess PORNOGRAPHY or other explicit written or graphic sexual material, an adult is generally considered to be eighteen years of age or older.

The COMMUNICATIONS DECENCY ACT (1996), which the Supreme Court found unconstitutional in *Reno v. American Civil Liberties Union* (1997), declared that a person had to be at least eighteen years of age to legally view pornography on the INTERNET. The CHILD ONLINE PROTECTION ACT (1998) tried to lower the limit to seventeen years of age, but it was likewise held unconstitutional by the Supreme Court in several decisions beginning in 2002, culminating in *Ashcroft v. American Civil Liberties Union* (2002, 2004). Among other constitutional problems found with the legislation during the extended litigation, a lower court cited the act's ambiguous definition of a minor.

The *Miller* Case

Use of the term *adult materials* is relatively new as far as the U.S. Supreme Court is concerned. In *MILLER V. CALIFORNIA* (1973) and the companion case *Paris Adult Theatre I v. Slaton* (1973), the Supreme Court handed down one of its key decisions on OBSCENITY. Writing for the Court, Chief Justice Warren E. Burger noted that the appellant had "conducted a mass mailing campaign to advertise the sale of illustrated books, euphemistically called 'adult' material."

At issue were unsolicited brochures advertising books entitled *Intercourse, Man-Woman, Sex Orgies Illustrated,* and *An Illustrated History of Pornography,* as well as a film named *Marital Intercourse.* A restaurant manager and his mother received and opened the materials. The defendant was convicted under a California law making it a misdemeanor to knowingly distribute obscene matter.

In a footnote to his dissenting opinion, Associate Justice WILLIAM O. DOUGLAS quoted a two-year study published in 1970 by the U.S. Commission on Obscenity and Pornography: "Society's attempts to legislate for adults in the area of obscenity have not been successful. Present laws prohibiting the consensual sale or distribution of explicit sexual materials to adults are extremely unsatisfactory in their practical application. The Constitution permits material to be deemed 'obscene' for adults only if, as a whole, it appeals to the 'prurient' interest of the average person, is 'patently offensive' in light of 'community standards,' and lacks 'redeeming social value.'"

Constitutional Development

Later Supreme Court cases also referred to so-called adult materials. *United States v. R. Enterprises, Inc.* (1991), for example, involved a "distributor of sexually oriented paperback books, magazines, and videotapes. R. Enterprises . . . distributes adult materials," said the Court. In *United States* v. *Playboy Entertainment Group, Inc.* (2000), the Court noted that legislatures maintain a limited power to protect children by restricting access to, but not banning, adult materials.

Then in *City of Los Angeles v. Alameda Books, Inc.* (2002), the Supreme Court dealt with the distinction between "content-based regulation" (laws that aim to ban certain subject matter) and restrictive ZONING regulation "of businesses based on their sales of expressive adult material." Content-based regulation calls for "strict scrutiny," the highest standard used by the Court to determine if a law infringes the First Amendment freedom of expression. Different levels of scrutiny place ascending burdens on the government to prove the necessity for a law challenged on constitutional grounds. In free-speech cases where the government has sought to criminalize the content of a person's expression, the government must meet a higher standard of proof than when it is merely regulating some aspect of expression, as in the case of zoning regulations affecting distributors of adult materials. Strict scrutiny is also used by the Supreme Court to analyze laws that discriminate on the basis of race or national origin.

In *Alameda Books,* the Supreme Court concluded that, while "the city certainly bears the burden of providing evidence that supports a link between concentrations of adult operations and asserted secondary effects [such as an increased risk of crime] . . . it may rely on any evidence reasonably believed to be relevant." In other words, zoning regulations aimed at restricting the location of adult businesses are not attempting to regulate the content of the adult material purveyed; therefore, a state or a municipality will be allowed greater leeway in proving that such regulations are based on the fear that harmful secondary effects might occur were it not for the restrictive regulations.

More recently, in *City of Littleton, Colorado v. Z. J. Gifts D-4, LLC* (2004), the Supreme Court confirmed the proposition that business licensing and zoning requirements should not have the effect of suppressing adult materials. In this case, the Court held that an ordinance requiring the licensing of adult businesses "considered on its face, is consistent with the First Amendment's demands" and "does not seek to *censor* material."

Effect of Restrictions

Legal restrictions on adult materials have implications for many forms of communication. Providers of content on the Internet, including bloggers, for example, are protected by the First Amendment with respect to most adult materials, except for items that are defined in laws or by the courts as obscene or that involve child pornography. Such items, even if termed adult materials, have consistently been held to be outside the protection of the First Amendment guarantees of free expression.

Libraries have also been affected by laws and rulings regarding adult materials. The Children's Internet Protection Act, passed by Congress in 2000, requires libraries that receive federal funding—most school and public libraries—to install software to block adult materials, thus preventing access by minors on library terminals; the penalty is loss of federal funding. In *United States v. American Library Association* (2003), the Supreme Court held that the act did not infringe the First Amendment's protection of free speech and did not impose unconstitutional conditions on libraries. Unlike other attempts by CONGRESS to stifle access to adult materials on the Internet—by regulating content providers through the Communications Decency Act in 1996 and the Child Online Protection Act in 1998—this law was found to

be a valid exercise of congressional authority. The Court concluded that the aim of preventing the dissemination of harmful material to children was a compelling government interest and that Congress has wide latitude to attach conditions to the receipt of federal assistance. In addition, children are often free from direct parental supervision in libraries.

Businesses and citizens are also trying to cope with other restrictions on adult materials. In retail outlets defined by local government as adult bookstores, for instance, merchandise is limited to adults. Since 2003 bookstores and librarians have successfully challenged an Arkansas law requiring an adults-only section in bookstores; while the state supreme court has ruled favorably for the plaintiffs, the battle may not be over. Under a city zoning ordinance, however, a federal court, in *Pensack v. City and County of Denver* (1986), upheld the use of the term *adult bookstore* applied to a bakery that sold theme cakes with sexual designs and messages—even though no books were sold there.

Adult materials may still be a euphemism for pornography, as Chief Justice Burger suggested in the *Miller* decision. The concept nonetheless seems to have come to stand for the right of adults to distribute, view, and possess sexually explicit materials that are not otherwise illegal. To what extent such items may be regulated will undoubtedly continue to be an issue that polarizes many Americans: from those who see adult materials as a constitutional-rights issue to others who see them as a moral issue and urge more vigorous government attempts to restrict them.

See also CENSORSHIP; PRURIENT INTEREST; SEXUALLY ORIENTED BUSINESSES.

ADULTERY

Voluntary sexual relations between a person who is married and someone who is not his or her spouse are called adultery. According to the Bible, a Hebrew wife was required to share her husband with lesser wives and concubines but could be stoned to death herself for adultery. In medieval times women were locked into chastity belts when their husbands were away to prevent marital infidelity. The Puritans came to America in part because of their failure to change English laws that allowed ecclesiastical courts to selectively prosecute for fornication (unlawful consensual sexual intercourse between two unmarried persons) only the poorest citizens while looking the other way for sexual dalliances among the upper classes. The strict morality of the early English colonists is reflected in the 1850 novel *The Scarlet Letter* by Nathaniel Hawthorne (1804–64). In it an unmarried woman who had sex and a child out of wedlock was required to wear the letter *A* (for adulterer) when she went out in public; her lover was not so tagged, pointing up the fact that women were punished more often than men for adultery, especially when they had a child as evidence.

Protection of Public Safety and Morals

Traditionally MARRIAGE was the only accepted institution for legitimizing the right of a man and a woman to have sexual relations. Under common law, adultery is sexual intercourse by a man, married or single, with a married woman other than his wife. It has been regulated under a state's police power to protect the public's safety and morals. In some jurisdictions today, if one person is married and the other person is not, the former is considered to be committing adultery while the latter is committing fornication. Other jurisdictions cast both persons as adulterers if the woman is married. Therefore, in some situations the same act may be punishable as either adultery or fornication. In a few jurisdictions the accuseds' behavior must be open and notorious—generally recognized by the public—to be criminally prohibited.

Adultery is no longer a crime in many states. Where it is still on the books, in about half the states and the District of Columbia, adultery is generally not enforced. State laws have variously defined adultery as any sexual intercourse by a married person other than with that person's spouse (Colorado); voluntary sexual intercourse by a married person with a person other than his spouse (Georgia); sexual intercourse by a married person with a person not his spouse or by an unmarried person with a married person (Massachusetts); and sexual intercourse of two persons, either of whom is married to a third person (Michigan). Kansas defines adultery as "engaging in sexual intercourse or sodomy with a person who is not married to the offender if: (a) The offender is married; or (b) The offender is not married and knows that the other person involved in the act is married." Usually these are misdemeanors with relatively small fines. Where a homicide results from one spouse's catching another in the act of adultery, the charge may be reduced from first-degree murder to manslaughter because the killing was committed in the heat of passion.

The rationale behind making adultery a crime is to prevent the spread of SEXUALLY TRANSMITTED DISEASES, protect the institution of marriage, and safeguard the morals of the community. Many state courts, however, have questioned the relationship between these goals and laws on adultery. It is said that the fear of sexual disease is more of a deterrent to extramarital sex than is the law and that the institution of marriage as well as community morals have both changed, such that a large number of spouses now admit in polls that they have been unfaithful.

A Massachusetts court held in *Commonwealth v. Stowell* (1983) that prosecutions for adultery were not inconsistent with the right of PRIVACY under the federal and state constitutions. Then in *Marcum v. McWhorter* (2002), relying on the U.S. Supreme Court's since-overruled decision in *Bowers v. Hardwick* (1986), the U.S. Court of Appeals for the Sixth Circuit upheld the firing of an employee of the Pulaski County, Kentucky, sheriff's office because the employee was carrying on an adulterous affair with a married woman. Although the employee argued that his right to cohabit with a married woman was protected by the right to freely associate with whomever he wished, the court found no evidence to establish that entering "into an intimate, sexual relationship and cohabitation with a married woman is a fundamental right deeply rooted

In the 1870s, Henry Ward Beecher (1813–87), a nationally influential minister who was the brother of the author Harriet Beecher Stowe (1811–96), became embroiled in a legal scandal over his adulterous affair with Elizabeth Tilton but was acquitted. Today state laws criminalizing adultery are either not enforced or have been eliminated entirely.

in the Nation's history and tradition or implicit in the concept of ordered liberty." The opinion concluded that, while it is "perhaps unfair, [the employee's] dismissal did not infringe his right of association as guaranteed by the First and Fourteenth Amendments."

Fornication Laws

With respect to state laws criminalizing fornication, a New Jersey court in *State v. Barr* (1970) declared that such a law was not an unconstitutional interference with the privacy rights protected under the due

process clause of the Fourteenth Amendment (1868) to the U.S. Constitution. However, in the wake of *LAWRENCE v. TEXAS* (2003)—in which private SODOMY by consenting adults, in this case homosexuals, was upheld by the U.S. Supreme Court—the implication is that laws criminalizing fornication, which technically involves only nonmarried people, may have been made unconstitutional.

A Virginia law making it a crime for unmarried couples to have sex had been on the books since the early 1800s but had not been enforced since 1847; in 2005 the state's supreme court ruled that the law was unconstitutional as an improper abridgment of "a personal relationship that is within the liberty interest of persons to choose." That same year the AMERICAN CIVIL LIBERTIES UNION filed a lawsuit to have North Carolina's cohabitation law declared unconstitutional after a woman was fired from her job for living with her boyfriend out of wedlock. The ACLU's executive director, obviously referring to cases following the *Lawrence* decision, said, "The Supreme Court has made it clear that the government has no business regulating relationships between two consenting adults in the privacy of their own home."

Changing Mores

Adultery and fornication laws may one day be abrogated altogether because of the right of privacy on which the *Lawrence* decision was based. However, the fact that adultery involves the state-regulated institution of marriage makes it more difficult to predict how states will continue to treat it under their laws. Noncriminal avenues of redress have been available for injured parties, including DIVORCE proceedings, and some states permit civil claims, such as for alienation of affection, by a married person injured by a spouse's adultery. The availability of no-fault divorce decrees has made reliance on accusations of adultery less common. But in divorce cases based on the fault of one or both parties, adultery has traditionally been one of the grounds available; evidence of adultery may affect an award of ALIMONY in those jurisdictions where fault is still recognized by the courts. Adultery has also been used as grounds for forfeiting dower rights and for making charges of libel or slander for false accusations.

Clearly the morality of the times has changed from when laws criminalizing adultery and fornication were first enacted. Attempts by society to enforce morality in private consensual sexual relationships may no longer be acceptable except in voluntary religious, moral, and cultural subgroups. Yet the recent resurgence of moral issues in state and national politics—reflected in the recent movement to restrict

the institution of marriage to heterosexual couples—could signal a return to a stricter sense of morality in America and a return to stricter laws against sex outside marriage.

See also PREMARITAL SEX; UNMARRIED COHABITANTS.

AFFIRMATIVE ACTION

See DISCRIMINATION.

AIDS-HIV

According to the Centers for Disease Control and Prevention, nearly 525,000 persons have died from Acquired Immune Deficiency Syndrome (AIDS) since the outbreak in the United States began in 1981. Today more than 1 million persons in the country have the Human Immunodeficiency Virus (HIV), the precursor of AIDS. Worldwide it is estimated that about 3.1 million persons died of AIDS in 2004 alone. More people across the globe have the HIV virus than live in California, whose population is about 35.5 million.

HIV attacks the cells of the body. After the initial infection, which causes the fevers and aches typical of a viral infection, the virus continues to attack an increasing number of cells until, near the end, it has invaded billions of cells. In the body's fight against HIV, each day it may produce hundreds of millions of defense cells called lymphocytes that die in the struggle and are replaced the next day. Other antibodies produced to fight the virus kill individual virus particles called virons before they can infect more cells. AIDS is the second phase of the viral attack, after the HIV has reduced the immune system to the point where it can no longer provide effective protection from infection.

AS SEXUALLY TRANSMITTED DISEASES, AIDS and HIV have been at the center of political and legal policy battles in the United States primarily because of their connection to HOMOSEXUALITY. At the end of 2004, 58 percent of adults and adolescents with AIDS were men who had sex with men. (Around the world, however, the disease is spread more through heterosexual sexual activity. Of American women with AIDS, 64 percent were exposed through heterosexual contact, while the remainder acquired the disease through injections of DRUGS.) The U.S. Code contains some two hundred subentries under the heading Acquired Immune Deficiency Syndrome that range from "Abandonment, children and minors, assistance" and "Blood banks" to "Drug addicts," "Notice, Partner," and "Reports, Medical wastes," all of which confirm the extent to which the disease has come to have legal implications nationwide.

Discrimination Against Victims

Several factors may contribute to DISCRIMINATION against victims of AIDS-HIV in employment and other daily activities. Fear of contracting the disease is a major factor, especially by those who lack sufficient information about it. Even U.S. Senator Bill Frist of Tennessee, a medical doctor, was criticized in 2005 for stating on television that HIV can be transmitted through saliva. Some people also believe that AIDS-HIV is evidence of gay or promiscuous sexual behavior or even of divine punishment for some sin.

Employment. The U.S. Supreme Court has established that in the case of diseases such as AIDS-HIV, where an employee poses little risk to others in a workplace, he or she is covered by antidiscrimination provisions of the Rehabilitation Act of 1973, which prohibits discrimination by the federal government or those who receive federal funds. Its ruling came in *School Board of Nassau County v. Arline* (1987). The law's coverage was extended under the Americans with Disabilities Act (1990) to encompass all private-sector employment, except employers with fewer than fifteen employees.

Americans with Disabilities Act (1990). The ADA, which declares that "homosexuality and bisexuality are not impairments" under the act, applies to privately owned and operated public accommodations, including professional offices of health care providers

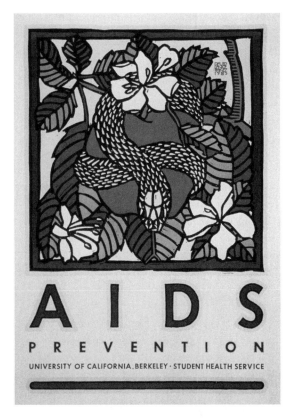

A worldwide health problem of major proportions, AIDS is linked to unprotected sexual activity. To educate the public at risk, the University of California at Berkeley in 1985 commissioned the popular artist David Lance Goines to design a distinctive poster.

and hospitals; religious organizations and entities controlled by them are exempt from the key antidiscrimination provisions of Title III of the act, even if their activities would otherwise make them a public accommodation. The antidiscrimination provisions apply to all stages of AIDS-HIV and even to cases of discrimination based on the mistaken belief that a person has the virus.

In *Bragdon v. Abbott* (1998), the Supreme Court dealt with one form of discrimination against AIDS-HIV victims under the Americans with Disabilities Act. The case involved a dentist who refused to fill the cavity of a patient who had informed him that she was infected with HIV; he agreed to perform the procedure at a hospital if the patient would pay for the use of the hospital's facilities. The Supreme Court agreed with the plaintiff that the HIV infection made her eligible for protection under the ADA. The Court, however, declared that the trial record did not conclusively prove that the dentist's fears of "a direct threat to the health or safety to others" (language in the ADA allowing discriminatory treatment) were unfounded. On remand, the plaintiff was again granted summary judgment based on additional evidence from the Centers for Disease Control's dentistry guidelines and other professional groups. The conclusion was that HIV-infected patients did not present a risk of transmitting the disease based on the dental treatment required in this case. As litigated in *Bragdon*, an exception to the ADA's antidiscrimination coverage is made in cases where the disease may pose a direct threat to the health and safety of others.

Health Insurance. Where an employer offers health insurance to employees, federal courts have held that persons with AIDS-HIV cannot be excluded unless the employer can show that covering them would cause an undue hardship. Courts have also held that the coverage limits may be reduced if based on the increased risk posed by the employees with the virus and not on a policy of discrimination. If individuals become too ill to work, then the ADA no longer protects them or requires that they be allowed to participate in their employer's health insurance plan.

Immigration. Ostensibly because of a fear of contagion, people with AIDS-HIV may be banned from entry into the United States and U.S. citizenship, as are sex workers, who may also carry sexually transmitted diseases. In 1993 the U.S. DEPARTMENT OF HEALTH AND HUMAN SERVICES proposed removing HIV infection from the list of communicable diseases that could require expulsion of aliens who were diagnosed with it. Yet that same year, Congress passed the National Institutes of Health Revitalization Act, which excluded any alien "who is determined ... to have a communicable disease of public health significance, which shall include ... [HIV-AIDS]." Although worded in a general way, to some extent this language acts as a renewal of an

earlier immigration policy in effect between 1952 and 1990 that excluded homosexuals and drug addicts, who were considered to be afflicted with a "constitutional psychopathic inferiority."

Privacy

The need to protect the public from infection may conflict with a patient's right to confidentiality after testing positive for AIDS-HIV. State legislatures have decided that some form of confidentiality is needed to ensure that potential carriers of the virus are not afraid to be tested. A number of states—among them California, Illinois, and Wisconsin—have enacted laws that regulate the disclosure of persons who have tested positively, but the statutes do not offer broad protection.

California law provides that "any person who negligently discloses the results of a blood test [for AIDS] to any third party ... shall be assessed a civil penalty." In *Urbaniak v. Newton* (1991), a state court noted that the law's language did not cover someone who was not involved in the testing process, partly because the purpose of the law was to impose confidentiality in the testing process to encourage testing and treatment. An analogous Wisconsin statute was similarly held, in *Hillman v. Columbia County* (1991), not to apply to jail employees who opened an envelope with test data and then disseminated the information to inmates. Other cases have held that an HIV test of a defendant may not be ordered by a court in a RAPE or SODOMY prosecution only to help the victim "relieve and recover from her emotional trauma," but it may be ordered if the test relates to the development of evidence for the prosecution's case. In Illinois the disclosure by a television station that a person was charged with the criminal transmission of the virus was held not to violate that state's AIDS confidentiality statute.

Safe-Sex Education

Legislators and policymakers have disagreed on how to promote education to help stem the tide of AIDS transmission—without seeming to promote homosexuality or offending some segments of society by sanctioning the practice of safe sex. In 1987 U.S. Senator Jesse

Helms of North Carolina began introducing language in federal spending bills banning any "promotion of homosexuality," provisions that impacted education policy in areas including AIDS-prevention programs. In 1989 CONGRESS specified that AIDS-education programs funded by the Centers for Disease Control and Prevention, an agency of the Department of Health and Human Services, "shall not be designed to promote or encourage, directly, intravenous drug abuse or sexual activity, homosexual or heterosexual."

In *Gay Men's Health Crisis v. Sullivan* (1992), a federal district court reviewed a language change by the CDC in its requests for grant applications relating to AIDS-HIV education. The language stated: "Written materials, audiovisual materials and pictorials should not include terms, descriptors, or displays which will be offensive to a majority of the intended audience or to a majority of adults outside the intended audience unless, in the judgment of the [CDC's] Program Review Panel, the potential offensiveness of such material is outweighed by the potential effectiveness in communicating an important HIV prevention message."

The court rejected the need for the review panel to make ad hoc determinations about this language, finding that, among other things, "[e]vidence of self-censorship by AIDS education groups ... provides evidence of the vagueness of the [new language]."

At the state level, laws have been enacted to set the tone of AIDS-HIV discussions in SEX EDUCATION classes. For example, an Arizona statute passed in 1991 and amended in 1995 provides in part:

A. Each common, high and unified school district may provide instruction to kindergarten programs through the twelfth grade on [AIDS and HIV].

B. Each district is free to develop its own course of study for each grade . . . [but]

C. No district shall include in its course of study instruction which:

1. Promotes a homosexual life-style.

2. Portrays homosexuality as a positive alternative life-style.

3. Suggests that some methods of safe sex are safe methods of homosexual sex.

Speech Restrictions

The frankness about sexual practices—especially male homosexual activity—resulting from the fear of an AIDS-HIV epidemic led to a rash of court cases under the FIRST AMENDMENT (1791) that challenged the use of sexually explicit language. However, the only successful case alleging OBSCENITY was *Rees v. State* (1995), brought in Texas. *Rees* involved a sex-information program on cable television that showed actual sexual relations between two men. In 1996 the U.S. Supreme Court denied a petition for review of the ruling by a Texas appeals court that the conviction for promoting obscenity was justified.

In Massachusetts an AIDS organization's advertisements were banned from subway and trolley cars because of a public policy prohibiting ads containing sexually explicit and patently offensive language. In *AIDS Action Committee of Massachusetts v. Massachusetts Bay Transportation Authority* (1994), a federal court of appeals found that this denial constituted discrimination in violation of the First Amendment because the authority did display ads for a movie with sexually explicit words and photographs. The court added that great damage is done if the government, in regulating access to public property, even appears to be discriminating in unconstitutional fashion.

Crime Victims

Crimes involving sex or other close contact may infect victims with AIDS-HIV, resulting in a consequent increase in the severity of the crime and the punishment. In *Scroggins v. State* (1990), Georgia's supreme court upheld a conviction for aggravated assault with intent to murder and aggravated assault with a deadly weapon because the defendant, knowing that he was infected with AIDS, bit a police officer. In a Texas case the same year, *Zule v. State*, a conviction for aggravated SEXUAL ASSAULT was upheld after the defendant had anal intercourse with a fifteen-year-old victim, infecting him with HIV.

GENDER-based violence, such as HATE CRIMES and attacks against women, also increases the risk of AIDS-HIV infection because the victim cannot negotiate safe sex, including the use of condoms. Women are two to five times more likely than men to become infected with HIV during unprotected vaginal intercourse; physical injuries from sexual assault can increase the risk of infection.

While seemingly under control, AIDS-HIV continues to touch many Americans and still poses problems for parents and CHILDREN, teachers and students, health care providers and patients, employers and employees, participants in contact sports, law enforcement and correctional officers, and just about anyone who can expect to come in contact with the bodily fluids of another person. Easy transmission during sexual behavior makes the disease an even more difficult subject for the law and society at large to deal with. Yet it is something taxpayers must deal with. In the 2006 federal budget, $21 billion was proposed for AIDS-HIV programs, of which $18 billion was allocated for domestic spending; of this, some $12.6 billion was targeted for the care of victims.

ALIMONY

The state not only is a party to the MARRIAGE contract, it has also set the rules for getting married and terminating a marriage. In the traditional model of marriage, the husband was the breadwinner and the wife and CHILDREN were dependent on him for the necessities of life. State rules have thus included provision of alimony (financial maintenance) for the wife after a DIVORCE as well as CHILD SUPPORT payments where the husband and sole bread winner does not obtain custody of the children when the marriage is terminated.

In divorce proceedings today, a court may still order one person to pay a suitable allowance to the other party. Such alimony payments may be for life or a limited period of time, and they may be modified as the parties' circumstances change. Alimony may be paid in the form of a single lump sum or spread out over some period of time. It may also be granted temporarily pending a divorce and include a reasonable amount for the legal fees and court costs involved.

Types of Alimony

There are two basic types of alimony: permanent and temporary (restitutional and rehabilitative).

Permanent. A spouse may be awarded permanent maintenance if he or she is not economically self-sufficient or able to maintain after a divorce the lifestyle that the court decides is appropriate given the parties' financial resources. Sometimes alimony is awarded even if both spouses are employed but one of them may never be able to earn as much as the spouse who has the better-paying job. To warrant permanent alimony, its need and the other party's ability to pay it must be proven. Such support may be modified later and even terminated, in the case of remarriage or cohabitation without marriage.

Restitutional. Restitutional or reimbursement alimony is always awarded for a specified period of time and may be given to pay back a debt. It is used to award one spouse who has supported the other through professional training, such as for a doctor or a lawyer. This type of alimony is a compromise by legislatures and courts between simply refusing to grant such relief and trying to value, on the same basis as other assets acquired during the marriage, a professional degree or license.

Rehabilitative. Rehabilitative alimony is also paid for a specific period and may be awarded to cover the cost of education or training to enable one party in the divorce to become self-supporting. Some factors considered by a court in awarding rehabilitative alimony include the educational or employment opportunities one party gave up during the marriage, the amount of time spent out of the job market, and the amount of education or training necessary to make the party self-sufficient.

Alimony is no longer tied to the traditional model of marriage, so a party's sex is no longer a factor in determining the right to alimony. In *Orr v. Orr* (1979), the U.S. Supreme Court invalidated state laws that imposed the obligation to pay alimony on husbands but not their spouses. This decision was in line with the evolution of federal law and the Supreme Court's rulings in DISCRIMINATION and PRIVACY cases that enforced the equality of men and women in the economic sphere while shifting the law's focus from the traditional marital unit to the rights of the individual parties in sexual relationships.

Private Agreements

Since the 1960s, with the arrival of no-fault divorce laws that essentially permitted marriage partners to privately determine the grounds for a divorce, the states have begun to recognize private divorce settlements, including PRENUPTIAL AGREEMENTS and postnuptial agreements. These agreements change the way in which marital property is divided under state law and may limit alimony. A prenuptial or premarital agreement is entered into before the marriage, while the postnuptial or postmarital agreement is made during a marriage. A court may refuse to enforce an unconscionable agreement that is clearly unfair to one party.

For unmarried couples who part after living together for some time, the high-profile separation of the actor Lee Marvin and his partner, Michelle Marvin, set a precedent that most states have followed. In *Marvin v. Marvin* (1976), the California supreme court held that "the judicial barriers that may stand in the way of a policy based upon the fulfillment of the reasonable expectations of the parties to a nonmarital relationship should be removed." The equivalent of alimony was thus extended to a former party in a close but nonmarital relationship—ever since popularly referred to as "palimony."

California, Hawaii, and New Jersey are among the states with laws allowing domestic partnerships that extend to unmarried heterosexual and same-sex couples many of the rights and benefits generally reserved to married couples; they may or may not include a right similar to that of palimony for one party in a homosexual relationship. However, in *Robertson v. Reinhart* (2003), a California court held that a palimony claim was not established by a lesbian partner for several reasons: no implied contractual arrangement was proven, no evidence was given that the women pooled their financial resources, and no evidence existed of an agreement to treat their property as jointly owned.

If states continue the recent trend of allowing marriage and divorce to become private matters in which government plays a decreased role in setting the rules, alimony may become negotiable between the parties rather than automatically imposed on one party or the other; an exception would be where there is no legal agreement to that effect. The recent wave of amendments to state constitutions restricting marriage and its privileges to heterosexual couples, however, may herald a shift away from extending alimony to partners in same-sex relationships, except in those states that recognize such marriages, civil unions, or domestic partnerships.

See also DEFENSE OF MARRIAGE ACT; FEDERAL MARRIAGE AMENDMENT; HOMOSEXUALITY; SAME-SEX MARRIAGE.

AMERICAN CIVIL LIBERTIES UNION

In 1971 the American Civil Liberties Union represented two gay men who sought a marriage license in Washington State but were turned down because a state court held that MARRIAGE was intended for the procreation and rearing of children and therefore was not applicable to homosexual couples. In 2005, as SAME-SEX MARRIAGE became a national issue, the ACLU again represented homosexual couples who wanted to get married in Washington. That same year, the organization also sought the release of U.S. Department of Justice records that might shed light on why hospitals are not advised to consider emergency CONTRACEPTION when treating RAPE victims.

The ACLU—which was founded in 1920 by Roger Baldwin, Crystal Eastman, Albert DeSilver, and others as the National Civil Liberties Bureau—is a nonprofit and nonpartisan legal organization that promotes and

THE AMERICAN CIVIL LIBERTIES UNION
Illustrated Guide to the
★ BILL OF RIGHTS ★

An abridged version* of those rights which the government may not abridge, as set forth by the Bill of Rights and certain later Amendments to the Constitution. To wit:

I. FREE SPEECH...

A FREE PRESS...

NO MIXING OF CHURCH AND STATE

IV. NO UNREASONABLE SEARCH OR SEIZURE

V. DUE PROCESS OF LAW

VI. A JURY TRIAL AND A LAWYER

VIII. NO CRUEL AND UNUSUAL PUNISHMENT

XIV. STATE GOVERNMENTS MAY NOT DENY YOUR RIGHTS NOR EQUAL PROTECTION OF THE LAWS.

XV. THE RIGHT TO VOTE REGARDLESS OF RACE... XIX. ...OR SEX

*For an unabridged leaflet, "The Bill of Rights," and for information about how you can help defend your rights through membership in the ACLU, write to your local ACLU branch or the national office:

AMERICAN CIVIL LIBERTIES UNION
22 East 40th Street
New York, N.Y. 10016

Designed & Illustrated by
LIONEL KALISH

defends civil liberties. Today it has more than four hundred thousand members and supporters and a number of regional and state affiliates. It participates in close to six thousand court cases a year nationwide and champions the notion that civil liberties must be respected at all times, even during national emergencies.

The union often represents in legal forums the most vulnerable citizens on issues relating to PRIVACY and freedom from unwarranted government intrusion. It works to protect the rights of those who have traditionally been denied their rights in America: women, lesbians, gays, bisexual and transgender persons, and prisoners. When not directly representing a party in a court case, the ACLU may file an *amicus curiae* (friend of the court) brief in support of one or the other litigants. Major issues that the ACLU addresses in its legal representation include free speech, AIDS-HIV, homosexual rights, rights of PRISONERS, REPRODUCTIVE RIGHTS, and WOMEN'S RIGHTS.

Some of the important cases in which the union has participated are household names. In 1925 it persuaded a Tennessee teacher, John Scopes, to defy the state's ban on teaching evolution—an issue that has come around again in the current decade. Scopes lost, but the famous case in which Clarence Darrow, a preeminent defense attorney and ACLU member, represented him became a national event. The ACLU also attacked the federal government's policy of internment for Japanese Americans after the bombing of Pearl Harbor on December 7, 1941, and played a major role in the case *Brown v. Board of Education of Topeka* (1954), which ended segregation in America's public schools. While normally an apolitical entity, the organization began the drumbeat for the impeachment of President Richard Nixon in 1973, and it has consistently challenged the USA PATRIOT Act, passed after September 11, 2001—a stance that by

December 2002 had increased the number of ACLU supporters by 20 percent.

The ACLU has been instrumental in defending the FIRST AMENDMENT to the U.S. Constitution from congressional challenges via CENSORSHIP laws. In *Reno v. American Civil Liberties Union* (1997), the U.S. Supreme Court held that the COMMUNICATIONS DECENCY ACT (1996), a law intended to protect CHILDREN from OBSCENITY on the INTERNET, was too broad and too vague to accomplish its goal without infringing the right of free expression guaranteed by the First Amendment. Six years later, in *Ashcroft v. American Civil Liberties Union* (2002, 2004), the Court again struck down as unconstitutional a federal law, the CHILD ONLINE PROTECTION ACT (1998), aimed at protecting children from Internet smut.

In 2005 the ACLU's Reproductive Freedom Project was instrumental in cutting off government funds for the Silver Ring Thing program, which in effect paid religious activists to counsel young people on ABSTINENCE as a form of SEX EDUCATION. Objecting to the use of taxpayer money to bring "unchurched" students to the Christian RELIGION in the guise of an objective sex education program, the union filed a lawsuit alleging the misuse of more than $1 million awarded by the U.S. DEPARTMENT OF HEALTH AND HUMAN SERVICES for programs that included three-hour sessions of testimony about the value of accepting Jesus Christ and quoting from the Bible.

The organization has taken some controversial stands by defending the free-speech rights of Ku Klux Klan members, neo-Nazi groups, and supporters of legalizing pederasty. Because of its unwavering stand to protect the rights of all citizens, the ACLU has critics as well as supporters across the political spectrum as it defends the U.S. Constitution against the erosion of citizens' rights.

The American Civil Liberties Union takes legal action to protect the fundamental constitutional rights of citizens under the Bill of Rights (1791). Its activities have targeted issues from censorship and privacy to contraception and abortion to the rights of homosexuals, women, and prisoners.

Contact: American Civil Liberties Union, 125 Broad Street, 18th Floor, New York, NY 10004 (212-549-2500). www.aclu.org.

See also HOMOSEXUALITY.

AMERICAN FERTILITY ASSOCIATION

Sexual behavior is innately directed toward reproduction, however else it may manifest itself. But the ability to reproduce depends on fertility. There have always been people who want to have CHILDREN but for some physical reason cannot do so.

The American Fertility Association was founded as the American Infertility Association in 1999 to educate, support, and advocate for men and women concerned about reproductive health, maintaining fertility, problems of infertility, and all forms of family creation. Although a basic mission of the AFA is to assist people confronting infertility, the organization's name change reflects its desire to emphasize the potential for overcoming this condition rather than to focus on the negative aspects of reproductive dysfunction or disease. Since its inception, the association has expanded its membership from three thousand to some twenty-one thousand persons.

The AFA works in the United States and around the world to dispel the stigma of infertility, raise public consciousness about reproductive disease and its prevention, improve reproductive medicine and health, and promote and protect the use of donated egg and sperm cells. It provides a range of services offering information about medical treatment, options for building a family, and techniques for coping with infertility problems, as well as about insurance issues and the law. A major goal is to help women and couples make informed decisions throughout the entire process of overcoming infertility.

The organization supports various forms of ASSISTED REPRODUCTIVE TECHNOLOGY. It takes the position that embryos created during the process of in vitro fertilization (outside a woman's body) carry the potential for human life but are not yet entitled to the same legal protection as more mature human fetuses. In commenting on a recent court ruling in favor of a couple who sued a laboratory for wrongful death in the negligent loss of an embryo, an AFA spokesperson said, "Elevating an embryo to the status of a living and breathing child has implications on issues of choice.... The judge's ruling is an affront to reproductive rights and could place limits on the treatment options available."

The AFA also supports adoption procedures. This is an important option, especially for individuals and couples for whom assisted reproduction does not work and for those who have reached a point where they are ready to consider alternative methods of bringing children into the family. Adoption has been known to affect a couple's fertility in a positive way—making it possible for normal conception when it was not possible before a child was adopted.

To further its mission, the AFA provides information and assistance to federal and state governments and conducts workshops and seminars around the country. It also works with MEDIA outlets to present the views of its members to the public, policymakers, and others who can help support the AFA's interests. It has made its free information and services available online. The association is governed by a board of directors and has an advisory board. A number of board members are physicians, as are all of the advisory board members.

Contact: American Fertility Association, 666 Fifth Avenue, Suite 278, New York, NY 10103 (888-917-3777). www.theafa.org.

See also FAMILY PLANNING; REPRODUCTIVE RIGHTS; STEM-CELL RESEARCH AND CLONING; UNBORN, RIGHTS OF THE.

AMERICAN MEDICAL ASSOCIATION

The medical profession plays a significant role with respect to sexual behavior in America. Doctors advise and educate patients and the general public on a range of sex-related concerns, from CONTRACEPTION and ABORTION to PREGNANCY and ASSISTED REPRODUCTIVE TECHNOLOGY, prenatal care, childbirth, and postnatal care. They also treat a host of sex-related diseases and conditions, including AIDS-HIV, SEXUALLY TRANSMITTED DISEASES, impotency, and cervical cancer. The American

Medical Association, the largest medical association in the country, has as its mission promoting scientific advancement, ensuring standards for medical education, developing and promoting a system of medical ethics, and improving public health.

The AMA was founded in 1847 by Nathan Smith Davis, a thirty-year-old doctor who had received his degree a few days after turning twenty, following training at the Medical College of Western New York and serving apprenticeships with practicing physicians. As a member of the New York Medical Society, Davis worked on improving medical education and licensing. In 1845 he introduced a resolution endorsing a national medical association, which two years later became a reality. Nathaniel Chapman was named the organization's first president, a position Davis would fill in 1864.

In its first year of existence, the AMA drafted and published a code of ETHICS, and by 1858 it had created a committee on ethics; ten years later the committee advocated recognition of qualified female physicians. Sarah Hackett Stephenson became the first woman president in 1876. The *Journal of the American Medical Association* (JAMA) was first published in 1883, with Nathan Davis as its editor.

Over the years the AMA would become an authoritative source of medical information for both doctors and the general public. For example, in 1982 the first edition of the *AMA Family Medical Guide* was published. Then in 1984 it provided guidelines for the diagnosis and treatment of cases involving CHILD ABUSE and neglect. Beginning in 1985 the association encouraged more research and studies on AIDS, supported increased funding for AIDS research, and published guidelines for a physician's personal, clinical, and public conduct with respect to AIDS. In 1988 the AMA established an office dealing with AIDS-HIV and a year later recommended that confidential HIV testing be made available for anyone wishing to be tested.

The AMA recognizes that improper ethical behavior may constitute or lead to illegal sexual behavior. For example, its guidelines state, "At a minimum, a physician's ethical duties include terminating the physician-patient relationship before initiating a dating, romantic or sexual relationship with a patient." Clearly, having sexual relations with a patient could lead to a allegations of a sexual offense based on the physician's using his professional status to take advantage of a victim.

The organization also actively lobbies for government policies and laws that it supports. In the summer of 2004, for instance, the association approved a resolution opposing the Food and Drug Administration's policy banning over-the-counter sales of the "morning-after pill" and urging doctors to write advance prescriptions for patients who want to have access to this form of contraception. Plan B, one of these contraceptives, remains unavailable without a prescription except in some pharmacies in California and New Mexico and online; approval for its nonprescription sale was delayed over concerns about its use by minors.

The AMA's litigation center also becomes involved in court cases. In 2002 the center filed an *amicus curiae* (friend of the court) brief in the U.S. Supreme Court case *Scheidler v. National Organization for Women* (2006). The association supported women's right of access to abortion clinics and opposed violence and acts of intimidation against doctors who perform abortions. Although the Supreme Court rejected a jury's finding in the lower court that some organizations opposed to legal abortions violated the Racketeer Influenced and Corrupt Organizations Act of 1970 (RICO), the case was returned to the Court in 2005. The appeal came after an award of more than $250,000 in damages and a nationwide injunction barring the defendants from using violence or the threat of violence against abortion clinics. In 2006 the Supreme Court decided that RICO was not intended to apply to threats or violence against abortion providers.

The AMA is governed by a board of trustees, but the organization's house of delegates is the principal policymaking body. Other affiliated groups include the AMA Foundation, which is its philanthropic branch, and the AMA International, which coordinates the association's long-standing involvement in international health.

Contact: American Medical Association, 515 North State Street, Chicago, IL 60610 (800-621-8335). www.ama.org.

ANNULMENT

Under state law an annulment is a court declaration that a formerly lawful MARRIAGE never existed as far as the law is concerned. A DIVORCE, in contrast, is the legal termination of a marriage that recognizes the fact of the marriage up until a court order of dissolution is entered. The Roman Catholic Church, which considers a marriage to be for life and thus does not recognize a civil divorce for certain purposes—for example, to remarry in the Church—also grants annulments in a process separate from the American legal system. By far the most annulment requests the Church receives come from the United States.

When no-fault divorces were difficult to obtain under state laws, annulments were a more popular option. Although annulment seems today to be an archaic way to deal with the dissolution of a marriage, for some people annulment remains preferable to divorce because of divorce's stigma—that of a failed marriage. It preserves the illusion of "virginity" for women. In addition, annulment may make remarriage easier in some religions, such as the Catholic Church; it helps avoid some states' long residency requirements for a divorce; it may restore benefits lost as a result of the marriage, such as ALIMONY from a former divorce; and it keeps the unwanted marriage essentially a legal secret.

Grounds for Annulment
State laws vary somewhat, but a majority generally set fraud and duress as grounds for annulment. In stricter jurisdictions, the fraud must be related to the "essentials" of marriage, which courts have interpreted as sexual intercourse and procreation. Both fraud and duress are considered to taint the CONSENT that must be freely and knowledgeably given to enter into a valid marriage.

Fraud. Fraud consists of an intentional deception by one spouse of the other, calculated to induce him or her to enter into the marriage. The subject matter of the fraud must be of a substantial nature, and it must have caused the other party to act on it; corroboration by a third party may also be required. The fraud must have occurred before the marriage and must have been discovered afterward. A time limit of several years in which to request an annulment may be required; it usually begins running at the time the fraud is discovered.

Duress. A marriage is voidable and may be annulled under state law if a party was forced into the marriage under duress. This usually means physical force or the threat of such force sufficient to overcome the will of the particular person, not just the average reasonable individual. A "shotgun" wedding because of a PREGNANCY would be the basis for an annulment on the grounds of duress. Some courts have ruled that the mere threat of criminal prosecution may be sufficient to prove duress, but mental distress might be sufficient if it overcomes the party's ability to freely enter the marriage.

Misrepresentation. Misrepresentations that can lead to annulment include deceiving one's potential spouse about the legal age of consent to be married or withholding information about an existing marriage to someone else. Lying about one's ability to have CHILDREN is another. In 1973 a New Jersey court granted an annulment based on the defendant's misrepresentation that he was a practicing Orthodox Jew, holding that the fraudulent misrepresentation meant that the plaintiff could not properly perform her duties as a wife and mother in the manner prescribed by her RELIGION.

Concealment. Another basis for annulment in some states is concealment, such as withholding information from a potential spouse about a serious addiction, a felony conviction, children from another relationship, impotency, or having SEXUALLY TRANSMITTED DISEASES.

Misunderstandings. The fact that one person wants children and the other does not may also constitute a reason for which an annulment is justified. A misunderstanding about children and other issues such as the state in which the couple would reside after marriage were the grounds for the 2004 annulment of the hasty marriage of the celebrity Britney Spears to her childhood sweetheart in Nevada.

Nevada law is more expansive than most other states and allows an annulment if there is a close blood relationship between the parties, insanity or intoxication at the time of the wedding, or any grounds that could be used to void a contract under equity law, as long as the parties were married or lived in Nevada and have not resided together. New York, in contrast, does not allow annulments for failure to consummate the marriage (have sexual intercourse), failure to live together, mistakes, mutual consent, or even if one of the parties is already married. Under New York law a bigamous marriage cannot be annulled because it was always *void ab initio* (not legal from the beginning). However, a court can render a judgment that the marriage is simply void.

Annulments have been granted for failure to consummate a marriage, given that these unions have traditionally served as a basis for procreation and that consent to marriage is taken to mean consent to having sexual relations. In contrast, some judges have been reluctant to annul a marriage that has been consummated because of the traditional notion that the loss of virginity is disadvantageous to a woman.

Effects of an Annulment

When fraud or duress form the basis for annulling a marriage, the marriage is voidable rather than void from the beginning, as in the case of a bigamous marriage. If a defrauded spouse does not wish to have the marriage annulled because of the fraud, the marriage is legal. The legal declaration of an annulment, however, makes the marriage void from the beginning. Under the legal doctrine of "relation back," this means that in addition to the restoration of the spouses' rights and interests, as if the marriage had never happened, the children of the annulled marriage may become illegitimate. Some state statutes have modified this stigmatization of obviously innocent children.

California law requires the following notice in petitions for a legal separation, nullification, or dissolution of a marriage: "Dissolution or annulment of your marriage may automatically cancel your spouse's rights under your will, trust, retirement benefits plan, power of attorney, pay on death bank account, transfer on death vehicle registration, survivorship rights to any property owned in joint tenancy, and any other similar thing . . . [except] rights as beneficiary of your life insurance policy." California urges parties seeking dissolution or annulment to review these and other matters such a credit reports to determine what action should be taken to protect each party's interests.

Usually courts award alimony only in the case of divorce, although some states allow spousal support after an annulment. A Virginia woman who was receiving alimony after a divorce forfeited it on remarrying, but the court held that she had no right to have the alimony reinstated after her second marriage was annulled on the grounds of fraud.

See also BIGAMY; CHILD SUPPORT; ILLEGITIMACY.

SUSAN B. ANTHONY

In San Francisco in 1871—amid hisses and boos from the audience—Susan B. Anthony (1820–1906) spoke out fearlessly: "I declare to you that woman must not depend upon the protection of man, but must be taught to protect herself, and there I take my stand!" Reviled at the beginning of her long campaign for WOMEN'S RIGHTS, including the right to vote, she would be honored later in life by many, including President Theodore Roosevelt at a White House reception on the occasion of her eighty-fourth birthday in 1904. A tireless fighter for the abolition of slavery, education reform, and worker's rights, in addition to EQUAL RIGHTS for women, she died on March 13, 1906,

For much of her life, Susan B. Anthony led the struggle to attain equal rights for women. Her efforts led to the adoption of the Nineteenth Amendment (1920) to the U.S. Constitution, which prohibits the denial or abridgment of the right to vote on account of sex.

fourteen years before ratification of the Nineteenth Amendment (1920) to the U.S. Constitution finally gave women the right to vote.

Susan Brownell Anthony was born on February 15, 1820, in Adams, Massachusetts, into a working-class Quaker family. In the colonial period and during the American Revolution, some women had been able to legally protect their property rights, inherit property in their own name, and manage farms and conduct businesses; a few women property owners had even been extended the right to vote. But after the war, such rights were eroded. State laws developed following the principles laid down in the *Commentaries on the Laws of England* (1765–69) by the English jurist William Blackstone (1723–80), who noted that "the very being or legal existence of the woman is suspended during the marriage, or at least is incorporated and consolidated into that of the husband; under whose wing, protection and cover, she performs every thing."

Her childhood coincided with the presidency of Andrew Jackson from 1829 to 1837, and the ideals of Jacksonian democracy—which emphasized the "self-made man" imbued with natural rights transcending one's class or station—served as a major influence on Anthony as a girl. She became a teacher, but after fifteen years she started to work in the temperance movement to support restrictions on the use of alcoholic beverages; because she was a woman, she was not permitted to speak at temperance rallies.

In 1845 Anthony's family became interested in the abolition movement, whose goal was to abolish slavery, and in 1856 she began working for the American Anti-Slavery Society. Before the end of the Civil War in 1865, many women believed that once the slaves were freed and given equal rights with white Americans, the stage would be set for adoption of the women's rights agenda, including the right to vote. Anthony had already met Elizabeth Cady Stanton (1815–1902), who induced her to join the women's rights movement in 1852. Stanton had helped organize the 1848 Women's Rights Convention in Seneca Falls, New York, which had adopted a resolution demanding the right to vote for women.

In the 1850s Anthony spoke often at teachers' conventions, urging that women be allowed into professions reserved for men and that female teachers be given better pay. She also campaigned during this period for changes in New York state law to accord married women property rights; the state legislature, in large part because of her lobbying efforts, passed the New York State Married Women's Property law in 1860. She also spoke out against PROSTITUTION and promoted equality of rights for women in MARRIAGE and the workplace, in addition to the voting booth.

After the Civil War and the adoption of the Thirteenth (1865), Fourteenth (1868), and Fifteenth (1870) Amendments to the U.S. Constitution, it became obvious that no action would be taken on rights for women. She and other feminists became more militant, and Anthony was arrested in 1872 for voting illegally. At her trial the judge ordered the jury to find her guilty; he fined her $100 but no imprisonment, in order to deny her the opportunity to appeal. She continued to work tirelessly at the grass-roots level for women's suffrage and, with Stanton and others, on the *History of Woman Suffrage* (1881–86). With Stanton, she also helped lead the National American Woman Suffrage Association, organized from other similar groups in 1887; Anthony became president in 1892, when Stanton retired.

The first women in the world to gain voting rights were residents of Wyoming Territory, which in 1869 extended suffrage to its women in order to increase the territory's perceived population as a precursor to statehood. (In 1893 New Zealand became the first nation to follow suit.) One of Anthony's campaigns was to ensure that western territories in which women had been granted the vote, like Wyoming, were not blocked from admission to the Union. Her goal of extending full voting rights to all American women was finally reached in 1920 with the ratification of what became known as the "Susan B. Anthony Amendment." The suffragist was honored later in the century as the first woman featured on a U.S. coin, the Susan B. Anthony dollar.

See also BRADWELL V. ILLINOIS; DISCRIMINATION; FEMINISM.

ART

See CENSORSHIP; NUDITY.

ARTIFICIAL INSEMINATION

See ASSISTED REPRODUCTIVE TECHNOLOGY.

ASHCROFT v.
AMERICAN CIVIL LIBERTIES UNION

See CHILD ONLINE PROTECTION ACT.

ASSISTED REPRODUCTIVE TECHNOLOGY

Since the first "test-tube" baby, LOUISE BROWN, was born in 1978, the use of assisted reproductive technology (ART) has helped overcome problems of infertility and other impediments to conceiving and giving birth. ART, which has been defined by the National Conference of State Legislatures as any fertility treatment in which "pregnancy is attempted through external means," provides ways for infertile heterosexual couples to have children of their own. It is also increasingly used as an option to give single persons and homosexual couples the means to have a genetically related child. In addition to in vitro fertilization (IVF), the process by which Brown was conceived, such treatments include artificial insemination as well as surrogacy, in which a woman gives birth to a baby on behalf of another person or couple.

The most recent information reported by the Centers for Disease Control and Prevention of the U.S. DEPARTMENT OF HEALTH AND HUMAN SERVICES shows that in 2003 the number of live babies born that year from ART procedures was 48,756. About three-fourths of these procedures involved use of fresh eggs from the mother. Fourteen percent used frozen eggs, while 11 percent used donated eggs. In 2006 the CDC estimated that ART births represented just over 1 percent of total U.S. births. The country's more than four hundred ART clinics are most heavily represented in the eastern states.

In the last several decades, while reproductive technology has progressed to provide a greater range of options for overcoming infertility and satisfying the biological urge to reproduce, the law has been struggling to catch up in any consistent way. These new techniques raise novel social, religious, and legal concerns along with some new demands for government regulation, although so far they have not attracted much public demand for government intervention. However, the President's Council on Bioethics called for greater regulation of infertility procedures in its 2004 report *Reproduction and Responsibility: The Regulation of New Biotechnologies.*

The U.S. Supreme Court has not yet ruled on whether there is a constitutional right to use assisted reproductive technology, as it has with regard to CONTRACEPTION and ABORTION. However, the Court has identified a general constitutional right to bear CHILDREN and to rear a family. The law relating to ART has evolved to include less traditional, non-nuclear families. A lower federal court held, in *Lifchez v. Hartigan* (1990), that the right to make decisions about reproduction extends to an infertile couple's right to use ART, such as IVF and donated embryos. If the decision to use contraceptives and thus not to have children is equally applicable to married and unmarried persons, as the Supreme Court held in *Eisenstadt v. Baird* (1972), then it would seem logical that the right to decide to have children should legally be available to married and unmarried persons as well. But to date the law has not reached this definitive conclusion.

In addition to the issues of citizens' constitutional right to have children by ART procedures, a number of other challenging legal issues have arisen. These include the legitimacy of the children produced, the legal rights of egg and sperm donors, the legality of CHILD SUPPORT claims against a husband who consents to the artificial insemination of his wife, inheritance rights of children conceived by artificial insemination but born after the sperm donor dies, the right of prisoners to procreate by artificial insemination during incarceration, and conflicts between an egg-donor mother and a surrogate mother over who is the "mother" for purposes of the birth certificate. Any implication that conceiving by artificial insemination constitutes ADULTERY as grounds for DIVORCE has been almost uniformly rejected by the courts.

Infertility

Many people resort to ART procedures because of infertility, which may stem from genetic defects, SEXUALLY TRANSMITTED DISEASES, physical trauma, or exposure to damaging chemicals. According to Connecticut law relating to health insurance, infertility is "the condition of a presumably healthy individual who is unable to conceive or produce conception, or retain a pregnancy during a one-year period." If the condition persists, it is generally considered sterility, although the medical profession recognizes both temporary and permanent infertility. An estimated 10 percent of all married couples in the United States are sterile, meaning that one or both partners are affected, and an additional 15 percent may be infertile, or unable to conceive for some period of time.

Although infertility can be a problem for females or males, women are more directly affected by state laws regarding infertility and ART; they are by nature involved to a far greater extent than men in the reproductive process, from PREGNANCY to child rearing, and they often feel a greater biological and social pressure to reproduce. The federal government and many states typically promote fertility and child bearing over the personal desires of some citizens to limit the size of families.

Federal Law. Infertility is dealt with primarily under state laws, but the condition is addressed in federal law in a few instances. In the U.S. Code, Title 42, The Public Health and Welfare, the secretary of health and human services, acting through the director of the Centers for Disease Control and Prevention, is authorized to make grants to the states and other public and private entities "regarding any treatable sexually transmitted disease that can cause infertility in women." Under this same title, basic health services are described as including "preventive health services (including . . . infertility services)." The secretary is also authorized by law to make grants and enter into contracts to assist in the establishment and operation of voluntary FAMILY PLANNING projects that include infertility services.

In 2005 Representative Anthony Weiner of New York introduced the Family Building Act, which would require insurance coverage for infertility treatments, as some states (discussed below) now do. If enacted the law would mandate that all group health plans that offer obstetrical benefits include up to four in vitro fertilization attempts. The Employee Income Security Act of 1974 (ERISA), which sets minimum standards for most voluntarily established pension and health plans in private industry, currently exempts self-insured plans from such state-mandated benefits.

In *International Union, UAW v. Johnson Controls, Inc.* (1991), the U.S. Supreme Court ruled unanimously in a DISCRIMINATION case that an employer could not establish a bona fide occupational qualification that might exclude women who would otherwise be qualified for jobs that involve a risk of causing infertility. In this case the company claimed that it was not discriminating against the women, but rather protecting their fetuses from exposure to lead used in the manufacture of batteries. In contrast, in *Saks v. Franklin Covey Co.* (2003), a federal court of appeals held that a female employee was not subjected to unlawful discrimination because her employer's self-insured health plan did not provide infertility treatments, specifically artificial insemination, IVF, and *in utero* insemination. The court ruled that the lack of coverage did not violate any federal law, including Title VII of the Civil Rights Act of 1964, and that her claims under the laws of New York State were precluded by ERISA rules.

State Law. State laws refer to infertility in a number of diverse contexts, including the practice of veterinary medicine. Mississippi, Nebraska, and Texas require that women seeking an ABORTION be informed that, among other things, it may lead to infertility. Virginia law specifies that certain information be provided to patients undergoing treatment for infertility, including "the testing protocol used to ensure that [egg or sperm cell] donors are free from known infection with [HIV]." Ohio and neighboring West Virginia have laws mandating that infertility treatments be included in basic health care services. Thirteen states have laws addressing the coverage of infertility treatments in insurance plans. Connecticut law requires that infertility be ruled out by a court before it determines if STERILIZATION is in a person's best interests; state law also mandates that patients being treated for infertility be provided with timely, relevant, and appropriate information sufficient to allow a patient to make an informed and voluntary choice regarding the disposition of any embryos or embryonic stem cells remaining after an infertility treatment.

Artificial Insemination

Artificial insemination has a long history, beginning with experiments in 1779 by Lazzaro Spallanzani, an Italian priest who proved that male semen is necessary for fertilization. The process became accepted for animal breeding because it made the selection of mates more accurate and conception more efficient. In mammals, including humans, artificial insemination generally involves introducing male sperm cells into the upper part of a female vagina or uterus at an auspicious time. In most mammals, except primates, this time is when the female is in estrus, or heat. For humans, the auspicious time is related to the female menstrual cycle and ovulation.

State laws dealing with artificial insemination vary widely. In all states, men who provide sperm as an unknown donor have no legal responsibilities for any children born as a result. Many state laws legitimize the children born by means of artificial insemination, and a husband's consent to the procedure gives rise to an obligation to support the child. Florida law creates an absolute legal presumption regarding PATERNITY in favor of the husband for any child conceived by "artificial or in vitro insemination" and born to a married couple, if both husband and wife consented in writing to the procedure. Ohio law requires signed, written CONSENT by the husband and wife before "non-spousal artificial insemination" can take place. Children conceived posthumously by artificial insemination may inherit from the donor father if he consented to the procedure and agreed to support the offspring. A federal court, in *Gillet-Netting v. Barnhart* (2004), found that posthumously conceived twins were entitled to participate in Social Security survivors' benefits.

About two-thirds of the states require that sperm donated for insemination be given to a physician or that the procedure be performed by a physician. Georgia law, for example, provides: "Physicians and surgeons licensed to practice medicine . . . shall be the only persons authorized to administer or perform artificial insemination." Anyone else is guilty of a felony.

A major issue under many state laws is whether artificial insemination of an unmarried woman is permitted. Alabama, Connecticut, Missouri, and North Carolina are among a dozen states that lack specific provisions regarding unmarried women. Missouri law, with certain exceptions, provides that with regard to "a child born to a married woman as the result of artificial insemination, [if] the mother was married at the time of either conception or birth, or between conception and birth, the name of the husband shall be entered on the certificate as the father of the child." States including California, Minnesota, New Hampshire, and New Mexico, however, make provision for unmarried women. According to New Hampshire law, in matters relating to the birth certificate, if "the mother is unwed, an affidavit of paternity shall be executed when the donor of the sperm can be identified and is willing to be identified on the birth record or, otherwise, the phrase 'not stated' shall be entered for the father's name."

A related issue concerns the right of lesbians and gays to have children genetically related to them through ART procedures. No state has a law prohibiting the use of artificial insemination for homosexuals; however, except for Massachusetts, a homosexual couple cannot marry under the laws of forty-nine states, thus making it impossible in those states with provisions covering only married women for lesbians to be assured that their rights will be enforced as they are for married women. Even in states that expressly permit unmarried women to conceive by artificial insemination, prejudice against homosexuals may be shown by the physicians who are authorized by the state to perform the procedure.

Lesbians also face the risk that a sperm donor may try to assert his parental rights if state law does not expressly protect the mother. This is especially true in states where the law criminalizes artificial insemination by anyone other than a doctor. A court in Oregon, however, in *McIntyre v. Crouch* (1989), interpreted its donor law to preclude the donor from having any parental rights even if a physician was not involved in the artificial insemination. The Uniform Parentage Act of 1973, which was revised in 2000 and 2002, provides that an unrelated donor of an egg or a sperm

in an ART procedure may not be declared the legal parent, but less than a handful of states, including Texas and Washington, have adopted the act.

PRISONERS are generally denied the right to procreate by artificial insemination. In *Gerber v. Hickman* (2002), a federal appeals court ruled that there is no such right under federal or state law. According to the opinion, prisoners' right to marry, confirmed by the U.S. Supreme Court in *Turner v. Safley* (1987), does not include the right to provide semen for the artificial insemination of a wife, and even though some prisoners may be granted conjugal visits, this policy against allowing artificial insemination is not a violation of the equal protection clause of the U.S Constitution or the Eighth Amendment (1791) prohibition against cruel and unusual punishment.

As far as the assertion of parental rights by sperm donors is concerned, the law has developed in the context of how it has treated UNMARRIED PARENTS and children born out of wedlock. In *Lehr v. Robertson* (1983), the Supreme Court took a major step forward by holding that an out-of-wedlock father must prove "a full commitment to the responsibilities of fatherhood" before his parental rights can be protected by the Constitution. Following this line of reasoning, a lower court in New York, in *Thomas S. v. Robin Y.* (1994), found that the fact that a sperm donor had waited ten years to assert his parental rights and had signed an agreement relinquishing all such rights precluded him from establishing legal paternity. A higher New York court reversed the decision because it determined that the letter of the state law regarding the insemination procedure had not been followed. But in *L.A.L v. D.A.L.* (1998), a Florida court refused to order a paternity test because both its state law, as noted above, and a written agreement precluded a sperm donor from asserting any parental rights.

In Vitro Fertilization

During the process of in vitro fertilization (from the Latin *vitreus,* meaning made of glass), the fertilization of an egg by a sperm cell (conception) takes place in a laboratory vessel and not inside a woman. In the process, an egg is taken from the mother-to-be or an egg donor and fertilized using fresh or frozen sperm from a male donor, who may be a husband, someone known to the woman, or anonymous. The fertilized egg (the embryo) is then inserted into the recipient's uterus to be carried to term.

One problem that has arisen with this technology concerns the legal status of frozen embryos when a couple is divorced. Courts have generally allowed ex-husbands to have them destroyed, because the potential father's desire not to become a parent outweighs the former spouse's interest in using them herself or donating them to childless couples. As with abortion, questions have been raised by the destruction or donation of frozen embryos for uses other than reproduction, such as in STEM-CELL RESEARCH AND CLONING; many pro-life supporters, for example, believe that a human being comes into existence at the moment of conception, whether inside or outside the body, and warrants state protection at that point.

Surrogacy

A surrogate is a substitute, and a surrogate mother is one who carries a baby to term and gives birth to it for another person or couple. The concept came to public notice in 1976, when a wife placed an advertisement in a Berkeley, California, newspaper looking for a woman to have her husband's child. The first surrogate mothers used their own eggs, a procedure known as traditional surrogacy. Later, as technology advanced, surrogate mothers began giving birth to babies who were not genetically related to them, using another woman's eggs; this is called gestational surrogacy. Legal implications of surrogacy arrangements and the rights of the parties involved, as well as of the children born, have been evolving in the states, although not always consistently.

An early, notorious decision by the New Jersey supreme court in *In re Baby M.* (1988), finding surrogacy contracts unenforceable, triggered a cascade of legislation in many states. The *Baby M.* case involved Holocaust survivors who were desperate to reproduce, but the woman feared that a pregnancy might exacerbate her multiple sclerosis. The couple paid a woman $10,000 to give birth to their child after a fertilized egg was implanted in her womb. Following the birth, the surrogate mother refused to give up the baby. A lower court found for the couple, but the decision was reversed on appeal. "We invalidate the surrogacy contract," said the New Jersey supreme court, "because it conflicts with the law and public policy of this State." The court indicated that it found "the payment of money to a 'surrogate' mother illegal, perhaps criminal, and potentially degrading to women."

Shortly after the *Baby M.* decision, most states simply extended bans on baby selling to cover surrogate-mother contracts, although these laws typically did not distinguish between traditional and gestational surrogacy. Since then, however, states have taken various approaches. Kentucky, Michigan, Utah, and Washington are among the states that permit only uncompensated surrogacy. Indiana, Nebraska, and North Dakota do not enforce surrogacy contracts, while Florida, Nevada, New Hampshire, and Virginia permit them with restrictions.

Although a model law called the Uniform Status of Children of Assisted Conception Act was proposed in 1988, it was later abandoned. Today the model law is the Uniform Parentage Act, as revised in 2000 and 2002, which provides rules for determining the parentage of children born by means of ART and pursuant to gestational surrogacy agreements. State legislatures have varied widely in adopting provisions of the model law, and states such as Delaware, North Dakota, and Wyoming ignore it.

State courts thus have often had to deal with surrogacy issues on an ad hoc basis. The California supreme court, in *Johnson v. Calvert* (1993), affirmed that a gestational contract was enforceable. In *In re Adoption of Baby Girl L. J.* (1986), a court in New York upheld a surrogacy contract in part because the adoption was in the child's best interests. In 1998 the *Johnson* decision was extended in *In re Marriage of Buzzanca* to cover the case of surrogacy even where the parents who contracted with the surrogate mother were not biologically linked to the child. A Connecticut court was faced with a complicated case involving a genetic father and his wife who were raising a child produced by a surrogate mother; the court held in *Doe v. Doe* (1998) that, although in a divorce the biological father was presumed by statute to be entitled to custody, this presumption could be rebutted based on a determination of what was in the best interests of the child.

Conflict can also occur when there is a dispute between the gestational surrogate mother and the genetic mother with respect to the embryo. In a California case, *Adoption of C. C.* (1997), a lesbian couple conceived a child by zygote intrafallopian transfer, in which eggs are fertilized and placed in the surrogate mother's fallopian tube rather than through implantation of an embryo in the uterus, the normal IVF procedure. The California court ruled that the woman carrying the child was the legal parent but that the genetic mother, who had furnished the egg, also was a legal parent; thus the birth certificate should list both women as the mother. A court in Colorado came to the same conclusion in a similar case involving a dispute between a lesbian couple and a gestational surrogate mother.

The law is finding its way step by step in dealing with issues involving assisted reproduction. The end sought by these procedures is salutary—giving individuals and couples the opportunity to have a child and raise a family. Only the complicated procedures and relationships involved, as well as the overriding principle of what is in a child's best interests, make it difficult for legislators and judges to agree on a uniform policy for dealing with this new frontier in sexual behavior.

Contact: RESOLVE: National Infertility Association, 7910 Woodmont Avenue, Suite 1350, Bethesda, MD 20814 (301-652-8585). www.resolve.org.

See also AMERICAN FERTILITY ASSOCIATION; BIOETHICS; ILLEGITIMACY; MOTHERHOOD; PATERNITY; REPRODUCTIVE RIGHTS; UNBORN, RIGHTS OF THE.

b

BANNED MATERIALS

See CENSORSHIP.

BARNES v. GLEN THEATRE, INC.

In 1991, the year in which the U.S. Supreme Court decided the case *Barnes v. Glen Theatre, Inc.,* Indiana had a public indecency law broadly prohibiting all public NUDITY. The statute defined nudity as "the showing of the human male or female genitals, pubic area, or buttocks with less than a fully opaque covering, the showing of the female breast with less than a fully opaque covering of any part of the nipple, or the showing of the covered male genitals in a discernibly turgid state."

Two establishments in South Bend, Indiana—the home of Notre Dame University—sued to stop the law's enforcement against them so that their dancers could appear completely nude rather than wear pasties and a G-string. Glen Theatre offered printed materials, movies, and live adult entertainment at a "bookstore" with coin-operated booths. The Kitty Kat Lounge presented "go-go dancing" but wanted to provide nude dancers.

The two venues argued that the law as applied to performances was a violation of the freedom of expression guaranteed by the FIRST AMENDMENT (1791) to the U.S. Constitution. The Supreme Court, however, found 5–4 that the state's traditional police power permitted

regulation of morals, including the banning of nudity, and that the impact on free expression or expressive conduct was merely incidental. In an opinion written by Chief Justice William H. Rehnquist, the Court replied that "the perceived evil that Indiana seeks to address is not erotic dancing, but public nudity."

Although the First Amendment does not cite freedom of expression in those words, the Supreme Court has dealt with a number of cases involving symbolic speech and expressive conduct encompassed in the stated rights of free speech, a free press, freedom to worship, and freedom to assemble and petetition the government for a redress of grievances. Whether a particular form of expression—flag burning or organizing sit-ins to protest government policies, for example, or even nude dancing—is protected has been a matter of legal interpretation.

In deciding *Barnes,* the chief justice referred to *Paris Adult Theatre I v. Slaton* (1973), in which the state police power to provide for "the public health, safety, and morals" was upheld as a basis for legislation. Then, addressing the proposition that the law is often based on moral choices, he referred to *Bowers v. Hardwick* (1986), which had upheld a state law criminalizing consensual homosexual sodomy *(Bowers* would be overruled by LAWRENCE V. TEXAS in 2003 when the Court decriminalized adult consensual homosexual sex in the privacy of one's own home.)

The *Barnes* opinion then noted that in *United States v. O'Brien* (1968), the Supreme Court had upheld a law making draft-card burning illegal. Chief Justice Rehnquist concluded that not all expressive conduct must be protected as free speech. The *O'Brien* decision had set forth certain criteria for laws that impinged on expressive conduct: the government must demonstrate that it has a valid interest in prohibiting the conduct, such interest must be unrelated to the suppression of free speech, and the restrictions must be "no greater than is essential" to the furtherance of the government's interest.

The Court then found that Indiana's interest in protecting public morals was both valid and unrelated to the suppression of free expression. Because the statute contested in *Barnes* met all of the above criteria, the chief justice reasoned that its requirement "that the dancers wear at least pasties and G-strings is modest, and the bare minimum necessary to achieve the State's purpose." The Indiana law thus survived the Supreme Court's test for constitutionality given that it was broadly drawn to address all forms of public nudity and not just nude dancing.

The opinion also distinguished the Indiana law from that in *Schad v. Borough of Mount Ephraim* (1981), a case in which the Court had ruled that barroom-type nude dancing had some claim to First Amendment protection. In *Schad* the law had banned nudity in all live performances and thus inappropriately singled out protected expressive conduct (a distinction that may be lost on the average citizen).

Associate Justice Antonin Scalia, in a circuitous concurring opinion, declared that Indiana could regulate conduct but not necessarily expression; therefore, those who wished to express themselves by conduct should choose only conduct that was not otherwise proscribed. In his concurring opinion, Associate Justice David H. Souter focused on the state's argument that the law sought to minimize the secondary effects of nude dancing—PROSTITUTION, SEXUAL ASSAULT, and related crimes—and that such valid objectives rendered the law constitutional. In a dissent in which three other justices joined, Associate Justice Byron R. White noted that nudity itself was a key element in the performers' dance. He added that "it cannot be said

that the statutory prohibition is unrelated to expressive conduct."

Obviously the Supreme Court was still some distance away from an understanding of how OBSCENITY and the First Amendment should interact. The Court continued to shift ground to include greater constitutional protection for sexual expression and sexual behavior in later cases. However, in *City of Erie v. Pap's A.M.* (2000), it again upheld the regulation of nude dancing without reaching a clear consensus on exactly where to draw the line on such expressive behavior.

See also INDECENT EXPOSURE; SEXUALLY ORIENTED BUSINESSES.

BASTARDS

See ILLEGITIMACY; UNMARRIED PARENTS.

BATTERED-WOMEN'S SYNDROME

See DOMESTIC VIOLENCE.

BESTIALITY

"If a man lies with a beast," says the Bible, "he shall be put to death; and you shall kill the beast. If a woman approaches any beast and lies with it, you shall kill the woman and the beast." Bestiality, also called zoophilia, is a psychological condition in which one's preferred method of sexual arousal and gratification is with animals; some limit the term to copulation between a human and an animal of the opposite sex. Bestiality has also been linked with SODOMY (nonreproductive human-to-human sexual activity) under the rubric "crimes against nature," and both have been known as buggery. At common law (the generally unwritten case law of England that became a part of American law at the time the United States was formed), bestiality was considered a form of sodomy. Many early American laws against sodomy made "the abominable crime against nature with man or beast" a criminal offense.

To a large extent, *bestiality* is an old-fashioned term for sexual perversions of various kinds. The U.S. Code under Title 18, Crimes, section 2423, Transportation of Minors (since amended), once defined "prohibited sexual conduct" of minors to include "(A) sexual intercourse, including genital-genital, oral-genital, anal-genital, or oral-anal, whether between persons of the same or opposite sex; [and] (B) bestiality." The current language simply proscribes the transportation across state lines of individuals under the age of eighteen years to engage in sexual activity or PROSTITUTION.

Many states—including Alabama, Alaska, Florida, Hawaii, Illinois, Iowa, Maine, Nevada, New Jersey, Ohio, Tennessee, and Vermont—do not have statutes expressly prohibiting bestiality, but some state laws still proscribe it. For example, the Delaware code, title 11, Crimes and Criminal Procedure, section 777, Bestiality, provides: "A person is guilty of bestiality when the person intentionally engages in any sexual act involving sexual contact, penetration or intercourse with the genitalia of an animal or intentionally causes another person to engage in any such sexual contact with an animal for purposes of sexual gratification." The crime is a felony under Delaware law, as is, under section 1103, permitting or promoting an exhibition of a child engaging in any act of bestiality or simulation of such an act. In Kansas oral or anal copulation between a person and an animal is a misdemeanor, along with the knowing exhibition or display of such an actual or simulated contact. The District of Columbia makes it a felony "for a person to take into that person's mouth or anus the sexual organ of an animal or to place that person's sexual organ in the mouth or anus of an animal."

In Michigan, whose 1902 statute characterizes as a felon anyone who commits "the abominable and detestable crime against nature with any animal," a court held in *People v. Carrier* (1977) that the crime of bestiality encompasses a broader range of acts than sodomy between two humans and includes a sexual connection between a human and an animal. A court in Minnesota, which has a statute prohibiting carnal knowledge of an animal or a bird, noted in *State v. Bonynge* (1990) that the general language of sodomy statutes has been interpreted to encompass all sexual contact between a human and an animal.

Whether originally prohibited because sexual congress with anything other than another human being is nonreproductive sexual behavior or because the act carries religious or moral concerns, bestiality may still be treated as a crime and punished under laws in the United States. Human sodomy between consenting adults in private was found by the U.S. Supreme Court in *LAWRENCE V. TEXAS* (2003) to be protected under the U.S. Constitution.

BIGAMY

In 2005 a man who had married a woman in Virginia while still married to a woman in Utah was charged with bigamy (MARRIAGE to more than one person at a time), which is a felony that carries a minimum two-year prison sentence. The Virginia wife learned of the other marriage while checking with the Internal Revenue Service about a delay in receiving a refund due under a joint tax return that had been sent to the other wife. The Virginia wife then discovered on the INTERNET that her husband was looking for other women to date. It soon came to light that he had been married to five other women and did not obtain a DIVORCE for three of those marriages.

According to legal theory, marriage is a contract and the government is always a party to any marriage contract. This is because it has important interests in the consequences of sexual behavior, the most significant of which involve CHILDREN. The government, therefore, can regulate the legality of the institution of marriage. Laws regarding marriage are primarily within the purview of the states, not the federal government. As the Oklahoma court of appeals pointed out in *Hendricks v. Hendricks* (1998), "Marriage and divorce are creatures of statute with the State having exclusive control over the establishment, maintenance and termination of the marital relationship."

In addition to prescribing the conditions of a legal marriage—the age of CONSENT, need for a license, and blood tests, among others—government can also prohibit certain types of marriage. In several cases, including *Reynolds v. United States* (1879), the U.S. Supreme Court made it clear that POLYGAMY (multiple marriage, of which bigamy is one form) was illegal and not protected by the establishment of RELIGION clause in the FIRST AMENDMENT (1791) to the U.S. Constitution. Some states had enacted laws banning interracial marriage before the Supreme Court's decision in *Loving v. Virginia* (1967) overturned them. Recently twenty states have adopted constitutional amendments prohibiting SAME-SEX MARRIAGE, and most other states have at least statutory provisions banning marriage between two men or two women.

Some of the arguments against bigamy often sound like those used against same-sex marriage: that the monogamous heterosexual family unit is the basic structure of the state, that it ensures the proper support and development of children, that it minimizes the spread of SEXUALLY TRANSMITTED DISEASES, and that it is the product of lengthy Western culture and the Jewish and Christian religions. Both the Muslim and Hindu religions, however, permit bigamy and polygamy.

Bigamy is a crime in all states and the District of Columbia, with little variation among these laws. Although it is generally a serious crime punished as a felony, bigamy is often not prosecuted unless it also involves an intent to defraud or some other felony. The Model Penal Code (1962) recommended that bigamy be considered a misdemeanor.

New York State's code, article 255, Offenses Affecting the Marital Relationship (which includes "unlawful solemnizing a marriage," "unlawful procuring a marriage license," and "incest") provides: "A person is guilty of bigamy when he contracts or purports to contract a marriage with another person at a time when he has a living spouse, or the other person has a living spouse.... In any prosecution for

At the turn of the twentieth century, "dime novels" (some of which cost 25 cents) entertained a reading public looking for romance and escape. A titillating contest between vice and virtue, *The King of Bigamists* was one title that captured attention with a melodramatic threat to the traditional institution of monogamous marriage.

... bigamy ... , it is an affirmative defense that the defendant acted under a reasonable belief that both he and the other person to the marriage or prospective marriage or to the sexual intercourse, as the case may be, were unmarried." The law in Utah states: "A person is guilty of bigamy when, knowing he has a husband or wife or knowing the other person has a husband or wife, the person purports to marry another person or cohabits with another person." Virginia similarly defines the crime of bigamy, specifying that the "[v]enue for a violation of [the bigamy statute] may be in the county or city where the subsequent marriage occurred or where the parties to the subsequent marriage cohabited."

Some states have "Enoch Arden statutes" that permit a spouse to remarry without any criminal penalty after about five years—based on a good-faith belief that a spouse is dead after disappearing. This protects the remarried spouse should the presumably deceased husband or wife reappear. Enoch Arden was a character in a poem by the English poet Alfred Lord Tennyson (1809–92) who is presumed dead but returns to find that his wife has remarried.

The legal presumption is that a couple's most recent marriage is valid, leaving the burden of proof in bigamy cases on the party asserting that a valid earlier marriage is still in existence. This is especially true if the second marriage is of long duration and has produced children. A federal district court held in 1983, for example, that where the widow of a spouse to whom she had been married for thirteen years and with whom she had a child contests a wife from an earlier marriage over annuity benefits from the deceased spouse's employment, the presumption that the most recent marriage is valid defeats the earlier wife's claim.

Associate Justice Antonin Scalia has suggested that a recent Supreme Court decision might open the floodgates against state laws banning bigamy as well as same-sex marriage and other laws criminalizing sexual behavior. This forecast in a dissent was designed to raise an outcry against potential negative outcomes unleashed by the majority opinion in LAWRENCE v. TEXAS (2003), which cited an individual's constitutional right of privacy to strike down a state law criminalizing consensual adult homosexual relations in the privacy of one's home. Post-*Lawrence*, several cases have been filed in state and federal courts challenging laws against both bigamy and polygamy, although to date none has risen to the level of a Supreme Court review of these laws. However, in *State v. Holm* (2006), the Utah supreme court, in confirming a conviction under the state's bigamy statute, dismissed the argument that the seemingly sweeping language of the *Lawrence* opinion had any effect on bigamy laws. The court said that these laws protect the institution of marriage and that in *Lawrence* the Supreme Court had expressly noted that its ruling did not protect conduct that causes "injury to a person or abuse of an institution the law protects."

BIOETHICS

Bioethics is the systematic study of the moral dimensions of the life sciences and health care, including medicine, biology, physiology, and psychology. The term (from the Greek words for life and ETHICS) was coined in 1970 by Van Rensselaer Potter (1911–2001), a biochemist at the McArdle Laboratory for Cancer Research, University of Wisconsin. The field grew out of the horrors of human experimentation conducted under the Nazi regime in Germany during World War II. Today many aspects of scientific research and medicine depend on testing of humans, raising a need for guidelines for scientists and doctors in order to protect against the unethical lapses of the Nazi era.

Informed consent, confidentiality, privacy, and respect for human life and dignity are some of the important rights that must be observed in the process of testing new products and procedures on humans. Bioethicists become involved in the formulation of proposed legislation. In addition, they provide scientific and ethical advice to legislatures on the subject matter of proposed laws related to sexual behavior, to administrators who execute such laws, and to judges and juries who apply them. The President's Council on Bioethics (discussed below) assists the PRESIDENT in making policy decisions on relevant matters such as stem-cell research and cloning.

Reputable scientists and doctors have voluntarily drawn a fairly bright bioethical line, which has to some extent been codified into laws that protect citizens from immoral and unethical practices related to modern biotechnology research and practices. Questions that bioethicists, politicians, and the public wrestle with include whether doctors and scientists working to save lives and prevent suffering should be hindered in their mission in any way? Should people who would benefit from their efforts be denied the freedom from disease or disability by what may be arbitrary, archaic, and illogical practices or laws?

"We need to realize that there is more at stake in the biological revolution than just saving life or avoiding death and suffering," suggested Leon Kass, chairman of the President's Council on Bioethics, in 2002. "We must also strive to protect and preserve human dignity and the ideas and practices that keep us human." Public debate continues about how much religious and moral input is necessary to determine precisely, for example, when a human life begins or whether such a determination is even possible or desirable in every biotechnological and medical context. As in the case of the asserted RIGHTS OF THE UNBORN, many people are eager to act on behalf of those who cannot speak for themselves.

Bioethical Issues

One major area of bioethical concern centers on reproduction, especially in relation to ASSISTED REPRODUCTIVE TECHNOLOGY and the rapidly developing field of stem-cell research and cloning. However, the discipline of bioethics has implications for many areas related to sexual behavior: ABORTION, ABSTINENCE, adolescent behavior, AIDS-HIV and other SEXUALLY TRANSMITTED DISEASES, CHILD ABUSE, circumcision of males and females, CONSENT for medical research, CONTRACEPTION, DOMESTIC VIOLENCE, DNA testing, DRUGS, eugenics, FAMILY PLANNING and population control, fertility and infertility, fetal treatment, GENDER identity and associated disorders, GENETICS, HOMOSEXUALITY, MARRIAGE, MOTHERHOOD, PREGNANCY, PRIVACY, treatment of PRISONERS, PROSTITUTION, REPRODUCTIVE RIGHTS, SEX EDUCATION, sex therapy and research, SEXUAL ENHANCEMENT, STEM-CELL RESEARCH AND CLONING, and WOMEN'S RIGHTS. A sample of some of the ethical questions raised by these issues follows.

Abortion. When does life begin? Is abortion an ethical method of family planning, or does it destroy viable human life?

AIDS-HIV. Are methods of disease prevention such as distribution of condoms and clean needles for drug users ethical? Should students be taught how to avoid catching the disease? How can the privacy of sufferers be preserved? Should medical personnel be forced to treat victims?

Circumcision. Is male circumcision a valuable or healthful practice irrespective of its religious basis? Should female circumcision be accepted because it is rooted in the cultural traditions of some religious or ethnic communities? Should victims of female genital mutilation be awarded political asylum?

Cloning. What are the ethical implications of cloning humans? Is it ethical to clone just body parts?

Contraception. Does contraception interfere with a grand plan for human life? Should it be restricted to married couples, or not allowed at all? Does its availability encourage sexual activity by unmarried persons?

DNA Testing. Should suspects or prisoners be forced to give DNA samples? Should results of private DNA testing be made available to employers, insurance companies, and others with power to affect a person's rights?

Drugs. Is it ethical for pharmacists to refuse to fill a prescription on moral or religious grounds?

Infertility. Is assisted reproductive technology such as artificial insemination, in vitro fertilization, and surrogate motherhood an ethical way of aiding persons who wish to have and rear children? Or are such techniques unnatural and thus immoral?

Gender. Should all laws be gender neutral, or are there times when discrimination on the basis of gender is acceptable? Is it ethical to want to change one's biological gender?

Homosexuality. Is this a genetic condition or a lifestyle choice? Can it be immoral? Should homosexuals, bisexuals, and transsexuals enjoy the full rights of other citizens?

Medical Procedures. Do doctors have an ethical obligation to advise patients of all possible risks from medical procedures? Who has rights to a person's tissue samples after they have been removed from the body, and should anyone profit from their use?

Pregnancy. Should an expectant mother be punished and incarcerated for misusing alcohol or drugs during pregnancy, thereby potentially harming her fetus? Is testing to determine such use ethical?

Stem-Cell Research. Is it ethical to use embryos discarded from infertility treatments to advance medical science and save or improve other lives? Should new lines of cells be created?

Unborn, Rights of the. Do fetuses not yet viable have rights, and, if so, what are they?

Like RELIGION, ethics and bioethics are concerned with private rules of behavior, although many religious adherents and ethicists attempt to codify such rules into law. In themselves they are not legally enforceable except to the extent that lawmakers, executive branch officials, and judges use them to make decisions about the law. For example, some bioethicists may assert that performing an abortion is an unethical practice of medicine; yet abortion is not illegal, even though Congress and many state legislatures have greatly circumscribed the constitutional right of abortion by enacting onerous requirements and denying public funding for abortions for women who cannot afford them.

Major questions remain: How are ethical and bioethical determinations arrived at? By peer-group agreement, popular majority, consensus of religious and moral leaders, or ad hoc, by those actually involved in the activity under scrutiny? In a secular society of culturally, religiously, and morally diverse citizens, from where does the authority emanate for setting ethical, as opposed to legal, standards that may nevertheless have legal implications?

President's Council on Bioethics

A National Bioethics Advisory Commission created by President Bill Clinton in 1995 expired on October 3, 2001. The next month, on November 28, 2001, President George W. Bush established the President's Council on Bioethics by Executive Order 13237. The move came several months after he had advised the nation that he was limiting federal funding for stem-cell research, citing ethical grounds related to his belief that human life begins at conception and that thereafter the fertilized cells that develop into a fetus and later into a human baby are entitled to the same legal protection as any viable human.

The council's mission is to "advise the President on bioethical issues that may emerge as a consequence of advances in biomedical science and technology." Its responsibilities include "to undertake fundamental inquiry into the human and moral significance of developments in biomedical and behavioral science and technology; to explore specific ethical and policy questions related to these developments; to provide a forum for a national discussion of bioethical issues; to facilitate a greater understanding of bioethical issues; and to explore possibilities for useful international collaboration on bioethical issues." The council is authorized to "study ethical issues connected with … embryo and stem cell research, assisted reproduction, cloning, uses of knowledge and techniques derived from human genetics. … In establishing priorities … [it] shall consider the urgency and gravity of the particular issue; [and] the need for policy guidance and public education on the particular issue."

The council may request information from the heads of federal agencies and hold hearings. It has issued several reports, including ones on alternative sources of human stem cells and the regulation of new biotechnologies entitled *Reproduction and Responsibility: Monitoring Stem Cell Research* and *Human Cloning and Human Dignity: An Ethical Inquiry.* A 2004 report specifically called for a ban on the creation of human embryos from cells obtained from a human fetus.

Membership in the council is limited to eighteen persons appointed for two-year terms by the president, who also designates its chairperson. No member may be an officer or an employee of the federal government; members are compensated for their work. The U.S. DEPARTMENT OF HEALTH AND HUMAN SERVICES provides administrative support to the council, which was to terminate after two years but was extended by the president in 2003 and again in 2005.

Predecessor organizations include the National Commission for the Protection of Human Subjects of Biomedical and Behavioral Research (1974–78), President's Commission for the Study of Ethical Problems in Medicine and Biomedical and Behavioral Research (1980–83), and Human Embryo Research Panel of the National Institutes of Health, formed in 1994. Similar bodies in other countries include the Ethics Office of the Canadian Institutes of Health, French National Consultative Committee for Health and Life Sciences, and German National Ethics Commission.

Federal Law

Even in areas of bioethics where there is general consensus, translating an approach into law is not always easy. Although there has been general agreement that cloning human beings is unethical, for instance, CONGRESS has failed to pass the Human Cloning Prohibition Act (2005). A form of the law, which would ban human cloning, has been introduced in Congress several times in the past without success.

In other cases, policymakers have rushed to judgment on bioethical issues. Before naming his own bioethics council, and despite objections from many members of the scientific and medical communities, in 2001 President Bush limited federal funding for stem-cell research; he approved work only on existing lines of stem cells (twenty-two eligible lines) rather than allowing researchers to use new supplies of stem cells. (Stem cells are undifferentiated embryonic cells that, if implanted in a womb, could produce a child.) However, stem-cell research using cells other than those authorized by the president has proceeded with private and state funding.

The only significant U.S. Supreme Court decision in which bioethics has played a role is *Washington v. Glucksberg* (1997), which involved a state law making the promotion of a suicide attempt a felony. The Court found that the law prohibiting anyone from "causing" or "aiding" a suicide did not violate the due process clause of the U.S. Constitution. Both the majority opinion and a concurring opinion by Associate Justice John Paul Stevens referred to briefs submitted by bioethicists to aid the Court's decision making.

State Law

Some states have laws regarding bioethics as well as institutions such as bioethical boards that set guidelines for procedures from assisted reproductive techniques to abortion, stem-cell research, and cloning. California, a leader in the field of biomedical and biotechnology research, requires doctors and other health care providers to provide information to individuals regarding the disposition "of any human embryos remaining following [a] fertility treatment." The options available under state law include "storing [them], donating them to another individual, discarding the embryos, or donating the remaining embryos for research." Florida civil rights law regarding health care directives (instructions regarding medical procedures in the event an individual becomes incapable of making informed decisions) provides in some situations for a proxy, selected by the health care provider's bioethics committee, to make decisions on behalf of an incapacitated person.

Case law in this new area is sparse, but some decisions deal with the use of health care providers' bioethics committees when a conflict arises over instructions related to medical procedures, such as removing a patient from life-support systems. In *In re Martin* (1993), which involved a dispute between the guardian of a legally incapacitated person and family members over withdrawal of medical support, a Massachusetts court of appeals remanded the case for additional findings; it noted the role of the hospital's bioethics committee "for the purpose of determining whether [the patient's] life-sustaining medical treatment should be withdrawn."

Although private enterprise is not limited by federal ethics concerns if no federal funding is involved, the chilling effect on research caused by reduced government funding and public pressure created by government officials is obvious. Technological advances in other countries where the ethical and moral issues are not as restrictive may have a negative long-term impact on America's global leadership in science, technology, and medicine. Also to be considered is the prolongation of pain and suffering by millions of persons in the absence of progressive research and treatment.

BIRTH CONTROL

See CONTRACEPTION; FAMILY PLANNING; REPRODUCTIVE RIGHTS.

BISEXUALITY

A bisexual person is sexually attracted to members of his or her own sex as well as to those of the opposite sex. Many bisexuals consider themselves homosexuals or at least allied with the homosexual cause for EQUAL RIGHTS and freedom from DISCRIMINATION. In the abbreviation GLBT referring to sexual minorities, the *B* signifies bisexuals. The term *bisexual* may also refer to a person known as a hermaphrodite who has the reproductive organs of both sexes (now usually called an intersexual person).

As acknowledged by a federal court in *Underwood v. Archer Management Services, Inc.* (1994), the term *sexual orientation* is generally considered to include heterosexuality, homosexuality, and bisexuality. Bisexual behavior, historically less stigmatized than purely homosexual behavior, has not been as definitively dealt with by the law as HOMOSEXUALITY, TRANSSEXUALISM, or TRANSVESTISM. For the most part, aspects of the law applied to homosexuals are transferred to any homosexual sexual behavior of bisexuals.

The expression of socially and legally acceptable bisexuality has been documented throughout history in many cultures and countries, including ancient Greece and Rome, some Arab countries, and China and Japan. The young Greek who conquered the known world in the fourth century B.C., Alexander the Great (356–323 B.C.E.), had many wives and also a male lover. In the ancient Greek city-state of Sparta around the same time, a young soldier was required to have a sexual relationship with an older, even married, warrior as a way to instill devotion and heroism in battle.

Like other sexual minorities in America, bisexuals have been discriminated against by laws and law enforcement officers, as well as by private citizens. Literature and art catering to them have been censored, and they have been excluded from MILITARY service, barred from government employment, denigrated in educational settings, prevented from adopting CHILDREN or retaining custody of their own offspring, kept from having intimate relationships recognized under the law, or stopped from immigrating to the United States or obtaining citizenship. In 1998 President Bill Clinton issued an executive order prohibiting discrimination against homosexuals in the federal government, and a number of states have revoked laws that discriminated against sexual minorities. But the nation as a whole remains sharply split on whether sexual differences are hard-wired or only lifestyle choices or the extent to which sexual minorities should be extended the same rights as heterosexuals in all arenas of life.

Studies such as *Sexual Behavior in the Human Male* (1948) and *Sexual Behavior in the Human Female* (1953) by ALFRED KINSEY indicate that a majority of people may be bisexual to some extent. The actual number is of course difficult to determine—as President Jimmy Carter once implied, it is one thing to lust in one's heart and yet another to act on that feeling. A further difficulty in categorizing men or women as bisexual arises from how one views the range of human sexuality. Is it divisible into discrete types? Or does each individual's orientation lie on a continuum from total heterosexuality at one end to total homosexuality at the other? Bisexuality may appear in youth and never be expressed again later in life. Some homosexuals have suggested that bisexuals may simply be homosexuals who have not fully come to terms with their sexuality, as summed up in the slogan, "bi now, gay later."

Federal Law

Several attempts have been made to use Title VII of the Civil Rights Act of 1964 to redress bisexual discrimination or harassment in the workplace. In this context, bisexual behavior may refer to an individual's attraction to members of both sexes or to an individual's discrimination against members of both sexes. Under Title VII it is an "unlawful employment practice for an employer ... to discriminate against any individual ... because of such individual's ... sex." The obvious wrong that this law was intended to address is discrimination against women by male employers who either treat them less favorably than male employees or who harass them and thus make it more difficult for them to do their work.

In *Meritor Savings Bank v. Vinson* (1986), the U.S. Supreme Court found that "when a supervisor sexually harasses a subordinate because of the subordinate's sex, that supervisor discriminates on the basis of sex" and therefore is guilty under the language of Title VII. But a lower federal court, in *Barnes v. Costle* (1977), had distinguished as outside the scope of Title VII "the case of the bisexual superior [whose] insistence upon sexual favors would not constitute gender discrimination because it would apply to male and female employees alike."

Clearly the *Barnes* decision illustrates a strict constructionist view of the law. Here the court looked to the intent of Title VII's language and found that the purpose was to remedy the disparity between men and women in the workplace and not to generally redress all forms of discrimination there. Using this rationale, if a bisexual employer harassed both male and female employees, Title VII would simply not be applicable. The fact that a supervisor would be guilty under the law if he or she harassed only employees of the opposite sex—but not guilty of harassing employees of both sexes—seems illogical and unjust. The ironic argument has been made that a heterosexual supervisor who wanted only to harass employees of the opposite sex might do so with impunity so long as he or she also harasses some employees of the same sex.

There may be some support for a more expansive reading of Title VII's reach in the reasoning of the Supreme Court in *Olmstead v. Zimring* (1999), a case that did not involve sexual behavior. The Court found that with respect to the Americans with Disabilities Act (1990), CONGRESS had a broader view of prohibited discrimination against disabled persons than was encompassed in a literal reading of the law. Using the same logic, any type of harassment based on sex or sexual orientation might constitute illegal discrimination under Title VII.

But in *Holman v. Indiana* (2000), a case more directly on point, the U.S. Court of Appeals for the Seventh Circuit affirmed a lower court's dismissal of a case involving blatant sexual harassment of a married couple by their supervisor. The court held that because discrimination under Title VII is to be determined on a "gender-comparative basis" (behavior to which the other sex is not exposed), "inappropriate conduct that is inflicted on both sexes, or is inflicted regardless of sex, is outside the statute's ambit. Title VII does not cover the 'equal opportunity' or 'bisexual' harasser, then, because such a person is not *discriminating* on the basis of sex. He is not treating one sex better (or worse) than the other; he is treating both sexes the same (albeit, badly)." As this case illustrates, the term *bisexual* may refer to an individual or a pattern of behavior directed against persons not of the same sex. This dual aspect of the term makes it difficult to put *bisexual* into a precise category when analyzing laws against discrimination on the basis of sexual orientation.

State Law

The waters are even muddier in state law. Only about nineteen states—including Alaska, Hawaii, Montana, and Texas—have a constitutional provision addressing sex discrimination. The New Hampshire constitution, for one, states in its bill of rights, "Equality of rights under the law shall not be denied or abridged by this state on account of race, creed, sex or national origin." In about half the states—including Arizona, Idaho, Missouri, Oklahoma, and Wisconsin—sexual discrimination is barred by law. And six states—Alabama, Iowa, Minnesota, Mississippi, Nevada, and North Carolina—have no provisions against discrimination on the basis of sex.

Just as the federal courts have been grappling with the issue of discrimination against bisexuals, state courts have had to interpret their constitutional and statutory rules to determine if they apply to individual situations in which bisexuals, as well as other sexual minorities, are involved. In *Equifax Services, Inc. v. Cohen* (1980), the supreme court of Maine held that a provision of the state's fair credit reporting act prohibiting the inclusion of a consumer's race, religion, and sexual orientation infringed a business's constitutional right to commercial speech. However, a California court, in *Kovatch v. California Casualty Management Co.* (1998), found that harassment based on sexual orientation that rises to the level of outrageous behavior may be grounds for a suit for the intentional infliction of emotional distress.

The level of scrutiny that state courts will bring to gender-classification laws (ones that grant or deny rights based on GENDER) bears on the degree to which those courts will go to expand or narrow such rights for heterosexual men and women and sexual minorities. In *Hewitt v. State Accident Insurance Fund Corp.* (1982), the supreme court of Oregon said that the suspicion that a gender classification may be unconstitutional can be overcome if it is based on specific biological differences between men and women but not if based on "other personal characteristics or social roles assigned to men and women because of their gender and for no other reason." Oregon's constitution states, "No law shall be passed granting to any citizen or class of citizens privileges, or immunities, which, upon the same terms, shall not equally belong to all citizens." Strictly followed, this provision would mean that bisexuals—like homosexuals, transsexuals, transvestites, and others whose sexuality or gender is beyond an individual's control—should not form a constitutionally acceptable category of discrimination.

See also SEXUAL HARASSMENT.

A BOOK NAMED "JOHN CLELAND'S MEMOIRS OF A WOMAN OF PLEASURE" v. ATTORNEY GENERAL OF THE COMMONWEALTH OF MASSACHUSETTS

The battle between advocates of free expression and citizens opposed to indecency that would rage throughout the SEXUAL REVOLUTION in the late 1960s and early 1970s was just getting up a head of steam in 1966.

That was the year in which the U.S. Supreme Court rendered its decision in the case *A Book Named "John Cleland's Memoirs of a Woman of Pleasure" v. Attorney General of the Commonwealth of Massachusetts*, whose subject was an eighteenth-century British novel purporting to be the memoirs of a former prostitute named Fanny Hill. Two years earlier the Illinois supreme court had overturned the conviction of the comedian LENNY BRUCE for using obscene language; it based its judgment on the Supreme Court's decision in *JACOBELLIS V. OHIO* (1964), in which the Court had broadly defined community standards for judging OBSCENITY. In 1965 numerous antipornography groups demonstrated against free sexual expression. The next year the Court in "*Memoirs*" declared that this erotic novel (1748), first published in the United States by G. P. Putnam's Sons in 1963, was not obscene and thus deserved FIRST AMENDMENT protection from CENSORSHIP or any criminal penalty for selling or distributing it.

Defining Obscenity

Nine years earlier, in *ROTH V. UNITED STATES* (1957), the Supreme Court had for the first time spelled out how it would judge what was and was not obscene. The *Roth* test for obscenity required that the dominant theme of a work as a whole must appeal to the PRURIENT INTEREST; be patently offensive because it goes beyond contemporary community standards; and be "utterly without redeeming social importance." Because the justices had already held that obscenity was not protected by the First Amendment (1791) to the U.S. Constitution, Roth's conviction for sending obscene material through the mail was not reversed. The decision nonetheless narrowed the definition of obscenity to avoid constraining the rights of free speech and freedom of the press protected by the amendment.

Then in *GINZBURG V. UNITED STATES* (1966), a five-member majority of the Court agreed that in "close" cases, the scales would be tipped toward a finding of obscenity if a seller of questionable material pandered or exploited the weaknesses of his audience, thus demonstrating an attempt to appeal to their prurient interest. Here the Court was looking beyond the nature

John Cleland's eighteenth-century *Memoirs of a Woman of Pleasure* (1748), also known as *Fanny Hill,* was the object of censorship in the United States before the book was cleared of obscenity charges in 1966. To set the scene for a 1769 farcical British cartoon, an open copy of the ribald book was shown on the floor near the bed.

of the material itself to how it was being distributed. On the same day that the Court upheld Ralph Ginzburg's obscenity conviction, it also let stand another obscenity conviction in *Mishkin v. New York* (1966) by applying the PANDERING test. The new logic of those two decisions, however, would come apart when the Court dealt with *Fanny Hill* on the same day.

In 1930 Massachusetts had found Theodore Dreiser's *An American Tragedy* (1925) and D. H. Lawrence's *Lady Chatterley's Lover* (1928) to be obscene. In 1933, however, a federal district court reversed an obscenity conviction for selling James Joyce's *Ulysses* (1922) on the grounds that the book had to be considered as a whole—an approach later adopted by the Supreme Court in *Roth*—and not merely censored because of

selected passages. Then, in 1966, the U.S. Supreme Court was asked to uphold a finding under Massachusetts law that *Memoirs of a Woman of Pleasure,* written by John Cleland (1710–89) and more popularly known as *Fanny Hill,* was obscene. The case had been brought by the commonwealth's attorney general against the book itself, not against any person.

Redeeming Social Importance

Associate Justice William J. Brennan Jr. delivered the Court's opinion. The obscenity case, as he described it, arose out of a civil equity suit brought by the attorney general under Massachusetts law to have the book declared obscene. "Thus the sole question before the state courts was whether *Memoirs* satisfies the test of obscenity established in *Roth v. United States.*" The opinion then dismissed the finding by the Massachusetts supreme judicial court that *Memoirs* was obscene under the *Roth* tests: whether to the average person, applying community standards, the dominant theme of the material taken as a whole appealed to the prurient interest. The opinion focused on the Massachusetts court's misinterpretation of the "redeeming social value" requirement in the *Roth* opinion.

Because a book cannot be proscribed or banned unless it is *"utterly"* (Brennan's emphasis) without redeeming social importance, to find that *"Memoirs"* was obscene would require evidence that the work had no redeeming value, even to those who sought it for historical and literary purposes. As this was not established in the record, and the Court was being asked to make a determination of obscenity "in the abstract," a redeeming value overrides the possibility that the work might also be "exploited by panderers because it so pervasively treats sexual matters." Accordingly, the state court's finding that *"Memoirs"* was obscene under the criteria in *Roth* was reversed.

In a concurring opinion, Associate Justice WILLIAM O. DOUGLAS pointed out that after the American edition of *"Memoirs"* was published in 1963, "an unusually large number of orders were placed by universities and libraries; the Library of Congress requested the right to translate the book into Braille." On a historical note, he added that he had found an absence of any federal obscenity cases or laws passed immediately after the First Amendment's adoption in 1791; CONGRESS in fact passed no such laws until the mid-nineteenth century. Therefore, he reasoned, no contemporaneous evidence proves that it was the framers' intent to exclude any particular class of expression from the protection of the First Amendment.

On the heels of *Fanny Hill*, the Supreme Court dealt summarily with close to three dozen obscenity cases in the next few years, reversing all but one. Although the individual justices had different approaches to the obscenity question, enough would agree that "[w]hichever of the constitutional views is brought to bear upon the cases before us, it is clear that the judgments [findings of obscenity] cannot stand." By 1973, when the Court revisited the definition of obscenity in MILLER V. CALIFORNIA and *Paris Adult Theatre I v. Slaton,* the requirement that the prosecution prove that questionable material was "utterly without redeeming social importance" would be abandoned for a less liberal approach. Today the INTERNET, motion pictures, rap music, magazines, and books are pervaded by what in earlier eras would no doubt have been considered obscene and might even have made Fanny Hill blush.

See also ADULT MATERIALS; PORNOGRAPHY.

BRADWELL v. ILLINOIS

The Comstock Act to prohibit the sending of lewd or obscene material through the U.S. mail, named after the antivice zealot ANTHONY COMSTOCK, was passed in 1873. In the wake of this new federal statute, local laws began to ban the wearing of clothes of the opposite sex—a setback to women trying to pass as men to advance themselves professionally. That same year the U.S. Supreme Court, in *Bradwell v. Illinois,* decided the case of a Chicago resident, Myra Bradwell (1831–94), who hoped to practice law but happened to be not only a woman but married as well.

The opinion of the Supreme Court in *Bradwell* was written by Associate Justice Samuel F. Miller. Associate Justice Joseph P. Bradley, with whom two other justices joined, wrote a concurring opinion in which he expressed sympathy with the "humane movements of modern society, which have for their object the multiplication of avenues for woman's advancement, and of occupations adapted to her condition and sex." But he was not "prepared to say that it is one of her fundamental rights and privileges to be admitted into every office and position, including those which require highly special qualifications and demanding special responsibilities."

Bradwell had applied to the state supreme court for admission to the bar so that she could practice law.

She was eminently qualified, having studied law with her attorney husband, James B. Bradwell, and founded in 1868 what became the Midwest's foremost legal publication, the *Chicago Legal News*. She passed the bar examination with high honors in 1869 and was "found to possess the requisite qualifications" but was nonetheless denied admission to the Illinois bar. In her affidavit in support of her application to practice law in the state, she requested that the license be approved in accordance with Article IV, section 2, of the U.S. Constitution and its Fourteenth Amendment (1865).

According to section 2, "The Citizens of each State shall be entitled to all Privileges and Immunities of Citizens in the several States." The relevant language of the Fourteenth Amendment, section 1, states: "All persons born or naturalized in the United States, and subject to the jurisdiction thereof, are citizens of the United States and of the state wherein they reside. No state shall make or enforce any law which shall abridge the privileges or immunities of citizens of the United States; nor shall any state deprive any person of life, liberty, or property, without due process of law; nor deny to any person within its jurisdiction the equal protection of the laws."

Earlier in 1873 the Supreme Court had determined in the *Slaughterhouse* cases that the Thirteenth (1865), Fourteenth (1865), and Fifteenth (1870) Amendments were intended to ensure the freedom of former slaves and did not extend to the rights of other citizens, who derived their civil rights from state citizenship and were therefore not protected by the Fourteenth Amendment. This narrow reading of the Fourteenth Amendment would be relied on by the Court to thwart cases of DIS- CRIMINATION on the basis of sex until *Reed v. Reed* (1971); in this case, the equal protection clause, rather than the Constitution's privileges and immunities clause, was used as the basis for striking down a state law that gave preference to males as administrators of the estates of decedents lacking a will.

Regarding Bradwell's application, the Illinois supreme court had concluded that the law setting forth the criteria for the practice of law in the state left to

Myra Bradwell founded the *Chicago Legal News* and passed the state bar examination in 1869, only to be denied a license to practice law by the State of Illinois because she was a woman. The U.S. Supreme Court upheld the state supreme court's decision declaring that the law was no job for a woman.

the court the question of whether to admit a woman. That law, and the common law of England (adopted by the state years earlier), did not contemplate women practicing as attorneys. At the time these laws were enacted, according to the court's opinion, "That God designed the sexes to occupy different spheres of action, and that it belonged to men to make, apply, and execute the laws, was regarded as an almost axiomatic truth." Accordingly, the Illinois court declared that it had no authority to act otherwise than to deny admission to Bradwell.

As for the contention on appeal to the U.S. Supreme Court that the right or privilege of practicing law in a state was encompassed in the privileges and immunities clause of the U.S. Constitution, Justice Miller simply noted that the right to practice law was not one of the federal privileges and immunities in Article IV, section 2. With respect to Bradwell's argument that practicing law was a privilege or an immunity enforceable through the Fourteenth Amendment, he referred to the Court's decision in the *Slaughterhouse* cases to conclude that "the right to control and regulate the granting of [a] license to practice law in the courts of a State is one of those powers which are not transferred for its protection to the Federal government." He thus found it not enforceable through the Fourteenth Amendment.

The *Bradwell* case is most remembered for Justice Bradley's singular contention: "The paramount destiny and mission of woman are to fulfill the noble and benign offices of wife and mother. This is the law of the Creator." In arriving at this conclusion, he cited the Illinois court's determination that a married woman in particular would, as Bradley paraphrased it, be "incompetent fully to perform the duties and trusts that belong to the office of an attorney and counsellor." He pointed out that under common law, man was seen as woman's protector and defender and that the "natural and proper timidity and delicacy which belongs to the female sex evidently unfits it for many of the occupations of civil life." The most significant issue, however, was that "a married woman is incapable, without her husband's consent, of making contracts which shall be binding on her or him." An unmarried woman would not have had the same duties or "incapacities arising out of the married state."

Chief Justice Morrison R. Waite "dissented from the judgment of the court, and from all the opinions," but the basis for his dissent was not reported. Undoubtedly it would have been almost impossible for any of the justices on the Supreme Court in 1873 to have imagined that one day not only would the majority of law school students be women but that members of the delicate sex would sit on their own august bench.

Myra Bradwell was permitted to run her business under a special charter allowing a married woman to do so. She used the pages of the *Chicago Legal News* to advocate for WOMEN'S RIGHTS, speaking out for suffrage and property rights. She also pressured the State of Illinois to give every citizen access to a profession. Bradwell also befriended and assisted Mary Todd Lincoln (1818–82) in the years following her husband's assassination. An award has been named in Bradwell's honor by the Gonzaga University School of Law Women's Law Caucus in Chicago.

See also EQUAL RIGHTS.

BREAST IMPLANTS

See SEXUAL ENHANCEMENT.

BREASTFEEDING

The sexualization of women's breasts has created legal problems in dealing with the natural and beneficial activity of breastfeeding babies. That feeding must take place about every three hours means that nursing mothers outside the home sometimes have to be able to breastfeed in public or at their place of work. The history of breastfeeding in these locations is replete with tales of DISCRIMINATION.

Breastfeeding is not the only method by which a mother can feed her baby. However, because it provides health benefits to the child (according to many studies and the SURGEON GENERAL OF THE UNITED STATES), helps with mother-child bonding, and can have salutary effects for mothers after giving birth, it is now encouraged by most doctors in most situations. (But even mother's milk may contain toxic chemicals. A flame retardant known as PBDE, which was banned in the late 1970s, for example, has been found in many animals and humans. The milk of American women has the world's highest level of this substance.)

State Laws
The states have chosen to deal with breastfeeding in several ways. Thirty-five states—including California, Florida, Illinois, New York, South Dakota, and Virginia—allow mothers to breastfeed in virtually any

State Breastfeeding Laws

State	Protected in Public	Protected in Workplace	Exempt from Public Indecency	Exempt from Jury Duty	Education Programs	Other Provisions
Alabama	•					
Alaska			•			
Arizona	•		•			
Arkansas						
California	•	•		•	•	Expressing milk
Colorado	•					
Connecticut	•	•				
Delaware	•					
Florida	•		•			
Georgia	•	•				
Hawaii	•	•				Child custody
Idaho				•		
Illinois	•	•	•	•	•	Private right of action
Indiana	•					
Iowa	•			•		
Kansas	•			•		
Kentucky	•		•			
Louisiana	•					Day Care
Maine	•					Parental rights
Maryland	•					Sales tax
Massachusetts						
Michigan			•			
Minnesota	•	•		•		
Mississippi						
Missouri	•				•	
Montana	•		•			
Nebraska				•		
Nevada	•		•			
New Hampshire	•		•			
New Jersey	•					
New Mexico	•					
New York	•					
North Carolina	•		•			
North Dakota						
Ohio						
Oklahoma	•		•	•		
Oregon	•			•		Employer option for breaks
Pennsylvania						
Rhode Island	•	•	•			Mercury alerts

State	Protected in Public	Protected in Workplace	Exempt from Public Indecency	Exempt from Jury Duty	Education Programs	Other Provisions
South Carolina	•		•			
South Dakota	•		•			
Tennessee		•				
Texas	•	•				Expressing milk
Utah	•		•			
Vermont	•				•	
Virginia	•		•	•		
Washington		•	•			
West Virginia						
Wisconsin			•			
Wyoming						

Source: La Leche League International, 2006

public or private place. California's civil, health and safety, and labor codes all make reference to breastfeeding. The civil code permits a mother to breastfeed her child in any location, public or private, where the mother and child are otherwise authorized to be present, except in another person's private residence. The health and safety code requires hospitals to make available a breastfeeding consultant or to provide information to mothers on where to receive breastfeeding information. The labor code specifies that employers must allow a break and provide a room for a mother who wants to breastfeed in private.

Some eighteen states—among them Alaska, Florida, Illinois, New Hampshire, and Wisconsin—expressly exempt breastfeeding from public indecency laws. The Illinois law, found under Criminal Offenses in the state code, declares, "Breastfeeding of infants is not an act of public indecency." Alaska goes further and explains that terms such as LEWD BEHAVIOR, lewd touching, immoral conduct, and indecent conduct do not include a woman's breastfeeding of a child. Nine other states—including Connecticut, Hawaii, Tennessee, and Washington, like California—have laws relating to breastfeeding in the workplace. Illinois, Missouri, and

Vermont, in addition to California, encourage breastfeeding. In California, Idaho, Iowa, Kansas, Oklahoma, and five other states, nursing mothers are exempt from jury duty. Louisiana prohibits child care facilities from discriminating against breastfed babies.

Recognizing studies showing that breastfed children are generally healthier and that breastfeeding mothers are better employees with less absenteeism, the Washington legal code makes it state policy that breastfeeding is (1) an important contributor to infant health; (2) provides a range of benefits for an infant's growth, immunity, and development; (3) improves maternal health; and (4) contributes economic benefits to the family, health care system, and workplace.

In California a mother reached a settlement with Borders Books after being told to stop breastfeeding in the children's section, and the company agreed to educate its employees about women's right under the state's civil code to breastfeed in public. However, in Ohio a court held that discrimination against breastfeeding women was not sex discrimination in violation of the state's public accommodation laws; a woman can breastfeed in public, said the court, but it is not illegal for another person to harass her while she is feeding her baby.

NURSE THE BABY
YOUR PROTECTION AGAINST TROUBLE
INFORM YOURSELF THROUGH THE HEALTH
BUREAU PUBLICATIONS

Traditional strictures against breastfeeding an infant in public are gradually being replaced by state laws expressly permitting it. As early as 1938, a Federal Art Project poster by Erik Hans Krause promoted maternal nursing as one means of proper child care.

Federal Antidiscrimination Laws

At the federal level, the Right to Breastfeed Act (1999) made it permissible for women to breastfeed on any federal property where women and CHILDREN otherwise have a right to be. The sponsor of the bill in the House of Representatives, Carolyn B. Maloney of New York, said: "It is a shame that we need this law to protect such a natural choice, but women were being harassed, told to leave national parks and museums and intimidated off of federal grounds simply for breastfeeding."

State laws have tended to fill the gaps in federal antidiscrimination laws that the courts have generally excluded from application to breastfeeding issues, such as the Americans with Disability Act (1990), Family Medical Leave Act (1993), Pregnancy Discrimination Act (1978), and Title VII of the Civil Rights Act of 1964. With respect to Title VII, for example, in *General Electric v. Gilbert* (1976), the U.S. Supreme Court, using some contorted logic, upheld an employment disability program that excluded PREGNANCY benefits on the grounds that, because only women can become pregnant, there was no discrimination in a plan that denies them benefits for something that men could not get benefits for anyway. Dissents by Associate Justices William J. Brennan Jr. and John Paul Stevens pointed out, among other things, that Title VII prohibits classification by sex and that mothers are women and thus one of the two sexes.

Agreeing with the dissent in *General Electric,* CONGRESS amended Title VII by enacting the Pregnancy Discrimination Act. The amendment redefined *sex* to "include, but ... not be limited to pregnancy, childbirth, or related medical conditions." However, when women discriminated against for breastfeeding their babies sought relief in federal courts under the Pregnancy Discrimination Act, they were told—without any factual or legislative basis—that the act covered only illnesses that were incapacitating. In *Wallace v. Pyro Mining* (1990; affirmed 1991), a woman who was having difficulty weaning her child was denied additional maternity leave by her employer; a federal court agreed with the employer, declaring that breastfeeding and weaning were not "medical conditions" related to pregnancy and childbirth.

Today millions of working women, who contribute significantly to the economic support of their families, are encouraged to breastfeed their children. In comparison with other major countries, the United States lacks uniform laws that require workplace accommodation for breastfeeding. America—the land of baseball, mom, and apple pie—is only slowly coming to grips with the notion that the working mother should be treated with more respect for the role in which she has been cast by biology and society.

Contact: La Leche League International, 1400 North Meacham Road, Schaumburg, IL 60173-4808 (847-519-7730). www.lalecheleague.org.

See also INDECENT EXPOSURE; MOTHERHOOD; WOMEN'S RIGHTS.

LOUISE BROWN

An accident of birth has brought fame to Louise Joy Brown, the first successful "test-tube" baby. In 2003, twenty-five years after her birth and twenty-one years after being told by her parents of her unique status, she could still recall all of the questions she was asked as a child about who she was and what made her special. Then a postal worker in England, Brown said: "I thought it was something peculiar to me. I thought I was abnormal." More than one million children have since followed her route to birth, including her own sister, Natalie.

The pattern of human sexual behavior resulting from millions of years of evolution has not always worked effectively to produce offspring—the prime imperative for survival of the species. Some couples who want a child created from their own DNA are thwarted by problems such as a low sperm count or a blockage in the fallopian tubes, hindering the female's eggs from traveling down to be fertilized by the male sperm.

Lesley and John Brown, a couple living in Bristol, England, had tried unsuccessfully for nine years to have a child. In 1976 the couple was referred to Dr. Patrick Steptoe, a gynecologist who had been experimenting with in vitro fertilization techniques. Using an illuminated tube called a laparoscope, Dr. Steptoe extracted an egg from one of Lesley Brown's ovaries and gave it to his colleague, Dr. Robert Edwards, a physiologist, who fertilized the egg with John

Louise Brown, born in 1978 as the first "test-tube" baby, was destined for international celebrity from the moment she was conceived by in vitro fertilization. This and similar processes have since been used successfully to allow many people to have genetically related children.

Brown's sperm and placed it in a solution where the cells began to divide.

Steptoe and Edwards had begun working in 1966 to achieve a successful in vitro fertilization, but none of the resulting pregnancies lasted more than a few weeks. Unlike earlier attempts, in which the two scientists had waited four or five days, this time the fertilized egg was implanted in the mother's uterus only two and one-half days afterward. "Baby Louise," as she was soon dubbed by the press, was carried almost to term, being delivered by Caesarean section nine days before the due date, when her mother developed high blood pressure. At her birth at Oldham General Hospital in Oldham, England, at 11:47 P.M. on July 25, 1978, the healthy baby weighed five pounds, twelve ounces.

Louise Brown's generally normal gestation and birth were a breakthrough for couples with infertility problems. In addition to spawning a host of new developments in reproductive technology, the successful procedure raised a host of ethical and legal questions: When does human life begin? Would these babies be healthy? Can unused embryos be discarded or used for experimentation? Human intervention in nature's sexual reproductive processes, which undoubtedly began many centuries ago in the selection and breeding of plants and animals, is still evolving.

After the emergence in 1997 of a sheep named Dolly, the first mammal to be cloned, President Bill Clinton issued a directive banning the use of federal funds for research on human cloning. Legal implications of the new field of ASSISTED REPRODUCTIVE TECHNOLOGY continue to be dealt with at the federal and state levels in the United States. The same year that Dolly was born, the National Bioethics Advisory Commission, a predecessor of the President's Council on Bioethics, recommended continuing a moratorium on federal funding for research to create a child using somatic-cell nuclear transfer, a process that combines chromosomes from cells other than reproductive sperm and eggs.

Although today fewer than 5 percent of couples with infertility problems use in vitro fertilization, it is the accepted treatment for women with blocked or damaged fallopian tubes or men with low sperm counts. It also remains the treatment of last resort when other procedures such as artificial insemination fail. In this brave new world of technologically assisted reproduction, Louise Brown unwittingly became a pioneer.

See also AMERICAN FERTILITY ASSOCIATION; BIOETHICS; STEM-CELL RESEARCH AND CLONING.

LENNY BRUCE

When his last record album came out around the end of 1965, the comedian Lenny Bruce said: "The Supreme Court is concerned with one thing: the First Amendment. And here's their concern . . . not with anybody saying 'shit.' . . . They're concerned with the *information*, that there's no bar to the communication system." Whether he was just using foul language and sexual imagery in his routines to further his career, which got him hauled into court on seven charges of OB-SCENITY, or whether he really believed that he was putting CENSORSHIP to the test, Bruce changed how the ENTERTAINMENT INDUSTRY and the law would ever after view obscenity and portrayals of sexual behavior.

Leonard Alfred Schneider was born on October 13, 1925, in Mineola, New York. Shortly after his dishonorable discharge from the navy in 1946 for asserting that he was a homosexual, he changed his name to Lenny Bruce. His mother, who was divorced from Lenny's father when her son was just a child, had changed her name to Sally Marr when she became a dancer; she later worked as a stand-up comic under the name Boots Malloy. Bruce acknowledged his mother's influence on his sense of humor.

In the summer of 1946, Bruce won a drama contest doing a send-up of Hamlet's soliloquy "To be, or not to be. . . ." He soon began appearing at amateur talent events, winning on the nationally televised *Arthur Godfrey and His Talent Scouts* in 1949 with impersonations of Hollywood actors such as James Cagney, Edward G. Robinson, and Peter Lorre. His star in ascendancy, he was soon playing clubs in New York and other cities around the country. Bruce was arrested in 1951 but never sentenced for posing as a priest to solicit funds for an African leper colony. That same year he married a stripper named Honey Harlowe.

Bruce's career took him to many venues where he honed his comedy routines as probably the first modern comic, moving away from vaudeville jokes to social criticism. He tackled politics, religion, the law, race, and sex. Bruce once appeared naked on stage, and in 1957 he was fired for obscene language—his use of

A stand-up comic, Lenny Bruce pushed the envelope regarding sexually explicit and obscene language in his on-stage performances during the 1960s. Seen raising a V for victory sign in 1964, he saw himself as a defender of the constitutional right of free speech guaranteed by the First Amendment.

"blue material" using sexual terms. His MARRIAGE also ended in DIVORCE in 1957. That same year, a San Francisco municipal judge applied the new U.S. Supreme Court standards for obscenity set forth in ROTH V. UNITED STATES (1957) to declare that *Howl,* a poem by the Beat Generation poet Allen Ginsberg (1926–97), was not obscene because it had some "socially redeeming importance." Albert M. Bendich, the AMERICAN CIVIL LIBERTIES UNION counsel who represented the defendant in this case, later represented Bruce in a similar obscenity trial, as would the flamboyant legal celebrity Melvin Belli.

Arrested in September 1961 in Philadelphia for possession of narcotics, Bruce was arrested again the following month for violations of California and San Francisco obscenity laws. Represented by Albert Bendich, the comedian testified in his own defense at trial. Although some of the jurors said that they wished they could convict him, they had to find him not guilty according to the law regarding obscenity, as instructed by the judge. A part of the judge's instruction was that "a necessary element [of the crime] is the existence in the mind of the defendant knowing that the material used ... was obscene.... In determining whether the defendant had such knowledge, you may consider reviews of his work which were available to him, stating that his performance had artistic merit and contained socially important ideas."

In October 1962 Bruce was again arrested on obscenity charges, this time in Los Angeles after a performance at the Troubadour in West Hollywood. This time his trial was consolidated with another one on a charge based on a performance at another Los Angeles club, the Unicorn. It ended in a mistrial, but in a second trial the jury convicted Bruce after less than an hour's deliberation. He was fined $250, given a suspended one-year sentence, and placed on two years' probation. Bruce was also charged with obscenity for 1962 performances in Chicago (a guilty verdict was overturned, citing *JACOBELLIS V. OHIO*) and additional shows in Los Angeles (a charge that was dismissed on the basis of *ROTH V. UNITED STATES*).

Having now been convicted of obscenity charges and warned by judges in a number of cities that his routines using lewd language and spoofs of RELIGION could be considered obscene, Bruce began to lose bookings at many clubs and was deported from London and banned from performing in Australia. After another conviction in 1964 in New York City based on a performance at the Cafe au Go Go in Greenwich Village, in which Bruce used a now-familiar four-letter word, Allen Ginsberg sought support for the comedian; a hundred prominent people in the arts and literature were asked to sign a statement comparing him to the great social satirists Jonathan Swift (1667–1745) and Mark Twain (1835–1910). In voting 2–1 to find him guilty, the city court, in an opinion written by its chief justice, declared that Bruce's performances "were obscene, indecent, immoral and impure.... [W]ords such as 'ass,' 'balls,' 'cock-sucker,' 'cunt,' 'fuck,' 'mother-fucker,' 'piss,' 'screw,' 'shit,' and 'tits' were used about one hundred times in utter obscenity. The monologues also contained anecdotes and reflections that were similarly obscene."

Following a series of hospitalizations and a declaration of bankruptcy in 1965, Lenny Bruce died of a morphine overdose on August 3, 1966, at his home in the Hollywood Hills. In 2003 he was finally pardoned by the governor of New York, the first such posthumous pardon in the state's history. Governor George Pataki declared that the action was "a declaration of New York's commitment to upholding the First Amendment."

Bruce, branded as a "dirty comic," became an early casualty of his times, which started with the Beat Generation and the countercultural revolution and extended to the anti-Vietnam War movement, civil rights protests, demonstrations for EQUAL RIGHTS, and the SEXUAL REVOLUTION of the 1960s and 1970s. He wondered publicly why it was acceptable to say the word *kill* in front of an audience but not words used to describe love. In 1963 an interviewer in *Cavalier* magazine called him not a political revolutionary but an "authentic hipster hero of the sexual and moral revolution." For better or worse, the American entertainment industry today owes its openness in large part to the antic and allegedly obscene comic routines of Lenny Bruce and his willingness to push the boundaries of freedom of speech.

See also FIRST AMENDMENT.

BURLESQUE

See ENTERTAINMENT INDUSTRY.

BURLINGTON INDUSTRIES, INC. v. ELLERTH

The movement to expand the rights of American women in the 1960s, concomitant with the extension of civil rights to blacks, brought the enactment of several federal laws protecting women from sex DISCRIMINATION, including SEXUAL HARASSMENT, in the workplace. In the years preceding its finding in *Burlington Industries, Inc. v. Ellerth* (1998) that employers can be held vicariously responsible for harassment, the U.S. Supreme Court applied those laws in several key decisions; among them were *Meritor Savings Bank v. Vinton* (1986) and *Harris v. Forklift Systems, Inc.* (1993).

In *Meritor,* the Supreme Court held that under Title VII of the Civil Rights Act of 1964, which made sex discrimination in the workplace a federal offense, both the creation of a hostile work environment and a supervisor's quid pro quo unwelcome sexual advances and demands for sexual favors constituted prohibited sexual harassment. The justices went on to say that the best evidence of a hostile work environment was the psychological damage done to the complainant, which resulted in a failure to do her job properly. The decision laid out four conditions that must be met by a successful plaintiff: she must belong to the group the law was intended to protect, she must have been subjected to unwelcome sexual harassment, the harassment must have been based on sex, and the employer must have or should have known about the harassment and failed to act to stop it.

In the *Harris* case, the Supreme Court refashioned the standards it set in *Meritor.* The plaintiff, a thirty-five-year-old woman who had been divorced four times, filed a complaint two months before she quit, alleging that the company president had created a hostile environment. The lower courts concluded that she was not protected by Title VII because she had not suffered any psychological injury on the job from being called a "dumb-ass woman" and being asked to retrieve coins from the president's front pants pockets. In an opinion written by Associate Justice Sandra Day O'Connor, the Court concluded that the plaintiff did not have to suffer psychological damage to establish a hostile work environment and that her job performance did not have to suffer because of the harassment. The decision made it easier for subsequent victims to prove harassment.

But because this area of federal law was still evolving, some confusion developed in the lower federal courts as to the extent to which employers could be held responsible for sexual harassment by their supervisors or mangers. How much did the management of a company have to know about the harassment? What did it do to stop it? Did it have a well-disseminated policy against harassment? What internal remedies were available for dealing with sexual harassment? Questions such as these were often raised but resolved differently in lower-court decisions.

In *Burlington Industries, Inc. v. Ellerth*, the female complainant had quit her job as a salesperson, alleging that her male supervisor had constantly harassed her because of her sex and had demanded that she provide him with sexual favors in return for being promoted. This type of sexual harassment is called quid pro quo because something is offered in exchange for sex. She claimed that she had never provided the sexual favors demanded, but there was no solid evidence that she had suffered any retaliation, and she did receive one promotion. She never reported the harassment to the company, which had in place a policy that encouraged such reporting.

In a 7–2 opinion written by Associate Justice Anthony M. Kennedy, the Supreme Court held: "An employer is subject to vicarious liability to a victimized employee for an actionable hostile environment created by a supervisor with immediate (or successively higher) authority over the employee. When no tangible action is taken, a defending employer may raise an affirmative defense to liability or damages, subject to proof by a preponderance of the evidence."

A companion case, *Faragher v. City of Boca Raton*, was also decided by 7–2 majority on the same day in 1998. In this case, whose opinion was written by Associate Justice David H. Souter, a female lifeguard alleged that two male supervisors created a hostile work environment for her and other female lifeguards by uninvited and offensive touching, lewd remarks, and an offensive manner of speaking about women. In both cases, the complainants had resigned their jobs and brought actions in federal court for sexual harassment under Title VII. The *Faragher* decision contains language virtually identical to *Burlington* regarding harassment in a hostile workplace environment.

The decisions have established two elements for the defense against such charges: (1) "the employer exercised reasonable care to prevent and correct promptly any sexually harassing behavior"; and (2), "that the plaintiff employee unreasonably failed to take advantage of any preventive or corrective opportunities provided by the employer or to avoid harm otherwise." The need to promulgate an antiharassment policy was advised if the employer wanted to avoid liability, as was the "corresponding obligation" of the victim to use "reasonable care to avoid harm" and to "use any complaint procedure provided by the employer" in order to prevail in court. According to both cases, "No affirmative defense is available, however, when the supervisor's harassment culminates in a tangible employment action such as discharge, demotion, or undesirable reassignment."

In another 1998 case, *Oncale v. Sundowner Offshore Services*, the Supreme Court held that the federal law also applies to same-sex harassment in the workplace. But in *Ulane v. Eastern Airlines, Inc.* (1984), the U.S. Court of Appeals for the Seventh Circuit refused to extend the law to cover discrimination against transsexuals.

All of these cases have clarified employers' liability for sexual harassment in the workplace. Because many of the lower federal court rulings had been more restrictive to plaintiffs, these cases also opened up possibilities for more successful lawsuits by victims subject to sexual harassment in their places of employment.

See also EQUAL RIGHTS; TRANSSEXUALISM.

C

MARY S. CALDERONE

Dr. Mary Steichen Calderone, the cofounder of the
Sexuality Information and Education Council of the
United States (SIECUS) in 1964, was dubbed by *Time*
magazine the "Grandmother of Sex Education." Like
Alfred Kinsey, Calderone helped take the mystery and
shame out of sexual behavior, declaring, "We must
block our habit of considering sex as a 'problem' to
be 'controlled.' Emphasis must be on sex as a vital life
force to be utilized." For Calderone, "Sex is what it
means to be a man or a woman."

Born in New York City on July 1, 1904, Mary
Steichen lived with her family in France from the age
of two years until their return to the United States in
1914 at the start of World War I. When her mother and
younger sister went back to France, Mary opted to stay
in the country with her father, the noted photographer
Edward Steichen (1879–1973), who was born in Luxem-
bourg; her parents divorced in 1922. Mary attended
the private school Brearley and later Vassar College,
where she majored in chemistry. She was the niece of
the Pulitzer Prize–winning American poet and Lincoln scholar Carl Sandburg (1878–1967).

While pursuing a theater career in New York City,
in 1926 she met and married an actor, W. Lon Martin. Two years later, after the birth of their second
daughter, she abandoned her career in the theater;
eventually she divorced her husband. She began taking premedical courses at Columbia University in 1934,

**A champion of people's right to obtain accurate information
about sexual behavior, Mary Calderone believed that sex
education could not begin too early. In 1964 she co-
founded the Sex (later Sexuality) Information and Education Council to promote sex education nationwide.**

graduated from the Rochester School of Medicine in
1939, completed an internship in pediatrics at New
York's Bellevue Hospital, and then continued her
education in public health. In 1941 she married Dr.
Frank Calderone, who was to become the deputy
health commissioner of New York City and then the

director of medical services for the United Nations secretariat. The couple had two daughters and later separated in 1979 but never divorced.

In 1953 Mary Calderone took the part-time job of medical director of the PLANNED PARENTHOOD FEDERATION OF AMERICA, a position she held until 1964. In 1955 she organized a conference on ABORTION that included Alfred Kinsey. The result was the first thorough, clinical report on the relationship between abortion and women's health, *Abortion in the United States*, published in 1958. But her focus soon began to shift from CONTRACEPTION TO SEX EDUCATION. In addition to other writings on the subject, she published *Release from Sexual Tension* in 1960.

After leaving Planned Parenthood, she organized SIECUS to disseminate information on sexual behavior and to promote sex education, although the council itself did not sponsor courses. SIECUS served as an umbrella organization of sex educators and social scientists working to avert teen pregnancies and SEXUALLY TRANSMITTED DISEASES through scientific education. Its overriding goal was "to establish man's sexuality as a health entity . . . to dignify it by openness of approach, study and scientific research designed to lead toward its understanding and its freedom from exploitation."

The mission she had chosen, however, was not without obstacles. Some organizations, such as the Ku Klux Klan and the John Birch Society (a politically conservative group), opposed her efforts by analogizing SIECUS's liberal attitude toward and open discussion of sexual behavior to communism, pedophilia, and child PORNOGRAPHY. Her support for HUGH HEFNER, the controversial publisher of *Playboy* magazine and organizer of Playboy Clubs in major U.S. cities, also drew condemnation from the religious right and made members of the feminist movement uneasy. Her speeches were often picketed.

Calderone later began to expand her field of interest to sexuality of the disabled and older people. As an adjunct professor at New York University after leaving SIECUS in 1982, she taught courses on human sexuality and promoted scientific research on the subject.

A victim of Alzheimer's disease, she died on October 24, 1998, in Kennett Square, Pennsylvania. SIECUS maintains the Mary S. Calderone Library of books and other materials on human sexuality and sex education, subjects to which she had devoted her life's work.

Calderone was inducted into the National Women's Hall of Fame in Seneca Falls, New York, in 1998. She was also honored with awards from institutions and organizations such as the American Public Health Association. She received the Margaret Sanger Award from Planned Parenthood and the Elizabeth Blackwell Award for distinguished services to humanity. Along with pioneers such as MARGARET SANGER and Alfred Kinsey, Mary Calderone helped usher in the modern era of openness about sexual behavior that has changed public policy and the law.

See also FAMILY PLANNING; REPRODUCTIVE RIGHTS.

CASTRATION

See SEX OFFENDERS; STERILIZATION.

CENSORSHIP

In 23 B.C.E. Augustus Caesar, the first Roman emperor, granted himself new powers; although he did not officially assume the position of censor, he took on the power to exercise general responsibility for public morals. Censorship (named for a Roman official called the censor) is the process of deciding what other people may see and hear. England had official censors, including the poet John Milton (1608–74), who, ironically, was an advocate of freedom of the press.

Following suit, in 1798 the new nation's CONGRESS enacted An Act for the Punishment of Certain Crimes Against the United States. Called the Sedition Act, this law, among other things, criminalized malicious writings that defamed the government, the PRESIDENT, or Congress; that brought them into contempt or disrepute; or that excited the hatred of the people. About two dozen persons, include newspaper editors, were prosecuted under the act before it automatically expired in three years, without giving the U.S. Supreme Court time to pass judgment on it. James Madison, known as the "Father of the Constitution," had no doubt how the Court should have ruled had it been given the opportunity. Madison, according to the Court's later opinion in *New York Times Co. v. Sullivan* (1964), believed that in a republican government "the censorial power is in the people over the Government, and not in the Government over the people."

The Supreme Court would have a number of other opportunities to decide whether the government could act as a censor, including issues involving matters relating to sex.

Sexual Behavior Czars

The first significant federal law instituting censorship over sexual matters was the Tariff Act of 1842, which authorized customs officials to prohibit the importation of obscene items. An increased public fervor against vice and indecency led to the passage of the Comstock Act of 1873, named after the antiobscenity crusader ANTHONY COMSTOCK; in addition to prohibiting the interstate transportation of contraceptives, this law banned obscene materials, including birth control information.

In *Ex parte Jackson* (1878), the Supreme Court upheld the government's power to censor the U.S. mail this way and would continue to do so; the Court avoiding saying directly that Congress—under its power in Article I, section 8, of the U.S. Constitution "To establish Post Offices"—had absolute authority over the content of the mail. However, in 1964, in *Hannegan v. Esquire*, the Court ruled that the Post Office could not exclude *Esquire* magazine from the mail because of what it deemed to be the poor taste and vulgarity of its contents. Then, in *Lamont v. Postmaster General* (1965), the justices noted that Congress did not have to run the postal service, but as long as it did it was subject to honor the protections of the FIRST AMENDMENT (1781).

A key case involving a state law that tried to impose censorship by banning publication is *Near v.*

Minnesota (1931). Here the Supreme Court in a 5–4 decision held that a Minnesota statute aimed at stopping the publication of any "malicious, scandalous and defamatory newspaper, magazine, or other periodical" was an infringement of the First Amendment's guarantee of freedom of the press. This decision did not conclude that any publication was immune from being sued for libel, only that the government could not impose prior restraint on publication.

Printed Matter. Printed materials were once subject to state censorship through censorship boards that—based on finding some offense in even a single passage—might ban works such as *The Red Badge of Courage* (1895), written by Stephen Crane (1871–1900), or *Leaves of Grass* (1855), written by the poet Walt Whitman (1819–92). A lesbian novel, Radclyffe Hall's *The Well of Loneliness* (1928), was declared obscene in New York State in 1929. But a federal district court found in *United States v. One Book Called "Ulysses"* (affirmed by a federal court of appeals in 1934) that "we believe that the proper test of whether a given book is obscene is its dominant effect."

In *ROTH V. UNITED STATES* (1957), the Supreme Court created for the first time a definition of OBSCENITY that focused on a work as a whole, rather than on individual parts, and set contemporaneous community standards as the test for whether the government could impose censorship. Obscenity, the Court affirmed, was outside the scope of First Amendment protections. In *Roth* the Court concluded that obscenity depended on whether the average person, applying contemporary community standards, would find that the work, taken as a whole, appeals to the PRURIENT INTEREST; that the work depicts or describes, in a patently offensive way, sexual conduct specifically defined in the applicable state law; and that the work, taken as a whole, lacks serious literary, artistic, political, or scientific value. Although the Court has massaged and refined these criteria in later cases, the basic definition crafted in this case remains the test of what may and may not be censored by the government.

Motion Pictures. Censorship of the movies traces its history to the inventor Thomas Edison (1847–1931), whose film *Fatima's Serpentine Dance* was censored in 1895 by blacking out the sensual parts of the actress's clothed body. The movie *Orange Blossoms* was censored by a New York court in *People v. Doris* (1897) because it contained a wedding night scene. In 1908 the mayor of New York City shut down all the movie theaters because he believed that they were immoral; four years later, police raided a showing of pornographic films in Manhattan. In 1930 the nascent motion picture industry developed a code of self-censorship (discussed below) and in 1968 adopted the PG, R, and X rating system (signifying parental guidance, restricted, and adults only).

According to the Supreme Court's decision in *Times Film Corp. v. City of Chicago* (1961), although motion pictures are included within the free-speech and free-press guarantees of both the First Amendment and the Fourteenth Amendment (1868), there is no absolute freedom to publicly exhibit any motion picture without prior restraint. *Bantam Books, Inc. v. Sullivan* (1963) involved Supreme Court review of a Rhode Island commission created by law "to educate the public concerning any book ... or other thing containing obscene, indecent or impure language, or manifestly tending to the corruption of the youth...." The Court held that the Fourteenth Amendment required that such an agency conform to procedures that will not curtail constitutionally protected expression. Then in *Freedman v. Maryland* (1965), the Court set forth specific requirements: the government has the burden of showing that nonobscene material is protected; a prompt judicial proceeding for challenging censorship decisions must be provided; and the government must either approve the publication or display or justify its refusal in court. Finally, in *Vance v. Universal Amusement Co.* (1980), the Court imposed a heavy burden on government censors to justify enjoining future exhibitions of films not yet found to be obscene simply because of past exhibitions of obscene films.

In *Paris Adult Theatre I v. Slaton* (1973)—a companion case to Miller v. California (1973), in which obscene materials were sent through the mail—the Supreme Court ruled that the exhibition of obscene material, in this case films, in places of public accommodation

The First Amendment guarantees of freedom of speech and the press contain no limitations, but the U.S. Supreme Court has consistently held that obscenity falls outside that protection. *Censored,* a three-act comedy by Conrad Seiler, tested limits of the day and shocked Hollywood when it was released in 1936.

is not protected by any constitutional doctrine of privacy. The Court's opinion in *Miller,* however, had refined the definition of obscenity, so the *Paris* case was remanded for review by the Georgia courts. But in 1974, in *Jenkins v. Georgia,* the Court rendered its opinion that the mainstream film *Carnal Knowledge* did not appeal to the prurient interest and was not patently offensive, regardless of the views of the courts or the community at issue in Georgia.

Governments have also been given permission to proscribe where adult films may be shown. In *Young v. American Mini Theatres* (1976), the Supreme Court upheld a Detroit ZONING regulation that limited the location of sex-related businesses, including adult movie theaters.

Other Media. Censorship of radio and television has been more pervasive, in part because of the limited number of stations that can be licensed by the government—government control of license renewals makes compliance with censorship more enforceable. The openness of these media to anyone in the family, including CHILDREN, has further set them up for government control. With the advent of cable and satellite programming, the role of the FEDERAL COMMUNICATIONS COMMISSION has been limited to the public-access stations. A person or a household is free to subscribe or not to cable programming that contains material that may be considered obscene; blocking procedures help limit exposure to children.

Telephone communication, as with other forms of regulated communication, has been subject to some censorship. For example, in 1988 Congress enacted the Telephone Indecency Act to ban obscene interstate commercial telephone calls—TELEPHONE SEX. But in *Sable Communications of California, Inc. v. Federal Communications Commission* (1989), the Supreme Court held that an absolute ban on indecent telephone messages violates the First Amendment.

The INTERNET has similarly been kept relatively free of censorship by Supreme Court decisions in such cases as *Reno v. American Civil Liberties Union* (1997) and *Ashcroft v. American Civil Liberties Union* (2002, 2004), both of which struck down federal laws intended to censor the Internet to protect children from obscenity.

Government censorship of sexual matters has largely been limited by the Supreme Court to obscenity in the public arena and to keeping ADULT MATERIALS away from children; child pornography is treated more strictly, even in the private arena. Attempts nonetheless continue to be made to censor sexual materials and information, especially in the case of TEENAGERS. Federal SEX EDUCATION programs for students have been accused of withholding information about CONTRACEPTION and ABORTION, and some school

boards have made attempts to edit out or cast doubt on material in science books that explains evolution. In 2005 a state representative in Alabama introduced a bill banning literary works by homosexual authors or about homosexual characters.

Self-Censorship

Parents, teachers, and libraries; publishers of books, magazines, and newspapers; producers of films, radio, television, plays, art exhibitions, and other forms of entertainment all make decisions every day about what information other people will see and hear. Although there are no laws protecting the public from some forms of self-censorship—such as in movie production, newspaper editing, and writing—certain laws do inform those decision makers. Among them are laws against libel and slander, obscenity, PORNOGRAPHY, and other forms of indecency not protected by the First Amendment.

Just the fear of new and stricter laws may influence private decisions. After several scandals in Hollywood involving people in the motion picture industry in the 1920s and 1930s, for example, the Motion Picture Producers and Distributors of America (later the Motion Picture Association of America) brought in a "censorship czar," William Harrison Hays (1879–1954). Born in Sullivan, Indiana, Hays was a lawyer and an elder in the Presbyterian Church and had been chairman of the Republican National Committee in 1918 and postmaster general of the United States in 1921 and 1922. His new job was to administer a production code drawn up by the leaders of the motion picture industry in 1930. Known as the Hays Code, it aimed to avoid anything that would "lower the moral standards" of picture viewers and set standards for the depiction of sex, vulgarity, obscenity, dress, violence, and criminal punishment.

Budget laws and government policies and actions can also influence private decisions, leading to self-censorship. Government funding may be used as a carrot or a stick to influence private actions, such as federal funding for sex education programs that mandate what may and may not be taught. How the government funds the arts has also proved controversial. In

1989 and 1990 U.S. Senator Jesse Helms of North Carolina argued that he found one work of art supported by the National Endowment for the Arts was pornographic and another was blasphemous; as a result the Senate voted to bar funding for "obscene and indecent" works of art and terminate funding for the offending exhibitions. Then in *National Endowment for the Arts v. Finley* (1998), the Supreme Court held that a federal decency requirement was not unconstitutional on its face, but that each case would have to be judged on its own merits. Supporters of Helms's viewpoint suggested that the issue was not one of government censorship but of sponsorship, as artists were free to do what they wanted without government funding.

Public libraries are constantly under pressure from individuals, parents, and interest groups to restrict or discard what some people consider obscene materials or matter unsuitable for the general public, young adults, or children. The American Library Association, for one, received 547 challenges or requests to ban books in 2004. In *Board of Education v. Pico* (1982), the Supreme Court affirmed a lower court judgment that a school board's removal of books from high school and junior high school libraries—over the objections of a committee of parents and school staff—because they were deemed to be "anti-American, anti-Christian, anti-Sem[i]tic, and just plain filthy" violated the First Amendment.

Self-censorship tries to draw the line at what can legally be protected under the Constitution and what makes money. Foul language, sexual innuendo, and soft pornography are readily available in all forms of the media and the ENTERTAINMENT INDUSTRY. Some self-censorship measures that seem to have real effect, without overburdening First Amendment freedoms, are the rating system for movies, warnings on television programs, and tools for blocking cable programming and Internet sites. Some cable companies are also offering family programming packages aimed at keeping censorship in the hands of the consumer.

See also CHILD ONLINE PROTECTION ACT; COMMUNICATIONS DECENCY ACT; MEDIA.

CHILD ABUSE

"Child sexual abuse is a national health problem—it is a national crisis," said Robert Bennett, one of the authors of a 2004 report on the child sexual abuse scandal in the Roman Catholic Church. It is estimated that as many as five hundred thousand incidents of child sexual abuse occur annually in the United States, a rough guess because the vast majority of cases are never reported. Only about 3 percent of offenders—most of them family members or acquaintances, not strangers—are ever convicted.

In addition to child sexual abuse by priests, allegations of child molestation gained worldwide media attention in 2005 during the trial of the pop singer Michael Jackson. An indictment handed down by a California grand jury charged the performer with ten felony counts related to lewd acts committed on a boy under the age of fourteen years with the intent of arousing the sexual desires of the defendant and the child. Jackson was acquitted of the charges, for which he could have been sentenced to almost twenty years in prison.

According to the American Academy of Pediatrics, "Sexual abuse occurs when a child is engaged in sexual activities that the child cannot comprehend, for which the child is developmentally unprepared and cannot give consent, and/or that violate the law or social taboos of society." Various types of inappropriate sexual behavior cited by the organization include touching abuses, such as "oral-genital, genital, or anal contact by or to the child" and "nontouching abuses, such as exhibitionism, voyeurism, or using the child in the production of pornography. Sexual abuse includes a spectrum of activities ranging from rape to physically less intrusive sexual abuse."

In U.S. law, abuse (mistreatment of a person) was traditionally limited to the RAPE of a female child or injury to her genital organs in an attempt at carnal knowledge. Today the term is used to connote a range of behaviors in which the abuser has power or a superior relationship over the person who is abused—not only by an adult over a child (child abuse or molestation), but also by a husband over a wife (spousal abuse) or a caregiver over an invalid or an elderly person. Actions taken may include sexual abuse as well as nonsexual violence or maltreatment. The term does not generally include sex between adolescents or TEENAGERS; however, state laws protect underage females from improper sexual activity, which the U.S. Supreme Court upheld in *Michael M. v. Superior Court of Sonoma County* (1981) on the grounds that the state has a legitimate interest in stemming the incidence of teenage PREGNANCY.

At the federal level, sex crimes against children may be prosecuted under Title 18, Crimes and Criminal Procedure, subsection 2241(c), which deals with crossing state lines to engage in sex acts with children under the age of twelve years; subsection 2422(b), which addresses inducing or coercing a person under eighteen years of age to "engage in prostitution or any sexual activity for which a person can be charged with a criminal offense"; and subsections 2423(a) and (b), which cover the transportation of minors and travel with the intent to engage in a sex act with a juvenile. In *United States v. Brockdorff* (1997), subsection 2423(b) was held to be constitutional against challenges that it exceeded Congress's authority under the commerce clause of the U.S. Constitution and that it was an impermissible burden on the right of interstate travel.

Reporting Abuse

CHILDREN who are victims of sexual abuse sometimes fail to report it until later in life, which may allow abusers to claim that the alleged abuse was fabricated. In 1983 Dr. Roland C. Summit explained that such behavior is based on the fact that the child is often threatened or feels that the abuser will cause some harm if the incident is not kept secret; that children generally feel subordinate to adults and fear confrontation; that if a child feels helpless, he or she often believes that accepting the situation is the only option; and that the difficulties in talking about abuse tend to break down as the child reaches adulthood. Boys are often less likely to report sexual abuse by males because of the stigma attached to being called a homosexual. Faced with a

delayed claim of child abuse, courts have not been consistent in whether they allow the elements of the syndrome to be introduced into evidence at trial.

Although states may not set a time limit on filing criminal charges against child abusers, they do limit civil suits that require a lesser standard of proof—a preponderance of the evidence, as opposed to evidence that seems beyond a reasonable doubt. In 2006 an attempt in Maryland to remove restrictions on lawsuits by victims against abusers and their employers (originally limited to victims twenty-five years of age or younger) faced strong opposition and intense lobbying by the Catholic Church; a legislative compromise would allow victims under the age of twenty-five to bring actions until they become forty-two, based on evidence that many victims typically wait until their thirties or forties to report childhood abuse.

Victims' Testimony

States also have laws against child abuse, but a major barrier to enforcement is the uncertain testimony of child victims. As noted in *Pennsylvania v. Ritchie* (1987), child sexual abuse is "one of the most difficult crimes to detect and prosecute, in large part because there often are no witnesses except the victim." Children may not be good witnesses for many reasons: they may be scared or ashamed, feel intimidated, be unable to communicate well, or want to protect a family member or other trusted person, such as a priest.

In the Sixth Amendment (1791), the U.S. Constitution provides that a defendant has the right "to be confronted with the witnesses against him." This right as well as rules against hearsay evidence (testimony of someone who is not in court) allow a defendant to test a witness's credibility and evidence against him. To address this problem, about half of the states have enacted "general child hearsay" exceptions, and they may permit the videotaped testimony of a child to avoid intimidation by the defendant in a face-to-face courtroom confrontation.

In *Idaho v. Wright* (1990), the U.S. Supreme Court held that for a child's statement to be admitted in court under an exception to the prohibition against hearsay, there must be a finding that the statement is supported by "particularized guarantees of trustworthiness." But in *White v. Illinois* (1992), the Court opined that the constitutional right of confrontation does not necessarily require the child to appear in court if the victim's testimony is based on the spontaneous declaration or medical examination exceptions to the hearsay rule. (A spontaneous declaration is a statement related to a startling event or condition or a statement made under the stress of emotion caused by an event or a condition; a medical examination exception allows statements that are reasonably pertinent to diagnosis or treatment, for example, the general character of a patient's symptoms, pain, or feelings.)

Prenatal Abuse

An emerging area of the law concerns prenatal abuse during a woman's PREGNANCY. When a newborn baby tests positive for toxic DRUGS, courts may order the child to be taken into custody and placed with a state facility on the grounds that the drug level constitutes child abuse per se (by itself). However, they are divided on the question of whether drug abusers should be subject to civil or criminal liability for causing harm to a child before it is born. A civil action would require the government to take the child into custody, but a criminal action might require that the mother go to jail. Some state courts have ruled that child abuse and neglect proceedings do not apply to unborn children.

Federal, state, and private programs, including a federal grant program for child abuse and neglect prevention and treatment under Title 42, section 5106a, of the U.S. Code, now target the full range of DOMESTIC VIOLENCE, including child sexual abuse, to help prevent this damaging behavior. The law can come into play only after an incident has occurred. Even then the relationship of the victims to their abusers can make it difficult for justice to be done in many cases.

See also HUMAN TRAFFICKING; MOTHERHOOD; PORNOGRAPHY; PROSTITUTION; RELIGION; SODOMY; VICTIMS' RIGHTS; VOYEURISM.

CHILD CUSTODY

See CHILD SUPPORT; DIVORCE.

CHILD ONLINE PROTECTION ACT

The use of personal computers has spread rapidly into homes, offices, schools, and libraries in the past two decades. With this proliferation has come the ability of not only adults but also CHILDREN and TEENAGERS to connect to the INTERNET at home and in libraries. Well over half the U.S. population now uses the Internet. This form of communication was obviously not envisioned when the framers of the U.S. Constitution crafted the protections for speech and the press in the FIRST AMENDMENT (1791). But the similarity between the importance to a democratic society of the right of free speech and a free press and the uncensored exchange of information and ideas over the Internet has not been lost on the U.S. Supreme Court. Twice it has struck down the Child Online Protection Act (1998), once in 2002 and again in 2004.

In an earlier case, *Reno v. American Civil Liberties Union* (1997), the Supreme Court ruled 9–0 that the COMMUNICATIONS DECENCY ACT (1996) was an unconstitutional violation of the First Amendment. That act made it a crime to use a computer to transmit indecent material to anyone under eighteen years of age or to display such material in a way that made it available to someone in that age group. According to the Court, CONGRESS had not clearly defined the term *indecent* in the act, simply referring to it as "patently offensive" descriptions or images of sexual or excretory activities. Punishment for violations, however, could range up to a fine of $250,000 or two years in jail or both. The justices found the law both too vague and too broad and declared that it would inevitably lead to the suppression of speech among adults and children.

A year after the *Reno* decision, Congress tried again to protect children from the Internet's pernicious evils by passing the Child Online Protection Act. "Congressional Findings" cited at the beginning of the act declared that "the protection of the physical and psychological well-being of minors by shielding them from materials that are harmful to them is a compelling government interest." The operative language begins: "Whoever knowingly and with knowledge of the character of the material, in interstate or foreign commerce by means of the World Wide Web, makes any communication for commercial purposes that is available to any minor and that includes any material that is harmful to minors shall be fined not more than $50,000, imprisoned not more than 6 months, or both."

The material considered by the lawmakers to be harmful to minors is described using language from Supreme Court decisions, such as ROTH V. UNITED STATES (1957). Included is "any communication, picture, image, graphic image file, article, recording, writing, or other matter of any kind that is obscene." The description continues by citing anything that "the average person, applying contemporary community standards, would find, taking the material as a whole and with respect to minors, is designed to appeal to, or . . . pander to, the PRURIENT INTEREST." To counter the lack of specificity in the Communications Decency Act, the new law singled out material that "depicts, describes, or represents, in a manner patently offensive with respect to minors, an actual or simulated sexual act or sexual contact, an actual or simulated normal or perverted sexual act, or a lewd exhibition of the genitals or post-pubescent female breast . . . [which] taken as a whole, lacks serious literary, artistic, political, or scientific value for minors. . . . The term 'minor' means any person under 17 years of age."

Soon after the act's passage in 1998, the AMERICAN CIVIL LIBERTIES UNION and the Electronic Privacy Information Center asked a federal district court to issue an injunction preventing the government from enforcing the new law. The court did so, holding that adults' protected speech was burdened by the attempt to keep harmful material from minors. Among its reasons were that costs would be imposed on adults to access otherwise free material, that adults without credit cards would be penalized, that interactive speech (even speech not harmful to minors) would

be placed behind verification screens, and that self-censorship would occur to avoid penalties. An appeals court upheld the sanction, finding, "Because of the peculiar geography-free nature of cyberspace, [the law's] community standards test would essentially require every web communication to abide by the most restrictive community's standards."

An appeal by the U.S. Department of Justice put the case, *Ashcroft v. American Civil Liberties Union* (2002), before the Supreme Court. While not directly deciding any of the case's core legal issues, the Court ordered the appeals court to decide it in the context of a broad range of First Amendment concerns. That court then ruled in *American Civil Liberties Union v. Ashcroft* (2003) that the lack of national standards for determining the harmful materials proscribed in the act, along with other defects, made the law unconstitutional. The other defects included the ambiguous definition of a minor, which could apply both to a young child and a seventeen-year-old sitting in front of a computer screen. In 2004 the Supreme Court, on appeal from the lower court, confirmed the unconstitutionality of the Child Online Protection Act on the grounds that the government had not shown that there are no "less restrictive alternatives" to the act's language and that should the law become effective "there is a potential for extraordinary harm and a serious chill upon protected speech."

The law also established a commission to study ways to reduce children's access "to material that is harmful to minors on the Internet." Before the law was voided, the commission on October 20, 2000, submitted its final report. This made recommendations to protect children from OBSCENITY online through public education, consumer empowerment efforts, aggressive law enforcement, and voluntary actions by the online providers. The report concluded that the "child-protective technologies and methods evaluated . . . provide an important but incomplete measure of protection from harmful to minors material online."

More and more, lawmakers and courts are having to grapple with the dramatic changes wrought in American society by advancements in science and technology. Whether the Internet will be subjected to some new form of CENSORSHIP cannot be predicted. For the time being, however, this worldwide and nearly instantaneous communication system is being allowed to flourish without undue restraint.

CHILD PORNOGRAPHY

See CHILDREN; PORNOGRAPHY.

CHILD SUPPORT

All states have laws obligating parents to support their CHILDREN, who are a natural outcome of reproductive sexual behavior. Biological and adoptive parents must care for a child to the age of majority, generally eighteen years, or twenty-one in some states. They may be required to continue this support longer, for example, if the child is in college or has special needs. A parent is exempt from this obligation if the child is on active MILITARY duty, the parental relationship is terminated (as in the case of adoption), or a court declares a child emancipated from his or her parents.

Legal issues regarding child support generally arise in cases where the parents are separated or divorced and the parent with the custody of the child depends on monetary aid from the absent, or noncustodial, parent. Custody of a child following a DIVORCE is determined by a court under state law, although federal courts may interpret that law. In *Elk Grove Unified School Dist. v. Newdow* (2004), the U.S. Supreme Court affirmed that parental and custodial relationships between a child and a parent are "defined by state law," noting that "this Court customarily defers to the state-law interpretations of the regional federal court." The case in question involved the right of a father to bring a suit on behalf of his daughter, whose mother had been given *"sole* legal custody" and was "authorized . . . to 'exercise legal control' over her daughter." The Court found that the father, an atheist, had no legal standing to file a lawsuit on his daughter's

behalf. Newdow was asserting that the words "under God" in the Pledge of Allegiance, which his daughter was required to recite in school, was religious indoctrination prohibited by the FIRST AMENDMENT (1791) to the U.S. Constitution.

Parents of a child born in a MARRIAGE are generally considered joint guardians and have equal rights to the child's custody if they separate or obtain a divorce. Courts base the amount of child support due from each parent on their relative income and the percentage of time the child spends with each. The amount of the payment may be adjusted by the court when there is a substantial change of circumstances, such as when the income of a parent who has been ordered to pay support is significantly reduced or increased.

Under Missouri law, to take one example,

[T]he court may order either or both parents . . . to pay an amount reasonable or necessary for the support of the child . . . after considering all relevant factors including: (1) The financial needs and resources of the child; (2) The financial resources and needs of the parents; (3) The standard of living the child would have enjoyed had the marriage not been dissolved; (4) The physical and emotional condition of the child, and the child's educational needs; (5) The child's physical and legal custody arrangements, including the amount of time the child spends with each parent and the reasonable expenses associated with the custody or visitation arrangements; and (6) The reasonable work-related child care expenses of each parent.

In Utah the law requires courts to include in the divorce decree, among other things, "an order assigning responsibility for the payment of reasonable and necessary medical and dental expenses of the dependent children," and, if available "at a reasonable cost, an order requiring the purchase and maintenance of appropriate health, hospital, and dental care insurance" for them. A court may also provide "an order assigning financial responsibility for all or a portion of child care expenses ... necessitated by the employment or training of the custodial parent."

Some parents—nicknamed "deadbeat dads"—fail to pay their court-ordered child support, a fact that has led to federal and state laws intended to help enforce such orders. The federal Child Support Recovery Act (1992), for one, makes it a crime to willfully fail to pay support for a child who lives in another state if the amount due has not been paid for more than one year or exceeds $5,000. Punishment includes imposition of fines and imprisonment, as well as garnishment of the delinquent parent's wages. The Child Support Enforcement Amendments (1984) require each state to have its own guidelines, under which the following factors may be taken into consideration: needs of the child, such as health care, education, day care, and special needs; income and needs of each parent; number of children being supported; and the child's standard of living before the family's dissolution. The Full Faith and Credit for Child Support Orders Act (1994) requires states to enforce child support orders issued in other states. Federal prosecutors can help bring actions that involve interstate cases.

A study reported in 2005 found that one result of stricter state laws and enforcement of child support orders was a reduction in the number of out-of-wedlock births for the period 1980–93. It was not clear whether the drop came because pregnancies were prevented or would-be parents were encouraged to marry. Nonetheless, the change bodes well for their offspring, because children of single parents have a greater probability of poverty, academic failure, and social problems.

The rule in dealing with children in a court of law is to first seek to do what is in the best interests of the child. In some cases, separation or divorce may be in a child's best interests if a parent is abusive or otherwise may do a child more harm than good. Child support is a means by which the law ensures that a child whose parents do not live together receives at least the basic necessities to which any child is entitled.

Contacts

Office of Child Support Enforcement, U.S. Department of Health and Human Services, 370 L'Enfant Promenade, SW, Washington, DC 20447 (202-401-9383). www.acf. dhhs.gov/programs/cse.

National Child Support Enforcement Association, 444 North Capitol Street, Suite 414, Washington, DC 20001-1512 (202-624-8180). www.ncsea.org.

See also ALIMONY; ILLEGITIMACY; PATERNITY; UNMARRIED PARENTS.

CHILDREN

Children are both the product of sexual activity and the subjects of many laws regulating sexual behavior; they may also become victims of sexual misbehavior or SEX OFFENDERS themselves. State laws require that they be protected and supported to ensure the preservation of the species. A child or a minor (generally under the age of eighteen years) is given special legal protection, for example, by statutory rape laws that hold a child under a certain age (variable by state) incapable of giving CONSENT to sexual relations; efforts are also made to reduce children's exposure to sexually explicit materials.

Special state courts, generally called juvenile courts, have jurisdiction over certain cases involving children, such as CHILD ABUSE and neglect, adoption, juvenile misconduct, and delinquency. Some states have established family courts that handle a broader range of legal issues and provide a broader range of remedies, especially those tailored to minors. A primary rule adopted by the courts for deciding cases that involve children is to give priority to the best interests of the child.

Parents and the State

The child, the parents or family, and the state are intricately entwined in the process of protecting children, including victims of illegal sexual behavior, and also punishing them as sex offenders.

Responsibilities. Whatever the legal connection of a child to a parent or a guardian—whether born into a traditional nuclear family of mother and father, conceived by one of several ASSISTED REPRODUCTIVE TECHNOLOGY methods or by surrogate MOTHERHOOD, or adopted—the law imposes an obligation of maintenance and CHILD SUPPORT. States have enacted laws that incorporate the common law duty of parents to provide their children with necessary food, clothing, and shelter; many states have family-expense acts that require both spouses to support their children, although at common law only the father was typically held to be responsible. State laws also deal with the obligations of support for children when the parents separate or DIVORCE.

Rights. Parents also have certain legal rights regarding their children. After noting the state's authority to compel school attendance and set the curriculum, the U.S. Supreme Court held in *Meyer v. Nebraska* (1923) that a state law requiring the teaching of English only for children up to the eighth grade was an unconstitutional interference with the parents' right to "establish a home and bring up children"; in this case, the parents had hired a German teacher for their children. Then the Court, in *Pierce v. Society of Sisters* (1925), by striking down a state law that required all children between eight and sixteen years of age to attend public schools, upheld parents' right to send their children to private or parochial schools.

Children's rights were acknowledged by the Supreme Court in *Prince v. Massachusetts* (1944). The opinion for the Court, written by Associate Justice Wiley B. Rutledge, concluded that "the custody, care, and nurture of the child reside first in the parents," noting that there was a "private realm of family life which the state cannot enter." This decision also recognized the "rights of children to exercise their religion," pointing out that "children have rights, in common with older people," but that the "state's authority over children's activities is broader than over like actions of adults." In *Bellotti v. Baird* (1979), the Court observed that the special vulnerability of children, their inability to make critical decisions, and the role of parents in child rearing all limit children's rights; the state consequently may adjust its legal system to take this into account.

Child Victims

Children, like adults, may be the victims of SEX OFFENSES such as sexual abuse, SEXUAL ASSAULT, and rape, but certain sex offenses specifically involve child victims. Among these are child molestation, statutory rape, and child pornography. Child sexual abuse, as a court in Pennsylvania stated in *Pennsylvania v. Ritchie* (1987), is "one of the most difficult crimes to detect and prosecute, in large part because there often are no witnesses except the victim"; child witnesses are generally not fully capable of understanding the nature of the crime committed against them.

Most sex offenses against children are prosecuted at the state level. However, some federal laws in the U.S. Code, Title 18, sections 2241(c) and 2422(b), respectively, make it a crime to cross a state line with the intent to engage in an illegal sex act with a minor or to coerce or entice a minor across state lines to engage in PROSTITUTION or HUMAN TRAFFICKING. The federal government also assists individuals, organizations, and state governments in combating sex crimes against children, including crimes involving use of the Internet, and the Federal Bureau of Investigation includes a CRIMES AGAINST CHILDREN UNIT.

Child Molestation. Child molestation (to accost or harass sexually) can cover a variety of sexual offenses, including improper touching or fondling, lewd and lascivious conduct such as indecent exposure, sexual intercourse, and oral-genital, oral-anal, and genital-anal contact. States use various terms for describing crimes related to child molestation, from conduct and assault to sexual abuse. New York law refers in varying degrees to "sexual conduct against a child" and a "course of sexual conduct against a child" (conduct over a period of time). Under Illinois law, child molestation is encompassed in "sexual exploitation of a child": "Any person commits sexual exploitation of a child if in the presence of a child and with intent or knowledge that a child would view his or her acts, that person: (1) engages in a sexual act; or (2) exposes his or her sex organs, anus or breast for the purpose of sexual arousal or gratification of such person or the child."

INCEST, a crime that does not necessarily involve a child, may occur when a child is molested by a family member. All states outlaw incest, defined as marriage or sexual relations between close blood relations. Some states extend the prohibition against incest to certain nonblood relatives. It is also generally a crime for an adoptive parent to have sexual relations with an adopted child.

Statutory Rape. Statutory rape laws penalize sexual intercourse with a partner who is less than an age limit set by statute; in various states this age ranges between twelve (Alabama) and eighteen (California, Idaho, and Wisconsin) years, although the majority set it at sixteen years. In most states, such illegal sexual relations with a child, especially relations between an underage girl and an adult male, are treated as a crime that, unlike RAPE, may not be defended against by proving that the victim consented to the sex act. Even a mistake by the perpetrator as to the age of the victim may not be a defense. Besides making the adult responsible for knowing the other person's correct age, this type of strict liability protects the victim and generally eliminates the requirement that a victim testify against a defendant. Some states, however, allow a defense based on a mistake as to the victim's age; others allow it for older but not younger victims. Colorado, for example, permits such a defense for minors of more than fifteen years of age.

Most states have gender-neutral laws regarding statutory rape. In *Michael M. v. Superior Court of Sonoma County* (1981), however, the Supreme Court reviewed a California statutory rape law under which a seventeen-year-old-male could be guilty of the crime but a fourteen-year-old female could not. The Court said that such a distinction in age was not unconstitutional given that the state has a legitimate interest in protecting against unwanted PREGNANCY; this threat did not affect the male partner as much as the female partner.

Pornography. Laws regulate two major areas involving children and PORNOGRAPHY: (1) children who come in contact with pornography, which is protected by the U.S. Constitution's FIRST AMENDMENT

(1791) if it is not obscene; and (2) children who are used in the production of pornography. With respect to the first area, the FEDERAL COMMUNICATIONS COMMISSION exercises CENSORSHIP over the broadcast media to keep indecent materials away from children, and violators may be fined. Cable and satellite television are outside its control because access to these MEDIA is by subscription. The film industry has adopted a rating system for parents to monitor the level of sexually explicit material their children might be exposed to in the movies. And despite congressional efforts, the INTERNET, like cable and satellite television, is basically uncensored, except for OBSCENITY, because access by children can similarly be restricted by parents.

State laws typically prohibit the distribution or sale of sexually explicit materials to minors. North Dakota, for one, makes it a crime to "produce, direct, manufacture, issue, sell, lend, mail, publish, distribute, exhibit, or advertise" obscenity to minors. It is similarly a crime to admit a minor onto premises "where a performance harmful to minors is exhibited or takes place." Such crimes are felonies. The law, however, charges as a misdemeanor any action to willfully display "at newsstands or any other business establishment frequented by minors, or where minors are or may be invited as a part of the general public, any photograph, book, paperback book, pamphlet, or magazine, the exposed cover or available content of which exploits, is devoted to, or is principally made up of depictions of nude or partially denuded human figures posed or presented in a manner to exploit sex, lust, or perversion for commercial gain." According to Kansas law, promoting obscenity to minors is outlawed "where the recipient of the obscene material or obscene device or a member of the audience of an obscene performance is a child under the age of 18 years."

When it comes to pornography depicting children engaged in sex acts, the Supreme Court has held that a state law making it a crime to distribute child pornography was not unconstitutional. In *New York v. Ferber* (1982), the justices declared that the government

In 1908 the mayor of New York City shut down all the movie theaters on the grounds that they were immoral (a closure that lasted just two days). As attendance increased, reformers engineered ordinances to prohibit children under sixteen years of age from entering a theater without a parent and banned the depiction of crime on the screen.

has a legitimate interest in protecting children from sexual exploitation and abuse, that child pornography bears a direct relationship to such exploitation and abuse, that there is little or no social value to child pornography, and that the Court's precedents have found such material to lack First Amendment protection. In *Stanley v. Georgia* (1969), the Court held that private possession of obscene material was constitutionally protected. But in *Osborne v. Ohio* (1990), the Court made an exception for child pornography, which it said contributed to the sexual exploitation of children. In *Ashcroft v. Free Speech Coalition* (2002), the Court granted constitutional protection for possession

of "virtual" child pornography, in which no real children are involved but in which adults may instead pose as children or animations are used.

Child Sex Offenders

About one-third of sexual assaults on children are committed by other children. As a result of the same act, one child may be a victim and another an offender. For this reason, most courts apply statutory rape laws against a child offender when the victim is also a child, whom the law was intended to protect; an Illinois court followed this reasoning in *In re T. W.* (1997). But child SEX OFFENDERS, depending on their age and the nature of their crime, tend to be treated differently than adults in the legal system.

In *In re Gault* (1967), the Supreme Court ruled that juvenile offenders, regardless of the salutary need for special treatment in the legal system, are nonetheless entitled to certain due process rights during the adjudication of a juvenile delinquency proceeding. The *Gault* case involved the commitment of a fifteen-year-old-boy to an industrial school in Arizona for up to six years for making an obscene telephone call while on probation for another juvenile offense. The entire adjudicatory process took only a week, and many due process procedures were not afforded the defendant because he was a juvenile. The Court declared that, at a minimum, a child accused of a crime must be given adequate and timely notice of the charges and any hearings, the right to counsel, the right to confront and cross-examine witnesses, and the right not to incriminate himself—all guarantees found in the Bill of Rights (1791) of the U.S. Constitution.

A report entitled *Understanding Juvenile Sexual Offending Behavior*, issued by the Center for Sex Offender Management of the U.S. Department of Justice in 1999, indicated that "juveniles account for up to one-fifth of all rapes and almost one-half of all cases of child molestation." Although prosecution of child sex offenders is discretionary and the age of the accused and the nature of the crime are important factors, the center's National Task Force on Juvenile Sex Offending in 1993 recommended that prosecution should be a component of most interventions in juvenile sex offenses. Idaho, Illinois, New Jersey, and North Carolina are among a number of states that now require juveniles convicted of sex offenses, like adult perpetrators, to register as sex offenders.

Homosexuality

A number of issues relating to HOMOSEXUALITY involve children, among which are parenting by homosexuals, whether achieved by artificial insemination, in vitro fertilization, surrogate motherhood, or adoption; disparaging references to homosexuality in SEX EDUCATION

or no references at all; and SEXUAL HARASSMENT in school based on sexual orientation. Same-sex dates at school-sponsored social events may involve First Amendment rights, as may displaying gay pride symbols or clothing. In a case involving students wearing armbands to protest the Vietnam War, *Tinker v. Des Moines Independent Community School District* (1969), the Supreme Court concluded that as long as the symbols cause no disruption, freedom of expression should be allowed in public schools.

Children's transition from prepubescence into sexually mature and active adults poses many problems for law enforcement, legislatures, and the courts. Laws regarding sexual behavior, as the sex researcher ALFRED KINSEY noted, are intended more to protect social custom than to provide justice. His observation applies even more accurately to sexual behavior involving children. While people are expanding their knowledge of the world through advancements in science and technology, our basic understanding of how to rear our children in a challenging environment still remains largely intuitive, rather than logical.

See also CHILD ONLINE PROTECTION ACT; DOMESTIC VIOLENCE; ENTERTAINMENT INDUSTRY; LEWD BEHAVIOR; SINGLE-SEX EDUCATION; TEENAGERS; TELEPHONE SEX; UNMARRIED PARENTS; VICTIMS' RIGHTS.

CIVIL UNIONS

See SAME-SEX MARRIAGE.

CLONING

See STEM-CELL RESEARCH AND CLONING.

COHABITATION

See ADULTERY; MARRIAGE; PREMARITAL SEX; UNMARRIED COHABITANTS; UNMARRIED PARENTS.

COMMUNICATIONS DECENCY ACT

The law has had a particularly difficult time dealing with PORNOGRAPHY, OBSCENITY, and indecency on the INTERNET. Congress has made several attempts to pass legislation that would keep improper materials away from CHILDREN, including the Communications Decency Act in 1996 and the CHILD ONLINE PROTECTION ACT in 1998. These efforts have been thwarted by the U.S. Constitution's FIRST AMENDMENT (1791) and the U.S. Supreme Court.

The Communications Decency Act made it a crime to allow someone under eighteen years of age to have access to indecent or obscene materials on the Internet. The act prohibited the posting of "indecent" or "patently offensive" materials in a public forum on the Internet, including on Web pages or in chatrooms. Relevant provisions criminalized the "knowing" transmission of "obscene or indecent" messages and the sending or display of any message "that, in context, depicts or describes, in terms patently offensive as measured by contemporary community standards, sexual or excretory activities or organs." An affirmative defense involved taking "good faith, . . . effective . . . actions" to restrict access by minors to prohibited communications.

Although couched in terms of protecting children from obscenity, pornography, and stalking on the Internet, these activities were in fact already crimes under existing laws. Therefore, the motivation for the new law was viewed as political—a demonstration to legislators' constituents that their elected officials were doing as much as they could to protect children from inappropriate materials on computer screens in homes, schools, and libraries.

The act was criticized for imposing content regulations—CENSORSHIP—on the Internet, which was open and decentralized, as is encouraged in a free society. Because the law was considered a threat to the existence of the Internet as another venue for free expression, education, and political debate, a number of organizations, including the Citizens Internet Empowerment Coalition and the AMERICAN CIVIL LIBERTIES UNION, opposed it as an infringement of citizens' rights under the First Amendment.

The U.S. Supreme Court in *Reno v. American Civil Liberties Union* (1997) unanimously affirmed a lower federal court's finding that the Communications Decency Act was unconstitutional. The opinion written by Associate Justice John Paul Stevens was based on the premise that the Internet was similar to newspapers and books in our democratic society and thus deserved the highest level of constitutional protection under the First Amendment. The opinion pointed out that unlike the Internet, no technical skill or expertise is required to receive material via broadcast and cable television; therefore, more regulation of those MEDIA may be allowed to prevent children's inadvertent exposure to indecent material.

A crucial consideration of the decision was that because Internet service providers were unable to identify the end users of their products to determine whether they were under the age of eighteen years, the providers would in all likelihood be put out of business under the law. The Court concluded that, while the goal of protecting children from obscenity and indecency was commendable, the means to that end were in this case unconstitutional. The act's "indecent transmission" and "patently offensive display" provisions were found to abridge the First Amendment's protection of freedom of speech. Without comment the Court allowed the act's general prohibition against obscenity to remain the law because, as the line of Supreme Court cases beginning with *ROTH V. UNITED STATES* (1957) has held, obscenity is outside First Amendment protection.

Also left in effect in the act was an important protection for Internet service providers that insulated them from lawsuits based on information originating with a third-party user. As an example, a computer dating service was held not liable by a federal appeals court in 2003 for the identity theft involving an actress who had appeared on the television shows *Star Trek: Deep Space Nine* and *General Hospital*. Information about Christianne Carafano, acting under the name of Chase Masterson, had been supplied to the dating service without her knowledge or permission. Such immunity, however, does not apply to federal criminal liability or intellectual-property lawsuits involving the Internet.

In 1998, by enacting the Child Online Protection Act, CONGRESS would again try to censor the Internet under the guise of protecting children from obscenity. Even though this later piece of legislation was more precise in the definition of the evils to be eliminated and the law reduced the penalties for violations, the Supreme Court rejected it as well in 2002 and 2004.

See also INDECENT EXPOSURE.

COMMUNITY STANDARDS

See OBSCENITY; *ROTH V. UNITED STATES*.

ANTHONY COMSTOCK

A crusader against vice in many forms, Anthony Comstock campaigned for passage of a strict federal law against sending obscene materials, including information about contraceptives, through the U.S. mail. The 1873 law made it a misdemeanor to mail any "obscene, lewd, or lascivious, or filthy book, pamphlet, picture, paper, letter, writing, print, or other publication of an indecent character." After its enactment, he was appointed a special U.S. postal agent and given authority to prosecute violators of what became known as the Comstock Act—a position he held until his death on September 21, 1915, in Summit, New Jersey.

Born in New Canaan, Connecticut, on March 7, 1844, Anthony Comstock attended public schools and served for two years in the Union Army after his older brother had died at Gettysburg. Following his discharge in 1865, he wound up in the New York City area. There he became concerned about the government's indifference to what he perceived as a lack of morality, evidenced by prostitution and OBSCENITY, including erotic literature and information on CONTRACEPTION. Taking matters into his own hands, he

The quintessential public censor, Anthony Comstock crusaded against vice and obscenity as he saw it and spearheaded a drive for a national law, called the Comstock Act, to help him accomplish his goals. The 1873 law prohibited the interstate transportation of obscene materials, including contraceptives.

helped apprehend two pornographers; one of them later attacked him with a knife, after which he grew bushy whiskers to hide the scar.

With support from several influential friends, Morris Jessup and William E. Dodge, Comstock organized an antivice committee of the Young Men's Christian Association in 1871. When some YMCA members became offended by his overzealous methods of entrapping alleged lawbreakers, he set up a separate organization called the New York Society for the Suppression of Vice (modeled after the seventy-five-year-old London Society for the Suppression of Vice); he served as secretary and the most active member. Comstock's crusade came at a time that cities around the nation were rallying to eradicate PROSTITUTION.

"Purity" (antiprostitution) advocates and suffragists supported his efforts for a time, although his stridency finally turned away many of them.

In 1880 he published a report of his personal efforts to stamp out vice as he saw it. In addition to obscenity and contraception, *Frauds Exposed; or, How the People Are Deceived and Robbed and Youth Corrupted, Being a Full Disclosure of Various Schemes Operated through the Mails, and Unearthed by the Author* focused on gambling, real estate scams, astrological forecasts, and many other forms of fraud uncovered by Comstock. Some years later, his activities to enforce moral purity—still including forms of entrapment and strong-arm tactics—were praised by a special committee of the New York legislature as "vitally essential to the safety and decency of the community."

Among the items Comstock criticized were sexual hygiene publications published by MARGARET SANGER, the SEX EDUCATION and birth control advocate. The Comstock Act prohibited the interstate transportation of contraceptives, considering them to be obscene materials. In 1914 Sanger was prosecuted under the postal agent's namesake law for distributing her magazine, *The Woman Rebel;* she fled to Europe, but her estranged husband was jailed in her place. The federal charges were later dropped to avoid making her a martyr to her own cause. Comstock was also an active antiabortionist. When Madame Restell, a New York woman who provided contraceptives and performed abortions, committed suicide after he had begun prosecuting her, he was reported to have been elated.

By one account Comstock was responsible for the destruction of some 160 tons of obscene literature and pictures. He protested exotic dancing at the World's Columbian Exposition in Chicago in 1893, tried to ban the play *Mrs. Warren's Profession* by the British playwright George Bernard Shaw (1856–1950) in 1905, and threatened to arrest the artist Paul Chabas, who displayed his nude painting *September Morn* (1912) in New York City in 1913. An annual government report in 1914 assessed the number of people he was responsible for arraigning on charges in federal and state courts at 3,697.

After his death, Comstock's legacy of federal and state laws, as well as the private organizations he helped create in his never-ending battle against his concept of vice in America, continued for many years. Threatened himself by this relentless crusader, George Bernard Shaw helped etch Comstock's name in the nation's vocabulary. Writing to the *New York Times* in 1905, he declared: "*Comstockery* is the world's standing Joke at the expense of the United States. . . . It confirms the deep-seated conviction of the Old World that America is a provincial place, a second rate country-town civilization after all." Today most of the activities that Comstock railed against—contraception, ABORTION, PORNOGRAPHY—are no longer considered crimes.

See also ADULT MATERIALS; FAMILY PLANNING.

CONGRESS

Article I of the U.S. Constitution (1789) establishes the Congress of the United States as the legislative branch of the federal government. The other two branches, the executive (led by the PRESIDENT) and the JUDICIARY, are coequal and independent in their own spheres of authority. Yet it is clear, from Congress's location in the Constitution's first article, that the framers intended the legislature to be the lead institution in governing the nation, granting it the power to translate the concept of majority rule into written laws.

Under the Constitution today, as it has evolved by amendment, Congress is the branch most representative of and accountable to the people. Only the members of Congress are directly elected by citizens; the president is elected indirectly by an electoral college, and the members of the federal judiciary are appointed for life. Members of Congress are also accountable to the electorate on a regular basis, with elections held every two years; the president can be reelected only once after four years, and federal judges are not subject to election at any time.

The American government established by the Constitution differs in two important ways from the constitutional monarchy of its mother country, the United Kingdom: (1) Congress is a coequal branch of the national government, whereas the Parliament of the United Kingdom is the supreme branch; and (2) the U.S. government is a federal system of limited powers, whereas the United Kingdom is a unitary government not subject to any constitutional limitations or required to share power with semisovereign states. The United Kingdom has an unwritten constitution based on tradition, documents of constitutional stature such as Magna Carta (1215), and the laws of Parliament. The United States, in contrast, has a written constitution that is supplemented by tradition—for example, the role of political parties in the government—and by decisions of the federal judiciary—for example, the presumption of innocence, which no court would deny is a fundamental and unalterable right despite the fact that nowhere is it expressly guaranteed in the written Constitution.

How Congress Works

Congress consists of an upper house, the Senate, and a lower house, the House of Representatives. Whereas the Senate is composed of two senators from each state, reflecting the equal sovereignty of each state, the members of the House are apportioned among the states on the basis of population; the more populous states have more representatives, but no state has fewer than one representative. Other important differences include the fact that senators are elected for six-year-terms, one-third of them every two years, but each member of the House is elected every two years. The Senate has authority to approve presidential nominees for key positions, including all federal judgeships, and it must ratify important treaties, which, according to the Constitution, become the law of the land just as does other congressional legislation. Any proposed law to raise revenues must be initiated in the lower house, a requirement based on the theory that representatives are more closely responsible to the people (standing for election every two years) than are the members of the Senate, which must approve any such revenue measures.

The Constitution provides some guidance on how Congress functions to make laws, but the process has actually developed into a much more complex interaction among the political leadership, executive branch officers, lobbyists, special-interest groups, and constituents than was ever envisioned. Almost all of the members of Congress are members of the Democratic or Republican parties, for instance, and the party that has a majority of members in each house controls the body, although at times bipartisanship may come into play.

A major factor driving much of the business of Congress today is getting reelected, which means appeasing constituents and soliciting campaign funds. Being reelected also means attaining seniority, which in turn generally produces more power within the party leadership and in committee assignments and chairmanships. Committees play an important role in Congress's work, given that all legislative proposals introduced in either house are assigned to a committee for consideration before any action is taken by the entire body. Some committees and subcommittees have responsibilities for matters relating to sexual behavior; among them are Senate and House committees with oversight and budgetary responsibilities for key executive branch agencies and programs dealing with ABORTION, AIDS-HIV and other SEXUALLY TRANSMITTED DISEASES, CHILDREN, communications and the FEDERAL COMMUNICATIONS COMMISSION, constitutional rights, DRUGS, ETHICS, families, federal prisons, the MILITARY, and SEX EDUCATION.

Much of the time of senators and representatives and their staffs is taken up with providing services to constituents and dealing with special-interest groups and lobbyists for powerful business and political constituencies, who can afford professional representation. Bills are often drafted by people in the executive branch or by lobbyists, so that members of Congress often vote on measures that they have not read personally and that they may understand only in broad outline. Congress today works more like the floor of the New York Stock Exchange, with votes and interests and money being aggregated and traded, rather than like the deliberative legislative body often described in civics classes.

Legislating Sexual Behavior

Laws that have emerged from this chaotic process relating to sexual behavior can have a significant impact on the lives of many citizens. A sample of laws of this type, chosen to demonstrate the scope of congressional involvement in areas related to sexual behavior, are set forth below. Many other types of legislation, such as tax laws that allow a deduction for dependent children, can indirectly affect sexual behavior by making it easier to support and thus have more children.

Comstock Act (1873). Named for the antivice crusader ANTHONY COMSTOCK, this law made it a federal crime to send obscene materials, including information about CONTRACEPTION, through the U.S. mail.

White Slave Traffic Act (Mann Act) (1910). This law criminalized interstate transportation of a female for PROSTITUTION or other immoral purposes.

Sheppard-Towner Maternity and Infancy Act (1921). To promote child and maternal health services, this act provided matching federal grants to the states.

Federal Communications Act (1934). With this law Congress established the Federal Communications Commission, which among other responsibilities oversees the decency of material broadcast over the airwaves.

Title VII of the Civil Rights Act (1964). The purpose of this law is to curb sex DISCRIMINATION in the workplace.

Family Planning Services and Population Research Act (1970). The law authorized funding to coordinate and expand FAMILY PLANNING and population research by the federal government.

Title IX of the Education Amendments of 1972. The provisions of TITLE IX prohibit sex-based discrimination in education programs or activities that receive federal funding.

Equal Rights Amendment (1972). Congress passed this constitutional amendment to give women EQUAL RIGHTS with men. In accordance with the provisions of Article V of the Constitution, the amendment was sent to the states for approval, but it failed to obtain the necessary ratification by three-fourths of the states during the original seven-year period and a three-year extension granted by Congress.

Child Abuse Prevention and Treatment Act (1974). This law provided federal aid for the prevention and treatment of CHILD ABUSE and neglect.

Hyde Amendment (1976). Beginning with the federal budget for fiscal year 1977, Congress has continually precluded any federal funding for abortion through Medicaid, the health program for the needy. This law, named after its sponsor, Representative Henry J. Hyde of Illinois, was upheld by the U.S. Supreme Court in *Harris v. McRae* (1980).

Adolescent Family Life Act (1981). This law provided prenatal care and counseling for pregnant TEENAGERS and funds for programs to discourage teenage sexual activity.

Violence Against Women Act (1994). The VIOLENCE AGAINST WOMEN ACT was intended to assist federal and state jurisdictions in preventing DOMESTIC VIOLENCE, prosecuting offenders, and assisting victims by strengthening criminal laws, enlisting the help of health care professionals, and providing support for children who are the victims of abuse or witnesses to such mistreatment.

Defense of Marriage Act (1996). The DEFENSE OF MARRIAGE ACT established a federal definition of MARRIAGE that excludes homosexual couples and limits federal privileges and benefits to the traditional married couple consisting of one man and one woman.

Megan's Law (1996). Named after a seven-year-old victim of RAPE and murder by a twice-convicted pedophile, MEGAN'S LAW required all fifty states to set up a public notification system to identify dangerous SEX OFFENDERS.

Communications Decency Act (1996) and *Child Online Protection Act (1998).* Disturbed by underage children's access to PORNOGRAPHY on the INTERNET, Congress sought to rein in such material with these laws. However, the Supreme Court in several decisions found both to be unconstitutional restrictions on the FIRST AMENDMENT freedoms of adults.

Federal Marriage Amendment (2002). Reintroduced unsuccessfully in 2004 and 2006—both election years in which the Republican Party worked to energize its base of conservative voters—this proposed constitutional amendment would restrict marriage to "the union of a man and a woman," thereby placing the mandates of the Defense of Marriage Act within the body of the Constitution itself. If eventually passed and ratified by the states, although this is now deemed unlikely, the FEDERAL MARRIAGE AMENDMENT would be the only constitutional amendment other than Prohibition (1919, repealed in 1933) to diminish, rather than increase, rights of U.S. citizens.

Just as sex scandals have ensnared presidents of the United States, they have not bypassed members of Congress. In 1983 two members of the House of Representatives—Daniel B. Crane, a Republican from Illinois, and Gerry E. Studds, a Democrat from Massachusetts—were officially censured for sexual misconduct with congressional pages. Then in 1998, the same year the House of Representatives voted to impeach President Bill Clinton, the speaker-designate of the House resigned after admitting to having had several extramarital affairs. That lawmakers often err in matters of sexual behavior is probably just a mirror of the total population and proves how difficult it can be for laws and social constraints to effectively control the sexual behavior of citizens.

See also CHILD ONLINE PROTECTION ACT; COMMUNICATIONS DECENCY ACT.

CONSENT

The concept of consent—agreement or, more simply, saying yes or I do—is found in many legal contexts from contract and tort law to criminal law. In contract law, consent (agreement) to the terms of a contract makes it legally binding; in tort law, consent (acquiescence) to a person's entrance onto one's property negates an action for trespass; and in criminal law, consent to waive a constitutional right, such as to representation by counsel, can make a defendant more vulnerable to prosecution. The notion of consent implies an act of reason and deliberation—a true choice between alternatives—and may not be influenced by duress or intimidation. Giving one's agreement is no less an important factor with regard to legal aspects of sexual behavior. A recent landmark U.S. Supreme Court decision, *LAWRENCE V. TEXAS* (2003), for example, found that the U.S. Constitution protects homosexual SODOMY conducted by consenting adults in private.

Sexual Relations

Consent lies at the heart of many sex-related issues. Among them are consent of a person to have sexual relations with another; of two parties to marry, or in the case of minors, consent provided by their parents; of a woman or parents to give up a child for adoption; of a woman to carry the child of others to term; of a minor's parents for her to have an ABORTION; of patients to release of private medical or genetic information; and of minors to treatment for SEXUALLY TRANSMITTED DISEASES and for abuse of DRUGS. In other legal situations, consent is often provable by physical evidence, such as a signed document, an oral statement in front of witnesses, or merely a handshake. But when it comes to sexual behavior, what constitutes consent is often harder to prove under the law. Questions may arise about a person's legal age for consent, mental capacity to give consent, and extent of the informed consent (requiring sufficient reliable information to make assent meaningful). A concept that makes perfect sense in other legal contexts becomes more complicated when sex is involved.

Marriage. MARRIAGE, the traditional basis for agreeing to sexual relations and making a commitment to a partner and a family for life, is based on consent that is epitomized in the "I do" of the marriage vows. Consent alone does not create a legal marriage, however, because state laws require that certain formalities also be observed; the legal adage is that marriage is a contract between two persons and the state. The words used in marriage ceremonies may vary, but the law presumes that a legally married person has consented to several important commitments and to a change in legal status from an individual to a married partner, including shared property, mutual support, and consent to sexual relations. Laws regarding both marriage and DIVORCE have changed radically in the last fifty years. What before was regarded as irrevocable consent by a wife to sexual relations with her husband is now generally considered revocable, so that a husband may be guilty of the crime of raping his wife.

Consent also plays a role under state laws in determining eligibility for marriage, because these laws determine the age of consent to marry. All states except one require that a person be at least eighteen years of age or older to be issued a marriage license and to consent to marriage on their own; Mississippi makes the age of consent, without parental approval, seventeen years for males and fifteen for females. As for the threshold for minors to marry with parental consent, the age of the intended spouses varies under state law between eighteen for males in several states, to fourteen in Alabama for males and females, to twelve for females in Kansas and Massachusetts, to no age limit in Mississippi.

Rape. RAPE involves nonconsensual sexual relations and has long been a crime under Anglo-American law; under common law, the act had to be carried out by force and against the victim's will, meaning without consent. In his *Commentaries on the Laws of England* (1765–70), William Blackstone (1723–80) noted that although a victim might give evidence under oath as to the lack of consent, "if the place, where the fact was alleged to be committed was where it was possible she might have been heard, and she made no outcry; these and the like circumstances, 'if unexplained,' carry a strong, but not conclusive, presumption, that her testimony is false or feigned."

Even today, despite the evolution of the law regarding proof of consent since Blackstone's time, a major consideration in rape trials may be whether the victim consented to the sexual activity. Kentucky law regarding sexual offenses, including rape and other types of SEXUAL ASSAULT and abuse, provides in part: "(1) Whether or not specifically stated, it is an element of every offense defined in this chapter [Sexual Offenses] that the sexual act was committed without consent of the victim. (2) Lack of consent results from: (a) Forcible compulsion; (b) Incapacity to consent; or (c) If the offense charged is sexual abuse, any circumstances in addition to forcible compulsion or incapacity to consent in which the victim does not express or impliedly acquiesce in the actor's conduct." According to Kentucky law, victims are presumed incapable of giving consent if they are younger than sixteen years of age, mentally retarded or suffering from mental illness, or otherwise mentally incapacitated or physically helpless.

The California case *People v. Vela* (1985) provides some insight into the traditional approach to the issue of consent as a defense to a charge of rape. This decision held that where the victim consents to intercourse at the time of penetration but thereafter withdraws her consent, any use of force by her assailant past that point does not constitute rape. But in *In re John Z.* (2003), the California supreme court criticized the *Vela* decision on several grounds, including the conclusion that a woman could not revoke her consent during the act. The court also rejected the defense's arguments that, "By essence of the act of sexual intercourse, a male's primal urge to reproduce is aroused [and it] is therefore unreasonable for a female and the law to expect a male to cease having sexual intercourse immediately upon her withdrawal of consent." The defense's suggestion that a male needed "a reasonable amount of time in which to quell his primal urge" was also disputed.

As in Kentucky, the laws in states such as Alaska, Montana, Washington, and Wisconsin specify that a lack of consent is an element of the crime of rape. Arizona, Colorado, and Delaware are among other states that have determined that once force is proven, a lack of consent can be assumed. An Illinois court found in *People v. Borak* (1973) that the force necessary to establish rape may be implied when the victim is not given the opportunity to consent; in this case the rape occurred during a gynecological examination. The same implication may be made if a victim is intoxicated, drugged, or otherwise rendered incapable of rationally consenting to a sex act.

Although federal laws relating to sex crimes such as aggravated sexual abuse are limited to "the special maritime and territorial jurisdiction of the United States or in a Federal prison," Title 18, section 2241, of the U.S. Code addresses a lack of consent or impaired capability of providing consent by requiring evidence of force or threats that cause another person to engage in a sex act. Section 2241 also defines similar crimes when committed by a person who knowingly renders "another person unconscious and thereby engages in a sexual act with that other person"; in such a case, a victim is unable to give meaningful consent to the sexual activity.

Statutory Rape. A victim's age is the determining factor in a charge of statutory rape, which occurs when a victim is below the statutorily set age of consent; the defense may not assert that the victim consented because she or he is presumed to have been too young to understand the meaning of consent to a sex act. In Ohio having sex with a child under the age of sixteen years is considered statutory rape, while in Utah the age is fourteen. Some states have gender-neutral laws, although others specify female or male victims. In some states "Romeo and Juliet laws" treat youthful offenders more leniently than adults. Most statutory rape provisions are found in state laws, but, uniquely, South Carolina's constitution addresses the subject: "No unmarried woman shall legally consent to sexual intercourse who shall not have attained the age of fourteen years." At common law, as Blackstone noted, the statutory age was ten.

Marital Rape. Because at one time marriage vows were considered sufficient to constitute consent forever after to sexual relations with one's spouse, rape within marriage was not legally possible. Since the SEXUAL REVOLUTION of the 1960s and 1970s, however, WOMEN'S RIGHTS in many areas of the law have grown. Today most states have either done away with the traditional marital exemption for rape or have specifically made marital rape a separate crime. With regard to questions about consent in marital rape, the New York

court of appeals explained, in *People v. Liberta* (1984), that rape "is not simply a sexual act to which one party does not consent. Rather, it is a degrading, violent act which violates the bodily integrity of the victim and frequently causes severe, long-lasting physical and psychic harm."

Sex-Related Behavior

Consent may become an important element with respect to sex-related activities such as abortion and testing for sexually transmitted diseases. Here an individual's right to PRIVACY and confidentially often must be balanced with the government's role in enforcing the law and protecting the general welfare.

Abortion. Most states have enacted requirements that parental consent be secured before a minor is able to obtain an abortion, although such requirements can be avoided—for example, by a court order. This requirement may pit the interests of the minor against those of the state in ensuring that parental rights and responsibilities are taken into account and that the minor's decision is being made under the best possible conditions. In PLANNED PARENTHOOD OF SOUTH-EASTERN PENNSYLVANIA V. CASEY (1992), the U.S. Supreme Court upheld a state law requiring parental consent for minors but struck down a provision that made a woman notify her husband (implying a consent requirement) before having an abortion. Twenty-six states mandate counseling before a woman obtains an abortion, usually followed by a waiting period; such provisions indirectly imply that the patient is giving consent after being informed about abortion alternatives and potential side effects.

Confidentiality. In medical areas such as GENETICS studies, AIDS-HIV testing and treatment and care of other sexually transmitted diseases, and mandated DNA testing, records relating to patients or test subjects are considered confidential. State laws require an individual's consent for the release of information to others. Kentucky, for one, requires the written consent of a person determined to be infected with a sexually transmitted disease before this information can be released, except in cases such as a medical emergency or for statistical uses if the individual is not identified. Delaware law similarly prohibits the release of information regarding an individual with a sexual disease or HIV without his or her consent.

As the *Lawrence* decision seemed to declare, consent to sexual activity by adults negates any role for the state in issuing regulations for private consensual sexual conduct, except to protect minors. If men and women are equal under the law, their sexual relationships should be private matters beyond the reach of the law. However, the notion that consent legalizes sexual relations between a man and a woman is not without its critics. According to one feminist view, the unequal status of men and women in society makes it difficult for women to bargain on an equal footing with men. Catherine MacKinnon has written in *Toward a Feminist Theory of the State* (1989) that the "law of rape divides women into spheres of consent according to indices of relationship to men." A female's consent to sexual relations thus cannot always be assumed to have been freely given.

Whichever theory one subscribes to, mutual consent to sexual relations inside or outside marriage remains an important element of the law. Consent is particularly important where children could be the product of sexual activity, because they must be assured of their parents' commitment to their care and support. As with many aspects of sexual behavior, individuals want an unfettered right to enter into and leave sexual relationships as they see fit, although the state has a legitimate obligation to society to ensure that even consensual sexual behavior does not harm innocent victims.

See also BIOETHICS; DATE RAPE; FEMINISM.

CONTRACEPTION

Evidence from the paleolithic era (between 750,000 and 15,000 years ago, before the development of farming) shows that women were already using plant-based drugs to prevent PREGNANCY. The effectiveness of such contraceptive potions has been established based on plant drugs used today by women in the central forests of Paraguay. Ancient Romans also experimented with various methods of contraception, including wool plugs and astringents that helped secure the plugs and kill or reduce the efficacy of sperm.

Christianity reflected the teachings of St. Augustine (354–430 C.E.) that sex in MARRIAGE was a sin unless procreation was the goal; most adherents thus believed that contraception to prevent pregnancy was morally wrong. But something happened in Britain in 1798 to make citizens and government leaders reconsider the social ban on contraception: Thomas Malthus (1766–1834) published his *Essay on the Principle of Population,* in which he theorized that a growing population would inevitably surpass the development of resources to support it. Underscoring his prediction, a British census in 1801 showed a startling rise in population.

Although the American colonists brought their Christianity with them in a number of denominations, contraception was used—if not openly spoken about—and undoubtedly contributed to the drastic decline in the American birth rate; it fell from approximately seven CHILDREN per married woman in 1800 to 4.24 in 1880 and 3.56 by 1900. The two chief means of contraception were coitus interruptus and crude condoms, both leaving women at men's mercy. At the turn of the twentieth century, contraception became a hot political issue. President Theodore Roosevelt, who served from 1901 to 1909, used his "bully pulpit" to condemn the trend toward smaller families. He characterized any woman who avoided having children as "criminal against the race" and the "object of contemptuous abhorrence by healthy people."

A number of factors later led to an increased interest in contraception, including the 1920 constitutional amendment giving women the right to vote, the flood of women into the workforce to maintain the home front during World War II (1941–45), and the increased availability of contraceptive information and devices, including the birth control pill beginning in 1960. Backing them up were the nascent SEXUAL REVOLUTION, sparked by the reports of ALFRED KINSEY in

1948 and 1953 on male and female sexuality; the civil rights movement; the modern WOMEN'S RIGHTS movement; and efforts to stop the Vietnam War. Spurred by new freedoms, women began to push for the ability to control their reproductive process without giving up sexual relations.

Contraceptive Rights

MARGARET SANGER opened a medically supervised FAMILY PLANNING clinic, the first of many such PLANNED PARENTHOOD FEDERATION OF AMERICA centers, in Brooklyn, New York, in 1916. First she had to contend with laws that made contraceptives and information about them illegal. In *United States v. One Package* (1936), however, a federal appeals court ruled that doctors were exempt from the federal ban on the importation of contraceptives. But many states, such as Connecticut and Massachusetts, still prohibited the private use of contraception.

Estelle Griswold, the executive director of the Planned Parenthood League of Connecticut, was convicted in 1961 of violating an 1879 Connecticut law, passed during the heydey of ANTHONY COMSTOCK, banning the use of contraceptives. "Any person who uses any drug, medicinal article or instrument for the purpose of preventing conception," it read, "shall be fined not less than fifty dollars or imprisoned not less than sixty days nor more than one year or be both fined and imprisoned." She was charged along with the league's medical director, a Yale Medical School professor, with giving contraceptive information and medical advice to married persons at a New Haven clinic, which was open only ten days in 1961 before it was closed. In *GRISWOLD V. CONNECTICUT* (1965), the U.S. Supreme Court ruled that, under a newly fashioned right of PRIVACY gleaned from several provisions of the Bill of Rights (1791), the U.S. Constitution protects the use of contraceptives by married couples in their own home. Later, in *Eisenstadt v. Baird* (1972), the right was extended to nonmarried couples.

Unlike the right of ABORTION declared by the Supreme Court in *Roe v. Wade* (1973), the right to use contraceptives has not provoked much organized opposition.

TO MARRIED WOMEN—MADAME RESTELL, *Female Physician*, is happy to have it in her power to say that since the introduction into this country, about a year ago of her celebrated Preventive Powders for married ladies, whose health forbids a too rapid increase of family; hundreds have availed themselves of their use, with a success and satisfaction that has at once dispelled the fears and doubts of the most timid and skeptical; for, notwithstanding that for twenty years they have been used in Europe with invariable success, (first introduced by the celebrated Midwife and Female Physician, Madame Restell, the grandmother of the advertiser, who made this subject her particular and especial study,) still some were inclined to entertain some degree of distrust, until become convinced by their successful adoption in this country. The results of their adoption to the happiness, the health, nay, often the life of many an affectionate wife and a fond mother, are too vast to touch upon within the limits of an advertisement—results which affect not only the present well-being of parents, but the future happiness of their offspring. Is it not but too well known that the families of the married often increase beyond the happiness of those who give them birth would dictate? In how many instances does the hardworking father, and more especially the mother, of a poor family, remain slaves throughout their lives, tugging at the oar of incessant labor, toiling to live and living but to toil; when they might have enjoyed comfort and comparative affluence; and if care and toil have weighed down the spirit, and at last broken the health of the father, how often is the widow left, unable, with the most virtuous intentious, to save her fatherless offspring from becoming degraded objects of charity or profligate votaries of vice? And even though competence and plenty smile upon us, how often, alas! are the days of the kind husband and father embittered in beholding the emaciated form and declining health of the companion of his bosom, ere she had scarce reached the age of thirty fast sinking into a premature grave—with the certain prospect of himself being early bereft of the partner of his joys and sorrows, and his young and helpless children of the endearing attentions and watchful solicitude which a mother alone can bestow, not unfrequently at a time when least able to support the heart-rending affliction! Is it desirable then —is it moral for parents to increase their families, regardless of consequences to themselves or the well being of their offspring when a simple, easy healthy and certain remedy is within our control? The advertiser feeling the importance of this subject and estimating the vast benefits resulting to thousands by the adoption of means prescribed by her, would respectfully arouse the attention of the married, by all that they hold near and dear to its consideration. Is it not wise and virtuous to prevent evils to which we are subject by simple and healthy means within our control? Every dispassionate, virtuous, and enlightened mind will unhesitatingly answer in the affirmative. This is all that Madame Restell recommends or ever recommended. Price Five Dollars a package, accompanied with full and particular directions. For the convenience of those unable to call personally, "Circulars" more fully explanatory, will be sent free of expense (postage excepted) to any part of the United States. All letters must be post-paid, and addressed to MADAME RESTELL, Female Physician. Principal office, 148 Greenwich street, New York. Office hours from 9 A.M. to 9 P.M. Philadelphia office, 39½ South Eighth street.

ap10 1m*

By 1840 Madame Restell, "female physician," was advertising in the *New York Herald* her "preventative powders for married ladies, whose health forbids too rapid increase of family." She also had offices in Newark and Philadelphia but committed suicide after being entrapped by Anthony Comstock. In 1965 the U.S. Supreme Court declared unconstitutional state laws banning the use of contraceptives by married persons.

Some churches—the Roman Catholic Church, for one—remain officially opposed to contraception, however. Some pharmacists, notably members of Pharmacists for Life International, refuse to fill contraceptive prescriptions, contending that preventing a child is immoral. States such as Arkansas, Georgia, South Dakota have taken action to protect pharmacists who refuse to fill contraceptive prescriptions. The rules of the American Pharmacists Association say that although pharmacists may refuse to fill such a prescription on moral grounds, they must make arrangements for patients to get the prescription elsewhere. Some pharmacies and stores have also recently begun keeping condoms in locked cases, allegedly to prevent thefts.

One of the same questions that inflames the debate over abortion can also be asked about contraception: When in the development of a human embryo or a fetus does it attain the status of a person? The answer goes to the government's interest in protecting the RIGHTS OF THE UNBORN. Contraception is sometimes described as any method that prevents conception (the fertilization of the female egg cell by the male sperm cell). But according to the American College of Obstetricians and Gynecologists, contraception is "a procedure that terminates the development of a fertilized egg prior to completed implantation" in the uterine wall.

In *Webster v. Reproductive Health Services* (1989), Associate Justice Sandra Day O'Connor, dissenting in part but concurring in the judgment of the U.S. Supreme Court, stated, "It may be correct that the use of post-fertilization contraceptive devices [as encompassed by the definition of the obstetricians' group] is constitutionally protected" by Supreme Court decisions beginning with *Griswold*. However, the Code of Federal Regulations (2001), under Public Protection of Human Subjects, provides that pregnancy begins with the implantation of a fertilized egg in the uterine wall. The prevention of conception—the fertilization of the egg—therefore differs from the prevention of pregnancy—the implantation of the fertilized egg in the womb.

In *Catholic Charities of Sacramento, Inc. v. Superior Court of Sacramento County* (2004), the California supreme court ruled that the Catholic Charities organization must provide contraceptive coverage in its employee health care programs. California is one of more than twenty states that require employers to include such coverage for prescription contraceptives, regardless of the Church's position against contraception. As for the Catholic Charities' argument that the FIRST AMENDMENT (1791) to the U.S. Constitution protects its religious beliefs, the court said that the organization could still express its beliefs by encouraging employees not to use birth control.

Minors' Rights

Compared to those of adults, the rights of minors with respect to contraception are less absolute. The Supreme Court in *Carey v. Population Services International* (1977) recognized that minors also have constitutionally protected rights to make reproductive choices. In that case the Court struck down a New York law that prohibited the distribution of nonprescription contraceptives to anyone under the age of sixteen years. And a federal court in *Planned Parenthood Association of Utah v. Matheson* (1983) voided a state law requiring parental notification before a minor could obtain contraceptives, noting that the provision would interfere with the minor's constitutional right to contraception.

As to whether public institutions should give young people access to contraception, however, the public seems to be split. Some parents want their children to be able to obtain contraception for the obvious reasons of preventing pregnancy and the spread of SEXUALLY TRANSMITTED DISEASES. Yet other parents do not, perhaps because of moral concerns or the belief that the availability of contraception leads to promiscuity.

Some states allow parents to let their children opt out of health or SEX EDUCATION programs that also distribute contraceptive devices, such as condoms. New York and California laws require parental CONSENT for the distribution of health services by schools. Consent requirements have been upheld by the courts as a parental right under the U.S. Constitution to raise their children as they see fit. A New York case, *Alfonso v. Fernandez* (1993), noted, "The Constitution gives parents the right to regulate their children's sexual behavior as best they can." As of 2002, twenty-two states required parental consent for the use of government-sponsored contraceptive services, although state parental consent statutes have been invalidated when federal funds are involved.

Emergency Contraception

Many birth control clinics and hospitals in the United States provide emergency contraception to victims of SEXUAL ASSAULT and RAPE and other women who have had unprotected sex. Because measures taken to prevent pregnancy in these cases may interfere with the implantation of a fertilized egg in the womb, some religious groups such as the Catholic Church believe that it is immoral to provide a service tantamount to abortion. Recent scientific studies seem to indicate, however, that rather than inhibiting an egg's implantation, postcoital contraceptives destroy the egg. Emergency contraceptive measures carry a 20 percent failure rate.

Plan B, called the "morning-after pill," uses a synthetic hormone to block ovulation (the natural expulsion of the female egg from the ovary) and fertilization of the egg. It is not a form of abortion, in which a fertilized embryo is removed, but it can be used after sexual intercourse rather than before to prevent pregnancy. In only some states are Plan B and a similar drug, Preven, available without a prescription. In 2005, ignoring the 24–3 recommendation of its advisory panel, the Food and Drug Administration delayed deciding whether Plan B could be sold over the counter nationwide. Opponents of easier availability of the pill fear that it will lead to greater promiscuity and increase the spread of disease.

Plan B differs from RU-486, the "abortion pill," which can be taken up to forty-nine days after the beginning of a woman's last menstrual cycle. This pill blocks hormones needed for a pregnancy to continue. RU-486, whose generic name is mifepristone, was developed by Roussel Uclaf and first made available in France. The FDA withheld approval of the drug, which is sold in the United States under the trade name Mifeprex, until 2000. "We have always understood that the battles about abortion were just the tip of a larger ideological iceberg," says Gloria Feldt, president of Planned Parenthood Federation of America, "and that it's really birth control that they're after also."

Should the natural outcome of sexual intercourse—pregnancy—be left to chance when the means are readily available to prevent an unwanted pregnancy? The law has come down on the side of allowing people to have sexual relations yet avoid the added responsibility of raising an unwanted child. If as Americans we value our freedom, the courts have said, then a significant element of that freedom is the freedom to choose if and when to have children.

Contact: Guttmacher Institute, 120 Wall Street, New York, NY 10005 (212-248-1111). www.guttmacher.org.

See also ETHICS; FEMINISM; REPRODUCTIVE RIGHTS.

CRAIG v. BOREN

A state law allowing girls to buy beer at an earlier age than boys constitutes DISCRIMINATION on the basis of sex, ruled the U.S. Supreme Court in *Craig v. Boren* (1976). In a 7–2 decision written by Associate Justice William J. Brennan Jr., the Court held that such unequal treatment of males and females in Oklahoma was unconstitutional under the equal protection clause of the Fourteenth Amendment (1878) to the U.S. Constitution. The case's significance lies in the justices' explication, for laws incorporating GENDER-based discrimination, of an "intermediate" standard of judicial scrutiny—as differentiated from a "strict" standard reserved for cases involving racial discrimination or from a "rational basis test" or ordinary scrutiny used for other less suspect categories of legislative classifications. It is ironic, however, that such an important decision ultimately affecting the EQUAL RIGHTS of women was based on discrimination against males.

Discrimination had previously been upheld by the Supreme Court in many cases involving racial and sexual distinctions in the law. In the famous case *Plessy v. Ferguson* (1896), the Court let stand a Louisiana statute requiring railroads to provide "equal but separate accommodations for the white and colored races." But a half century later, with *Brown v. Board of Education of Topeka* (1954), the Court laid to rest this untenable "separate but equal" doctrine. Nonetheless, WOMEN'S RIGHTS under the U.S. Constitution, according to a 1947 Supreme Court ruling, were long seen to consist only of the hard-won right to vote guaranteed by the Nineteenth Amendment (1920).

Not until a year before CONGRESS sent to the states the Equal Rights Amendment (1972), an unsuccessful attempt to constitutionally guarantee equality between men and women, did the Supreme Court break its own precedent by ruling in *Reed v. Reed* (1971) that statutory sex discrimination could violate the Constitution. Referring to a "rational basis test," the Court held that an Idaho law giving preference to males over females as administrators of intestate decedents' estates violated the Fourteenth Amendment's equal protection clause. In *Reed* the Court noted that the objectives of the state law—"reducing the work of the probate courts" and "avoiding intrafamily controversy"—were of insufficient importance to sustain the use of an overt gender criterion.

Then in *FRONTIERO V. RICHARDSON* (1973), the Supreme Court declared that a federal statute allowing different treatment for male spouses of female military personnel violated the Fifth Amendment's due process clause. The law required a female member to prove her husband's dependence in order to receive benefits, although the spouses of male servicemen did not have to offer proof of such dependency. As in *Reed*, the argument in support of classification on the basis of sex—in this case for administrative convenience—was found inadequate to support the constitutionality of the law in question.

Three years later, the Supreme Court's opinion in *Craig* began "with the reminder that *Reed* emphasized

that statutory classifications that distinguish between males and females are 'subject to scrutiny under the Equal Protection Clause.'" The contested classification in *Craig* involved an Oklahoma law that prohibited the sale of "nonintoxicating" beer with a 3.2 percent alcohol content to females under the age of eighteen years but to males under the age of twenty-one.

Justice Brennan built on the level of judicial scrutiny that the Court would apply in sex- or gender-based discrimination cases. The constitutional standard to be met by a law based on gender classification is that the law "must serve important government objectives and must be substantially related to those objectives." Because this standard was less strict than in the case of race-based classifications, which were "suspect" to begin with, it became known as an "intermediate" level of judicial scrutiny. Although Oklahoma's intent to reduce drunk driving was an important government objective, it had not proven that this goal was clearly served by differentiating between males and females in the sale of 3.2 percent beer. Thus, the second part of the test—that the law must be substantially related to the objective—had not been met.

In a concurring opinion, Associate Justice John Paul Stevens opined that he was not convinced that "the two-tiered analysis of equal protection claims" accurately described "a completely logical method of deciding cases." Instead he found the basis of the classification objectionable as "an accident of birth [and] because it is a mere remnant of the now almost universally rejected tradition of discriminating against males in this age bracket." (In 1971 the right to vote was extended to all citizens eighteen years of age or older by the Twenty-sixth Amendment.)

In his dissent, Associate Justice William H. Rehnquist expressed concern over the addition of a new level of judicial scrutiny as well as to its use to protect male plaintiffs, whom he believed did not need special protection. He proposed that a rational test could be devised based on statistical evidence of discrimination. Chief Justice Warren E. Burger generally agreed with Justice Rehnquist but questioned the plaintiff's standing, based on "her status as a sa-loon keeper to assert the constitutional rights of her customers."

Craig v. Boren has been much discussed and has been applied in many subsequent cases. Its test for evaluating sex-based legal classifications was reaffirmed a year later in *Califano v. Goldfarb* (1977). In that case the Court upheld a challenge to a Social Security provision that denied benefits to widowers unless they had received at least half of their support from their wives, while granting such benefits to widows without such a condition.

While the ruling in *Craig* still stands, the Supreme Court has found ways to uphold legally sanctioned discrimination in some cases. Those decisions have generally been based on arguments used to defeat the Equal Rights Amendment (which was approved by Congress in 1972 but failed to achieve ratification in the allocated ten-year period): doubts about the wisdom of ensuring the rights of homosexuals, fully integrating women into the MILITARY, and relaxing statutory RAPE laws and bans against SAME-SEX MARRIAGE. For example, in *Rostker v. Goldberg* (1981), the Court saw no problem in upholding the exclusion of women from military registration.

The Supreme Court has also given wide latitude to legislative determinations of gender classifications under Congress's immigration and naturalization powers. In *Nguyen v. Immigration and Naturalization Service* (2001), the Court approved the government's discrimination against a biological father (a U.S. citizen) of a child born out of wedlock outside the United States in favor of the biological mother; there was, the justices reasoned, a significant difference in the respective relationships to the potential citizen (the child) of unmarried fathers—who may have to establish PATERNITY—and unmarried mothers. The difference was enough to meet the requirements in *Craig v. Boren* that the law must be substantially related to achieving governmental objectives and serve an important government interest.

See also HOMOSEXUALITY.

CRIMES AGAINST CHILDREN UNIT (FBI)

Over the past several decades, federal and state governments have created laws and institutions to deal with crimes against CHILDREN, the most vulnerable members of society. According to federal law, a child is a minor under the age of eighteen years. The Crimes Against Children Unit was established in the Violent Crimes and Major Offenders Section, Criminal Investigation Division, of the Federal Bureau of Investigation in 1997 to provide a quick and effective response to all incidents of crimes against children.

In 2000 nearly two million juveniles between birth and seventeen years of age were the victims of violent crime, and in that year 89,000 cases of child sexual abuse were substantiated. Although the overall rate of all crimes dropped in the last decade of the twentieth century, the exploitation and abuse of children, including sexual acts, are still dramatically high; the rate remained basically unchanged statistically for the four years ending in 2003. According to statistics from the Administration for Children and Families in the U.S. DEPARTMENT OF HEALTH AND HUMAN SERVICES, the youngest age group of children—up to three years old—has the highest rate of maltreatment, including sexual abuse: 16.4 victims per 1,000 children. The rate of child sexual abuse through age seventeen has remained at approximately 1.2 victims per 1,000 children each year for 2000 through 2003. With the proliferation of the computer and access to the INTERNET, the avenues for such crimes against children have expanded.

The FBI's responsibilities for crimes against children involve the sexual exploitation of children, including on the Internet and with respect to the possession, production, and distribution of child PORNOGRAPHY; interstate transportation of obscene materials or children for sexual purposes; child abduction and parental kidnaping of children; physical or sexual abuse of a child in a federal jurisdiction; the National Sex Offender Registry (MEGAN'S LAW); and violations of the Child Support Recovery Act (1992).

To assist in accomplishing its mission, the Crimes Against Children Unit has created an Innocent Images

National Initiative to investigate and prosecute cases of child pornography and child sexual exploitation facilitated through the use of computers online. This initiative targets people who are willing to travel interstate for the purpose of engaging in sexual activity with a minor, as well as major producers and distributors of child pornography. In 1998 the agency began a national Internet Crimes Against Children Task Force to help state and local law enforcement officials develop effective responses to cybersex enticements and the production and distribution of child pornography over the Internet.

A number of federal statutes provide the FBI with authority to address crimes against children. For one, Title 18, section 2251(a), of the U.S. Code provides:

Any person who employs, uses, persuades, induces, entices, or coerces any minor to engage in, or who has a minor assist any other person to engage in, or who transports any minor in interstate or foreign commerce, or in any Territory or Possession of the United States, with the intent that such minor engage in, any sexually explicit conduct for the purpose of producing any visual depiction of such conduct, shall be punished under subsection (d), if such person knows or has reason to know that such visual depiction will be transported in interstate or foreign commerce or mailed, or if such visual depiction has actually been transported in interstate or foreign commerce or mailed.

According to subsection (d), punishment for a first offense is a fine or imprisonment for no fewer than ten years nor more than twenty years, or both.

In addition to statutes regarding kidnaping and CHILD SUPPORT, other provisions under Title 18 of the U.S. Code relating to sexual behavior that involve the FBI and its Crimes Against Children Unit include the following:

(1) Section 1462, Importation or Transportation of Obscene Matters.

(2) Section 1465, Transportation of Obscene Matters for Sale or Distribution.

(3) Section 1466, Engaging in the Business of Selling or Transferring Obscene Matter.

(4) Section 1470, Transfer of Obscene Materials to Minors.

(5) Section 2241(a) (c), Aggravated Sexual Assault.

(6) Section 2243, Sexual Abuse of a Minor or Ward.

(7) Section 2251(a)(b)(c), Sexual Exploitation of Children.

(8) Section 2251A(a)(b), Selling or Buying of Children.

(9) Section 2252, Certain Activities Relating to Materials Involving the Sexual Exploitation of Minors.

(10) Section 2252A, Certain Activities Relating to Material Constituting or Containing Child Pornography.

(11) Section 2260(a)(b), Production of Sexually Explicit Depictions of a Minor for Importation into the United States.

(12) Section 2423(a), Transportation of Minors with Intent to Engage in Criminal Sexual Activity.

(13) Section 2423(b), Interstate or Foreign Travel with Intent to Engage in a Sexual Act with a Juvenile.

(14) Section 2425, Use of Interstate Facilities to Transmit Information about a Minor.

Under Title 42 of the code, additional laws relevant to the unit's activities include section 13032, Reporting of Child Pornography by Electronic Communication Service Providers, and section 14072, the Pam Lychner Sexual Offender Tracking and Identification Act (1996).

It remains to be seen if the federal government's response to the challenge of protecting children with new laws, reorganization, and modern techniques will improve the crime statistics. Individual FBI field offices are the primary source of information and help for people requiring assistance with crimes against children. Information on the appropriate field office to contact can be obtained from FBI headquarters.

Contact: Crimes Against Children Unit, Federal Bureau of Investigation, U.S. Department of Justice, 935 Pennsylvania Avenue, NW, Washington, DC 20535-0001 (202-324-3000). www.fbi.gov/hq/cid/cac/federal.htm.

See also CHILD ABUSE; CHILD SUPPORT; HUMAN TRAFFICKING.

CYBERSEX

See INTERNET.

d

DATE RAPE

According to U.S. Department of Justice statistics, well over half of the rapes and sexual assaults reported are committed by someone acquainted with or related to the victim. More than 80 percent of women who were the victims of such acquaintance rape, also called date rape, knew their attacker; in other cases, a male date may have been introduced by someone else, and males other than a woman's own date may take advantage of her. Women who are between sixteen and twenty-four years of age are four times as likely as other females to become the victims of date rape and forced to have sex against their will.

Date rape, like RAPE and SEXUAL ASSAULT, is a crime that can be traumatic and destructive to both the victim and the rapist. Statistics show that close to half of date rape victims have considered committing suicide. A conviction for rape can carry a stiff penalty and ruin the life of the perpetrator.

Some studies have compared date rape and rape by strangers. One finding is that the perception of the crime of rape is influenced by two varying views of sexual behavior: hostile sexism and benevolent sexism. In short, the first view is a stereotypical antipathy towards women traditionally associated with sexual prejudice. The second view divides women into good and bad and then condemns women who are perceived to be bad, so that a rape victim is more likely to be blamed for what happens to her. Thus, some jurors at trial may judge the perpetrator of a rape as less to blame than the victim. Studies show that the latter view results in shorter sentences for the acquaintance rape perpetrator than for stranger rapists.

Alcohol and Drug Use

Often date rape is facilitated by alcohol or so-called date rape DRUGS that reduce a victim's ability to meaningfully consent to the sex act or to resist the attacker. Rape carried out by means of drugs is also known as drug-facilitated sexual assault and is included in the criminal laws of many states. In some jurisdictions the use of drugs aggravates the crime and increases the punishment because it is evidence of premeditation to commit rape.

Rape-facilitating drugs include GHB (gamma hydroxybutyric acid), Rohypnol (flunitrazepam), and Ketamine (ketamine hydrochloride). GHB—which is odorless and colorless and comes in the form of a liquid, white powder, or pill—can cause relaxation, drowsiness, and unconsciousness. Rohypnol, which is available in pill form but can be dissolved in a liquid, induces sleepiness, confusion, loss of consciousness, and inability to remember what happened while under its influence. Ketamine, a white powder, can cause hallucinations, a loss of control, numbness, and memory problems. Although Rohypnol is not legal in the United States, the other two drugs have been approved for restricted use as an anesthetic and treatment for narcolepsy, a sleeping disorder.

The Issue of Consent

Successful prosecutions for date rape, like stranger rape, hinge on the question of CONSENT. Sexual intercourse that occurs with the consent of both adult partners is not rape. In the case of acquaintance rape, there is a subtle presumption that if a victim knows the accused rapist, a consensual relationship may have existed—in contrast to the situation with a total stranger. Moreover, some people may see the rape of an acquaintance as wrong yet the result of an irresistible urge, rather than as an act of hostility.

The introduction of date rape drugs, however, goes a long way to dispel this view. Their use shows premeditation to negate the victim's ability to consent to or remember the incident, rendering her a poor witness. If the victim is unable to understand what is going on, there is no way she can grant or withhold consent; and if the victim cannot clearly remember the incident, her credibility can be questioned because typically only the accused and the victim are witnesses to the act.

Attempted Remedies

Under current law, acquaintance rape is often harder to prove and harder for authorities to take as seriously as violent rape by a stranger. At the federal level, an attempt by CONGRESS to provide a civil remedy allowing private suits to redress gender-motivated violence was foiled by the U.S. Supreme Court in *United States v. Morrison* (2000). In this case, the Court considered an appeal under the VIOLENCE AGAINST WOMEN ACT (1994) and TITLE IX of the Education Amendments of 1972 that involved the assault and rape of Christy Brzonkala, a student at Virginia Polytechnic Institute, by two members of the varsity football team thirty minutes after she had met them. In 1995 she filed a complaint under the school's sexual assault policy provisions. One of the men, Antonio Morrison, was suspended for two semesters; the other was not punished by the school for lack of sufficient evidence.

Brzonkala then sought to prove her case in court. On appeal, however, the Supreme Court referred to its decision in *United States v. Lopez* (1995), which held that Congress did not have authority under the commerce clause in Article I, section 8, of the U.S. Constitution to keep guns out of areas around schools. It thus found that the civil remedy crafted by Congress to permit suits under the Violence Against Women Act was an unconstitutional arrogation of power. The Court also affirmed the lower court's dismissal of the challenge under Title IX as an ineligible claim for relief in a rape case. Thus the rape victim had no private cause of action against her assailants under federal law.

Some states have recognized the problem of date rape. For example, the Donahoe Higher Education Act (1991) in California contains legislative findings and declarations regarding sexual assault and rape on college campuses. It states: "Resident life student staff and all students living in campus recognized housing should receive acquaintance rape training every semester."

Like DOMESTIC VIOLENCE, date rape often goes unpunished because of an absence of training and resources with which to investigate and prosecute it—a problem that the Violence Against Women Act attempted to correct by allowing a private remedy.

DEFENSE OF MARRIAGE ACT

Beginning with a 1993 case in Hawaii that ended with a decision by the state's supreme court in *Baehr v. Miike* (1999), holding that MARRIAGE licenses could not be denied to same-sex couples, the attack on the institution of marriage, according to many citizens and legislators, was under way. Hawaii soon moved to limit marriage to heterosexual couples by amending the state constitution to empower its legislature "to reserve marriage to opposite-sex couples." Many states have similarly acted since then to amend their constitutions or enact statutes to deny any marriage-related rights to homosexual couples. Massachusetts, in contrast, permits SAME-SEX MARRIAGE, and Connecticut and Vermont allow gay and lesbian couples to enter into civil unions that approximate the institution of marriage.

CONGRESS also enacted legislation in 1996 to limit the right of marriage to heterosexual couples, passing a sweeping law against homosexual rights called the Defense of Marriage Act (DOMA). This law establishes a federal definition of marriage as a union between a man and a woman for purposes of federal actions—such as government benefits including Social Security, immigration, income taxes, and so forth. The act leaves it up to the states to determine for themselves whether or not to recognize same-sex marriages.

One Man, One Woman

DOMA's key provisions, as set forth in the U.S. Code, are:

(1) Title 28, Judiciary and Judicial Procedure, part V, Procedure, chapter 115, Evidence; Documentary, section 1738C, Certain acts, records, and proceedings and the effect thereof:

No State, territory, or possession of the United States, or Indian tribe, shall be required to give effect to any public act, record, or judicial proceeding of any other State, territory, possession, or tribe respecting a relationship between persons of the same sex that is treated as a marriage under the laws of such other State, territory, possession, or tribe, or a right or claim arising from such relationship.

(2) Title 1, General Provisions, chapter 1, Rules of Construction, section 7, Definition of "marriage" and "spouse":

In determining the meaning of any Act of Congress, or of any ruling, regulation, or interpretation of the various administrative bureaus and agencies of the United States, the word "marriage" means only a legal union between one man and one woman as husband and wife, and the word "spouse" refers only to a person of the opposite sex who is a husband or a wife.

(3) Article IV, section 1, U.S. Constitution:

Full Faith and Credit shall be given in each State to the public Acts, Records, and judicial Proceedings of every other State. And the Congress may by general Laws prescribe the Manner in which such Acts, Records, and Proceedings shall be proved, and the Effect thereof.

It is the second sentence of the Constitution's Article IV, section 1, on which the proponents of DOMA base the constitutionality of its provisions. But opponents of the act—those who think that it unconstitutionally restricts states that recognize the right of same-sex couples to marry, as Massachusetts does, or that recognize the right of civil unions for same-sex couples, as Connecticut and Vermont do—argue that the sentence does not give Congress the power to limit the full faith and credit clause but only to prescribe how the clause will be implemented equally in the states.

Issues of Constitutionality

To date the U.S. Supreme Court has not ruled on the act's constitutionality. But preparing themselves should the law be held unconstitutional, opponents of same-sex marriage and civil unions have already proposed a constitutional amendment. The FEDERAL MARRIAGE AMENDMENT, in its most restrictive form, would prohibit federal and state governments from recognizing same-sex marriage or any similar status for nonheterosexual couples. The Supreme Court's ruling in LAWRENCE V. TEXAS (2003), in which adult consensual homosexual sodomy in the privacy of one's home was held to be constitutionally protected, has raised questions as to whether the right of PRIVACY relied on in that case might be grounds for finding DOMA unconstitutional.

Unless and until the Defense of Marriage Act is tested for its constitutionality in the Supreme Court, it will continue to raise a number of questions: If constitutional, how does it affect civil unions in Connecticut and Vermont, which are not defined as marriage but which extend many of the same rights and privileges? How will domestic partnerships, some of which use the term *spouse* to refer to a partner, be treated, as they do not purport to be long-term commitments and can be terminated at will? How will the act affect reciprocity between nations if same-sex marriages in other countries (Canada, Denmark, and the Netherlands, for example) are not recognized in the United States?

The problems with DOMA must be worked out over time, but meanwhile the status of same-sex marriages and similar arrangements for homosexual partners will to some degree be in legal limbo. For now, the Defense of Marriage Act is the law by which other federal laws are interpreted and government agencies carry out their mandates. The basic issue remains whether the traditional institution of marriage—under attack from relaxed DIVORCE procedures, abrogated or unenforced laws against unmarried cohabitation as well as ADULTERY and fornication, and the same-sex marriage movement—can be defended or preserved by laws alone.

See also HOMOSEXUALITY; UNMARRIED COHABITANTS.

DEFINITION OF MARRIAGE LAWS

See DEFENSE OF MARRIAGE ACT; FEDERAL MARRIAGE AMENDMENT; SAME-SEX MARRIAGE.

DEVIANT BEHAVIOR

Sexual behavior has differed widely during various human cultures and within each culture. Deviant or variant sexual behavior is activity that does not comport with the legal or social norms of a group or a community and thus lies outside an acceptable range; a sexual deviate, sometimes called a sexual pervert, is a person whose behavior differs from aceptable social or moral standards. But who considers a particular sexual behavior deviant, and what harm does such behavior cause? In the United States today, the meaning of deviant sexual behavior to theologians, high school students, sex therapists, psychologists, producers of PORNOGRAPHY, and homosexuals may vary significantly, even within each category of individual.

Any human activity that furthers procreation can be viewed as sexual behavior; but some of this behavior—rape, for example—is proscribed by law as unacceptably deviant. Procreative sex is generally condoned, as long as it is conducted according to the law. Sexual intercourse between a legally married husband and wife is not deviant sexual behavior by nearly any standard in the United States. Sexual intimacy between unmarried consenting heterosexuals, however, may be considered by some citizens to constitute immoral or deviant behavior. So too may sexual intimacy between consenting adult homosexuals, including SODOMY, although this behavior is generally no longer illegal. The U.S. Supreme Court's decision in *LAWRENCE v. TEXAS* (2003), which declared unconstitutional a Texas law that criminalized consensual homosexual sodomy in the PRIVACY of one's own home, led a dissenting justice to opine that states could not in the future prohibit any kind of variant sexual behavior between consenting adults.

Stimulative sexual behavior—action intended to arouse or give pleasure—may or may not be procreative. It may be engaged in by individuals who for various reasons do not want to have or cannot have children. Many people, married and unmarried, have sex far more often for physical stimulation than to create progeny. But forcing such sexual behavior on someone against her or his will or performing it other than in the privacy of one's home is generally illegal. Even overly graphic pictures or descriptions of reproductive or otherwise stimulative sexual behavior may be considered obscene and therefore the subject of criminal prosecution because OBSCENITY is by definition beyond the scope of protection of the FIRST AMENDMENT (1791) to the U.S. Constitution.

Private deviant sexual behavior may not create social or legal problems. Masturbation in private, for example, while contravening some religious and moral teachings, is not illegal. Sexually molesting CHILDREN or committing INCEST, whether in private or not, is deviant behavior that is proscribed by law in all states. INDECENT EXPOSURE and other LEWD BEHAVIOR in public are considered deviant activities and are outlawed in all states. BESTIALITY (sex with animals) remains proscribed in numerous states. Necrophilia (sexual relations with a corpse) is specifically prohibited in some states, while in others general provisions regarding treatment of the dead can be read to encompass sexual acts. Alaska's statute, enacted in 1978, reads: "It is a misdemeanor to engage in sexual penetration of a corpse."

State laws generally break down SEX OFFENSES into traditional terms, such as RAPE, SEXUAL ASSAULT, CHILD ABUSE, and so forth, but they may also list categories of deviant behavior. For example, Oregon has a prohibition against sexual assault of animals, and Massachusetts punishes "unnatural and lascivious acts . . . by a fine of not less than one hundred nor more than one thousand dollars or by imprisonment in the state prison for not more than five years or in jail or the house of correction for not more than two and one half years." The Indiana code defines deviant sexual conduct as "an act involving: (1) a sex organ of one person and the mouth or anus of another person; or (2) the penetration of the sex organ or anus of a person by an object." Under Pennsylvania law, "voluntary deviant sexual intercourse" is a second-degree misdemeanor, whereas "involuntary deviant sexual intercourse" is a first-degree felony. Elements that distinguish involuntary from voluntary actions include "forcible compulsion" or the threat thereof and a victim who is "unconscious," "mentally deranged or deficient," or "less than sixteen years of age."

Courts are often left to decide which actions constitute "lascivious acts" or other deviant sexual behavior. For some time many state laws have equated various forms of deviant sexual behavior with the term *sodomy*. A federal appeals court in 2004, however, held that the constitutional right of privacy relied on by the Supreme Court in *Lawrence* does not apply to the sale of sexual devices prohibited under Alabama law. This form of deviant sexual behavior may still be regulated by the states, at least until the Supreme Court has a chance to rule on this issue.

Trying to differentiate between "deviant sexual assault" and "rape," an Illinois appellate court heard a case, *People v. Borak* (1973), in which it was asserted that during a gynecological examination, a doctor asked the patient improper questions and appeared to be in a state of arousal. The court held that these actions did not remove the element of surprise when

he placed his tongue in the victim's vaginal area. It was thus found that she did not CONSENT to the act, satisfying the statutory requirement that force was necessary to sustain the charge of deviant sexual assault. But the subsequent penetration of the victim by the defendant's organ did not come as a surprise, the court held, so her failure to resist amounted to consent, thus invalidating a conviction for rape.

Deviant sexual *conduct* and *assault*—as opposed to merely atypical sexual behavior—are terms that have acquired specific legal meaning over many years and refer to sex offenses proscribed by law. Such offenses are being pared down as social mores change. In the end, deviant sexual behavior is simply what someone in authority or a majority of citizens through their representatives say is not normal.

See also BISEXUALITY; HOMOSEXUALITY; MISCEGENATION; NUDITY; UNMARRIED COHABITANTS; VOYEURISM.

DISCRIMINATION

The first woman to sit on the Supreme Court, Sandra Day O'Connor, wrote in a concurring opinion in *Roberts v. United States Jaycees* (1984) that a "shopkeeper has no constitutional right to deal only with persons of one sex." At issue was whether the right of association contained in the FIRST AMENDMENT (1791) to the U.S. Constitution would protect the Minnesota Junior Chamber of Commerce from a state law barring discrimination against women. Justice O'Connor's conclusion that it did not could be extended to any human activity. The question may fairly be asked: What gives anyone the right to discriminate against another person in any activity?

Democracies are based on the premise that all citizens have EQUAL RIGHTS, with certain reasonable exceptions, such as for minors, criminals, and the mentally incompetent. Discrimination is behavior that treats people differently even if there is no reasonable distinction among them. Lawmakers may discriminate between citizens on what they believe are logical and reasonable grounds. Judges and juries, government officials, and private individuals may discriminate on the basis of race, national origin, RELIGION, disability, appearance, and so forth. Discrimination because of GENDER (sex) or sexual orientation (HOMOSEXUALITY) are other prejudices that have long been a part of many human cultures. There remains a pervasive notion that innate or physical differences justify treating people differently in the political, economic, and social arenas.

Discrimination by Sex

Judicial review of allegedly discriminatory laws or actions generally addresses two questions: Is the basis of the discrimination reasonable or unreasonable? And is the government's interest so important as to warrant some form of discrimination? With respect to discrimination on the basis of sex, medical benefits for prenatal and maternity care may reasonably be denied to men, and women may reasonably be denied a position on a male basketball team; in the latter instance, the law requires only that equal opportunities be made available to women, such as to play on a female basketball team. Although scientific studies have recognized many differences in the way that men and women process information and emotions, there is no evidence that such differences justify discrimination in most aspects of daily life.

Unacceptable discrimination on the basis of sex has often arisen in the context of employment and education. In an important early U.S. Supreme Court case, *BRADWELL V. ILLINOIS* (1873), an otherwise well-qualified married woman, Myra Bradwell, was denied the right to practice law solely because she was a woman, and a married woman at that. According to the Court's opinion, the "law, as well as nature herself, has always recognized a wide difference in the respective spheres and destinies of man and woman." Bradwell's unsuccessful appeal was based on the privileges and immunities clause of the Constitution. Later successful challenges were grounded in the Constitution's due process and equal protection clauses.

In the workplace today, the fact that men earn about one-fourth more than women is at least circumstantial evidence that some sex discrimination may be taking place. Arguments have been put forward that other factors—such as women's lack of aggressiveness, different personal goals, and absences to care for family—may contribute to this outcome. Information announced in 2005 by the U.S. Bureau of Labor Statistics that women now hold nearly one-half of all the nonfarm payroll jobs, an increase of almost one-third since 1964, shows that discrimination in hiring on the basis of sex may be less prevalent today. A $72.5 million settlement in 2004 of a sex discrimination lawsuit against Boeing, however, indicates that discrimination on the basis of sex in wage and promotion policies can be a costly practice.

As far as higher education is concerned, it was not until 1970 that the federal district court judge Robert R. Merhige Jr. would order the University of Virginia to admit female students. In 2005 the president of Harvard University, Lawrence Summers, suggested that the shortage of elite female scientists might stem in part from the innate differences between men and women—thereby touching off a firestorm about the effects of gender and discrimination.

Sex discrimination, both overt and subtle, has taken place in many other areas. For example, women were long systematically excluded from serving on juries, despite the U.S. Supreme Court's ruling in *Neal v. Delaware* (1880), indicating that such discrimination was unconstitutional under the Fifteenth Amendment (1870) to the U.S. Constitution. It would not be until 1975, when a male defendant challenged the lack of women on his jury in *Taylor v. Louisiana,* that women's constitutional right to be jurors was confirmed by the Supreme Court. Legalizing women's right to vote and to hold political office required the adoption of the Nineteenth Amendment (1920), although even today a much greater percentage of men than women hold elective or appointed government positions. The right of women to administer the estate of a decedent who left no valid will would not be confirmed by the Supreme Court until *Reed v. Reed* (1971).

Sex has been the basis of both illegal and legal discrimination. One example of the former is SEXUAL HARASSMENT, while affirmative action laws (see below) are an example of the latter. In CRAIG V. BOREN (1976), the Supreme Court reviewed a case in which women received more favorable, rather than less favorable, treatment. At issue was an Oklahoma law that permitted females to purchase beer with a 3.2 percent alcohol content at the age of eighteen, while males were prohibited from drinking any beer until the age of twenty-one. Although the state argued among other things that the distinction was aimed at reducing the incidence of drunk driving, the Court held that the resulting discrimination violated the equal protection clause of the Fourteenth Amendment (1868) to the U.S. Constitution.

Constitutional Law. The word *sex* appears in the U.S. Constitution only once: in the Nineteenth Amendment (1920) prohibiting the denial of the right to vote on the basis of sex. After the adoption of the Fourteenth (1868) and Fifteenth (1870) Amendments to the Constitution, which extended civil rights to freed black men, women who had worked for abolition as well as women's suffrage were distressed that they still could not vote. The American suffrage movement had gotten its start with efforts to abolish slavery before the Civil War, but as early as 1792 Mary Wollstonecraft (1759–97), an Englishwoman, had advocated the vote for women in *A Vindication of the Rights of Woman*. In MINOR V. HAPPERSETT (1875), the Supreme Court held that it was not unconstitutional for states to deny women the right to vote. By 1914, however, women in eleven states could vote in state and local elections. The drive for women's suffrage nationwide culminated in the 1920 constitutional amendment.

The only significant Supreme Court case dealing with the Nineteenth Amendment is *Breedlove v. Suttles* (1937), which held that a Georgia poll tax exempting women who did not register to vote did not discriminate against men's right to vote. The Court went on to state that the amendment "applies to men and women alike and … supersedes inconsistent measures, whether federal or State." Then in *Fay v. New York* (1947), the Court declared that the right to vote was the only right granted to women by the Constitution.

The evolution of Supreme Court decisions regarding sex discrimination is complex. Before the Nineteenth Amendment, the all-male court had a tradition of treating women as "the weaker sex" who needed to be protected. Three years later, in *Adkins v. Children's Hospital* (1923), the justices struck down a District of Columbia law that gave women and minors a minimum wage not guaranteed to men; the Court's reasoning was that this was a violation of the due process clause of the Fifth Amendment (1791) and that the Nineteenth Amendment placed women and men on an equal footing in bargaining for wages. As late as 1948, the Supreme Court held in *Goesaert v. Cleary* that a woman had no right to work as a bartender because of the unsavory nature of the job. Associate Justice Felix Frankfurter declared: "The Constitution does not require legislatures to reflect sociological insight, or shifting social standards, any more than it requires them to keep abreast of the latest scientific standards."

By 1976, when the court decided *Craig v. Boren*, much had changed in the country in the wake of the SEXUAL REVOLUTION and the WOMEN'S RIGHTS movement. In his opinion for the Court, Associate Justice William J. Brennan Jr. spelled out the standard of scrutiny the justices had been applying since 1971: sex-based classifications were subject to "intermediate scrutiny"—rather than simply "rational" (ordinary) scrutiny—to determine if discrimination was unconstitutional under the Fourteenth Amendment's equal protection clause. A three-tier level of scrutiny had been created: race-based classifications would receive the strictest scrutiny, sex-based the next level, and other less obviously discriminatory classifications would be given the lowest level of scrutiny. To be upheld, wrote Brennan, a statute that classified by gender "must serve important governmental objectives and must be substantially related to those objectives."

Federal Statutory Law. Two important federal laws protect against arbitrary discrimination on the basis of sex: Title VII of the Civil Rights Act of 1964, which prohibits discrimination "because of … sex" in the workplace; and TITLE IX of the Education Amendments of 1972, which bans discrimination "on the basis of sex" in education programs and activities receiving federal aid.

In *Price Waterhouse v. Hopkins* (1989), the Supreme Court concluded that "when a plaintiff in a Title VII case proves that her gender played a motivating part in an employment decision, the defendant may avoid a finding of liability only by proving by a preponderance of the evidence that it would have made the same decision even if it had not taken the plaintiff's gender into account." This case involved a woman denied partnership in the accounting firm, but it could also apply to a male who was evaluated on the basis of sexual stereotyping. The basic issue revolved around the "gender" of the job (does it require masculine or feminine qualities?) and how does the employer require the employee, whether a man or a woman, to act (more masculine or more feminine)?

On the other side of the coin, in *Equal Employment Opportunity Commission v. Sears, Roebuck and Co.* (1986), a federal district court found that the employer could challenge the statistical disparity in pay and promotions between men and women with evidence that the disparity was the result of the different employment goals of men and women employees, rather than discriminatory company policy. The record in this case established that selection for more lucrative commissioned sales jobs went more often to men, because women at the company expressed a preference for keeping their less competitive noncommission jobs.

State courts also apply federal statutory law regarding discrimination. For example, in *Penhollow v. Board of Commissioners for Cecil County* (1997), Maryland's court of special appeals held that it was not bound by a federal court of appeals decision as to whether Title VII liability would be imposed on individual employees. The court also declared that in a claim based on SEXUAL HARASSMENT under Title VII, an employee must sufficiently assert that the offending conduct was of a sexual nature, which was not the case where a coworker simply said: "I don't need you in here. Go sit in booking and look nice."

Enforcement of sex discrimination claims is carried out through the U.S. Department of Justice, Equal Employment Opportunity Commission (EEOC), nongovernmental legal assistance organizations, and private actions brought by victims. The Civil Rights Act of 1991, enacted partly in response to the Supreme Court's decision in *Griggs v. Duke Power Co.* (1971)—involving systematic racial discrimination by an employer—and subsequent cases, allows victims of intentional discrimination to recover damages proportional to the size of the employer. The act generally requires the complaining party to demonstrate "that an employment practice [or group of such practices] results in a disparate impact on the basis of . . . sex," and the respondent must fail to show that such practice or practices are required by "business necessity." The term *disparate impact* was a concept developed by the EEOC to extend the protections of Title VII beyond just "disparate treatment" of employees to more subtle discriminatory practices that were not job related.

State Law. In about half the states, discrimination on the basis of sex is outlawed by statute, but only about nineteen state constitutions have provisions barring discrimination on the basis of sex. (Six states—Alabama, Iowa, Minnesota, Mississippi, Nevada, and North Carolina—have no provisions against sex discrimination.) The scope of constitutional protection varies widely. Since 1972 Maryland's constitution has declared: "Equality of rights under the law shall not be abridged or denied because of sex." That same year Alaska's constitution was amended to provide: "No person is to be denied the enjoyment of any civil or political right because of race, color, creed, sex, or national origin."

Twenty years after the U.S. Supreme Court's *Bradwell* decision, Indiana's supreme court held in 1893 that language in its constitution prohibiting the legislature from granting "to any citizen, or class of citizens, privileges or immunities which, upon the same terms, shall not equally belong to all citizens" meant that the denial of admission to the state bar on account of sex was unconstitutional.

Without any specific language prohibiting sex discrimination in New Jersey's constitution, the state's supreme court in *Peper v. Princeton University Board of Trustees* (1978) validated a claim for sex discrimination under a provision in the constitution's article on rights and privileges; this states in part: "All persons [have the right] of acquiring, possessing, and protecting property." California's supreme court declared in 1976 that "the court deals not so much with a statute's neutral language as with its practical impact.... A seemingly neutral statute which actually disqualifies a disproportionate number of one sex is discriminatory."

In *Darrin v. Gould* (1975), the supreme court of Washington determined that the specific language of its equal rights amendment meant that sex discrimination is simply forbidden, thus eliminating the need to treat sex as a suspect class or use a strict standard of scrutiny. The case involved the right of girls in high school to participate on the football team with boys. In Massachusetts boys' right to play on girls' teams was upheld in *Attorney General v. Massachusetts Interscholastic Athletic Association* (1979). In 1987 the Washington supreme court ruled in *Blair v. Washington State University* that a set percentage of a university's athletic funds must be devoted to women's sports programs.

In Texas, however, the constitutional guarantee of equality under the law was held to apply only to public affairs and some egregious private actions linked with state functions; thus, the right of a peewee football team to exclude girls was upheld as purely private discrimination. In *State ex rel. Tompras v. Board of Election Commissioners* (2004), the Missouri supreme court held that a law reserving an elected position of "committeewoman" of a political party was not unconstitutional because party offices were not public positions to which the language of the constitution expressly referred in requiring equality of the sexes.

Discrimination by Sexual Orientation

Discrimination on the basis of sexual orientation has generally arisen in four areas: with respect to laws that (1) criminalize homosexual sodomy between consenting adults in private, which were struck down by the Supreme Court in LAWRENCE V. TEXAS (2003); (2) in employment; (3) in attempts to legalize relationships such as SAME-SEX MARRIAGE, civil unions, or domestic

partnerships; (4) and in the MILITARY. The Supreme Court gives "strict scrutiny" to laws discriminating on the basis of race, and it has held the government to a lesser standard for laws that permit discrimination on the basis of sex. But in the case of discrimination because of sexual orientation, the Court has not imposed even an intermediate standard of scrutiny on the government and has been somewhat inconsistent in applying constitutional protections to victims of discrimination. This situation emanates from a variety of potential reasons, from a male-dominated society's fear of a loss of "maleness" to an inability to make rational distinctions on the basis of various gradations of sexuality and gender (compared to simple classifications into male and female). The law thus does not currently protect homosexuals or other sexual minorities to the same extent as it does women and racial minorities.

Federal Law. After World War II the threat of communism was used to fire homosexuals in the federal government. In 1950, shortly after Senator Joseph McCarthy of Wisconsin claimed that two hundred communists were working in the State Department, it was announced that ninety-one homosexual employees had been fired as security risks. But when FRANKLIN KAMENY was let go from his civil service job, he appealed all the way to the Supreme Court. Although the justices unanimously refused to hear his appeal in 1961, he made the case that he and fifteen million more American citizens were being persecuted not for any illegal conduct but for their sexual identity.

Not until 1969, in *Norton v. Macy*, did the U.S. Court of Appeals for the District of Columbia rule that firing a federal civil servant simply because his sexual orientation might prove an embarrassment to the government—based on an alleged "homosexual advance" toward another employee—was arbitrary and therefore illegal. The court held that due process limited the government's discretion in firing, even for employees whose employment status is unprotected by statute. In 1998 President Bill Clinton prohibited discrimination against homosexuals in the federal civil service through an executive order.

Five years earlier President Clinton announced that he would lift the ban on homosexuals in the military, using an executive order, but military leaders balked at this. A compromise policy was then adopted to allow homosexuals to serve as long as they were not open about their sexual orientation. A year later, a federal appeals court in *Steffan v. Perry* (1994) upheld the discharge of a naval officer who admitted that he was gay; the court stated that regardless of whether homosexuality is genetically determined, the military requirement that openly homosexual members be discharged for the good of the service is no worse than maintaining a height requirement for military service, because height is also genetically determined.

The law enshrining this "don't ask, don't tell" policy is found in Title 10 of the U.S. Code, section 654, which states in part:

(14) The armed forces must maintain personnel policies that exclude persons whose presence in the armed forces would create an unacceptable risk to the armed forces' high standards of morale, good order and discipline, and unit cohesion that are the essence of military capability.

(15) The presence in the armed forces of persons who demonstrate a propensity or intent to engage in homosexual acts would create an unacceptable risk to the high standards of morale, good order and discipline, and unit cohesion that are the essence of military capability.

The U.S. Court of Appeals for the Ninth Circuit held in 1979 that discrimination on the basis of sexual orientation—for signs of homosexuality, effeminacy, or TRANSSEXUALISM—using any reason other than the traditional definition of the female and male sexes, was not covered by Title VII of the Civil Rights Act of 1964. A dissent in the case seemed to indicate that a claim based on discrimination against a male, regardless of the reason, might "protect males generally" and thus be encompassed in the language of Title VII. Other ways in which the federal government legally discriminates against sexual minorities include language in appropriations bills for SEX EDUCATION in the schools and materials regarding prevention and treatment of AIDS-HIV that bars statements condoning homosexuality. The DEFENSE OF MARRIAGE ACT (1996) prohibits any government benefits for married couples unless they are heterosexual.

State Law. As of 2005, fourteen states, with the recent addition of Illinois, had laws banning discrimination on the basis of sexual orientation; a similar measure before the Delaware legislature has been hotly debated. The California supreme court's watershed decision in *Gay Law Students Association v. Pacific Telephone and Telegraph Co.* (1979) established that discrimination by a public utility against employees and potential employees on the basis of sexual orientation violated their right of political freedom. The decision noted that "one important aspect of the struggle for equal rights is to induce homosexual individuals to 'come out of the closet,' acknowledge their sexual preferences, and to associate with others in working for equal rights."

More recent cases, however, highlight the polarization that is taking place in the country around this issue. In *Opinions of the Justices to the House of Representatives* (1998), the supreme court of Massachusetts confirmed the extension of health care benefits to domestic partners of employees of the city of Boston. In *Mack v. City of Detroit* (2002), however, the Michigan supreme court overruled a lower court's recognition of a private cause of action against the city government for discrimination based on sexual orientation.

Homosexuals are also being accorded different treatment in terms of MARRIAGE rights. In 1998 Alaska amended its constitution to add language that effectively forecloses to same-sex couples the rights and privileges of marriage: "To be valid or recognized in this State, a marriage may exist only between one man and one woman." The recent spate of amendments to other state constitutions, defining marriage as between one man and one woman (thirteen in 2004 alone), deny the same status to homosexual couples. Such a groundswell indicates how strongly many citizens continue to believe in the reasonableness of discrimination on the basis of sexual orientation.

Enforcement by state courts is just catching up with enforcement at the federal level; in many cases remedies depend on the state in which the alleged discrimination occurs. Civil actions to obtain equitable relief or money damages are generally less successful. To recognize an implied right of action for discrimination, some states have used the federal court ruling in *Bivens v. Six Unknown Named Agents of the Federal Bureau of Narcotics* (1972), which held that government agents have no immunity from damage suits alleging violations of constitutional rights.

Affirmative Action

President Lyndon Johnson first used the term *affirmative action* in a 1965 executive order designed to ensure that federal contractors treat job applicants and employees "without regard to their race, creed, color, or national origin." Many federal and state laws and regulations as well as the policies of private employers and colleges have since followed suit, incorporating affirmative measures to be taken in recruitment, hiring, job assignment, and promotion. The goal is to make a special effort to give members of certain historically disadvantaged groups—minorities and women, in particular—an equal opportunity at educational and job-related benefits.

Some citizens who, because of affirmative action, believe that they have lost a similar opportunity assert that they are victims of reverse discrimination. In *Regents of the University of California v. Bakke* (1978), the U.S. Supreme Court found a state medical school's affirmative action policy unconstitutional because it discriminated against a white male applicant to the school; he had argued that he was not admitted so that room could be made for a less qualified minority applicant. The Court, however, did not rule that any affirmative action policy would be unconstitutional. Later, in *United Steelworkers v. Weber* (1979), it approved an affirmative action employment plan.

Yet the policy of affirmative action by the federal and state governments has been under attack. The country remains divided over the constitutionality of any measure that accords one group of citizens special treatment in work and educational opportunities. In some political circles, calling for "a color-blind Constitution" is code for an antiaffirmative action policy.

"Equal means getting the same thing, at the same time and in the same place," said U.S. Supreme Court Associate Justice Thurgood Marshall—no stranger to discrimination himself. Anything else is discrimination. Legalized discrimination may be rationalized, but for those discriminated against on the basis of sex or sexual orientation, the technical distinctions on which their suspect classifications are based—whether related to employment, education, legal rights, or any other privileges and benefits extended to other citizens—may seem to thwart rather than promote the concept of justice for all.

See also Bisexuality; Breastfeeding; Hate Crimes; Pregnancy; Transvestism; *Virginia, United States v.*

DISEASES

See AIDS-HIV; Sexually Transmitted Diseases.

DIVORCE

It is estimated that between 43 and 50 percent of first marriages end in divorce. Divorce is the legal termination of a MARRIAGE, in some states called a dissolution of marriage. Just as marriage affects the parties' legal rights relating to sexual behavior, so does divorce. For example, the right to cohabit or live together in the same house as husband and wife and be sexually intimate ceases in a divorce or a separation.

A separation occurs when a husband and a wife begin living apart from each other, perhaps for a trial period holding out the possibility of a reconciliation. Some states require a period of separation before a no-fault divorce is granted. A separation may be an informal arrangement or may be based on either a written agreement or a court order. In the case of a permanent separation, many states require that the parties' assets and debts also become separate; in

For much of American history, parties to a divorce, especially the woman, were often stigmatized. Thanks partly to the many divorces and remarriages of celebrities such as the movie legend Marilyn Monroe, who wed the baseball great Joe DiMaggio and then the playwright Arthur Miller, divorce no longer brings social opprobrium.

some states this can happen only after divorce proceedings are begun. A legal separation is like a divorce in that a court divides the marital property and rules on questions of ALIMONY (sometimes called separate maintenance), the custody of children, and CHILD SUPPORT.

The legal nature of divorce has changed greatly since the end of the nineteenth century, when marriage was intended to be a permanent, "until death do us part" relationship. Marriage laws, as well as religious and social pressure, made it extremely difficult for a woman to obtain a divorce, because in marriage she was under the custody of her husband and had few, if any, individual rights of her own. The Nineteenth Amendment (1920) to the U.S. Constitution gave women the right to vote and hold office, ushering in an era of greater autonomy for wives in marriage. The fact that women

held many traditionally male jobs during World War II, while men were in MILITARY service, followed by the 1960s civil rights and WOMEN'S RIGHTS movements, fueled an expansion of EQUAL RIGHTS for women in the legal, economic, and social spheres. It was almost inevitable that changes in marital and SPOUSAL RIGHTS AND DUTIES would follow. One of the first significant changes was what is sometimes described as the private ordering, as opposed to the public regulation, of marriage, including a general recognition by courts of private arrangements affecting both marriage and divorce, such as PRENUPTIAL AGREEMENTS and postmarital agreements.

Like marriage, the legal concept of divorce is wholly the creation of the government, and states have the sole authority to set the rules of disengagement, so to speak. In *Pennoyer v. Neff* (1877), the U.S. Supreme

State Divorce Laws

State	Grounds			Judicial Separation Available	Division of Property		
	No-Fault Only	No-Fault Plus Traditional	Incompatibility		Community Property	Separate Property Excludable	Statutory Considerations
Alabama		•	•	•		•	
Alaska		•	•	•	•[1]		•
Arizona	•	•[2]			•	•	
Arkansas		•[2]		•		•	•
California	•			•	•	•[3]	
Colorado	•			•		•	•
Connecticut		•		•			•
Delaware		•		•		•	•
Florida	•			•		•	•
Georgia		•				•	
Hawaii	•			•		•	•
Idaho		•			•	•	•
Illinois		•		•		•	•
Indiana	•			•			•
Iowa	•			•			•
Kansas			•	•			•
Kentucky	•			•		•	•
Louisiana		•[2]		•	•	•[2]	
Maine		•		•		•	•
Maryland		•		•			•
Massachusetts		•		•			•
Michigan	•			•		•	
Minnesota	•			•		•	•
Mississippi		•[4]					
Missouri	•			•		•	•
Montana	•			•			•
Nebraska	•			•			•
Nevada			•	•	•	•	
New Hampshire		•		•			•
New Jersey		•		•			
New Mexico		•	•		•	•	
New York		•		•		•	•
North Carolina		•		•		•	•
North Dakota		•		•			
Ohio		•	•			•	•
Oklahoma			•	•		•	
Oregon	•			•			

State	Grounds			Judicial Separation Available	Division of Property		
	No-Fault Only	No-Fault Plus Traditional	Incompatibility		Community Property	Separate Property Excludable	Statutory Considerations
Pennsylvania		•				•	•
Rhode Island		•		•		•	•
South Carolina		•		•		•	•
South Dakota		•		•			
Tennessee		•		•		•	•
Texas		•			•	•	
Utah		•		•			
Vermont		•					•
Virginia		•		•		•	•
Washington	•				•		•
West Virginia		•		•		•	•
Wisconsin	•			•	•	•	•
Wyoming		•		•			•

1. By contract the parties may make some or all marital property community property.

2. Covenant marriage has different rules.

3. Community property must be divided equally.

4. No-fault grounds available only with a joint petition.

Source: American Bar Association, *Family Law Quarterly,* 2006

Court declared: "The State ... has [the] absolute right to prescribe the conditions upon which the marriage relation between its own citizens shall be created, and the causes for which it may be dissolved." The decision in that case also established the rule that a state does not have to have personal jurisdiction over a defendant in a divorce case if that person is domiciled (has legal residence) in the state. The normal rule in civil actions is that personal jurisdiction is required in order for the state to acquire jurisdiction.

Divorce is a civil, not a criminal, matter. Some states have created a family court system to deal with divorce as well as with other family problems; among these are civil abuse proceedings to remove a child from a home for his or her protection, criminal cases involving juvenile delinquency, and the prosecution of adults for CHILD ABUSE. A unified family court system allows CHILDREN to be given special treatment not available in the regular court system and involves social service agencies that can provide extrajudicial assistance to families and family members in the process of administering justice.

Types of Divorce

States began passing laws in the 1960s permitting no-fault divorce. Before then, certain grounds had to be specified for a marriage to be legally dissolved: marital offenses such as abandonment or desertion, ADULTERY, inability to engage in sex, insanity, imprisonment, physical or mental cruelty, habitual drunkenness, or addiction to DRUGS. Before the 1960s, a divorce would not be granted when both spouses were at fault because the courts could find no blameless party; the narrow logic of such decisions no longer prevails.

No-Fault Divorce. Most states and the District of Columbia allow a divorce without a determination of which party is at fault. About twenty states—including California, Colorado, Minnesota, and Oregon—have no-fault divorce as their only option. In other states, a spouse may choose fault or no-fault as the basis for seeking a divorce. A spouse cannot prevent a no-fault divorce if the other spouse wants it.

Fault-based Divorce. A divorce based on a marital offense may be defended against by proving to the court that the ground alleged is baseless or by using other reasons such as a condonation (the faultless spouse's willingness to look the other way with respect to the at-fault spouse's offense). Basing a divorce on fault may shorten the separation time.

The nature and extent of the marital offense can alter the terms of a court-ordered settlement. A few states exclude evidence of fault in the allocation of property and only to a limited extent consider fault in determining the amount of alimony to be paid by one spouse to another. Several states, including Arkansas, Kansas, and New York, except in rare or egregious cases, disregard the fault entirely. Some states allow trial courts to consider fault only in alimony determinations. About fifteen states permit courts to consider fault in both property allocations and alimony payments. Federal entitlements, such as pensions and veterans' benefits, may be an exception.

The Constitution does not grant the federal government any involvement in divorce, except under Article III, section 2, in relation to foreign diplomats. The Court has dealt with tangential issues, however; for example, in the WILLIAMS V. NORTH CAROLINA I and II cases, decided in 1942 and 1945, respectively, the Court ruled that the Constitution's full faith and credit clause requires a legitimate establishment of domicile in a state before a divorce decree in one state must be legally recognized in another. In *Sosna v. Iowa* (1975), the Court upheld a one-year residency requirement before a divorce could be granted; and in *Boddie v. Connecticut* (1971), the Court held that the Constitution's due process clause prohibits a state from denying divorces to indigents just because they cannot pay court costs and fees.

Alternatives to Divorce

A number of other legal procedures have evolved to handle special relationships and circumstances.

Annulment. An ANNULMENT of a marriage is based on the legal fiction that the union never took place; in essence, the parties are returned to their premarital status. Courts grant annulments typically on the grounds of fraud or misrepresentation, such as a failure to disclose an infectious disease or a prior marriage that ended in divorce.

Covenant Marriage. Arkansas, Arizona, and Louisiana are among the states that provide an option called covenant marriage that makes it harder for partners to obtain a divorce. In covenant marriage they waive their rights to no-fault divorce and some of the grounds used to obtain a fault-based divorce.

Nonmarital Relationships. Divorcelike proceedings are sometimes available to nonmarried couples. In *Marvin v. Marvin* (1976), a California court upheld a six-year "palimony" agreement entered into by an opposite-sex couple, reasoning that a contract to provide for a spouse, in which sexual services were not a consideration, was enforceable. Some courts have even recognized implied contracts of this nature. Meretricious contracts of cohabitation, ones involving the provision of sexual relations, were historically unenforceable in a court of law because such a consideration for the contract—a willingness to have sex with the other contracting party—was against public policy as being too much like a contract for PROSTITUTION.

Same-Sex Relationships. Some courts apply the same standards of divorce to the termination of same-sex relationships. Vermont grants same-sex partners in a civil union benefits identical to those conferred on married couples, but an issue in such cases may be whether or not the sole consideration was sexual services. A couple who were partners in a Vermont civil union were perfunctorily granted a divorce in 2003 by a judge in Iowa, who did not realize at the time that they were both women. When he learned of the mistake, he let the settlement stand; but it raised questions in Iowa—a state that bans SAME-SEX

MARRIAGE—whether granting the divorce was somehow implicitly sanctioning same-sex marriage. Massachusetts, which currently recognizes same-sex marriage, treats divorce basically the same for homosexual and heterosexual spouses.

The traditional rules for marriage and its termination have changed drastically in the last several decades. This trend toward privatizing the marital structure—by allowing personal rather than state-mandated choices—has caused a backlash by some Americans who long for the days when the state could be counted on to supervise all aspects of the institution of marriage. Yet it would seem to follow that as the capitalist economic system offers a plethora of choices for consumers, more choices should also be available in terms of individual social rights. An interesting study publicized after the 2004 election found that divorce was less prevalent in the "blue" (more liberal) states than in the "red" (more conservative) states, in which moral values were deemed to be of strong concern. Differences in RELIGION as well as higher education and income levels have been found to correlate with lower rates of divorce.

Notably, the divorce rate has seen a steady decline since 1992, when it was 0.48 percent per capita. In 2003, based on provisional estimates from the National Vital Statistics System, the per capita annual divorce rate in the United States was about 0.38 percent (doubled for the two persons involved). Just under one million American marriages are annually severed by divorce.

DNA

In January 2005 the police in the small Massachusetts town of Truro on Cape Cod asked local men to voluntarily provide DNA samples from cheek swabs for the investigation of the stabbing death of a woman on whose body semen had been found. Some men complied with the request, but others opted out. The Massachusetts chapter of the AMERICAN CIVIL LIBERTIES UNION asked that the DNA sweep

Deoxyribonucleic acid (DNA)—the constituent of human genes that plays a part in transmitting genetic information from one generation to another—forms a double-helix configuration. DNA can now be used to identify the perpetrators of crimes and to determine a child's paternity.

be halted as a serious invasion of personal PRIVACY; officials refused, saying that DNA testing is a useful method of solving crimes. Crime-detection dragnets such as this have little chance of success, however, because it is doubtful that a perpetrator will voluntarily incriminate himself. In Baton Rouge, Louisiana, law enforcement officials got lucky in 2003 when DNA collected in a seemingly unrelated case led them to a suspect in five brutal rape-murder cases.

DNA (deoxyribonucleic acid) is the substance contained in the cells of living organisms that carries genetic information passed on to offspring during reproduction. In sexual reproduction, genetic material is contributed by both the male and the female, and it determines much about who we are or will be. Sexual reproduction requires an egg cell and a sperm cell. These specialized cells are haploid—that is, they have a single strand of DNA, or half of the genetic material of a diploid somatic cell, the kind of cell that makes up the rest of the human body; at conception each haploid cell, one from the male and one from the female, forms one-half of the double strand of DNA that will produce a new human being. The British scientists James Watson (b. 1928) and Francis Crick (1916– 2004), along with their New Zealand colleague, Maurice Wilkins, first identified DNA's double-helix structure in 1953, unlocking its secrets. They shared a Nobel Prize in 1962 for this discovery.

DNA has become a useful tool—akin to fingerprints and blood typing—in identifying individuals and their genetic relationships, particularly in criminal law and paternity cases; it can also help match organ donors and transplant recipients, identify plant and animal species, and detect bacteria and other harmful organisms. Semen, which carries sperm cells, holds the DNA of the male who produced it. Other cells in the body—such as hair, skin, blood, and saliva—can also provide DNA information. Like fingerprints, each person's DNA is unique and can be compared against another DNA sample with great precision. Analysts look at several locations on a person's genome, a complete haploid set of chromosomes contained in a strand of DNA. If matches are found in at least five locations, then this is a rare enough occurrence that the identification can be considered beyond a reasonable doubt. Identification can be made with very few possibilities of error, not counting human error in the testing procedures.

The history of DNA technology began with experiments by an Austrian monk and biologist, Gregor Mendel (1822–84); he is considered the founder of GENETICS because of his pioneering work in discovering the inheritance of genetic traits by living organisms such as pea plants. After the groundbreaking work of Crick and Watson, ALEC JEFFREYS at the Lister Institute in England and the Lifecodes Corporation in the United States began work on genetic probes that

could find a human gene and discern differences in individuals based on the genetic information found. In 1984 Jeffreys's team became the first to develop genetic probes that could be used to identify people.

Criminal Law

The DNA-profiling or "fingerprinting" techniques developed by Jeffreys were used for the first time two years later, in 1986, to help solve the Enderby murders in Leicestershire, England. Although 4,582 genetic samples were provided by men in the area in response to a police request, no match was found for the semen left at the scene of one rape-murder. The perpetrator was caught, however, when the police discovered that he had asked another man to provide a sample of DNA on his behalf.

The first U.S. case in which DNA was used successfully in a criminal trial occurred in Orlando, Florida, in 1987. A man accused of burglary and rape as well as sexual assaults in the Orlando area was identified as the rapist through DNA testing. Since then, the method has been used in countless criminal cases.

DNA comparisons are also used to exonerate people wrongly accused or convicted of crimes. One difficulty is the length of time that may have passed since the data were collected, which can affect the condition of the samples. A man sentenced to death in Virginia in 2005 appealed his conviction after it was discovered that a DNA sample that might have proved his innocence was mistakenly destroyed; he was cleared of the crime. A year earlier, the U.S. Senate passed a bill to ensure postconviction access to DNA testing for PRISONERS on death row and any inmates who assert their innocence. As of 2005 at least twelve prisoners sentenced to death have been exonerated through this testing. The Justice for All Act (2004) promotes access to DNA testing for RAPE victims as well as convicted felons.

DNA tests are not perfect but have a high percentage of accuracy. In a 1992 SEXUAL ASSAULT case in Texas, for example, it was determined that the frequency of the DNA material introduced into evidence was one in fifty-four billion in North America. Various factors may account for wrongful identification, including problems in collecting (such as in the Enderby case above), handling, and testing the DNA material. The U.S. Supreme Court has not directly addressed questions raised by DNA sampling and analysis, but in its decision in *Daubert v. Merrell Dow* (1993), the Court opened the door for evidence of DNA identification by broadening the rules for the admission of scientific evidence into the courtroom.

A number of federal court cases, including *United States v. Shea* (1997), have recognized that DNA identification is generally admissible in determining a criminal perpetrator's identity and that a test's statistical results (as in the Texas case above) are admissible. The Indiana supreme court, in *Overstreet v. State* (2003), held that the following criteria must be established for admissibility: that the scientific principles on which the DNA identification expert's testimony rests are reliable; that the witness is qualified; and that the testimony's probative value is not substantially outweighed by the dangers of unfair prejudice.

The federal government provides funds for the training and education of law enforcement, correctional, and court officers that includes DNA collection and anaylsis. DNA analysis in federal criminal cases is carried out by the Federal Bureau of Investigation. In the U.S. Code, Title 42, The Public Health and Welfare, chapter 136, subchapter IX, part A, DNA Identification, section 14133, mandates: "Personnel at the Federal Bureau of Investigation who perform DNA analyses shall undergo semiannual external proficiency testing by a DNA proficiency testing program ... , [and] ... the Director of the [FBI] shall arrange for periodic blind external tests to determine the proficiency of DNA analysis performed at the [FBI] laboratory."

To build a DNA database, states in the 1980s and 1990s began collecting samples from criminals; by the end of the century, all states had passed laws to establish such databases, and information on about three million persons had been collected. Each state and the District of Columbia also has a law that allows DNA to be taken from certain individuals who have come in contact with the justice system, such as prisoners, parolees, and others taken into custody for some reason. Such programs are not always funded at a useful level, however, and the laws vary as to the subjects of the samples and what can be done with them. For example, all states authorize samples from SEX OFFENDERS and other violent criminals, but only about half call for samples from individuals convicted of felonies and crimes against property. Louisiana, Texas, and Washington State permit samples to be taken from persons arrested but not convicted. Most states allow research to be done on samples collected from convicts and authorize the removal of data from the records if a person is acquitted. A majority of states also include juveniles in their database. In 2006 researchers proposed that DNA additionally be taken from close relatives of known criminals, as has been done in England; New York and Massachusetts already expressly allow this.

States vary on how they deal with legal issues surrounding DNA collection, in part because taking a suspect's blood, other bodily fluids, and hair without CONSENT may raise allegations of unconstitutional searches and seizures under state and federal law. In *State v. Clark* (1982), Hawaii's supreme court found that a forcible search of a suspect's vagina required a search warrant and was not legal simply as a search incident to an arrest. In reviewing a grand jury action in *In re May 1991 Will County Grand Jury* (1992), the Illinois supreme court ruled that the constitutional right of privacy plays a role in the jury's authority to subpoena evidence from a person's body and that there is a higher standard—probable cause—for obtaining evidence from a person's private areas; evidence from parts of the body that are publicly exposed, such as hair or fingerprints, may be obtained based on reasonable suspicion alone, a lower standard.

Relationship Identification

All living humans are descended from one mother in the very distant past, according to evidence from mitochondrial DNA (cell parts that generate energy, rather than a cell nucleus). There are times, however, when it is important to legally establish closer relationships between two persons. The first recorded use of DNA identification techniques for this purpose occurred in England shortly after the process for probing human DNA was first described by Alec Jeffreys in the science journal *Nature* in 1985. In an immigration matter, the United Kingdom government had questioned the relationship of a boy and a woman who claimed to be his mother, but the test proved her claim.

DNA can also be used to establish PATERNITY and other family relationships. The Supreme Court in *Rivera v. Minnich* (1981) held that determining paternity by just a preponderance of the evidence—rather than beyond a reasonable doubt—was sufficient and does not violate constitutional due process protections. In *Little v. Streater* (1981), the Court held that due process requires extending the right to a blood test to indigent defendants to prove or disprove paternity. The Uniform Parentage Act (2002) authorizes courts to refuse to order genetic testing in some cases in paternity disputes, such as where a parent has been living with a child for more than two years and thus may be considered a de facto parent regardless of any biological connection or where the parents do not want to know if their baby has a different father.

DNA has become a useful tool in the legal arsenal to determine the truth of life-and-death issues as well as fairness and equity. But the use of DNA technology is not without its problems, among which are the competence of those who perform the comparisons, the integrity of the chain of custody and security procedures for the samples, and the possible misuse of the data obtained, given that DNA can tell much about the person who has given the sample, including race, family relationships, and any propensity for certain diseases. Perhaps most important, as more evidence of wrongful convictions is brought to public attention, this new forensic tool has helped resurrect questions about the fairness of the death penalty in the United States.

See also BIOETHICS; STEM-CELL RESEARCH AND CLONING.

DOMESTIC PARTNERSHIPS

See MARRIAGE; SAME-SEX MARRIAGE.

DOMESTIC VIOLENCE

Under the English common law inherited by the states when the United States became a nation, a husband was permitted to moderately chastise his wife, but any beating had to be with a rod no thicker than his thumb. Today all states have laws that criminalize such domestic battering, regardless of the legal relationship between the parties. Domestic violence—abuse within the home or between family members—is most often carried out by males against females and CHILDREN. It includes physical behavior, such as slapping or punching; coerced sex or sex-related acts, from sexual jokes and insults to RAPE, other types of SEXUAL ASSAULT, and INCEST; threats of abuse, in some cases with a weapon, including CHILD ABUSE; psychological abuse, including intimidation and controlling behavior; stalking, including cyberstalking, to cause emotional distress; and even murder.

It is estimated that some 960,000 incidents of domestic violence occur every year, with abuse among homosexual partners about the same as among heterosexuals. Although women are less likely than men to be victims of violent crimes overall, they are five to eight times more likely than men to be victimized by an intimate partner. Approximately 31 percent of American women have reported being physically or sexually abused by a husband or a boyfriend at some time in their lives. As many as 324,000 women each year experience violence from partners while they are pregnant. On average more than three women in the United States are murdered every day by their husbands or boyfriends. Only about 15 percent of the victims of domestic violence are men.

In an attempt to combat such destructive behavior, CONGRESS enacted the VIOLENCE AGAINST WOMEN ACT in 1994. Although this act has many provisions directed at assisting abused, battered, and assaulted women regardless of whether they stem from domestic violence, the act's teeth were pulled by the U.S. Supreme Court in its decision *United States v. Morrison* (2000). In this case the Court ruled that the commerce clause in Article I, section 8, of the U.S. Constitution does not empower Congress to legislate a national right of action for violence against women as it does for civil rights violations. Congress was thus found to lack authority to extend to victims, including women experiencing domestic violence, a private cause of action to seek justice when federal and state systems fail them. The act still provides remedies for related crimes that involve crossing state lines, and it offers grants to state law enforcement agencies to improve their ability to deal with domestic violence and other violent crimes against women.

Recourse to State Law

Domestic violence, including sexually related acts, is generally covered under state law. But, as the *Morrison* case illustrates, the path to protecting women and bringing perpetrators to justice is not without legal and cultural obstacles. Until recently law enforcement officers often did not take domestic violence reports seriously enough, with the result that more serious crimes ensued. Even judges, who have the power to grant protective orders to restrain abusive spouses and partners, may take such matters too lightly. In Maryland, for example, a judge's refusal in 2005 to continue such a protective order led to the wife's being set afire by an abusive husband.

The laws themselves may have some built-in limitations with respect to domestic violence. In *Crawford v. Washington* (2004), the Supreme Court upheld the hearsay evidence rule against the admission of testimony where a witness is unavailable for cross-examination. The videotaped testimony of the victim's six-year-old daughter, who had witnessed her mother's being beaten and choked by a former boyfriend, had been introduced into evidence at the trial, but because the child was unable to testify the conviction was reversed on appeal. Other prosecutions have been unsuccessful because of intimidation of witnesses or even victims.

Before the *Crawford* case, many state laws made exceptions to the hearsay evidence rules for cases involving domestic violence. These laws reflected a recognition that domestic violence cases—in which the parties are known to each other, family members may take sides, and intimidation and false remorse are likely—produce a high rate of victims who recant their initial stories or who refuse to cooperate with law enforcement or prosecutors after initially reporting the incidents. In 2003 the Pennsylvania state constitution was amended to allow closed-circuit television in criminal trials involving child victims or witnesses, a problem similar to the one involved in the *Crawford* case. This amendment, designed to remove the "face-to-face" requirement to facilitate testimony by a child victim or witness, was found the next year not to infringe a criminal defendant's right to confront witnesses. The difference in the Pennsylvania law and the *Crawford* case lies in the defendant's right to cross-examine the witness in the closed-circuit session, which he could not have done if merely presented with a videotape of a witness's untested statement.

Many states are recognizing the special problems involved in preventing, reporting, and adjudicating crimes of domestic violence. On their own and in partnership with the federal government, they are taking steps to improve. In 2003, for example, New Jersey passed a law directed at educating citizens about domestic violence and child abuse. This law provides in part that instructions on these types of crime may be included in public school curriculums and "shall enable pupils to understand the psychology and dynamics of family violence, dating violence and child abuse, the relationship of alcohol and drug abuse to such violence and abuse, ... and to learn methods of non-violent problem solving." Vermont law authorizes its center for crime-victim services to grant awards "for the purpose of providing shelter, protection or support for battered or abused spouses." Private organizations also offer shelter and aid to victims of abuse, and women's advocacy groups can help with obtaining legal protection.

Because earlier domestic violence and abuse cases were often not prosecuted, women began relying on civil protective orders in the 1970s to keep abusers away. Such court orders may be called protection orders, restraining orders, temporary protection orders (TPOs), or, more commonly, temporary restraining orders (TROs). A victim has to request the order and appear in court to present evidence to a judge to establish the need for such an order. It is not necessary that the party against whom the order is being sought be notified or present at the hearing. Some states, however, provide for a follow-up hearing after the abuser is notified of the order or if the abuser challenges the order.

Battered-Women's Syndrome

Many wives or partners in a relationship may submit to persistent spousal abuse and not report it or leave the abusive relationship. To explain this phenomenon, Lenore Walker, a psychologist, has argued that battered women are victims of "learned helplessness," a condition that allows them to stay in a violent relationship because the abuse creates a state of depression negating any motivation to respond rationally to such abuse. For women who murder their abusive partners, this battered-women's syndrome has become the basis for their legal defense. The syndrome may trigger an act of violence against the abuser by a woman who legitimately feels that her life is threatened. To prove this, she must demonstrate that she reasonably feared that she was in imminent danger of bodily harm, which in turn depends on an assessment by the judge or the jury as to the reasonableness of her perception of the danger.

The California evidence code, as amended in 2004, provides: "In a criminal action, expert testimony is admissible by either the prosecution or the defense regarding intimate partner battering and its effects, including the nature and effect of physical, emotional, or mental abuse on the beliefs, perceptions, or behavior of victims of domestic violence." A 2000

The victims of family or domestic violence are generally women and children. To help raise awareness of this often hidden form of abuse, Congress asked the U.S. Postal Service to issue a fundraising stamp on the subject. These stamps cost more than regular first-class postage, with the difference donated to the cause depicted.

case, tried under California's former battered-women's syndrome language before it was amended in 2004, found two major components in the analysis of battered-women's syndrome: "First, there must be sufficient evidence in the particular case to support a contention that the syndrome applies to the woman involved; second, there must be a contested issue as to which the syndrome testimony is probative." In other words, the woman must be shown to suffer from the syndrome, and the syndrome's effect must be shown to have caused the harm.

Little by little, domestic violence is no longer simply ignored as lovers' spats or typical arguments in personal relationships. Political leaders, law enforcement officers, and judges are being urged to abandon the notion that violence in MARRIAGE and other significant relationships is somehow not as serious as crime on the streets. The OFFICE ON VIOLENCE AGAINST WOMEN in the U.S. Department of Justice provides assistance, training, and grants to the states and other U.S. jurisdictions, such as Native American tribal justice systems, to improve their handling of domestic violence issues and cases.

Contacts

National Coalition Against Domestic Violence, 1633 Q Street, NW, Suite 210, Washington, DC 20009 (202-745-1211). www.ndvh.org.

National Domestic Violence Hotline (800-799-SAFE).

WILLIAM O. DOUGLAS

William O. Douglas, who served on the U.S. Supreme Court for thirty-six years and seven months, from 1939 to 1975—the longest continuous service of any member—was instrumental in laying the groundwork for still-controversial decisions regarding sexual behavior, among them *Roe v. Wade* (1973) on ABORTION rights and *LAWRENCE V. TEXAS* (2003) on homosexual SODOMY rights. In *GRISWOLD V. CONNECTICUT* (1965), his opinion for the 7–2 majority created the constitutional right of privacy by what might be called a structural reading of the Bill of Rights (1791), one that focused on the document's overall intent rather than on a word-by-word, line-by-line, or clause-by-clause analysis.

William Orville Douglas was born in the town of Maine, Minnesota, on October 16, 1898. As a boy he contracted polio; to strengthen his weakened legs, he hiked in the mountains around Yakima, Washington, where he grew up, developing a love of the outdoors and a special concern for the environment. After graduating from Whitman College in Walla Walla, Washington, and Columbia University Law School, he worked for two years as a Wall Street lawyer.

A strong defender of First Amendment freedoms, Supreme Court Associate Justice William O. Douglas was instrumental in developing several key constitutional concepts that have had a lasting impact on the law relating to sexual behavior, among them the right of privacy and the definition of obscenity.

In 1936 President Franklin D. Roosevelt, who had also been stricken with polio, appointed Douglas to the newly created Securities and Exchange Commission, and a year later Douglas became the agency's chair. Three years later Roosevelt named him to the Supreme Court and almost picked him as his running mate in 1944, which would have made Douglas president when Roosevelt died in 1945.

Even before Douglas joined the Supreme Court in 1939, its decisions were finding more room in the Constitution for the economic and social programs that Roosevelt and CONGRESS devised to solidify the economic recovery from the Great Depression. In one of his first opinions, Douglas upheld federal authority to fix coal prices. Sanctioning a greater national power also gave Douglas a basis for expanding individual rights and protections against government authority. Many of the dissents written by Associate Justices Oliver Wendell Holmes Jr. and Louis D. Brandeis in the earlier decades of the twentieth century became the basis of majority decisions during Douglas's tenure; his own early dissents would also become the basis for later majority decisions.

Justice Douglas was a creative force in two main areas of the law relating to sexual behavior: OBSCENITY and PRIVACY.

Obscenity

In *ROTH V. UNITED STATES* (1957), the first case in which the Supreme Court addressed the constitutionality of obscenity under the FIRST AMENDMENT (1791) to the U.S. Constitution, Douglas filed a dissenting opinion. The majority in *Roth* held that because obscenity was beyond the scope of free-speech protection, federal and state laws making it a crime were constitutional. Douglas, however, thought that much of how obscenity was defined and how it was perceived as a cause of antisocial behavior was too arbitrary to ignore the Constitution's clear prohibition against infringing the rights of free expression. "The absence of dependable information on the effect of obscene literature on human conduct should make us wary," he said. "It should put us on the side of protecting society's interest in literature, except and unless it can be said that the particular publication has an impact on action that the government can control.... I would give the broad sweep of the First Amendment full support. I have the same confidence in the ability of our people to reject noxious literature as I have in their capacity to sort out the true from the false in theology, economics, politics, or any other field."

Douglas also wrote dissents in two other obscenity cases, *Byrne v. Karalexis* (1969) and *Paris Adult Theatre I v. Slaton* (1973), a companion to *MILLER V. CALIFORNIA* (1973); both cases involved the showing of adult films—*I Am Curious Yellow* in *Byrne* and *Magic Mirror* and *It All Comes Out in the End* in *Paris Adult Theatre I.*

He concurred in the majority opinion in *A BOOK NAMED "JOHN CLELAND'S MEMOIRS OF A WOMAN OF PLEASURE" V. ATTORNEY GENERAL OF THE COMMONWEALTH OF MASSACHUSETTS* (1965), stating, "Whatever may be the reach of the power to regulate *conduct*, I stand by my view in *Roth v. United States* ... that the First Amendment leaves no power in government over *expression of ideas.*"

Today the regulation of obscenity by government has devolved mainly to protecting CHILDREN and preventing their sexual exploitation in PORNOGRAPHY. As attested to by the availability on the INTERNET and other MEDIA outlets of what was once considered hard-core pornography, Justice Douglas's view of the First Amendment has basically been accepted, if only by default.

Privacy

In a dissent in *Public Utilities Commission v. Pollack* (1952), Douglas presaged his concern with privacy rights under the Constitution by opining: "Liberty in the constitutional sense must mean more than freedom from unlawful government restraint; it must include privacy as well, if it is to be a repository of freedom. The right to be let alone is indeed the beginning of all freedom." Thirteen years later, in the *Griswold* case, he expanded on this notion of liberty and conjured up out of pieces of the Bill of Rights, as well as from that document's general tenor, the right of privacy.

In *Griswold* the Supreme Court declared unconstitutional a long-standing Connecticut law against CONTRACEPTION practiced by married couples. In his opinion for the majority, Douglas adroitly pointed to earlier Court precedents that had carved out new rights not expressly mentioned in the Constitution, such as the right of association and the right of parents to educate their children in a school of their choice. In similar fashion, he found a right of privacy for the individual citizen. Drawing on parts of the First, Third, Fourth, Fifth, and Ninth Amendments, he posited a right of privacy lurking in the secondary shadows of those provisions, in the "penumbras," as he called them. Douglas wrote that the right of privacy in the MARRIAGE relationship is "older than the Bill of Rights–older than our political parties, older than our school system." He later filed a concurring opinion in *Eisenstadt v. Baird* (1972), which extended the right of contraception to couples who were not married.

In a concurring opinion in *Doe v. Bolton* (1973), a companion case to *Roe v. Wade* that struck down a Georgia law banning abortion, Douglas noted that the NINTH AMENDMENT (1791), although it did not specifically create enumerated liberties, does protect certain "customary, traditional, and time-honored rights, amenities, privileges, and immunities . . . [such as] *freedom of choice in the basic decisions of one's life respecting marriage, divorce, procreation, contraception, and the education and upbringing of children.*" Georgia's law against abortion, he reasoned, was overbroad and thus unconstitutional, in part, "because it equates the value of an embryonic life immediately after conception with the worth of a life immediately before birth." The question of exactly when a human life becomes entitled to state protection as a person is still at issue in today's debate over the right of abortion.

William O. Douglas retired from the Supreme Court in 1975, because of ill health. He left a legacy of 1,306 majority, concurring, and dissenting opinions—a number surpassed only by Associate Justice William J. Brennan Jr., who wrote 1,360. Douglas also bequeathed a history of constitutional development that championed the individual against government intrusion into private and personal aspects of daily life—especially those aspects of sexual behavior, he argued, that the government has no legitimate interest in controlling. Justice Douglas died in 1980.

DRUGS

Just as humans develop technology to enhance their ability to improve themselves and control the world around them, for many centuries they have also used natural and synthetic drugs and chemicals to change themselves. Attitude adjustment, heightened sexual experiences, and protection from pregnancy are just some of the ways in which drugs affect sexual behavior. A drug is a biologically active substance used for medicinal purposes or for its pleasurable, stimulating, or corrective effects. Drugs used primarily for their pleasurable effects, sometimes called mind-altering drugs, include alcohol; nicotine; marijuana; sedatives such as barbiturates and tranquilizers; stimulants such as caffeine, cocaine, and amphetamines ("speed"); psychedelics such as LSD (lysergic acid diethylamide) and mescaline; and narcotics, such as heroin, morphine, and opium.

What effects do drugs have on sexual activity? While many people may have different reactions, LSD is said to increase sexual awareness, cocaine in small doses can increase sexual arousal and facilitate erections and orgasms, amphetamines can stimulate the libido, marijuana can reduce inhibitions and stimulate sensory perceptions, Ecstasy can increase both arousal and a sense of empathy for a sexual partner, and alkyl nitrites ("poppers") are reported to provide a brief and intense rush to the brain and then a relaxing effect. Alcohol or barbiturates such as Amytal, Luminal or Phenobarbital, and Nembutal reduce inhibitions about engaging in sexual activity. In addition, the human body produces its own sexual stimulants; for example, sexual desire may be stimulated by the release of dopamine, a neurohormone produced in the hypothalamus, which then induces the release of testosterone to enhance the sex drive. The use of manufactured drugs to enhance sexual activity or experiences may have harmful side effects, especially if taken in large doses and over a long period of time. Opiates including heroin, morphine, and codeine are painkillers and have little if any effect on sexual activity,

Drugs may be used legally to increase sexual pleasure, to facilitate lawful sexual activity, to practice CONTRACEPTION, to cause a medical ABORTION, and to treat sexual dysfunction as well as SEXUALLY TRANSMITTED DISEASES (STDs). By the same token, drugs may be used illegally to carry out SEXUAL ASSAULT or to create a dependency that facilitates sexual exploitation. Drug abuse may have an adverse effect on a MARRIAGE and may become grounds for DIVORCE, or it can interact with a PREGNANCY, causing damage to the mother and the fetus. Drug users who share hypodermic needles may transmit AIDS-HIV and other STDs.

Government Regulation

The Food and Drug Administration, an agency of the U.S. DEPARTMENT OF HEALTH AND HUMAN SERVICES, plays an important role in regulating the legal use of drugs of all kinds. In 1938 CONGRESS passed the Food, Drug, and Cosmetic Act to prohibit the adulteration or mis-branding of "any food, drug, device, or cosmetic." The intent of the act was to protect the public's health and safety by preventing deleterious, adulterated, or mis-branded articles from entering interstate commerce. Those who violate the act are subject to penalties that include injunctions against distributing improper goods, seizure of those goods, and prosecution for a misdemeanor or a felony.

The Controlled Substances Act of 1970 forms the basis for federal regulation of the manufacture, importation, possession, and distribution of drugs in the United States. The use of contraband drugs and the misuse of legally obtained drugs are considered of such importance that the executive office of the PRESIDENT includes a President's Drug Policy Council, on which the vice president and cabinet members serve, to provide overall policy guidance. An Office of National Drug Control Policy develops policies, priorities, and objectives to meet the goal of reducing illicit drug use, manufacturing, trafficking, drug-related crime, violence, and adverse health consequences.

States also have drug-related laws, but they vary widely from state to state. Some states, for example, have recommended life sentences for any crime involving the use of a certain amount of an illegal drug; in another state, a similar crime might carry a maximum one-year sentence. State laws also address various aspects of drug activities. North Carolina insurance law, for one, provides that "every insurer providing a health care benefit plan that provides coverage for prescription drugs or devices shall provide coverage for contraceptive drugs or devices." The

state's criminal laws, however, make it a felony for anyone to "willfully administer to any woman, either pregnant or quick with child, or prescribe for any such woman, or advise . . . such woman to take any medicine, drug or other substance whatever, or . . . use or employ any instrument or other means with intent thereby to destroy such child."

Legal Use

Drugs are used legally in contraceptives, including emergency contraception, and to enhance potency and sexual activity. The legality of such drugs affecting sexual behavior has changed drastically in the last fifty years, as strict morality gave way during the SEXUAL REVOLUTION of the 1960s and 1970s to greater sexual freedom, especially for women. Yet some people and groups still seek to impose the strict moral codes of the past on the public through laws such as those banning abortion by any means, including drugs, and limiting drug-based contraceptive options that they believe endanger the RIGHTS OF THE UNBORN. Laws especially at the state level reflect this state of flux in public opinion on the use of sex-related drugs.

Contraceptives. Contraceptive chemicals, devices, and pills have been legalized, but oral contraceptive pills (generally a combination of the synthetic hormones estrogen and progestin) must be prescribed by a doctor. The "minipill" contains a small dose of a progestogen and must be taken every day; it eliminates some of the negative side effects that may occur with the synthetic estrogens in the original birth control pill, which was developed by Gregory Pinkus with funding from the PLANNED PARENTHOOD FEDERATION OF AMERICA. In 1952 he confirmed that progesterone worked as an antiovulent in rabbits; human tests were later conducted by the Harvard obstetrician John Rock. By late 1959, following the Food and Drug Administration's approval of Searle's drug Enovoid for theraputic purposes, more than half a million American women were on the Pill—even though states could then still ban contraception.

The introduction of the birth control pill helped women begin a systematic campaign to gain control of their own reproductive activities. At a press conference in 1959, President Dwight D. Eisenhower commented that birth control was "not a proper political or government activity or function or responsibility," adding that it was "not our business." Laws regarding all forms of contraception soon caught up, developing in accordance with two landmark U.S. Supreme Court decisions: GRISWOLD V. CONNECTICUT (1965) and *Eisenstadt v. Baird* (1972), which extended the right to use contraceptives to married couples and then to unmarried couples, respectively.

Emergency Contraception. A new emergency contraceptive drug known as the "morning-after pill" (Plan B) has so far not been approved by the Food and Drug Administration for over-the-counter distribution because the manufacturer could not prove that young teenage girls would be able to use it safely without the help of a doctor. In only some states are Plan B and a similar drug, Preven, available without a prescription. Ignoring the 24–3 recommendation of its advisory panel in 2003, the FDA in 2005 continued to delay deciding whether Plan B could be sold without a prescription nationwide. Opponents of the pill's easier availability fear that it will lead to greater promiscuity and increase the spread of disease. The FDA's delay has spurred legislatures in some states to expand access and in others to restrict the drug's use; more than sixty bills were pending in the states in 2006.

Abortion. Drugs can be used to terminate a pregnancy medically rather than surgically. RU-486, known as the "abortion pill," can be taken up to forty-nine days after the beginning of a woman's latest menstrual cycle to block hormones needed for a pregnancy to continue. The FDA withheld its approval until 2000, because of the general controversy surrounding abortion in America as well as the usual need to verify a drug's safety. Now sold in the United States under the trade name Mifeprex (mifepristone), RU-486 was developed by Roussel Uclaf and first made available in France. Medical abortions are subject to the same legal limitations as surgical abortions; because a dose of the drug sufficient to cause an abortion is said to cost less than $2, however, it provides an affordable alternative to the increasingly restricted surgical procedure. Some unexplained deaths among users of this pill have heightened calls by abortion opponents to remove it from the market.

Sexual Enhancement. Recently developed drugs to enhance men's sexual performance include the widely advertised Viagra, Cialis, and Levitra, all used to combat erectile dysfunction. The first on the market, the blue pill named Viagra (sildenafil citrate) was created in England after being studied for use in controlling high blood pressure and certain types of cardiovascular disease. Patented by the Pfizer Company in 1996 and approved by the Food and Drug Administration two years later, the drug had sales in the period 1999–2001 that exceeded $1 billion. In 2005 Congress took steps to prohibit Medicare and Medicaid coverage of these drugs, noting that the money spent on such "recreational" medications should instead be used to pay for life-saving drugs. That same year they were the subject of a warning by the FDA that their use may cause an ocular condition resulting in sudden blindness. The search continues for a Viagra for women. Some products, including a blue tablet marketed as Estravil, purport to restore a lack of sex drive in women.

Illegal Use

As with many beneficial products that humans develop, there is always a potential downside. The illegal use of recreational and pleasure-enhancing drugs became highly visible during the era of the Vietnam War protests and the sexual revolution. With the problem approaching epidemic proportions, Congress in the Anti-Drug Abuse Act (1988) created a position that has been dubbed the nation's "drug czar." In 1993 the Office of National Drug Control Policy was raised to cabinet status to reflect the seriousness of its mission. Illegal drugs continue to affect sexual behavior in a number of ways.

Sexual Assault. Some drugs—among them GHB (gamma hydroxubutyric acid), Rohypnol (flunitrazepam), and Ketamine (ketamine hydrochloride)—may be used to facilitate DATE RAPE or acquaintance RAPE;

they render the victim incapable of being able to withhold CONSENT to engage in a sex act and may distort or eliminate the victim's memory of the assault. Massachusetts law, to cite one state, provides that anyone who "applies, administers to or causes to be taken by a person any drug, matter or thing with the intent to stupefy or overpower such person so as to enable any person to have sexual intercourse with such person shall be punished by imprisonment in the state prison for life or for any term of years not less than ten years." Under New York law, facilitating a sex offense with a controlled substance is a felony.

Sex for Drugs. Highly addictive opiates such as morphine and heroin may be used to keep prostitutes on the job by feeding their drug habits. Addicts who may have originally used heroin to induce a state of euphoria are often reduced to selling sexual services to obtain enough money to sustain their habit. Illegal sexual behavior then becomes the means to the end—feeding their drug addiction. The link between drugs and PROSTITUTION was noted by a Maryland court in *Speaks v. State* (1968), in which it upheld the discovery of illegal narcotics during a warranted police search for marked money related to PANDERING. In two recent Ohio cases, *State v. Hill* (2005) and *State v. Hopkins* (2006), women were charged with offering sex for drugs. In one case, the allegation was used as a defense against a sexual assault charge; the defendant stated that rather than having sexually assaulted the victim, she had offered to exchange sex for drugs. The other case involved the offer of sex for drugs as a method of entrapment by a female undercover law enforcement officer.

Drug Abuse. In some of the states that have not completely abandoned fault-based DIVORCE, abuse of drugs can be grounds for divorce. In Alabama, for example, a divorce can be granted for, among other things, "becoming addicted after marriage to habitual drunkenness or to habitual use of opium, morphine, cocaine or other like drug."

Fetal Abuse. Drug abuse during pregnancy may adversely affect the fetus as well as the mother. The supreme court of South Carolina, in *State v. McKnight* (2003), upheld a homicide conviction in the case of a stillborn child who had cocaine in her system; the sentence of twenty years, to be suspended after twelve years, was held not to constitute cruel and unusual punishment of the mother. In contrast, a Florida court, in *Johnson v. State* (1992), refused to allow prosecution of a mother for "delivering a controlled substance to a minor" based on the transmission of cocaine to her fetus through the umbilical cord. This phrase used in drug laws is typically intended to apply to drug dealers and pushers.

In *Ferguson v. City of Charleston* (2001), the Supreme Court held that South Carolina had violated the Fourth Amendment (1791) rights of a group of pregnant women by targeting them in the state's medical school for cocaine use. Tests on the women's urine were performed without their consent, and on the basis of positive reports the police arrested some thirty women over a period of five years. The state's interest in prosecuting cocaine use by pregnant women in order to deter it, suggested the Court, was not sufficient to override the constitutional protection against warrantless, nonconsensual searches.

Contact: National Alliance for Model State Drug Laws, 700 North Fairfax Street, Suite 550, Alexandria, VA 22314 (703-836-6100). www.natlalliance.org.

See also ETHICS; MOTHERHOOD; REPRODUCTIVE RIGHTS.

e

EDUCATION

See SEX EDUCATION; SINGLE-SEX EDUCATION; TITLE IX.

EMERGENCY CONTRACEPTION

See CONTRACEPTION; DRUGS.

ENTERTAINMENT INDUSTRY

The entertainment industry encompasses all types of live, broadcast, recorded, descriptive, and virtual forms of entertainment produced for commercial profit. Although the industry includes some SEXUALLY ORIENTED BUSINESSES such as topless bars and adult video stores, sex also sells CDs, video games, and tickets to the movies, just as it does drinks in bars and X-rated DVDs. Even entertainment businesses that are not specifically sexually oriented often try to push the envelope to include greater sexuality to attract more customers.

The industry's major protection is the FIRST AMENDMENT (1791) to the U.S. Constitution, but the U.S. Supreme Court has ruled that the First Amendment does not protect OBSCENITY or all forms of free expression—for example, total nudity in public. In cases such as *MILLER V. CALIFORNIA* (1973), which confirmed the states' power to regulate obscenity that is beyond First Amendment protection, the Court has indicated that the government may have greater regulatory power with respect to representations of sexual behavior than with the behavior itself. This power follows from the Court's decisions in *GRISWOLD V. CONNECTICUT* (1965), which struck down a state law banning the use of contraceptives; *Loving v. Virginia* (1967), which negated a state law prohibiting interracial MARRIAGE; and *LAWRENCE V. TEXAS* (2003), which eviscerated a state law against homosexual SODOMY by consenting adults in private. Where CENSORSHIP is upheld, the underlying motive is the desire to keep legal, sexually explicit ADULT MATERIALS away from CHILDREN.

Laws regarding the entertainment industry's depiction of sexual behavior have changed radically since the first showing in New York City of the short film *The Kiss* (1896), one of the earliest films from the Edison Manufacturing Company. Its showing inspired editorials proclaiming that a descent into immorality had begun; by 1907 Chicago had passed the first U.S. law censoring movies. Throughout its history, the motion picture industry has created celebrities whose sexual behavior has run afoul of the law and made for sensational headlines. The "trial of the century" (*State of California v. Roscoe Arbuckle*), as it was billed in the media in 1922, involved the movie star Roscoe Conkling, known as "Fatty" Arbuckle (1887–1933), who was accused of raping and killing a showgirl, Virginia Rappe. The twenty-first-century equivalent involved the pop singer Michael Jackson,

Sexual titillation has been a component of many forms of commercial entertainment, from live burlesque and striptease shows to movies. In 1937 the famous Minsky's Burlesque in New York City was closed after a city commissioner refused to renew its license.

who faced trial in 2005 on ten counts relating to child molestation. Like Jackson, Arbuckle was acquitted, but the notoriety of his lifestyle—wild parties and a Rolls-Royce with a commode in the back seat—helped feed the notion that the entertainment industry, or at least the movie industry portion, was another Babylon, if not a Sodom or a Gomorrah.

Live Entertainment

Stand-up comics such as LENNY BRUCE, striptease artists, and fellow burlesque performers, as well as producers and performers in the legitimate theater and in musicals such as *Hair* (1967) and *Oh! Calcutta!* (1969), have had run-ins with the law over the sexually explicit nature of their performances. In 1927 the stage and screen actress Mae West (1893–1980) was arrested and sentenced to ten days in jail for public obscenity because city officials did not regard her play *Sex* as art (she got two days off for good behavior). The "high-class" stripper Gypsy Rose Lee (1911–70) was frequently arrested for her performances at burlesque theaters in the early days of her career; H. L. Mencken later conjured up a snake shedding its outer skin when he coined the word *ecdysiast* to characterize

Lee's intellectualized stripping routine. Today the First Amendment's protection of free speech and expression is recognized to permit just about any kind of public routine in an adult consensual setting, although the provocative excesses of nudity and sexually explicit live performances of the 1960s and 1970s have since abated, the battle seemingly won—a victim of easily accessible DVDs to watch at home, fear of sexual diseases, and a change in social mores.

However, some legal restrictions are permitted on performances involving NUDITY. The U.S. Supreme Court, in *Barnes v. Glen Theatre, Inc.* (1991) and *City of Erie v. Pap's A.M.* (2000), upheld laws banning nudity in public and requiring professional nude dancers to wear a G-string and pasties. As these decisions reasoned, the law's impact on free expression is considered negligible where nonpolitical speech is concerned and where the state has a legitimate interest in reducing any harmful side effects of totally nude dancing, such as crime and other public health and safety issues; the minimal covering requirement for dancers is considered only a small step toward that goal. The Supreme Court has also upheld ZONING restrictions on adult entertainment establishments based on the government's interests in controlling crime and urban blight.

Broadcast Entertainment

Entertainment transmitted via broadcasting on radio and television has always been regulated by the federal government. In 1934 CONGRESS passed the Federal Communications Act, establishing the FEDERAL COMMUNICATIONS COMMISSION with authority to punish broadcast licensees for transmitting indecent programming. Broadcast radio and television remain subject to regulation, even though satellite and cable channels are exempt; the theory is that subscribers to paid cable or satellite communications, unlike broadcast communications that come into the home or car free and can be easily accessed by children, have control over programming and can unsubscribe if they are offended by the programming. In *United States v. Playboy Entertainment Group, Inc.* (2000), the Supreme

Court struck down provisions of the Telecommunications Act of 1996 that attempted to regulate adult material on cable television; the measures proposed were found to be a restriction of the First Amendment right of free speech.

Because broadcast entertainment has always been subject to government regulation, communications law has tended to induce self-censorship by broadcasters to avoid fines or license suspensions. Nevertheless, television has transmitted sensational examples of willful attempts by performers to shock the public, from the "wardrobe malfunction" on the 2004 Super Bowl halftime show to the repeated antics of the radio "shock jock" Howard Stern. These lapses draw heavy fines—the Fox network was fined $1.2 million in 2004 for sexually graphic scenes in a reality series, *Married by America,* and Viacom settled for $3.5 million in the same year for indecency on the radio, including shows by Howard Stern—but the publicity value may mitigate the punishment. In 2006 Congress increased fines tenfold for airing indecent and sexually explicit material.

Recorded Entertainment

Nudity and explicit sexual activity or expression in the movies and recorded music are generally more protected under the Supreme Court's decisions related to obscenity and the First Amendment than are live performances, especially when the latter take place in bars or adult clubs and not in legitimate theater productions. Federal courts have tended to uphold First Amendment protection for the recorded entertainment industry. In *Kingsley Pictures Corp. v. Regents of the University of the State of New York* (1959), the Supreme Court invalidated a state education law that required the denial of a license to show a motion picture "presenting adultery as being right and desirable for certain people under certain conditions," even though such a portrayal was in violation of the industry's own self-imposed code of conduct. In *Luke Records, Inc. v. Navarro* (1992), a federal appeals court refused to find that the lyrics of a rap song, "As Nasty as They Wanna Be," recorded by 2 Live Crew, were obscene under the

Miller test; the government did not refute evidence that the work, taken as a whole, had some artistic merit.

The battle over censorship of recorded entertainment, however, has been fought and won to a large extent out of court—public pressure for government regulation has been headed off by industry self-censorship.

Motion Pictures. In terms of tolerance for sexual expression in recorded entertainment, perhaps the apex was achieved with the showing of the hard-core pornographic film *Deep Throat* (1972) in public theaters nationwide. The film has become a PORNOGRAPHY classic; a documentary about the making of this low-budget movie, entitled *Inside Deep Throat*, was released in 2005 and grossed approximately $600 million. The evolution from prudery to pornography in this division of the entertainment industry is the result of several key Supreme Court decisions.

In 1915 the Supreme Court ruled in *Mutual Film Corp. v. Ohio Industrial Commission* that motion pictures were not protected by the First Amendment's free speech and free press provisions. Just a year after the Arbuckle trial, the film industry in 1922 brought in a church official and former chairman of the Republican National Committee, William Harrison Hays (1879–1954), to shore up its image and protect producers from some form of official government censorship. As president of the Motion Picture Producers and Distributors of America, he administered a morality code established by agreement of the heads of the movie industry. The so-called Hays Code he developed was the forerunner of the voluntary film-rating system put into effect in 1968 by the Motion Picture Association of America and the National Association of Theater Owners.

Provisions of the Code to Govern the Making of Talking, Synchronized and Silent Motion Pictures, first promulgated in 1930, mandated that ADULTERY, while often necessary to a movie plot, must not be explicitly treated, justified, or presented attractively; excessive and lustful kissing, lustful embraces, and suggestive postures and gestures were not to be shown; sexual hygiene and venereal diseases were not to be the subjects of motion pictures; and obscenity in word, gesture, reference, song, joke, or by suggestion was forbidden. In 1968 the Motion Picture Association of America, under the presidency of the former presidential adviser Jack Valenti, instituted a new system of rating films. With some modifications, it remains in place today. The system used G for general audiences, M for mature (changed in 1969 to PG for parental guidance suggested), R for restricted, and X for adults only (changed in 1990 to NC-17). In 1984 PG-13 was added to depict movies for children aged thirteen years and older.

In 1952 the Supreme Court overruled its decision in the *Mutual Film* case, declaring in *Burstyn v. Wilson* that expression by means of motion pictures is included in the free-speech and free-press guarantees of the First Amendment, as made applicable to the states by the Fourteenth Amendment (1868). In subsequent decisions, such as *Paris Adult Theatre I v. Slaton* (1973) and *Young v. American Mini Theatres, Inc.* (1976), however, the Court reaffirmed that reasonable state restrictions on adult movies and sexually explicit material were not unconstitutional. As the Court declared in *Miller* and ROTH V. UNITED STATES (1957), obscene material, in any form, lies outside the First Amendment's protection.

Popular Music. Although the Hays Code forbade obscenity in songs used in motion pictures in the 1930s, several decades passed before popular music attracted public concern over sexually explicit lyrics. Rock-and-roll music in the 1950s drew criticism over some of its lyrics and presentations—when Elvis Presley appeared on *The Ed Sullivan Show* in 1956, the television camera remained focused above the singer's gyrating hips. In the early 1960s, a musical group called the Fugs came under suspicion by the Federal Bureau of Investigation for using obscenity in its lyrics, and its magazine, *Fuck You! A Magazine of the Arts,* became the basis for obscenity charges against a bookstore where it was sold. The lyrics were later declared by the FBI not to be obscene, and the AMERICAN CIVIL LIBERTIES UNION successfully defended the bookstore. The lyrics to the inscrutable popular song "Louie, Louie" were also investigated by the Bureau in 1964, but the conclusion was that no one could tell if they were obscene or not.

Motion Picture Production Code (Hays Code), 1930

General Principles

- No picture shall be produced that will lower the moral standards of those who see it. Hence the sympathy of the audience should never be thrown to the side of crime, wrongdoing, evil, or sin.

- Correct standards of life, subject only to the requirements of drama and entertainment, shall be presented.

- Law, natural or human, shall not be ridiculed, nor shall sympathy be created for its violation.

Sex

- Adultery, sometimes necessary plot material, must not be explicitly treated, or justified, or presented attractively.

- Scenes of Passion
    a. They should not be introduced when not essential to the plot.
    b. Excessive and lustful kissing, lustful embraces, suggestive postures and gestures are not to be shown.

- Seduction or Rape
    a. They should never be more than suggested, and only when essential for the plot, and even then never shown by explicit methods.
    b. They are never the proper subject for comedy.

- Sex hygiene and venereal diseases are not subjects for motion pictures.

- Scenes of actual childbirth, in fact or in silhouette, are never to be presented.

Obscenity

- Obscenity in word, gesture, reference, song, joke, or by suggestion (even when likely to be understood only by part of the audience) is forbidden.

Vulgarity

- The treatment of low, disgusting, unpleasant, though not necessarily evil, subjects should always be subject to the dictates of good taste and a regard for the sensibilities of the audience.

Costume

- Complete nudity is never permitted. This includes nudity in fact or in silhouette, or any lecherous or licentious notice thereof by other characters in the picture.

- Undressing scenes should be avoided, and never used save where essential to the plot.

- Indecent or undue exposure is forbidden.

Repellent Subjects

The following subjects must be treated within the careful limits of good taste:

- Actual hangings or electrocutions as legal punishments for crime.

- Third-degree methods.

- Brutality and possible gruesomeness.

- Branding of people or animals.

- Apparent cruelty to children or animals.

- The sale of women, or a woman selling her virtue.

- Surgical operations.

Source: Excerpted from General Principles and Applications, Code to Govern the Making of Talking, Synchronized and Silent Motion Pictures, adopted by Association of Motion Picture Producers and Motion Picture Producers and Distributors of America, March 1930

Parental advisory labels for music were suggested during a 1984 U.S. Senate hearing. Elizabeth "Tipper" Gore, the wife of Senator Al Gore of Tennessee, testified on behalf of the Parents Music Resource Center that the explicit lyrics of certain recording artists, among them Twisted Sister and 2 Live Crew, called for the industry to step in. The following year, the Recording Industry Association of America agreed to a rating system that required placing "explicit lyrics" warning stickers on objectionable products as a form of parental advisory. Producers of the music requiring the labels actually hoped that these labels would increase sales to young people, who would use them as a way to identify products containing sexual material. In 2002, in the wake of a second movement to lobby Congress for even stricter censorship laws, BMG, RCA, and several other recording companies began voluntarily putting parental advisory stickers on products containing strong language.

The Internet

The INTERNET, which has begun to change the culture of communications around the world, has so far been protected from government regulation by the Supreme Court, which has upheld the First Amendment right of freedom of expression. Challenges in the form of congressional legislation to punish distribution to minors of indecent and sexually explicit materials—the COMMUNICATIONS DECENCY ACT (1996) and the CHILD ONLINE PROTECTION ACT (1998)—were foiled in *Reno v. American Civil Liberties Union* (1997) and *Ashcroft v. American Civil Liberties Union* (2002, 2004), when the Court struck down their provisions as not narrowly tailored enough to escape infringement of the First Amendment. However, Congress has been successful in limiting access to such materials on computers in many libraries that receive some federal funding.

Video Games

Another technological change in the entertainment industry is the popularity of video games, which appeal especially to TEENAGERS. The Supreme Court addressed the censorship of video games along with other industry aspects in *Ashcroft v. Free Speech Coalition* (2002). This case involved a challenge to the constitutionality of the Child Pornography Prevention Act (1996), which attempted in part to ban "virtual" child pornography (representations not using actual children). The Court noted that "many things innocent in themselves, . . . such as cartoons, video games, and candy, . . . might be used for immoral purposes, yet we would not expect those to be prohibited because they can be misused." It nonetheless found that certain key sections of the act were "overbroad and unconstitutional" under the First Amendment and noted that, under its ruling in *Ginsberg v. New York* (1968), adults were still liable for punishment for providing unsuitable materials to children.

Faced with the constant threat of laws that might be held constitutional, producers of these games, like the movie and recording industries, have adopted a rating system mainly for parents who want to keep explicit sexual material and intense violence away from their children. These ratings, which were promulgated by the Entertainment Software Ratings Board, are more comprehensive and detailed than those used by the film industry. The current ratings are E for everyone; EC for early childhood (three years of age and older); T for teen (thirteen years of age and older); M for mature (seventeen years of age and older); AO for adults only (not intended for anyone under eighteen years of age); and RP for rating pending, covering games not yet released for sale.

In 2001 Senator Joseph Lieberman of Connecticut introduced a bill to prohibit the marketing of adult-rated entertainment—movies, music, and computer games containing violent or sexual material—to teenagers under the age of seventeen years. This Media Marketing Accountability Act would authorize the Federal Trade Commission to regulate the advertising of entertainment products to young people. To date this attempt at regulating the marketing of adult entertainment to minors has not become law. Neither this nor the earlier alarm raised by Tipper Gore in the mid-1980s over violent and vulgar language in popular music lyrics has resulted in any laws regulating the entertainment industry. Yet they have brought about the rating and parental advisory systems adopted by the industry to allow adult materials to continue to be sold while meeting parental concerns. Based on past Supreme Court decisions, it is doubtful that extensive government regulation of the industry would pass constitutional muster in any case.

Contacts

Cyber Angels (parental advisories), P.O. Box 3171, Allentown, PA 18106 (610-377-2966). www.CyberAngels.org.

Entertainment Software Ratings Board, 317 Madison Avenue, 22nd Floor, New York, NY 10017 (212-759-0700). www.esrb.org,

See also HEFNER, HUGH; MEDIA.

EQUAL RIGHTS

Just as the term *civil rights* became identified with the movement to ensure political and legal equality for blacks in America in the 1960s, the concept of *equal rights* has come to embrace the movement to achieve the equality of women and men. This movement is based on the premise that the biological differences between men and women should not be used to condone DISCRIMINATION, including SEXUAL HARASSMENT, against women. In 1972 CONGRESS submitted to the states for ratification the Equal Rights Amendment to make this goal a part of the nation's supreme laws. The amendment, however, received the approval of only thirty-five of the thirty-eight states required under Article V of the U.S. Constitution by the end of the ten-year period allowed by Congress (seven years plus a three-year extension). The movement has nonetheless continued in various other legal settings.

Men and women have been treated unequally before the law for at least as long as recorded history. Women, minors, slaves, and foreigners were not permitted to vote in ancient Athens, home of the world's first democracy. New Zealand was the first country to give women the right to vote in 1893. Not until 1920 did the Nineteenth Amendment to the U.S. Constitution permit American women to vote, declaring: "The right of citizens of the United States to vote shall not be denied or abridged by the United States or by any state on account of sex. Congress shall have power to enforce this article by appropriate legislation."

But women still did not receive equal treatment in many areas, including property rights, MARRIAGE, DIVORCE, education, employment, and the MILITARY. Discrimination took a range of forms: making married women's property and other legal rights dependent on their husbands, denying women a divorce except on proof of a husband's marital offense, denying women admission to institutions of higher learning, denying women jobs in fields such as the law that were reserved to males, and excluding women from job opportunities in the military. A commission on the status of women created by President John F. Kennedy reached this seminal conclusion in 1962: "Equality of rights under the law for all persons, male or female, is so basic to democracy and its commitment to the ultimate value of the individual that it must be reflected in the fundamental law of the land."

Federal Law
Some strict constructionists believe that the only right granted to women by the U.S. Constitution is the right to vote—and no others. But in addition to the Nineteenth Amendment ensuring women this right of suffrage, the Constitution contains other language that the Supreme Court has used to secure WOMEN'S RIGHTS. For example, in *Reed v. Reed* (1971), the Court set a precedent by finding that the equal protection clause of the Fourteenth Amendment (1868) prohibits GENDER discrimination. This case involved a state law in Idaho giving preference to males in administering the estates of decedents. Chief Justice Warren E. Burger, who wrote the majority opinion, concluded that the discrimination presented in this case was "the very kind of arbitrary legislative choice forbidden by the Equal Protection Clause."

In *Frontiero v. Richardson* (1973), the Supreme Court declared that a federal statute that accorded different treatment for male spouses of female military personnel violated the Fifth Amendment's due process clause insofar as it required a female member to prove her husband's dependency in order to receive benefits, whereas spouses of male servicemen did not have to offer proof of such dependency.

In *United States v. Virginia* (1996), a case involving the exclusion of women from the Virginia Military Institute, the Supreme Court, while making a finding of discrimination on the basis of sex, did not place such discrimination on the same level as discrimination on the basis of race or national origin, for which the Court reserves the highest scrutiny. By *scrutiny*, the Court means the degree to which the law in question is suspected of being unconstitutional; the legislature must have a compelling reason for disparate treatment of members of a class based on race or nationality, but in the case of a class based on sex, the Court will be more lenient in scrutinizing the legislature's reasons for treating members of the class differently. (Other allegations of unconstitutional discrimination in which the complainant is not a member of a suspect class such as race or sex receive the lowest level of judicial scrutiny.)

Initially the Supreme Court decided that allegations of unequal treatment of the sexes should receive "heightened" or special scrutiny. Later the level of scrutiny—under which a defendant's burden to show a rational basis for the alleged discrimination is weighed—would be lowered to an "intermediate" level; the Court reasoned that there could be a rational basis for treating men and women differently under the law. The result was that discrimination on the basis of sex was deemed reasonable and permissible in some cases. Yet, as the Court pronounced in *Frontiero*, sex "frequently bears no relation to ability to perform or contribute to society."

Although the Equal Rights Amendment failed to become a part of the U.S. Constitution, Congress has acted to accomplish some of its goals through legislation. For example, Title VII of the Civil Rights Act of 1964 prohibits discrimination "because of . . . sex" in the workplace. Similarly, Title IX of the Education Amendments of 1972 provides: "No person in the United States shall, on the basis of sex, be excluded from participation in, be denied the benefits of, or be subjected to discrimination under any educational program or activity receiving Federal financial assistance."

Enforcement relies on government agencies such as the U.S. Department of Justice and the Equal Employment Opportunity Commission, nongovernmental legal assistance organizations such as the American Civil Liberties Union, and private legal actions brought by victims. Remedies may include monetary damages and injunctive relief (a court order requiring that some action be taken or stopped), such as restoration of an employment position or other status lost as a result of the illegal discrimination.

State Law

To date nineteen states—Alaska, California, Colorado, Connecticut, Hawaii, Illinois, Louisiana, Maryland, Massachusetts, Montana, New Hampshire, New Mexico, Pennsylvania, Rhode Island, Texas, Utah, Virginia, Washington, and Wyoming—have added equal rights provisions or prohibitions against sexual discrimination to their constitutions, and most other states have similar language in statutes. In *Cannon v. Cannon* (2004), the Maryland court of special appeals countered the argument that there was a legally recognized "natural dominance of the husband over the wife" by citing the state's constitutional provision, which provides: "Equality of rights under the law shall not be abridged or denied because of sex."

Language in the Massachusetts constitution is also broad in scope. It says: "Equality under the law shall not be abridged because of sex." California's constitution states in article I, Declaration of Rights, section 7: (a) "A person may not be denied life, liberty, or property without due process of law or denied equal protection of the law." (b) "A citizen or class of citizens may not be granted privileges or immunities not granted on the same terms to all citizens." Section 8 provides: "A person may not be disqualified from

In 1977 demonstrators gathered in front of the White House to show their opposition to the proposed Equal Rights Amendment (1972), which was intended to recognize the equality of male and female citizens under the law. The measure failed to obtain the necessary ratification by three-fourths of the states in the ten years allotted by Congress.

entering or pursuing a business, profession, vocation, or employment because of sex."

Some state constitutions do not specifically refer to sex or women. For example, Michigan's document simply declares: "No person shall be denied the equal protection of the laws; nor shall any person be denied the enjoyment of his civil or political rights or be discriminated against in the exercise thereof because of religion, race, color or national origin." But Michigan has statutory provisions prohibiting discrimination on account of sex, addressing the "opportunity to obtain employment, housing and other real estate, and the full and equal utilization of public accommodations, public service, and educational facilities." Washington's constitution includes responsibilities along with rights that "shall not be abridged on account of sex."

The evolution of the Supreme Court's analysis of equal rights violations has influenced state courts. Indiana and Oregon courts, however, have been more independent in their review of this issue. Oregon courts draw a distinction between "true" classes, which include gender, and "pseudo" classes, which, rather than having members with immutable personal characteristics, include people whose only similarity is having been disadvantaged by the law or other action by the state. Indiana, whose equal protection–type constitutional guarantee was the model for Oregon's, avoids creating levels of scrutiny by simply declaring that the provision applies to any improper grant of privileges or immunities.

Some examples of state statutory provisions related to equal protection under the law follow.

Illinois: "It is the public policy of this state: (A) . . . To secure for all individuals . . . the freedom from discrimination against the individual because of his or her . . . sex . . . in connection with employment, real estate transactions, access to financial credit, and availability of public accommodations. (B) . . . To prevent sexual harassment in employment and . . . in higher education."

New Jersey: "No employer shall discriminate in any way in the rate or method of payment of wages to any employee because of his or her sex."

Wisconsin: "(1) Women and men have the same rights and privileges under the law in the exercise of suffrage, freedom of contract, choice of residence, jury service, holding office, holding and conveying property, care and custody of children and in all other respects."

Indiana's supreme court found discrimination in a state teachers' health and retirement plan that paid women less than men because statistically females live longer than men. In *Arp v. Workers' Compensation Appeals Board* (1977), the California supreme court, unlike the federal courts, used "strict scrutiny" of a state law that discriminated against women on the basis of sex. Reminiscent of the situation in the *Frontiero* case, California did not presume that a widower, unlike a widow, was a dependent of his wife for purposes of death benefits under the state worker's compensation law. The state court concluded that the law's presumption was a denial of equal protection. Other states that have applied the "strict scrutiny" level of review in sex discrimination cases include Hawaii, Illinois, and West Virginia. Also interpreting California's statutory provision regarding equal rights, a state court of appeals held in *Rotary Club of Duarte v. Rotary International* (1986) that membership in an organization related to business is clearly an advantage or a privilege; exclusion from or arbitrary termination of membership on the basis of sex, therefore, is prohibited.

Not all court cases involve victims in a suspect class such as race, national origin, or sex. Reverse discrimination cases, such as *Lewis v. State* and *Sharp v. Lansing* (both 2001) from Michigan concluded that victims complaining of injury from affirmative action policies

favoring women or minorities could sue for declaratory or injunctive relief for violations of the state's equal protection guarantees; however, no right to sue for monetary damages could be inferred by the courts.

Some states designate institutions to assist in enforcement of equal rights provisions. For example, in New Jersey the commissioner of labor and industry is authorized to enforce provisions relating to inequality in pay. Illinois has both a department of human rights and a human rights commission. Yet prejudice, tokenism, reverse discrimination, and double standards all influence the degree to which inequality continues to be tolerated before the law as well as in the workplace, the family, and society at large.

See also Breastfeeding; Motherhood; Pregnancy; Reproductive Rights.

EROTIC DANCING

See Barnes v. Glen Theatre, Inc.; First Amendment; Nudity; Sexually Oriented Businesses.

ETHICS

Sexual behavior may be influenced not only by the law, government policies, and court decisions but also by personal and professional ethics, morality, religion, social context, and personal psychology. Whereas the law, at least in theory, applies equally to all citizens, ethics is the purview of the professions such as doctors, psychiatrists, pharmacists, lawyers, judges, and accountants. Ethics are rules of conduct deemed by some consensus among professional peers to be appropriate or acceptable behavior among themselves and in contact with the public.

Many organizations and professions have adopted codes of ethics to help members make decisions that will be in the best interests of the group and their clients or patients. These private rules, some of them including restrictions on sexual behavior, are generally self-enforced or monitored by the associations of which a person is a member, such as the American Bar Association or a state bar, a church, or a civic club. Some provisions of ethics codes for various professions such as doctors, lawyers, and judges have also influenced the enactment of statutes and court decisions regarding legal behavior.

The usual sanction for unethical, as opposed to illegal, behavior generally comes from the peer group. The law may become involved when a sanction for a breach of ethics is challenged by an accused professional, who may file a lawsuit to have the matter legally reviewed. In some cases the procedures for determining the infraction may be challenged along with the appropriateness of the punishment. A reprimand or a loss of one's license to practice can be a significant punishment for any professional.

Legislators and courts regularly look to professional codes of ethics to inform their decisions. In *Jaffee v. Redmond* (1996), for example, the U.S. Supreme Court ruled that psychotherapists are entitled to the same privilege of confidentiality concerning their counseling as the traditionally recognized attorney-client, husband-wife, and priest-penitent privilege. In his dissent in *Jaffee*, Associate Justice Antonin Scalia referred to several professional codes of conduct and ethics in the field to support his conclusion that the profession had no consensus on the privilege issue.

Morality, which is often associated with ethics, is a personal code of conduct and is sometimes based on religious tenets. A person may believe that it is immoral to have sex before MARRIAGE or to have or perform an ABORTION, even though there is no ethical or legal prohibition against such behavior.

Government Employees

Federal and state governments have ethics rules for officials and employees. The Ethics in Government Act (1978) primarily addresses financial disclosure and abuse or misuse of public office. For a time an ad hoc federal tool for investigating unethical or illegal sexual conduct by high officials involved the appointment of an independent counsel. Kenneth W. Starr, a former

U.S. solicitor general, was chosen in 1994 to investigate alleged improprieties by President Bill Clinton and his wife, Hillary Rodham Clinton, with respect to Arkansas property known as Whitewater. The counsel's authority was amended in 1998 to allow him to investiage charges that the PRESIDENT had had sex with a White House intern, Monica Lewinsky, and had lied under oath about it, which led to Clinton's subsequent impeachment by the House of Representatives (he was acquitted in the Senate). The Illinois Governmental Act (1972) generally prohibits improper influences, prescribing a code of conduct for legislators and requiring disclosure of economic interests. Most other states have similar provisions.

The International Association of Chiefs of Police has had a code of ethics since 1957, under which police officers are required to "perform all duties impartially, without favor or affection or ill will and without regard to status, sex, race, religion, political belief or aspiration." In many cases involving crimes against women such as RAPE, SEXUAL ASSAULT, and DOMESTIC VIOLENCE, however, charges of prejudice have been leveled against law enforcement officials. In recognition of this problem, provisions of the VIOLENCE AGAINST WOMEN ACT (1994) authorize grants and assistance to state and local law enforcement agencies to raise awareness of all types of behavior that can lead to unequal enforcement of the law.

The Legal Profession

Lawyers and judges are subject to the laws and rules of a supervisory court, usually the supreme court of the jurisdiction. The American Bar Association, which is a voluntary organization, has promulgated model rules of professional conduct that have been adopted by law in many states. The organization has its own canon of ethics (rules of conduct) addressing the attorney-client relationship. State bar organizations that admit attorneys to practice have similar canons of ethics that can be used to discipline lawyers and judges; sanctions may include censure, suspension, or even disbarment. In many cases, unethical conduct is also illegal conduct and may be the basis for a lawsuit for damages.

A conflict of interest might arise in the case of an attorney who has represented a family but must avoid any conflict, or the appearance thereof, should the husband and wife decide to DIVORCE. When the interests of the family are identical, an attorney representing the husband and wife may be acting in a perfectly ethical manner. In a divorce proceeding, however, the individual spouses are assumed to be distinctly different clients and in many cases so too are their interests.

Other major concerns are sexual improprieties with clients and violations of confidentiality. In the ABA's Model Rules of Professional Conduct, rule 8.4, Misconduct, under Maintaining the Integrity of the Profession, states in part that it is professional misconduct for a lawyer to "engage in conduct involving dishonesty, fraud, deceit, or misrepresentation; [or] in conduct that is prejudicial to the administration of justice." Most instances of lawyer-client sexual relationships are dealt with under this rule, but other rules may also apply. In *In re Piatt* (1997), an Arizona attorney was found to have violated the conflict-of-interest provisions by making lewd remarks and requesting sexual relations from clients instead of charging them "a lot more money" for his services.

A lawyer's sexual relations with a vulnerable client going through a divorce warrant disbarment under ethics rules, declared the Kansas supreme court in *In re Berg* (1998), even though the rules did not expressly prohibit such behavior. The Oklahoma Bar Association's legal ethics committee similarly found that same year that a lawyer's sexual relationship with a client was unethical even without a specific ethical rule on the subject. In 1989 a New Hampshire court, in *Bourdon's Case,* noted that a lawyer's "physical and emotional involvement with [a client in a divorce proceeding] adversely influenced his professional decisions."

As for jurists, canon 2 of the ABA's Model Code of Judicial Conduct provides: "A Judge shall avoid impropriety and the appearance of impropriety in all of the judge's activities." The commentary here specifically addresses membership in organizations that practice invidious DISCRIMINATION "on the basis of race, sex, religion or national origin."

The Medical Profession

Like the American Bar Association, the AMERICAN MEDICAL ASSOCIATION has a code of ethics for practitioners, as do the American Nurses Association and the American Pharmacists Association. While the general tenor of these codes is directed at promoting caring, compassionate, nondiscriminatory, and confidential medical assistance for patients, unprofessional sexual behavior would also be a breach of professional ethics as well as a potential basis for criminal and civil liability.

Medical ethics and sexual behavior intersect at many points. The physician-patient relationship involves discussions about sex and sexuality, physical examinations of a patient's body and sexual organs, PRIVACY interests concerning sex-related health matters (such as AIDS-HIV and other SEXUALLY TRANSMITTED DISEASES), and medical procedures relating to sex and reproduction, from SEXUAL ENHANCEMENT to CONTRACEPTION and ABORTION to fertility and ASSISTED REPRODUCTIVE TECHNOLOGY. The AMA's Principles of Medical Ethics provide, for instance, that a physician is not prohibited from performing an abortion in accordance with good medical practice and under circumstances that do not violate the law.

Pharmacists lately have been wrestling with their personal morality over prescriptions they are asked to fill. Asserting a "right of conscience," numerous pharmacists (many of them members of Pharmacists for Life International) have begun refusing to dispense contraceptives, the "abortion pill" RU-486, and emergency contraceptives such as Plan B (the "morning-after pill"). Some emergency-room hospital staff have also refused to provide the "morning-after pill" to prevent a PREGNANCY that may have resulted from RAPE or DATE RAPE.

Refusal to provide certain medical services because of personal religious, ethical, or moral considerations is generally not a crime. A number of states have moved variously to require that pharmacists ensure that such prescriptions are filled or—in states such as Arkansas, Georgia, and South Dakota—to support them in their boycott of DRUGS with which they disagree. California requires pharmacists to fill prescriptions regardless of their personal beliefs, and Illinois does so by regulation. Several other states—including New York, Minnesota, and Wisconsin—have pending legislation addressing this issue. The rules of the American Pharmacists Association say that although pharmacists may refuse to fill such prescriptions on moral grounds, they must make arrangements for patients to obtain the prescription elsewhere.

BIOETHICS is a subset of ethics that deals primarily with the treatment of people who are receiving medical or clinical care or are used for testing new biomedical techniques. This profession's ethics call for according such subjects dignity, honesty, and confidentiality and obtaining informed CONSENT from them before treatment or testing. With respect to infertility treatments, California's health and safety code provides that a "physician and surgeon . . . or other health care provider delivering fertility treatment shall provide his or her patient with timely, relevant, and appropriate information to allow the individual to make an informed and voluntary choice regarding the disposition of any human embryos remaining following the fertility treatment."

Many other professions and professional and business organizations promulgate codes of ethics, especially in those professions where there is a fiduciary or trust relationship between the professional and another person, such as between teachers and students or ministers and parishioners. If sexual behavior may be involved, ethical conduct calls for professionals— who have a duty to protect the interests of their clients—to act above reproach even beyond the strict letter of the law. Although private ethics codes, like general moral principles and religious beliefs, are separate from legal regulations governing sexual behavior, they undoubtedly influence both such behavior and the laws governing it.

EXHIBITIONISM

See INDECENT EXPOSURE; LEWD BEHAVIOR; NUDITY.

EXPLOITATION

See CHILDREN; HUMAN TRAFFICKING; PORNOGRAPHY.

EXPRESSION, FREEDOM OF

See CENSORSHIP; FIRST AMENDMENT; NUDITY; OBSCENITY; PORNOGRAPHY.

EXTRAMARITAL SEX

See ADULTERY; PREMARITAL SEX; UNMARRIED COHABITANTS.

f

FAMILY PLANNING

A natural outcome of sexual behavior is the procreation of CHILDREN. Throughout history women
and men have sought ways to avoid or at least reduce the possibility of unwanted pregnancies, but
family planning is a relatively new concept that
refers to steps to control the number and spacing of
children. Methods include ABSTINENCE, CONTRACEP-
TION, the "rhythm" method, male withdrawal before ejaculation, DRUGS such as the "morning-after pill,"
surgical STERILIZATION and vasectomies, and ABOR-
TION. In a broader sense, family planning encompasses
overall control of the process of having children
and includes efforts to increase the number of children in a family by means such as ASSISTED REPRO-
DUCTIVE TECHNOLOGY and adoption.

Family planning in the United States was promoted in the first part of the twentieth century by MAR-
GARET SANGER. At this time contraceptives and information about contraception were considered obscene
under federal law and were banned in the states under similar OBSCENITY statutes. Publication in 1914 of
Sanger's pamphlet *Family Limitation,* which described
contraceptive methods, led to the arrest of her husband that year on charges brought by the antivice crusader ANTHONY COMSTOCK. Sanger, who was out of the
country at the time, returned in 1915, but charges
against her were dropped to prevent her from using
a trial to publicize her mission: to provide women with

information about family planning. In 1916 she opened
the first American birth control clinic in Brooklyn, New
York, the forerunner of clinics now run by the PLANNED
PARENTHOOD FEDERATION OF AMERICA.

Many benefits accrue from family planning in a
modern, postindustrial society, where, unlike in agri-
cultural societies, there is no direct benefit from having a large family. Women are spared health risks from
a large number of pregnancies. With fewer children,
mothers also have greater freedom to develop personally, and their children benefit from having a
mother who can spend more quality time with each
child. Family finances are less strained with fewer
mouths to feed and children to school; mothers who
can work outside the home also contribute to a higher
economic status for the family. Not least, the world's
resources at some point will be unable to sustain unlimited population growth.

Constitutional Law

In 1918 the U.S. birth control movement won a victory of sorts in *People v. Sanger,* when a New York court
declared that doctors could discuss matters relating
to PREGNANCY with patients; an appeal to the U.S.
Supreme Court was dismissed in 1919. Later, in *United
States v. One Package* (1936), a federal court of appeals
ruled that doctors were also exempt from the ban on
the importation of contraceptives. A small step toward
giving all citizens access to contraception came in a
dissent by Supreme Court Associate Justice John

Marshall Harlan II in *Poe v. Ullman* (1961). Harlan argued that tradition is a "living thing" and thus any interests involving individual liberty—such as marital privacy—"require particularly careful scrutiny of the state needs asserted to justify their abridgment."

The precedent set in *Griswold v. Connecticut* (1965) to allow married couples access to contraceptives opened the door for the free flow of information and contraceptive devices, helping make family planning not only an individual right but also leading to federal and state laws promoting the practice. In its *Griswold* decision, the Supreme Court struck down a state law that made the use of contraceptives illegal, calling the ban an unconstitutional infringement of married couples' right of PRIVACY. In *Eisenstadt v. Baird* (1972), the Court extended the same right to unmarried couples.

Abortion as a family planning option has been more controversial. In *Roe v. Wade* (1973), the Supreme Court—again referencing the right of privacy gleaned from several provisions in the Bill of Rights (1791)—ruled that states could not ban abortions. In that case and subsequent decisions, however, the Court has allowed states to place restrictions on abortion rights. Three Supreme Court justices, two of whom are still on the Court, have suggested that *Roe* was wrongly decided, thus indicating that if the opportunity arises they may vote to overrule that decision. Restrictions on abortion have been upheld in several cases, including *Planned Parenthood of Southeastern Pennsylvania v. Casey* (1992), in which a twenty-four-hour waiting period and parental consent for minors seeking an abortion were approved by the Court.

Title X Programs

In 1969 President Richard Nixon vowed that "no American woman should be denied access to family planning assistance because of her economic condition." A year later CONGRESS passed Title X of the Public Health Service Act, originally enacted in 1944. The act authorizes federal funding for a national network of approximately 4,600 clinics—including affiliates of the Planned Parenthood Federation of America, university and hospital health care centers, state and local health departments, independent clinics, and other public and nonprofit agencies—that deliver family planning and reproductive health care to five million persons each year.

Federal family planning programs are administered by the Office of Family Planning in the Office of Public Health and Science, U.S. DEPARTMENT OF HEALTH AND HUMAN SERVICES. According to Title 42, The Public Health and Welfare, section 300: "The Secretary [of HHS] is authorized to make grants to and enter into contracts with public or nonprofit private entities to assist in the establishment and operation of voluntary family planning projects which shall offer a broad range of acceptable and effective family planning methods and services (including natural family planning methods, infertility services, and services for adolescents)." Funding has increased from $62 million in 1971 to some $288 million in 2005. Title X services are available regardless of a person's ability to pay for them; a majority of clients are members of ethnic and racial minorities who have no income or incomes below the poverty level; others are charged a fee based on their income.

Contraceptive counseling is provided to help couples space births and plan intended pregnancies. For nearly a decade, the Office of Family Planning and the Office of Population Affairs, also in HHS, have addressed family planning and reproductive health information and services to males; one part of the program promotes responsible sexual behavior. As with other related federally funded programs, however, no funds may be used to promote or perform abortions, and no one can be required to perform an abortion or a sterilization if such a procedure would be "contrary to his religious beliefs or moral convictions."

State Law

All states have laws dealing with some aspects of family planning and birth control, and sixteen states have family planning programs for women who would not otherwise be eligible for them under the federal

Medicaid program, which provides medical and health care to people who cannot afford to pay for it.

Public health laws in North Carolina, for example, list family planning under the mission and essential health services of the state. Pennsylvania law declares that its medical assistance program "provides payment for family planning services provided to eligible recipients." The Oregon code, under a section entitled Birth Control; Termination of Pregnancy, provides in part: "The Department of Human Services and every county health department shall offer family planning and birth control services within the limits of available funds. The Director of Human Services or a designee shall initiate and conduct discussions of family planning with each person who might have an interest in and benefit from such service."

In Maryland a minor who is married or the parent of a child is legally granted the same capacity as an adult to consent to "treatment for or advice about contraception other than sterilization." According to a 1991 state attorney general's opinion, the law also permits an eligible minor to choose the provider of such treatment. An attempt by HHS in the 1980s to require parental notification when contraceptives are prescribed to minors was struck down by a federal court in *New York v. Heckler* (1983); the court noted that Title X was the cornerstone of the nation's effort to promote family planning and curb adolescent pregnancies.

The attempt by some states to limit abortions has spilled over into the family planning arena. In Texas the legislature in 2003 cut off federal funding to family planning organizations that also provided abortions under both Title X of the Public Health Service Act and Title XX of the Social Security Act (1935), which funds block grants to the states for social services, even though the abortions were privately funded. A federal district court heard objections by several Planned Parenthood organizations in the state whose funds would be eliminated, granting an injunction on the grounds that Texas law conflicted with the federal preemption of the law in this area. In *Planned Parenthood of Houston and Southeast Texas v. Sanchez* (2005),

however, a federal appeals court ruled that the state law could stand because the Planned Parenthood facilities could create independent affiliates to perform abortions, making the parent organizations eligible for the federal funding.

Other attempts to challenge family planning programs on religious or moral grounds have failed. In *Civic Awareness of America, Ltd. v. Richardson* (1972), a federal court rejected a challenge to federal funding for abortion, artificial contraception, and vasectomies, citing the FIRST AMENDMENT (1791) prohibition against the establishment of RELIGION; the opinion noted that the purpose of the law in question, the Family Planning Services and Population Research Act of 1970, was to assist in making comprehensive, voluntary family planning services readily available to all persons desiring such services.

Family planning in the United States—at least as far as methods that do not involve terminating pregnancies, such as abortion—is now generally taken for granted. Abortion, in contrast, is considered by many citizens and politicians on religious and moral grounds to be outside the scope of reasonable family planning methods. The federal government's policy has been to restrict in any way possible the funding of abortions with taxpayer money. This policy has led to a prohibition of abortion as a family planning option in both domestic and foreign or international family planning programs. The so-called Mexico City policy, first developed in 1984 during the Reagan administration, denies any U.S. funding to international family planning organizations that use even their own funds to "perform or actively promote" abortion. The theory behind this prohibition—which did not escape the Texas legislators who passed the law that became the subject of the *Sanchez* case—is that money that is freed up by U.S. funding might be used for abortion activities. The Mexico City policy was countermanded by President Bill Clinton two days after taking office in 1993 but was reinstated by President George W. Bush after he entered office in 2001.

See also ETHICS; MOTHERHOOD; UNMARRIED PARENTS.

FEDERAL COMMUNICATIONS COMMISSION

An independent federal agency, the Federal Communications Commission was established by Congress in the Communications Act of 1934. A successor to the Federal Radio Commission, it is responsible for regulating all nonfederal government uses of the radio spectrum, including radio and television broadcasting, and all interstate telecommunications whether by wire, satellite, or cable. International communications that originate in or terminate in the United States also come under its jurisdiction.

The agency is directed by five commissioners appointed by the president and confirmed by the Senate for five-year terms. The president designates one member to be the chairperson, and only three commissioners can be of the same political party. A commissioner may not have a financial interest in any business regulated by the agency.

One aspect of the FCC's regulatory authority is its power to police the airwaves for OBSCENITY and indecency. Federal law prohibits broadcasting obscene programs at any time and restricts indecent programming to certain hours (a "safe harbor" from 10:00 P.M. to 6:00 A.M.). The agency is charged by CONGRESS with the enforcement of Title 18, section 1464, of the U.S. Code, which prohibits the utterance of "any obscene, indecent, or profane language by means of radio communication." To be considered obscene, the material must describe or depict in a "patently offensive" way sexual conduct specifically defined by law that, taken as a whole and applying community standards, appeals to the PRURIENT INTEREST and lacks any serious literary, artistic, political, or scientific value (*see MILLER V. CALIFORNIA*). So far it has enforced indecency and profanity regulations only against conventional broadcast services, not against subscription services such as cable and satellite.

The agency's enforcement powers include issuing warnings, assessing fines, and revoking a station's license to broadcast. In 2004, for example, the FCC received 1,405,419 indecency complaints involving 145 radio, 140 television, and 29 cable programs. The number of complaints received in prior years totaled 166,683 in 2003; 13,922 in 2002; 346 in 2001; and 111 in 2000. Mass e-mail and letter campaigns have helped increase some of the totals. In 2004 the FCC singled out twenty CBS-owned television stations for the Super Bowl halftime "wardrobe malfunction" that exposed Janet Jackson's breast to millions of prime-time viewers. Fines levied that year totaled $3,658,000, although the agency took in $7,928,080 including voluntary settlements. Until 2006 the statutory maximum fine was $32,500 per violation, based on factors such as the nature, extent, and gravity of the violation and the violator's history of prior offenses; that year, however, Congress raised the figure tenfold, to $325,000.

Monitoring and policing the tens of thousands of licensed broadcasters whose authority to stay on the air must be renewed by the FCC every eight years is a daunting task. The burden of proof that a broadcaster's license should be revoked lies with the complainant, resulting in automatic renewal of more than 99 percent of the licenses. Of those not automatically renewed, only a few are actually denied. Some cases go to court to be resolved.

A policy statement issued in 2001 noted that *Federal Communications Commission v. Pacifica Foundation* (1978), in which the U.S. Supreme Court held that it was not unconstitutional for the federal government to regulate indecent broadcasts, "provides the judicial foundation for FCC indecency enforcement." In this case the Court accepted the agency's definition of indecency, which is "language or material that, in context, depicts or describes, in terms patently offensive as measured by contemporary community standards for the broadcast medium, sexual or excretory activities or organs." For the commission to make a finding of indecency, the material in question must come under the above definition and must be patently offensive to the average listener and not necessarily to the sensibilities of any individual complainant.

An indecency warning was issued in 1987 against Howard Stern's radio show, for example, because the cited material was found to consist of "vulgar and lewd references to male genitals and to masturbation and sodomy," among other explicit sexual talk. Infinity Broadcasting, the network that carried the "shock jock," incurred the largest cumulative fine to date, $1.7 million, for airing graphic references to sex by Stern and his guests such as strippers and pornographic movie stars. (In 2006 Stern moved to satellite radio to try to escape enforcement of FCC indecency regulations.) Sexually oriented rap lyrics have also been targeted; for example, in 2001 two radio stations were fined $7,000 each for indecent hip-hop songs shortly after President George W. Bush made new appointments to the FCC.

With respect to indecency on television, the commission in 1990 reviewed a television show, *Teen Sex: What About the Kids?*, which broadcast portions of a high school SEX EDUCATION class. Although it included realistic models of sex organs, demonstrated various methods of birth control, and offered frank discussions of sexual topics, the show was not considered indecent. "[T]he material presented," said the FCC, "was clinical or instructional in nature and was not presented in a pandering, titillating or vulgar manner." Protecting CHILDREN from easily accessible sexually inappropriate material on television lies at the heart of much of the FCC's regulatory mission.

In *Reno v. American Civil Liberties Union* (1997), the Supreme Court struck down an indecency standard for the INTERNET but did not question the FCC's broadcast standard. The Court recognized the "special justifications for regulation of the broadcast media that are not applicable to other speakers." Other constitutional challenges of the commission's regulation of indecency on the airwaves have been turned back, although it has been required to identify the compelling government interests that warrant regulation.

Without staff to monitor all broadcasts, the FCC relies on viewers and listeners to bring potentially indecent broadcasts to its attention. To file a complaint, the commission requires the call sign of the station involved and information regarding what was actually said or depicted during the allegedly indecent, profane, or obscene broadcast.

Contact: Federal Communications Commission, 445 12th Street, SW, Washington, DC 20554 (888-225-5322). www.fcc.gov.

See also CENSORSHIP; MEDIA; PORNOGRAPHY.

FEDERAL MARRIAGE AMENDMENT

In debating a bill in the Delaware legislature to enact a state constitutional ban on SAME-SEX MARRIAGE in 2004, a proponent suggested: "Marriage is the foundation of our society, and has always been between one man and one woman. We must do everything we can to preserve the institution." An opponent of the measure, who had wed his life partner in a same-sex marriage ceremony in Canada, countered: "Where are you going to put it—in a new Bill of Wrongs? It could not go in the Bill of Rights, which were written to protect our freedoms."

Thus the lines have been drawn throughout the nation over the issue of limiting the institution of MARRIAGE to heterosexual couples. Nearly all states have laws defining marriage as being between one man and one woman, of which thirty-seven are the states' version of the federal DEFENSE OF MARRIAGE ACT. Only six states—Connecticut, Massachusetts, New Jersey, New Mexico, New York, and Rhode Island—and the District of Columbia have no explicit prohibition against same-sex marriage. As of 2006 twenty states had adopted constitutional amendments along these lines; proposed amendments were to be on the ballots in six to eight other states, including Arizona, Colorado, Idaho, South Carolina, South Dakota, Tennessee, Virginia, and Wisconsin. Eleven states, including California and even Massachusetts, have pending similar legislative or ballot initiative measures. Massachusetts now allows same-sex marriage, a move the California legislature made in 2005 only to have the law vetoed by Governor Arnold Schwarzenegger. Connecticut and Vermont permit civil unions, which extend to homosexual couples at the state level basically the same rights as marriage.

Senator Samuel D. Brownback of Kansas was one of nineteen senators to sponsor Senate Joint Resolution 40 in 2004 to amend the U.S. Constitution to define marriage as "only the union of a man and a woman." The amendment, which has failed several times to gain Senate approval, would make same-sex marriage unconstitutional.

In 1996 CONGRESS passed the Defense of Marriage Act (DOMA), which defined marriage for the purposes of federal law—income taxes, employee benefits, Social Security, and the like—as "only a legal union between one man and one woman as husband and wife." The act also provided that no state is required to give full faith and credit (as mandated by Article IV, section 1, of the U.S. Constitution) to "any public act, record, or judicial proceeding of any other State ... respecting a relationship between persons of the same sex that is treated as a marriage under the laws of such other State ... or a right or claim arising from such relationship." As yet the U.S. Supreme Court has not ruled on the question of whether Congress can constitutionality limit the scope of the full faith and credit clause through such legislation.

DOMA's questionable constitutionality lies behind the pursuit of an amendment to the U.S. Constitution that would limit marriage to heterosexual unions. If such an amendment were ratified, federal and state governments would be bound by it and federal laws made pursuant to it would override any current constitutional limitations.

The proposed Federal Marriage Amendment, first introduced in Congress in 2002, was revised and reintroduced in 2004 and 2006. The original version stated: "1. Marriage in the United States shall consist only of the union of a man and a woman. 2. Neither this constitution or the constitution of any state, nor state or federal law, shall be construed to require that marital status or the legal incidents thereof be conferred upon unmarried couples or groups."

The 2004 version reads: "Marriage in the United States shall consist only of the union of a man and a woman. Neither this Constitution, nor the constitution of any State, shall be construed to require that marriage or the legal incidents thereof be conferred upon any union other than the union of a man and a woman."

This new version was intended to avoid problems with the second section of the first version, which it was thought might restrict courts in interpreting antidiscrimination and equal protection laws as they may apply to nonmarried couples regardless of sexual orientation. The phrase "unmarried couples or groups" was thus replaced with "any union other than the union of a man and a woman," which would protect unmarried couples in common law marriages. (A common law marriage is one that has not been legally formalized but which a state may nonetheless recognize under certain conditions.) The revised language would presumably also allow civil unions between same-sex couples like those that are legal in Vermont and Connecticut. Some conservatives, therefore, believe that the proposed amendment should be rewritten again to ban all unions except marriage between a man and a woman.

Proponents of this constitutional amendment offer a variety of reasons for supporting it: (1) marriage is a privileged union and not a civil right, thus it is not subject to constitutional protection; (2) government and businesses should be absolved of any responsibility for providing rights, privileges, or benefits to same-sex partners; (3) same-sex unions are immoral, so to accord them a status equal to that given to heterosexual married couples is to legislate immorality; (4) churches that might refuse to perform same-sex marriages fear lawsuits; and (5) the judiciary should be restricted in expanding rights that a majority of the citizens do not believe are deserved.

Opponents argue that the proposed amendment would constitutionally protect DISCRIMINATION against lesbians and gays and their families, because many homosexual couples have CHILDREN. Homosexual rights groups see the movement for the Federal Marriage Amendment as part of a campaign to foment antigay bigotry and to encourage hatred of homosexuals by branding them as not worthy of the same rights and privileges as heterosexuals. States' rights advocates oppose a law that would federalize marriage, which has always been under the control of individual states. Some critics unfavorably compare civil unions to the "separate but equal" doctrine that was used to maintain racial segregation until the Supreme Court's decision in *Brown v. Board of Education of Topeka* (1954). Perhaps the strongest argument against such an amendment is that the U.S. Constitution is a document that was intended to protect citizens from government abuses—not to enshrine in law deprivations of rights for a minority of Americans. The amendment failed again in 2006 to gain the votes required for passage by Congress.

Behind the serious concerns of equality raised by this battle over who will define marriage lies a key issue: the hundreds of rights and benefits at the state and federal levels that accrue to married persons and the money to be saved by governments and businesses if they do not have to extend the rights of marriage to a new class of citizens.

See also HOMOSEXUALITY.

FEMALE GENITAL MUTILATION

See BIOETHICS; SEX OFFENSES.

FEMINISM

There is no "masculine mystique." Throughout history men have defined the world we all live in and have thus defined the opposite sex. The Declaration of Independence (1776) suggested that "all Men" are created equal, but it took 131 years after the U.S. Constitution was ratified before men deigned to allow all American women to vote and hold political office. Yet other WOMEN'S RIGHTS gained toward the end of the twentieth century—especially the right to choose whether to end a PREGNANCY—are still not beyond attack.

Feminism can be defined briefly as a doctrine that advocates for women the same rights as men have in the political, economic, and social spheres, as well as the right to control their own bodies and reproductive choices. Mary Wollstonecraft (1759–97) was an early British feminist who wrote *A Vindication of the Rights of Woman* in 1792, in which she called for equal educational opportunities for women. She argued that men had incorrectly relegated women to second-class citizenship based solely on what they believed to be females' "sexual character." Wollstonecraft was a member of a radical group that included Thomas Paine (1737–1809), whose incendiary pamphlet *Common Sense* (1776) helped spark the American colonies' revolt against Britain.

Whether called such, the feminist movement in the United States began in earnest with the women who worked to abolish slavery before the Civil War. As part of the crusade to free the slaves, these women saw an opportunity to expand their own civil and legal rights. The first convention on women's rights in America was held in Seneca Falls, New York, in 1848, and it adopted a resolution demanding the vote for women. The resolution was drafted by Elizabeth Cady Stanton (1815–1902), who, along with SUSAN B. ANTHONY (1820–1906) would become a leader of the early suffragist movement in the United States. But after the Civil War, the impetus for women's rights, including suffrage, went unrewarded.

With the ratification of the Nineteenth Amendment to the U.S. Constitution in 1920, granting women the right to vote, came political equality with men at the national and state levels. Yet women, like African Americans, were still discriminated against and treated as less than equal in the law, education, and employment. The civil rights movement in the early 1960s sparked the feminist movement anew, as evidenced by Betty Friedan's book *The Feminine Mystique* (1963) and the founding of the NATIONAL ORGANIZATION

FOR WOMEN in 1966. Issues that organized groups and individuals took on ranged from equal pay and maternity leave to DISCRIMINATION and SEXUAL HARASSMENT in the workplace, REPRODUCTIVE RIGHTS and ABORTION, and DOMESTIC VIOLENCE, as well as larger intellectual issues such as patriarchy and sexual objectification.

The movement for EQUAL RIGHTS culminated in the passage by Congress of a proposed Equal Rights Amendment to the U.S. Constitution, which was sent to the states in 1972. But the ERA's failure over ten years to garner enough support in the states to become a part of the Constitution—only thirty-five of the thirty-eight necessary states ratified it by the deadline—took the momentum out of the movement. It was already becoming fragmented over which direction to take. Some women saw the feminist movement as a threat to those who wanted to stay at home and raise a family and did not necessarily want to pursue a career. Other women who are nonwhite and outside the middle class felt neglected until efforts sought to focus on related issues of race, culture, RELIGION, and social class.

Since the 1970s several theories of feminism and antifeminism have been proposed. One approach draws on Marxism to conclude that women's sexuality has been historically expropriated by men in the same way that the labor of workers has been exploited by the capitalist system. Such a view influences how some proscribed sexual behavior may be analyzed. A proponent of this view, Catharine MacKinnon, has argued that sexuality is a form of power and that crimes such as INCEST and sexual harassment are simply the applications of male power over women—serving as "the linchpin of gender inequality." Or as she phrased it: "Man fucks woman; subject verb object."

An alternate take on feminism is based on historical religious definitions of good and bad sexual behavior, constituting a hierarchy of social values. According to Gayle Rubin, an anthropologist interested in sexual subcultures, married reproductive heterosexuals represent the highest form of sexual arrangement, followed by unmarried monogamous heterosexual couples, with homosexuals, transsexuals,

As president of the National Organization for Women, Betty Friedan (1921–2006) led a campaign in the 1960s to have the New York legislature "put sex into section 1 of the New York constitution." The document now contains gender-neutral language that encompasses both men and women.

transgender individuals, prostitutes, and, finally, child molesters, at the bottom. In this view, the CONSENT required by law for sexual relations empowers those at the top of the erotic pyramid but even if given does not lessen the impropriety of sexual behavior at the bottom. Perhaps the radio talk-show host Rush Limbaugh's characterization of feminists as "feminazis" sums up the opposition of many to the movement.

Feminism is ultimately about expanding choices. The commercial world, steeped in capitalist theory, declares that choice—in products, distributors, and services, all of which flow from competition in the marketplace—is good for the consumer and for business. As for choices in other areas of life—such as family arrangements, sexual lifestyle, sexual morality, reproductive rights, and economic independence—some people seem to regard fewer choices as better than more. This may be a symptom of the inevitable struggle between

past traditions and the changes rampant in modern society. But if sex is power, as some feminists argue, then those who determine the context in which sexual behavior is permissible have a share in that power and are probably reluctant to give it up without a fight.

Contacts

Feminist Majority Foundation, 1600 Wilson Boulevard, Suite 801, Arlington, VA 22209 (703-522-2214). www.feminist.org.

National Organization for Women, 733 15th Street, NW, Washington, DC 20005 (202-331-0066). www.now.org.

See also GENDER; MARRIAGE; MOTHERHOOD; PREGNANCY; RAPE.

FERTILITY

See ASSISTED REPRODUCTIVE TECHNOLOGY.

FETAL HOMICIDE

See UNBORN, RIGHTS OF THE.

FIRST AMENDMENT

The Bill of Rights (1791), which comprises the first ten amendments to the U.S. Constitution, became effective two years after the Constitution itself was ratified in 1789. This document prohibits the government from infringing certain rights of the people relating to religion, speech, the press, public assembly, gun ownership, searches and seizures, due process, and criminal proceedings. The Bill of Rights has been emulated around the world in many forms. Among other nations, Canada's constitution includes a Charter of Fundamental Rights and Freedoms, adopted in 1982; part 3 of India's 1950 constitution sets out Fundamental Rights; and Russia's 1993 constitution has a chapter entitled Human and Civil Rights and Freedoms. A wide gulf may separate a constitutional statement of rights and effective enforcement of those rights. But the need for governments to spell out individual liberties that are beyond their power to diminish has become a fundamental element of almost all constitutional democracies.

The 1688 English Bill of Rights served as an inspiration for the American version, even though that constitutional document guaranteed rights only of the English Parliament, not of the people. The constitutions of some of the original thirteen colonies served as a second major source for the Bill of Rights—for example, the 1776 Virginia constitution's forceful declaration of rights written by George Mason (1725–92). During the first Congress in 1789, James Madison (1751–1836), called the "Father of the Constitution," introduced twelve amendments to allay public fears over preserving the people's rights and help obtain ratification of the Constitution. The original first amendment has never been approved, and the second was ratified only in 1992, making the last ten of the twelve measures the Bill of Rights upon ratification by the states.

The Constitution's First Amendment is probably the most well known to Americans. It states: "Congress shall make no law respecting an establishment of religion, or prohibiting the free exercise thereof; or abridging the freedom of speech, or of the press; or the right of the people peaceably to assemble, and to petition the Government for a redress of grievances." This amendment was written to permit and encourage the unfettered expression of beliefs and ideas that are necessary for a democratic citizenry to make informed choices about their lives and their government.

Of the ten amendments, regulation of sexual behavior is most closely tied to the First Amendment. Reproductive rights and marital practices such as polygamy, for instance, raise issues that relate to freedom of RELIGION. CENSORSHIP, production and use of ADULT MATERIALS, OBSCENITY, PORNOGRAPHY, and HATE CRIMES involve activities to which freedom of speech and the press may apply. Freedom of association, which the U.S. Supreme Court has derived from the right of assembly contained in the First Amendment, impacts the legality of laws attempting to regulate intimate sexual relations that cover a spectrum running from ADULTERY to SODOMY. Taken together, First Amendment rights encompass the broader legal notion of freedom of expression. Along with other constitutional rights found in the Third, Fourth, Fifth, and Ninth Amendments, they have provided the basis for the constitutional right of PRIVACY first upheld by the Supreme Court in *GRISWOLD V. CONNECTICUT* (1965).

The Bill of Rights was intended to protect against infringement of personal freedoms by the federal government. But in a series of cases, the Supreme Court extended some of these protections to the states by a process known as the doctrine of incorporation. As for the First Amendment freedoms of speech, the press, and assembly, as well as the free exercise of religion and the prohibition against the establishment of a state religion, each was made applicable to the states in 1927, 1931, 1937, 1940, and 1947, respectively.

Freedom of Religion

Madison's original draft of language to guarantee religious freedom stated: "The civil rights of none shall be abridged on account of religious belief or worship, nor shall the full and equal rights of conscience be in any manner, or on any pretense, infringed." During debate on the amendment in the first term of the House of Representatives, Madison indicated that he meant "that Congress should not establish a religion, and enforce the legal observation of it by law, nor compel men to worship God in any Manner contrary to their conscience." The language was consequently changed. In *Everson v. Board of Education* (1947), the Supreme Court restrictively construed this statement, citing Thomas Jefferson to the effect that the establishment clause was intended to erect "a wall of separation between church and State."

Courts have often had to balance constitutionally protected religious freedom with important governmental interests that may infringe on that right.

Polygamy. In *Davis v. Beason* (1890), the Supreme Court held that protecting the monogamous family unit trumped the religious beliefs exhibited by some Americans in the practice of POLYGAMY. "BIGAMY and polygamy are crimes by the laws of all civilized and Christian countries," declared the opinion. "To call their advocacy a tenet of religion is to offend the common sense of mankind." In an earlier polygamy case, *Reynolds v. United States* (1879), the Court had made a clear distinction between beliefs, which were protected under the First Amendment, and actions that were not if they violated criminal laws.

Reproductive Rights. U.S. law with respect to REPRODUCTIVE RIGHTS, especially those of women, was greatly liberalized in the twentieth century. At the beginning of the century, the strict morality that many religions sought to impose on adherents and others meant that matters related to SEX EDUCATION, CONTRACEPTION, and ABORTION were often considered obscene; contraceptive materials could not be distributed or sent through the mail. Gradually changes were made to shore up the wall of separation between church and state and allow individual choice.

In *Civic Awareness of America, Ltd. v. Richardson* (1972), a federal court rejected a suit filed to block funding of federal FAMILY PLANNING services. The plaintiffs had argued that providing contraceptive information and procedures violated the First Amendment's establishment clause, because it was tantamount to government support for the "religion of secular humanism." Although federal and state governments continue to refuse to fund abortions to protect the so-called RIGHTS OF THE UNBORN, contraception itself is generally now considered legal. Religious groups nonetheless organize politically to deny or restrict access to sex education and abortion, promoting ABSTINENCE until MARRIAGE over provision of complete and accurate information on protection from PREGNANCY and SEXUALLY TRANSMITTED DISEASES.

Freedom of Speech and the Press

With respect to the freedom of speech guaranteed in the First Amendment, the lines drawn by the Supreme Court over the years have not been particularly straight. In *Cohen v. California* (1971), the Court upheld the right of a draft protester to wear a jacket in public emblazoned with the words *Fuck the Draft*. In contrast, the Court ruled in *Federal Communications Commission v. Pacifica Foundation* (1978) that the FEDERAL COMMUNICATIONS COMMISSION could prohibit the comedian George Carlin from performing his "Filthy Words" routine, noting that the indecent language might be heard by CHILDREN. Yet, as Associate Justice Oliver Wendell Holmes Jr. wrote in *Schenck v. United States* (1919), to be outside the protection of the First Amendment, speech must "create a clear and present danger," such as shouting "Fire!" in a crowded theater and causing a panic.

Censorship and Obscenity. Whether the government can restrict publication of questionable materials, rather than punish such behavior after the fact, was settled in the Supreme Court case *Near v. Minnesota* (1931). Here the Court found prior restraint (prepublication censorship) to be an infringement of the First Amendment. *Near* did not involve indecent or obscene material, however, so when the Court first seriously tackled the question of obscenity under the First Amendment, it had to develop a new method of analysis.

In *ROTH V. UNITED STATES* (1957), the Supreme Court reaffirmed that obscenity is beyond the scope of First Amendment protection and that any definition of obscenity must take into account the material in question as a whole, not just selected passages; the material must appeal to the PRURIENT INTEREST of the average person, not the most vulnerable persons; and it must be utterly without socially redeeming value. Later, in *MILLER V. CALIFORNIA* (1973) and other cases, the Court continued to refine the definition of obscenity in the arts and the ENTERTAINMENT INDUSTRY. The most recent forays by the Supreme Court into constitutional protection for sexually explicit or adult materials came in *Reno v. American Civil Liberties Union* (1997) and *Ashcroft v. American Civil Liberties Union* (2002, 2004), in which laws enacted by CONGRESS to protect children from sexually explicit material on the INTERNET were struck down as infringements of the First Amendment.

Another area of First Amendment jurisprudence related to sexuality involves expressive conduct; besides

"PUT THIS ON – YOU'RE OBVIOUSLY NOT COVERED BY THE FIRST AMENDMENT"

RULING THAT LOCAL GOVTS. CAN REQUIRE NUDE DANCERS TO WEAR G-STRINGS AND PASTIES

U.S. SUPREME COURT

©2000 HERBLOCK

The *Washington Post's* political cartoonist, Herbert Block (known as Herblock), responded to a 2000 decision by the U.S. Supreme Court in the case *City of Erie v. Pap's A.M.* In this important obscenity case, the Court held that local governments can demand that nude dancers wear G-strings and pasties without infringing the First Amendment.

obscenity, this includes nude dancing, homosexuality, and protests against abortion. Two key elements of analysis in these types of case revolve around what is permissible state regulation of expressive speech or conduct and whether government regulations are neutral with respect to conduct or are based on actual conduct. Conduct-neutral regulations are those that control the time, place, and manner of expressive conduct. Because such regulations presum-

ably do not seek to regulate a specific message, the Supreme Court gives government more leeway than if the regulations attempt to censor the message itself.

Nude Dancing. In upholding First Amendment protection for "virtual" (as opposed to actual) child pornography, the Supreme Court in *Ashcroft v. Free Speech Coalition* (2002) noted that it was well established that speech cannot be prohibited because it concerns subjects offensive to the Court's sensibilities. But in *City of Erie v. Pap's A.M.* (2000) and several earlier decisions, the Court indicated that expressive conduct such as nude dancing in legitimate theater or artistic performances may be more protected than similar expressive conduct in bars and cabarets; therefore, the latter performances may be regulated more restrictively than the former. This distinction has been criticized as an irrational, elitist analysis of the First Amendment's protection of expressive conduct.

Homosexuality. In *Gay Students Organization of the University of New Hampshire v. Bonner* (1974), a federal appeals court found that restrictions placed on a gay campus organization by the school were unconstitutional under the First Amendment. "Communicative conduct," said the court, "is subject to regulation as to 'time, place, and manner' in the furtherance of a substantial governmental interest, so long as the restrictions . . . are unrelated to the content and subject matter of the message communicated." In *Acanfora v. Board of Education of Montgomery County* (1974), however, another federal appeals court held that by failing to indicate his HOMOSEXUALITY on a job application or membership in a gay college campus organization, an employee was not able to challenge his employer's policy of discriminating against gays.

Some state laws have attempted to prohibit speech relating to GENDER issues by members of the gay, lesbian, bisexual, and transgender communities, contending that such speech advocates violating laws against homosexual sex acts. The Supreme Court's decision in *LAWRENCE V. TEXAS* (2003), giving constitutional protection to homosexual sodomy by consenting adults in the privacy of their own home, may have taken the wind out of this argument. Most federal and state courts have found that when such speech—sometimes referred to as "out speech" or "coming-out speech"—promotes political objectives such as individual autonomy and self-identity in the struggle for equal treatment, it is protected by the First Amendment. A leading case is *Gay Law Students Association v. Pacific Telephone and Telegraph Co.* (1979). The California supreme court declared that the company's discriminatory policy based on sexual orientation violated the "political freedom" of employees and potential employees, because "one important aspect of the struggle for equal rights is to induce homosexual individuals to 'come out of the closet,' acknowledge their sexual preferences, and to associate with others in working for equal rights."

Cross-Dressing. Laws against cross-dressing (wearing clothes generally associated with the opposite sex), a characteristic of TRANSVESTISM, have generally been declared unconstitutional under the First Amendment, especially in cases where a person is undergoing sex-reassignment surgery for TRANSSEXUALISM and where medical authorities establish that such behavior is the result of an irresistible impulse or loss of will power. Suits alleging DISCRIMINATION against cross-dressers in prisons, schools, and the workplace have not fared as well.

Abortion Protests. Because of the potential for violence at abortion clinics where antiabortion protesters attempt to interfere with patients and clinic staff, protective legislation has been passed. The Freedom of Access to Clinic Entrances Act (1994) nonetheless raised First Amendment issues regarding an individual's right to protest. Provisions of the law prohibit such acts as "using force, the threat of force, or physical obstruction to intentionally injure, intimidate, or interfere with persons" seeking an abortion and make violations a crime. Federal courts have uniformly found the law to be constitutional. The Supreme Court refused to review the leading case on this question, *United States v. Gregg* (2000), which declared that the act "does not regulate speech and expression protected by the First Amendment."

Freedom of Assembly and Association

The right of assembly is linked in the First Amendment to the right "to petition the Government for a redress of grievances," but it has been broadened by the Supreme Court to undergird an unexpressed right of association. The threat of communism after World War II and the civil rights movement in the 1960s gave rise to calls to stem government infringement of the right to associate with people of one's choosing. This right went beyond the traditional concept of an ad hoc assembly of citizens protesting government policies or actions. The Supreme Court would use this right of association to protect some groups, such as minorities, while narrowing its scope to allow integration, especially of women into all-male institutions.

In *National Association for the Advancement of Colored People v. Alabama* (1958), the Supreme Court declared a freedom of association that protected the NAACP from having to divulge its membership list to the state. But in *City of Dallas v. Stanglin* (1989), the Court noted that under the First Amendment there is no general right of social association, only the right of "expressive association" for political purposes, such as in political parties or interest groups seeking specific political objectives.

In *Stoumen v. Reilly* (1951), California's supreme court determined that the fact that a restaurant was a known hangout for homosexuals was not a basis for indefinitely suspending its liquor license. In *Roberts v. United States Jaycees* (1984), the U.S. Supreme Court heard a case that pitted the Minnesota Human Rights Act, which barred discrimination on the basis of sex, against the male-only membership rules of a business organization. Associate Justice William J. Brennan Jr. wrote in the opinion for the Court that the right of association was not absolute. Given that the association concerned, the U.S. Jaycees (an organization of junior chambers of commerce), was a large, general group without a narrow, specific interest, it did not fall within the ambit of the First Amendment's right of association. Associate Justice Sandra Day O'Connor, in a concurring opinion, argued that associations could rationally be divided into expressive—requiring constitutional protection—and nonexpressive—which nonetheless may not unreasonably discriminate in membership.

That the First Amendment protects aspects of sexual behavior and the expression of sexuality is a byproduct of the need in a democratic society for a free exchange of ideas—even concepts that may offend the sensibilities of some citizens. The twentieth century's expansion of sexual rights culminated in 2003 in the Supreme Court's decision in *Lawrence v. Texas*. The First Amendment, which is one of the constitutional amendments on which the right of privacy invoked in the *Lawrence* case is based, has played a major role in this evolution.

See also EQUAL RIGHTS; NINTH AMENDMENT; NUDITY.

LARRY FLYNT

An outspoken supporter of liberal causes and candidates, Larry Claxton Flynt Jr., the founder of *Hustler* magazine—the blue-collar version of *Playboy*—has been involved in three U.S. Supreme Court cases involving portrayals of sexual behavior. The publisher lives in constant pain as the result of being shot in 1978 outside a county courthouse in Georgia, where he was involved in an OBSCENITY trial. He went on to parody the television evangelist Jerry Falwell in his magazine and in 1983 was forcibly removed from a Supreme Court hearing and arrested for contempt of court after he reportedly called the justices "nothing but eight assholes and a token cunt."

Born in poverty in Salyersville, Kentucky, on November 1, 1942, Flynt enlisted in the army at the age of fifteen. Leaving before his first year was up, he later joined the navy and served on the aircraft carrier USS *Enterprise*. In 1964 he quit the navy and opened a striptease club in Dayton, Ohio. Ten years later he owned several clubs and began publishing the pornographic magazine *Hustler*. Flynt has been married five times and has five children.

Hustler pushed the envelope of obscenity in 1974 with photographs showing women with open vaginas; in 1975

the magazine published nude photographs of Jacqueline Kennedy Onassis taken by *paparazzi*. Today Larry Flynt Publications, Inc., publishes some twenty magazines, and Flynt has been involved in a number of other businesses, including the Hustler Casino, which opened outside Los Angeles in 2000; the Hustler Club; and the Hustler Store, owned by his brother Jimmy.

Larry Flynt's fight for the right to publish PORNOGRAPHY set him against the Supreme Court's decision in MILLER V. CALIFORNIA (1973), which affirmed that obscenity, as defined by the Court, was not protected by the U.S. Constitution. The argument that the speech and press protections of the FIRST AMENDMENT (1791) were absolute—except perhaps for recklessly shouting "Fire!" in a crowded theater—had been rejected earlier by the Court in ROTH V. UNITED STATES (1957).

One of several Flynt cases to reach the Supreme Court was *Flynt v. Ohio* (1981). Here he raised the question whether he had been "subjected to selective and discriminatory prosecution in violation of the equal protection clause of the Fourteenth Amendment [1868]" to the Constitution for disseminating obscenity proscribed by an Ohio statute. The appeal to the Supreme Court was dismissed because the lower court's ruling was not final. Although Flynt was sentenced to up to twenty-five years, he served only six days because the decision was overturned on a technicality.

Keeton v. Hustler Magazine, Inc. (1984) was based on a derogatory cartoon published in *Hustler* in 1976 showing Kathy Keeton, the girlfriend of the rival publisher of *Penthouse* magazine, Bob Guccione. After her civil suit for damages in Ohio was dismissed because it was filed after the statutory deadline, Keeton sought to file the suit in New Hampshire, where the deadline was longer but where *Hustler's* monthly sales were only ten to fifteen thousand copies. Nevertheless, the Supreme Court held that "New Hampshire jurisdiction over a complaint based on this circulation of magazines satisfies the Due Process Clause's requirement that a State's assertion of personal jurisdiction over a nonresident defendant be predicated on 'minimum contacts' between the defendant and the State." (The decision became a

The defendant in several cases involving his pornographic magazine *Hustler* to reach the U.S. Supreme Court, Larry Flynt chats with some of his supporters outside a courthouse in Cincinnati, Ohio, in 1978. He had just posted bond on charges of disseminating information harmful to juveniles and selling obscene materials.

law-school case study for the issue of a state's personal jurisdiction over a nonresident.)

In *Hustler Magazine, Inc. v. Falwell* (1988), Flynt took on not only the law but also RELIGION—or at least a nationally known conservative religious leader, the Reverend Jerry Falwell. This case grew out of the Supreme Court's decision in *New York Times Co. v. Sullivan* (1964), which held that a public figure was fair game for public discussion and, except where "actual malice" could be proved, could not succeed in a suit for slander or libel. Falwell had sued *Hustler,* seeking damages because of a parody on a national liquor advertising campaign that portrayed him as having had sex with his mother in an outhouse. The Supreme Court held in *Falwell* that public plaintiffs such as Falwell who are public officials or public figures cannot recover for

the tort of intentional infliction of emotional distress by reason of the publication of a caricature such as the ad parody at issue without showing in addition that the publication contains a false statement of fact which was made with "actual malice," i.e., with the knowledge that the statement was false or with reckless disregard as to whether or not it was true. The State's interest in protecting public figures from emotional distress is not sufficient to deny First Amendment protection to speech that is patently offensive and is intended to inflict emotional injury when that speech could not reasonably have been interpreted as stating actual facts about the public figure involved.

Larry Flynt would continue to have run-ins with the law over PANDERING and the sale of sex videos to young people, but he would weather these attacks and go on to take an active part in politics. In 1998, for example, during the impeachment trial of President Bill Clinton after he had a sexual affair with the White House intern Monica Lewinsky, Flynt offered a reward of $1 million for evidence of sexual improprieties by Republican lawmakers; among other things, this offer led to the resignation of the designated new speaker of the House of Representatives, Robert Livingston. Then in 2003, Flynt came in seventh of more than one hundred candidates in the California recall election won by the movie actor Arnold Schwarzenegger.

Larry Flynt has been a gadfly in the commercial sex and pornography business and has become wealthy in the process. Today many mainstream MEDIA companies have interests in pornographic television, videos, DVDs, and related productions, and magazines such as *Hustler* are available at most newsstands and through the mail. Like HUGH HEFNER, the founder of *Playboy* magazine; LENNY BRUCE, the off-color comedian; and HENRY MILLER, the author of erotic literature, Flynt is part of the movement in America to expand the market for and the public's acceptance of sexually explicit material.

See also ADULT MATERIALS; CENSORSHIP; ENTERTAINMENT INDUSTRY; SEXUAL REVOLUTION.

FOOD AND DRUG ADMINISTRATION

See U.S. DEPARTMENT OF HEALTH AND HUMAN SERVICES.

FORNICATION

See ADULTERY; PREMARITAL SEX; UNMARRIED COHABITANTS.

FRONTIERO v. RICHARDSON

When a married air force officer was denied increased benefits for her dependent spouse, which were routinely granted to male officers for their wives,

she challenged the basis for this discriminatory treatment. The U.S. Supreme Court, by an 8–1 vote in *Frontiero v. Richardson* (1973), held that different classifications for male and female spouses of MILITARY personnel in federal statutes for the purpose of determining entitlement to benefits are "inherently suspect" and "so unjustifiably discriminatory as to violate the Due Process Clause of the Fifth Amendment" to the U.S. Constitution. *Frontiero* represents the culmination of a long line of challenges alleging DISCRIMINATION against women solely because of their sex and not for rational reasons or important public policy goals.

In *Ballard v. United States* (1946), a bare majority of the Supreme Court overturned a woman's conviction by a federal court in California because of the systematic exclusion of women from the jury. A federal law required federal juries to be drawn from the same type of pool or "community" as those of the highest state court, and California state law made women eligible for jury duty. As a matter of practice, however, the state courts excluded women, and the federal court in the *Ballard* case had simply followed the same practice. In his opinion Associate Justice WILLIAM O. DOUGLAS explained why the illegal exclusion of women from a jury was wrong. "Women and men," he said, are "not fungible; a community made up of one is different from a community composed of both. If the shoe were on the other foot, who would claim that a jury was truly representative of the community if all men were intentionally and systematically excluded from the panel?"

In *Ballard*, the Supreme Court was enforcing a federal statute. A year later, however, in *Fay v. New York* (1947), the question was whether the Constitution prohibits exclusion of women, as well as working-class people, from a state "blue ribbon" jury panel—a panel for which only certain citizens were qualified and on which women were not required to serve. In a 5–4 decision, with Justice Douglas dissenting, the Court refused to find that such discrimination against women and other citizens violated the equal protection clause of the Fourteenth Amendment (1868) to the U.S.

Constitution. Acknowledging the *Ballard* decision, the Court declared: "The contention that women should be on the jury is not based on the Constitution, it is based on a changing view of the rights and responsibilities of women in public life ... [and it] has achieved constitutional compulsion on the states only in the grant of the franchise by the Nineteenth Amendment."

In 1971, however, in *Reed v. Reed*, the Supreme Court in a 7–0 decision (two seats on the Court were vacant) found that an Idaho statute that discriminated against women in their eligibility for appointment as administrators of the estates of intestate decedents violated the equal protection clause. This case set the stage for *Frontiero*, which would challenge discrimination on the basis of sex in a federal law.

Sharron Frontiero, a lieutenant in the air force, requested an increase in her quarters allowance as well as housing and medical benefits for her husband, who was her dependent spouse. In the case of female dependents of male officers, such requests were automatically granted, but because Lieutenant Frontiero was a woman, her request was denied on the grounds that she had failed to prove that her husband was dependent on her for more than one-half of his support. She and her husband then brought suit on the grounds that the laws making this distinction unreasonably discriminated against her and her husband on the basis of sex and thus violated the due process clause of the Fifth Amendment (1791) to the U.S. Constitution.

On appeal from a determination adverse to the plaintiff, the Supreme Court looked at a number of precedents, including the *Reed* case, which was based on a state, rather than a federal, law. The violation in *Reed* fell under the Fourteenth Amendment, which applies to the states, rather than the Fifth Amendment, which applies to the federal government. With respect to *Reed*, the plurality opinion (one agreed to by less than the majority of members, who nevertheless agreed with the outcome of the case) written by Associate Justice William J. Brennan Jr. noted that by classifying applicants for administrators of estates on the basis of sex, Idaho had established "'a classification

subject to scrutiny under the Equal Protection Clause.'"

Justice Brennan pointed out that "under 'traditional' equal protection analysis [by the Court], a legislative classification must be sustained [found to be constitutional] unless it is 'patently arbitrary' and bears no rational relationship to a legitimate government interest." The classification on the basis of sex was like those based on race or national origin—other immutable characteristics "determined solely by the accident of birth." It therefore differed from nonsuspect statuses such as intelligence or physical disability because the characteristic of sex "frequently bears no relationship to ability to perform or contribute to society."

The plurality of four justices went on to declare "that classifications based on sex," like classifications by the government "based upon race, alienage, or national origin, are inherently suspect" categories. Any such classification thus must be given heightened scrutiny by the courts to ensure that reasons for it are justified and not constitutionally discriminatory. The justices concluded that by according differential treatment to male and female members of the uniformed services for the sole purpose of achieving administrative convenience, the challenged statutes violated the Fifth Amendment's due process clause insofar as they required a female member to prove the dependency of her male husband.

In a concurring opinion Associate Justice Lewis F. Powell Jr., joined by Chief Justice Warren E. Burger and Associate Justice Potter Stewart, agreed that the law was unconstitutionally discriminatory but suggested that in deference to the other branches of government and to the constitutional amendment process—the Equal Rights Amendment had been sent to the states for ratification in 1972—the Court should postpone finding legislative classifications based on sex "suspect."

A major precedent in the drive for EQUAL RIGHTS for women, the *Frontiero* decision still did not garner a majority of the justices in support of making classifications based on sex suspect for the purpose of determining if a law was discriminatory under the Constitution, as proposed in Justice Brennan's opinion. That next step would come in 1976 in another opinion written by Justice Brennan: *CRAIG V. BOREN*.

g

GAYS

See Discrimination; Gender; Homosexuality; Same-Sex Marriage; Transsexualism; Transvestism.

GENDER

The words *gender* and *sex* have become linked in the English language and sometimes in the public mind. For example, under the listing Gender in the index to the U.S. Code is a cross-reference: "See Sex and Sexual Matters." (The indexes of state legal codes differ widely in how gender and sex or sexual matters are referenced.) The term *gender* has actually been appropriated from grammar, where it refers to the classification of nouns as masculine or feminine.

What is now considered gender behavior is not always the same as sexual behavior. Gender or sexual identity, sometimes called core gender, results from how a person's sense of his or her own masculinity or feminity develops as he or she matures. The outward expression of a person's self-awareness of that identity is called a gender role. People thus have both an internalization of their gender and external actions expressing their concept of gender. Sexual behavior, in comparison, is the way in which a person acts in regard to sex and sexual matters. The sometimes subtle semantic differences between sexuality, sexual behavior, and gender identity and gender roles have

occasionally muddied the logic behind many laws and court decisions regarding sexual behavior.

A human's sexuality is a complicated matter. We begin life being designated male or female on a birth certificate and then spend many years developing into an adult who is the product of complex genetic and environmental forces that can greatly affect our sense of gender. Almost daily, scientific research reveals new information about sexuality and gender from the womb into old age. In a presentation at the annual meeting of the American Association for the Advancement of Science in 2005, for instance, researchers announced a finding that gender depends on more than just anatomy and hormones; it stems from the earliest brain development. The finding was supported by the identification of fifty-four genes that work differently in the brains of male and female mouse embryos just ten days after conception.

Gender Identity

Sex is the biological distinction between the male and the female of a species, a product of billions of years of evolution leading to sexual reproduction. Today the biological distinction between male and female humans remains fixed. However, the concept of gender identity (named by the noted sex researcher Dr. John Money) has become complex because no person is absolutely male or female, and many people have disassociated conditions in which the biological sex determinates conflict with their gender identity.

The chromosomes that determine a human's sex—X and Y—are only part of the process of sexual development. Other factors include hormonal development, social and cultural influences, and even artificial acts such as sex-change operations. In *Richards v. United States Tennis Association* (1977), for example, a New York court agreed that a male professional tennis player, who had undergone a sex-change operation to become a female and now sought to be allowed to qualify in the women's division, was discriminated against by being required to take a sex-chromatin test to prove that she was a woman; the court held that other evidence was sufficient to accord her that status.

Sexual identity relates to one's sexual orientation and is usually restricted to considering oneself to be heterosexual (attracted to the opposite sex), homosexual (attracted to the same sex), or bisexual (attracted to both sexes). Sexual preference, like sexual orientation, concerns the chosen sex of one's sexual partner. Sexuality generally refers to all the aspects of one's makeup and behavior related to sex; in a broader context, the term may refer to tangential matters, such as love or strong affection, that are not intrinsically sexual in nature.

Whereas *male* and *female* are strictly biological classifications, the words *masculine* and *feminine* indicate perceived characteristics: how a person acts or appears according to accepted concepts of how males and females act or appear. Binary gender norms are accepted concepts of how a person may be identified as either male or female. A hermaphrodite is a person with both male and female genitalia. Individuals with both male and female characteristics or ambiguous sexual characteristics are called intersexuals. A transsexual is a person who has male or female genitalia but whose sexual identity is the opposite. A transsexual male may be called a genetic or biological male; after a sex-change operation (which generally includes psychological counseling and therapy as well as hormone treatments), the transsexual is called a reassigned female; transsexuals are also sometimes referred to as transgender or transidentified persons.

Gender Discrimination

Although sex and gender are two separate aspects of an individual's identity, in many legal contexts the terms are used interchangeably. What used to be called simply sex discrimination has now evolved in many cases into gender discrimination, which includes sex discrimination based strictly on biology. Some states expressly prohibit DISCRIMINATION on the basis of gender, or the sexual persona adopted by an individual as opposed to simply his or her biological sex.

For example, the Virginia Human Rights Act declares: "Unlawful discriminatory practice and gender discrimination [is defined as conduct] that violates any Virginia or federal statute or regulation governing discrimination on the basis of.... sex, pregnancy, childbirth or related medical conditions.... The terms 'because of sex or gender' or 'on the basis of sex or gender' or terms of similar import ... include 'because of on the basis of pregnancy, childbirth or related medical conditions.'" California law also prohibits sex- or gender-based discrimination, but it provides that "[n]othing ... relating to gender-based discrimination affects the ability of an employer to require an employee to adhere to reasonable workplace appearance, grooming, and dress standards ... provided that an employer shall allow an employee to appear or dress consistently with the employee's gender identity."

In two other states, Kentucky and Pennsylvania, the governors have issued executive orders prohibiting discrimination based on gender identity. In the Delaware code, section 223, Words of Gender or Number, under General Provisions Concerning Offenses in title 11, Crimes and Criminal Procedure, provides that "words denoting the masculine gender may, and where necessary shall, be construed as denoting the feminine or the neuter gender."

Gender-based classifications in both state and federal statutes have been the subject of important court decisions involving women, men, and various sexual minorities. The standard used by courts to review statutory gender-based classifications is evolving. In *Reed v. Reed* (1971), for instance, the U.S. Supreme Court was still applying what was called the "rational basis test" in sex or gender discrimination—meaning that discrimination against women would be tolerated only if it bears some rational relationship to the reason for exclusion. In *Reed* the Supreme Court found that there was no rational reason to prefer men over women in the selection of an administrator of the estate a decedent who died without leaving a valid will. The Court, however, would later raise the level of scrutiny because it came to realize that, like classification by race, classification by gender or sex was inherently suspect. Judgments were then based on an "intermediate" level of scrutiny, less than that given to actions affecting race. In other words, the Supreme Court has accepted that the inherent biological differences in men and women and their perceived roles in society allow some legal discrimination, such as separate restroom facilities, which would no longer be tolerated for blacks and whites in America.

American culture had previously assigned certain firmly established traits, characteristics, and behavior to each of the sexes, a differentiation often reflected in Supreme Court cases. In Bradwell v. Illinois (1873), the Court's opinion announced that when the law in question was enacted it was understood that "God designed the sexes to occupy different spheres of action, and that it belonged to men to make, apply, and execute the laws." A concurring opinion by Associate Justice Joseph P. Bradley added, "The paramount destiny and mission of woman are to fulfill the noble and benign offices of wife and mother." As late as 1948, a Supreme Court decision excluded women from the occupation of bartender because of their perceived unsuitability for this type of work.

Before the U.S. Supreme Court, in *United States v. Morrison* (2000), struck down women's right to bring private suits under the Violence Against Women Act (1994), federal courts had permitted civil remedies for sexual assaults on women under the act's gender-motivated violence provisions. A federal district court in *Crisonino v. New York City Housing Authority* (1997) found that a claim could be established under both VAWA and Title VII of the Civil Rights Act of 1964 for the alleged conduct of a supervisor who called a female employee a "dumb bitch" and later pushed her to the floor. The questions addressed in *Crisonino* also involved the power of Congress under the commerce clause of the U.S. Constitution to provide for civil remedies under VAWA. While the court found the act constitutional, it noted that the question of the impact of a regulated activity on interstate commerce is a matter of degree (an impact that the Supreme Court found unconstitutional in *Morrison).*

Sexual Minorities

The situation with respect to discrimination against sexual minorities has been even less progressive, although several states—including California, Minnesota, New Mexico, and Rhode Island—now have laws prohibiting discrimination against persons classified as transgender; laws against HATE CRIMES in even more states encompass transgender persons. The law is gradually expanding to address the nuances of human sexual behavior that are beyond an individual's ability to control, just as it has with respect to the basics of binary sex classification—male and female—and other traditional bases for unreasonable discrimination.

One example of how federal courts in the past dealt with claims of alleged discrimination against a transgendered person involves Kenneth Ulane, a licensed pilot who had served in the army until 1968 and became an Eastern Airlines pilot that same year. He was diagnosed in 1979 as a transsexual, a person whose gender was based on a sexuality other than his biological sex. A year later he underwent sex-reassignment surgery that changed him to a her. After returning to work, Karen Ulane was fired by Eastern in 1981. She filed a complaint with the Equal Employment Opportunity Commission, which supported her in bringing a suit against Eastern under Title VII of the Civil Rights Act of 1964 on the grounds that she was discriminated against because she was a woman and a transsexual.

The U.S. Court of Appeals for the Seventh Circuit held in *Ulane v. Eastern Airlines* (1984) that the evidence was clear that, if Eastern discriminated against Karen Ulane, it was not because she was a female but because she was a transsexual. Transsexuals, the court found, are not covered under Title VII, which prohibits discrimination by employers on the basis of sex. As the court noted, "It is a maxim of statutory construction that, unless otherwise defined, words should be given their ordinary, common meaning." Therefore, the language of Title VII, said the court, does not cover "a person who has a sexual identity disorder." Note the finding that Ulane's condition as a transsexual is described as a "disorder," implying that it was a condition that could be cured rather than simply a manifestation of a gender distinction beyond the control of the transsexual.

In *Enriquez v. West Jersey Health Systems* (2001), the supreme court of New Jersey found that TRANSSEXUALISM could be considered a handicap under the state's antidiscrimination law. The reason cited was that the transsexualism was clinically diagnosed as gender dysphoria, a "mental disorder occurring in an estimated frequency of 1:50,000 individuals." A New York court, in *Jean Doe v. Bell* (2003), dealt with the case of a person born male but who grew up to have a female gender identity. Forced to wear boys' clothing, she developed a condition called gender-identity disorder. The court found that this condition should allow her special accommodation to dress as a female and to use certain feminine accessories such as makeup and breast enhancements in the boys' foster-care facility in which she lived. To make Jean Doe wear boys' clothing, the court concluded, would constitute discrimination under the state human rights law.

Continuing stereotypes of distinctions between the sexes in the law and the workplace perpetuate outdated notions of a hierarchical structure based on sex—keeping women, for example, from attaining equal pay for equal work and being accepted in leadership roles in business and the professions. Added to this is the difficulty of shedding the typecasting of homosexual males and females, bisexuals, and transsexuals. It is thus little wonder that the law, which in the courts is grounded in the use of precedent, is often tragically unable to reach just and logical conclusions in cases involving sexual behavior and gender-based classifications.

See also BISEXUALITY; EQUAL RIGHTS; HOMOSEXUALITY; SAME-SEX MARRIAGE; SEXUAL HARASSMENT; TRANSVESTISM; WOMEN'S RIGHTS.

GENETICS

Genetics is the biology of heredity—the study of how specific traits are passed on from a parent to an offspring. The basic unit of genetics is the gene, the carrier of genetic information called DNA that is located on the chromosome (the linear part or strand) of a cell of a living organism. The Human Genome Project was launched in 1990 to identify each gene on the twenty-three human chromosomes making up a single strand of DNA and was declared complete on April 14, 2003.

Human sexual behavior is largely determined by our genes. Sexual reproduction combines genetic material from two parents, information that then becomes the blueprint for the child that develops from the union of a female egg cell and a male sperm cell. The difference between a male and a female offspring depends on the combination of X and Y chromosomes, with two Xs determining a female and an X and a Y determining a male. Variations also exist: Some children are born with two X chromosomes and one Y, a condition known as Klinefelter's syndrome. Others may be born with one X and two Y chromosomes. Such people are sometimes referred to as intersexual, as are true hermaphrodites—those who have both female and male characteristics, including ambiguous external genitalia.

Some commentators on biology, such as Richard Dawkins and E. O. Wilson, have suggested that almost all of our activities have as their ultimate goal the acquisition of a suitable partner with whom to propagate our genes. This view makes a human little more than a mechanism for ensuring the survivability of some of our own genes through generations to come. But humans have also taken sexual activity beyond mere biological imperatives. Wealthier members of society generally have fewer CHILDREN, and many sexually related activities from contraceptive use to homosexual sex do not have reproduction as a goal or even a byproduct.

In our new technological universe, genetics and the law are becoming entwined in many ways. Genetic information is used in forensic science, such as in DNA typing of suspects, determinations of maternity and PATERNITY, and identification of victims of disasters, as well in medicine, such as in ASSISTED REPRODUCTIVE TECHNOLOGY and STEM-CELL RESEARCH AND CLONING. The law is also called on to deal with PRIVACY rights occasioned by the collection, use, and dissemination of genetic material; discrimination on the basis of genetic information; and property rights in altered or created genetic material. In *Arizona v. Youngblood* (1988), a case involving the recovery of semen from a victim of SEXUAL ASSAULT, the U.S. Supreme Court noted, "As technology develops, the potential for this type of evidence to provide conclusive results on any number of questions will increase. Current genetic testing measures, frequently used in civil paternity suits, are extraordinarily precise."

State Law

Most states have moved to protect genetic information, treating it differently from other types of health information—a policy called genetic exceptionalism. Some observers contend that genetic data should instead be considered on a par with other health data. To date Washington is the only state that treats it the same, including genetic information in the definition of health care information under the state's health privacy law.

State genetic privacy laws generally restrict parties such as insurers and employers from using genetic information without a person's CONSENT. According to the National Conference of State Legislatures, sixteen states require informed consent for a third party to perform or require a genetic test or to obtain genetic data. Twenty-six states mandate informed consent to disclose genetic information. Alaska, Colorado, Florida, Georgia, and Louisiana regard genetic information as personal property, and Alaska incudes DNA samples in this category (a right that Oregon repealed in 2001). Only nineteen states have set civil or criminal penalties for violating genetic privacy laws. The use of genetic information in applying for employment or insurance may be covered in separate state laws.

Privacy

Genetic information can tell a lot about a person, including sexual characteristics and the disposition to certain types of sexual behavior. In addition to indicating whether a person is male or female, genetic information can reveal sexual abnormalities. Some evidence also indicates that one's genetic makeup may create the potential for HOMOSEXUALITY, although the jury is still out on whether homosexuality is linked to genetic anomalies—hardwired—or whether it is simply influenced by genetics and developmental conditions, a mix of nature and nurture. Genetic information may also reveal information about a person's health conditions or a family history with implications for individual health risks. Because of the potential harm that such information may cause and because the samples used are small and may be obtained without a person's knowledge—from skin, hair, or saliva—the rights of PRIVACY and confidentiality come into play in the collection and use of genetic information.

Accident and health insurers generally do not have to obtain a person's consent for disclosure of genetic information. Wisconsin law, however, while not addressing other aspects of genetics, prohibits

State Genetic Privacy Laws

State	Consent Required for				Considered Personal Property		Specific Penalties for Violations of Genetic Privacy
	Genetic Testing	Access to Information	Retention of Information	Disclosure of Information	Information	DNA	
Alabama							
Alaska	•	•	•	•	•	•	•
Arizona	•			•			
Arkansas				•			
California				•			•
Colorado[1]				•	•		•
Connecticut							
Delaware		•	•	•			•
Florida	•			•	•		•
Georgia	•			•	•		•
Hawaii				•			
Idaho							
Illinois				•			•
Indiana							
Iowa							
Kansas							
Kentucky							
Louisiana				•	•		•
Maine							
Maryland				•			
Massachusetts	•			•			•
Michigan	•						
Minnesota							
Mississippi							
Missouri				•			•
Montana							
Nebraska	•						
Nevada		•	•	•			•
New Hampshire				•			
New Jersey		•	•	•			•
New Mexico	•	•	•	•			•
New York	•		•	•			•
North Carolina							
North Dakota							
Ohio							
Oklahoma							
Oregon		•	•	•			•
Pennsylvania							

State	Consent Required for				Considered Personal Property		Specific Penalties for Violations of Genetic Privacy
	Genetic Testing	Access to Information	Retention of Information	Disclosure of Information	Information	DNA	
Rhode Island				•			
South Carolina	•			•			•
South Dakota	•						
Tennessee							
Texas				•			
Utah							•[2]
Vermont	•			•			•
Virginia				•			
Washington				•[3]			
West Virginia							
Wisconsin							
Wyoming							

1. May apply only to life and individual disability insurance.
2. Limits disclosures of and access to genetic information by employers and insurers.
3. Requires written authorization only.

Source: National Conference of State Legislatures, 2006

insurers from requiring or requesting any member of an individual's family to obtain a genetic test or an individual to reveal whether a family member has obtained such a test.

Chapter 39 of the South Carolina legal code addresses Privacy of Genetic Information, stating, "All genetic information obtained ... must be confidential and must not be disclosed to a third party in a manner that allows identification of the individual tested without first obtaining the written informed consent of that individual or a person legally authorized to consent on behalf of the individual." Exceptions to these privacy rules include criminal cases, investigations of deaths, determinations of paternity, actions pursuant to a court order, instances where information "will assist in medical diagnosis of blood relatives of [a] decedent," or where "specifically authorized or required by a state or federal statute."

In a key legal case, the Burlington Northern Santa Fe Corporation in 2002 settled with thirty-six employees for $2.2 million for allegedly secretly testing them for a genetic predisposition to carpal tunnel syndrome. Among the issues raised in the initial lawsuit were the victims' fears about not knowing whether they were being tested or for what, their lack of consent for such a procedure, and the potential damage, such as stigmatization and discrimination, that disclosure of the results might engender. In contrast, a Massachusetts court, in *Viriyhiranpaiboon v. Department of State Police* (2001), refused to allow a man convicted of the murder of a pregnant woman to obtain redacted genetic information that the state police had tested along with three other samples related to the crime scene's forensic evidence, which they deemed not related to his case. "Numerous statutes were cited indicating legislative concern for privacy in medical matters," the court noted. "An especially sensitive area of medical data is genetic information."

Discrimination

DISCRIMINATION on the basis of genetic information can occur in several ways. Employers may want to screen out job applicants to avoid investing time and money training an individual whose genetic makeup indicates that he or she is at risk of becoming significantly disabled. A company may also want to protect its health care program from a large liability or to spare the firm from liability for an injury to others as a result of an employee's becoming progressively disabled. An employer may also want to protect an at-risk employee if the employee's job could put her or him at greater risk.

Such genetic discrimination has not been addressed in a comprehensive way by CONGRESS, although several bills have been introduced over the past few years. One, entitled the Genetic Information Nondiscrimination Act of 2005, was passed by the Senate on a vote of 98–0. The act would prohibit insurance companies from discriminating on the basis of genetic information, protect the privacy of such data, and ensure that genetic information is not used to discriminate in employment. In 2000 President Bill Clinton signed Executive Order 13145, prohibiting federal employers or any business receiving federal funds from discriminating on the basis of protected genetic information.

The major federal law that relates to discrimination of this type is the Americans with Disabilities Act (1990). This law defines a disability as "(A) a physical or mental impairment that substantially limits one or more of the major life activities of such individual; (B) a record of such impairment; or (C) being regarded as having such an impairment." Although some people opposed to a comprehensive genetic antidiscrimination law argue that the ADA is sufficient to cover such cases, little precedent for this conclusion can be found.

The ADA has not proved helpful in protecting employees from adverse actions taken by employers based on medical—if not specifically genetic—information. For example, in the U.S. Supreme Court case *Chevron USA v. Echazabal* (2002), Mario Echazabal, an employee of a Chevron contractor, applied for a job with Chevron, but a required physical exam indicated a condition that would be exacerbated by environmental toxins. He was denied the job, and Chevron further asked the independent contractor for whom Echazabal worked to remove him from his existing position. The Supreme Court upheld Chevron's actions under the ADA, agreeing that an employer might want to protect an individual even if he himself was willing to take the risk for the sake of keeping his job. A comparison can be made with the Court's decision in *Lochner v. New York* (1905), later overruled in *West Coast Hotel v. Parrish* (1937), in which workers' absolute right to bargain for their labor was declared. The decision in *Echazabal* seems to again give employers the right to decide against whom they may discriminate on the basis of information about the health of an employee or a prospective employee.

Another Supreme Court decision, *Sutton v. United Airlines* (1999), also appears to indicate that employers may escape liability under section (C) of the ADA. Here the Court found that "an employer is free to decide that physical characteristics or medical conditions that do not rise to the level of an impairment—such as one's height, build, or singing voice—are preferable to others, just as it is free to decide that some limiting, but not *substantially* limiting, impairments make individuals less than ideally suited for a job."

The fear that information from DNA testing will be used by insurance providers to discriminate against customers or will be released without a person's authorization has led to new state laws. Massachusetts prohibits insurers from discriminating on the basis of genetic information. Rhode Island bars insurance administrators, health plans, and providers "from releasing genetic information without prior written authorization of the individual." Vermont prohibits any insurance policy "underwritten or conditioned on the basis of: (1) any requirement or agreement of the individual to undergo genetic testing; or (2) the results of genetic testing of a member of the individual's family." Violations are considered "an unfair method of competition or unfair or deceptive act or practice" and are enforced under state banking and insurance laws.

Collection of Material

Two theories of legal liability for unauthorized possession or use of genetic material have emerged. The first is based on tort law. A second theory is based on the more narrow legal field of misappropriation of trade secrets.

In *Greenberg v. Miami Children's Hospital Research Institute, Inc.* (2003), a federal district court, applying Florida law, found that there were no grounds in tort law or under the state's misappropriation of trade secrets statute for a claim against a doctor who used human tissue and fluid samples, given voluntarily, as well as a list of people suffering from a specific disease in order to conduct research on the condition. A contrary conclusion was reached in *Midwest Oilseeds, Inc. v. Limagrain Genetics Corp.* (2002), a case in which a marketer was charged with breaching an agreement with a breeder not to make illicit seed lines using the germ plasm the breeder had developed. Here the federal district court, applying Iowa law, found that genetic information could be considered property and thus the basis of a tort claim as well as an action for misappropriation of trade secrets.

Intellectual Property Rights

Rights to inventions and other types of intellectual property—which today include the creation of new life forms and medical and genetic processes—may be legally protected for a period of time under patent and related laws. These laws allow those who create something new and useful to benefit from their genius and labors. Much of the progress that comes in science and technology is built on the sharing of information, however, so balances must be struck to resolve these competing interests.

In Article I, section 8, the U.S. Constitution gives Congress exclusive authority to control the patenting of inventions and discoveries. Since the 1970s, the U.S. Patent Office has issued patents on newly cloned genes, many of which involve DNA sequencing, and since the 1980s, other patents have been granted for genetic sequencing and information derived from reading genetic material. States regulate other aspects of genetic research and information.

The announced policy of the National Institutes of Health, an agency of the U.S. Department of Health and Human Resources, is that protection should be given to intellectual property based on discoveries of useful products, but that there should be free dissemination of research tools whenever possible. After receiving a request from NIH to tighten the criteria for issuing patents in the field of biotechnology, the Patent Office at the beginning of 2001 revised its guidelines regarding patents on DNA sequencing and other intellectual property derived from such sequencing. By raising the bar for establishing the utility of products on which patent applications are based, the agency essentially made it more difficult to obtain such patents. International licensing of genetic applications and products is likely to be addressed by the courts in the future.

An emerging area of legal conflict involving genetic information concerns the question of who has rights to a person's tissue samples after they have been removed from the body. Until now, the law has not been well developed in this area. For the most part, researchers have considered removed tissue or DNA to be without ownership and thus available for their own work, even uses in which the samples may acquire a high monetary value. The resolution of lawsuits over this issue and efforts by bioethical and biomedical ethics groups to come up with agreed-on legal standards may help bring some order to this currently chaotic interface between medical research and the law of property rights.

Compared to blood typing and fingerprinting, genetics is a relatively new science and will undoubtedly continue to evolve. So too will the laws that govern who has rights to the information contained in human genes and how this information can be obtained and used. We are on the threshold of an era in which we will not only know more about how genes affect our behavior but also how we can manipulate them to determine who our children will be and how they will behave.

See also AIDS-HIV; Bioethics.

GINZBURG v. UNITED STATES

The obscenity conviction of Ralph Ginzburg (1929–2006), publisher of *Eros* magazine—imposed for sending sexually arousing materials through the U.S. mail—was upheld in 1966 by the U.S. Supreme Court despite recent softening of legal and social views toward obscenity. On the same day, the Court in *A Book Named "John Cleland's Memoirs of a Woman of Pleasure" v. Attorney General of the Commonwealth of Massachusetts* (1966) refused to find the eighteenth-century erotic novel *Fanny Hill* obscene, and William H. Masters and Virginia E. Johnson published their clinical study *Human Sexual Response*. The Court's decision in Ginzburg's case essentially held that the context of commercial exploitation, or pandering, can tip the scales in determining whether questionable materials are obscene or protected by the First Amendment (1791) to the U.S. Constitution. In 1962 the Supreme Court had held in *Manual Enterprises v. Day* that the U.S. Post Office could not keep homosexual magazines out of the mail.

Associate Justice William J. Brennan Jr. delivered the opinion for the Court in *Ginzburg v. United States* (1966). The publisher had been convicted of violating a federal obscenity law for mailing his expensive hard-cover magazine, *Eros;* a sexual newsletter, *Liaison;* and a short book purporting to be a sexual autobiography, entitled *The Housewife's Handbook on Selective Promiscuity.* According to the federal obscenity statute: "Every obscene, lewd, lascivious, indecent, filthy or vile article, matter, thing, device, or substance; [and] ... Every written or printed

In 1966 the U.S. Supreme Court held that regardless of whether or not Ralph Ginzburg's erotic hard-cover magazine *Eros* contained obscene material, the manner in which he promoted it—such as mailing it from Blue Ball, Pennsylvania, and Middlesex, New Jersey—violated a federal law criminalizing obscene advertising.

card, letter, circular, book, pamphlet, advertisement, or notice of any kind giving information ... where, or how, or from whom, or by what means any of such mentioned matters ... may be obtained ... [i]s declared to be nonmailable matter." The penalty for knowingly violating the law was a fine of not more than $5,000 or imprisonment of not more than five years, or both, for the first offense.

Justice Brennan announced at the outset that the Court, as in *Mishkin v. New York* (decided the same day), would "view the publications against a background of commercial exploitation of erotica solely for the sake of their prurient appeal." This was a deviation from *Roth v. United States* (1957) and subsequent obscenity cases decided on the basis of *Roth,* in which the Court determined obscenity solely on the basis of the materials in question.

Some of the contextual factors that influenced the *Ginzburg* decision included "the deliberate representation of [the materials] as erotically arousing." Ginzburg's own expert witness agreed that, "If the object [of a work] is material gain for the creator through an appeal to the sexual curiosity and appetite," the work is pornographic. As additional evidence of pandering, *Eros* had sought mailing privileges from the towns of Intercourse and Blue Ball, Pennsylvania. Unmentioned by the Court was the fact that Ginzburg retained as his attorney Sidney Dickstein.

As Justice Brennan summed up the case: "By animating sensual detail to give the publication a salacious cast, petitioners reinforced what is conceded by the Government to be an otherwise debatable conclusion." In the Court's view, materials that may or may not be obscene per se (by themselves) become clearly obscene in the context of pandering, "the business of purveying textual or graphic matter openly advertised to appeal to the erotic interests of their customers." Said the opinion, "We perceive no threat to First Amendment guarantees in thus holding that in close cases evidence of pandering may be probative with respect to the nature of the material in question and thus satisfy the *Roth* test."

Associate Justice Hugo L. Black, who held a fairly absolutist position on constitutional protections— when the Constitution says "no law," it doesn't mean "except for some laws"—wrote a strong dissent. By making the *Roth* test only a starting point in determining obscenity, he said, his colleagues in the majority were adding new elements that no one, including Ginzburg, could have foreseen as the basis for being incarcerated for five years. For Justice Black, the First Amendment required recognition of the fact "that sex at least as much as any other aspect of life is so much a part of our society that its discussion should not be made a crime."

Although the Court in *Roth* had attempted to clarify the line between protected material and obscenity,

for many constitutional scholars the *Ginzburg* decision seemed to further blur the line. Seven years later, in *MILLER v. CALIFORNIA* (1973), the Supreme Court would once again try to redraw the line more clearly by making the basic test of obscenity hinge on whether the materials in question "depict or describe patently offensive 'hard core' sexual conduct." The notion of how less-than-hard-core pornographic material was marketed was for the most part abandoned. Today Ginzburg's materials would be subject to restrictions only if distributed to minors.

When the Supreme Court refused to hear an appeal of his sentence, Ginzburg served eight months in a federal prison in 1972. " 'Obscenity' or 'pornography' is a crime without definition or victim," he said later in his book, *Castrated: My Eight Months in Prison* (1973). "It is a bag of smoke used to conceal one's own dislikes with regard to aspects of sex."

See also ADULT MATERIALS; CENSORSHIP; PORNOGRAPHY; PRURIENT INTEREST.

GRISWOLD v. CONNECTICUT

Brown v. Board of Education of Topeka (1954), which ended the legality of "separate but equal" schools for black Americans, may have been the U.S. Supreme Court's most important case in the last half of the twentieth century. *Griswold v. Connecticut* (1965) is probably the next in importance because of the far-reaching implications of the right of PRIVACY the Court conjured up in this case. In *Griswold* the justices perceived the potential for a major threat to liberty: the forced disclosure of citizens' private and intimate lives through pervasive surveillance and investigations that would be needed to enforce laws of the type at issue here.

Estelle Griswold, the executive director of the Planned Parenthood League of Connecticut, had been convicted of violating an 1879 Connecticut law banning the use of contraceptives. "Any person who uses any drug, medicinal article or instrument for the purpose of preventing conception," read this Comstock-era law, "shall be fined not less than fifty dollars or imprisoned not less than sixty days nor more than one year or be both fined and imprisoned." Anyone abetting a violator would "be prosecuted and punished as if he were the principal offender." Along with the organization's medical director, a Yale Medical School professor, Griswold was charged with giving contraceptive information and medical advice to married persons at a New Haven clinic, which was open just ten days in 1961.

Consensual, intimate sexual behavior between a married couple in their bedroom would seem to be nobody else's business. However, state legislatures were emboldened in the late nineteenth century to pass laws against various activities perceived as threats to a moral and virtuous life—from PROSTITUTION and PORNOGRAPHY to CONTRACEPTION. A key instigator of this popular movement to enforce strict standards of morality was the antivice crusader ANTHONY COMSTOCK, who influenced passage of the Comstock Act (1873). This law made it illegal to send obscene materials, including contraceptives, through the mail. Comstock and his followers feared that the use of contraceptives would lead to loose sexual morals, particularly among women.

The Supreme Court's opinion in the 7–2 *Griswold* decision was delivered by Associate Justice WILLIAM O. DOUGLAS. He began by citing some of the Court's decisions regarding the due process clause in the U.S. Constitution's Fourteenth Amendment (1868)—a line of decisions starting with *Lochner v. New York* (1905) and ending with *West Coast Hotel v. Parrish* (1937). In *Lochner,* the Court had upheld the unstated constitutional right of citizens, both employers and employees, to purchase and sell labor without arbitrary interference from the government. But as in *Parrish,* the *Griswold* ruling rejected any notion of a right to unbridled liberty as the basis for determining the constitutionality of the Connecticut law. Instead it acknowledged that liberty is subject to reasonable regulation in the interest of the community. The Court, however, went on to declare that it does

"not sit as a super-legislature to determine the wisdom, need, and propriety of laws that touch economic problems, business affairs, or social conditions."

Justice Douglas surveyed the Court's expansion of rights under the Bill of Rights, noting that many of these are not expressly stated in the Constitution—such as the rights of citizens to associate with others, to teach, to educate a child in a school of the parents' choosing, to "utter or print," as well as the right to distribute, receive, and read without government CENSORSHIP. These are considered "peripheral rights" without which "the specific rights would be less secure." Just as the Court had already found a peripheral right of association implied by the right of free speech in cases involving the National Association for the Advancement of Colored People and political parties, the Court began to carve out a "zone of privacy" from the "penumbras" (secondary shadows) of the First, Fourth, Fifth, and Ninth Amendments. If the unexpressed but intended purpose of provisions in these amendments is to safeguard citizens' privacy against government intrusion, then whenever their privacy is invaded the Constitution may be used to determine if such an action is permitted or not.

Applying this analysis to Connecticut's law banning the use of contraceptives, Justice Douglas concluded that by "forbidding the *use* of contraceptives rather than regulating their manufacture or sale," the government had overstepped the bounds of the Constitution's protection against invasion of privacy. "Would we allow the police to search the sacred precincts of marital bedrooms for telltale signs of the use of contraceptives? The very idea is repulsive to the notions of privacy surrounding the marriage relationship." The Court thus ruled that the Connecticut law was unconstitutional because it violated the right of privacy.

Associate Justice Arthur J. Goldberg, with whom Chief Justice Earl Warren and Associate Justice William J. Brennan Jr. joined, wrote a concurring opinion. In it the justices found that the Connecticut law violated a fundamental right that, although not expressly protected by the Constitution, is nevertheless retained by the people under the NINTH AMENDMENT (1791) and applicable to the states under the due process clause of the Fourteenth Amendment (1868). A dissenting opinion by Associate Justice Hugo L. Black, with whom Associate Justice Potter Stewart joined, focused on the exact language of the Constitution, which Justice Black had traditionally adhered to and which, according to him, precluded the federal courts from vetoing laws of CONGRESS or the states that were "based on their own judgment of fairness and wisdom."

The *Griswold* decision was influential in many subsequent decisions, among them *Eisenstadt v. Baird* (1972), in which the Supreme Court extended to unmarried individuals the right to contraception. Undoubtedly the most important and controversial cases following *Griswold* are *Roe v. Wade* (1973), in which the Court used the right of privacy to recognize the constitutional right to ABORTION, and *LAWRENCE V. TEXAS* (2003), in which it recognized the right of homosexual adults to consensual SODOMY in private.

The right of privacy has been criticized as an instrument to expand protection for supposedly immoral acts and also as a hindrance to a state's ability to control the sexual behavior of its citizens. At the other end of the cultural spectrum, others have worried about basing sexual freedom on the "found" right of privacy rather than on citizens' inherent rights under the Constitution, contending that such a reading might give support to those who would try to limit such rights. As a case in point, legal attacks on the right of abortion have included the argument that the right is not based on any specific language in the Constitution and thus may be rescinded by the Supreme Court. The Court has upheld a number of abortion limitations, such as statutory waiting periods and parental notification for minors, that seem to water down the right.

In the battle on and off the Supreme Court regarding "strict construction" of the Constitution and an individual's right to be left alone when it comes to sexual behavior, the expansive nature of the *Griswold* decision will undoubtedly continue to spur debates about the role of the Court in interpreting the Constitution.

See also FAMILY PLANNING; REPRODUCTIVE RIGHTS; SANGER, MARGARET.

h

HATE CRIMES

The categorization of certain offenses as hate crimes is relatively new. Such offenses are viewed as products of hatred, bias, or prejudice against a member of a definable group and are punished more severely under the law. To target crimes based on race, color, RELIGION, or national origin, CONGRESS passed the first hate crimes statute in 1968, the year in which the civil rights leader Martin Luther King Jr. was assassinated. More recently, in 1994 sexual orientation and GENDER were added to the list of protected categories under a federal hate crime sentencing law to reflect similar laws being passed in the states.

Females, homosexuals, transsexuals, and transvestites are often the victims of prejudicial criminal acts, especially acts of violence. Yet the level of bias exhibited against people because of their sex or sexual orientation may not have reached the level of racial hatred that resulted in lynching, burning, and dragging to death of African Americans. Local law enforcement officials, however, have often shown a lack of concern with crimes against gays, lesbians, and transsexuals.

The Hate Crimes Statistics Act, passed in 1990, requires the U.S. attorney general to compile data on crimes motivated by bias based on race, religion, and ethnicity as well as sexual orientation. In 2003 the number of victims of hate crimes based on sexual orientation, as reported in the FBI's Uniform Crime Reports, was 1,479, compared with 4,754 victims of hate crimes based on race and 1,489 based on religion. One incident that rose to national prominence occurred in Wyoming in October 1998, when two men beat Matthew Shepard and tied him to a fence post so badly bruised that he appeared to have been burned, a crime for which each was sentenced to life in prison. Similar incidents have not received the same widespread attention.

Proponents of hate crime laws see them as a means to deter such crimes by permitting an increase in punishment, which exacts additional societal vengeance because of the moral reprehensibility of the perpetrator's motivation. Opponents view the special nature of hate crimes as dividing the citizenry into classes and giving victims a special status. Their arguments include the observation that to a victim, an injury is the same whether committed with the intent to rob or to vent prejudice.

Several kinds of hate crime laws exist at the federal and state levels. The intent of some is to enhance the degree of a generic crime in order to increase the penalty. Other laws move directly to enhance the sentence where prejudice against the victim is a factor. For example, with the traditional crime of assault and battery (a felony), the level might be enhanced from a class D felony to a class B felony if the crime was motivated by prejudice against a protected group, such as a member of a racial minority or a religious group. A third alternative is that a hate crime law may say simply that the penalty for a crime may be increased, leaving the decision about additional punishment to a judge or a jury. Guidelines may specify how the sentence is to be increased; for example, an additional year may be added in one class of crime and two years in another.

Federal Law

A predecessor of the modern hate crime law was the Ku Klux Klan Act (1871), also known as the Civil Rights Act of 1871, which was passed by Congress in the wake of the Civil War (1861–65); the act prohibited two or more persons from conspiring to deprive any person or class of people "of equal protection of the laws, or of equal privileges and immunities under the laws." During the height of the civil rights movement, two years after *Miranda v. Arizona* (1966) provided new rights for those accused of crimes, Congress moved to protect victims of prejudicial crimes. Its 1968 law, under Title 18, section 245, of the U.S. Code, provides, "Whoever … by force or threat of force willfully injures, intimidates or interferes with … any person because of his race, color, religion or national origin" who is engaged in specified activities—"enrolling in or attending any public school or public college" or "travelling in or using any facility of interstate commerce, or using any vehicle, terminal, or facility of any common carrier by motor, rail, water, or air"— is to be fined or imprisoned for not more than one year.

To cover crimes based on a person's gender or sexual orientation, legislation was passed by Congress in 1994 to extend federal hate crime protection to these additional groups. The Hate Crime Sentencing Enhancement Act, part of the 1994 crime bill, was spurred by state laws addressing this issue. The act required the U.S. Sentencing Commission to increase the penalties for crimes in which the victim was selected because of his or her "actual or perceived race, color, religion, national origin, ethnicity, gender, disability, or sexual orientation." The measure applies to attacks that occur on federal property and in national parks. In 1995 the sentencing commission implemented a three-level system for punishing such crimes.

Although the Gender Motivated Violence Act was included in the VIOLENCE AGAINST WOMEN ACT (1994), the remedy envisioned in the law (private civil suits) was declared unconstitutional by the U.S. Supreme Court in *United States v. Morrison* (2000).

State Law

A little more than half of the states as well as the District of Columbia have categorized as hate crimes any offenses based on sexual orientation, and almost as many have added crimes based on gender. Most state laws do not explicitly define either gender or sex to mean only a person's biological status and often use the terms interchangeably. States that do not have such laws include Alabama, Arkansas, Georgia, Idaho, Indiana, Montana, Ohio, Oklahoma, South Carolina, South Dakota, Utah, Virginia, and Wyoming.

The 1968 federal hate crime law is a "specifics acts" type of statute—that is, a defendant may be charged with a separate offense if the victim was chosen because of prejudice against him or her. Some of the states that have enacted hate crime statutes have used this same concept of a stand-alone offense. The California penal code, for one, provides that no person by force or threat of force may "willfully injure, intimidate, interfere with, oppress, or threaten any other person in the free exercise or enjoyment of any right or privilege secured … by the Constitution or laws of this state … because of one or more of the actual or perceived characteristics of the victim"; included among these are disability, gender, race or ethnicity, religion, and sexual orientation. The Illinois hate crime law also includes gender and sexual orientation and encompasses harassment by telephone in the specific acts covered. Some state laws outlaw only physical violence that is motivated by prejudice or hatred. Minnesota law addresses assault based on the "actual or perceived race, color, religion, sex, sexual orientation, disability …, age, or national origin" of the victim; the penalty for conviction is "imprisonment for not more than one year or … a fine of not more than $3,000 or both."

State Hate Crime Laws

State	Criminal Penalty	Civil Action	Based on Gender	Based on Sexual Orientation	Data Includes Gender/Sexual Orientation	Law Enforcement Training
Alabama	•					
Alaska	•		•			
Arizona	•		•	•	•	•
Arkansas		•				
California	•	•	•	•	•	•
Colorado	•	•		•		
Connecticut	•	•	•	•	•	•
Delaware	•			•		
Florida	•	•		•	•	
Georgia		•				
Hawaii	•		•	•	•	
Idaho	•	•			•	
Illinois	•	•	•	•	•	•
Indiana						
Iowa	•	•	•	•	•	•
Kansas	•			•		
Kentucky	•			•	•	•
Louisiana	•	•	•	•	•	•
Maine	•	•	•	•	•	
Maryland	•			•	•	
Massachusetts	•	•		•	•	•
Michigan	•	•	•		•	
Minnesota	•	•	•	•	•	•
Mississippi	•		•			
Missouri	•	•	•	•		
Montana	•					
Nebraska	•	•	•	•	•	
Nevada	•	•		•		
New Hampshire	•		•	•		
New Jersey	•	•	•	•	•	•
New Mexico	•		•	•	•	•
New York	•		•	•		
North Carolina	•	•	•			
North Dakota	•		•			
Ohio	•	•				
Oklahoma	•	•			•	
Oregon	•	•		•	•	•
Pennsylvania	•	•	•	•	•	

State	Criminal Penalty	Civil Action	Based on Gender	Based on Sexual Orientation	Data Includes Gender/Sexual Orientation	Law Enforcement Training
Rhode Island	•	•	•	•	•	•
South Carolina						
South Dakota	•	•				
Tennessee	•	•	•	•		
Texas	•	•	•	•	•	
Utah	•[1]					
Vermont	•	•	•	•		
Virginia	•	•			•	
Washington	•	•	•	•	•	•
West Virginia	•		•			
Wisconsin	•	•		•		
Wyoming						

1. The Utah statute ties penalties for hate crimes to violations of a victim's consitituional or civil rights.

Source: Anti-Defamation League, 2005

Other states reclassify criminal acts motivated by prejudice to increase the level of a crime and, accordingly, its punishment. For example, Florida law provides that the penalty for felonies and misdemeanors "shall be reclassified ... if the commission [of the crime] ... evidences prejudice" based on sexual orientation, among other categories, but not on sex or gender. The law goes on to reclassify a misdemeanor of the second degree to one of the first degree, and so on, up to a felony of the first degree, which is "reclassified to a life felony."

In *Wisconsin v. Mitchell* (1993), the U.S. Supreme Court reviewed the constitutionality of a Wisconsin statute authorizing increased sentences when a criminal intentionally selects a victim or a property to harm based on race, religion, color, disability, sexual orientation, national origin, or ancestry. The Court held that a racially motivated crime, as in this case, could be the basis of an increased sentence. While thoughts are protected by the FIRST AMENDMENT (1791) to the U.S. Constitution, said the justices, a physical assault is not.

Nebraska has added sexual orientation to the list of crimes for which a penalty may be enhanced. Its 1997 law provides: "Any person who commits one or more of the following criminal offenses against a person or a person's property because of the person's race, color, religion, ancestry, national origin, gender, sexual orientation, age, or disability or because of the person's association [with such persons] shall be punished [with some exceptions] by the imposition of the next higher penalty classification than the penalty prescribed for the criminal offense." There follows a list of crimes from manslaughter to criminal trespass in the second degree. The state's supreme court, in *Brandon v. County of Richardson* (2001), held law enforcement officials liable for not protecting a young girl who had been attacked and raped by several men because she assumed the sexual identity of a male. She had suffered a gender-identity disorder after being sexually abused as a child. Following the SEXUAL ASSAULT the victim, who had reported the crime to the police, was murdered along with several friends by the same assailants, who had not been apprehended by the local sheriff's office even though they had been identified.

Texas permits judges to require perpetrators of hate crimes to attend an education program designed to further acceptance and tolerance of others. Two dozen states require the collection of statistics on crimes based on gender and sexual orientation; while not including sexual orientation as a hate crime, Michigan has a similar a requirement.

Legality of Increased Sentences

The method by which sentences are increased for hate crimes has proved to be unacceptable to the courts in some cases. The Supreme Court, in *Apprendi v. New Jersey* (2000), invalidated a sentence enhancement because the state's hate crime law mandated only that judges find a defendant guilty based on a preponderance of the evidence rather than by proof beyond a reasonable doubt, as would be required for a prosecution before a jury. In *Blakely v. Washington* (2004), the Supreme Court again invalidated an additional sentence beyond the statutory maximum imposed by a state trial judge, but in this case it was because the decision had not been made by a jury. And then in *United States v. Booker* (2005), the Court ruled that under federal sentencing guidelines allowing judges to increase sentences based on evidence considered by a judge but not by a jury or admitted by the defendant, such enhancement violates the guarantees of the Sixth Amendment (1791) to the U.S. Constitution; the amendment protects the right to have an impartial jury determine one's guilt or innocence.

This line of Supreme Court decisions, besides requiring a revamping of federal sentencing guidelines to conform to the Sixth Amendment standard, will produce some impact on those states whose hate crime laws most closely follow the federal model. To conform to these decisions, they will have to redraft their laws to require that a sentence enhancement, if the defendant demands, be made by a jury and not solely by a judge. Another possible impact was considered by a federal district court in *United States v. Siegelbaum* (2005); the issue here was whether the

Court's decision in *Booker* is retroactive, so that those convicted under a sentence enhancement scheme of the type found by the Court to be unconstitutional can challenge the imposition of additional punishment.

The traditions of Anglo-American jurisprudence are clearly incompatible with punishment of thoughts, but where is the line between thoughts and criminal motivations to be drawn, and by whom? American law has long recognized degrees of criminality; crimes of passion, for instance, have generally received lesser punishment. To deter hate crimes, society has allowed itself to send a message to those who would act on their dislike of minorities. The Supreme Court has at least required that sentence enhancements under such hate crime laws be made in accordance with constitutional guarantees for criminal trials. Broader questions include whether all states will ultimately adopt hate crime laws and which victim classifications will be included. As with many areas of sexual behavior, there is little consensus on these issues.

See also Homosexuality; Sex Offenses; Sexual Harassment; Telephone Sex; Transsexualism; Victims' Rights.

HAYS CODE

See Entertainment Industry.

HEALTHY MARRIAGE INITIATIVE

President George W. Bush announced in 2001 that his administration was "committed to strengthening the American family." By the next year a so-called Healthy Marriage Initiative aimed at establishing federal programs to promote marriage, especially among low-income citizens, had been launched. It remains unclear whether Americans' decreased interest in marriage and relatively high divorce rate—about one million marriages are terminated each year—are due to irreversible social changes or a failure of education about marriage and lack of support for the traditional two-parent family.

The initial Healthy Marriage proposal called for at least $1.5 billion for training to help couples develop interpersonal skills that sustain "healthy marriages." At the beginning of 2004, a presidential election year, the Bush administration announced plans to strengthen the Healthy Marriage Initiative as part of the Personal Responsibility, Work and Family Promotion Act of 2005, an expanded reauthorization of a 1996 welfare reform law. Implementation of the initiative is currently being overseen by the Administration for Children and Families in the U.S. DEPARTMENT OF HEALTH AND HUMAN SERVICES. The program funds public advertising campaigns on the value of a healthy marriage, education about marriage and relationship skills, premarital education for couples, marriage enhancement training, divorce reduction programs, and efforts to reduce the disincentives to marriage in means-tested government aid programs. It also encourages state-run programs to promote marriage, discourage divorce, and create "mentorship" programs for struggling families. The education programs are directed primarily to the high school level.

A government report on the initiative's accomplishments for the years 2002 through 2005 pointed to progress in carrying out the initiative "in coordination with many public, faith- and community-based organizations and private partners." The report noted increased "access to marriage strengthening services and awareness about the value of healthy marriage for children, adults, and communities." During the period, 170 grants totaling $61 million were awarded, and two programs worked with African American and Latino communities. However, there is as yet no evidence that the continuing decline of marriage has been stemmed: the percentage of married Americans over the age of eighteen years decreased from 72 percent in 1970 to 59 percent in 2002.

A year before the Healthy Marriage Initiative was launched, the Supreme Court handed down its decision in LAWRENCE V. TEXAS (2003), ruling that state governments could not criminalize private consensual sexual activity by adult homosexuals. Clearly the government was sending two different messages: one, that the federal government should be involved in encouraging heterosexual couples to marry and stay married (the DEFENSE OF MARRIAGE ACT of 1996 defines marriage for the purpose of federal activities as only between a man and a woman); and two, that state governments may not criminalize sexual behavior between consenting adults—married or not, heterosexual or not.

From the beginning the Healthy Marriage Initiative has been linked with the proposal by political conservatives to ban SAME-SEX MARRIAGE at the state and federal levels. Although the Defense of Marriage Act limits federal programs to heterosexual couples, a spate of state constitutional amendments to the same effect has emboldened a movement, supported by President Bush, to add a ban on same-sex marriage to the U.S. Constitution (unsuccessful in CONGRESS in both 2004 and 2006). These efforts were intensified by a decision from Massachusetts's highest court, which ruled in *Goodridge v. Department of Public Health* (2003) that the Commonwealth of Massachusetts could not deny the privilege of marriage to a same-sex couple.

Contact: Healthy Marriage Initiative, Administration for Children and Families, U.S. Department of Health and Human Services, 200 Independence Avenue, SW, Washington, DC 20201 (202-619-0257). www.acf.hhs.gov/healthymarriage/funding/index.html.

See also FEDERAL MARRIAGE AMENDMENT; HOMOSEXUALITY; SEX EDUCATION.

HUGH HEFNER

The first issue of *Playboy* magazine in December 1953 featured Marilyn Monroe and an editorial by its founder and editor in chief, Hugh Hefner, explaining, "We enjoy . . . inviting in a female acquaintance for a quiet discussion on Picasso, Nietzsche, jazz, sex . . . , [and if] we are able to give the American male

Publication of Hugh Hefner's *Playboy* magazine helped fuel the sexual revolution in the 1960s and 1970s. "Hef" parlayed his "*Playboy* philosophy" into a sexual entertainment industry, with Playboy Clubs, a cable television channel, and other media products. Here he is surrounded in 1962 by Playmates of the Month.

a few extra laughs and a little diversion from the anxieties of the Atomic Age, we feel we've justified our existence." The first issue sold out its 51,100 copies and ushered in a new era of sexual freedom for male fantasies. Today, with some three million subscribers, *Playboy* remains among the top magazines in terms of circulation.

Hugh Marston Hefner was born on April 9, 1926, in Chicago. He completed high school in 1944 and was honorably discharged from the army two years later. With a reportedly high I.Q. and natural management skills, Hefner left his job as a copywriter for *Esquire* magazine after two years to create a new type of periodical. Based on an idea he developed at the University of Illinois, he wanted to incorporate photographs of nude women, articles by noted writers (as in *Esquire*), and interviews with leading celebrities and world figures. The first name proposed for the new magazine was *Stag Party*, which conjures up beer, smoke, and pornographic movies. But Hefner wanted a more sophisticated image, as suggested by *Playboy*—a name that reflected his own personality.

The magazine's initial success catapulted its founder into a business empire that grew to include a nationwide chain of Playboy Clubs, whose waitresses wore the sexy "bunny" outfits made famous by the parent publication. (Before she became a feminist icon, the journalist Gloria Steinem went underground as a Playboy Bunny in 1963 to write an exposé for *Show* magazine. Some of the bunnies disputed her characterization of them as unhappy, naive, exploited victims.) Hefner even hosted *Playboy's Penthouse* on television in 1959, a weekly talk show set in a bachelor pad with celebrities such as the singers Ella Fitzgerald and Nat King Cole and the comedian LENNY BRUCE. His Playboy Mansion in Chicago, purchased in 1959, became the scene of lively parties once Hefner became a bachelor following his divorce that year. In 1963 he was acquitted of OBSCENITY in Chicago over a charge involving a publication entitled *The Nudest Jayne Mansfield.*

Playboy spawned competition, such as *Penthouse* magazine, that pushed the envelope of sexual explicitness. Soon even more candid periodicals began appearing on newsstands and in stores open to the general public. To Hefner, *Playboy's* theme was antipuritanical, "[n]ot just in regard to sex, but the whole range of play and pleasure." It was in *Playboy* that President Jimmy Carter made his now-famous admission that he had lusted in his heart. In 1988 Hefner turned over the operations of Playboy Enterprises to his daughter, Christie, giving his attention to more modern MEDIA, including an electronic version of the magazine.

The Playboy Entertainment Group's entrance into the cable television market was followed by an attempt by CONGRESS to censor the Playboy cable channel and similar entertainment under section 505 of the Telecommunications Act of 1996. The legislation targeted shows that were "primarily dedicated to sexually oriented programming," and it required television operators such as the Playboy Group to "fully scramble or otherwise fully block" transmissions during hours when CHILDREN might be viewing.

In 2000 the U.S. Supreme Court, in *United States v. Playboy Entertainment Group, Inc.,* struck down the act. The Court declared that "a content-based speech restriction . . . can stand [under the FIRST AMENDMENT to the U.S. Constitution] only if it satisfies strict scrutiny." This meant that the government must prove a compelling interest in requiring the restriction of free speech, that the law must be "narrowly tailored to promote" that interest, and that no "less restrictive alternative," such as subscriber blocking procedures, is available. Because parental blocking was in fact available for cable channels, unlike most broadcast channels, the section of the law was held to be unconstitutional. "Simply put," wrote Associate Justice Anthony Kennedy for the Court, "targeted blocking is less restrictive than banning, and the Government cannot ban speech if targeted blocking is a feasible and effective means of furthering its compelling interests."

According to Hefner, his own philosophy mirrors the Supreme Court's language in the *Playboy* case. He has stated that, as a parent himself, he believes that parents should be empowered with blocking devices to keep ADULT MATERIALS away from children. Subsequent Supreme Court decisions in cases such as *Reno v. American Civil Liberties Union* (1997) and *Ashcroft v. American Civil Liberties Union* (2002, 2004) extended the Court's "strict scrutiny" of congressional attempts to restrict First Amendment guarantees in order to protect children from obscene material on the INTERNET.

A pioneer in the movement to open American society to greater sexual freedom, Hefer has lent his name to the Hugh M. Hefner First Amendment Awards, established in 1979 by Christie Hefner "to honor individuals who have made significant contributions in the vital effort to protect and enhance First Amendment rights for Americans." Hefner, recovered from a stroke in 1985, has purchased a crypt in Westwood Village Memorial Cemetery in Los Angeles. It is next to where Marilyn Monroe is interred so that he can be buried beside her.

See also CHILD ONLINE PROTECTION ACT; ENTERTAINMENT INDUSTRY; FEDERAL COMMUNICATIONS COMMISSION; NUDITY; PORNOGRAPHY; WOMEN'S RIGHTS.

HOMOSEXUALITY

A homosexual (from the Greek *homos,* meaning same) is a person who is sexually attracted to members of his or her own sex. *Gay* is the term generally used to refer to male homosexuals or sometimes to the entire homosexual community, while female homosexuals are typically called lesbians. Homosexuals are one of the groups considered to be sexual minorities—anyone who is not heterosexual. Others include bisexuals, people who are attracted to persons of either sex; and transsexual and transgender persons, individuals who have the reproductive organs of one sex but who consider their GENDER to be the other sex (most often biological men with the self-image of females). Sexual minorities sometimes use the initials GLBT (gay, lesbian, bisexual, and transgender) or LGBT to refer to themselves as a group.

Homosexuality has been recognized throughout recorded history and has been accepted openly in some cultures but vilified in others. In the United States, a person's assertion that he or she is a homosexual has various consequences, depending on the person and the context. Barney Frank, a member of the U.S. House of Representatives from Massachusetts "came out of the closet" some years ago and continues to be reelected from his district. In contrast, James McGreevey, the married governor of New Jersey and a father, reluctantly acknowledged his homosexuality in 2004 and quickly announced his resignation from office, in part because of an extramarital affair with a gay lover. Federal and state laws mirror this ambivalence about homosexuality, resulting in legalized DISCRIMINATION against homosexuals and denial of rights accorded heterosexual citizens.

Gay Rights

The civil rights and WOMEN'S RIGHTS movements in the mid-twentieth century helped spark a similar effort by sexual minorities to publicly declare their sexual orientation and to work toward complete integration into the mainstream of American society. To a large extent, blacks and women today enjoy EQUAL RIGHTS under federal and state law. Sexual minorities, whose largest membership encompasses those who profess to be homosexuals, have been less successful.

A number of reasons for this failure can be cited:

(1) Lawmakers and the courts, especially the U.S. Supreme Court, have identified grounds for maintaining legal discrimination against homosexuals, for instance, in restricting military service, denying marriage and partnership rights, and standing in the way of child custody and adoption.

(2) Many religious leaders argue that homosexual sex acts, more generally referred to as sodomy, are immoral and should not be condoned.

(3) People often fear, whether rationally or not, that homosexuality is a learned response and that CHILDREN thus should be protected from hearing about homosexuality or being exposed to the homosexual "lifestyle."

Homosexuals have obtained specific legal recognition of some rights, however. One is the right to equal treatment by the federal government with regard to hiring, firing, and promotion; this change was due in part to the pioneering efforts of FRANKLIN KAMENY, who challenged his firing in 1957 from the U.S. Army Map Service for being a homosexual. The right of adult homosexuals to engage in consensual sexual activity in private was finally upheld by the Supreme Court in LAWRENCE V. TEXAS (2003) as a constitutional guarantee of PRIVACY.

A few states extend to homosexuals the right to have families by adopting children or using some form of ASSISTED REPRODUCTIVE TECHNOLOGY. Ohio's supreme court in *In Re Adoption of Charles B.* (1990), for example, reinstated a trial court determination that a gay man could adopt a child under Ohio law. But Utah in 2000 amended its adoption laws to provide, "The Legislature specifically finds that it is not in a child's best interest to be adopted by a person or persons who are cohabiting in a relationship that is not a legally valid and binding marriage under the laws of this state." Thus, because homosexuals cannot marry in Utah, they are precluded from adopting; however, the law does not prohibit "the court's placement of a child with a single adult who is not cohabiting."

Because all states except Massachusetts now prohibit SAME-SEX MARRIAGE, most homosexuals cannot marry and may be precluded from adopting or having children by means of assisted reproduction under some state laws. Lesbians, of course, can have children by artificial means, just as can heterosexual women, married or unmarried. Surrogacy laws in Washington State do not require the intended parents to be a married couple; therefore, an unmarried man may become a parent through the use of a surrogate mother. Arkansas, a progressive state regarding parenting via surrogacy, goes even further and expressly permits an unmarried man to contract with a surrogate mother for a child, allowing intended parents to be a married couple or an unmarried male or female. New Hampshire and Washington, while not limiting parents to married couples, discriminate against single men by not allowing a biological or birth mother to contract away her parental rights.

In addition to the right of homosexuals to marry recognized by Massachusetts, Vermont and Connecticut have created civil unions that provide many of the same benefits of marriage. Some states and municipalities and private businesses recognize domestic partnerships between members of the same sex for the purpose of extending rights and benefits usually reserved to heterosexual married couples. Although some 7,500 employers in the United States offer health insurance to employees through domestic partnerships, Virginia is the only state that specifically prohibits private employers from including anyone other than a legal spouse or a dependent child in an employee's health plan.

Some state laws against HATE CRIMES include actions against homosexuals. In 2004 Colorado added to the state's hate crime law a measure extending protection to homosexuals; at the same time the governor vetoed a bill that would have extended protection against workplace discrimination to gays and lesbians. New Jersey has a so-called bias crime statute that allows an enhanced sentence if a trial judge finds, by a preponderance of the evidence, that a defendant committed a crime to intimidate a person or because of factors such as gender or sexual orientation; the punishment can reach 110 years' imprisonment. Such maximum penalties are rarely applied, however; in 2005 a man charged with fatally stabbing a fifteen-year-old lesbian was allowed to plead guilty to aggravated manslaughter "with bias intimidation," which carries a penalty of only twenty to twenty-five years in jail.

Homosexual Discrimination

At the federal level the two major areas of discrimination against homosexuals involve marriage and employment.

Marriage and Personal Relationships. The issue of allowing homosexuals to marry and be accorded all the rights, privileges, and obligations that heterosexual couples have under the law with respect to personal rights, property, pensions, and tax benefits has been hotly contested recently. In 1996 the DEFENSE OF MARRIAGE ACT was passed by CONGRESS to bar recognition of a MARRIAGE or a similar relationship except those between one man and one woman. This law affects all federal rights and obligations, including benefits under federal programs and tax laws. A movement, supported by President George W. Bush, has also been launched to amend the U.S. Constitution to ban homosexuals from enjoying any marriage rights or privileges. With the exception of Massachusetts, all states currently discriminate against homosexuals with regard to the right to marry, although alternate relationships have been offered in Vermont and Connecticut.

Employment. Regarding discrimination in employment, sexual minorities have been far less successful than blacks and women in invoking statutory or constitutional law to counteract blatant discrimination. Federal courts have been fairly consistent in ruling that discrimination claims by sexual minorities are not covered under Title VII of the Civil Rights Act of 1964, a section added to make sex as well as race, color, RELIGION, and national origin a protected class in the workplace. A federal appeals court, in *DeSantis v. Pacific Telephone and Telegraph Co.* (1979), concluded, "We ... hold that discrimination because of effeminacy, like discrimination because of homosexuality ... or transsexualism ..., does not fall within the purview of Title VII."

However, in *Shahar v. Bowers* (1998), another appeals court seemed to indicate that cases of discrimination against homosexuals in the workplace may turn on the nature of the job. Here the court found that a woman who symbolically married another woman and was fired from her job by the attorney general of Georgia had no recourse; the nature of the position on the attorney general's staff, reasoned the court, required a certain element of discretion, thus no provisions of the U.S. Constitution barred the attorney general from exercising his personal discretion in making the personnel decision in question.

As for the MILITARY, the policy that was adopted in 1993 during President Bill Clinton's first year—often referred to as "don't ask, don't tell"—allows gays and lesbians to serve in the military as long as they do not acknowledge or announce their sexual orientation. Five years later President Clinton in 1998 signed Executive Order 11478, adding sexual orientation to the list of classifications such as race and national origin to be protected from discrimination in federal employment. (The Civil Service Commission had barred discrimination against homosexuals in 1975.) A policy instituted by the administration of George W. Bush in 2005, however, could make it more difficult for homosexuals to obtain security clearances for government work; whereas previous guidelines barred sexual orientation from being used as a "disqualifying factor," the new rules, among other changes, say merely that it cannot be the sole basis for rejecting a candidate.

Some states have laws protecting homosexuals in the workplace. New Mexico, for instance, makes it unlawful for an employer to discriminate on the basis of an "employee's sexual orientation or gender identity . . . if the employer has fifteen or more employees"; exceptions are based on bona fide occupational qualifications or a statutory prohibition. New York law provides some protections; under the state's human rights law, the "opportunity to obtain employment without discrimination because of age, race, creed, color, national origin, sexual orientation, military status, sex or marital status is hereby recognized as and declared to be a civil right." In 2000 Maine voters narrowly rejected a referendum to approve an act by the state legislature extending to all citizens, regardless of their sexual orientation, the same basic rights against discrimination guaranteed to other citizens in employment, housing, public accommodation, and credit.

Obviously there is little consistency among the states on this issue. California's highest court, in *Gay Law Students Association v. Pacific Telephone and Telegraph Co.* (1979), ruled that as a matter of civil rights a state may not exclude homosexuals as a class from employment opportunities without showing that their homosexuality renders them unfit; the decision was based on the equal protection clauses of both the state and federal constitutions, which prohibit any state or government entity from discriminating against any class of individuals in employment decisions.

AIDS-HIV. Acquired immunodeficiency syndrome and human immunodeficiency virus (AIDS-HIV) have disproportionally impacted the male homosexual community. According to congressional testimony during debate in the House of Representatives on the Americans with Disabilities Act in 1990, some 70 percent of Americans who had then contracted the HIV virus were male homosexuals; as of late 2004, the percentage had dropped to 58. Because of the fear by many members of Congress that they would be rewarding behavior they consider to be immoral, the ADA contains a provision that "homosexuality and bisexuality are not impairments, and as such are not disabilities under this Act."

After the AIDS-HIV epidemic came to public attention in the 1980s, some religious leaders declared that this infection, which often leads to death, was a punishment of male homosexuals sent by God. Undoubtedly a widespread belief remains that the homosexual way of life is responsible for this most horrific of SEXUALLY TRANSMITTED DISEASES. AIDS-HIV has been linked with homosexuality, such that homosexual males in particular are discriminated against on the grounds that they may carry the virus. This is a problem especially in occupations involving physical contact or exposure to bodily fluids such as blood.

Sex Education. Nearly twenty years ago, a conservative U.S. senator, Jesse Helms of North Carolina, began adding "no promo homo" language to bills in an effort to cut off any federal funding that might appear to condone or promote homosexuality. SEX EDUCATION programs including information on homosexuality began to come under close scrutiny. Although independent studies have concluded that teaching efforts that honestly and openly address homosexuality benefit all students, the federal and state governments have in some instances refused to include information on homosexuality in taxpayer-funded education programs. Alabama, Arizona, Texas, and Utah are among the states that restrict what may be taught about sexual minority issues. The Arizona statute, for example, provides: "No [school] district shall include in its course of instruction [language] which: 1. Promotes a homosexual lifestyle. 2. Portrays homosexuality as a positive alternative lifestyle. 3. Suggests that some methods of sex are safe methods of homosexual sex."

Other Issues. With respect to social, political, and community life, the Supreme Court in *Boy Scouts of America v. Dale* (2000) held that the protection of "expressive" association afforded by the FIRST AMENDMENT (1791) to the U.S. Constitution permitted the Boy Scouts to reject as a leader an avowed homosexual adult who was a gay-rights activist. In *Hurley v. Irish-American Gay Group of Boston* (1995), the Court also held that the organizers of Boston's St. Patrick's Day Parade were under no obligation to include a homosexual group in their activities.

However, in *Romer v. Evans* (1996), the Supreme Court found unconstitutional an antihomosexual constitutional amendment to a state constitution. The voter-approved Colorado amendment barred any state or local agency from offering homosexuals special protection, such as the 2004 inclusion of crimes against homosexuals in the state's hate crime law. Giving the opinion of the Court, Associate Justice Anthony M. Kennedy declared that "we cannot accept the view that [the] ... prohibition on specific legal protections does no more than deprive homosexuals of special rights. To the contrary, the amendment imposes a special disability upon those persons alone."

Extrapolating from information collected during the 2000 census about homosexual partners living together, in a nation of some 300 million persons somewhat over 10 million are gays and lesbians. The rights of this many citizens would seem to be an important matter for the legal system of a constitutional democracy to deal with openly and consistently. Yet the U.S. legal system does anything but that. Part of the difficulty seems to be rooted in the view of many Americans that homosexuality is not genetically determined, as are the biological differences between men and women; it is often viewed as a "lifestyle" choice that is immoral. To date no scientific evidence conclusively proves or disproves the theory that homosexuality is genetically determined; some studies do indicate that genetic factors in male homosexuals inherited from their mothers, together with triggering experiences in the early stages of development, may influence a propensity toward homosexual behavior. Genetic determination would mean that homosexual behavior is not a choice but rather an inherent and immutable behavioral trait—one that should no more be the basis for discrimination than blue eyes or brown skin.

See also BISEXUALITY; FEDERAL MARRIAGE AMENDMENT; GENETICS; TRANSSEXUALISM; TRANSVESTISM.

HUMAN RIGHTS CAMPAIGN

With nearly 600,000 members, the Human Rights Campaign is the largest gay, lesbian, bisexual, and transgender (GLBT) organization in the United States. It was founded as the Human Rights Campaign Fund in 1980 to counter the successful organizing activities of politically conservative groups such as the National Conservative Political Action Committee and the Moral Majority. The HRC seeks to ensure EQUAL RIGHTS and protection for GLBT citizens at work, at home, and in the community.

In 1982 the organization adopted as a part of its bylaws the avowed purpose of advancing "the cause of lesbian and gay civil rights by supporting and educating candidates for federal elective office." Later that year it held a fundraiser in New York City at which Walter Mondale, the former U.S. vice president, was the keynote speaker, and by November $800,000 in contributions had been collected. To increase its effectiveness and influence on lawmakers, the group merged with the Gay Rights National Lobby in 1985 (it dropped "Fund" from its name in 1995).

In addition to contributing to political candidates and lobbying for changes in laws regarding sexual minorities, the organization worked with other groups to defeat the 1987 Supreme Court nomination of Robert H. Bork. It has also been active in supporting funding and research related to the AIDS epidemic as well as protecting rights of victims of the debilitating disease. The organization's efforts also contributed to the passage by CONGRESS of the Hate Crimes Statistics Act of 1990, which requires the federal government to keep track of HATE CRIMES committed each year; in recognition of those efforts the Human Rights Fund was invited by President George H. W. Bush to the signing of the law. In 1994 Congress passed the Hate Crime Sentencing Enhancement Act, providing greater punishment for those who perpetrate federally defined hate crimes, including those who target gays and lesbians.

Not all of the HRC's efforts have been successful. The Employment Non-Discrimination Act, first introduced in Congress in 1994 and sponsored by Representatives Barney Frank and Gerry Studds (both homosexuals), has not been enacted. The act would have prohibited DISCRIMINATION in employment based on sexual orientation. Currently some thirty-four states permit the firing of a person because of his or her sexual orientation, and forty-four states allow a person to be fired based on GENDER identity. In 1998, however, President Bill Clinton signed an executive order prohibiting discrimination against homosexuals in the federal civil service; HRC acted to prevent attempts by members of Congress to water down the executive order's effect.

Today the HRC's mission includes supporting health issues such as AIDS-HIV and special concerns relating to lesbian health; inclusion of crimes based on sexual orientation in the definition of hate crimes; public education about discrimination faced by the transgender community; changes in the military's treatment of homosexuals and transsexuals; and opposition to judicial nominees who would deny basic justice and equality for GLBT Americans.

The HRC is governed by a board of directors. The Human Rights Campaign Foundation, an affiliated organization that does research and provides public education and programming, has its own board. An additional HRC board of governors is responsible for coordinating fundraising and volunteer activities.

Contact: Human Rights Campaign, 1640 Rhode Island Avenue, NW, Washington, DC 20036-3278 (800-777-4723). www.hrc.org.

See also BISEXUALITY; HOMOSEXUALITY; TRANSSEXUALISM; TRANSVESTISM.

HUMAN TRAFFICKING

Slavery, a form of trafficking in humans, was condoned under the U.S. Constitution until it was abolished by the Thirteenth Amendment (1865), although under Article I, section 9, the importation of slaves into the country was protected only until 1808. Slavery still exists in many forms around the world. As one example, after the Union of Soviet Socialist Republics was dissolved in 1991, trafficking for sexual purposes greatly increased in Eastern Europe. The International Labor Organization, which is associated with the United Nations, recently reported that of the approximately 12.3 million persons who are subjected to some form of forced labor, 11 percent, or nearly 1.4 million, are being sexually exploited.

As for the magnitude of the problem in the United States, reports vary depending on the source. In 2003 the U.S. Department of State estimated the annual number of victims of human trafficking for sexual purposes to be about twenty thousand persons, including males as well as females. For the most part, these are immigrants brought into the United States under false pretenses.

Coerced sexual behavior, including kidnapping and transportation of women and CHILDREN for sexual slavery or PROSTITUTION, is probably as old as human history. In 1877 the first meeting of the International Abolitionist Federation began focusing world attention on the "organized trafficking in women." The threat posed by the importation of women into the United States for prostitution led CONGRESS to federalize the immigration laws in 1875 and prohibit the "importation into the United States of women for the purposes of prostitution."

Later reports of international prostitution rings that lured young women into "white slavery," as this form of prostitution was often described, resulted in the White Slave Traffic Act of 1910. This law became known as the Mann Act after U.S. Representative James R. Mann of Illinois, who introduced the legislation. It criminalized the transportation of a woman or a girl in interstate commerce "for the purposes of prostitution or debauchery, or for any other immoral purpose, or with the intent and purpose to induce, entice, or compel such woman or girl to become a prostitute."

Federal laws on the subject evolved into a cumbersome process under many uncoordinated criminal, labor, and immigration statutes. A man who drove a woman across a state line for personal relations might be ensnared in the net. The U.S. Code under Title 18, Crimes, section 2423, Transportation of Minors, has since been amended to read: "Whoever knowingly transports any individual under the age of 18 years in interstate or foreign commerce, or in any Territory or Possession of the United States, with intent that such individual engage in prostitution, or in any sexual activity for which any person can be charged with a criminal offense, shall be fined under this title or imprisoned not more than ten years, or both."

In 1999 several bills were introduced in Congress to address the problem of increased human trafficking. On October 28, 2000, the Victims of Trafficking and Violence Protection Act, which included most provisions of several separate bills, was signed into law to prevent trafficking, protect victims, and punish those engaged in sexual slavery. The act, which was hailed as the most significant human-rights legislation of the 106th Congress, was proposed by Senator Paul Wellstone of Minnesota, who died in a 2002 airplane crash. The new law created a single definition of sex trafficking that cures the previous problem of having to prosecute cases under several separate laws. This definition includes aspects of forcible RAPE but also notes that sex trafficking includes "violations of other laws, including labor and immigration codes and laws against kidnapping, slavery, false imprisonment, assault, battery, pandering, fraud, and extortion."

The act also increased the penalties—in some cases from ten to twenty years' imprisonment—and made a life sentence the punishment for aggravated sexual abuse or attempted murder. Other features include protection for women victims of violence and special immigration visas that allow alien victims of "severe forms of trafficking" to stay in the United States. Public education is an important element of the law, and victims are rewarded for cooperating in the prosecution of those who engage in this degrading business.

A major drawback of the act, however, is the lack of enforcement, which requires a commitment of government resources to punish violators. There is also no guarantee that victims who cooperate with law enforcement will be adequately protected or that some women who are eager to immigrate to the United States will not attempt to make false claims to obtain protection and special immigration treatment. Some feminist groups argue that a ban on all voluntary and involuntary commercial sex acts is a better solution, while yet others argue for legalizing prostitution, unionizing sex workers, and letting the government regulate and tax such businesses.

The Victims of Trafficking and Violence Protection Act was reauthorized by Congress in 2003 with enhanced features, making convictions and sentencing as important as investigations and prosecutions in evaluating how countries are doing in their efforts to stem human trafficking throughout the world. Changes emphasized better monitoring and greater access to law enforcement data related to trafficking. Another federal law passed in 2003, the PROTECT Act, addresses international sex tourism, the commercial exploitation of children, and federal offenses such as CHILD ABUSE, kidnapping of children, and child torture.

In 2003 a federal court of appeals, in *United States v. Martinez-Candejas,* upheld enhanced sentencing guidelines for crimes involving, among other offenses, human trafficking and the smuggling of aliens for profit. The same year, in *United States v. Kil Soo Lee,* a jury in a federal district court trial convicted a defendant in American Samoa on several counts involving involuntary servitude, an offense related to sex trafficking, which the State Department, in its Trafficking in Persons Report released on June 14, 2004, has characterized as "the largest trafficking prosecution ever brought by the Department of Justice."

Contact: U.S. Department of State, Office to Monitor and Combat Trafficking in Persons, 2201 C Street, NW, Washington, DC 20520 (888-373-7888). www.state.gov/g/tip.

See also SEXUAL ASSAULT.

i

ILLEGITIMACY

Illegitimacy arises when a child is born to unmarried parents or when the MARRIAGE during which the child was born is annulled and therefore considered null and void from the beginning. An illegitimate child has also been variously called a bastard, an out-of-wedlock child, or a nonmarital child. In 1925 New York State decreed that the terms *bastard* and *illegitimate child* would henceforth no longer be used in public documents and would be replaced with *child born out of wedlock*.

Throughout much of American history, the illegitimate child was an outcast stigmatized for the sin of the father and the mother. Under the law illegitimate CHILDREN were generally denied the rights, privileges, and benefits extended to legitimate children. A major change occurred when the U.S. Supreme Court held for the first time in *Levy v. Louisiana* (1968) that illegitimate children were "persons" for purposes of applying the equal protection clause of the Fourteenth Amendment (1868) to the U.S. Constitution. In this case, the Court ruled that the states were precluded from denying illegitimate children some of the same rights granted to legitimate children.

In *Levy*, which involved a claim for the wrongful death of a mother on whom several illegitimate children were dependent, the Supreme Court said: "Why should the illegitimate child be denied rights merely because of his birth out of wedlock? He certainly is subject to all the responsibilities of a citizen, including the payment of taxes and conscription under the Selective Service Act. How under our constitutional regime can he be denied correlative rights which other citizens enjoy?"

Inheritance

Since the *Levy* decision, the Supreme Court has extended its ruling to include a number of benefits legally available to legitimate children, such as CHILD SUPPORT and Social Security benefits. But the right of illegitimate children to inherit property has been more difficult to equalize. For example, in *Labine v. Vincent* (1971), the Court upheld Louisiana's denial of an illegitimate child's right to intestate succession, even though she was publicly acknowledged by her father. However, in *Trimble v. Gordon* (1977), the Court went the other way and found a violation of the equal protection clause in an Illinois law allowing nonmarital children to inherit from their fathers only if the fathers had subsequently married the mothers or had acknowledged their PATERNITY.

The Supreme Court's difficulty with inheritance by illegitimate children became more clear when in *Lalli v. Lalli* (1978) it upheld New York State's statutory requirement that a determination of paternity be made by a court before the right to inherit would be extended to a nonmarital child. In this case the Court noted that the state has a legitimate interest in requiring sufficient proof of the right to inherit "to provide for the just and orderly disposition of property at death."

Citizenship

The same problem—proof of paternal relationship—was again evident in *Nguyen v. Immigration and Naturalization Service* (2001). The question in *Nguyen* involved a child born out of wedlock in Vietnam to a Vietnamese mother and an American father. Different rules exist regarding how an illegitimate child born overseas can obtain U.S. citizenship, depending on whether the mother or the father is a U.S. citizen. U.S. law makes a person born in the country a citizen by birth, but someone born outside the United States is subject to certain rules with respect to obtaining U.S. citizenship. These rules are relaxed where there is a special bond between a child born outside the country, as in the case of a child born to a U.S. citizen mother or father.

Tuan Anh Nguyen was being threatened with deportation after pleading guilty in a Texas court to two counts of SEXUAL ASSAULT on a child. His claim of U.S. citizenship through his U.S.-citizen father was rejected in the deportation proceedings. Nguyen appealed, alleging that different treatment for children seeking U.S. citizenship based on the mother's or father's citizenship was sex DISCRIMINATION and therefore a violation of the Constitution's equal protection clause.

In *Nguyen* the Supreme Court concluded that the immigration law's GENDER-based classification served important governmental objectives. It requires that one of three steps—legitimization (marriage), a declaration of paternity under oath by the father, or a court order of paternity—be taken when the nonmarital father is a U.S. citizen. When the mother is a U.S. citizen, these steps are not required because her relationship to the child seeking U.S. citizenship, the Court noted, is verifiable from the fact of having given birth to the child; the father's paternity is not so easily proven. If the U.S.-citizen father has not in some way established a bond with the nonmarital child, then proof is lacking that a connection with the United States was established sufficient to allow special treatment for the child in obtaining citizenship (as opposed to the naturalization

process available to other immigrants). The Court concluded that there is nothing irrational or improper in recognizing that at the moment of birth—a critical event in the tradition of citizenship law—the mother's knowledge of the child and the fact of parenthood have been established in a way not guaranteed to the unwed father.

Some state laws have requirements similar to those set forth in the *Nguyen* decision. For the purposes of inheritance in New York State, a nonmarital child may be considered the legitimate child of his father: "he and his issue inherit from his father and his paternal kindred" if a court order declares paternity; or "the father of the child has signed an instrument acknowledging paternity"; or "paternity has been established by clear and convincing evidence and the father . . . has openly and notoriously acknowledged the child as his own;" or "a blood genetic marker test had been administered to the father which together with other evidence establishes paternity by clear and convincing evidence."

Assisted Reproduction

Another legal aspect of illegitimacy involves ASSISTED REPRODUCTIVE TECHNOLOGY. State statutes generally deny a third-party sperm donor any parental rights with respect to children born as a result of assisted reproduction. In some cases, however, a donor may have such rights. In *Tripp v. Hinckley* (2002), a New York court allowed the male donor parental rights, even though by written agreement he was permitted only limited visitation rights. This agreement between the gay male donor and the lesbian mother provided that his name would be put on the birth certificate as the father and that the two children born would view him as their father. Most important, the court found that that it would be in the best interests of the children to extend parental rights to the father.

Although the laws denying rights to illegitimate children have been relaxed in the last several decades, nonmarital children are still at a disadvantage in a society that treats marriage as the only legal and proper institution for procreating and rearing children. Just as the stigmatization of citizens born with a homosexual orientation is being questioned today, so too is the morality of treating as second-class citizens children who are illegitimate through no fault of their own.

See also ANNULMENT; MOTHERHOOD; UNMARRIED PARENTS.

IN VITRO FERTILIZATION

See ASSISTED REPRODUCTIVE TECHNOLOGY.

INCEST

For the ancient rulers of Egypt, having sexual relations with a relative was not an uncommon practice. Pharaoh Ikhnaton, who reigned from 1385 to 1358 B.C.E., for example, married his maternal cousin, Nefertiti. But throughout history, incest (from the Latin *in*, meaning not, and *castus*, meaning pure) has been one of the strongest human taboos, prohibited by custom or law. A list in the Old Testament of the relatives with whom sexual relations are forbidden extends to the maternal grandmother's paternal brother's wife. The father of psychoanalysis, Sigmund Freud (1865–1939), reached back to the ancient Greek story of a man who unwittingly killed his father and married his mother to describe the Oedipus complex: a male child's strong and persistent attachment to his mother.

The English playwright William Shakespeare (1564–1616) has the character Hamlet, whose mother has married his uncle, declaim: "Let not the royal bed of Denmark be [a] couch for luxury and damned incest." Some forms of incest may seem to be victimless crimes, as in *Hamlet*, in which a man marries his deceased brother's wife, or when an adopted son marries his adoptive mother's sister. Nonetheless the taboo against incest and the disruptions and traumas that may be associated with it have led lawmakers and judges to treat various forms of this sexual behavior as a serious crime.

The Universal Taboo

Incest is a crime in all states. For example, the West Virginia code declares that a "person is guilty of incest when such person engages in sexual intercourse or sexual intrusion with his or her father, mother, brother, sister, daughter, son, grandfather, grandmother, grandson, granddaughter, nephew, niece, uncle or aunt." Adopted CHILDREN and their parents are included. A person convicted of incest in the state is subject to a five- to fifteen-year sentence, a fine of $500 to $5,000, or both. If the victim is a minor, the offender may also be ordered to pay for "the cost of medical, psychological or psychiatric treatment of the victim."

Cousins can marry in twenty states and the District of Columbia; six states allow MARRIAGE of first cousins only under certain circumstances. Twenty-four states bar all marriage between first cousins.

As recounted by a state court of appeals for Washington in *State v. Kaiser* (1983), incest was once prohibited by church law but is now a statutory crime barring sexual relations between people related by blood and marriage. According to the court, the prevention of birth defects (because of participants' close genetic relationship) is only one reason for the prohibition. Other rationales include the protection of family harmony and of children from the abuse of parental authority. "[S]ociety cannot function in an orderly manner," it added, "when age distinctions, generations, sentiments and roles in families are in conflict." Incest differs from RAPE when mutual CONSENT is involved.

Blood Relationships. The Washington statute involved in the *Kaiser* case declared that a "person is guilty of incest if he engages in sexual intercourse with a person whom he knows to be related to him, either legitimately or illegitimately, as an ancestor, descendant, brother, or sister of either the whole or the half blood. . . . As used in this section, 'descendant' includes stepchildren and adopted children under eighteen years of age." This language was amended in 2003 to make it GENDER neutral and to make engaging in incestuous sexual intercourse a class B felony,

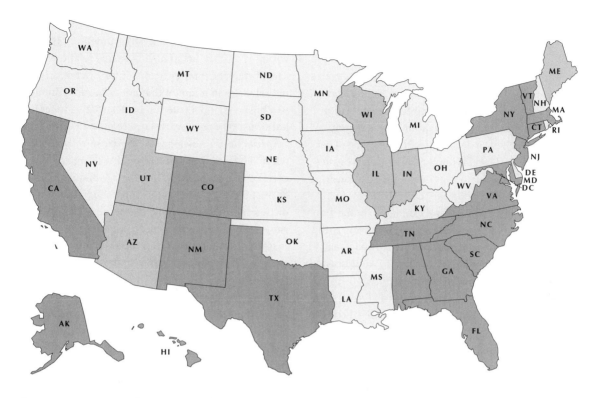

State Laws on Marriage to Cousins

Twenty states and the District of Columbia allow cousins to marry, while six permit marriage of first cousins only under certain circumstances. Twenty-four states bar any marriage between first cousins. North Carolina permits first-cousin marriage, although it prohibits double-cousin marriage. (If two brothers from one family marry two sisters from another and if each couple has a child, those children would be double cousins.) On the map above, dark gray indicates that first-cousin marriage is legal, light gray that it is prohibited, and medium gray that it is legal under certain circumstances.

Source: National Conference of State Legislatures, 2005

bringing a maximum of ten years in a state correctional facility or a fine of not more than $20,000, or both. Conviction for engaging in "sexual contact" is a lesser, class C, felony.

Affinity Relationships. In the case of incest based on affinity—by marriage, as opposed to a blood relationship—the incestuous act must occur during a time when the affinity relationship exists in order to be deemed illegal. Such a relationship generally terminates with DIVORCE or the death of the blood relation. After the death or divorce of a wife, for in-

stance, it is not considered incest for a man to have sexual relations with his stepdaughter or the sister of his former spouse. Where knowledge of the relationship is required for incest, as in the Washington statute, only the party charged with the offense must have such knowledge.

State courts seem to deal with incest on a case-by-case basis. A Colorado case, *Israel v. Allen* (1978), involved a petition to have a marriage certificate issued to two persons who became members of the same family at the ages of eighteen and thirteen years, when the boy's father married the girl's mother; both parents approved of the marriage, and the Roman Catholic bishop of Denver filed an affidavit approving their union. In granting their petition, the court acknowledged that the "objections that exist against consanguineous marriages [between blood relations] are not present where the relationship is merely by affinity. The physical detriment to the offspring of persons related by blood is totally absent." The court ignored other possible objections to the relationship, such as the potential damage to family harmony referenced in the *Kaiser* case in Washington. In the Tennessee case *Rhodes v. McAfee* (1970), however, the court annulled a marriage between a man and his stepdaughter, citing the likelihood that it "would result in discord and disharmony in the family."

Child Abuse. In some states, incest is linked with CHILD ABUSE and neglect, but in the Iowa legal code it is found under the heading Protection of Family: "A person ... who performs a sex act with another whom the person knows to be related to the person, either legitimately or illegitimately, as an ancestor, descendant, brother or sister of the whole or half blood, aunt, uncle, niece, or nephew, commits incest." An Iowa court has declared that even when nonviolent, crimes such as incest that take "base advantage of a young person who is entitled to protection rather than exploitation" may be punished by the legislature without violating the constitutional guarantee of equal protection of the law, such as by denying the offender any right to probation.

Legal Assumptions
Incest rests on several long-held assumptions and legal bases: (1) There is the scientifically unsupported assumption that children of people who are genetically closely related are more likely to be abnormal or somehow impaired. (There is evidence, however, that certain diseases, such as Tay-Sachs disease in Ashkenazi Jews and "Maple Syrup" disease in Amish children, can be perpetuated in closed, inbreeding societies.) (2) When intergenerational sex is involved, it is assumed, rightly or wrongly, that the older family member is imposing his or her will on a younger, more vulnerable member. (3) It is assumed, rightly or wrongly, that the act of having sexual relations with a family member may be traumatic for a victim. (4) Sexual relations in a family that are not strictly limited to a husband and a wife can be destructive to family harmony. (5) Some incest laws require that the participants have knowledge of the close relationship, while others may penalize even unwitting acts of incest. Furthermore, what may be a violation of laws against incest may also constitute child abuse, rape, or indecent liberties with a minor, and the more serious crime may be the one charged.

As with rape, incest may be difficult to defend against. The fact that a victim had prior sexual relations or even a reputation for being promiscuous is no defense, nor is consent, drunkenness, certain types of insanity, or uncontrollable impulses. A New York court held that the unsworn and uncorroborated testimony of an infant victim was sufficient evidence. In fact, corroboration is generally not necessary to prove incest, because the jury has a duty to determine if the victim's statements describing the alleged acts are credible. In *People v. Soulia* (1999), a New York appeals court found valid inferences to support the defendant's conviction with respect to his daughter on each of eight counts of first-degree SODOMY, eight counts of incest, four counts of first-degree sexual abuse, and eight counts of second-degree sodomy; testimony at the trial also indicated that the defendant had twice subjected his son, before the age of eleven years, to sexual contact.

Incest is a good example of how difficult the subject of sexual behavior is for laws to deal with. Acts of love and affection may be proper under certain circumstances but not under others. In the *Israel* case, for instance, two unrelated young persons who wanted to get married were precluded by the letter of the law, even though the spirit of the law was allowed to prevail. As with DATE RAPE or marital rape, incest requires that the law recognize a wide range of sexual behavior and make the difficult distinctions between the benign and the malignant.

INDECENT EXPOSURE

Indecent exposure is a form of SEXUAL ASSAULT, one that might seem to be nothing more than a harmless prank—such as "mooning" (exposing one's bare buttocks) from a car window at hapless passersby. But a charge of indecent exposure can be a serious crime on a person's record and may affect future job opportunities. The act, which is a crime in all states, or even the intent to commit such an act, which is also a crime in Michigan and some other states, can go awry: in spring 2004 a flasher (someone who publicly exposes his genitals) was tackled and beaten so badly by a group of schoolgirls in Philadelphia that he had to be treated at a hospital.

State criminal laws generally define the nature of indecent exposure. For example, the Pennsylvania legal code, under chapter 31, Sexual Offenses, provides: "A person commits indecent exposure if that person exposes his or her genitals in any public place or in any place where there are present other persons under circumstances in which he or she knows or should know that this conduct is likely to offend, affront or alarm." The law makes the act a misdemeanor in the first degree if "any of the persons present are less than 16 years of age"; otherwise, it is a second-degree misdemeanor.

Nebraska's law, in contrast, focuses on the age of the perpetrator: "(1) A person, eighteen years of age or over, commits public indecency if such person performs or procures, or assists any other person to perform, in a public place and where the conduct may reasonably be expected to be viewed by members of the public: ... (b) An exposure of the genitals of the body done with intent to affront or alarm any person." This public indecency is considered a misdemeanor, as it is in Maryland. That state's criminal code declares, "A person convicted of indecent exposure is guilty of a misdemeanor and is subject to imprisonment not exceeding 3 years or a fine not exceeding $1,000 or both." A misdemeanor is a lesser crime than a felony and is punishable by a fine or incarceration in a county jail, usually for up to one year.

A 1981 court decision in Maryland held that indecent exposure was neither an "infamous crime" nor a "crime of moral turpitude."

In *City of Tucson v. Wolfe* (1996), Arizona's court of appeals addressed a case involving a challenge to a city ordinance prohibiting females, but not males, from exposing the nipples and areolas of their breasts. The court found that the ordinance was substantially related to the important government interest of regulating public decency and narrowly drawn so as not to be unduly burdensome. Therefore, it was found not to violate either the equal protection clause of the Fourteenth Amendment (1868) to the U.S. Constitution or article 2, section 13, of the Arizona constitution, which states, "No law shall be enacted granting to any citizen, or class of citizens, or corporation other than municipal, privileges or immunities which, upon the same terms, shall not equally belong to all citizens or corporations."

The Arizona case might just as easily have been one involving NUDITY. But the difference between nudity and indecent exposure has to do with the nature of the underlying act. Nudity is a natural state of undress for which society has carved out areas of acceptance in public—in the arts, motion pictures, and technical or medical materials. Indecent exposure presupposes that the act is intended to shock or offend the viewer or that the person exposing himself or herself should have reason to know that the act would be offensive to those present. Recalling the language of U.S. Supreme Court decisions on OBSCENITY, it might be said that indecent exposure, unlike limited forms of public nudity, has no socially redeeming value.

Indecent exposure may also be accompanied by other prohibited sexual behavior. As one example, a man was arrested in Delaware in 2004 for indecent exposure in the vicinity of a shopping center and also charged with performing lewd acts, endangering an incompetent person, and engaging in disorderly contact. Some may argue that the fear of being publicly confronted with another person's exposed genitals is puritanical or excessively prudish. Clearly, however, there are some areas of sexual behavior—

such as indecent exposure—that are not as potentially harmful as RAPE or sexual assault but nonetheless require laws enforcing a modicum of decency in public places, especially with regard to exposure to CHILDREN.

Thirty-five states to date have enacted laws guaranteeing a mother the right to breastfeed her child in public, and eighteen have further declared that BREASTFEEDING is not an act of public indecency. In 2006 Arizona amended its statutes to state, "Indecent exposure does not include an act of breast-feeding by a mother." A Kentucky law passed the same year asserts, "In a municipal ordinance, indecent exposure, sexual conduct, lewd touching, obscenity, and similar terms do not include the act of a mother breastfeeding a child in a public or private location where the mother and child are otherwise authorized to be."

See also LEWD BEHAVIOR.

INFERTILITY

See ASSISTED REPRODUCTIVE TECHNOLOGY.

INTERNET

In 1969 the musical revue *Oh! Calcutta!,* in which performers were totally nude, opened in New York for what would be a run of 1,314 performances; humans landed on the moon for the first time; and what would become the Internet—the largest worldwide computer network—was created when computers at several universities in the United States were successfully linked. The first internet, called Arpanet by its founders, was shut down in 1990, but the NSFnet, developed by the National Science Foundation in 1986, evolved into the Internet that now spans the world, linking many millions of users.

A feature of any internet is cyberspace, the electronic medium of computer networks through which online communications operate. Coined by the cyberpunk author William Gibson, the term is derived from *cybernetics,* which refers to the theoretical study of control processes in electronic, mechanical, and biological systems, especially the mathematical analysis of the flow of information in such systems. Cyberspace is a form of virtual reality populated by information in the form of digital data that can be accessed by computer terminals and other electronic devices and displayed as words, numbers, pictures, and sounds.

This new form of interpersonal and commercial communication lies beyond traditional means of communication with a corporeal existence, such as printed matter and audiovisual materials. Those media may be banned or seized if they constitute illegal OBSCENITY as defined by federal and state laws and as interpreted by the courts. Internet users feel freer to distribute sexually explicit materials that can be viewed and copied by anyone else. Because people online can communicate with each other in the privacy of cyberspace, sexual predators, including child molesters, can easily engage potential victims and arrange opportunities to meet them to commit a variety of SEX OFFENSES.

First Amendment Issues

A previously unimaginable form of mass communication, the Internet soon became the subject of debate about whether the government should try to regulate it—as it does with other electronic MEDIA, such as radio and television—or whether it should be protected along with other forms of free speech and freedom of the press under the FIRST AMENDMENT (1791) to the U.S. Constitution. A variety of First Amendment issues have been raised in the Internet's relatively short life.

Obscenity. According to the National Academy of Sciences, in 2005 approximately 500,000 commercial Web sites worldwide were devoted to PORNOGRAPHY; additional noncommercial sources include file exchanges, chatrooms, Web cameras, and unsolicited e-mail. According to a report entitled *Youth, Pornography, and the Internet,* issued in 2002 by the Committee to Study Tools and Strategies for Protecting Kids from Pornography and Their Applicability to Other

Inappropriate Internet Content, *pornography* is an inexact term. *Obscenity,* which may include certain hard-core pornography and child pornography, is a more precise legal term, one that the U.S. Supreme Court has addressed beginning with ROTH V. UNITED STATES (1957). The Court has developed criteria that define obscenity and has consistently held that sexually explicit or other indecent material or activity that meets its definition is outside First Amendment protection.

Several general principles generated by the Supreme Court's obscenity decisions apply as well to material on the Internet:

(1) The government may not constitutionally restrict speech or expression simply because the government or a majority of citizens believe certain expressions of ideas, opinions, or values to be wrong or improper. In a democracy it is a citizen's right to be exposed to all forms of expression and arguments in order to decide what is wrong or improper.

(2) Except in extreme circumstances—for example, where there is evidence of a clear and present danger of some real harm—the government may not constitutionally restrict expression of ideas that may cause those exposed to such expression to engage in unlawful or socially objectionable conduct.

(3) As reflected in the Supreme Court's opinion in *Chaplinsky v. New Hampshire* (1942), certain types of expression, including obscenity—as defined by laws and the Court's interpretations—and traditionally actionable wrongs such as libel and slander, have a reduced value as far as First Amendment protections are concerned. The harm caused by such actions clearly outweighs the need for constitutional protection. Trademark law is also an area that may conflict with First Amendment rights on the Internet. For example, in 2004 a federal appeals court sided with Playboy Enterprises by allowing protection for the terms *playboy* and *playmate,* which had been used by a search engine along with nearly four hundred other suggestive words to trigger sex-oriented ads on the Internet.

In recent years, prosecutions for violations of obscenity laws have been extremely rare at the state and federal levels. Particularly during the 1970s, the Supreme Court began to define *obscenity* as encompassing only the most hard core of pornography. In MILLER V. CALIFORNIA (1973), the justices ruled that for material to be deemed obscene depends on whether the average person, applying contemporary community standards, would find that, taken as a whole, it appeals to the PRURIENT INTEREST; depicts or describes in a patently offensive way sexual conduct specifically defined by law; and as a whole lacks serious literary, artistic, political, or scientific value. The "community," according to the Court's line of cases, is a local one. But with respect to the Internet, the Court held in *Reno v. American Civil Liberties Union* (1997) that "the 'community standards' criterion as applied to a nationwide audience will be judged by the standards of the community most likely to be offended by the message."

Children's Access to Pornography. According to Nielsen/NetRatings, a national Internet rating service, nearly 16 percent of the visitors to adult-oriented or pornographic Web sites in February 2002 were under the age of eighteen years. Other sources have asserted a much higher percentage. Although adult-oriented sites represent only about 2 percent of the Web's overall content, they remain accessible and inviting to CHILDREN.

As a medium of communication, the Internet has a number of unique aspects. One is that it requires an intentional act and some skill to access sites on it, and another is that sufficient measures can be taken to block access by children to offensive material online. These characteristics have complicated the crafting of laws to censor or criminalize the distribution of pornographic material via the Internet. However, to keep children away from pornography online, several unsuccessful attempts have been made at the federal level to do so.

In 1996 CONGRESS passed the COMMUNICATIONS DECENCY ACT, which authorized CENSORSHIP of material on the Internet by making it a crime to allow someone under eighteen years of age to have access to indecent or obscene materials. But in *Reno v. American*

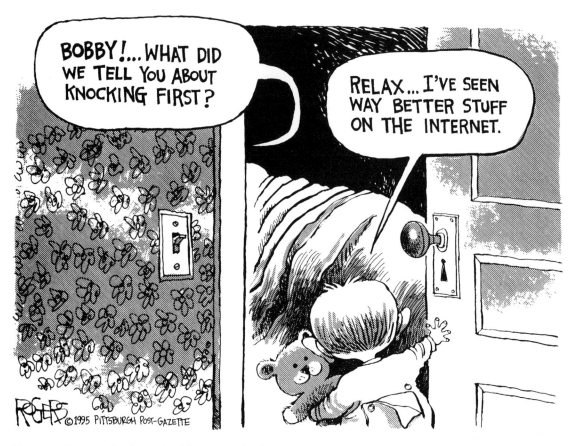

The generally unregulated growth of the Internet has led to federal laws aimed at protecting children from adult materials online. The first such law, the Communications Decency Act (1996), inspired this cartoon. Both this legislation and the later Child Online Protection Act (1998) were found to unconstitutionally infringe the First Amendment.

Civil Liberties Union (1997), the Supreme Court ruled unanimously that the law was unconstitutional under the First Amendment. The Court declared that the Internet, like newspapers and books in a democratic society, deserved the highest level of constitutional protection against censorship.

Two years later Congress again tried to rein in the Internet by passing the CHILD ONLINE PROTECTION ACT (1998). The act made the posting of content harmful to minors on the World Wide Web punishable by a fine of up to $50,000 and six months in prison. Again, the Supreme Court held—twice, in 2002 and 2004—that this attempt was unconstitutional as well. In their decision in *Ashcroft v. American Civil Liberties*

Union (2002, 2004), the justices concluded that the government had failed to show that less restrictive alternatives were not available, stating that in its present form the law had "a potential for extraordinary harm and a serious chill upon protected speech."

More success came with the Children's Internet Protection Act, passed by Congress in 2000 to prevent minors' access to pornographic Web sites on library terminals, where they may be free from direct parental supervision. This law requires libraries that receive federal funding—most school and public libraries—to install blocking software; the penalty is loss of federal funding. In *United States v. American Library Association* (2003), the Supreme Court held that the act did not infringe the First Amendment's protection of free speech and did not impose unconstitutional conditions on libraries. Unlike the attempts to regulate content providers through the Communications Decency Act and the Child Online Protection Act, this legislation was found to be a valid exercise of congressional authority. The Court concluded that the aim of preventing the dissemination of harmful material to children was a compelling government interest and that Congress has wide latitude to attach conditions to the receipt of federal assistance.

It is also a federal offense to use misleading domain names on the Internet to deceive children into viewing material that is harmful to minors, regardless of whether the material meets the legal definition of obscenity. It has been proposed that pornographic sites be designated with an "xxx" Web domain to visually segregate them from other addresses.

Child Pornography. Child pornography—any visual depiction of a child under the age of eighteen years engaged in sexually explicit conduct—is a federal offense under Title 18, Crimes, section 2256, of the U.S. Code; the manufacture, possession, and distribution of it are all a crime. States also have laws that address online child pornography. For example, the criminal law of Maryland requires that an "investigative or law enforcement officer who receives information that an item of alleged child pornography resides on a server or other storage device controlled or owned by an interactive computer service provider" request that the item be voluntarily removed or make application for a court order to compel its removal. Failure to remove the material in a timely manner is a crime punishable by a fine up to $30,000 for multiple violations.

Blogs and E-mail. The Internet has become the new printing press of the twenty-first century, allowing virtually anyone with access to a computer linked online to communicate ideas to many others nearly instantaneously. It may be too early to tell to what extent this new form of mass communication will change society, as the printing revolution did, but the aspects of this new technology related to sexual behavior are creating concerns that legislatures and courts are beginning to address.

According to Technorati, a search engine that tracks blogs (personal Web logs), in 2006 some fifteen thousand blogs were added daily to the existing five million blogs. They are subject to the same protections and prohibitions regarding sexual materials as commercial distributors. A significant federal law, under the U.S. Code, Title 18, section 2257, imposes a record-keeping requirement applicable to a wide range of producers of sexually explicit material; it includes maintaining at the producer's place of business the identification of all names used by performers, including professional names, and their date of birth. However, such onerous requirements may not withstand a challenge under the First Amendment.

E-mail (electronic mail) is a form of personal communication and, as such, has some constitutional protections. Once an e-mail is sent through the Internet, a copy may be retained and accessed by other parties not intended to receive the communication. In 2003 the Federal Trade Commission reported that some 17 percent of unsolicited pornographic offers sent via spam (e-mail distributed to a multitude of e-mail addresses for commercial purposes) contained images of NUDITY. In 2005 the FTC ruled under a federal antispam law that beginning on May 19 of that year sexually explicit e-mail must bear the label "Sexually Explicit" and that the messages themselves may not contain graphic images.

Cybersex

The technological creation of cyberspace has spawned a new form of virtual interaction known as cybersex. This sexual behavior encompasses personal interaction with Web sites online and other people in chatrooms and e-mail, activities that may be analogous to physical sexual relationships. In addition to viewing sexually related material alone, Internet users can interact with one another to send sexually explicit messages and play roles in games and fantasies that mimic actual sexual contact. While cybersex among consenting adults is not a legal problem, sexual predators can use the Internet to harm others, especially children, and their actions may be criminal under federal and state laws.

A recent study of Internet users between the ages of ten and seventeen years indicates that one out of five received a solicitation regarding sex during the year, of which about a third requested a meeting, telephoned, or sent gifts and money. One out of five children was exposed to unsolicited sexually explicit pictures, and a smaller number were actually threatened or harassed. Most of these types of cybersex offenses were not reported to law enforcement agencies or Internet service providers or documented through telephone hotlines available for this purpose, such as the CyberTipline operated by the NATIONAL CENTER FOR MISSING AND EXPLOITED CHILDREN in cooperation with the Office of Juvenile Justice and Delinquency Prevention in the U.S. Department of Justice. The number of cases of sexual exploitation of children online has dramatically increased, as reflected in CyberTipline reports that went up 36 percent from 2003 to 2004; Federal Bureau of Investigation cases increased more than tenfold between 1996 and 2002.

Prosecution is not always easy, however. In 1999 a federal court of appeals, in *United States v. Burgess*, reversed the conviction of a man who had exchanged sexually explicit messages online with a twenty-six-year-old man posing as a thirteen-year-old girl in order to turn in cybersex predators to the police. The defendant offered to meet the "girl" but was confronted at the rendezvous site by the local police and arrested. The court, however, criticized the trial court's failure to instruct the jury that the defendant's failure to testify at the trial was not to be given any adverse inference. Other issues raised by the defendant on appeal but not dealt with by the court included that he was entrapped—he would not have acted as he did if he had not been led on—and that he had not in fact believed that the "girl" he was meeting was really only thirteen years old.

Americans have lived for many years with government regulation and censorship in other areas of communication such as television, radio, and the movies. So far, howver, the technological revolution in communications wrought by the Internet, World Wide Web, and e-mail has been left virtually unregulated as far as private use is concerned. As the reach and the power of this new technology increase, however, there will undoubtedly be more attempts to curb it.

Contacts

CyberTipline (800-843-5789). www.cybertipline.com.

Child Pornography Tipline (800-843-5678).

See also ENTERTAINMENT INDUSTRY; TELEPHONE SEX.

j

JACOBELLIS v. OHIO

During the same year in which the U.S. Supreme Court handed down its decision in *Jacobellis v. Ohio* (1964), the Federal Bureau of Investigation began an inquiry into possible obscenities in the lyrics of the popular song "Louie, Louie," and some citizens attacked the literature of the SEXUALITY INFORMATION AND EDUCATION COUNCIL OF THE UNITED STATES as pornographic. Nico Jacobellis of Cleveland Heights, Ohio, had been charged with possessing and exhibiting an allegedly obscene French film, *The Lovers* (*Les Amants*). When Jacobellis's case reached the Supreme Court, Associate Justice Potter Stewart wrote in a concurring opinion his now-famous statement about the difficulty of defining hard-core PORNOGRAPHY: "I know it when I see it."

Representations of sexual behavior—from literary descriptions and photographs in books and magazines to motion pictures and live performances—are all subject to some limitations under FIRST AMENDMENT (1791) protections for freedom of speech and the press. In *Jacobellis* the Supreme Court looked specifically at a motion picture that an Ohio court had determined to be obscene. *The Lovers* had been rated by two critics of national stature as among the best films produced that year, and it had been exhibited in a hundred cities in the United States larger than Cleveland Heights.

The film, as the Supreme Court was to explain, contained one "explicit love scene in the last reel," to which the state of Ohio objected. Based on its finding

of OBSCENITY, an Ohio trial court convicted the theater manager under a statute that made "selling, exhibiting, and possessing obscene literature or drugs for criminal purposes" punishable by a fine of "not less than two hundred nor more than two thousand dollars or imprison[ment for] not less than one nor more than seven years, or both." Ohio's highest court affirmed the conviction.

Associate Justice William J. Brennan Jr. delivered the 6–3 opinion for the Supreme Court in favor of the defendant. Justice Brennan's opinion acknowledged at the outset that in *ROTH v. UNITED STATES* (1957), the Court had held that obscenity was not subject to First Amendment protections. Thus, for the Ohio obscenity law to be properly applied, "ascertainment of the 'dim and uncertain line' that often separates obscenity from constitutionally protected expression" was required. He further noted that the *Roth* decision required a finding that the material in question "goes substantially beyond customary limits of candor in description or representation of such matters" and that such a judgment must be based on "contemporary community standards." Such standards, said the Court, should be those of the particular community in which the case arises. But what was the extent of such a community?

In addition to concluding that "society at large" is the "community" to be used in determining obscenity, the Supreme Court dismissed any notion that somehow local community standards could be used under a federal constitution that applies equally throughout the nation. The Court also revisited *Butler v. Michigan* (1957), in which a definition of obscenity based on the material's possible effect on a minor was rejected as effectively reducing adults' reading matter to the level of CHILDREN—a conclusion that a lower court judge had reached in 1913.

The opinion concluded that the film was not obscene under the criteria in *Roth* and the companion case *Alberts v. California* (1957) decided at the same time. The concurring opinion of two associate justices, Hugo L. Black and WILLIAM O. DOUGLAS, concluded that "conviction of . . . [anyone] . . . for exhibiting a motion picture abridges freedom of the press as safeguarded by the First Amendment." A separate concurring opinion by Justice Stewart noted that in such cases, the Court "was faced with the task of trying to define what may be indefinable." He then concluded with his view that only "hard-core pornography" can be the subject of criminal penalties—and "the motion picture involved in this case is not that," declared Stewart.

Taking up Justice Stewart's concern about defining obscenity, Chief Justice Earl Warren, joining with Associate Justice Tom Clark, dissented on the grounds that because there was at least some evidence of obscenity in the record on which the Ohio courts had made their decisions, "society's right to maintain its moral fiber and the effective administration of justice require that this Court not establish itself as an ultimate censor."

As the decision in *Jacobellis* demonstrates, the Supreme Court has often had to balance protection for the free expression of ideas against the moral outrage of those who make the laws. The definition of community standards would be revised in later Supreme Court decisions to refer to local community standards, but with a narrow range of variances. However, the basic right of the average adult American citizen to be free to choose the level of sexual expression with which he or she is most comfortable has persisted in the Court's subsequent decisions involving obscenity.

See also CENSORSHIP; ENTERTAINMENT INDUSTRY.

ALEC JEFFREYS

In 1975 Alec Jeffreys began work in the field of mammalian molecular genetics at the University of Amsterdam. While there he and his colleagues discovered a technique for detecting single-copy genes—the basis of inheritable traits in organisms. Two years later at the University of Leicester in England, he moved on to work with DNA (deoxyribonucleic acid), the strands of genetic material that carry the information making each of us who we are, or will become, as we grow into a complex individual from a single cell formed as a result of sexual reproduction. Then in 1984 he and his associates developed a genetic probe for detecting specific areas or patterns in DNA. As Jeffreys wrote in 1993 about that accomplishment, "It was clear that these . . . DNA patterns offered the promise of a truly individual-specific identification system."

The modern-day crime-detection arsenal that has helped popularize television shows such as *CSI* and its myriad clones about crime-scene investigation includes the ability to identify perpetrators of crimes using DNA. This new forensic science was made possible by Jeffreys's discoveries. DNA evidence, especially semen left by rapists, is increasingly used to identify the guilty party with a high degree of precision. Many people owe their freedom to DNA testing, which may exonerate them of crimes, and in addition many CHILDREN learn who their fathers are by means of such testing.

Alec John Jeffreys, now Sir Alec Jeffreys, was born on January 9, 1950, in Luton in Bedfordshire, England, and educated at Oxford University, where he earned a degree in biochemistry in 1972 and his Ph.D. in 1975. After his postdoctoral work in Amsterdam, he joined the University of Leicester and became a full professor in 1987. Jeffreys was elected a fellow of the Royal Society in 1986, a year after his groundbreaking paper, entitled "Hypervariable Minisatellite Regions in Human DNA," was published in 1985. About the paper Jeffreys said that "almost as an accidental byproduct, it suggested approaches for not only developing genetic markers for medical genetic research, but for

For Alec Jeffreys, his Eureka! moment came in 1984 when he examined an x-ray of a blot of DNA developed in a darkroom and realized that he was seeing "a level of individual specificity that was light years beyond anything that had been seen before." The process of DNA "fingerprinting" has revolutionized criminal investigations around the world.

opening up the whole field of forensic DNA typing."

The first man to be exonerated of a crime using the forensic DNA typing pioneered by Jeffreys was Richard Buckland, who had been a suspect in the RAPE and murder of two fifteen-year-old girls in England, one in 1983 and another in 1986. Buckland's DNA did not match the DNA evidence found on the victims. Law enforcement officials then attempted to collect DNA samples from five thousand local men, but this effort failed to turn up the culprit. However, after a man was overheard admitting that he had given a DNA sample for his colleague, Colin Pitchfork was arrested and in 1988 was sentenced to life imprisonment for the crimes.

The first use of forensic DNA testing in the United States came in the Orlando, Florida, trial of an accused

rapist in 1987. This type of evidence was accepted, even by defense lawyers, as unassailable when properly presented in court. Some doubt was first cast on the process in 1989 over the protocols regulating DNA testing and interpretation of the results. Problems relating to improper DNA testing methods led to defense lawyers' ability to successfully challenge evidence in court. Since then, a number of irregularities that have come to light, among them mistakes and deliberate misconduct by forensic experts, have resulted in convictions being overturned based on improper DNA testing. Yet today the basic process, when conducted properly, is still a potent weapon for crime investigation and prosecution.

Jeffreys has continued to work in the field of DNA research and to publish many scientific papers on GENETICS and DNA. Knighted in 1994 for his contributions to science, he was also awarded the Albert Einstein World Award of Science in 1996, the Australian Prize in 1998, and the Royal Medal of the Royal Society in 2004. In 2005 he split the Lasker Prize for clinical research with Sir Edwin Southern of Oxford University, another pioneer in DNA research.

See also PATERNITY; SEX OFFENDERS; SEX OFFENSES.

JUDICIARY

The United States is a federal nation, in which political power is distributed between a national government and the constituent states. Over the country's two centuries, the line between federal and state power has shifted and continues to be altered by legislation and court decisions. But in one way the state and federal governments are alike: all are divided into three coequal branches—the executive, the legislative, and the judicial—to achieve a separation of powers. With this organization, no branch dominates another, and checks and balances protect the states and the people from arbitrary and unconstitutional actions. The judiciary, which forms the judicial branch of the federal and state governments, is charged under its respective federal or state constitution with interpreting and applying laws that are passed by the legislative branch and enforced by the executive branch.

The Federal Judiciary

The first tier in the American judicial system is occupied by the U.S. Supreme Court, which has authority to decide certain legal issues in accordance with Article III of the U.S. Constitution (1789). This article vests the "judicial Power of the United States ... in one supreme Court, and in such inferior Courts as the Congress may from time to time ordain and establish." It also declares, "The judicial Power shall extend to all Cases, in Law and Equity, arising under this Constitution." Although the document does not expressly empower the Supreme Court to declare acts of CONGRESS unconstitutional, the Court under Chief Justice John Marshall held in the famous case *Marbury v. Madison* (1803) that it is "essential to all written constitutions, that a law repugnant to the constitution is void" and therefore unenforceable.

The *Marbury* decision began the Supreme Court's process of judicial review, by which it declares both federal and state laws to be either constitutional or not. In this regard, the text of the Constitution and precedents established by Supreme Court rulings become the primary references for the Court's decisions. For example, in MINOR V. HAPPERSETT (1874), Missouri had denied a woman the right to vote because she was a woman, and the state's supreme court upheld this denial. The matter was appealed to the U.S. Supreme Court on the grounds that the denial of voting rights violated the privileges or immunities clause of the Constitution's Fourteenth Amendment (1868). The Supreme Court affirmed the Missouri court's decision, and so the matter stood until the Nineteenth Amendment (1920) finally granted American women the right to vote.

In addition to the Supreme Court, the federal court system contains a second tier of courts called courts of appeal. These courts were created by Congress and have no original jurisdiction; they decide cases only

It fell to Associate Justice Harry A. Blackmun to write perhaps the most polarizing opinion in the recent history of the U.S. Supreme Court: *Roe v. Wade* (1973). His service as counsel for the Mayo Clinic in Rochester, Minnesota, is thought to have influenced his reasoning regarding the need to protect abortion rights.

on appeal from the third tier of courts, the federal district courts. The United States is divided geographically into eleven circuits, each with its own appeals court, and there are additional courts for the District of Columbia and special federal cases. The U.S. Court of Appeals for the First Circuit, for example, covers the states of Maine, Massachusetts, New Hampshire, and Rhode Island as well as Puerto Rico.

Federal district courts have original jurisdiction in federal criminal and civil cases. There are ninety-four district courts in the United States and four in the U.S. territories, including Puerto Rico, Guam, the Virgin

Islands, and the Northern Mariana Islands, plus one for the District of Columbia. They conduct trials from which appeals may be taken to the federal appeals courts and ultimately to the Supreme Court.

Other federal courts not created under the authority of Article III of the Constitution include the U.S. Court of International Trade, Court of Federal Claims, Tax Court, Court of Appeals for the Armed Forces, Court of Veterans Appeals, Armed Services Board of Contract Appeals, and bankruptcy courts.

The chief justice of the United States, the other eight justices of the Supreme Court, and all Article III federal judges are appointed by the PRESIDENT and confirmed by the U.S. Senate to serve for life or, as the Constitution phrases it, "during good Behavior." Like other officers of the government, justices and judges may be impeached and removed from office.

Federal Decision Making

Decisions of the federal judiciary with respect to laws governing sexual behavior may have wide impact. The *Happersett* decision mentioned above is a case in point, as the Supreme Court denied to women the important civil right to vote; women then had to mount a campaign to amend the Constitution to secure that right. Since then, the Court's direction with respect to issues involving sexual behavior has been erratic at best.

Yet the finality of Supreme Court decisions is often illusory, because Congress can limit and the voters can ultimately overrule the Court's rulings. With respect to a woman's right to vote, *Happersett* was overruled by the Nineteenth Amendment in 1920, and with respect to the right of abortion, Congress has limited the scope of the Supreme Court's approval of the procedure in *Roe v. Wade* (1973) by consistently denying federal funding for abortions, making this reproductive choice unavailable to many women who cannot afford it.

The Supreme Court has developed two key concepts in analyzing cases involving sexual behavior. The first is the right of PRIVACY, which a Court majority created in 1965 from various related provisions of the Bill of Rights (1791), the first ten amendments to the U.S. Constitution. Under the right of privacy, citizens are free from government interference with activities in which it has no legitimate business being involved— such as what transpires in a married couple's bedroom concerning the use of CONTRACEPTION or what intimate consensual relations an adult couple may engage in.

The other concept involves judicial scrutiny, meaning the level of proof the courts require the government to present in order to discriminate against some citizens while not transgressing constitutional protections. In cases alleging DISCRIMINATION based on race or national origin, the Supreme Court has consistently held the government to the highest level, called "strict scrutiny." Likewise the Court has ruled that government regulation of the content of sexually explicit materials—as opposed to the ZONING of adult bookstores or other SEXUALLY ORIENTED BUSINESSES—is subject to the same strict scrutiny in light of the protection of free speech and expression contained in the FIRST AMENDMENT (1791). Yet, given certain distinctions between the sexes, the Court has permitted a secondary level of review, called "intermediate scrutiny," in analyzing government discrimination on the basis of biological sex. In other cases, the Court may use a "rational basis test" to give legislators the benefit of the doubt.

Notable Decisions

Federal decisions on sexual behavior do not stand alone but instead tend to be built on precedents that relate to other issues. Dissents in earlier cases and even seemingly obscure footnotes can become the basis of future precedents. Some key cases summarized below in reverse chronological order represent noteworthy judicial precedents in the evolution of sexual behavior and the law. (Many of these are discussed in more detail as separate entries in this book.)

Ashcroft v. American Civil Liberties Union (2002, 2004). Because the attempt made in the CHILD ONLINE PROTECTION ACT (1998) to protect CHILDREN from ADULT MATERIALS on the INTERNET was overbroad and infringed the freedom of speech guaranteed by the First Amendment, the Supreme Court declared it unconstitutional.

Lawrence v. Texas (2003). Here the Supreme Court overruled its own earlier decision in *Bowers v. Hardwick* (1986), finding instead that the vital interests of liberty and privacy protected by the Fourteenth Amendment's due process clause made unconstitutional a state law criminalizing homosexual SODOMY by consenting adults in the privacy of their own home.

United States v. Morrison (2000). Congress unconstitutionally overreached its authority under the commerce clause in Article I, section 8, of the Constitution, said the Supreme Court, when it enacted a provision in the VIOLENCE AGAINST WOMEN ACT (1994) that allowed private suits (analogous to suits allowed for civil rights violations) for acts of gender-motivated violence such as RAPE. The decision effectively pulled the teeth out of a law that had been supported by attorneys general of thirty-eight states because of the inadequacy of state and local remedies for violence against women.

United States v. Virginia (1996). According to the Supreme Court, the male-only student policy of the Virginia Military Institute violated the Constitution's equal protection clause. Although the decision was viewed at the time as the death-knell for SINGLE-SEX EDUCATION, some single-sex schools continue to be established on the theory that during their formative years, students can benefit from an educational environment free of interaction with the opposite sex.

Thomasson v. Perry (1996). The U.S. Court of Appeals for the Fourth Circuit upheld the constitutionality of a law permitting the navy to discharge an exemplary officer who presented a letter to four admirals stating, "I can remain silent no longer. I am gay." The letter was offered several months after Congress and the president had blessed a new "don't ask, don't tell" policy regarding homosexuals in the MILITARY.

Planned Parenthood of Southeastern Pennsylvania v. Casey (1992). In this case, the Supreme Court upheld two of three conditions on the right of ABORTION mandated by state law; one required a twenty-four-hour waiting period, during which information including alternatives to abortion must be presented, and the other mandated a parent's CONSENT before a minor could obtain an abortion. The Court struck

down as unconstitutional a third condition—that a married woman tell her husband of her intent to have an abortion—declaring that such a provision presumed that a wife required her husband's permission to obtain an abortion.

Roe v. Wade (1973). A state law prohibiting abortion was an unconstitutional infringement of a woman's right of privacy to make decisions about her own reproductive choices in consultation with her physician, said the Supreme Court in this landmark decision. The ruling treated the three trimesters of PREGNANCY differently, progressively restricting the right to an abortion in the second and third trimesters to protect the fetus.

Miller v. California and *Paris Adult Theatre I v. Slaton* (1973). The Supreme Court built on its line of decisions beginning with *Roth v. United States* (below) to craft a definition of OBSCENITY, which it confirmed was beyond the protection of the First Amendment. The Court's test for obscene material required determinations of whether the average person, applying contemporary community standards, would find that the material, taken as a whole, appeals to the PRURIENT INTEREST; that it depicts or describes, in a patently offensive way, sexual conduct specifically defined by applicable law; and that it lacks serious literary, artistic, political, or scientific value.

Reed v. Reed (1971). Here the Supreme Court struck down a state law that preferred males over females in court appointments of administrators of decedents' estates. The Court, ignoring its own precedents to the contrary, declared that such a law was "the very kind of arbitrary legislative choice forbidden" by the Fourteenth Amendment's equal protection clause.

Griswold v. Connecticut (1965) and *Eisenstadt v. Baird* (1972). A state law prohibiting any person from using any drug, article, or instrument to prevent conception was held by the Supreme Court in *Griswold* to be an unconstitutional invasion of a newly minted right of privacy. Although the decision was based on a marital right of privacy, in *Eisenstadt* the Court extended it to include unmarried couples.

Roth v. United States and *Alberts v. California* (1957). The Supreme Court began its analytical evolution of obscenity by discarding the notions that obscenity can be found in portions of materials and that such material must be judged on the basis of the most vulnerable members of society, such as children. However, once identified, obscenity was declared to be beyond First Amendment protection. *Roth* involved a federal antiobscenity law, whereas the companion *Alberts* case questioned a similar state law.

State Courts

A state's judiciary is one of the three branches of every state government. It often mirrors to a greater or lesser degree the federal judiciary's structure—with trial courts, appellate courts, and a supreme court. There are many exceptions, such as in Oklahoma and Texas, which have a separate court of criminal appeals. Many states have other types of courts, including family courts that deal with juvenile and domestic law issues as well as traffic courts. Unlike jurists in Article III federal courts, however, justices and judges of many state courts may be elected for fixed terms rather than appointed for life.

State court decisions that relate to sexual behavior may be limited in effect to the jurisdiction of a particular court. Decisions of a state's highest court, in contrast, apply throughout the state and may indirectly influence federal court decisions, simply because of the logic of their opinions. The ten state court cases described below are examples of noteworthy decisions regarding sexual behavior. They have been chosen to reflect some of the issues with which state courts deal every day.

Goodridge v. Department of Public Health (2003, Massachusetts). In the wake of the *Baehr* decision (discussed below), *Goodridge* has made Massachusetts the only state to declare SAME-SEX MARRIAGE legal. The supreme judicial court of Massachusetts ruled that the "Massachusetts Constitution [which is nine years older than the U.S. Constitution] protects matters of personal liberty against government incursion as zealously, and often more so, than does the Federal Constitution." Therefore, said the ruling, "barring an individual from the protections, benefits, and obligations of

civil marriage solely because that person would marry a person of the same sex violates the Massachusetts Constitution."

In re John Z. (2003, California). Here California's supreme court held that "forcible rape occurs when the act of sexual intercourse is accomplished against the will of the victim by force or threat of bodily injury and it is immaterial at what point the victim withdraws her consent, so long as that withdrawal is communicated to the male and he thereafter ignores it."

Enriquez v. West Jersey Health Systems (2001, New Jersey). The superior court of New Jersey, appellate division, held that "gender dysphoria [a condition related to TRANSSEXUALISM, having a gender personality, usually female, that is different from one's biological sex, usually male] is a recognized mental or psychological disability that can be demonstrated psychologically by accepted clinical diagnostic techniques and qualifies as a handicap under the New Jersey Law Against Discrimination." According to the decision, an employer or a prospective employer may not discriminate against a person with such a condition.

People v. Garcia (2000, California). The California court of appeals, fourth district, held that although the sexual orientation of a juror may become known and considered by the contending parties in "their jury selection decisions, just as they factor in occupation, education, body-language, and whether the juror resembles their stupid Uncle Cletus . . . there is no reason to allow inquiry about" the sexual orientation of a prospective juror.

Alfonso v. Fernandez (1993, New York). Because parents have a constitutional right "to regulate their children's sexual behavior as best they can," the New York supreme court, appellate division, second department, held that a condom distribution program in New York City's public high schools "excluding parental involvement . . . impermissibly trespasses on [those] parental rights." In this case, students "are not just exposed to talk or literature on the subject of sexual behavior; the school offers the means for students to engage in sexual activity at a lower risk of pregnancy and contracting sexually transmitted diseases."

Baehr v. Lewin (1993, Hawaii). Hawaii's supreme court held in this case that the provision of the state constitution declaring that no person "shall be denied the equal protection of the laws, nor be denied the enjoyment of a person's civil rights or be discriminated against in the exercise thereof because of . . . sex" does not establish a fundamental right of marriage for same-sex couples. Nevertheless, said the court, a statute restricting marital relations to males and females establishes a sex-based classification that is subject to the "strict scrutiny" test for equal protection challenges. In 1998 the Hawaiian constitution was amended to forestall such challenges, stating: "The legislature shall have power to reserve marriage to opposite-sex couples."

Thoreson v. Penthouse International, Ltd. (1992, New York). The New York supreme court, appellate division, first department, held that a former *Penthouse* magazine Pet of the Year was entitled to compensatory damages for being forced by her employer to engage in sexual activity with his business associates and others. The court noted that the fact that the complainant had embarked on a career to exploit her sexuality did not preclude her from being able to recover damages for being forced to engage in nonconsensual sexual activity. Moreover, said the court, medical treatment was not a precondition for recovery, and mental injury could be proved by her own testimony.

Gay Law Students Association v. Pacific Telephone and Telegraph Co. (1979, California). The California supreme court held that discrimination by an employer against openly gay people in hiring, firing, and promotion violated their fundamental rights, because "one important aspect of the struggle for equal rights is to induce homosexual individuals to 'come out of the closet,' acknowledge their sexual preferences, and

to associate with others in working for equal rights."

Whaley v. Whaley (1978, Ohio). The Ohio court of appeals held that even though a mother who had been given custody of her four-year-old daughter in a DIVORCE proceeding had subsequently been involved romantically with a married man (criminal adultery in Ohio), a court could not transfer her custody to the father. As the court noted, the proof of "immorality" and a "moral norm" against which to measure such immorality "in light of the diversity of religious and moral practice in this country [is] simply an unworkable standard beyond the realm of legitimate judicial inquiry."

Marvin v. Marvin (1976, California). In this original "palimony" case, California's supreme court held that unmarried adults "who voluntarily live together and engage in sexual relations are nonetheless as competent as any other persons to contract respecting their earnings and property rights." It added: "So long as the agreement does not rest upon illicit meretricious [sex for money] consideration, the parties may order their economic affairs as they choose, and no policy precludes the courts from enforcing such agreements."

In the United States, the role of protecting citizens' rights rests primarily in the hands of the courts, which are charged with making sure that laws and law enforcement do not commit tyrannies in the name of democracy. Unchecked, majority rule may trample with impunity the rights of minorities. Many of the rights and freedoms that citizens now enjoy with respect to sexual behavior, whether unmarried cohabitation or viewing PORNOGRAPHY on the Internet, result from vigilant federal and state judiciaries.

See also ALIMONY; CONTRACEPTION; EQUAL RIGHTS; GENDER; HOMOSEXUALITY; REPRODUCTIVE RIGHTS; WOMEN'S RIGHTS.

k

FRANKLIN KAMENY

Considered one of the fathers of the gay rights movement, Franklin Kameny did not meekly accept his dismissal from the U.S. civil service in 1957, which was based solely on the grounds that he was a homosexual. "My dismissal amounted to a declaration of war against me by the government," he said, taking his case all the way to the U.S. Supreme Court. Although the Court dismissed his appeal in *Kameny v. Brucker* (1961), his brief was a landmark statement on behalf of persecuted homosexuals and a major first step in the homosexual rights movement.

Born on May 21, 1925, in New York City, Franklin Edward Kameny was a largely self-taught prodigy who was admitted to Queens College at age fifteen and majored in physics. After serving in World War II, he resumed his studies and obtained a Ph.D. in astronomy from Harvard University in 1956. After a year teaching at Georgetown University in Washington, D.C., he was hired as an astronomer with the U.S. Army Map Service.

One night in 1957 Kameny was arrested on a morals charge in Lafayette Park, a popular gay meeting place across the street from the White House. He was released, but several months later he was questioned by an investigator from the Civil Service Commission about rumors that he was homosexual. Beginning in 1950, Senator Joseph McCarthy of Wisconsin had begun making accusations and holding hearings on alleged communists in government that touched off a wave of firings of homosexuals; they were believed to be security risks because they could be blackmailed during the cold war to keep their sexual orientation a secret. Although McCarthy was censored by the Senate in 1954, the scare continued to influence government personnel decisions.

Before the end of 1957, Kameny was fired by the Map Service. Because of the security implications, he was effectively barred from any other government employment that required a security clearance. Kameny fought back through the courts but lost. Finally, in desperation, he filed a petition for review of his case with the Supreme Court. He argued in his brief that the federal government's blanket exclusion of homosexuals "makes of the homosexual a second-rate citizen, by discriminating against him without reasonable cause." The American government, he continued, "exists to protect and assist *all* its citizens, not, as in the case of homosexuals, to harm, to victimize, and to destroy them."

The Supreme Court unanimously denied Kameny's petition. And then in *Boutilier v. Immigration and Naturalization Service* (1967), the justices noted that the phrase *psychopathic personality*, on which a contested deportation order was based and which refers to having a severe mental disorder, was intended to include "such types of pathological behavior as homosexuality or sexual perversion." The Civil Service Commission, after later decisions altering the view declared in *Boutilier*, in 1975 revised its antigay policy, however.

Franklin Kameny, second from the right, was fired from his federal government job in 1957 because he was a homosexual. His unsuccessful legal battle to protest his dismissal led to later changes in the U.S. civil service. During a 1971 campaign for Congress, he joined other gay activists: Lige Clarke, Jack Nichols, and Barbara Gittings.

Four decades after Kameny's arrest, President Bill Clinton used an executive order in 1998 to add sexual orientation to the list of classifications, along with race and national origin, that were to be protected from discrimination in federal employment.

Besides legally pursuing the matter of discrimination against gays, in 1961 Kameny also helped establish the District of Columbia chapter of the Mattachine Society, a gay rights organization founded in Los Angeles in 1950; the society was named after a character in Italian theater named Mattacino—a sort of court jester who could speak the truth to the king when others were afraid to. The Mattachine Society, dedicated to liberating the oppressed homosexual community, persuaded the AMERICAN CIVIL LIBERTIES UNION to take up its cause and in 1965 organized the first gay demonstration at the White House.

Although Kameny lost his appeal to get his job back and the Mattachine Society disbanded in 1987, to be reorganized in 2005 in Shreveport, Louisiana, his mission to bring EQUAL RIGHTS and dignity to all U.S. citizens regardless of sexual orientation has continued. Whether or not legalized DISCRIMINATION against gays and lesbians in the MILITARY and in MARRIAGE will some day be reversed, the nation has begun the process of making all citizens equal before the law—changes due in part to Kameny's willingness to fight for what he believed in.

See also HOMOSEXUALITY; SAME-SEX MARRIAGE.

KANSAS v. HENDRICKS

At one time a person convicted of a crime who had paid his debt to society by serving his sentence was considered to be "a free man." But in the late twentieth century, a backlash against the U.S. Supreme Court's expansion of rights for those accused of crimes spawned various movements to promote VICTIMS' RIGHTS. Victims of violent SEX OFFENSES, especially those committed against CHILDREN, sought ways to protect themselves and others from further SEXUAL ASSAULT. MEGAN'S LAW (1996), for example, requires some SEX OFFENDERS to make their whereabouts known for the public's protection. Such postincarceration requirements have been upheld by the courts as constitutional.

In addition to Megan's Law provisions, most states also have sex offense commitment statutes that provide for the involuntary confinement of certain violent sex offenders and sexual predators after they have completed any sentence imposed for their crimes. In 1994 Kansas enacted the Sexually Violent Predator Act, which sets up procedures for the civil commitment of persons who, because of a "mental abnormality" or a "personality disorder," are likely to engage in "predatory acts of sexual violence." Although Kansas already had a law addressing the involuntary commitment of mentally ill persons, its state legislature did not believe that this provision was adequate to deal with the risks presented by sexually violent predators.

Leroy Hendricks, a self-proclaimed pedophile (an adult attracted to children) with a long history of molesting children, was convicted in 1984 of taking indecent liberties with two thirteen-year-old boys. After serving almost ten years of his sentence, he was approved for release to a half-way house, but the state filed a court petition to have him confined as a sexually violent predator. Although Hendricks challenged the proposed civil (not criminal) confinement in a mental institution, the court ordered that he undergo an evaluation to determine his condition.

Hendricks then requested a jury trial on the question of whether he was legally a sexually violent predator who could be committed under the act. During the trial, Hendricks testified to his history of pedophilia and characterized previous treatments for it as "bull——." He admitted that only his death would stop his urge to molest children. The jury found him to be a sexual predator as defined in the act, a verdict he appealed. The Kansas supreme court, however, decided that for him to be involuntarily committed to a mental institution, it had to be established that he had a mental illness and not just a mental abnormality as permitted under the law.

By a 5–4 majority, the U.S. Supreme Court disagreed in 1997, with Associate Justice Clarence Thomas writing the opinion for the Court. After citing a 1905 Supreme Court case, *Jacobson v. Massachusetts*, which rejected an absolute right of liberty under the U.S. Constitution, and a 1788 New York law permitting the confinement of the "furiously mad," the Court examined the Kansas act. *Amicus curiae* (friend of the court) briefs filed by mental health organizations, including the Association for the Treatment of Sexual Abusers and the Menninger Foundation, asserted that "sex offenders can be treated" and that such treatment can "significantly reduce recidivism." Therefore, Justice Thomas concluded, involuntary civil commitment was not an additional punishment for Hendricks's crime but a form of treatment. Accordingly, the Kansas law was deemed constitutional.

The decision negated arguments that civil confinement in this case violated the U.S. Constitution's prohibitions against double jeopardy and ex post facto (after the fact) punishment, both applicable to the states under the due process clause of the Fourteenth Amendment (1868). The majority opinion noted that the Kansas law had in fact built in some procedural protections; among them was the use of legal counsel to present evidence on behalf of a sex offender and to cross-examine witnesses against him.

In his concurring opinion, Associate Justice Anthony M. Kennedy agreed that the Kansas law "conforms to our precedents" but warned the states against using civil commitment as "a mechanism for retribution or general deterrence"—for example, by mandating civil confinement to increase a sentence reduced through a plea bargain. "We should bear in mind," he wrote, "that while incapacitation is a goal common to both the criminal and civil systems of confinement, retribution and general deterrence are reserved for the criminal system alone."

The dissenters (Associate Justices Breyer, Ginsburg, Souter, and Stevens) challenged the majority opinion because no treatment was actually required under the law, despite Justice Thomas's characterization of the involuntary confinement as a form of treatment.

As our understanding of aberrant sexual behavior improves, legislatures and the courts undoubtedly will continue to grapple with the problem of how to treat habitual sex offenders within the framework of constitutional protections against arbitrary and unjust denials of liberty. However, *Hendricks* stands for the moment as the U.S. Supreme Court's stamp of approval on preventive and protective civil confinement of potentially dangerous sex offenders.

ALFRED KINSEY

Alfred Charles Kinsey's published works on human sexuality in America—in particular, *Sexual Behavior in the Human Male* (1948) and *Sexual Behavior in the Human Female* (1953)—were an important impetus in launching the SEXUAL REVOLUTION in the 1960s. Reactions by the public and his peers to his findings regarding human sexuality, which were based largely on some 18,500 personal interviews, were both positive and negative. It is uncontested, however, that Kinsey helped open the door to the free discussion and study of human sexuality that had been closed for centuries. The Kinsey reports remain the largest study ever undertaken of human sexual behavior.

Born in Hoboken, New Jersey, on June 23, 1894, Kinsey was graduated magna cum laude from Bowdoin College in Brunswick, Maine, with a degree in biology and psychology. After obtaining his doctorate

in biology from Harvard University in 1919, he went the next year to Indiana University in Bloomington as an assistant professor of zoology. In 1938 he became the coordinator for a MARRIAGE course at the university. Discovering that little scientific data existed on human sexual behavior, he began gathering case histories, using in-depth face-to-face interviews. In 1940 he made the decision to devote himself to expanding this effort into an ongoing sexual research project.

Kinsey incorporated the Institute for Sex Research in 1947, remaining as its director until his death on August 25, 1956. In his two groundbreaking books on male and female sexual behavior published between 1948 and 1953, he addressed topics such as NUDITY, PREMARITAL SEX and extramarital sex, foreplay, orgasm, anal and oral sex, fantasies, masturbation, sadomasochism, BISEXUALITY, and HOMOSEXUALITY. In *Sexual Behavior in the Human Male*, written with his research assistants Wardell Pomeroy and Clyde Martin, Kinsey developed a heterosexual-homosexual rating scale with seven gradations based on the notion that male sexuality cannot be represented by just two extremes.

During his lifetime Kinsey's reports were celebrated as a triumph of science over mystery and myth. He appeared on the cover of *Time* magazine, and his work was funded by the National Research Council and the Rockefeller Foundation. His institute won an important legal battle in federal court in *United States v. 31 Photographs* (1957), a decision that confirmed its right to import erotic and pornographic materials for use in research.

The mission of the institute, which changed its name in 1981 to the Kinsey Institute for Sex Research and a year later to the Kinsey Institute for Research in Sex, Gender, and Reproduction, is "to promote interdisciplinary research and scholarship in the fields of human sexuality, gender, and reproduction ... through: development of specialized collections of resources for scholars; programs of research and publication; interdisciplinary conferences and seminars; provision of information services to researchers; and graduate training."

Kinsey is credited with establishing the academic field of sexology, and his views were sought by policymakers. For example, he testified before the Subcommittee on Sex Crimes of the California General Assembly in 1949 and worked with the Columbia University law professor Herbert Wechsler to promote the American Law Institute's Model Penal Code (1962), in which the penalties for sex offenses were related to his findings.

Those who found fault with Kinsey's work often did so on the grounds that his sampling of subjects to interview did not reflect the general public, because he relied heavily on white, middle-class, college-educated persons. After publication in 1953 of *Sexual Behavior in the Human Female* (written with Wardell Pomeroy, Clyde Martin, and Paul Gephard), some women took issue with his conclusions that American women were either sexually repressed in marriage or highly promiscuous. Many argued that he denigrated MOTHERHOOD, misrepresented married couples, and defined American husbands and fathers as SEX OFFENDERS. Others viewed his conclusions as too permissive of harmful sexual behavior; for example, he recommended leniency for suspected child molesters, arguing that the hysteria surrounding such cases could be more harmful than the acts themselves. "We are the recorders and reporters of facts," he noted, "not the judges of the behaviors we describe." Kinsey's legacy includes studies of human sexuality conducted by later researchers, among them William H. Masters and Virginia E. Johnson, coauthors of *Human Sexual Response* (1966), and Shere Hite, whose more popular reports on female and male sexuality have included *The Hite Report on Female Sexuality* (1976) and *The Hite Report on Men and Male Sexuality* (1981).

Kinsey thought it important to establish a collection of library materials, films and videos, fine art, artifacts, photography, and other archives that "encompass the mundane, the arcane, the exquisite, and the scientific." Today that collection numbers some seven thousand artifacts and nearly fifty thousand images representing two thousand years of

One of Alfred Kinsey's major studies on sex in America, *Sexual Behavior in the Human Female* (1953), brought a barrage of media attention and criticism from women. The reception was later chronicled in an exhibition, *Oh! Dr. Kinsey! A Photographic Reaction to the Kinsey Report.*

human history. The Kinsey Institute continues to conduct research and publish its findings as well as sponsor workshops, symposiums, exhibitions, and training on topics ranging from sexual development to understanding high-risk sexual behavior. Books including *The Kinsey Institute New Report on Sex* (1990), *Peek: Photographs from the Kinsey Institute* (2000), and *Sex and Humor* (2002) were based on the institute's work.

Contact: Kinsey Institute for Research in Sex, Gender, and Reproduction, Morrison 313, Indiana University, Bloomington, IN 47405 (812-855-7686). www.indiana.edu/~kinsey.

I

LAWRENCE v. TEXAS

In 2002 many states, including Texas, had laws that made it a crime for two persons of the same sex to engage in "deviant sexual intercourse," or SODOMY. This was defined as "any contact between any part of the genitals of one person and the mouth or anus of another person; or the penetration of the genitals or the anus of another person with an object." To challenge the law's legality, a neighbor called the police and complained of a weapons disturbance. When the officers entered the house, they found instead John Geddes Lawrence and Tyron Garner engaged in intimate sexual activity. After paying a fine, the pair appealed their conviction on the grounds that the Texas sodomy law was an unconstitutional violation of protected PRIVACY rights and that it treated homosexuals unequally compared to heterosexuals, who were exempt from its provisions.

In its 6–3 decision in *Lawrence v. Texas* (2003), the U.S. Supreme Court held that the Texas statute was unconstitutional because it violated the due process clause of the Fourteenth Amendment (1868) to the U.S. Constitution. The majority opinion was written by Associate Justice Anthony M. Kennedy. In it the Court recognized that while history and tradition are the starting points for a substantive due process inquiry, the Fourteenth Amendment protections for intimate relationships first acknowledged in *GRISWOLD v. CONNECTICUT* (1965) were the overriding consideration.

The *Lawrence* case pitted two powerful social elements against one another: the political ideal of individual liberty protected by the Constitution versus the traditional religious and moral belief that sodomy is an abomination. According to the Bible, God destroyed the cities of Sodom and Gomorrah to end their perceived immorality. *Sodomy* came to mean anal intercourse or, more generally now, any type of supposedly unnatural sex act or perversion, whether engaged in by heterosexuals or homosexuals. For liberty in the form of the right to privacy to trump the state's power to proscribe certain types of "immoral" sexual behavior between consenting adults in private, the majority of the Court in *Lawrence* had to first deal with its decision in *Bowers v. Hardwick* (1986). In that case a majority of the justices refused to extend the constitutional right of privacy to protect consensual homosexual sodomy in one's own home.

According to the *Lawrence* opinion, the "most pertinent beginning point is our decision in *Griswold v. Connecticut*." The Supreme Court in that instance struck down an 1879 state law making it a crime for any person to use any drug, article, or instrument to prevent CONTRACEPTION. *Griswold* built on the principle announced by Associate Justice Louis D. Brandeis in his dissenting opinion in *Olmstead v. United States* (1928), which suggested that the Constitution confers on the people, "as against the government, the right to be let alone—the most comprehensive of rights and the right most valued by civilized men."

Justice Kennedy in *Lawrence* traced the development of the constitutional protections for "sexual conduct" and the "marital relationship" in several later cases, including *Roe v. Wade* (1973), all of which led to revisiting the Court's decision in *Bowers*. That case presented the issue of "whether the Federal Constitution confers a fundamental right upon homosexuals to engage in sodomy and hence invalidates the laws of many States that still make such conduct illegal and have done so for a very long time." The opinion went on to acknowledge that while for centuries powerful voices have condemned homosexual conduct as immoral, "there is no long-standing history in this country of laws directed at homosexual conduct as a distinct matter."

After considering the fact that many European nations have affirmed the right of adult homosexuals to engage in intimate sexual conduct, Justice Kennedy found that the rationale in *Bowers* could not withstand careful analysis. Quoting from the Court's decision in PLANNED PARENTHOOD OF SOUTHEASTERN PENNSYLVANIA *v. CASEY* (1992), the opinion noted, "Our obligation is to define the liberty of all, not to mandate our own moral code." Eschewing the argument that the case be decided on the basis of the Fourteenth Amendment's equal protection clause, the opinion declared that "the Due Process Clause gives them [homosexuals] the full right to engage in their conduct without intervention of the government." It cited *Planned Parenthood* for the proposition that "[i]t is a promise of the Constitution that there is a realm of personal liberty which the government may not enter."

Associate Justice Sandra Day O'Connor, in her concurring opinion, noted that the Fourteenth Amendment's equal protection clause "is essentially a direction that all persons similarly situated should be treated alike." Associate Justice Antonin Scalia dissented, arguing that in overruling *Bowers* the Court had created, without saying so, a fundamental right of homosexual sodomy, thus eviscerating any state's ability to regulate morality. Associate Justice Clarence Thomas joined in Scalia's dissent, adding, however, that the matter was one for state legislatures to decide

and that he could find no provision in the U.S. Constitution for a general right of privacy.

In the wake of *Lawrence*, state courts may reason that the only consensual sexual conduct by adults that can be proscribed is conduct that harms third parties. Yet citizens in a growing number of states are actively pursuing state constitutional amendments that at least limit a state's ability to recognize or grant to homosexual couples traditional rights such as MARRIAGE or similar rights such as civil unions and domestic partnerships. The *Lawrence* decision has taken the right of privacy with respect to intimate sexual conduct to its logical limit and will undoubtedly be revisited should a case involving the right of homosexuals to marry come before the Court. As with many watershed Supreme Court decisions, *Lawrence* may inspire those who disagree with it to increase their efforts to counteract its effect rather than to accept its logic.

See also HOMOSEXUALITY; SAME-SEX MARRIAGE.

LESBIANS

See HOMOSEXUALITY; SAME-SEX MARRIAGE.

LEWD BEHAVIOR

Originally meaning ignorant, *lewd* now commonly means licentious or lustful. It is a relatively old term. William Shakespeare (1564–1616) used it in his play *Henry VI, Part I,* in the sense of unchaste or lascivious when he has the duke of Gloucester say to the bishop of Winchester: "No, prelate. Such is thy audacious wickedness, Thy lewd, pestiferous and dissentious pranks. . . ." In 1971 a Maryland court found that *lewd* and *indecent* have been absorbed into the word *obscene* and thus have "no independent vitality of their own."

Many state laws relating to proscribed sexual behavior still include the terms *lewd* or *lewdness*. For example, Virginia has on its books the crime of lewd and lascivious cohabitation. Oklahoma City's municipal code makes "offering to engage in an act of lewdness" a crime and defines lewdness as: "(a) any lascivious, lustful or licentious conduct, (b) the giving or receiving of the body for indiscriminate sexual intercourse, fellatio, cunnilingus, masturbation, anal intercourse, or lascivious, lustful or licentious conduct with any person not his or her spouse, or (c) any act in furtherance of such conduct or any appointment or engagement for prostitution." The law was challenged in the case *Sawatzky v. City of Oklahoma City* (1995), but the Oklahoma criminal appeals court upheld it. The court concluded that "protecting citizens from solicitation for sexual acts [in this instance, SODOMY] is a legitimate governmental interest."

In *Osborne v. Ohio* (1990), the U.S. Supreme Court upheld a state law making the possession of child PORNOGRAPHY illegal, noting that the law was not constitutionally overbroad in being applied specifically to "depictions of nudity involving a lewd exhibition or graphic focus on a minor's genitals." As recently as 2000, in *City of Erie v. Pap's A.M.*, the Supreme Court considered the term *lewd* in the context of a city ordinance requiring erotic dancers to wear at least pasties and a G-string. In upholding the ordinance against a challenge under the FIRST AMENDMENT (1791) to the U.S. Constitution, the Court cited the preamble to the law. This stated that "the Council of the City of Erie has, at various times over more than a century, expressed its findings that certain lewd, immoral activities carried on in public places for profit are highly detrimental to the public health, safety and welfare, and lead to the debasement of both women and men, promote violence, public intoxication, prostitution and other serious criminal activity."

State governments have several rationales on which they tend to base their interest in regulating or prohibiting lewd behavior in public places. Among them are the prevention of violent reactions to offensive acts or overtures in the case of sexual solicitation, as was considered in the *Sawatzky* case, as well as a general interest in protecting citizens from offensive actions. Lewd activities may be considered to cause a general public nuisance or to be offensive because of where they are carried out; such activity in a residential neighborhood is more intrusive than in an urban business district where ZONING laws make it more acceptable, as was the case with the nude erotic dancing addressed in the *Erie* case. There is also the argument that lewd or obscene behavior attracts other, more harmful, criminal behavior, such as DRUGS, theft, and SEXUAL ASSAULT.

In quasi-public places, laws against lewdness, and the rationales for them, are less clear. The Pennsylvania supreme court, in *Commonwealth v. Bonadio* (1980), ruled that a statute prohibiting consensual sodomy was unconstitutional when applied to erotic dancers who performed oral sex on patrons in a private club. It was presumed that anyone who frequented the club would not likely be offended by that type of lewd behavior. A New Jersey court ruled in 1945 that neither ADULTERY nor fornication committed in secret—as opposed to in an open and public manner—constituted lewdness. In contrast, lewd behavior where CHILDREN are involved would clearly not be condoned under current state laws.

See also BARNES V. GLEN THEATRE, INC.; INDECENT EXPOSURE; NUDITY; PROSTITUTION; STATE AND LOCAL GOVERNMENT.

LIVE SHOWS

See ENTERTAINMENT INDUSTRY; NUDITY; SEXUALLY ORIENTED BUSINESSES; ZONING.

LOCAL GOVERNMENT

See STATE AND LOCAL GOVERNMENT.

MAGAZINES

See ADULT MATERIALS; CENSORSHIP; FLYNT, LARRY; *GINZBURG v. UNITED STATES;* HEFNER, HUGH; MEDIA; PORNOGRAPHY.

MARRIAGE

The concept of the family unit including a husband, a wife, and CHILDREN has prevailed for millennia. Aristotle (384–322 B.C.E.), the Greek philosopher, opined that the family—by which he meant master and slave, husband and wife, and father and children—was an integral part of the structure of the nation-state. After 1500 C.E., political theorists in Europe proposed that the family and the state were the only human associations rooted in natural law. Around the same time, European governments began exercising some control over the institution of marriage, which for some time had been the province of the Roman Catholic Church; because marriage was considered a sacred commitment, the Church required the consent of the parties. Before then arranged marriages had more often been the rule and are still prevalent in many parts of the world.

In the eighteenth century, England began requiring marriage licenses and regulating the time and place of marriage ceremonies. But the process was still one sided. The husband, after the marriage was formalized, became the head of the family and the owner of his wife's property, and she lost the right to enter into contracts in her own name. In the United States today, the partners in a marriage are, for the most part, considered equal under the law, although some residual social, economic, and religious DISCRIMINATION against married women remains.

The changes in the institution of marriage from the patriarchal model ruled by the husband and father, whose authority over his wife and children was virtually unquestioned, to the modern model came about because of a number of factors. Among them are the population movement from rural areas to the cities after the Industrial Revolution, the decrease in the social influence of RELIGION, the SEXUAL REVOLUTION and the concomitant expansion of WOMEN'S RIGHTS, liberalization of DIVORCE laws, and the increase in the number of women obtaining higher education and working outside the home.

The traditional married family is now being eclipsed by alternative living arrangements, from unmarried partners to single persons and same-sex households. According to the U.S. Census Bureau and the National Center for Health Statistics, some 2.3 million marriages took place in 2001. The percentage of unmarried to married cohabitants is steadily increasing, and projections show that the population of unmarried women will soon surpass that of married women. Half of all American children will spend part of their childhood in a family that does not consist of two married biological parents.

"Completely Under State Control"

The rules and regulations regarding marriage are still subject to the laws of the states and the interpretation of those laws by the courts. In *Boddie v. Connecticut* (1971), U.S. Supreme Court Associate Justice Hugo L. Black noted in his dissent: "Absent some specific federal constitutional or statutory provision, marriage in this country is completely under state control." In *Flores v. Flores* (1979), the supreme court of Alaska declared that "marriages and divorces are wholly creations of the state."

Aspects of marriage that are subject to state laws include the minimum age for legal CONSENT (because consent to marriage is consent to having sexual relations), authorization of officials to perform marriage ceremonies, establishment of waiting periods, and requirements for licenses, physical examinations, and blood tests. The laws of the states vary on these issues.

Consent. The range of the minimum age for consent with parental approval for males is fourteen to eighteen years old; without parental approval, it is from eighteen to twenty-one years of age. For females, the corresponding ranges are from twelve to eighteen years of age with or without parental approval. Most states allow a fourteen-year-old to marry with parental permission and a court order. Some states allow a couple under the age of eighteen years to marry, usually without the parents' approval, if the female is pregnant or has given birth to a child by the male partner.

Officiators. Although some states authorize governors and mayors to officiate at wedding ceremonies, marriages are more typically conducted by licensed or ordained members of the clergy as well as judicial officials, including judges, justices of the peace, and other civil magistrates.

Waiting Periods. The waiting period—to discourage rash decisions—between the application for a marriage license and its issuance may be three to five days. Florida withholds the issuance of a marriage license for three days unless the couple can present proof that they have completed a course preparing them for marriage.

Eximination. Many states also require a doctor's certification as evidence that both parties have been

The marriage certificate, whether a simple government form or a more elaborate keepsake document like this early-twentieth-century example from West Virginia, is evidence of the commitment a couple makes to live together and rear a family. It also serves as proof of the legitimacy of children born during the marriage.

examined, which generally includes a blood test, and that they are free of SEXUALLY TRANSMITTED DISEASES.

Failure to comply with procedural requirements such as licensing, physical exams, solemnization, waiting periods, and recordation of the certificate does not generally invalidate a marriage that is otherwise legal.

Prohibitions. The states prohibit certain parties from marrying. The INCEST taboo manifests itself in laws preventing marriage between members of the nuclear family—father, mother, and their children, as well as other relatives of close sanguinity such as grandparents. Some states prohibit marriage between first cousins and even more distant cousins. A legally certified mentally ill person or an extremely retarded person may be barred from marrying, as is a person who at the time is married to a living husband or wife. Marriage to more than one person at the same time (BIGAMY) is illegal in all U.S. jurisdictions. Homosexual couples are barred from marrying in all states except Massachusetts, a social taboo codified by the recent spate of constitutional amendments adopted so far in twenty states to prohibit SAME-SEX MARRIAGE; nearly all other states have statutory bans, and only Vermont and Connecticut to date allow civil unions of homosexual couples.

As state courts apply and interpret their unique state laws regarding marriage, sometimes unique cases test those laws. In *In re Estate of Gardiner* (2002), the Kansas court of appeals held that Kansas was required to recognize the birth certificate of a man born in Wisconsin who had changed his sex to female and then married a man. Some courts have followed the Kansas court's "once a man always a man" rule, while others have accepted arguments that the question of a person's sex is more complicated than simply judging by the physical evidence at birth.

In both *Loving v. Virginia* (1967), a case testing state laws against interracial marriage, and *Zablocki v. Redhail* (1978), involving denial of a marriage license because of failure to pay child support, the U.S. Supreme Court confirmed the constitutional right to marry and struck down state laws that unconstitutionally restricted that right. In 1987 the Court unanimously invalidated state regulations prohibiting marriage by PRISONERS. In her opinion in that case, *Turner v. Safley*, Associate Justice Sandra Day O'Connor explained that the right to marry was unaffected by the prison setting, where sex is prohibited. The "incidents of marriage, like the religious and personal aspects of the marriage commitment," she said, "are unaffected by the fact of confinement or the pursuit of legitimate corrections goals."

Rights and Obligations

The status of marriage confers certain rights as well as obligations on the partners under both federal and state law.

Legal Rights. Legally married spouses have the right to recovery for emotional stress and loss of consortium in certain types of lawsuits, standing to sue in the case of the wrongful death of a partner, the privilege of spousal immunity from testifying, and the right of privileged communication with a spouse. In some states, marriage remains a defense against charges of marital RAPE or fornication before the marriage.

Concerning the right of PRIVACY in marriage, the U.S. Supreme Court in *Griswold v. Connecticut* (1965) struck down a state law banning the use of CONTRACEPTION. In his opinion for the Court, Associate Justice WILLIAM O. DOUGLAS asked: "Would we allow the police to search the sacred precincts of marital bedrooms for telltale signs of the use of contraceptives? The very idea is repulsive to the notions of privacy surrounding the marriage relationship." In *Roberts v. United States Jaycees* (1984), Associate Justice William J. Brennan Jr. explained that one of the types of association protected by the Constitution is freedom of association related to marriage, procreation, conception, and family and children.

Property Rights. Property rights that are affected by marriage depend on state law. California and eight other states, for example, are community property states, which means that all property in a marriage is owned one-half by each spouse. Most states are title-based or separate property states, whereby each spouse owns his or her own property before marriage and as it is obtained or earned during marriage. Property such as a house may be owned jointly with the right of survivorship, meaning that the spouse who survives the death of another becomes the sole owner.

Marital status also extends rights in DIVORCE that include child custody and visitation rights as well as financial maintenance and ALIMONY.

Inheritance. Entitlements include the right of inheritance in the absence of a will; in some cases, a widow and children may have inheritance rights even if excluded from a will. One traditional reason for such laws was to keep the state from having to support destitute widows and children. Courts typically deny claims against an estate by an unmarried

State Marriage Laws

State	Common Law Marriage	Age With/Without Parental Consent	Medical Exam Required	Marriage License	
				Waiting Period Before License	Duration of License
Alabama	Yes	14/18	No	No	30 days
Alaska	No	16/18	No	3 days	3 months
Arizona	No	16/18	No	No	1 year
Arkansas	No	Male 17/18 Female 16/18	No	No	–
California	No	With[1]/18	Yes	No	90 days
Colorado	Yes	16/18	No	No	30 days
Connecticut	No	16/18	Yes	4 days	65 days
Delaware	No	Male 18/18 Female 16/18	No	24 hours	30 days
Florida	No	16/18	No	No	60 days
Georgia	No[2]	16/18	Yes	3 days	30 days
Hawaii	No	15/18	No	No	30 days
Idaho	No[2]	16/18	Yes	No	–
Illinois	No	16/18	Yes	1 day	60 days
Indiana	No[2]	17/18	Yes	No	60 days
Iowa	Yes	16/18	No	3 days	–
Kansas	Yes	Male 14/18 Female 12/18	No	3 days	6 months
Kentucky	No	18/18	No	No	30 days
Louisiana	No	18/18	Yes	No	–
Maine	No	16/18	No	3 days	90 days
Maryland	No	16/18	No	48 hours	6 months
Massachusetts	No	Male 14/18 Female 12/18	Yes	3 days	60 days
Michigan	No	16/18	No	3 days	33 days
Minnesota	No	16/18	No	5 days	6 months
Mississippi	No	Male[3]/17 Female[3]/15	Yes	3 days	–
Missouri	No	15/18	No	No	30 days
Montana	Yes	16/18	Yes	No	180 days
Nebraska	No	17/19	Yes	No	1 year
Nevada	No	16/18	No	No	1 year
New Hampshire	No	Male 14/18 Female 13/18	No	3 days	90 days
New Jersey	No	16/18	No	72 hours	30 days
New Mexico	No	16/18	Yes	No	–
New York	No	16/18	Yes[4]	24 hours	60 days

State	Common Law Marriage	Age With/Without Parental Consent	Medical Exam Required	Marriage License	
				Waiting Period Before License	Duration of License
North Carolina	No	16/18	No	No	–
North Dakota	No	16/18	No	No	60 days
Ohio	No[2]	Male 18/18 Female 16/18	No	5 days	60 days
Oklahoma	No[2]	16/18	Yes	[5]	30 days
Oregon	No	17/18	No	3 days	60 days
Pennsylvania	No[2]	16/18	Yes	3 days	60 days
Rhode Island	Yes	Male 18/18 Female 16/18	Yes	No	3 months
South Carolina	Yes	Male 16/18 Female 14/18	No	1 day	–
South Dakota	No	16/18	No	No	20 days
Tennessee	No	16/18	No	3 days	30 days
Texas	Yes	14/18	No	[6]	30 days
Utah	Yes	14/18	No	No	30 days
Vermont	No	16/18	Yes	1 day	–
Virginia	No	16/18	No	No	60 days
Washington	No	17/18	No[7]	3 days	60 days
West Virginia	No	18/18	Yes	3 days	–
Wisconsin	No	16/18	No	5 days	30 days
Wyoming	No	16/18	Yes	No	–

1. No age limit set for parental consent; other statutory requirements apply.
2. Recognizes earlier common law marriages.
3. No age limit; parental consent and/or a judge's permission required.
4. Test for sickle-cell anemia may be required.
5. Three-day waiting period if parental consent required.
6. Seventy-two-hour waiting period after issuance of license.
7. No exam required but venereal disease certificate mandated.

Source: Cornell University Law School, 2006

heterosexual or same-sex partner; the state supreme court of Washington held in *Vasquez v. Hawthorne* (2001), however, that the type of relationship between the life partner and the decedent could warrant an equitable division of the estate. A spouse has priority as executor of a decedent's estate. In Vermont, same-sex partners in civil unions have rights under probate law.

Other Benefits. Other benefits that flow from the status of marriage include health, accident, and disability insurance coverage through employer benefit plans; family leave; reduction in tax liability because of marital status (in 2003 the so-called marriage penalty was eliminated at the federal level from all but the highest and lowest income brackets); pension rights; worker's compensation rights; and hospital visitation rights.

Obligations. Obligations of marriage include each spouse's right to receive maintenance and support from the other, responsibility to jointly care for their children and provide CHILD SUPPORT, and to generally live up to the vows taken at the time of the marriage.

Marital-type Relationships

In addition to the typical marriage contract, several similar relationships are recognized in various states.

Common Law Marriage. Common law marriage (still sanctioned in a handful of states as well as the District of Columbia) is regarded as a regular marriage except without the benfit of a license or a legal ceremony; some states require that a couple cohabit and agree between themselves to be married. This common law arrangement allows a couple to live together openly in the community as husband and wife, acting as such by filing joint tax returns and referring to each other as a spouse on insurance applications and the like in order to be treated as married legally. A few states have set a moratorium on when a common law marriage must have been entered into. For example, in Georgia, it must have been created before January 1, 1997, and in Idaho before January 1, 1996.

Covenant Marriage. More than twenty states provide an option called covenant marriage. This makes it harder for partners to obtain a divorce because they waive their rights to no-fault divorce and some of the grounds used to obtain a fault-based divorce. Covenant marriage is just one of a number of steps, along with waiting and separation periods, that some states such as Louisiana and Arizona have taken to make it more difficult to obtain a divorce.

Domestic Partnerships. For partners who are precluded by law from marrying or for whom marriage would be an economic hardship, domestic partnerships provide privileges and benefits similar to those enjoyed by married couples. While most domestic partnership laws are aimed at same-sex couples, in some cases heterosexual domestic partnerships may be recognized. California, for one, recognizes unmarried heterosexual couples sixty-two years of age or older who are eligible for Social Security (and therefore might lose benefits). Hawaii recognizes couples including a brother and a sister or a widowed mother and her unmarried son under its provision for people who are "legally prohibited from marrying one another under state law." Where domestic partnerships are allowed, they represent an alternative to civil unions, which are legal in Vermont and Connecticut, as well as same-sex marriage.

Domestic partnerships are sometimes recognized for the purpose of treating an unmarried domestic partner like a spouse for employee benefits. In 1999, for example, the Chicago board of education extended spousal health benefits to domestic partners who were of the same sex, unmarried and unrelated, at least eighteen years of age, and "each other's sole domestic partner, responsible for each other's common welfare."

The face-off over traditional versus nontraditional marriage—same-sex marriage, civil unions, domestic partnerships, and plain unwed cohabitation—is a symptom of the pace at which cultural changes are occurring. Some people see the notion of a typical nuclear family as already an anachronism that fewer and fewer modern families can conform to. Although states are trying to deal with these conflicts in the institution of marriage, it may be a long time before a stable and just consensus is finally reached.

See also ADULTERY; ANNULMENT; HEALTHY MARRIAGE INITIATIVE; MISCEGENATION; POLYGAMY; SPOUSAL RIGHTS AND DUTIES; UNMARRIED COHABITANTS.

MATERNITY

See ASSISTED REPRODUCTIVE TECHNOLOGY; MOTHERHOOD; PREGNANCY.

MATERNITY LEAVE

See MOTHERHOOD.

MEDIA

A means of mass communication is called a medium; collectively newspapers, magazines, radio, and television have traditionally been known as the media, the plural form of *medium*. In 1791, when freedom of the press was guaranteed by the FIRST AMENDMENT (1791) to the U.S. Constitution, mass media took the form of just printed matter. Today electronic media from radio and television to the INTERNET also qualify as forms of mass communication.

As early as 1690, the Massachusetts Bay Colony confiscated a newspaper because it carried a story about the amorous affairs of the French king, Louis XIV. The founders of the United States were keenly aware of the importance in a democracy of allowing the dissemination of information, ideas, and opinions by means of a free press. The first ten amendments to the Constitution, making up the Bill of Rights, thus included protection of printed matter from government CENSORSHIP.

Libel (defamatory writing or publishing of items that are blasphemous, seditious, or immoral) remains outside First Amendment protections. Applicable to media communications since before the American Revolution (1775–83), libel laws have since been liberalized somewhat by the U.S. Supreme Court. In a landmark case, *New York Times Co. v. Sullivan* (1964), for example, the media's freedom to comment on public figures was expanded. This decision would protect LARRY FLYNT's *Hustler* magazine in 1988 from a damage suit filed by the Reverend Jerry Falwell. The evangelical minister, who had been depicted in *Hustler* as having had sex with his mother in an outhouse, was deemed a public figure because he had often commented on public affairs during his televised sermons.

Print Media

Faced with what appears to be an absolute constitutional prohibition against government interference with the press, the Supreme Court in 1957 began trying to balance this freedom with the publication of OBSCENITY. In *Kingsley Books, Inc. v. Brown* (1957), the Court upheld a New York law that allowed a court to enjoin distribution of and destroy booklets displayed for sale that were held to be clearly obscene. The majority decision, written by Associate Justice Felix Frankfurter, noted that this case differed from the situation in the Court's precedent, *Near v. Minnesota* (1931), in which it struck down a state law that amounted to prior restraint of publication. The restraint in *Kingsley* occurred only after a determination that the material was obscene. And obscenity, declared the Court in ROTH V. UNITED STATES in the same year of 1957, lacks First Amendment protection. Although *Kingsley* left the door open for some form of prior restraint of obscene books and periodicals, in several later cases, including *Freedman v. Maryland* (1965), the Court made clear the need for procedural safeguards, such as speedy appeals of adverse determinations, before obscenity can be restrained.

In *Richmond Newspapers, Inc. v. Virginia* (1980), the Supreme Court held that it was unconstitutional to bar newspaper coverage of a trial by closing it to the public on the assumption that not to do so would jeopardize the defendant's right to a fair trial. Then, in *Globe Newspaper Co. v. Superior Court* (1982), the Court extended the media's right to have access to trials in a case involving the testimony of a minor who was a witness in a sex offense case.

Electronic Media

Radio and television, unlike the press, have been regulated by the federal government through the FEDERAL COMMUNICATIONS COMMISSION since the agency's creation in 1934. At the time, it was thought that because only a limited number of frequencies were available for broadcasting, those who were permitted to use these public airwaves should be required to use them in the public interest.

The FCC is now often in the news because of its power to fine those who violate the law and the agency's rules regarding the dissemination of vulgar, indecent, or obscene language or portrayals. For example, twenty CBS-owned stations that broadcast the Super Bowl halftime show in 2004, during which a "wardrobe malfunction" exposed a female performer's breast, were fined $550,000 in 2004. Clear Channel Communications was fined $495,000 in 2004 based on allegations of eighteen indecency violations by the radio "shock jock" Howard Stern in a broadcast a year earlier. And then in 2006, the FCC levied one of its largest total fines ever—some $3.35 million—for the portrayal of group sex by TEENAGERS on the CBS drama *Without a Trace.* That year CONGRESS raised the maximum single fine for indecent broadcasts from $32,500 to $325,000.

Because radio and television are not specifically protected by the Constitution, as are the print media, the Supreme Court has upheld reasonable government restrictions. A key case in the development of the FCC's powers regarding indecency and obscenity is *Federal Communications Commission v. Pacifica Foundation* (1978). Here the Court upheld the FCC's sanction of a station for airing a monologue by the comedian George Carlin called "Filthy Words," in which he listed and repeated a variety of "words you couldn't say on the public airwaves"; Carlin's monologue had been recorded before a live audience in a California theater and later broadcast by a New York station. The Court noted that the FCC had found that the words—*shit, piss, cunt, fuck, cocksucker, motherfucker, and tits*—were used in a particularly offensive manner and were broadcast in the early afternoon "when children are undoubtedly in the audience." The FCC had concluded that the language as broadcast was indecent and prohibited under Title 18, section 1464, of the U.S. Code, which forbids the use of "any obscene, indecent, or profane language by means of radio communications."

Cable and satellite transmission of television and radio signals has been treated by the government as a special case because a person or a household must take action to subscribe to that form of media service. The theory is that there is little need for regulation of material transmitted by cable and satellite given that if people are offended by programs, they can simply cancel their subscription. In reality, most people today have cable or satellite television, and they exercise personal programming options to avoid objectionable material.

The Internet

The Supreme Court has accorded special status to the Internet, a newer form of electronic media. This is due in part to its function as a means of political communication among individuals through e-mail and to the fact that, unlike television and radio, it is not a passive medium but requires an active effort to seek material. Parents can use various methods to block access by CHILDREN to improper material or information on the Internet.

Congress has tried several times to criminalize the transmission of obscene materials on the Internet if they can be accessed by minors. In *Reno v. American Civil Liberties Union* (1997) and *Ashcroft v. American Civil Liberties Union* (2002, 2004), however, the Court struck down as unconstitutional the COMMUNICATIONS DECENCY ACT (1996) and the CHILD ONLINE PROTECTION ACT (1998), respectively, as unconstitutional infringements of the First Amendment's freedoms of speech and the press; the Court noted that there were less restrictive ways to protect children from improper material than criminalizing the distribution of such materials.

The media play a special role in the American democratic system: they have the ability to broadly disseminate information about what public figures are doing so that citizens can make informed decisions at the polls. Those who wish to stifle the media for any reason—no matter how incensed they might be by the nature of the information or material disseminated—bear a heavy burden under the First Amendment to justify censorship. Commercial interests that wish to advertise products and services to a large audience also have an important stake in keeping the various media avenues open to the public. The Supreme Court has made it clear that, except for instances in which children may be easily exposed to indecent or ADULT MATERIALS, the media are to be protected under the Constitution.

See also ENTERTAINMENT INDUSTRY; HEFNER, HUGH.

MEDICAL PROCEDURES

See SEXUAL ENHANCEMENT; TRANSSEXUALISM.

MEGAN'S LAW

In 1994 seven-year-old Megan Kanka was lured from her home in New Jersey, raped, and strangled by a twice-convicted sex offender who lived across the street. Megan's parents organized a movement to enact a law in New Jersey establishing a community notification system for convicted sex offenders. A subsequent federal law, known as Megan's Law (an amendment to the Violent Crime Control and Law Enforcement Act of 1994), was enacted in 1996 to require all fifty states to set up a similar notification system to pinpoint dangerous sex offenders. The act, introduced in 1995 by Representative Dick Zimmer of New Jersey, specfies that states must keep and maintain records of criminals guilty of violent sex crimes and crimes against CHILDREN and to release such information to the public. All states have enacted their own laws mandating the registration of certain SEX OFFENDERS and public dissemination of information on them, including their location.

Each state's Megan's Law is different. The Alaska Sex Offenders Act, for one, was described in the U.S. Supreme Court decision *Smith v. Doe* (2003) as follows:

Under the . . . Act, any sex offender or child kidnapper incarcerated in the State must register with the Department of Corrections within 30 days before his release, providing his name, address, and other specified information.

If the individual is at liberty, he must register with local law enforcement authorities within a working day of his conviction or of entering the State. If he was convicted of a single, nonaggravated sex crime, the offender must provide annual verification of the submitted information for 15 years. If he was convicted of an aggravated sex offense or of two or more sex offenses, he must register for life and verify the information quarterly.

The offender's information is forwarded to the Department of Public Safety, which maintains a central registry of sex offenders. Some data such as fingerprints, . . . anticipated change of address, and whether the offender has had medical treatment afterwards is kept confidential. The offender's name, aliases, address, photograph, physical description, driver's license number, motor vehicle identification numbers, place of employment, date of birth, crime, date and place of conviction, length and conditions of sentence, and a statement as to whether the offender is in compliance with the Act's updated requirements or cannot be located are, however, published on the Internet.

The Supreme Court held in *Smith v. Doe* that, because the act was not intended to be a punishment, the fact that it was made retroactive (applicable to offenders convicted before it went into effect) did not violate the U.S. Constitution's provision prohibiting ex post facto (after the fact) laws.

In addition to the issue disposed of in *Smith,* these notification laws have raised other constitutional and procedural issues. For example, in *Connecticut Department of Public Safety v. John Doe* (2003), the Supreme Court held that requiring the registration of a sex offender under Connecticut's Megan's Law without giving him a hearing does not deprive the offender of a "liberty interest" and thus does not violate the due process clause of the Fourteenth Amendment (1868) to the U.S. Constitution. The offender had argued that the injury to his reputation caused by the registration requirement entitled him to a hearing to determine if he was "currently dangerous."

Other federal laws related to Megan's Law include the Jacob Wetterling Crimes Against Children and Sexually Violent Offender Act (1994), which laid the groundwork for Megan's Law and establishment of the National Sex Offender Registry; and the Pam Lychner Sexual Offender Tracking and Identification Act (1996). These two laws are also named for victims of SEX OFFENSES. The National Sex Offender Registry Web site directs inquiries to state sex offender Web sites; each state has its own rules about how to access information regarding the whereabouts of registered sex offenders.

Laws that seek to warn citizens about sex offenders in their midst are extensions of the trend toward legal concern for VICTIMS' RIGHTS. These are an outgrowth of the Supreme Court's emphasis on the rights of the accused in the mid- to late twentieth

After Megan Kanka was murdered in 1994 by a convicted sex offender living across the street, her mother spearheaded a movement to require sex offenders to keep the public advised of where they live. Today all fifty states mandate sex-offender registries available to the public.

century, such as "*Miranda* warnings" for suspects emanating from its decision *Miranda v. Arizona* (1966). Victims' rights laws are to some extent politically driven by individuals and groups affected or shocked by heinous acts such as sex crimes, HATE CRIMES, and crimes against law enforcement officers. But at their root efforts such as Megan's Law evince a nearly universal desire to protect one of the nation's most vulnerable segments: its children.

Contact: National Sex Offender Registry, Crimes Against Children Unit, Federal Bureau of Investigation, U.S. Department of Justice, 935 Pennsylvania Avenue, NW, Washington, DC 20535-0001 (202-324-3000). www.fbi.gov/hq/cid/cac/registry.htm. www.nsopr.gov.

See also CRIMES AGAINST CHILDREN UNIT (FBI); RAPE; SEXUAL ASSAULT.

MILITARY

The U.S. Constitution places the military under civilian control in several ways. Article I, section 8, provides that CONGRESS has the power to "declare War . . . raise and support Armies . . . provide and maintain a Navy," and "make Rules for the Government and Regulation of the land and naval Forces." Article II, section 2, makes the PRESIDENT the "Commander in Chief of the Army and Navy of the United States." Given that the British sovereign had been in charge of Great Britain's armed forces (if only titularly since the ascendancy of Parliament), the drafters of the Constitution saw the wisdom in having the new nation's civilian president oversee the military forces; unlike a monarch, the elected head of state and government could be impeached by Congress or removed by regular elections for overstepping his bounds.

Two relationships have undergirded the nature of the military in America: citizenship and manhood. In one sense, the obligations of citizenship have created a willingness on the part of Americans (able-bodied males for most of our history) to serve in the military to protect the country. In *Scott v. Sandford* (1857)—the infamous Dred Scott case denying slaves the constitutionally guaranteed rights and privileges of citizenship granted to white citizens—the U.S. Supreme Court noted that in the 1790s Congress barred men of African descent from the armed forces; thus, it concluded, slaves could not be citizens of the United States because one of the indicia of citizenship is the ability to serve in the nation's military.

The other pillar of the American military has been the notion of service as proof of manhood—a recruiting slogan once proclaimed that the U.S. Marines were "looking for a few good men." A corollary is the military's need for cohesion and high morale among the troops, two elements that are believed necessary for an efficient and effective fighting force. Members of a military unit must be able to obey orders, rely on each other, and be loyal to the unit under extreme circumstances. For most of American history, blacks, women, and homosexuals have been considered by military leaders to be a detriment to achieving these goals.

Sex Discrimination

A major factor working against modern efforts to integrate the military—racially as well as by including women and sexual minorities—was the assumption by many military leaders and government officials that anyone other than a heterosexual white male soldier was bad for troop morale and the cohesion of the fighting unit. Controlling civilian antisocial sexual behavior is difficult enough, but in the military loneliness, alienation, rigorous discipline, and stress from combat conditions compound the problem. When the integration of women into some areas of the military and the inclusion of homosexuals, both male and female, were added to this previously all-male arena, the process of addressing proscribed sexual behavior in the military became even more complicated.

The first wave of military integration involved that of black men. When President Harry S. Truman began to contemplate integrating black and white troops in the 1940s, no top military officials favored it. Nevertheless, Truman issued Executive Order 9981 on July 26, 1948, doing just that. This move was a major step forward in permitting all U.S. citizens willing and able to serve in the armed forces to be treated equally. A year later, however, a report on the military's desegregation revealed that the "racist belief that the Negro was a natural coward was the real objection to integration by many in the Army."

Women have historically served in wartime as nurses. According to one nurse serving during the Civil War, some four hundred women also passed as males and fought alongside men; one private, who served with distinction in a regiment from Illinois, was discovered to be a woman when she was captured in the Battle of Chattanooga. Nurses were treated as civilian auxiliaries rather than as military personnel before World War I, in which thousands served in the nursing corps of various branches of the armed services. During World War II, well over two hundred thousand women came to serve in many skilled positions, other than as nurses, by 1945. Their participation led to enactment of the Women's Armed Services Act of 1948, which permitted women to serve as full members of the U.S. armed forces.

Although the racial discrimination that once pervaded the military has been abandoned, at least legally if not always in fact, DISCRIMINATION against women continues. The Defense Authorization Act of 1992 allowed women in the navy and the air force to fly in combat, but restrictions remain in areas of special operations forces, helicopter flights, and rescue missions. In 1993 President Bill Clinton signed a bill allowing women on ships in combat; since then at least ten navy women have taken command of ships, but women remain excluded from submarine warfare and special warfare assignments. The army has allowed women in limited combat roles and as helicopter pilots. As U.S. Representative Heather A. Wilson of New Mexico, the only female military veteran in Congress, pointed out on the floor of the House of Representatives in 2005, in connection with a failed attempt to further limit women's combat roles in the army, there are "men and women 6,000 miles from home [in Iraq] doing a very dangerous job, and we should not do anything to indicate we do not appreciate their service."

A major obstacle to the complete integration of women into the U.S. military, as with homosexuals, is the assumption that a heterosexual man can trust and understand only a fellow heterosexual male soldier under the intense conditions of combat. Another fear is that a woman, as a sexually attractive person, could be a distracting influence on a virile young heterosexual male soldier. A further concern is that if captured by the enemy, a woman could be sexually abused. Based on these concerns, the military has adopted special rules regarding women that otherwise might be inimical to citizens in a constitutional democracy. According to a 1980 Senate report, "The principle that women should not intentionally and routinely engage in combat is fundamental, and enjoys wide support among our people."

The Women's Armed Services Act passed in 1948, also referred to as the Integration Act, in fact severely restricted women in the military by limiting the number who could serve in any branch to 2 percent of the entire force and by creating separate promotion lists and setting higher minimum ages for women who wished to enlist than for men. Their duties were to be assigned as appropriate for them, and they were barred by law from combat missions, except in the army, where they were barred by regulation. In 1967, however, an amendment removed restrictions on the promotion of women. The combat role of women has since been gradually increased in the army. For example, in 1994 the secretary of defense approved a policy to allow army women to serve with some ground combat units. Yet in the few cases involving women military members to reach the Supreme Court, the justices have agreed that women are not entitled to be treated equally with men.

In the 1970s the Vietnam War and the failed drive to ratify the Equal Rights Amendment (1972) to the U.S. Constitution, which would have given women EQUAL RIGHTS with men, brought on new pressures for a greater role for women in the military. Women were admitted to the military academies for the first time in 1976. In 1980 President Jimmy Carter asked Congress for authority to register women for the military draft. "Both men and women are working members of our society," he said, "[and] ... women are now providing all types of skills in every profession. The military should be no exception." Congress rejected the request by a large majority.

In 1981 the Supreme Court addressed the question of "whether the Military Selective Service Act [1976] violates the Fifth Amendment to the Constitution in [requiring] the registration of males and not females." The Court held in *Rostker v. Goldberg* that the purpose of registration for the draft was to ultimately draft combat troops; because women were excluded from combat, there was no need for them to be registered, the justices reasoned. Such discrimination thus was found not to violate the equal protection clause of the Fifth Amendment (1791), as would an arbitrary classification, such as registering only blacks or Catholics or Republicans.

As indicated in *Rostker*, the Supreme Court has tended to be overly deferential to the military when it is challenged on constitutional grounds. But an important case involving discrimination and the rights of women in the military, an officer in this instance, was decided in *FRONTIERO V. RICHARDSON* (1973). Here the Court declared unconstitutional a federal law making it more difficult for a woman military officer to get a salary supplement based on her being married. Unlike the *Rostker* case, the distinction here was seen as having no reasonable purpose.

During congressional hearings in the 1970s, a Marine Corps commandant testified: "War is man's work. [Women] would be an enormous psychological distraction for the male who wants to think that he's fighting for that woman somewhere behind.... It tramples the male ego. When you get right down to it, you have to protect the manliness of war." A military directive has created the Defense Department

Military Equal Opportunity Program, which forbids discrimination and defines SEXUAL HARASSMENT as a form of sex discrimination that involves unwelcome sexual advances, requests for sexual favors, and other verbal or physical conduct of a sexual nature.

Numerous cases of sexual harassment in the military have been documented, including the highly publicized Tailhook Association convention sex scandal in Las Vegas, Nevada, in 1991. Later reports of sexual assaults and harassment at the Army Proving Grounds in Aberdeen, Maryland, in 1996 resulted in the Defense Department's setting up a free telephone number for sexual complaints. Scores of charges of SEXUAL ASSAULT were filed by female military service officers serving in Iraq and Kuwait.

Harassment at the military academies had become so serious, including sex scandals at the Air Force Academy in 2002, that a Department of Defense Task Force on Sexual Harassment and Violence at the Military Service Academies was set up in 2003. Its report, released in 2005, found that "harassment is the more prevalent and corrosive problem, creating an environment in which sexual assault is likely to occur." While acknowledging the problem is a step in the right direction, the question remains how seriously the military will take its responsibilities for changing the environment. The 2002 RAPE scandal at the Air Force Academy produced a court-martial for only one cadet; in 2004 another academy cadet who was facing charges of rape, sodomy, and indecent assault, which could have brought a life sentence, got off with a $2,000 fine and a reprimand.

Homosexuals in the Military

Homosexuals have been expressly banned from the military for some fifty years; any member of the armed services who disclosed that he or she was gay or lesbian could be summarily discharged. But after a naval officer publicly announced on television in 1992 that he was gay and discharge proceedings were initiated based on his announcement, he sued the navy and the Defense Department on the grounds that his dismissal would be unconstitutional under the equal

protection clause of the U.S. Constitution. In 1994 the U.S. Court of Appeals for the Ninth Circuit held in *Mienhold v. U.S. Department of Defense* that a dismissal because a member of the military made a public statement that he was a homosexual was not unconstitutional; however, the court held that such a person could not be discharged merely for professing a status. His statement would have to be accompanied by evidence of conduct or intent to engage in such conduct. The government agreed not to appeal the decision.

Department of Defense Directive 1332.14, issued in December 1993, states: "Homosexual conduct is grounds for separation from the Military Services." The directive sets forth elements of such conduct, including where a "member has made a statement that he or she is a homosexual or bisexual, or words to that effect." Exceptions are allowed for mistakes and even errant conduct by a heterosexual service member. This directive became the basis for the still-enforced policy known as "don't ask, don't tell." Its effect is that the military will not inquire into a person's sexual orientation, but if someone voluntarily divulges his or her HOMOSEXUALITY, he or she may be discharged from the service. In *Thomasson v. Perry* (1996), the U.S. Court of Appeals for the Fourth Circuit found that, in deference to the military's special requirements, statements of homosexuality are plausible evidence of illegal SODOMY and that openly declaring one's homosexuality may thus undermine morale and unit cohesion. Since then, the Supreme Court's decision in *LAWRENCE v. TEXAS* (2003) has overruled most state laws banning consensual, private acts of sodomy.

In 1993 another federal court heard a case involving a Naval Academy cadet who, six weeks before he was scheduled to graduate, told a classmate and a chaplain that he was gay. Rather than let himself be discharged, the cadet resigned and later sued to be reinstated. He asserted that he had been forced to resign not because of any misconduct, but because of his avowed status as a homosexual—the same grounds cited in the naval officer's suit. The academy's actions were upheld the following year by a federal appeals court, which reasoned that the ban on homosexuals was as rational as a height or an eyesight requirement. A dissent, however, suggested that to force a person into silence because of his sexual orientation was unconstitutional.

Sex Offenses

From rape scandals at the military academies to sexual assaults to torture techniques that involve sexually degrading activity, illegal sexual behavior in the military regularly appears in the news headlines. Sex offenses in the military are handled under the Uniform Code of Military Justice, outside civilian law and its court system. The UCMJ, in Title 10 of the U.S. Code, specifically addresses some sex offenses, including rape and carnal knowledge as well as sodomy, in addition to a catchall prohibition of "conduct unbecoming an officer."

Service members subject to the Uniform Code of Military Justice, according to article 2, section 802, include members of a regular component of the armed forces, volunteers, inductees, "and other persons lawfully called or ordered into, or to duty in or for training in the armed forces," as well as "cadets, aviation cadets, and midshipmen," and others, including prisoners of war "in custody of the armed forces." Members of the National Guard are exempt, except "when in Federal Service."

Members of the military subject to the UCMJ are permitted to be to be tried in military, as opposed to civilian, courts. The code provides in part that "all disorders and neglects to the prejudice of good order and discipline in the armed forces, all conduct of a nature to bring discredit upon the armed forces, and crimes and offenses not capital, of which persons subject to this chapter may be guilty, shall be taken cognizance of by a general, special, or summary court-martial, according to the nature and degree of the offense, and shall be punished at the discretion of that court." The U.S. Court of Appeals for the Armed Forces (formerly the U.S. Court of Military Appeal), which was created by Congress outside the Constitution's mandates for the federal JUDICIARY, reviews military decisions.

In two cases, *United States v. Frazier* (1992) and *United States v. Kroop* (1993), the U.S. Court of Appeals

for the Armed Forces upheld the power of the armed services to discharge an officer for committing ADULTERY, based on the UCMJ's prohibition against conduct unbecoming an officer. Service members can also be charged under the U.S. Code. *United States v. Brooks* (2005) involved an appeal from a general court-martial for engaging in a criminal sex act in violation of a provision of Title 18 of the U.S. Code, attempting to commit the offense of carnal knowledge of a child under the age of twelve years and wrongfully soliciting an individual under the age of eighteen years to engage in a criminal sexual act. The military appeals court found that the evidence introduced at trial strongly supported a conviction where the appellant knowingly induced a woman to bring her minor sister to a designated site for sex.

Sexually Transmitted Diseases

Disease is another factor that can affect troop morale and performance. During the Civil War (1861–65), prostitutes (known as "camp followers") made themselves available to soldiers as they traveled from battlefield to battlefield; yet in 1865 Congress felt compelled to pass a law aimed at keeping pornographic books from Union soldiers. The U.S. War Department later began providing condoms to sailors going on shore leave. In World War I, American soldiers serving overseas were also issued condoms, a measure credited with holding the number of cases of venereal disease reported in the army and navy between September 1917 and February 1919 to just over 280,000. The military continues programs to educate troops about ways to prevent SEXUALLY TRANSMITTED DISEASES.

To ensure an effective military, lawmakers, the courts, and presumably a majority of the American public have been willing to make certain tradeoffs by allowing it exceptions to the U.S. Constitution's equal protection requirements. To what degree such concessions—whether concerning women, homosexuals, or racial and ethnic minorities—truly serve that end will undoubtedly continue to be tested.

See also EQUAL RIGHTS; WOMEN'S RIGHTS.

Although Henry Miller's sexually provocative books *Tropic of Cancer* and *Tropic of Capricorn* were written in the 1930s, they played a key role in the evolution of the law regarding sexual behavior in the 1960s. The U.S. Supreme Court held in 1964, without issuing an opinion, that *Tropic of Cancer* was no longer regarded as obscene.

HENRY MILLER

The CENSORSHIP of and litigation over Henry Miller's literary works, including *Tropic of Cancer* (1934) and *Tropic of Capricorn* (1938), made him the most famous banned author in America. Finally, in 1964, in *Grove Press v. Gerstein*, the U.S. Supreme Court reversed a lower court judgment and its own ruling the year before that *Tropic of Cancer*—perhaps the most litigated book in history—was obscene.

The grandson of immigrants from Germany, Henry Valentine Miller was born in New York City on December 26, 1891. Always a dreamer, he longed for a life of adventure rather than that of a tailor like his father. He dropped out of college in 1909 and began a series of love affairs and adventures, marrying his second wife, June, in 1924 and sailing alone to Paris in 1930. Although he had tried to become a writer, success eluded him until at the depth of his despair he began to write a new type of book. He later described it as "a gob of spit in the face of Art, a kick in the pants to God, Man, Destiny, Time, Love, Beauty."

Despite its excessive emphasis on sexual behavior, the book, *Tropic of Cancer*, was soon hailed by important authors and critics, including the poets T. S. Eliot (1888–1965) and Ezra Pound (1885–1972) and the authors and critics George Bernard Shaw (1856–1950), Edmund Wilson (1895–1975), George Orwell (1903–50), and Norman Mailer (b. 1923). Funds to publish *Tropic of Cancer* were supplied by the emerging writer Anaïs Nin (1903–77), with whom Miller had been involved in a love triangle with his wife, who divorced him in 1933. Forty-two years old when the book (he denied that it was a novel) was published, Miller went on to write some sixty-five books, including the trilogy called *Rosy Crucifixion*, consisting of *Sexus* (1949), *Plexus* (1953), and *Nexus* (1960).

After Grove Press, a leading publisher of erotic books, published *Tropic of Cancer* in the United States in 1961, there ensued a series of legal battles over whether the work was obscene or protected under the First Amendment (1791) to the U.S. Constitution. The trials went on for two years but ended with the Supreme Court's *per curiam* ruling (without issuance of a written opinion) in the *Gerstein* case that the book was protected under the Constitution.

As the basis for their decision in *Gerstein*, several of the justices cited the opinion in *Jacobellis v. Ohio* (1964). In that case the Supreme Court had found a national standard applicable for determining obscenity for purposes of First Amendment protection against censorship. Miller's litigation made legal and intellectual history by removing the last vestiges of literary censorship and placed him as a major contributor to the social changes that have persisted to the present.

Idolized by some for his avant-garde literature and reviled by others for what they perceived as obscenity, Miller moved to southern California. There he married three more women and lived until his death on June 7, 1980. He believed that his work had always been about love in all its forms, or as he put it: "The one thing we can never get enough of is love. And the one thing we never give enough of is love." Henry Miller will, however, be remembered primarily for works that were banned from publication in the United States and that changed the law regarding art and PORNOGRAPHY.

See also ADULT MATERIALS.

MILLER v. CALIFORNIA

By 1973 the SEXUAL REVOLUTION was in high gear in America. The movies *Deep Throat* and *Behind the Green Door*, both hard-core pornographic films, were shown in theaters patronized by the general public. This invasion of mainstream public entertainment was due in part to U.S. Supreme Court decisions extending the envelope of constitutionally protected obscenity. *Stanley v. Georgia* (1969), for one, allowed the viewing of pornographic films in private. A movie-rating system put in place by the film industry limited such films to adults. Many U.S. cities also retained their old burlesque and adult or "art" film theaters.

In *Miller v. California* (1973), the Supreme Court revisited the question it had faced in *Jacobellis v. Ohio* (1964) and *Ginzburg v. United States* (1966): by what standards should obscenity be judged? *Miller* and a companion case decided the same day, *Paris Adult Theatre I v. Slaton*, reaffirmed the Court's ruling in *Roth v. United States* (1957) that obscenity—however defined in the context of the times—was beyond the protection of the U.S. Constitution. Mr. Miller was in the business of selling sexually explicit ADULT MATERIALS, while the *Paris* case involved sexually explicit films, which the Supreme Court held are not protected by the Constitution simply by being exhibited to consenting adults.

Chief Justice Warren E. Burger, who had been appointed to the Court by President Richard M. Nixon in 1969, delivered the opinion in the 5–4 *Miller* decision. The defendant was charged with mailing unsolicited, sexually explicit material in violation of a detailed California law making it a misdemeanor to knowingly distribute obscene matter. His conviction was based on five brochures advertising four books entitled *Intercourse, Man-Woman, Sex Orgies Illustrated,* and *An Illustrated History of Pornography* as well as a film entitled *Marital Intercourse.* The materials were mailed to a restaurant in Newport Beach, California, where they were opened by the manager and his mother.

Chief Justice Burger began by recognizing "that the States have a legitimate interest in prohibiting dissemination or exhibition of obscene material when the mode of dissemination carries with it a significant danger of offending the sensibilities of unwilling recipients or of exposure to juveniles." He then chose two cases, *Roth* and *A BOOK NAMED "JOHN CLELAND'S MEMOIRS OF A WOMAN OF PLEASURE" V. ATTORNEY GENERAL OF THE COMMONWEALTH OF MASSACHUSETTS* (1966), to illustrate "the somewhat tortured history of the Court's obscenity decisions." His analysis noted that in *Roth,* obscenity was presumed "to be 'utterly without redeeming social importance.'" In *"John Cleland's Memoirs,"* however, the Court required "that to prove obscenity it must be affirmatively established that the material is *'utterly* without redeeming social value.'" Therefore, after *"Memoirs,"* the prosecutions in such cases were required to prove a negative: that the material was *"utterly* without redeeming social value," which Chief Justice Burger termed "a burden virtually impossible to discharge under our criminal standards of proof."

Saying that no members of the Supreme Court—not even the decision's author, Associate Justice William J. Brennan Jr.—any longer supported the requirement formulated in *"Memoirs,"* the opinion turned to setting out "the permissible scope of . . . regulation [for] works which depict or describe sexual conduct. That conduct," the opinion continued, "must be specifically defined by the applicable state law . . . [and] must also be limited to works which, taken as a whole, appeal to the prurient interest in sex, which portray sexual conduct in a patently offensive way, and which, taken as a whole, do not have serious literary, artistic, political, or scientific value."

The chief justice closed by noting that, as the Court held in the *Roth* case, "obscenity is to be determined by applying 'contemporary community standards,' . . . not 'national standards.'" This issue had been decided differently in the *Jacobellis* and later cases. Although the Court permitted the determination of contemporary community standards by geographical area, in obscenity cases that followed *Miller* the standards in fact did not vary much from place to place.

In a dissent Associate Justice WILLIAM O. DOUGLAS emphasized that the majority opinion was making new law. It was redefining how obscenity was to be determined, he contended, and thus was permitting people to face imprisonment "when they had no 'fair warning' that what they did was criminal conduct." Associate Justice Hugo Black had made a similar argument in his dissent in the *Ginzburg* case, saying that the "harsh expedients used by bad governments to punish people for conduct not previously clearly marked as criminal [will] . . . put Mr. Ginzburg in prison for five years."

While the Supreme Court in *Miller* tried to clarify the analysis necessary to determine whether questionable material was obscene and therefore unprotected by the FIRST AMENDMENT (1791) to the U.S. Constitution, the majority's reasoning broke down when it was applied to child PORNOGRAPHY in *New York v. Ferber* (1982). In that decision, the Court ruled that the test for child pornography is different from the obscenity standard enunciated in *Miller.* In *Ferber* the Court required only that the conduct prohibited be adequately defined, that it be limited to visual depictions of sexual conduct by CHILDREN below a specified age, and that the category of sexual conduct proscribed be suitably limited and described.

The decision in *Miller* and its progeny—when compared to the Supreme Court's decisions in cases involving real-life sexual behavior (as opposed to descriptions or graphic portrayals), such as *GRISWOLD V. CONNECTICUT* (1965), *Loving v. Virginia* (1967), and *LAWRENCE V. TEXAS* (2003)—seems to permit more state regulation of representations of explicit sexual activity than of the activities themselves, as long as they are done in private. This is generally the opposite of how other types of criminal behavior are regulated;

murder, for instance, may be described or portrayed in motion pictures but not actually carried out without criminal consequences. Perhaps the dual nature of reproductive sexual behavior—a necessity for the survival of the species that is not publicly demonstrable—makes it difficult for our legal system to deal rationally with many of its aspects.

See also CENSORSHIP; PRURIENT INTEREST.

MINOR v. HAPPERSETT

In 1893 New Zealand became the first country to extend to its female citizens the right to vote. Female British subjects, those more than thirty years of age and otherwise qualified under the restrictive Representation of People Act (1918), were allowed to vote in 1918. American women followed suit in 1920, when the Nineteenth Amendment to the U.S. Constitution was ratified.

Aspects of the U.S. federal system of government sometimes helped to advance and sometimes to hold back the women's suffrage movement. The Wyoming Territory, needing to enhance its population to qualify for statehood, extended state voting rights to women in 1869 and included women's suffrage in its first state constitution in 1890, as did Utah in 1896. But at the national level, no doubt in part because of the U.S. Supreme Court's decision in *Minor v. Happersett* (1874), suffrage for women would be obtained only after a long and frustrating struggle.

As the Supreme Court's opinion in *Happersett* related: "On the 15th of October, 1872 (one of the days fixed by law for the registration of voters), Mrs. Virginia Minor, a native born, free, white citizen of the United States, and of the State of Missouri, over the age of twenty-one years, wishing to vote for electors for President and Vice-President of the United States, and for a representative in Congress, and for other officers, at the general election held in November, 1872, applied to one Happersett, the registrar of voters, to register her as a lawful voter, which he refused to do

[because] she was not a 'male citizen of the United States' [as required by Missouri law], but a woman." Minor then sued Happersett, and after losing in the state courts she appealed to the Supreme Court.

Chief Justice Morrison R. Waite delivered the Court's opinion. "There is no doubt that women may be citizens" and "persons" for the purposes of the Fourteenth Amendment (1868), he noted. This amendment extends to all persons and states the Constitution's protection with respect to due process and equal protection, providing, "No state shall make or enforce any law which shall abridge the privileges or immunities of citizens of the United States." But the Constitution does not define the rights and privileges associated with national, as opposed to state, citizenship. Looking to historic definitions, the Court adopted the narrowest characterization of citizenship, that of "conveying the idea of membership of a nation, nothing more."

Then, declaring that the Fourteenth Amendment conferred no substantive federal right of suffrage, which women had never before had under the Constitution, the Court concluded that states were free to continue their practice of denying voting rights to women. "No argument as to women's need of suffrage can be considered," Waite decreed. "We can only act upon her rights as they exist. It is not for us to look at the hardship of withholding. Our duty is at an end if we find it is within the power of a State to withhold." Not until the 1960s would the Supreme Court affirmatively change its position on the Constitution's protection of citizens' voting rights. It did so in cases involving fair apportionment for voting, such as *Baker v. Carr* (1962), which held that federal courts have jurisdiction in state legislative reapportionment cases that affect the proportional value of each citizen's vote; and others involving state poll taxes, such as *Harper v. Virginia State Board of Elections* (1966), which declared that poll taxes restricting voting rights were unconstitutional under the equal protection clause.

That a valuable right of citizenship—to vote and otherwise participate in the political process enshrined in America's national and state constitutions—should turn on the chance combination of X or X and Y chromosomes defies credulity today. But as the feminist slogan goes: "You've come a long way, baby!" The decisions in *Minor* and *BRADWELL V. ILLINOIS* (1873), a case denying women the right to practice law, may have been inevitable at the time they were handed down, but they are now only relics of discriminations past, in the category with the Supreme Court's decisions in cases upholding slavery, such as *Scott v. Sandford* (1857) (the Dred Scott case), or "separate but equal" accommodations for black citizens, such as *Plessy v. Ferguson* (1896).

See also DISCRIMINATION; EQUAL RIGHTS; WOMEN'S RIGHTS.

MISCEGENATION

In the nineteenth century speculation was rampant that there was a basic inequality in the races. Even *On the Origin of Species* (1859) by Charles Darwin (1809–82) was cited in support of the notion that a superior race resulted from natural selection. *Miscegenation* (from the Latin *miscere*, meaning to mix, and *gene*, meaning race, among other things) is defined as an interbreeding of the races or, legally, MARRIAGE between persons of different races. The word appeared in an 1864 political booklet, *Miscegenation: The Theory of the Blending of the Races, Applied to the American White Man and Negro*, which was intended to inflame the electorate against the party's opponents. In *United States v. Limehouse* (1932), the U.S. Supreme Court noted that personal attacks charging sexual immorality and "miscegenation and similar practices" were "unquestionably filthy within the popular meaning of that term."

But just as school segregation was upheld by the Supreme Court until the "separate but equal" doctrine on which it was based was renounced in *Brown v. Board of Education of Topeka* (1954), state miscegenation laws making it a crime for a black and a white person to marry were long condoned. The Court dealt with the unequal treatment of black and white sexual partners in *Pace v. Alabama* (1883). In this case an Alabama law that punished interracial fornication more severely than fornication by couples of the same race was upheld because both partners were being punished equally; according to this strained line of reasoning, no violation of the equal protection clause of the Fourteenth Amendment (1868) to the U.S. Constitution had occurred. The conclusion based on this reasoning would be referred to as the "equal application" exception to the equal protection clause.

In 1948, however, the Supreme Court found that orders by state courts enforcing private restrictive covenants barring blacks from holding real property in certain sections of Detroit and St. Louis violated the Fourteenth Amendment's equal protection clause. After *Brown*, the stage was set for the Supreme Court to review miscegenation laws under this clause, but the backlash in the South from that 1954 decision made the Court reluctant to add more fuel to the fire.

Finally, in 1967, in *Loving v. Virginia*, the Supreme Court addressed the case of Richard and Mildred Loving, a white man and an African American woman who had married in the District of Columbia in 1958 and returned to Virginia to live together as husband and wife. Shortly thereafter they were prosecuted under the state's law against miscegenation, which provided: "If any white person intermarry with a colored person, or any colored person intermarry with a white person, he shall be guilty of a felony and shall be punished by confinement in the penitentiary for not less than one nor more than five years." The Virginia statutes included Indians in the category of "colored persons."

The Lovings pleaded guilty, and a one-year jail sentence was imposed; however, the judge suspended the sentence for twenty-five years, conditioned on the couple's leaving the state. Appeals at the state level alleging that the law was unconstitutional were unsuccessful. Virginia's supreme court had upheld the law in 1955 in *Naim v. Naim* on the grounds that the state had a legitimate interest in maintaining the racial integrity of its citizens as well as in preventing "a mongrel breed of citizens."

Chief Justice Earl Warren wrote the opinion for the Court's 9–0 *Loving* decision. Noting that at the time sixteen states had laws banning miscegenation, the ruling declared that marriage was "one of the 'basic civil rights of man'" and a "fundamental freedom." Three years earlier the Court had concluded in *McLaughlin v. Florida* (1964), after the state could not show an overriding statutory purpose for a segregation measure, that the equal protection clause required "consideration of whether the classifications drawn by any statute constitute an arbitrary and invidious discrimination." Rejecting the "equal application" exception on which *Pace* had been decided, the chief justice summed up by saying, "Under our Constitution, the freedom to marry, or not marry, a person of another race resides with the individual and cannot be infringed by the State."

Marriage is a procedure whereby the government enters into a contract with two persons who wish to live together and typically have sexual relations and rear a family. Although today unwed cohabitation is not illegal, the right to have a marital relationship officially sanctioned by a state is important for many reasons; this imprimatur adds a sense of commitment to the arrangement and a measure of stability for CHILDREN who may be the product of the relationship. The state has legitimate interests in setting some rules for a couple wishing to marry—for example, age requirements and CONSENT by both parties—but arbitrary and discriminatory rules infringe on a traditional and constitutionally guaranteed right of all citizens.

See also UNMARRIED COHABITANTS.

MODEL PENAL CODE

See BIGAMY; RAPE; SEX OFFENSES.

MORALITY

See BIOETHICS; ETHICS.

MOTHERHOOD

Just as the idea of the family has undergone significant expansion, so too have the concept of motherhood and the laws that affect this vital biological and societal role. Society and the law are now beginning to embrace not only the iconic nuclear family consisting of a husband, a wife, and CHILDREN but also UNMARRIED COHABITANTS, UNMARRIED PARENTS, homosexual couples, homosexual parents, and even forms of polyparenting (in which more than two adults have some parental rights and responsibilities). Additional choices mean sometimes-difficult decisions about motherhood that can range from deciding to be a single mom, to cohabit with a partner, or to marry and, if married, to work outside the home or at home, full time or part-time, and even to separate or divorce, all of which can have legal ramifications on mothers, children, and families.

In 2006 census figures documented more than eighty million mothers in the United States, ten million of them single mothers with children under the age of eighteen years (more than triple the three million counted in 1970). Somewhat fewer mothers are now in the labor force, however, with the number at 55 percent for mothers with infants, compared to a record high of 59 percent in 1998. As for single mothers with children under eighteen years, some 70 percent work outside the home. More than five million women are stay-at-home moms.

Although PREGNANCY generally creates the state of motherhood, its concerns extend to mothers who give up their babies for adoption, adoptive mothers, and surrogate mothers who give birth to babies on behalf of other couples or single parents. An infertile woman or couple can spend close to $100,000 on in vitro fertilization attempts to conceive a child. Some homosexual women are having children of their own using donated sperm. Unwed fathers are claiming their rights to children they have sired but whom the biological mothers are putting up for adoption. Motherhood relates to the full spectrum of activities by which a woman nurtures, rears, and takes responsibility for

Motherhood is held in high regard in all societies, yet mothers' unique needs are often ignored in many countries when it comes to pregnancy and maternity leave, insurance, flexible employment, and child care. The famed Indian photographer Edward S. Curtis captured a close maternal bond on the Plains about 1905.

a child, however that burden devolves on her. "Due to the nature of the roles of men and women in our society," states the Family and Medical Leave Act (1993), "the primary responsibility for family caretaking often falls on women, and such responsibility affects the working lives of women more than it affects the working lives of men."

Rights and Responsibilities

With respect to their children, mothers have a number of legally protected parental rights that may or may not be shared with the father or husband. These rights include custody, naming a child, and rearing and educating children within the terms of state laws. Such rights, however, may be lost under certain circumstances. For example, custody of a child may

be terminated if a court finds that a mother is unfit or otherwise unable to care for her child. In *Roe v. Connecticut* (1976), a federal court held that the only basis for terminating parental rights is if "the child is subjected to real physical or emotional harm and less drastic measures would be unavailing."

The termination of parental rights may be based on CHILD ABUSE or abusive discipline. In several cases, such as *Meyer v. Nebraska* (1923) and *Pierce v. Society of Sisters* (1925), the U.S. Supreme Court confirmed the common law privilege of parents to discipline their children, ruling that parents have a constitutional right to the care and custody of their children. But in *Department of Social Services v. Father and Mother* (1988), a South Carolina court held that abuse of a child by a father who inflicts physical harm, in this case beating his thirteen-year-old daughter, compounded by the mother's neglect in failing to stop the abuse, provided a basis for state intervention and loss of parental rights.

Concomitant with rights regarding children, parents have a duty to provide the necessities of life for their children: food, shelter, and clothing. Many states require both spouses to support their children, although at common law only the father was typically held to be responsible. In the event of a separation or a DIVORCE, states have established presumptions regarding child custody. A century ago, fathers were favored given that they were charged by law with their children's support. However, there was a "tender years" presumption favoring the mother, depending on her fitness; sexual misconduct, such as ADULTERY, traditionally resulted in denial of custody. In the last half century, as mothers became equally responsible for their children's support, they became favored for custody. Beginning in the 1980s, some courts—for example, an Alabama court in *Devine v. Devine* (1981)—began finding that the presumption in favor of the mother denied equal protection for the father. Today most courts treat both parents equally in custody battles. The child's age is nonetheless considered relevant in determining custody, as is consideration of what is in the child's best interests.

State Family, Medical, and Maternity Leave Laws

State	Sector		Type of Leave		
	Public	Private	Family	Family and Medical	Maternity
Alabama	•				•
Alaska	•			•	
Arizona	•			•	
Arkansas	•				•
California	•	•		•	
Colorado	•	•			•
Connecticut	•	•		•	
Delaware	•	•			•
Florida	•			•	
Georgia					
Hawaii	•	•		•	
Idaho					
Illinois	•			•	
Indiana	•			•	
Iowa	•			•	
Kansas	•			•	
Kentucky	•			•	
Louisiana					
Maine	•	•		•	
Maryland	•	•		•	•
Massachusetts	•	•	•		•
Michigan	•				•
Minnesota	•	•	•		
Mississippi	•			•	
Missouri	•		•		
Montana	•	•	•		•
Nebraska	•				•
Nevada					
New Hampshire	•			•	
New Jersey	•	•		•	
New Mexico	•			•	
New York	•		•		
North Carolina	•	•	•		
North Dakota	•		•		
Ohio	•				•
Oklahoma	•	•		•	
Oregon	•	•		•	
Pennsylvania					
Rhode Island	•	•	•	•	

State	Sector		Type of Leave		
	Public	Private	Family	Family and Medical	Maternity
South Carolina	•			•	
South Dakota					
Tennessee	•	•	•		•
Texas	•	•		•	
Utah					
Vermont	•	•	•	•	
Virginia	•			•	
Washington	•	•		•	
West Virginia	•		•		
Wisconsin	•	•		•	
Wyoming					

Source: National Conference of State Legislatures, 2006

Maternity Leave

Before Congress passed the Pregnancy Discrimination Act in 1978, employers could adopt "no maternity leave" policies; these were justified under state laws that permitted wage supplements for all forms of disability except pregnancy. The act amended Title VII of the Civil Rights Act of 1964, which prohibits discrimination in employment, to include "pregnancy, childbirth, and related medical conditions." Women with these conditions, according to the act, must be treated the same as others who are disabled from work. The act was implicated in a challenge to a California law that required employers to provide four months of maternity leave; an employer alleged that Title VII preempted the state law. The U.S. Supreme Court, however, declared in *California Savings and Loan Association v. Guerra* (1987) that the federal law was meant to be a floor with regard to maternity rights and did not preclude states from providing additional rights.

Half of American women return to work within four months of giving birth to their first child. In 1993 the Family and Medical Leave Act extended unpaid leave benefits to employees for up to twelve weeks in the event of birth, adoption, or the need to care for a family member with a serious health problem. However, the act applies only to employers with at least fifty employees and to employees who have worked for more than a year. About 60 percent of workers who wish to take family leave are ineligible for it. Another criticism of the law is that it continues the traditional definition of a parent and family members and excludes lesbian coparents. Nonetheless, during eighteen months in 1999 and 2000, nearly twenty-four million Americans took leave from work for an FMLA-covered reason.

Most states now similarly have laws addressing pregnancy and maternity leave. As was held in the *Guerra* case, the Family and Medical Leave Act allows states to broaden the federal coverage. California, Minnesota, and Washington are the only states to offer paid leave. California law governs employers of five or more employees and provides for maternity leave of up to four months even if the employer's policy for disabilities does not normally cover that much. Hawaii's leave policy applies to employers with one or more employees, while the laws in Iowa and New York apply to employers of four or more. In 2006 a family leave bill was introduced in Massachusetts to pay workers their full salary up to $750 a week for a maximum of twelve weeks, to be funded by employee contributions.

Research conducted for Harvard University's Project on Global Working Families found that 164 of 168 countries studied guarantee paid maternity leave. The four that do not are Papua New Guinea, Swaziland, Lesotho, and the United States. In about forty-five nations, even fathers are granted some paid parental leave. Canada allows a mother fifteen weeks of partial paid parental leave for physical recovery plus thirty-five weeks of partial paid leave before a child turns one year old; the latter can be taken by the mother or the father or shared between them.

Discrimination

DISCRIMINATION may also occur on the basis of mothers' unique responsibilities. The traditional role assigned to women—as the primary caregiver of children—may cause conflicts between work and family. In *McCourtney v. Imprimis Technology, Inc.* (1991), a Minnesota court ruled that a woman was wrongfully denied unemployment compensation because she was fired for "misconduct"; in fact, she was discharged from her job because she could not find affordable child care that allowed her to maintain her work schedule. The court ruled that her inability to obtain child care compatible with her work schedule did not constitute misconduct.

Many large employers have initiated programs to help mothers cope with working and child care, including providing day care centers in the workplace and tailoring jobs to permit work at home. However, a report by the Center for Work Life Law at the University of California, Hastings, found that while flexible schedules are available to nearly two-thirds of workers who earn more than $71,000 a year, only a third of those who earn less than $28,000 are granted such a benefit. Half of working-class employees cannot take leave to care for sick children. In addition, a woman who wants to breastfeed her baby to promote its health is not always legally guaranteed the right to take time from work to do so; only about ten states have enacted laws protecting this right.

Wrongful Birth and Life

Wrongful pregnancy, wrongful birth, and wrongful life are relatively new legal concepts. They describe causes of action by parents as well as children for mistakes made by medical professionals that result in harm. Wrongful pregnancy may result from negligence in performing a STERILIZATION procedure to prevent pregnancy. When a lawsuit seeking damages is brought by the parents, it is called a wrongful-pregnancy or wrongful-birth action. A suit brought by a child or on his or her behalf is called a wrongful-life action.

Lawsuits for wrongful birth allege a failure of medical providers during the period of prenatal care to provide parents with information that their child might be born severely ill or handicapped. Such negligence, if defects could have been discovered by prenatal testing, prevents the mother from making an informed choice to terminate the pregnancy or not. This type of lawsuit relies on the legalization of ABORTION by the Supreme Court in *Roe v. Wade* (1973).

As yet, courts have generally refused to entertain lawsuits by children against their parents for simply bringing them without their CONSENT into a world that may hold pain, hardship, and suffering. A Maryland court, in *Kassama v. Magat* (2001), recognized that wrongful-life actions include claims by normal but unwanted children who seek damages from those responsible for their conception or birth. The court went on to deny all such claims, even by impaired children who seek damages because of the failure of their mothers to abort them.

Each type of suit has its own basis for damages: parents may sue to recover the extra cost of dealing with a severely handicapped child; and a child may sue for compensation for the added burden of going through life severely handicapped, on the basis that the disability could have been avoided were it not for his or her wrongful birth. These tort claims (private wrongs, as opposed to crimes that may be prosecuted by the state) are relatively new and still somewhat controversial. Wrongful death of the unborn is an even more ambiguous basis for a tort claim, one that various laws and state court decisions treat disparately.

"The paramount destiny and mission of woman are to fulfill the noble and benign offices of wife and mother," suggested a justice of the U.S. Supreme Court in 1873. In BRADWELL V. ILLINOIS, Joseph P. Bradley used the concept of motherhood to justify the Court's denial of the right of an otherwise well-qualified woman, Myra Bradwell, to practice law. Women today have the option to both work and raise children. Fulfilling the biological imperative to procreate can be far more complex than in Bradwell's day. Yet modern mothers have more control over their reproductive life and their child rearing and more legal rights to help them attain their personal goals as well as their goals for their children. However, a Work and Family Bill of Rights promoted in 2006 by a Georgetown University Law Center research group and others would include these components: paid family leave, negotiable flexibility in work hours, national health insurance, affordable quality elder and child care, and a living wage.

Contact: National Partnership for Women and Families, 1875 Connecticut Avenue, NW, Suite 650, Washington, DC 20009 (202-986-2600). http//:www.national partnership.org.

See also BREASTFEEDING; CHILD SUPPORT; FAMILY PLANNING; UNBORN, RIGHTS OF THE; WOMEN'S RIGHTS.

MOTION PICTURES

See CENSORSHIP; ENTERTAINMENT INDUSTRY; PORNOGRAPHY.

MULLER v. OREGON

Can chivalry coexist with EQUAL RIGHTS for women? Should women as a group be given special protection under the law, or does the concept of true equal rights preclude special treatment for women? The 1908 landmark U.S. Supreme Court decision in *Muller v. Oregon* became the touchstone for such concerns at least

until Title VII of the Civil Rights Act of 1964, which generally bans DISCRIMINATION against either sex in the workplace.

The *Muller* case vindicated the views of two former dissenters on the Supreme Court, Associate Justices Oliver Wendell Holmes Jr. and John Marshall Harlan, in a similar case from 1905, *Lochner v. New York.* In *Lochner* the Court had ruled that a New York statute setting a limit on the weekly working hours of bakers was unconstitutional, contending that the state's police power could not be used to unreasonably and arbitrarily interfere with individuals' right to contract out their work at whatever terms they wished. In his dissent, Justice Holmes argued that state legislation should be upheld unless a rational person would find that some fundamental principle of American law or tradition was being infringed. The right to contract out one's labor without restrictions, he said, is not a fundamental principle specifically enshrined anywhere in the Constitution.

Louis D. Brandeis, who later became a Supreme Court justice, was counsel for the winning side in *Muller.* His case was a model of modern courtroom strategy, based on the laborious accumulation of evidence to support the proposition that long hours of work in industry could be deleterious to women's health. Oregon had passed a law in 1903 that made it a crime for "any mechanical establishment, or factory, or laundry" to employ women for "more than ten hours during any one day." While on the surface the Oregon law might seem similar to the New York law struck down in *Lochner,* the Court treated them differently. To do otherwise would have meant acknowledging that "the difference between the sexes does not justify a different rule respecting a restriction of the hours of labor." In other words, the Court felt free to act in a chivalrous or protective manner toward women but not men.

According to the facts presented to the Supreme Court in *Muller,* the defendant "on said 4th day of September, A.D. 1905 . . . [required] a female, to wit, one Mrs. E. Gotcher, to work more than ten hours in said laundry." Curt Muller, the owner of the Grand Laundry in

Portland, Oregon, was then found guilty of violating the Oregon law. His conviction and the law's constitutionality were upheld by the Oregon supreme court.

The opinion for the U.S. Supreme Court's unanimous decision in the *Muller* case was written by Associate Justice David J. Brewer. The Court took note of the fact that the basic difference between *Lochner* and *Muller* was the sex of the party contracting out his or her labor. It concluded that a woman's physical well-being "becomes an object of public interest and care in order to preserve the strength and vigor of the race." A woman, wrote Justice Brewer, "is not an equal competitor with her brother." This supposition was seen to justify the "special legislation restricting or qualifying the conditions under which she be permitted to toil." Women should be protected "from the greed as well as the passion of man," the justice added. According to the Court, the two sexes are different and this difference warrants different types of legislation and outcomes in the courts.

Today the language in *Muller* seems sexist and paternalistic. Yet the decision became an important precedent for attempts throughout the so-called *Lochner* era, from 1905 until 1937, to overturn protective social and economic legislation. This stance was finally rejected in *West Coast Hotel v. Parrish* (1937), which upheld a statute regulating wages and hours of women and children. Although most laws aimed at ameliorating some of the ills of America's industrial society were rejected during the *Lochner* era, some—as in the *Muller* case—were upheld. Protection for working women is now integrated into federal and state employment laws applying equally to men and women and is no longer dependent on judicial interpretation. Rational distinctions between the sexes nonetheless remain the basis of laws granting women certain exclusive rights and privileges relating to PREGNANCY and MOTHERHOOD.

See also DISCRIMINATION; WOMEN'S RIGHTS.

n

NARAL PRO-CHOICE AMERICA

NARAL Pro-Choice America, formerly the National Abortion Rights Action League, has been the leading advocate for personal PRIVACY and a woman's right to choose to have an ABORTION since it was founded in 1969. The mission of the organization, described by *Fortune* magazine as "one of the top 10 advocacy groups in America," is to develop and sustain a constituency that uses the political process to guarantee every woman the right to make personal decisions regarding the full range of reproductive choices. These include making abortion less necessary by preventing unintended pregnancies, bearing healthy children, or choosing to have a legal abortion.

Originally named the National Association to Repeal Abortion Laws, NARAL's mission changed after the U.S. Supreme Court's decision in *Roe v. Wade* (1973). This decision struck down state laws criminalizing abortion, relying on a constitutional right of privacy to make a decision about abortion a matter for a woman and her doctor. "And yet, more than thirty years later," declares the organization, "the promise of *Roe* remains unfulfilled." It cites opponents in federal, state, and local offices, adding, "Congress has banned access to abortion for virtually every woman who depends on the federal government for her health care, including Medicaid recipients, women in the military and military dependents

stationed overseas, women in federal prisons, Native American women, federal employees, and even Peace Corps volunteers."

Among other NARAL issues are restrictions on late-term abortions, waiting periods for women seeking an abortion, and parental notification requirements for minors. "In 2004, states enacted twenty-nine new anti-choice measures," notes the organization. "The cumulative effect of enacted anti-choice legislation is staggering: more than four hundred anti-choice measures have been enacted since 1995."

Several justices on the U.S. Supreme Court have stated in subsequent opinions that they believe *Roe v. Wade* was wrongly decided, thus making it possible for new justices filling Court vacancies to side with them in overturning the decision and again permitting laws banning abortion. In 2005 NARAL aired what became a controversial national television advertisement urging that the confirmation of John G. Roberts Jr. as chief justice not be approved by the Senate based on this concern.

NARAL has three components: NARAL Pro-Choice America, a nonprofit organization that defends a woman's right to choose and lobbies for comprehensive reproductive health policies; NARAL Pro-Choice America PAC, a political action group that supports pro-choice political candidates; and the NARAL Pro-Choice Foundation, a charitable organization that performs research and legal work and organizes public education campaigns. It has more than two dozen state affiliates and nearly four hundred thousand members.

Contact: NARAL Pro-Choice America, 1156 15th Street, NW, Suite 700, Washington, DC 20005 (202-973-3000). www.naral.org. www.prochoiceamerica.org.

NATIONAL CENTER FOR MISSING AND EXPLOITED CHILDREN

Some 2,100 children are reported missing in America every day. In 2004 the National Center for Missing and Exploited Children, which was founded in 1984 to help solve this problem, received its 200,000th child sexual exploitation report through its twenty-four-hour hotline and INTERNET reporting system. Even in the face of increased sexual predation on CHILDREN, the center has developed techniques and a network of assistance that raised its missing children recovery rate to 94 percent in 2004.

A nonprofit organization, NCMEC pursues a public-private partnership to provide services nationwide and internationally to families and professionals for the prevention and recovery of abducted, endangered, and sexually exploited children in accordance with certain federal laws. Title 42 of the U.S. Code, chapter 72, Juvenile Justice and Delinquency Prevention, subchapter IV, Missing Children, presents a finding by Congress that the NCMEC has "(A) served as the national resource center and clearinghouse Congressionally mandated under the provisions of this subchapter; and (B) worked in partnership with the Department of Justice, Federal Bureau of Investigation, Department of the Treasury, the Department of State, and many other agencies in the effort to find missing children and prevent child victimization."

The center was given official responsibilities under Title 42 of the U.S. Code, chapter 121, International Child Abduction Remedies, and under Title 22 of the Code of Federal Regulations, part 94, International Child Abduction. Based on an agreement among the Department of State, Department of Justice, and

Posters and other public service projects help alert parents and caregivers to the dangers posed by some four hundred thousand known sexual predators who are at large in the United States. Since 1984 the National Center for Missing and Exploited Children has responded to nearly two million calls for assistance.

NCMEC relating to procedures for children abducted from the United States, the center receives applications seeking the return of a child abducted to the United States, confirms or ascertains the child's location, and facilitates the voluntary agreement for visitation rights or the return of the child.

NCMEC also operates the CyberTipline (called "a 911 for the Internet") to encourage public reporting of online child sexual exploitation from PORNOGRAPHY to

CyberTipline Reports

Type of incident	2004	1998–2005[1]
Child pornography	106,119	316,801
Child prostitution	559	3,079
Child sex tourism	248	1,337
Child sexual molestation (not family)	1,466	8,515
Online enticement for sexual acts	2,605	14,396
Unsolicited obscene material	533	2,124
Misleading domain names	487	1,039
Total	112,017	348,443

1. Through September 19, 2005

Source: National Center for Missing and Exploited Children, October 2005

enticement and molestation. A 1999 federal law requires Internet service providers to report child pornography and sexual exploitation directly to the CyberTipline. In 2001 the center began project AMBER (America's Missing: Broadcast Emergency Response) to provide technical assistance in conjunction with the Department of Justice. When an Amber Alert for a missing child is issued at the local law enforcement level, information about the individual is disseminated immediately through the media and on highway signs.

The center also conducts training programs for law enforcement and social services professionals, distributes photographs and descriptions of missing children worldwide, coordinates child-protection efforts with the private sector, networks with other nonprofit services and clearinghouses about missing-persons cases, and helps support effective state legislation to protect children.

A typical case handled by NCMEC began in 2003, with a report on its CyberTipline about online file sharing of pornographic images of children. The organization's Exploited Child Unit checked records and forwarded information to the Arizona State University police department. The police found the suspect's computer and noted messages between him and a thirteen-year-old girl in Pennsylvania whom the suspect was attempting to meet in person. The Delaware County, Pennsylvania, Internet Crimes Against Children Task Force was notified and checked on the girl's safety. The suspect was later apprehended and charged with three counts of sexual exploitation of a minor and one count of luring a minor for sexual exploitation.

Contact: National Center for Missing and Exploited Children, 699 Prince Street, Alexandria, VA 22314-3175 (703-274-2200). www.ncmec.org. www.missingkids.com. CyberTipline (800-843-5678). www.cybertipline.com.

See also CRIMES AGAINST CHILDREN UNIT (FBI); MEGAN'S LAW.

NATIONAL ORGANIZATION FOR WOMEN

Founded in 1966 by the author and feminist leader Betty Friedan (1921–2006), working with thirty other prominent Americans, the National Organization for Women is the largest association of feminist activists in the United States. The mission of NOW, which has some six hundred thousand contributing members and 450 chapters in all fifty states and the District of Columbia, is to work to eliminate DISCRIMINATION and SEXUAL HARASSMENT in the workplace, schools, the justice system, and all other sectors of society; secure the right to CONTRACEPTION and ABORTION, as well as other REPRODUCTIVE RIGHTS for all women; and end all forms of violence against women. Although NOW failed in its major goal of adding the Equal Rights Amendment (1972) to the U.S. Constitution by the congressional deadline of 1982, it has nonetheless remained instrumental in promoting WOMEN'S RIGHTS as well as EQUAL RIGHTS through the elimination of sexism, homophobia, and racism.

NOW's methods for pursuing its goals include extensive involvement in the election process, lobbying at federal and state levels, and bringing lawsuits to enforce women's rights. It also organizes rallies, marches,

Abortion rights are one of the many women's issues championed by NOW. In *Scheidler v. National Organization for Women* (2006), the organization supported women's right to use abortion clinics and opposed violence and intimidation of doctors who perform abortions.

and picketing as well as nonviolent civil disobedience activities. Marches were held in Washington, D.C., in 1978 for the Equal Rights Amendment, in 1989 for reproductive rights, and in 1992 for women's rights. In 2004 a March for Women's Life attracted more than 1.15 million persons to the nation's capital, making it the largest mass action of its kind in U.S. history.

The organization also helps elect feminist women to positions of political power; sues antiabortion terrorists; lobbies for the passage of laws such as those that require employers to provide family leave and that ensure strict enforcement of CHILD SUPPORT obligations; advocates for victims of RAPE, sexual harassment, and sex discrimination; and supports affirmative action, the government safety net for poor women and their children, civil rights for lesbian women and gay men, MARRIAGE equality, and women's rights in the MILITARY and in education under TITLE IX of the Education Amendments of 1972. NOW maintains a legislative action center that has supported approval by the Food

and Drug Administration of unrestricted over-the-counter emergency CONTRACEPTION; it has also called on CONGRESS to release data on the risks of breast implant surgery, to take stronger legislative action to stop violence against women, to support information and access by RAPE victims to emergency contraception, to oppose the proposed FEDERAL MARRIAGE AMENDMENT to the U.S. Constitution, and to repeal the DEFENSE OF MARRIAGE ACT. The last two actions are aimed at ensuring equal rights for same-sex couples.

Since 1983 the proposed Equal Rights Amendment has been reintroduced in Congress several times but has not been passed. Although ratification of the amendment would make NOW's work easier, the organization has built a strong base of support for women's rights that has translated into equal rights laws in a number of states. NOW's mission remains to encourage first-class citizenship for all.

Contact: National Organization for Women, 733 15th Street, NW, Washington, DC 20005 (202-331-0066). www.now.org.

See also FEMINISM; SAME-SEX MARRIAGE; VIOLENCE AGAINST WOMEN ACT.

NATIONAL SEX OFFENDER REGISTRY

See MEGAN'S LAW; SEX OFFENDERS.

NATURALISM

See NUDITY.

NINTH AMENDMENT

The debate over so-called strict constructionist versus activist judges revolves around the question whether the American people are better served by a literal (strict) interpretation of the U.S. Constitution or by an expansive (activist) interpretation. As the renowned U.S. Supreme Court Associate Justice Oliver Wendell Holmes Jr. once opined: "When we are dealing with words that also are a constituent act, like the Constitution of the United States, we must realize that they have called into life a being the development of which could not have been foreseen completely by the most gifted of its begetters." His choice of the words "a being" and "begetters" reflects the organic or growing nature of the Constitution as Justice Holmes viewed it.

Continuing the allusion to sexual reproduction and developing organisms, the U.S. Constitution's approximately 3,500 words can be seen as seeds for a growing body of constitutional law. Should the law focus only on the seeds or also on the body that develops from the seeds? The Ninth Amendment (1791) in the Bill of Rights contains a seed of explanation about how the founders of our nation viewed the constitutional document they "begat." It states: "The enumeration in the Constitution, of certain rights, shall not be construed to deny or disparage others retained by the people." The two key legal questions that flow from this language are: What are the unenumerated rights retained by the people? And what responsibility does the federal government have to protect them?

According to James Madison (1751–1836), known as the "Father of the Constitution," this seldom-used provision of our supreme law was added to the Bill of Rights to quell a key concern. This was the possibility that if a right was not expressly mentioned in the Constitution, it might later be assumed that it was unprotected from government infringement. Alexander Hamilton (1755–1804) and some of the document's other framers, however, did not see a need for a bill of rights at all. They argued that because the federal government was one of limited powers, those powers not expressly granted to it—such as CONGRESS's authority to deal with interstate commerce—were therefore prohibited. The Constitution as drafted in 1787 and ratified in 1789 made no grant of power to the federal government with respect to RELIGION; therefore, they reasoned, it could not infringe on religious concerns.

In fact, there is a long-standing rule of construction in the law that a thing not expressly mentioned in a legal document is, by definition, outside its scope. The Latin phrase is *inclusio unius est exclusio alterius* (inclusion of one thing means the exclusion of another). Nowhere does the U.S. Constitution guarantee the presumption of innocence of a person accused of a crime, but it has nonetheless been recognized as a sacred liberty throughout the nation's legal history.

The argument over the Ninth Amendment's language has continued into modern times. Robert H. Bork, the failed nominee for the U.S. Supreme Court in 1987, has called it an inkblot and said that judges were not permitted to make up what was underneath it. Others, however, have considered the Ninth Amendment the expression of a basic presumption of liberty, especially when read together with the Tenth Amendment (1791). The final amendment in the Bill of Rights states: "The powers not delegated to the United States by the Constitution, nor prohibited by it to the states, are reserved to the states respectively, or to the people." The Declaration of Independence (1776) speaks of "certain unalienable Rights" that belong to all of us. Taken together, this language supports the notion that the entire Bill of Rights is not a grant of rights by the federal government to the people but rather a limitation on the powers granted to the government by the states and the people. As such, it is the government that has the burden of proof not to infringe the liberty of the people—instead of the other way around.

With respect to sexual behavior, the Ninth Amendment has played an important supporting role from the landmark case *GRISWOLD V. CONNECTICUT* (1965) to *LAWRENCE V. TEXAS* (2003). In *Griswold*, for example, a majority of the Supreme Court, relying on a structural analysis of the Constitution—looking at the entire document to glean its overall intent—fashioned the right of PRIVACY. This is an unenumerated right not expressly mentioned in the document that is found in the secondary shadows cast by the First, Third, Fourth, Fifth, and Ninth Amendments. In *National Association for the Advancement of Colored People v. Alabama*

(1958), the Court had already affirmed that the language in the FIRST AMENDMENT included the right of association even though this right was not expressly mentioned in the Constitution.

Griswold extended the Constitution's protection to the bedrooms of married couples by declaring state laws banning CONTRACEPTION to be an unconstitutional invasion of privacy. Later cases—such as *Eisenstadt v. Baird* (1972), which extended to unmarried couples the same privacy regarding contraceptives, and *Roe v. Wade* (1973), which legalized ABORTION—continued to broaden the right of privacy. As Associate Justice WILLIAM O. DOUGLAS, the author of the Court's *Griswold* opinion, wrote in a concurring opinion in a companion case, *Doe v. Bolton* (1973): "The Ninth Amendment obviously does not create federally enforceable rights. [But it refers to] a catalogue of ... rights [including] customary, traditional, and time-honored rights, amenities, privileges, and immunities that come within the sweep of 'the Blessings of Liberty' mentioned in the preamble to the Constitution. Many of them, in my view, come within the meaning of the term 'liberty' as used in the Fourteenth Amendment."

In *Bowers v. Hardwick* (1986), however, the Supreme Court refused to extend the right of privacy to acts of consensual homosexual SODOMY performed in the privacy of one's own home. Associate Justice Harry A. Blackmun, in a strong dissent, countered that the case was not about a "fundamental right to engage in homosexual sodomy"; the subject was "'the most comprehensive of rights and the right most valued by civilized men,' namely, 'the right to be let alone.'" Among other specific criticisms of the majority opinion, he also took issue with it for failing to address the questions raised by denying the right of privacy under the Ninth Amendment.

Bowers would be overruled seventeen years later by *Lawrence v. Texas*, thus vindicating the Ninth Amendment's power: the notion that the government has just as much of a duty to protect citizens from the infringement of unenumerated rights as it does to protect them from infringement of the enumerated rights. As Chief Justice John Marshall had declared in his groundbreaking opinion in *Marbury v. Madison* (1803): "It cannot be presumed that any clause in the Constitution is intended to be without effect.... If any other construction would render the clause inoperative, that is an additional reason for rejecting ... [it]." For the past four decades the Supreme Court has seemed to agree with him by treating the Ninth Amendment as much more than just an inkblot to be ignored.

NUDITY

We are all born naked, yet humans have some innate need to cover their nakedness to function as social beings. The taboo against nudity (going without clothes or sufficient clothes in public) is an old one. When Europeans came to the New World, they were often shocked by the relative nudity of some Native Americans. In the Old World, public nudity was equated with wantonness or a lack of morality. But Roger Williams (?1603–83), the founder of the Rhode Island colony in 1636, wrote this in *A Key into the Language of America* about the natives' nakedness: "Custome hath used their minds and bodies to it, and [there is] a freedom from any wantonnesse."

Social and legal prohibitions against the free exercise of nudity may have evolved as a way to prevent sexual behavior that would disrupt other important activities. Because procreation is such a prime biological directive, without some societal restraints on when and where copulation may take place, humans might accomplish little else. Clothing is just one way of enforcing the old adage "out of sight, out of mind." Yet nude dancing, especially by women for men, has been a form of entertainment for a long time; Salome's Dance of the Seven Veils, for example, is recounted in the New Testament.

Anglo-American law traditionally dealt with nudity in public under the terms *exposure* or *indecent exposure*, defining it as the crime of intentionally exposing the naked body or private parts to "shock the feelings of chastity or to corrupt the morals of the community." In his *Commentaries on the Laws of England* (1765–70),

William Blackstone (1723–80) noted that "[b]y the Vagrant Act ... the exposure of the person with intent to insult a female, renders a person liable to be dealt with in a summary way as a rogue and vagabond."

What constitutes improper nudity is often difficult to pin down, and relevant laws appear somewhat inconsistent. Nudity, unlike OBSCENITY, can be perfectly acceptable both socially and legally. A nude model in a freehand drawing class or a nude statue in a museum is not considered offensive by most people. The same is true of passive nudity, which includes nudity in acceptable social contexts, such as on nude beaches or at private parties. But nudism or naturism is protected only when practiced in seclusion among like-minded people. Passive nudity in public has been found to be outside the bounds of constitutional protection. When nudity is used to shock or offend those who do not want to see it—almost exclusively engaged in by males—it is deemed INDECENT EXPOSURE: activities such as "mooning," "streaking," and "flashing." In unacceptable VOYEURISM, nudity is observed by stealth by peeping Toms or secret video cameras.

Nudity as a component of PORNOGRAPHY may be offensive if it fits the legal definition of obscenity. Hardcore pornography goes beyond passive nudity and becomes socially and legally objectionable with displays of some form of sexual activity, typically including various forms of perversion. Other forms of nudity, from nude dancing to nudity in movies, are merchandised to willing buyers. People pay money to see what they presumably want to see. Provocative nude or seminude dancing is accepted in many places, and similar public nudity in entertainment and the arts has gained constitutional protection. With the coming of the SEXUAL REVOLUTION beginning in the 1960s, how much public nudity would be protected under the U.S. Constitution became a question that had to be addressed by the U.S. Supreme Court.

Nudity in Public

Public nudity can have significant legal consequences. Although there is no federal law against nudity as such, many states and localities have

Paul Jennewein's Art Deco statue *Spirit of Justice* has stood in the Great Hall of the U.S. Department of Justice since it opened in 1936. After John Ashcroft became attorney general of the United States in 2001, the statue's exposed aluminum breasts were covered by a drape during press conferences. His successor, Alberto Gonzales, removed the drapery in 2005.

statutes criminalizing some types of nudity and indecent exposure. The U.S. Constitution addresses questions of nudity only indirectly in the free-speech and free-press rights guaranteed by the FIRST AMENDMENT (1791), from which the courts have derived a constitutional right of freedom of expression. Each citizen has also been found to have a zone of PRIVACY undergirded by the First, Third, Fourth, and Fifth Amendments. Arguments supporting "the right to be let alone" rely on the NINTH

AMENDMENT, which reserves to the people other rights not specified in the Constitution.

The Supreme Court has dealt with public nudity primarily in the context of whether nude dancing before an audience constitutes freedom of expression protected by the First Amendment. While this amendment was intended to guarantee individual rights against the national government, in *Gitlow v. New York* (1925), the Court extended its protection to actions of state governments. The Court has recognized that freedom of expression, like freedom of speech and freedom of the press, is not without limits, however. The right to express oneself by appearing nude in public or in a public performance is not necessarily guaranteed under the First Amendment.

The Supreme Court started to address local regulation of nude dancing in 1973, in *City of Kenosha v. Bruno,* but it got sidetracked by the question of whether it had jurisdiction in this type of situation to impose a civil liability on a municipality as it did on persons under the Civil Rights Act of 1871. Without granting hearings, the cities of Racine and Kenosha, Wisconsin, had denied the renewal of liquor licenses based on alleged nude dancing at the establishments involved. In *Monell v. New York City Department of Social Services* (1978), however, the Court reversed its prior rulings and agreed that it did have the jurisdiction required in cases such as *Bruno.* The Court thus opened the door to review challenges to local restrictions on nude dancing based on abitrary government actions and denials of due process.

In an earlier case, *California v. LaRue* (1972), the Supreme Court had hinted "that at least some [live sexual] performances . . . are within the limits of the constitutional protection of freedom of expression." Even earlier, the Court in *United States v. O'Brien* (1968) declared that government regulation could trump the Constitution's protection of freedom of expression if the government's interests were valid and important and unrelated to the suppression of free speech. *O'Brien* involved draft-card burning in public as a protest against the Vietnam War.

The stage was thus set for the Supreme Court to tackle the nudity issue head on in *Doran v. Salem Inn, Inc.* (1975). In this case, operators of bars in Hampstead, New York, complained that a city ordinance proscribing topless dancing was unconstitutional under the First and Fourteenth (1868) Amendments. The Court agreed, citing with approval the lower court's observation:

The local ordinance here attacked not only prohibits topless dancing in bars but also prohibits any female from appearing in "any public place" with uncovered breasts. There is no limit to the interpretation of the term "any public place." It could include the theater, town hall, opera house . . . [and therefore] would prohibit the performance of the "Ballet Africains" [in which female dancers perform topless] and any number of other works of unquestionable artistic and socially redeeming significance.

The Supreme Court had held in ROTH V. UNITED STATES (1957) that works with socially redeeming significance were not obscene and therefore were protected by the First Amendment.

That same year, in *Southeastern Productions v. Conrad* (1975), the Supreme Court invalidated the denial of use of a public auditorium for a production of the musical *Hair,* which had been declared obscene by a jury. The Court held that the action constituted prior restraint, or CENSORSHIP; the opinion did not answer the question whether the production, which contained group nudity and simulated sexual activity, was a constitutionally protected form of expression. Later Court opinions continued to grapple with public nudity.

In BARNES V. GLEN THEATRE, INC. (1991) and *City of Erie v. Pap's A.M.* (2000), a majority concluded that regulation of nudity in public, within limits, would pass constitutional muster. In *Barnes,* the Court held that Indiana's interest in protecting public morals through its public indecency law was both valid and unrelated to the suppression of free expression; the chief justice reasoned that the state's requirement "that the dancers wear at least pasties and G-strings is modest, and the bare minimum necessary to achieve the State's purpose." In *Pap's A.M.*, the city of Erie, Pennsylvania, had argued that its ordinance was aimed at combating nude dancing's negative secondary effects on public health and safety and was not an attempt to suppress freedom of expression. According to the Court, "Even if Erie's public nudity ban has some minimal effect on the erotic message by muting that portion of expression that occurs when the last stitch is dropped, the dancers . . . are free to perform wearing pasties and G-strings. Any effect on the overall expression is therefore de minimus."

In 2005 an enterprising owner of a strip club in Boise, Idaho, had his nude dancers remove what little they generally wore and promoted an "Art Club Night," inviting patrons to sketch the totally nude women. He cited a city ordinance that prohibited nudity in public except when the purpose had "serious artistic merit." The club owner was obviously in accord with the Court's finding in *Doran* as to the presence of "socially redeeming significance."

For the most part, state and local laws relating to nudity conform to the definitions and guidelines enunciated in U.S. Supreme Court decisions. Laws against indecent exposure typically prohibit the willful and lewd exposure of a person's genitals in public. The definition of obscenity in the Delaware criminal code, chapter 5, Specific Offenses, subchapter VII, Offenses Against Public Health, Order and Decency, for example, includes "[p]atently offensive representations or descriptions of . . . and/or lewd exhibitions of the genitals." For purposes of obscene literature deemed harmful to minors, this state code defines nudity as "the showing of the human male or female genitals, pubic area or buttocks with less than a full opaque covering, or showing of the female breast with less than full opaque covering of any portion thereof below the top of the nipple or the depiction of covered male genitals in a discernibly turgid state." The Delaware law makes exceptions for the possession of obscene nudity for persons with scientific, educational, governmental, or similar justification and for the noncommercial dissemination to personal associates who do not object to it. California is relatively tolerant of nonsexual nudity, having adopted a policy in 1972 that "nude is not lewd"; however, as in all other states, local ordinances outlaw public nudity.

Representational Nudity

Art, from the dawn of humankind, has found expression in the representation of the human form. The nude statue of the biblical David by Michelangelo (1475–1564)—regarded as one of the world's greatest works of art—does not offend community standards of decency. Even today the nudity that can be viewed on the INTERNET is not so offensive to most adults that it falls outside First Amendment protections for the free and uncensored exchange of ideas. Representational nudity, in sum, garners more protection from being classified as obscene than does live nudity.

Nudity in the arts, on television, in the movies, in print, and on the Internet more generally runs afoul of the law when it is deemed to be obscene. In addressing obscenity in *Roth v. United States*, the Supreme Court confirmed that anything judged obscene was outside the protection of the First Amendment and began a long series of opinions on the topic. For material to be found obscene, said the Court in *Roth*, it must, taken as a whole, be "utterly without redeeming social importance" before it loses constitutional protection. Today almost any representation of nudity, except hard-core pornography or pornographic child nudity, is protected.

Nudity displayed in films or still photographs, for example, cannot be presumed obscene. According to the Supreme Court in *Erznoznik v. City of Jacksonville* (1975), an ordinance making it a public nuisance and a punishable offense for a drive-in theater—whose screen was visible from a public street—"to exhibit films containing nudity" was an infringement of the First Amendment. The Court acknowledged that when claims of privacy and freedom of speech or the press collide, both sides may have arguments based on "the traditions and significant concerns of our society." It added that "when the government, acting as censor, undertakes selectively to shield the public from some kinds of speech on the grounds that they are more offensive than others, the First Amendment strictly limits its power." In *Erznoznik*, the ordinance was "not directed against sexually explicit nudity or otherwise limited." As for nudity in books and magazines, the continued unchallenged publication of *Playboy, Penthouse, Hustler,* and myriad other similar publications confirms that there are few or no social or legal limits to the representation of nudity in these types of printed MEDIA for adults.

Child Nudity

Constitutional protection for material containing child pornography is virtually nonexistent. Some representations of nude CHILDREN, however, may be permitted in medical treatises or textbooks or in artistic works with socially redeeming value. In *United States v. Dost* (1986), a federal district court set out six factors to use in determining "sexually explicit conduct" under the Protection of Children from Sexual Exploitation Act (1977). Among the six was consideration of "whether the child is fully or partly clothed, or nude." Under federal child pornography laws today, according to the U.S. Court of Appeals for the Third Circuit in *United States v. Knox* (2003), even when the pubic area of genitals of children—in this case teenage and preteen girls—were completely covered by underclothes or bikini bathing suits, such "non-nude visual depictions . . . can qualify as lascivious exhibitions, and . . . this construction does not render the [federal law in question] unconstitutionally overbroad." In other words, said the court here, objectionable nudity did not necessarily mean just naked.

In *New York v. Ferber* (1982), the Supreme Court suggested that the reason for protecting children from being shown in obscene situations was that CHILD ABUSE might be involved and that a permanent record of the child's participation would be created. In view of these possibilities, it was considered not too

much of a burden under the Constitution to require alternatives to children in pornographic works, such as adults portraying children or "virtual" representations, including cartoons. Following the *Ferber* decision, CONGRESS passed the Child Protection Act (1984), which prohibited distribution of nonobscene material depicting sexual activity by children and made it a crime to receive through interstate or foreign commerce materials showing minors engaged in sexually explicit conduct. Then in *Osborne v. Ohio* (1990), the Supreme Court upheld a state law that made it a crime to possess a photograph of a minor "in a state of nudity," even if there was no attempt to distribute the material. The Court declared that by "limiting the statute's operation to nudity that constitutes lewd exhibition or focuses on genitals [the Ohio supreme court] avoided penalizing persons for viewing or possessing innocuous photographs of naked children and thereby rendered the 'nudity' language permissible."

Nudism

Recreational nudism, also called naturism, is the practice of not wearing clothes for certain periods of time in private or secluded locations, ostensibly for comfort and better health. Naturism is often carried out communally, with both sexes and even families participating without any sexual activity. The practice had its origins in Germany at the beginning of the twentieth century as a rebellion against the strict moral codes of the Victorian era. After World War I, nudism spread to North America and garnered a limited following. The 1955 nudist colony film *Garden of Eden* was approved by the New York court of appeals based on the finding that nudity is not obscenity. The practice, however, is still considered improper by mainstream Americans.

Nude sunbathing in public places has generally not been tolerated under state law, although some resorts have set aside areas for it. In his dissent in the *Roth* obscenity case, the usually liberal-minded Associate Justice WILLIAM O. DOUGLAS opined, "No one would suggest the First Amendment permits nudity in public places, adultery, or other phases of sexual misconduct." More recently Chief Justice William H. Rehnquist, in his opinion in the *Barnes* nude dancing case, observed that indecent exposure laws "reflect moral disapproval of people appearing in the nude among strangers." But as long as it is done in private and there are no elements of sexual misconduct—especially with respect to children who might be subjected to the nudist experience—the law is pretty lenient toward the practice. In 2004, however, Virginia passed a law requiring that any children attending a nudist activity be accompanied by their parents, grandparents, or legal guardian.

The freedom to appear or perform in the nude, display nudity in photographs and films, and represent nudity in the arts probably reached a plateau in America before the end of the twentieth century. Since then the pendulum may, if anything, have begun to swing back again. Although there is now more nudity in the entertainment world than ever before, and women's thong bikinis leave little to the imagination, blatant public nudity is generally not acceptable. Evidence of this move toward conservatism can be found in the public outcry over the "wardrobe malfunction" that exposed the singer Janet Jackson's breast at the televised Super Bowl halftime event in 2004.

See also BREASTFEEDING; ENTERTAINMENT INDUSTRY; LEWD BEHAVIOR; SEXUALLY ORIENTED BUSINESSES; ZONING.

O

OBSCENE LANGUAGE

See BRUCE, LENNY; ENTERTAINMENT INDUSTRY; FEDERAL COMMUNICATIONS COMMISSION; MEDIA; OBSCENITY.

OBSCENITY

Legally defining obscenity in light of the U.S. Constitution's FIRST AMENDMENT (1791) guarantees regarding freedom of speech and the press has been difficult for lawmakers and the courts for the last fifty years. It was in 1957 that the U.S. Supreme Court, in *ROTH v. UNITED STATES,* first began the process of delineating what constitutes obscenity, including PORNOGRAPHY. The difficulty of reaching a consensus is illustrated in the famous comment in *JACOBELLIS v. OHIO* (1964) by Associate Justice Potter Stewart, who said simply about obscenity: "I know it when I see it."

One problem in crafting a legal definition of obscenity is that it may vary over time and within different contexts. In 1991, for example, Anita Hill testified before the Senate Judiciary Committee on the nomination of Clarence Thomas to the U.S. Supreme Court, accusing him of SEXUAL HARASSMENT. Her advisers argued over whether it would be proper for her to use the word *penis,* as it might offend the senators. But just two years later, when Lorena Bobbitt cut off her husband's penis in 1993, the word became widely and freely used in reporting the story in the press and on television.

Some guidance on the subject can be found in the technical report of the Commission on Obscenity and Pornography (1967), volume II, Legal Analysis. According to the report, obscenity can be analyzed in two major legal contexts. One involves general statutes in which *materials* in the abstract are prohibited as being obscene. The second concerns specific laws that limit the *distribution* of certain materials—to minors, for example—in public or in unsolicited mailings.

Obscenity is a term that has evolved from simply meaning improper behavior—such as obscene gestures or actions, speech, or publication of offensive materials—to specific violations of community standards of decency, as determined by the Supreme Court in its line of decisions regarding the First Amendment rights of free expression. Pornography, in contrast, is a term reserved for depictions in writing, pictures, or live performances of sexually explicit acts that may or may not be considered obscene, depending on the context and the audience.

In his *Commentaries on the Laws of England* (1765–70), William Blackstone (1723–80) denounced "the sale of immoral pictures and prints" as a "grossly scandalous and public indecency," noting that "the punishment 'at common law' is by fine and imprisonment." Although the authors of the U.S. Constitution were undoubtedly aware of Blackstone's *Commentaries,* there is no evidence of just which activities they might have considered to be outside the scope of the First

Amendment's guarantees of free speech and a free press. As Associate Justice WILLIAM O. DOUGLAS noted in a concurring opinion in *A BOOK NAMED "JOHN CLELAND'S MEMOIRS OF A WOMAN OF PLEASURE" V. ATTORNEY GENERAL OF THE COMMONWEALTH OF MASSACHUSETTS* (1966), while a handful of states had obscenity laws at the time the First Amendment was ratified in 1791, "there is an absence of any *federal* cases or laws relative to obscenity in the period immediately after the adoption of the First Amendment."

Evolution of Federal Law

The adoption of the Fourteenth Amendment in 1868 triggered the Supreme Court's power to enforce the protections of the Bill of Rights against infringement by the states—a process that took decades to develop under what became known as the doctrine of incorporation. In an English case, *Regina v. Hicklin*, the same year, the court accepted that "the test of obscenity is this, whether the tendency of the matter charged as obscenity is to deprave and corrupt those whose minds are open to such immoral influences, and into whose hands a publication of this sort may fall." The work in question was an anti-Roman Catholic pamphlet, half of which was found to be obscene because "it is quite certain that it would suggest to minds of the young of either sex, or even to persons of more advanced years, thoughts of the most impure and libidinous character."

The evolution of a modern American legal definition of obscenity at the federal level is generally said to begin with the *Roth* case. Before *Roth* the Supreme Court had not squarely faced the question, as asked in this case, "[w]hether obscenity is utterance within the area of protected speech and press" under the First Amendment. Some earlier cases, however, did address obscenity. In *Chaplinsky v. New Hampshire* (1942), the Court upheld a conviction for violating a state law prohibiting offensive speech or name calling in public. The opinion declared that "certain well-defined and narrowly limited" types of speech that do not contribute to the expression of ideas or have any "social value" are not

protected by the First Amendment. This included lewd, obscene, profane, and libelous utterances, and, as in *Chaplinsky*, insulting or "fighting" words that tend to incite an immediate breach of the peace.

In *Roth* the Supreme Court reaffirmed that obscenity was not protected by the Constitution—that it is a recognized exception to the freedoms of speech and the press under the First Amendment—because it is "utterly without redeeming social importance" or it does not convey ideas that the First Amendment is meant to protect. Citing the English decision in *Hicklin*, the Supreme Court fashioned a test for determining if material was obscene. This test required a determination of "whether to the average person, applying contemporary community standards, the dominant theme of the material taken as a whole appeals to the prurient interest." But the so-called *Roth* test would not end the problem of defining obscenity under the First Amendment.

Post-*Roth*

In 1962, in *Manual Enterprises v. Day*, the Supreme Court, without a clear majority opinion, declared unconstitutional a U.S. Post Office ban on certain magazines sent through the mail to homosexuals. The prevailing opinion in this case went beyond the PRURIENT INTEREST part of the *Roth* test and instead held that the determinant of obscenity was whether material was "patently offensive" and "affronts contemporary community standards of decency." This opinion declared that the community was the "national community." Based on these tests, the Court ruled that the materials in question were not obscene.

In *MILLER V. CALIFORNIA* (1973) and its companion case, *Paris Adult Theatre I v. Slaton*, the Supreme Court again confirmed that obscenity is not constitutionally protected under First Amendment. But here it revisited the problem of defining obscenity at the national level and came up with a few new wrinkles. In *Miller* the Court declared that the community standards to be used were not national but local and that the test for obscene material did not require proving a negative—that the material was "utterly without redeeming social value," as found in *"John Cleland's Memoirs of a Woman of Pleasure,"* also known as the *Fanny Hill* case.

With *Brockett v. Spokane Arcades, Inc.* (1985), the Supreme Court began giving state laws on obscenity the benefit of the doubt, rather than holding them to a strict standard to pass constitutional muster. In this case, a Washington statute that defined *prurient interest* to include lust, a normal and natural emotion, had been invalidated by a federal court of appeals. The Supreme Court reversed that decision, upholding the state law's constitutionality by reasoning that the term *lust* could be construed to refer only to that "which appeals to a shameful or morbid interest in sex." Moreover, the Court noted that the law had a severability clause, and only the portion that "proscribes materials that appeal to normal sexual appetites" should be invalidated, so that the rest of the statute would still be constitutional.

In the next decade, the Supreme Court renewed its vigilance with respect to federal laws aimed at censoring obscene material on cable television and the INTERNET. In *Reno v. American Civil Liberties Union* (1997), *United States v. Playboy Entertainment Group, Inc.* (2000), and *Ashcroft v. American Civil Liberties Union* (2002, 2004), the Court struck down laws aimed at keeping obscene material away from CHILDREN. These cases did not generally turn on the definition of *obscenity* but found that the ways in which offending materials would be limited were too restrictive of the Constitution's guarantee of free expression.

State Law

State constitutions, like the federal document, have language protecting the right of free expression. For example, in article I, section 3, Bill of Rights, the Minnesota constitution affirms that "the liberty of the press shall forever remain inviolate, and all persons may freely speak, write and publish their sentiments on all subjects, being responsible for the abuse of such right." In a landmark decision in *Near v. Minnesota* (1931), however, the U.S. Supreme Court

held that a Minnesota law that acted as a prior restraint—a form of CENSORSHIP that prevents publication rather than punishes a violation of the law after publication—was an infringement of citizens' freedom of the press.

The constitution of Virginia likewise guarantees freedom of speech and the press, but in the commonwealth's legal code *obscene* is defined as "that which, considered as a whole, has as its dominant theme or purpose an appeal to the prurient interest in sex, that is, a shameful or morbid interest in nudity, sexual conduct, sexual excitement, excretory functions or products thereof or sadomasochistic abuse, and which goes substantially beyond customary limits of candor in description or representation of such matters and which, taken as a whole, does not have serious literary, artistic, political or scientific value." Recent case law in Virginia has established that obscene conduct must violate contemporary standards of sexual candor (frankness of expression), but expert testimony as to what constitutes those standards is not required. In a 2000 case, *Copeland v. Commonwealth,* the Virginia supreme court found that evidence that the defendant, at approximately 11:30 P.M., was standing in the backyard of the home of a woman who could see him through a glass door and had his pants unzipped and had exposed his genitals, was clearly aroused, and was masturbating supported the jury's finding that his conduct went "substantially beyond" acceptable community standards and was obscene.

Obscene language is also addressed in many state laws, although they have been in accordance with the U.S. Supreme Court's relaxation of what constitutes obscenity. North Dakota, for example, includes under disorderly conduct "words" that are "intended to adversely affect the safety, security, or privacy of another person." Being careful to note that disorderly conduct "does not include constitutionally protected activity," California criminalizes the use of "offensive words." South Carolina makes it a misdemeanor to disturb religious worship by using "blasphemous, profane or obscene language" and includes under disorderly conduct the use of "obscene or profane language on any highway or at any public place or gathering or in hearing distance of any schoolhouse or church."

In *Gaithright v. City of Portland* (2006), however, a federal court upheld the right of a fundamentalist Christian to call women at a public event in a public park "whores," "sluts," Jezebels," and "daughters of Babylon," noting that a city ordinance permitting the exclusion of anyone who "unreasonably" interferes with an event being conducted in the public park by persons who have been issued a permit to hold the event there violated the First Amendment's guarantee of the right of free speech.

Obscene telephone calls are illegal in all states. Minnesota law provides that "Whoever, (1) by means of a telephone, (a) makes any comment, request, suggestion or proposal which is obscene, lewd, or lascivious . . . shall be guilty of a misdemeanor." Sexually explicit calls in which both parties consent to the obscene language is called TELEPHONE SEX, but obscene phone calls for sexual pleasure or gratification are a form of paraphilia (sexual arousal from objects or situations generally considered socially unacceptable) known as telephone scatalogia and may be related to SEXUAL HARASSMENT or stalking.

Despite concern that obscenity may inspire lewd and lascivious thoughts (which can be inspired in numerous other ways), all of the laws and cases regarding obscenity have at their core a determination as to what may offend. Yet the context always seems to be shifting. A pinup calendar in a car repair shop may offend only the most prudish, but in a politically correct society is there a need for such a display? Freedom of speech and the press presupposes a civil and respectful society whose members do not purposefully seek to offend minorities or more vulnerable citizens. In a public forum, limits on sexual behavior help maintain the communal discourse that a democracy needs to survive—even though we may not all agree on what is and is not offensive expression.

See also LEWD BEHAVIOR; VOYEURISM.

OFFICE ON VIOLENCE AGAINST WOMEN

The Office on Violence Against Women (formerly the Violence Against Women Office) of the U.S. Department of Justice was created in 1995 to implement the mandates of the VIOLENCE AGAINST WOMEN ACT (1994) and to spearhead the Justice Department's legal and policy operations with respect to crimes involving violence against women. Sex- or gender-motivated crimes are often a key element in the pathology of violence against women.

"Ending the terror of domestic violence is a top priority," stated the assistant attorney general heading the department's Office of Justice Programs in October 2002. Two years later, at a ceremony proclaiming October National Domestic Violence Awareness Month, President George W. Bush noted, "Hundreds of thousands of incidents of domestic violence are reported every year [and] many go unreported. About a third of women murdered each year in America are killed by this type of violence. And nearly half the households where domestic violence occurs also [have] a child under 12 years old. There's more than one victim." He continued: "Last year federal [prosecutions] for violence against women . . . increased by 35 percent."

In addition to implementing the provisions of the act, the office also has responsibilities under the Victims of Trafficking and Violence Protection Act of 2000, MEGAN'S LAW, the National Child Protection Act of 1993, and background checks for child care providers. It also provides information about SEXUAL ASSAULT, issues related publications, and administers grant programs authorized by the Justice Department and the Violence Against Women Act.

The grants assist the nation's criminal justice system in responding to the needs and concerns of women who either have been or are potentially likely to be victims of violence. Grants totalling more than $1 billion have been awarded by the office, including discretionary grants to the states and U.S. territories, including American Samoa, Guam, and Puerto Rico. Known as STOP (services, training, officers, and prosecutors) grants, the money helps state, tribal, and local governments and community-based agencies train personnel, establish specialized DOMESTIC VIOLENCE and sexual assault units, assist victims of violence, and hold perpetrators accountable for their crimes. Goals of the grant program include enhancing the delivery of assistance to victims, improving efforts to reach minorities and disabled women, and providing assistance to the Native American tribal justice system to deal with violent crimes against Native American women.

The office also provides technical assistance to state and tribal governments to improve the criminal justice system's response to violent crimes against women. In addition, it coordinates its activities with the U.S. DEPARTMENT OF HEALTH AND HUMAN SERVICES and the Bureau of Citizenship and Immigration Services of the U.S. Department of Homeland Security with respect to the provisions of the Violence Against Women Act regarding battered immigrant women.

Contacts

Office on Violence Against Women, U.S. Department of Justice, 810 Seventh Street, NW, Washington, DC 20531 (202-307-6026). www.ojp.usdoj.gov/vawo.

National Domestic Violence Hotline (800-799-SAFE).

p

PALIMONY

See ALIMONY.

PANDERING

In William Shakespeare's plays *Troilus and Cressida* and *Twelfth Night,* the character Lord Pandarus is referred to as a "go-between" for sexual liaisons. Pandering has come to mean catering to another person's baser desires, often exploiting their weaknesses—for instance, by enticing them with PORNOGRAPHY. The traditional legal definition of *pandering* is to pimp or procure a female for the purposes of PROSTITUTION, similarly catering to the gratification of someone's lust.

The term became important in cases such as GINZBURG V. UNITED STATES (1966), in which the U.S. Supreme Court sought to determine if the printed matter in question was obscene and thus if an offense had been committed by sending it through the U.S. mail. If the materials had been found not to be obscene, the FIRST AMENDMENT (1791) protection of the U.S. Constitution would bar a criminal prosecution. But the Court's opinion in *Ginzburg* noted that "there was abundant evidence to show that each of the accused publications was originated or sold as stock in trade of the sordid business of pandering—'the business of purveying textual or graphic matter openly advertised to appeal to the erotic interest of their customers.'"

In his dissent from the Supreme Court's decision in *City of Littleton, Colorado v. Z. J. Gifts D-4, LLC* (2004), Associate Justice Antonin Scalia asserted that the adult bookstore involved, which was denied a license because it was located in a place not zoned for adult businesses, was not "engaged in activity protected by the First Amendment." Citing his views in *FW/PBS, Inc. v. Dallas* (1990), he declared that "the pandering of sex is not protected by the First Amendment."

State laws also address pandering. For example, the Illinois criminal code provides: "(a) Any person who performs any of the following acts for any money, property, token, object, or article or anything of value commits pandering: (1) Compels a person to become a prostitute; or (2) Arranges or offers to arrange a situation in which a person may practice prostitution."

Although most states define pandering in the context of prostitution, state courts have also had to deal with OBSCENITY-related pandering. A New York case, *People v. Buckley* (1971), held that magazines whose covers boldly proclaim their appeal to sex, are openly displayed for sale, and might be freely purchased did not in themselves constitute pandering and therefore would not sustain a conviction for obscenity. The U.S. Supreme Court denied a request to review this decision, although with dissents by four members.

A Minnesota case, *City of Rochester v. Carlson* (1972), reviewed signs on a store that limited admission to persons over eighteen years of age and advertised sex-oriented literature. The owner also made statements that the city "is ready for this type of reading material" and "had a need for a store such as this." These facts were nonetheless held not to constitute pandering within the meaning of the *Ginzburg* decision.

Reliance on a finding of pandering as used by the Supreme Court in *Ginzburg* has been criticized for creating two classes of obscene material and making laws prohibiting obscenity inconsistent and unclear. They require a determination of obscenity not because of the material's content but because of the way in which the material is offered for sale or distributed. Today, however, obscenity findings are generally limited to truly hard-core material, so-called ADULT MATERIALS that are distributed or displayed in such a way that CHILDREN or minors might be exposed to them, or items that themselves portray children in a sexually offensive manner. Pandering to adults is no longer as important a legal issue as it was after the *Ginzburg* decision.

See also ENTERTAINMENT INDUSTRY; PRURIENT INTEREST; ZONING.

PARENTAL ADVISORIES

See ENTERTAINMENT INDUSTRY.

PARENTAL RIGHTS

See CHILDREN; MOTHERHOOD; UNMARRIED PARENTS.

PARTIAL-BIRTH ABORTION

See ABORTION; UNBORN, RIGHTS OF THE.

PATERNITY

In *Civilization and Its Discontents* (1930), the father of modern psychoanalysis, Sigmund Freud (1865–1939), declares that "the common man cannot imagine ...

Providence otherwise than in the figure of an enormously exalted father. Only such a being can understand the needs of the children of men and be softened by their prayers and placated by the signs of their remorse." As Freud was aware, the father figure throughout human history has often represented the chief religious deity—for example, the Greek god Zeus and the Roman god Jupiter (combining *Zeus* and the Latin *pater*, meaning father). The father also symbolizes the earthly intercessor between humankind and a religious deity—for example, *il Papa* (Italian for father), which refers to the pope of the Roman Catholic Church. As genetic technology creates new ways to shed light on paternity, more secular fathers are now the subject of new laws and policies related to their sexual behavior.

Fatherhood, or paternity, in America can be analyzed from either a strictly biological or a sociological point of view. A technical definition of paternity begins with the uniting of an egg cell and a sperm cell, resulting in the conception of a child. A male's contribution of the sperm cell establishes his paternity just as a female's contribution of an egg cell makes her the mother of the child. From a less purely biological point of view, the nuclear family—a father, a mother, and their CHILDREN—has been considered by political scientists since the time of the Greek philosopher Aristotle (384–322 B.C.E.) to be the basic unit of human society. For the most part, the nature of human societies, at least since the beginning of recorded history, has been patriarchal: headed by a male leader or a father figure.

The institution of MARRIAGE solemnizes and legalizes the nuclear-family relationship and provides a basis for the transfer of rights and interests from both parents to the children born of such union; today adopted and illegitimate children also have rights of inheritance under state laws. The basis of the family as a conduit for the transmission of property, religious beliefs, and social status—and even political status in the case of inheritable monarchies and lesser aristocratic titles in some countries—preceded the knowledge that parenting transmits genetic information from the biological parents to their children. However, the miracles of modern science in the field of GENETICS have made DNA (deoxyribonucleic acid) the new tool in legal battles over paternity. In fiscal year 2003, the Office of Child Support Enforcement in the U.S. DEPARTMENT OF HEALTH AND HUMAN SERVICES reported that paternity was established or acknowledged for more than 1.5 million children in order to pursue CHILD SUPPORT from their biological fathers.

Establishment of Paternity

Parenthood has been traditionally established by either a biological relationship or a legal adoption procedure. The biological fact of the maternity or mother-child relationship is fairly easy to establish accurately. A woman gives birth to a child in a hospital or other setting, attended by people assisting in the birth, and, barring some bureaucratic mix-up, the mother is identified on the child's birth certificate. Paternity for the purposes of the birth certificate is generally established simply by a statement from the mother and the putative father or by the mother alone. But today, using modern technology, the identity of either biological parent can be determined to a 99.9 percent probability.

A paternity test requires a DNA sample from the child as well as the putative father. Only a parent or a legal guardian can give permission to take the sample. The use of the test thus may depend on the cooperation of the parent or a legal guardian unless a court order is given for the child's sample. A sample taken in any other manner may not be admissible because of the possibility that other DNA might be fraudulently substituted.

A legal determination of paternity may be necessary for several reasons. As New York State's highest court declared in *Pamela L. v. Frank S.* (1983), "The primary purpose of establishing paternity is to ensure that adequate provision is made for the child's needs in accordance with the means of the parents." In most cases the child's best interests will thus be the court's primary concern.

Obligation to Support. While at common law a father had the duty only to support his legitimate children (those born in wedlock), today it is well established that he has a legal obligation to support an illegitimate child to the same extent as his legitimate children. First legal paternity must be established to allow a court to enforce the biological father's pre-existing duty to support his child and thus, in many cases, to relieve the state of this burden.

Since the U.S. Supreme Court's ruling in *Levy v. Louisiana* (1968), which held that illegitimate children are "persons" for the purposes of the U.S. Constitution's equal protection clause in the Fourteenth Amendment (1868), the states and the federal government have been prohibited from denying non-marital children the same benefits available to children born in wedlock, including child support. The *Levy* decision and Supreme Court cases following it that questioned the constitutionality of state laws regarding illegitimate children led to the drafting of the Uniform Parentage Act (1973). The act's primary concern is determining against whom the rights of non-marital children may be asserted. In most cases it is the child's father.

Most paternity proceedings are civil as opposed to criminal actions. Some states—including Alabama, Colorado, Kansas, and Montana—have adopted provisions of the Uniform Parentage Act. Each state has its own procedures, however. For example, a paternity action brought in Colorado under the act is governed by the state's rules for juvenile civil procedure, whereas the law in Virginia provides that paternity proceedings may be either a civil or a criminal matter depending on the section of the Virginia code under which the proceedings are brought.

The increased cost of welfare to the federal and state governments has been the driving force behind determining paternity and enforcing the obligations of child support. Federal child support programs require that states permit the establishment of paternity any time before the child reaches eighteen years of age. The act provides that when a child has no presumed, acknowledged, or adjudicated father, a paternity proceeding may be begun at any time, even when the child is an adult.

Presumption of Paternity. In the case *Michael H. v. Gerald D.* (1989), the Supreme Court, although sharply divided, upheld a California law that presumed the paternity of the husband living with his wife even against a challenge by the biological father, who requested an evidentiary hearing on his paternity claim. The Court noted that "the claim that a State must recognize multiple fatherhood has no support in the history or traditions of this country." The Court went on to approve the state law on the grounds that it did not make the child illegitimate but extended to her the same rights as other children to have a normal relationship with her legal parents.

Disestablishment of Paternity

A reverse of the *Michael H.* case occurs when a husband or another presumptive father suspects that he is not the biological father of a child and wishes to have that fact established legally. Some states are recognizing such requests to disestablish paternity when men wish to cease supporting a child that is not biologically theirs and thus terminate what they consider to be the bonds of parentage. These nonbiological fathers equate their putative paternity with being wrongfully convicted of a crime. The New Jersey Citizens Against Paternity Fraud has gone so far as to purchase space on highway billboards that depict a pregnant woman and declare: "Is It Yours? If Not, You Still Have to Pay!" Paternity fraud has become the basis of court petitions by suspicious and aggrieved men asking to have their lack of paternity legally established.

A major problem with such disestablishment petitions is that often their innocent victims are the children involved. In many instances, a significant parent-child relationship has already been established with the legal parent. State courts have acknowledged that the system with respect to establishing and disestablishing paternity is flawed and that the "father-child relationship encompasses more (and greater) considerations than a determination of whose genes the child carries. Sociological and psychological components should be considered," noted one judge.

State courts have also found that the "best interests of the child" analysis, although it may apply to decisions about custody and visitation rights in a separation or DIVORCE case, is not applicable to the determination of paternity itself. It has been held that the knowledge of genetic identity may be in the best interests of a child, even though this begs the question of whether the possibility of a new father-child relationship based on biology should be permitted to trump an existing satisfactory nonbiological father–child relationship. The U.S. Supreme Court has recognized that fatherhood's biological aspect must be supplemented by additional factors if biological fathers are to assert their rights with respect to their children against legal fathers. The Court therefore has developed a "biology plus" test, acknowledging that it takes more than simply a biological connection to be a parent in the legal sense.

The definition of a family is evolving rapidly in American society and law. Single-parent families, polyparenting families (in which more than two adults have parental responsibilities), and same-sex couples with children obtained by adoption, ASSISTED REPRODUCTIVE TECHNOLOGY, or surrogate mothers have transformed the traditional concept of the nuclear family. While 46 percent of married heterosexual couples are raising children, so are 34 percent of lesbian couples and 22 percent of gay male couples. In this brave new world of familial variations, the law is having to play a difficult game of catch-up.

See also ILLEGITIMACY; UNMARRIED PARENTS.

PEDERASTY

See SODOMY.

PEDOPHILIA

See CHILD ABUSE; CHILDREN; SODOMY.

PERVERSION

See BESTIALITY; DEVIANT BEHAVIOR; SODOMY.

PLAN B

See CONTRACEPTION.

PLANNED PARENTHOOD FEDERATION OF AMERICA

The Planned Parenthood Federation of America is the largest reproductive health care organization in the world. Founded in 1916 by MARGARET SANGER, the pioneer of the American birth control movement, the nonprofit organization promotes the rights of every person to choose whether or when to have a child, of every child to be wanted and loved, and of women to be in charge of their own destinies. What began as a visionary social reformer's birth control clinic in Brooklyn, New York, has become an association of nationwide affiliates in fifty states and the District of Columbia that promotes a number of activities related to human sexuality, education about sexuality, and maternal and infant health care; it also supports FAMILY PLANNING around the world to enable individuals to have CHILDREN when they are physically, emotionally, and financially ready.

By promoting access to information services related to sexuality, reproduction, contraception methods, fertility control, and parenthood, the organization seeks to ensure all individuals the freedom to make reproductive decisions. This freedom, according to Planned Parenthood, is based on the right to PRIVACY, especially in personal relationships; the right to education and information to make informed decisions about sexuality and reproduction; and the nondiscriminatory right of access to confidential and comprehensive reproductive health care services. These include CONTRACEPTION, STERILIZATION, ABORTION, ASSISTED REPRODUCTIVE TECHNOLOGY, and prevention and treatment of SEXUALLY TRANSMITTED DISEASES. Planned Parenthood supports medically safe and legal abortions as well as services for adolescents, including contraception and abortion.

The organization stresses efficient, effective, and innovative programs that preserve individual rights and privacy. Concern for each patient's rights requires Planned Parenthood personnel to respect personal privacy and individual dignity, obtain written and informed CONSENT from patients participating in research projects, provide understandable and balanced information and accurate answers to questions about health care and medical treatment, explain fees before services are provided, and offer channels within the organization for feedback from patients.

Planned Parenthood also promotes access to SEX EDUCATION, stressing that such instruction should increase an individual's understanding of sexuality as a normal, healthy, lifelong aspect of human development as well as enhance awareness that there are differences in sexual expression and that sexuality is a personal matter. It supports teaching that helps individuals understand their sexuality, communicate their sexual feelings and decisions to others, and accept responsibility for their sexual decisions. Lobbying activities include seeking funding for domestic and international family planning, supporting pro-choice candidates and political platforms, and advocating various birth control measures.

In 2001 Planned Parenthood set ten major goals for the first quarter of the twenty-first century. Among the initiatives planned for this "Vision for 2025" are ensuring that sexuality is understood as an essential, lifelong aspect and that it is celebrated with respect, openness, and mutuality; creating a new media company to prevent CENSORSHIP of reproductive and sexual health information; and developing the largest citizen activist base of any social movement in the United States. The organization continues to stress its policies to protect the right of each individual to facts about reproductive health and human sexuality and to affirm the fundamental right of each individual to manage his or her fertility free from coercion.

The path that Margaret Sanger paved a century ago has not always been a smooth one, and Planned Parenthood is not without its critics, especially among those who have moral or religious objections to interfering with the natural course of reproduction and childbirth. In 1992 the U.S. Supreme Court, in *PLANNED PARENTHOOD OF SOUTHEASTERN PENNSYLVANIA V.*

In 1941 the Planned Parenthood Federation, which was founded in 1916 by the birth control advocate Margaret Sanger, promoted family planning with a New York exhibition proclaiming, "Every baby wanted and loved." A half century later a chapter of the organization went to court to challenge a Pennsylvania law that restricted women's access to abortion.

CASEY, upheld many provisions of a Pennsylvania law aimed at making it more difficult for a woman to obtain an abortion, including a twenty-four-hour waiting period during which the abortion procedure would be described, the state of the fetus discussed, and alternatives to abortion explained. A five-member majority, however stopped short of overturning the Court's 1973 *Roe v. Wade* decision, which for the first time had extended the right of abortion to women in the United States. Today many women continue to rely on organizations such as Planned Parenthood for information and help in dealing with important aspects and consequences of their sexuality.

In addition to its headquarters in New York City, Planned Parenthood offices are located in San Francisco, Chicago, and Washington, D.C.; the international branch has regional offices in Nairobi, Kenya; Bangkok, Thailand; and Miami, Florida (for Latin America and the Caribbean). There is a board of directors, a chairman, and a president. One hundred and twenty-five affiliates manage 866 health centers, assisted by nearly twenty-one thousand volunteers and staff. The federation numbers its donors and activists at nearly two million persons. A separate Planned Parenthood Action Fund supports the organization with lobbying efforts and voter education programs.

Contact: Planned Parenthood Federation of America, 434 West 33rd Street, New York, NY 10001 (212-541-7800). www.plannedparenthood.org.

See also REPRODUCTIVE RIGHTS; SEXUALITY INFORMATION AND EDUCATION COUNCIL OF THE UNITED STATES.

PLANNED PARENTHOOD OF SOUTHEASTERN PENNSYLVANIA v. CASEY

The year the U.S. Supreme Court decided the ABORTION case *Planned Parenthood of Southeastern Pennsylvania v. Casey* (1992), the federal judiciary seemed to be continuing its vigilant protection of sexual behavior against restrictive laws and government actions. That same year federal courts overturned restrictions on allegedly obscene AIDS-HIV information as well as a Florida court ruling that an album by the pop group 2 Live Crew, *As Nasty as They Wanna Be,* was obscene. In *Jacobson v. United States* (1992), the Supreme Court threw out a federal case against a purchaser of child PORNOGRAPHY because government agents had been PANDERING to him for years, trying to entice him to buy it. The *Planned Parenthood* case, however, exposed the deep rift among the Supreme Court's members over the extent to which they thought the right of abortion first recognized in *Roe v. Wade* (1973) had gone too far.

The Supreme Court had been asked to overrule *Roe* in *Webster v. Reproductive Health Services* (1989). But, in an opinion approved by less than a majority, the Court balked at such an extreme step backwards; it nonetheless upheld a Missouri law requiring that, before an abortion could be performed, a fetus be tested for viability after the twentieth week of pregnancy. *Planned Parenthood* presented the Court with another opportunity to overturn *Roe*; this was again rejected, but, as in *Webster,* the Court upheld more state restrictions on abortion.

A woman's right to an abortion as recognized by the Supreme Court in its controversial *Roe* decision was not absolute. In that decision the Court acknowledged progressive limitations on abortions based on the trimesters of the average nine-month pregnancy. In the first three months, a pregnancy could be terminated by the woman in consultation with her doctor. In the second three-month period, an abortion had to be reasonably related to the woman's health. But during the last trimester, a state could regulate the right to an abortion except where it was necessary to preserve the woman's life or health.

In a joint opinion written by Associate Justices Sandra Day O'Connor, Anthony M. Kennedy, and David H. Souter, the Court in *Planned Parenthood* stepped back from *Roe.* Here it emphasized the state's interest in promoting fetal life along with measures to ensure that when a woman exercises her right to an abortion, she takes into consideration the consequences for the fetus. The Court's 5–4 decision went on to hold that only when state regulation of abortion imposes an "undue burden" on a woman's ability to decide whether to terminate her pregnancy (as established in *Webster*) does the state's power reach into the heart of the liberty protected by the due process clause of the Fourteenth Amendment (1868) to the U.S. Constitution.

The Pennsylvania law at issue required women to wait at least twenty-four hours after a doctor had given them specific information about the nature of the procedure and abortion alternatives. For a minor it also required the CONSENT of one parent, and married women were required to notify their husbands. Failure to obey the law made a person liable to a sentence of up to one year in jail. The Supreme Court upheld the first two provisions but found that requiring a wife to notify her husband was unconstitutional.

With respect to the waiting-period requirement, the Court in part overruled several earlier cases. According to the opinion, "Requiring that the woman be informed of the availability of information relating to the consequences to the fetus does not interfere with a constitutional right of privacy between a pregnant woman and her physician.... There is no evidence here that requiring a doctor to give the required information would amount to a substantial obstacle to a woman seeking an abortion."

The parental notification and consent provisions for a minor, the Supreme Court found, are constitutional as long as there is an adequate "judicial bypass" procedure, as there was in this case, to allow a court to "authorize the performance of an abortion upon a determination that the young woman is mature and capable of giving informed consent and has in fact given her informed consent, or that the abortion would be in her best interests."

As to the requirement that a woman notify her husband of her intent to have an abortion, the Court began by citing *Bradwell v. Illinois* (1873), a century-old decision that reaffirmed the principle at that time that "a woman had no legal existence separate from her husband." In *Planned Parenthood,* however, the Court concluded that in this day and age "a State may not give to a man the kind of dominion over his wife that parents exercise over their children."

The dissenting opinion by Chief Justice William H. Rehnquist—joined in by Associate Justices Byron R. White, Antonin Scalia, and Clarence Thomas—clearly stated: "We believe that *Roe* was wrongly decided, and that it can and should be overruled." Thus the *Planned Parenthood* decision represents another skirmish in the battle over the *Roe* decision, and the abortion issue may be decided a different way by the newly reconfigured Court. The two justices appointed by President Clinton after the *Planned Parenthood* decision, Ruth Bader Ginsburg and Steven G. Breyer, have both been reluctant to join in overturning *Roe v. Wade.*

POLYGAMY

"It is our ancient custom to have many wives at the same time," noted the Jewish historian Josephus in the first century C.E. King Solomon, who reigned nearly a thousand years earlier, was said to have had seven hundred wives and three hundred concubines. The practice of having more than one wife, husband, or mate at the same time is generically known as polygamy. Polygyny refers specifically to having multiple wives, and polyandry to multiple husbands.

Polygamy overlaps BIGAMY, the state of being married to more than one person at the same time, and both are crimes throughout the United States.

Polygamy is related historically to the religious practice of male members of the Mormon Church. Followers of Joseph Smith (1805–44), the church's founder, argued that having several wives was beneficial in providing for the family and raising children. In 1852 polygamy was officially declared a tenet of the church, many of whose members had settled in the Utah Territory between 1845 and 1849. In response the federal government in 1857 replaced the new Mormon leader, Brigham Young (1801–77), as governor, and in 1860 CONGRESS rejected Utah's petition for statehood and its draft of a state constitution because polygamy was allowed by the church. Two years later Congress passed a law prohibiting polygamy throughout the nation and revoked the church's corporate status; it later disenfranchised twelve thousand polygamists. A second draft constitution in support of a renewed application for statehood was rejected in 1872.

Then, in 1890, the Mormon Church rescinded its doctrine of plural MARRIAGE. In 1892 the legislature of the Utah Territory enacted a law "to punish polygamy and other kindred offenses," which, according to article XXIV, section 2, of the Utah constitution, is still in force. Utah finally became a state in 1896. Like Utah, some other western states where Mormons settled— Arizona, Idaho, New Mexico, and Oklahoma—have similar constitutional provisions prohibiting polygamy, written to assure Congress during the process of obtaining statehood that they would not permit the outlawed practice.

Polygamy is still practiced in the United States by some members of the Fundamentalist Church of Jesus Christ of Latter-day Saints, a group that split off from

Brigham Young, the second leader of the Mormon Church in America, promoted and practiced polygamy in Utah in the mid-1800s. In 1860 and again in 1872, when this cartoon was drawn, the territory's petitions for statehood were rejected because of its refusal to abandon plural marriage. Utah finally outlawed polygamy in 1892.

BRIGHAM YOUNG AND HIS WIVES—AN INTERESTING GROUP—NAMES AND LIKENESSES.

the Mormon Church after it officially renounced polygamy in 1890. In 2004 it was reported that the leader of a fundamentalist sect along the Arizona-Utah border was urging men in his flock to marry at least three women to improve their chances of reaching heaven.

First Amendment Issues

Unlike bigamy, polygamy has raised constitutional religious issues in addition to privacy concerns. The U.S. Supreme Court has ruled unanimously in two cases bearing on the Mormon Church's practice of polygamy. In *Reynolds v. United States* (1879), the Court upheld the use of force by the federal government to round up hundreds of Mormons in the Utah Territory for prosecution under the federal antipolygamy law. The church argued that the FIRST AMENDMENT (1791) to the U.S. Constitution protects religious freedom and the church's religious practices. They contended that polygamy was not bigamy—that it was religious-sanctioned plural marriage in line with mainstream American family values and neither destructive of the social structure nor a threat to the public peace. But the Court, noting Thomas Jefferson's phrase that there existed "a wall of separation between church and state," held that the government had a legitimate interest in making plural marriage a crime and that a crime was not protected by the First Amendment, even if it happened to be a religious practice. The government noted the practice's socially destructive nature and called Mormons a "moral menace."

In *Davis v. Beason* (1890), the Supreme Court defined polygamy as conduct rather than a belief and thus outside First Amendment protection. The Court, however, went on to uphold a Territory of Idaho law that denied the vote to anyone who advocated or practiced polygamy or belonged to an organization that did, which meant members of the Mormon Church. Its opinion emphasized that the preservation of the monogamous family was more important than the religious freedom to believe in or practice polygamy. The opinion by Associate Justice Stephen J. Field concluded that "crime is not the less odious because it is sanctioned by what a particular sect may designate as religion."

The Supreme Court in *Richardson v. Ramirez* (1974) cited *Davis v. Beason* for the principle that polygamy can be proscribed by law and can be taken into consideration by a state in determining who can vote. In *Brandenburg v. Ohio* (1969), however, the Court indicated that the mere belief in polygamy or promotion of it—as opposed to committing the prohibited act—was outside the power of the state to penalize.

State Interests

Most states' criminal laws deal with polygamy under provisions prohibiting bigamy. The 1910 compact with the United States that is a part of the New Mexico constitution, however, singles out the practice: "Perfect toleration of religious sentiment shall be secured, and no inhabitant of this state shall ever be molested in person or property on account of his mode of religious worship. Polygamous or plural marriages and polygamous cohabitation are forever prohibited." As mentioned, several other western states where Mormons settled have expressly prohibited polygamy, but Maine and Massachusetts simply declare polygamous marriages void, along with other bigamous marriages.

Like ADULTERY, a frequent outcome of polygamy is CHILDREN whom the parents cannot or will not support. This policy aspect is highlighted by a 1955 Utah case involving a man who had married three women and produced twenty-six children; a court found that not only had he violated the state's law against polygamy, he was also liable for neglect after the children became wards of the state.

During America's SEXUAL REVOLUTION in the 1960s and 1970s, many people formed communes and had sexual relations with various members, raising their ensuing children in an extended family context, as has been the custom in some island and other cultures for centuries. David Koresh (Vernon Wayne Howell), the leader of the Branch Davidian religious sect in Waco, Texas, openly advocated polygamy for himself and other select followers, among a variety of questionable practices. In 1993 Koresh and seventy-five others—seventeen of them under the age of twelve years—died in a fire during a raid on the Davidian compound by the Federal Bureau of Investigation and the Bureau of Alcohol, Tobacco, and Firearms.

Because the institution of the monogamous family unit is deeply rooted in Western culture and religion, polygamy—like SAME-SEX MARRIAGE—tends to trigger a strongly negative reaction in many Americans, far more so than with respect to adultery or DIVORCE. A 1985 federal case, *Potter v. Murray City,* found that the constitutional right of privacy used by the Supreme Court in cases such as GRISWOLD V. CONNECTICUT (1965) and *Roe v. Wade* (1973) to extend rights related to sexual behavior would not extend so far as to protect polygamous marriages. However, it is possible that, in light of the Court's decision in LAWRENCE V. TEXAS (2003)—which extended the constitutional right of privacy to consensual adult homosexual acts in the privacy of one's own home—new challenges could be mounted against the criminalization of polygamy as a violation of the constitutional right of privacy. In our pluralistic, secular nation, one that espouses the equality of all citizens, the practice of plural marriage might one day come to be seen as a matter of personal responsibility.

PORNOGRAPHY

Pornography, simply put, is material that depicts sexually explicit behavior in order to cause sexual stimulation. At least since the U.S. Supreme Court undertook in *ROTH V. UNITED STATES* (1957) to define OBSCENITY, lawmakers and judges have struggled with how to decide what the government can do to regulate or prohibit pornography without running afoul of the freedom of expression allowed by the FIRST AMENDMENT (1781) to the U.S. Constitution.

The law attempts to regulate two types of sexual behavior: physical and representative. The former is encompassed in statutes punishing SEX OFFENSES such as RAPE, INDECENT EXPOSURE, PROSTITUTION, and LEWD BEHAVIOR; also under this rubric are more private sex-related activities, among them ASSISTED REPRODUCTIVE TECHNOLOGY, CONTRACEPTION, ABORTION, PATERNITY, and SEX EDUCATION. As for representations of sex—what might be

considered virtual sexual behavior—laws regulate items and activities that are deemed too offensive or stimulative to be produced, displayed, distributed, or sold, at least in certain public venues. Pornography (from the Greek *pornè,* meaning harlot, and *graphos,* meaning writing) falls in the latter category of representational sexual behavior and may appear in printed or electronic materials, films, art, and sculpture.

In 1873 CONGRESS enacted the Comstock Act, named after the antivice crusader ANTHONY COMSTOCK, to ban obscene materials including pornography from being sent through the U.S. mail. More than a hundred years later, Attorney General Edwin Meese's Commission on Pornography in 1986 issued a much-criticized report that tried to document the harmful effects of pornography and link it to organized crime. The U.S. Department of Justice also created a National Obscenity Enforcement Unit. When the unit began using sting operations and forum shopping to convict pornographers, the AMERICAN CIVIL LIBERTIES UNION called it "a constitutionally renegade operation."

Today constitutionally protected forms of pornography are widely available in bookstores (particularly adult bookstores), at magazine stands, in video and DVD outlets, through the mail, and on the INTERNET. Banned pornography falls into two categories: obscene materials as defined under a three-step test in the U.S. Supreme Court's decision in MILLER V. CALIFORNIA (1973) and child pornography as addressed by the Supreme Court in its decisions in *New York v. Ferber* (1982) and *Osborne v. Ohio* (1990). As a footnote in the *Miller* decision noted, "Pornographic material which is obscene forms a subgroup of all 'obscene' expression, but not the whole."

Adult Pornography

Miller v. California held that for pornographic material to be considered obscene—and thus subject to legal prohibition—it must have three attributes: (1) It must appeal to the PRURIENT INTEREST of the average person, applying contemporary community standards and taken as a whole; (2) it must depict or describe, in a patently offensive way, sexual conduct specifically defined by the applicable law; and (3) when taken as a whole, it lacks serious literary, artistic, political, or scientific value. A year after *Miller*, in *Jenkins v. Georgia* (1974), nude scenes in the film *Carnal Knowledge* were found by the Supreme Court not to constitute hard-core sexual conduct.

The Supreme Court has not distinguished between heterosexual and homosexual pornography in cases involving First Amendment protection for free expression. Several years after the 1957 *Roth* decision, the Supreme Court in *Manual Enterprises v. Day* (1962) found that male physique magazines directed at gay men and sent through the mail were not obscene. The Court reasoned that appealing to the prurient interest was not the only test of obscenity; it had to be shown that the materials were "so offensive on their face as to affront current community standards of decency."

Pornography that depicts adults and that is not obscene may still offend many Americans. (The term *adult* refers to individuals more than eighteen years of age and includes those who may legally possess or view nonobscene pornography and those who are depicted in the pornography.) Many religious and morally strict individuals view even nonobscene pornography as improper to distribute or possess. Arguments have been made on both sides. Associate Justice WILLIAM O. DOUGLAS of the U.S. Supreme Court was generally of the opinion that the First Amendment, which makes no exception in its grant of free-speech and free-press protection, safeguards most if not all pornography with respect to adults. Some feminist theorists, in contrast, have argued that sexually explicit material objectifies, dehumanizes, and degrades women and encourages rape and sexual violence; they have urged that it be banned to protect women.

In recent decades, the legal battleground over pornography has switched from books and movies to television and the Internet. Relevant Supreme Court cases that addressed such pornography—among them *Reno v. American Civil Liberties Union* (1997), *United States v. Playboy Entertainment Group, Inc.* (2000), and *Ashcroft v. American Civil Liberties Union* (2002, 2004)—have affirmed extensive First Amendment

protection for adult pornography, despite attempts by Congress to limit access by adults to protect CHILDREN. The Court has generally found that overbroad regulation of subscription television or the Internet on the pretext of protecting young viewers from sexually explicit adult programming is unconstitutional.

Child Pornography

According to the Supreme Court, child pornography—at least pornography in which actual children participate, as opposed to "virtual" child pornography in which adults pose as children—is allowed essentially no constitutional protection. In *New York v. Ferber*, the Court in 1982 upheld a state law that prohibited knowingly promoting photographic or other visual reproductions of live performances of children engaged in nonobscene sexual conduct. Ignoring the obscenity tests set forth in the *Miller* decision, Associate Justice Byron R. White noted for the Court, "The prevention of sexual exploitation and abuse of children constitutes a government object of paramount importance." The state law in question, he said, "sufficiently describes a category of material . . . not entitled to First Amendment protection."

In *Osborne v. Ohio* eight years later, the Supreme Court allowed to stand a state law that punished the private possession of child pornography depicting "simple nudity." The Ohio supreme court had narrowed the law's reach to NUDITY that "constitutes a lewd exhibition or involves a graphic focus on the genitals." The Supreme Court tried to bolster its position for finding the overly broad law constitutional by arguing that making the private possession of child pornography illegal reduced the demand for it by destroying the market on which its production was based. The *Osborne* opinion was handed down in spite of a 9–0 opinion in *Stanley v. Georgia* (1969) that under several provisions of the Bill of Rights (1791) and the general concept of PRIVACY first used in *GRISWOLD V. CONNECTICUT* (1965), the law cannot punish a person for the purely private possession of obscene material such as a film at home.

New communications technology including cable and satellite television and the Internet brought attempts by Congress to restrict access to ADULT MATERIALS on the basis of protecting children. In 1996 the Child Pornography Prevention Act banned nonobscene "virtual" child pornography on the Internet. But the Supreme Court, in *Ashcroft v. Free Speech Coalition* (2002), rejected the virtual-image bans, leaving intact prohibitions against the use of real children. The Court countered the argument that pedophiles might use such materials to seduce children by saying that many things innocent in themselves, such as cartoons and candy, may be used for immoral purposes but should not therefore be banned. Other attempts to limit Internet access to adult materials to protect children from pornography, such as the COMMUNICATIONS DECENCY ACT (1996) and the CHILD ONLINE PROTECTION ACT (1998), were also struck down by the Court.

All states regulate obscenity and child pornography, and the lines have been sharply drawn by the courts to allow adult access to constitutionally protected material while permitting the government to prohibit it when it becomes obscene. The definition of constitutionally protected pornography no longer turns on subjective criteria that differ from state to state and judge to judge, as it did in 1964 when in *JACOBELLIS V. OHIO* Associate Justice Potter Stewart famously said that although he might not be able to succinctly define pornography, "I know it when I see it."

See also A BOOK NAMED "JOHN CLELAND'S MEMOIRS OF A WOMAN OF PLEASURE" V. ATTORNEY GENERAL OF THE COMMONWEALTH OF MASSACHUSETTS; CENSORSHIP; ENTERTAINMENT INDUSTRY; GINZBURG V. UNITED STATES; HOMOSEXUALITY; MEDIA.

POSTMARITAL AGREEMENTS

See ALIMONY; PRENUPTIAL AGREEMENTS.

PREDATORS

See MEGAN'S LAW; SEX OFFENDERS.

PREGNANCY

By law pregnancy (from the Latin *praegnans*) refers to a woman's condition that begins at conception and terminates with the birth of a child or the loss of the fetus before birth. Pregnancy and the law intersect in various ways, including with respect to issues involving CONTRACEPTION (preventing pregnancy), ASSISTED REPRODUCTIVE TECHNOLOGY (getting pregnant), ABORTION (terminating a pregnancy), DISCRIMINATION against pregnant women, and DRUGS (effect on pregnancy), as well as related topics such as MARRIAGE, SEX EDUCATION, TEENAGERS, UNMARRIED PARENTS, and RIGHTS OF THE UNBORN, among others.

The major areas of the law that specifically impact the state of pregnancy are workplace discrimination and prenatal care.

Workplace Discrimination

Before the modern era, many female employees simply expected to quit or be fired from their jobs once they became pregnant; pregnancy leave was not typically offered until the 1970s. When women began entering the workforce in great numbers, particularly during World War II, and when pregnancy became a part of the WOMEN'S RIGHTS movement in the 1960s and 1970s, discrimination against pregnant women came to be viewed as a pressing problem. The linking of discrimination on the basis of sex with discrimination against some women because they were pregnant tended to muddy the legal waters for a time, however.

In *Cleveland Board of Education v. LaFleur* (1974), the U.S. Supreme Court struck down school board regulations that required pregnant teachers to resign their jobs around five months before they were expected to give birth; the justices declared that such a policy violated the due process clause of the U.S. Constitution by using an irrefutable assumption that they could not perform their duties in such a condition. Although this seemed to be a blow to discrimination against pregnant women, in *Geduldig v. Aiello* the same year the Court upheld a California law that excluded health benefits

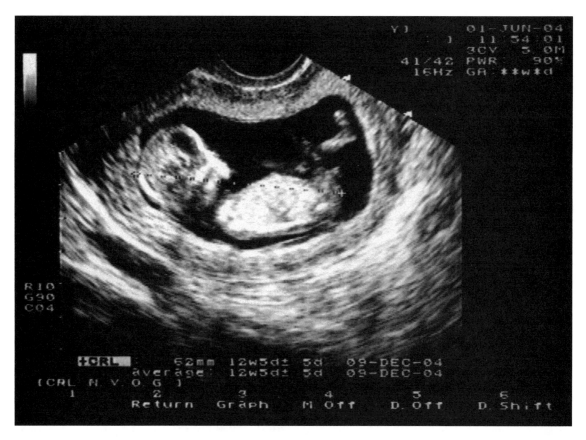

Ultrasound is part of the modern technology that now gives expectant mothers and their families reliable information on developing fetuses. Having such data during pregnancy permits the exercise of medical options, including abortion in the case of life-threatening deformities as well as treatment *in utero* or immediately after birth.

and hospitalization coverage for normal pregnancies; here it reasoned that the discrimination was not on the basis of sex—men were also denied such benefits for their wives—but on the basis of pregnancy, which was a legitimate basis for cutting costs.

Disappointed by the ruling in *Geduldig*, proponents of pregnant women's rights prevailed on CONGRESS to enact the Pregnancy Discrimination Act of 1978 as an amendment to Title VII of the Civil Rights Act of 1964, which prohibits sex discrimination in the workplace. The new federal law permitted an end run around the constitutional problem of sex discrimination versus discrimination against pregnant members of the same class—women.

In 1991 the Supreme Court had an opportunity to decide a landmark case under Title VII, as amended by the 1978 act. Women employees of a company that manufactured batteries challenged their employer's "fetal protection policy," which barred fertile women from high-paying jobs that involved exposure to lead. In *International Union, UAW v. Johnson Controls, Inc.* (1991), a Court majority reversed the lower courts' rulings against the women, holding that because the policy did not also apply to men, whose reproductive systems were just as liable to be damaged by exposure to lead, it was an example of disparate treatment based on sex prohibited under the law. Title VII permits an exception only if the discriminatory policy is based on a bona fide occupational qualification requiring men rather than women, but such a distinction was not established by the evidence in this case.

Another federal statute intended to give both parents the opportunity to provide care during pregnancy and afterward is the Family and Medical Leave Act, enacted by Congress in 1993. The act, which applies to employers with at least fifty employees and to employees who have been employed for at least one year, permits up to twelve weeks of unpaid leave for events related to the birth of a child, an adoption, or care of an ill family member.

The Equal Employment Opportunity Commission has estimated that between 1992 and 2004, the number of women in the workforce with CHILDREN under eighteen years of age increased by 5.2 percent; during the same period, claims against employers for pregnancy discrimination have risen by 33 percent. Discrimination against pregnant women obviously remains a problem. Federal and state laws, while available to redress valid cases of discrimination, have not yet created a general climate of accommodation for pregnant workers.

Prenatal Care

Many legal issues surround an injury to a fetus or a child as a result of negligence by a third party, such as a drug company or a doctor. Such issues are often associated with state medical malpractice laws or consumer rights and represent an enormous range of factual situations as well as medical and legal analyses. Legal implications of an expectant mother's actions on the health and well-being of the child she is carrying represent a more recent but developing area of the law.

Although no specific laws criminalize a pregnant woman's behavior that might be harmful to a fetus, from time to time various criminal statutes are used to prosecute expectant mothers. Scientific studies indicate that smoking during pregnancy can be detrimental to a developing fetus, yet as many as 20 percent of expectant mothers smoke during pregnancy, and such behavior—legal for adults—is not used as the

basis for prosecuting an expectant mother. Drug and alcohol abuse by an expectant mother, in contrast, can lead to charges of endangering a fetus. Several hundred cases of drug abuse during pregnancy have been prosecuted in more than half of the states.

Courts are divided on the legality of holding expectant mothers liable for drug abuse that may harm a developing fetus. Most have refused to sanction criminal prosecutions against expectant mothers under antidrug laws that prohibit "delivery of controlled substances to minors," noting that during pregnancy the drugs are "distributed" through the umbilical cord—not the delivery system intended by drug laws aimed at drug distributors. Florida's highest court held in *Johnson v. State* (1992) that the legislature had not meant to include the passing of cocaine through the umbilical cord in its prohibition against delivery of a controlled substance to a minor.

In South Carolina, conversely, the state supreme court, in *State v. McKnight* (2003), upheld a sentence of twenty years—suspended after twelve years—for a mother whose stillborn baby had cocaine in her system; the court found that the punishment was not cruel and unusual and that a urine sample taken in the hospital did not violate her Fourth Amendment (1791) constitutional right against unreasonable searches and seizures. The U.S. Supreme Court refused to review the case, even though, in *Ferguson v. City of Charleson* (2001), it had held that nonconsensual drug testing of urine from pregnant women violated the prohibition against unreasonable searches and seizures. Here the Court reasoned that the state's interest in prosecuting cocaine use by pregnant women in order to deter it was not sufficient to override the constitutional protection against warrantless, nonconsensual searches.

Legal drugs can also be harmful to a fetus during pregnancy and may produce consequences, such as civil suits against the manufacturer. In the 1950s and 1960s, for instance, the drug thalidomide, which was prescribed to combat morning sickness in pregnant women, was responsible for serious fetal damage and birth defects. In 2005 the Food and Drug Administration issued a warning to expectant mothers against taking Paxil, an antidepressant, because of an increased risk of birth defects; the action put the drug in the agency's highest-risk category for birth defects.

With regard to the right of a terminally ill pregnant woman to determine the course of her treatment and birth procedures, the courts have generally been lenient. In cases where a pregnant woman refuses medical treatment on religious grounds, however, courts have allowed doctors to perform a forced cesarean delivery to save the life of a viable fetus.

Pregnancy is a necessary condition for women if the human race is to survive, but the majority of lawmakers and judges are males who have no firsthand experience with it. Yet they bear significant responsibilities for making and interpreting laws that relate to pregnancy. As American society changes from the model nuclear family with a stay-at-home mom to a panoply of more diverse family models—including working mothers, single moms, and unwed mothers— the laws regarding the treatment of pregnant women will no doubt also continue to evolve.

See also Breastfeeding; Family Planning; Motherhood; Paternity; Unborn, Rights of the.

PREMARITAL SEX

Seventeenth-century court records from the Massachusetts Bay Colony reveal that women who had illegitimate children, their male partners, and couples whose first child was born less than eight months after the date of their marriage were generally prosecuted for fornication (sexual intercourse by an unmarried person with another, married or not). Fornication differs technically from adultery, which is voluntary sexual intercourse by a married person. However, if one party is married and the other is not, both crimes may be committed: adultery by the married person and fornication by the unmarried party.

Significant changes in American law regarding marriage have affected related issues such as divorce,

extramarital sexual relations, and premarital sex. At the beginning of the twentieth century, marriage—which is wholly a creation of the state as far as the law is concerned—was an institution through which government sought to ensure support and protection for women and children and to legalize the distribution of property from generation to generation. This policy was based on an idealized notion of a nuclear family consisting of a husband and a wife, plus their children conceived and born in wedlock. The husband was the breadwinner and authoritarian head of the family, while the wife was a helpmate who served the husband and was the mother of his children. A married woman had no independent rights apart from her husband. As Associate Justice Joseph P. Bradley declared in a concurring opinion in *Bradwell v. Illinois* (1873), a married woman was incapable of acting on her own without her husband's consent (making it legal for Illinois to deny an otherwise well-qualified married woman the right to practice law).

The marital bond was reinforced by divorce laws requiring commitment of an offense against a marriage—adultery, desertion, or cruelty, for example—before a decree could be granted. Sexual activity outside of marriage was discouraged for unmarried and married persons alike. It was public policy to limit sexual behavior to the institution of marriage to prevent illegitimate children and a general appearance of immorality in a community.

Among the factors that have led to independent rights for married women and the decriminalization of sexual activity outside marriage are the ratification of the Nineteenth Amendment (1920) to the U.S. Constitution, giving women the right to vote and hold political office; the urbanization of the country, with a shift from agriculture to factory and nine-to-five office jobs for women; the substitution of women in jobs left by men fighting in World War II; the women's rights movement that began in the 1960s; and the legalization of abortion and contraception, bringing wide availability of contraceptive devices and greatly reducing the fear of pregnancy and sexually transmitted diseases.

Support for laws criminalizing fornication, unmarried cohabitation, and premarital sex may have begun to erode more quickly after the landmark ruling by California's supreme court in *Marvin v. Marvin* (1976). In this case involving a claim for "palimony" against the Oscar-winning actor Lee Marvin by his live-in partner, Michelle Marvin, the court found that "adults who voluntarily live together and engage in sexual relations are nonetheless as competent as any other persons to contract respecting their … rights." The court added: "We are aware that many young couples live together without the solemnization of marriage, in order to make sure that they can successfully later undertake marriage. This trial period, preliminary to marriage, serves as some assurance that the marriage will not subsequently end in dissolution to the harm of both parties."

Most states have repealed laws against fornication, unmarried cohabitation, and premarital sex. However, seven states—Florida, Michigan, Mississippi, North Carolina, North Dakota, Virginia, and West Virginia—still have such statutes on the books. Even in these states, they are generally not enforced, especially since the U.S. Supreme Court's decision in LAWRENCE V. TEXAS (2003); this ruling struck down a state law prohibiting SODOMY, calling it an unconstitutional infringement of the right of PRIVACY. Under *Lawrence*, it is likely that any consensual sexual activity by adults in private is protected by the Bill of Rights (1791). Based on the *Lawrence* decision, in 2005 Virginia's supreme court, in *Martin v. Ziherl,* struck down its state law against unmarried cohabitation, although the North Dakota legislature's lower house defeated a challenge to its own cohabitation law that year.

North Carolina's law (in effect since 1805), to take one example, effectively makes criminals of the approximately 144,000 unmarried couples living together and anyone else who has engaged in premarital or unmarried sex in that state. The AMERICAN CIVIL LIBERTIES UNION in 2005 attempted to have the law overturned, but a spokesman for the conservative North Carolina Family Policy Council suggested, "We think that it's good to have a law against cohabitation because the studies show that couples that cohabitate before they're married … their marriages are more prone to break up."

Premarital sex between consenting adults may no longer be considered a social threat, but premarital sex between minors is a subject that states feel legally obligated to prohibit; some states, however, have adopted "Romeo and Juliet laws" that mitigate the penalties for sex between older minors or TEENAGERS. The physical and psychological trauma of sexual activity to young people below the age of CONSENT supports laws that proscribe this type of behavior. The age of consent ranges from sixteen to eighteen years, but the age of a rape victim may change the nature of the crime. For example, in Alabama the age of consent is sixteen; if a person over sixteen engages in sex with a person under twelve years, it is first-degree rape, but it is only second-degree rape if the victim is over twelve years.

Indulging in casual premarital sex may bring social and psychological consequences, such as a reputation for promiscuity and a lack of self-esteem. But the majority of states today seem to take the position that cohabitation by unmarried persons is just one of several lifestyle choices that should not be made illegal, even though it may not provide the same privileges and benefits of married cohabitation. The institution of marriage has undoubtedly served the human species well in many regards, but making sexual intimacy dependent solely on a pledge of a lifetime of commitment may be as undemocratic in theory as it is impractical in modern life.

See also ALIMONY; CHILD SUPPORT; ILLEGITIMACY; SPOUSAL RIGHTS AND DUTIES; UNMARRIED COHABITANTS; UNMARRIED PARENTS.

PRENUPTIAL AGREEMENTS

A prenuptial agreement, also called a premarital or an antenuptial agreement (and often colloquially referred to as a "prenup"), is a written contract entered into by two persons who intend to get married. Today's increase in the likelihood of DIVORCE and remarriage and the complicated issues that can arise in a divorce settlement have influenced many potential spouses to draw up a prenuptial agreement. Through this instrument they can decide before MARRIAGE, and a possible divorce, what each other's rights will be in the event the marriage is dissolved. Because a prenuptial agreement can also be viewed as a predivorce agreement, it can be entered into even during a marriage (when it is called a postnuptial or postmarital agreement).

Premarital agreements provide options for spouses, such as a woman who has more assets than her intended husband or a husband who is willing to put his career on hold while helping his wife through law or medical school. A prenuptial agreement also might be used in the case of a second marriage to protect assets that one or the other spouse wants to go to CHILDREN or grandchildren from a former marriage.

These agreements clarify the expectations and rights of the parties when future contingencies arise; remove doubts and worries about how property belonging to the married couple will be divided if the marriage fails; protect premarital assets of both parties; protect a family business in the event of death or divorce; ensure the passage of assets to family members from a previous marriage; and protect possible loss of credit eligibility for one partner by keeping the couple's assets separated during the marriage.

Prenuptial agreements, however, cannot preempt court decisions regarding child custody or financial support, which must be based on the best interests of the child. The Uniform Marital Property Act (1983), a model for state laws on marital property and prenuptial agreements, prohibits provisions in premarital agreements regarding CHILD SUPPORT. The act does not include any prohibition against including child custody provisions.

A prenuptial agreement differs from an ordinary contract in several ways: (1) The parties are related or intend to be related by marriage; therefore, such contracts are not made at "arm's length" or between individuals acting solely in their own self-interest. (2) Because state governments have certain legal and traditional interests in marriage, stricter rules apply to prenuptial agreements. Courts will examine them with an eye to determining the fairness of their provisions. (3) Prenuptial agreements are written to be carried out in the future, when circumstances may have changed and put one or the other party in a situation that is no longer fair and equitable. In such cases a court may intervene to change the terms.

Public Policy Changes

Prenuptial agreements are relatively new instruments. Until recently the parties to a marriage were legally precluded from determining their own rights and responsibilities. Before the 1970s, many state courts invalidated these marital agreements on the public-policy grounds that they encouraged divorce; they also suggested that the agreements changed the basic nature of the marriage contract, in which the state has various interests, such as ensuring support for children of the marriage and for a non-wage-earning spouse. Even courts that recognized premarital agreements might pick and choose the provisions they would allow. In 1916 a Kentucky court in *Stratton v. Wilson* upheld a provision in a prenuptial agreement dealing with a widow's benefit on the death of her spouse, but it rejected another one dealing with ALIMONY payments on divorce.

Courts have also voided some of these agreements because they reallocated what a legal treatise in 1932 called the "essential incidents of marriage." Although the treatise never described exactly what these "incidents" were, courts used the concept as the basis of decisions voiding prenuptial contracts that tried to alter the husband's duty to support his wife and children or the wife's duty to perform domestic services for her husband. In *Graham v. Graham* (1940), a Michigan court voided a contract between a husband and a wife that attempted to change the wife's obligation to accept the husband's choice of domicile and his responsibility to support her. As the Virginia supreme court stated in *Cummings v. Cummings* (1920), to enforce such agreements "would be to allow parties by private agreement to establish such marriage status as they wish.... There is but one marriage status known to the law."

However, the Florida supreme court, in *Posner v. Posner* (1970), upheld a prenuptial agreement based on the reasoning that there were other types of spousal contracts, such as contracts in contemplation of death, that were just as capable of encouraging divorce as a prenuptial contract. The court concluded that the increased incidence of no-fault divorce laws eliminated the JUDICIARY's obligation to protect the traditional form of marriage. The Florida court nonetheless directed that such contracts be scrutinized for changes in circumstances that might render them no longer equitable to the parties.

In *Lebeck v. Lebeck* (1994), a New Mexico court upheld a prenuptial agreement that went against the wife's interests. The court stated that "in keeping with the trend to apply traditional contract analysis to issues involving premarital agreements, [the agreement will be allowed] to stand, even if one party has given up all his or her rights in the property of the other." Community property states such as New Mexico have always permitted spouses to redefine their property rights, either from separate to communal or the reverse.

State Laws

States today generally follow the decision in the 1970 *Posner* case. Now all states and the District of Columbia recognize prenuptial agreements. More than half of them—including Arizona, Iowa, Maine, New Jersey, Texas, and the District of Columbia—have adopted the Uniform Premarital Agreement Act (1983), which provides guidance for people who want to draw up such an agreement. The act covers ownership, management, and control of property; the disposition of property in the case of separation, divorce, and death; alimony; wills; and life insurance beneficiaries. The act also provides for enforcement of prenuptial agreements unless they are fraudulent or unconscionable.

Because state laws on prenuptial agreements may differ somewhat, the rights and obligations under such contracts may change when a couple moves to another state. Some states do not permit the modification or elimination of the right to court-ordered alimony in the case of divorce. Maine makes any prenuptial contract null and void one and one-half years after the parties become parents, although the contract may be reinstated in writing.

The issue of privately negotiated arrangements is not yet completely settled, but the trend is towards fewer rather than more restrictions.

See also ANNULMENT.

PRESIDENT

In the United States, laws regarding sexual behavior are created and influenced in many ways by national, state, and local governments. At the national level, the U.S. Constitution (1789) assigns different responsibilities for laws and regulations to three institutions: CONGRESS, the president, and the federal JUDICIARY. Historically the president has not played as significant a role with regard to sexual behavior as have Congress and the U.S. Supreme Court. Laws involving sexual behavior and related subjects are often controversial. Congress, created as a reflection of the majority will of the citizens at any particular time, and the federal courts—the Supreme Court in particular—have assumed more active roles in this area.

Although the president is elected by members of a constituency that expect their candidate to promote their views, one reason that presidents have tended not to get involved in issues involving sexual behavior may be that under the Constitution, the president is both the head of state and the head of government. Like a prime minister who represents an electoral majority in a parliamentary system, the president leads the executive branch of government. But as the head of state—of the nation and all the people—the chief executive represents the United States both inside the country and outside to the other nations of the world. He must generally exercise care in taking sides on sensitive and divisive national issues, such as those involving sexual behavior. Nonetheless, the president can use the stature of the office to try to influence opinion at home and abroad.

Constitutional Powers

Article II of the Constitution sets forth the president's authority: "The executive Power shall be vested in a President of the United States of America." Section 2 makes the president "Commander in Chief of the Army and Navy of the United States, and of the Militia of the several States, when called into the actual Service of the United States." He is also given power to make treaties, with Senate approval, and to appoint ambassadors, judges, and other officers of the United States.

The president's constitutional role in making and enforcing laws includes proposing legislation to be considered by Congress, although technically the president must have bills formally introduced in each house of Congress by a member of that house. He also has the power to approve or veto bills passed by Congress; vetoes must be overridden by a two-thirds vote of both houses. Enforcement of federal laws and regulations is overseen by the president through the vast array of cabinet offices, especially the U.S. Department of Justice; other executive branch agencies are also under his supervision according to either the Constitution or laws that give the president increased supervisory authority not already conferred by the Constitution.

As the head of government, the president is responsible for developing overall federal policies, garnering support for these policies, and implementing them through oversight of executive branch departments, agencies, and other offices such as the Office of Management and Budget. The process involves developing the federal budget—recommending to Congress which programs should be funded and at what levels for the next fiscal year. Proposed budgets are likely to include many programs relating to sexual behavior, including scientific research as well as direct and indirect assistance through federal and state health and welfare services and other programs. Under the president's direction, the federal government deals with a variety of matters related to sexual behavior, among them research and education on AIDS-HIV and other SEXUALLY TRANSMITTED DISEASES, CENSORSHIP, CHILD ABUSE, DRUGS, DOMESTIC VIOLENCE, FAMILY PLANNING, GENETICS, the INTERNET, MOTHERHOOD, OBSCENITY, PORNOGRAPHY, PRISONERS, SEX OFFENSES,

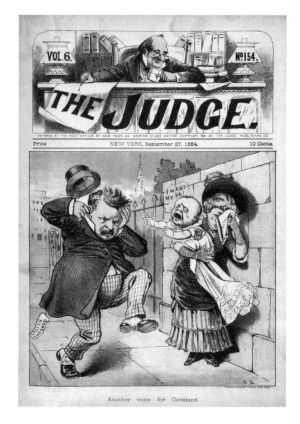

During his first campaign for president in 1884, Grover Cleveland was dogged by charges that he had fathered an illegitimate child. The cover of an issue of *The Judge* magazine that year featured a woman holding a baby crying out, "I want my pa." Cleveland provided child support, went on to win election in 1884 and 1892, and married Frances Folsom at the White House in 1886.

SEX OFFENDERS, SEXUAL HARASSMENT, STEM-CELL RESEARCH AND CLONING, and VICTIMS' RIGHTS, to name a few.

The appointment powers given to the president by the Constitution or Congress are another means of influence. For example, appointing a liberal or a conservative as attorney general will affect how the Justice Department enforces some laws regarding sexual behavior, such as crusading against OBSCENITY or prosecuting attacks on abortion clinics. The interpretation of laws can similarly be influenced by the president's constitutional powers to appoint federal judges, including the justices of the Supreme Court. During the confirmation process in 2005 and 2006 for two new Supreme Court members, Chief Justice John G. Roberts Jr. and Associate Justice Samuel A. Alito Jr., the question of how these men would rule on questions involving abortion rights took center stage, because the president had indicated that he disapproved of the right to ABORTION declared by the Supreme Court in *Roe v. Wade* (1973).

Following are some specific examples of the president's power to influence laws and policies regarding sexual behavior.

Chief Executive. By Executive Order 12968, President Bill Clinton in 1995 prohibited DISCRIMINATION on the basis of sexual orientation in the federal government's grants of security clearances. The 1995 order, however, allowed the continuance of Executive Order 10450, issued in 1953 by President Dwight D. Eisenhower; this directive requires investigations regarding security clearances to look into "notoriously disgraceful conduct" and "sexual perversion."

Legislation. In 1970 Title X of the Public Health Service Act was enacted in large part because of President Richard M. Nixon's promise in 1969 that "no American woman should be denied access to family planning assistance because of her economic condition."

Appointments. The president appoints a council on BIOETHICS to "study ethical issues connected with . . . embryo and stem cell research, assisted reproduction, cloning, uses of knowledge and techniques derived from human genetics." President George W. Bush appointed a new council in line with his own views several months after he had advised the nation that he was limiting federal funding for stem-cell research, citing ethical grounds related to his belief that human life begins at conception.

Commander in Chief. As the head of U.S. military forces, President Bill Clinton compromised with the Defense Department to allow it to issue Defense Directive 1332.14 in 1993, permitting homosexuals in the military to be separated for conduct that "includes homosexual acts, a statement by a member that demonstrates a propensity or intent to engage in homosexual acts, or a homosexual marriage or attempted marriage."

Delegated Authority. Under Title 22 of the U.S. Code, Foreign Relations and Intercourse, section 7103, the president is directed by Congress to "establish an Interagency Task Force to Monitor and Combat Trafficking" in humans in order to reduce international PROSTITUTION rings. The task force is directed to "[e]xamine the role of the international 'sex tourism' industry in the trafficking of persons and in the sexual exploitation of women and children around the world."

Extraconstitutional Influences

In addition to the president's executive and legislative roles under the Constitution, the chief executive also has extraconstitutional methods that he can use to influence laws and policies. The turnover of the White House to the Republican Party in 2001, for example, allowed President George W. Bush to use his position to support his party's more conservative agenda with regard to sexual behavior. His presidency brought an emphasis on faith-based programs sponsored by the federal government in areas such as ABSTINENCE-only SEX EDUCATION programs, opposition to SAME-SEX MARRIAGE and stem-cell research and cloning, appointment of individuals to the Supreme Court and other federal judgeships who are less supportive of WOMEN'S RIGHTS, including the right to abortion, and prohibition of the use of foreign aid funds for family planning.

As the leader of his political party, a president has the ability to influence the party's national platform. This may include positions on issues related to sexual behavior, such as REPRODUCTIVE RIGHTS, EQUAL RIGHTS, HOMOSEXUALITY, and sex education. The party's leaders and its platform in turn can influence the president's actions on policy and legislation. For example, in 2000 and 2004, the Republican Party had an antiabortion plank that reflected the views of George W. Bush, although more moderate members of the party had other views.

The office of the president further gives him access to a national forum or "bully pulpit" to speak out about political issues of all kinds. Theodore Roosevelt, who served as president from 1901 to 1909, railed against family planning that limited the size of families as "decadent" and "criminal against the race." More recently, George W. Bush spoke out in favor of a constitutional amendment to limit MARRIAGE to one man and one woman, and he indicated on more than one occasion that he supports a Supreme Court reversal of *Roe v. Wade*, which granted women abortion rights.

Setting an Example

The president's high visibility may make him a role model for citizens, even though some have suffered unwelcome attention to their own sexual behavior. Grover Cleveland, who served as president from 1885 to 1889 and again from 1893 to 1897, won his first election even after acknowledging that he had fathered a child out of wedlock; he admitted his PATERNITY and continued his financial support of the child. Other presidents—including Thomas Jefferson, Franklin Delano Roosevelt, and John F. Kennedy—reportedly had illicit sexual affairs both in and out of office. Earlier in the country's history, the press and insiders who knew about the affairs preferred not to publicize them.

Bill Clinton, who served from 1993 to 2001, was sued during his first term in office for SEXUAL HARASSMENT that allegedly occurred when he was governor of Arkansas. Then in 1998, after having had sexual relations with a female White House intern, he was impeached by the House of Representatives under the provisions of the Constitution, although in 1999 the Senate found him not guilty of any impeachable offenses. The aftermath of this process may have indirectly contributed to the success of the Republican Party in subsequent elections, bringing with it that party's agenda of more conservative laws and policies regarding sexual behavior. It will be interesting to see if the forays of President Bush into the arena of sexual policy will become the new rule for future presidents.

PRESIDENT'S COUNCIL ON BIOETHICS

See BIOETHICS.

PRESS, FREEDOM OF THE

See CENSORSHIP; FIRST AMENDMENT; MEDIA.

PRISONERS

When it comes to rights and protections, including those related to sexual behavior, the federal and state prison systems are worlds in themselves and worlds apart from that of the average citizen. There are many such systems: federal, state, and local prisons and jails; military and prisoner-of-war detention facilities; separate male and female institutions; maximum and minimum facilities, and some in between; juvenile and immigrant detention centers; and contract facilities that offer few federal legal protections. The Commission on Safety and Abuse in America's Prisons estimates that some 2.2 million prisoners (7 percent of them women) and 750,000 prison staff live and work in U.S. prisons on any given day. Like the MILITARY to some extent, these prison systems are special settings in which the constitutional and statutory legal rights and protections afforded ordinary citizens are greatly reduced.

Sex-Related Rights

A convicted felon customarily suffers a loss of substantial rights, noted the U.S. Supreme Court in *Estep v. United States* (1946). Yet a California court has pointed out, in *Yarish v. Nelson* (1972), that confinement to a penal institution does not strip a prisoner of all his or her constitutional rights. Prisoners' rights related to sexual behavior, however, are far more circumscribed than in the outside world. Florida is one state whose law includes the rights of inmates in the rules for the state's correctional system and establishes a prisoner grievance system. Elsewhere state legislatures and courts are reluctant to limit the discretion of prison officials.

Marriage. Prisoners have the right to marry, according to the U.S. Supreme Court in *Turner v. Safley* (1987). Associate Justice Sandra Day O'Connor acknowledged in her opinion for the Court that, although no right exists to consummate a MARRIAGE while in prison, there are other reasons for getting married besides sexual relations, such as legitimizing CHILDREN born out of wedlock or obtaining financial or other benefits. In *Gerber v. Hickman* (2002), a federal appeals court held that a prisoner's right to marry did not include the right to consummate the marriage or to have conjugal visits while in prison. There is also some authority for allowing prisoners to file for DIVORCE.

Obscene Materials. Prisoners do not have a right to receive obscene materials. Under California law, for example, inmates retain a right to correspond confidentially with an attorney or public officials, although incoming mail may be inspected for contraband; they also have the right to receive mail, books, and periodicals, except that "prison authorities may exclude ... obscene publications or writings, and mail containing information concerning where, how, or from whom this matter may be obtained." Texas officials only recently, in 2004, approved a prison ban on sexually explicit images, which are defined as "frontal nudity of either gender"; however, on a case-by-case basis they will permit exceptions for pictures in *National Geographic* magazines, materials concerning anatomy, and NUDITY related to art— but not *Playboy* or *Penthouse.*

DNA Testing. The U.S. Code, Title 42, The Public Health and Welfare, section 14135A, requires the director of the Bureau of Prisons to collect a DNA sample from each individual in the bureau's custody who has been convicted of a qualifying federal offense, such as murder, sexual abuse, or the attempt to commit a qualifying crime and authorizes the director to use "such means as are reasonably necessary to detain, restrain, and collect a DNA sample from an individual who refuses to cooperate." All states and the District of Columbia have similar laws to authorize the collection of DNA samples from certain types of prisoners and detainees as an aid in solving crimes.

DNA can also be used to exonerate wrongly convicted prisoners, although the condition of the evidence may be adversely affected if a long time has passed since the sample was collected. In 2005 the U.S. Senate passed a bill to ensure postconviction access to DNA testing for prisoners on death row and other inmates who assert their innocence. As of that year at least twelve prisoners on death row had been exonerated through this testing.

Equal Rights. As guaranteed under TITLE IX of the Education Amendments of 1972 as well as under some state laws, female inmates retain rights to participate in educational and vocational programs equal to those available to male inmates. A federal court of appeals found in *Jeldness v. Pearce* (1994) that disparate treatment whereby male prisoners were given "merit pay" for participating in a vocational training course but female inmates were denied it was a violation of Title IX. In *Women Prisoners of District of Columbia Department of Corrections v. District of Columbia* (1995), a federal court ordered the prison system to remedy violations of Title IX.

Abortion. In 2005 the U.S. Supreme Court, without issuing a written opinion or any indication of how the members voted, upheld a federal judge's order to a Missouri correctional officer to transport a pregnant inmate to a clinic to have an ABORTION, in spite of the state's policy of denying women prisoners any assistance in terminating a PREGNANCY. Missouri Governor Matt Blunt commented, "The decision is highly offensive to traditional Missouri values and is contrary to state law, which prohibits taxpayer dollars from being spent to facilitate abortions."

Pregnancy. As a report by Amnesty International brought to light in early 2006, the federal prison system and nearly half of the state prisons expressly permit the routine shackling of sick and pregnant women— even during childbirth—ostensibly as a precaution against escape. Only two states, California and Illinois, have laws regulating the use of restraints on pregnant women in prison; similar legislation is being considered in New York State. Corrections departments in Connecticut, Florida, Rhode Island, Washington, Wisconsin, Wyoming, and the District of Columbia have policies prohibiting restraints on women during labor and birth. In an editorial, the *New York Times* on March 5, 2006, stated, "The primitive practice of chaining women in childbirth should shame us all."

Protection from Assault

Consensual but illegal sexual relations occur in the country's prison systems, although unwanted sex is a bigger problem. A SEXUAL ASSAULT occurs when one prisoner or a group of prisoners attack another inmate or when an offense is committed by a prison official. The fact that the U.S. prison population has increased seven and one-half times between 1980 and 2004 is undoubtedly a factor in the sharp increase in sexual assaults. In many cases the ratio of prison staff to prisoners has grown larger—during night, morning, and weekend shifts, one correctional officer may oversee as many as four hundred prisoners, according to the president of the Council of Prison Locals of the American Federation of Government Employees. The sexual assault rate is ten times greater in juvenile facilities than in adult prisons: ten incidents of sexual contact were reported in 2004 for every two thousand young persons at state-run juvenile facilities.

On September 4, 2003, President George W. Bush signed into law the Prison Rape Elimination Act, which applies to all correctional and detention facilities, including federal, state, and local prisons; police lock-ups; private facilities; juvenile facilities; and immigration detention centers. The law's purpose is to establish a standard of zero tolerance for sexual assaults of any kind in prison systems; require collection of national data on the incidence of prisoner RAPE; provide funds for research and corrective programs; establish a federal commission to address the problem; and create a panel to review and rate detention facilities throughout the nation. The act also calls for a yearly report by the attorney general of the United States that includes "a listing of those institutions in [a] representative sample, separated into each category ... and ranked according to the incidence of prison rape ... ; and a listing of any prisons in the representative sample that did not cooperate with the survey."

According to section 10 of the act, *rape* is defined as "the carnal knowledge, oral sodomy, sexual assault with an object, or sexual fondling of a person, forcibly or against that person's will; or not forcibly or against the person's will, where the victim is incapable of giving consent ... or ... through the exploitation of the fear or threat of physical violence or bodily injury." Three categories of sexual violence are cited: completed nonconsensual sex acts, attempted nonconsensual sex acts, and abusive sexual contacts. The law addresses both inmate-on-inmate acts and sex involving prison staff.

States also have laws that address sexual violence in their prison systems. Assaults by state prisoners are dealt with by state correctional facilities, rather than by the police; the Prison Rape Elimination Act attempts to make these penal systems more accountable for preventing and punishing violations. Most states also have specific laws that deal with sexual offenses by prison staff against prisoners. For example, the Alabama law regarding custodial sexual misconduct makes it a felony for any employee to engage in sexual conduct with a person who is in the custody of the department of corrections, department of youth services, a sheriff, a county, or a municipality, as well as a person under the supervision of a parole officer; allegations that the person in custody gave CONSENT may not be raised as a defense. South Dakota has a similar law and also makes a misdemeanor of failure to separate prisoners by sex, except for a husband and a wife, and requires examination and treatment of all prisoners for venereal disease as appropriate.

Protecting the rights of sexual minorities in a prison setting, including the right to be free from sexual abuse, is an even greater challenge than safeguarding the average heterosexual prisoner. Two cases in point are *Maggert v. Hanks* (1997) and *Schwenk v. Hartford* (2000). In *Maggert* a federal appeals court found that the Eighth Amendment (1791) to the U.S. Constitution, which prohibits cruel and unusual punishment, did not entitle a transsexual prisoner to a curative treatment such as estrogen supplements or sex-reassignment surgery for TRANSSEXUALISM; however, the court noted that "as the cases have already established, he is entitled to be protected, by assignment to protective custody or otherwise, from harassment by prisoners who wish to use him as a sexual plaything, provided the danger is both acute and known to the authorities." *Schwenk* involved a "pre-operative male-to-female transsexual" prisoner who intended to have sex-reassignment surgery some day and was allegedly harassed sexually by a prison guard on a number of occasions. A federal court of appeals found that Douglas (Crystal) Schwenk was entitled to protection under a section of the VIOLENCE AGAINST WOMEN ACT called the Gender-Motivated Violence Act, which was struck down in 2000 in *United States v. Morrison;* protection was due, said the court, even though the GENDER harassment was caused by a person of the same sex. Other federal cases have held that prison authorities must provide treatment for gender-identity disorders, such as gender dysphoria.

The rapidly increasing number of inmates, escalating costs for maintaining them and staffing correctional facilities, and difficulty in recruiting and training professional custodial staff all make more difficult the problems of protecting prisoners and what few rights they have during incarceration. Deprived of normal human freedom and interactions, antisocial sexual behavior on the part of some prisoners is understandable—if not acceptable. And given the position of power that prison staff hold over those incarcerated, abuse of authority can also be expected. Perfecting the system for supervising both prisoners and staff is the key to preventing illegal sexual behavior in this type of environment.

See also HOMOSEXUALITY; OBSCENITY; PORNOGRAPHY; SEXUALLY TRANSMITTED DISEASES.

PRIVACY

Privacy (being secluded from others) plays an important role with respect to sexual behavior. Some sexual activity that may be carried out legally in private would be criminal if done in public. For example, sexual intercourse is generally not a crime when done out of the public eye by consenting adults. In *Lawrence v. Texas* (2003), the U.S. Supreme Court held that the constitutional right of privacy protects even consensual SODOMY between adult homosexuals in the privacy of one's own home.

This constitutional right of privacy, however, is not expressly stated in the U.S. Constitution. It was not recognized by the Supreme Court until its landmark decision *GRISWOLD V. CONNECTICUT* (1965), permitting the use of contraceptives. Since then, the concept of privacy has had a significant impact on U.S. law and policy regarding aspects of sexual behavior such as ABORTION, CONTRACEPTION, HOMOSEXUALITY, OBSCENITY, sexuality, and SPOUSAL RIGHTS AND DUTIES. Privacy rights also play a part in many related concerns, such as AIDS-HIV testing, the use of DNA information, the treatment of SEX OFFENDERS, the rights of CHILDREN, and crimes such as public NUDITY, INDECENT EXPOSURE, and VOYEURISM.

Found in the Penumbras

"Marriage and procreation are fundamental to the very existence and survival of the race," proclaimed the Supreme Court in *Skinner v. Oklahoma* (1942), a case involving a state law requiring the STERILIZATION of a certain class of criminal. It thereby laid the groundwork for an implied constitutional right of privacy, at least with respect to matters regarding marriage and the sexual behavior of a husband and a wife. Two decades later in the *Griswold* case, such a right of privacy was clearly identified by the Court within the structural implications of several provisions of the Bill of Rights (1791), including the FIRST AMENDMENT, Third Amendment, Fourth Amendment, Fifth Amendment, and NINTH AMENDMENT. Structural analysis of a legal document, especially a constitution, focuses on the document's intent instead of on the literal meaning of its words.

In his opinion for the Supreme Court in *Griswold*, Associate Justice WILLIAM O. DOUGLAS constructed a framework on which to build a constitutional right of privacy. He noted that the First Amendment protects not only the right to speak and publish but also the right to distribute and receive information. The right of association, recognized by the Court in *National Association for the Advancement of Colored People v. Alabama* (1958), is also not expressly mentioned in the Constitution; rather, it is derived on the basis of the framers' intent from the rights expressly included in the First Amendment, including the rights of assembly and religious freedom. The Third Amendment prohibits the government from quartering soldiers in a house without the owner's CONSENT. The Fourth Amendment protects the right of the people to be secure in their persons, homes, and personal effects against unreasonable searches and seizures. The Fifth Amendment guards against self-incrimination. The Ninth Amendment clearly states that even though a right is not expressly guaranteed in the Constitution it may nonetheless be retained by the people.

Justice Douglas thus found that in the "penumbras" (secondary shadows) of these specific constitutional rights was a zone that encompassed a broader implied right of privacy in other areas of human activity, one that the government could not transgress.

Constitutional Right of Privacy

The following is an overview of significant areas of sexual behavior that involve privacy, including the constitutional right of privacy as developed by the Supreme Court:

Contraception. In the 1965 *Griswold* case, the Supreme Court upheld a married couple's right to use contraceptives in the privacy of their own home. Reviewing a Connecticut law that since 1879 had made it a crime for any person to use any drug, article, or instrument to prevent conception, the Court declared the statute to be an unconstitutional invasion of a married couple's right of privacy. To enforce such a law, said the Court, would require invading the marital bedroom—an act the government had no rational basis for committing. In *Eisenstadt v. Baird* (1972), the right of privacy regarding contraception was extended to unmarried couples.

Abortion. Citing a woman's right to privacy regarding her body and reproductive functions, the Supreme Court in *Roe v. Wade* (1973) invalidated state laws banning abortion. This important case has been the subject of intense debate in America between advocates of a woman's right to choose whether or not to have an abortion and opponents who believe that a human being is created at the moment of conception. Anti-abortion proponents contend that the government's

duty to protect the life of an unborn child outweighs the mother's right to reproductive privacy. In subsequent cases such as *Planned Parenthood of Southeastern Pennsylvania v. Casey* (1992), the Court has signaled its willingness to permit state restrictions on abortion rights. It has also upheld federal laws that deny funding for abortions. Appointments in 2005 and 2006 to fill two seats on the Supreme Court by President George W. Bush, an avowed opponent of abortion rights, may create a new majority for overruling *Roe*, again allowing states to ban abortion.

Homosexuality. In its 2003 *Lawrence v. Texas* decision, the Supreme Court extended the constitutional right of privacy to protection of sexual activity between consenting adult homosexuals in the privacy of their own home. The case involved a Texas law that made it a crime for homosexuals to engage in sodomy. The Court held, however, that the government's interest in consensual sex between adults, whether heterosexual or homosexual, infringes the right of liberty protected by the Fourteenth Amendment (1868), as did the laws the Court invalidated in *Griswold* and *Roe*. This constitutional right of liberty includes the right of privacy.

Spousal Rights. In addition to the right of privacy protecting a married couple's sexual behavior, traditional spousal rights include confidentiality in communications between husband and wife. More often referred to as the marital communications privilege, this right of a husband or a wife to refuse to testify against the other was acknowledged by the Supreme Court in *Trammel v. United States* (1980). The principle is based on the rationale that permitting such testimony could disrupt marital harmony. The Court noted, however, that the modern trend in the states has been away from strict adherence to the principle, to allow a spouse-witness to decide whether or not to exercise the privilege.

Sexuality. A person has the general right to keep private his or her sexuality (as opposed to biological sex) and may not be required to disclose his or her GENDER identity or sexual orientation. In the MILITARY, however, a positive duty has been created not to disclose one's homosexuality, and failure to comply with this requirement can lead to discharge from the service. In *Thomasson v. Perry* (1996), a federal appeals court held that the military's special national requirements did not make DISCRIMINATION against self-proclaimed homosexuals illegal.

Nudity and Indecent Exposure. Nudity in private is legal, but nudity in public, except in certain places and under certain conditions—a live figure-drawing class, for example—is illegal. However, nudist or nature camps, in which adults and even families with children socialize in the nude, are not illegal, with some restrictions regarding maintaining privacy from the general public. Nude dancing as adult entertainment has been limited by the Supreme Court in *City of Erie v. Pap's A.M.* (2000), as a result of which dancers are required to wear a minimal covering such as pasties and a G-string. The Court's opinion presumably would allow total nudity in public performances in a legitimate theater. All states have laws prohibiting indecent exposure, making it a crime to expose one's genitals in public with the intent to affront or alarm another person.

Obscenity. The right of individuals to possess and view PORNOGRAPHY in the privacy of their own home has been upheld by the Supreme Court in *Stanley v. Georgia* (1969). However, in *Osborne v. Ohio* (1990), the Court indicated that its decision in *Stanley* did not necessarily apply with respect to child pornography featuring real children, as opposed to simulated images of children. As far as private use of the INTERNET is concerned, the World Wide Web and e-mail have been left virtually unregulated.

Voyeurism. State "peeping Tom laws" that make certain types of voyeuristic activity a crime also involve the notion of personal privacy. Kentucky law, for one, defines voyeurism as, among other things, observing or recording "the sexual conduct, genitals, or nipple of the female breast of another person without that person's consent," specifying that the "other person is in a place where a reasonable person would believe" that he or she will not be observed or recorded.

Sex Offenders. State laws now require sex offenders to register in accordance with MEGAN'S LAW provisions. These registration requirements apply even after completion of legal punishment and require publication of information including an offender's current residence. Courts have generally upheld these laws against challenges that they constitute an unconstitutional invasion of privacy. For example, an *Opinion of the Justices to the Senate* (1996) in Massachusetts (a state that permits advisory judicial opinions) found that a proposed community notification law regarding sex offenders did not violate either national or state constitutional guarantees of privacy; in *State v. Williams* (2000), an Ohio court held that a law classifying sexual offenders and requiring them to register did not violate the right of privacy. Victims of sex offenders, including children—especially in cases of child molestation, INCEST, and RAPE—are accorded consideration for their personal privacy in providing testimony, and many are the subjects of state VICTIMS' RIGHTS laws.

AIDS-HIV and Other Sexually Transmitted Diseases. Confidentiality and privacy play an important role in how laws deal with SEXUALLY TRANSMITTED DISEASES such as AIDS. Their intent is to protect people who have contracted the disease and to encourage them to be tested. Many states have passed laws specifically protecting the results of testing. In *Estate of Urbaniak v. Newton* (1991), a California court ruled that an AIDS patient had a cause of action under the privacy guarantee in the state's constitution. His infection had been disclosed by individuals examining him for a matter relating to an injury on the job.

DNA. Most state courts have held that taking DNA samples from persons convicted of crimes and maintaining a database of information is not an unconstitutional infringement of the right of privacy. Louisiana, Texas, and Washington State also permit samples to be taken from people who are arrested but not convicted. State privacy laws relating to GENETICS generally restrict insurers and employers from using genetic information without a person's consent, given the potential harm such information may cause and because samples may be obtained without a person's knowledge.

Children's Rights. The Supreme Court has recognized in several cases that children have some rights under the Constitution that are not coextensive with adult rights. In *Bellotti v. Baird* (1979), the Court identified a relatively narrow area of privacy for mature children, permitting minors seeking an abortion to obtain court approval directly without consulting or getting approval from their parents.

Several federal laws that address privacy do not directly relate to sexual behavior. Many states, however, have laws that prohibit invasions of privacy, which may involve criminal sexual behavior such as voyeurism. For example, Nebraska law provides that "any person, firm, or corporation that trespasses or intrudes upon any natural person in his or her place of solitude or seclusion, if the intrusion would be highly offensive to a reasonable person, shall be liable for invasion of privacy."

Protection of personal privacy has become an increasing concern in the modern world. An important pillar of privacy rights, especially for women of childbearing age, is the right of abortion, which is itself under attack in some states. Because the landmark *Roe v. Wade* decision is rooted in the constitutional right of privacy established in the *Griswold* case, the whole edifice of this right of privacy regarding sexual behavior—from SEX EDUCATION to contraception—could similarly be in jeopardy.

See also BIOETHICS; ETHICS; UNBORN, RIGHTS OF THE.

PROCREATION

See ASSISTED REPRODUCTIVE TECHNOLOGY; MOTHERHOOD; PATERNITY; PREGNANCY; REPRODUCTIVE RIGHTS; STERILIZATION; UNMARRIED PARENTS.

PROSTITUTION

Prostitution is sometimes called "the world's oldest profession." *Prostitute* is derived from the Latin *prostituere* (to expose publicly). In Latin the English word *prostitution* would be translated as *meretricius*. From this term comes the legal concept of a meretricious

MARRIAGE, one that is void because it is based on an exchange of some consideration for sex.

In most democratic countries, the exchange of sex for money is not a crime. Sex workers (a more politically correct term for prostitutes) are pursuing an agenda to establish their rights through the International Labor Organization, World Health Organization, and other groups affiliated with the United Nations. In the United States, however, prostitution is a crime in all states, even Nevada, although that state delegates to county governments its authority to prohibit or regulate prostitution, and some counties allow it.

Around the mid-nineteenth century, state and local governments in the United States began outlawing prostitution, making it a crime to operate a house of prostitution or to be associated with this form of commercial sex. During this period private organizations such as the Society for the Suppression of Vice, which the crusader ANTHONY COMSTOCK helped found, often assisted the police in enforcing laws against prostitution. In 1870 an attempt was made in St. Louis to regulate rather than criminalize prostitution by licensing brothels, restricting them to a specified area, and requiring regular medical inspections of prostitutes; the experiment sparked a backlash by groups such as the social purity movement, which saw prostitutes as a threat to the traditional role of wives as dependent on their husbands for economic support rather than independent sexual entrepreneurs.

Federal Law

The possibility that women might be imported into the United States for the purposes of prostitution led CONGRESS in 1875 to federalize the immigration laws (previously set by those states with ports) to prohibit the "importation into the United States of women for the purposes of prostitution." In construing the federal law, the U.S. Supreme Court, in *United States v. Bitty* (1908), characterized prostitutes as undermining "the idea of the family, as consisting in and springing from the union for life of one man and one woman in the holy estate of matrimony."

At the turn of the twentieth century, the prospect of young women being lured into "white slavery" by international prostitution rings resulted in the White Slave Traffic Act of 1910, which became known as the Mann Act after its chief sponsor, Representative James Mann of Illinois. Supporters were characterized as "men who reverence womanhood and who set a priceless value upon female purity." The law outlawed the interstate transportation of a female "for the purpose of prostitution or debauchery, or for any other immoral purpose, or with the intent and purpose to induce, entice, or compel such woman or girl to become a prostitute or to give herself up to debauchery, or to engage in any other immoral practice." The Mann Act was applied to cases in which women were "transported" not just for commercial sex but also for any "immoral" purpose. In *Bell v. United States* (1955), the Supreme Court ruled that transporting two women at the same time constituted only one offense under the act.

Those early efforts at controlling prostitution have since been codified in the U.S. Code. As amended through 1998, Title 18, Crimes and Criminal Procedure, part I, Crimes, chapter 117, Transportation for Illegal Sexual Activity and Related Crimes, section 2422, Coercion and Enticement, provides:

(a) Whoever knowingly persuades, induces, entices, or coerces any individual to travel in interstate or foreign commerce, or in any Territory or Possession of the United States, to engage in prostitution, or in any sexual activity for which any person can be charged with a criminal offense, or attempts to do so, shall be fined under this title or imprisoned not more than 10 years, or both.

(b) Whoever, using the mail or any facility or means of interstate or foreign commerce, or within the special maritime and territorial jurisdiction of the United States knowingly persuades, induces, entices, or coerces any individual who has not attained the age of 18 years, to engage in prostitution or any sexual activity for which any person can be charged with a criminal offense, or attempts to do so, shall be fined under this title, imprisoned not more than 15 years, or both.

Title 18, chapter 67, Military and Navy, restricts prostitution near any military or naval base or similar site. The law gives the secretaries of the army, navy, and air force the authority to punish any prostitution within a "reasonable distance" from a military facility by a fine, imprisonment for not more than one year, or both. Proscribed acts include keeping "a house of ill fame, brothel, or bawdy house."

State Laws

States differ widely in how they define and treat prostitution. Colorado, for example, defines prostitution as performing, offering, or agreeing to perform any act of sexual intercourse, fellatio, cunnilingus, masturbation, or anal intercourse in exchange for anything of value, a crime that is a misdemeanor (of lesser significance than a felony); however, engaging in prostitution or patronizing a prostitute with the knowledge that the offender has HIV is a felony. In Alabama prostitution is a loitering offense and charged as a misdemeanor. Georgia law makes pimping or PANDERING a misdemeanor of a high and aggravated nature, while Hawaii characterizes prostitution as a petty misdemeanor.

In many states, including Wisconsin and Wyoming, prostitution itself is a misdemeanor, but soliciting or promoting prostitution is a felony. In Connecticut it is a felony to advance or profit from prostitution, and in Florida it is a felony to procure a person under the age of sixteen years for prostitution. In Illinois pimping for a prostitute who is under the age of sixteen or who is institutionalized and severely or profoundly mentally retarded is a felony. Prostitution in New Jersey is treated as the mildest level of offense—as a "disorderly person"—but solicitation of a person to patronize a prostitute is a felony.

In New York State the courts have noted that prostitution as defined in state law does not preclude commercial agreements to engage in any and all kinds of sexual conduct, only those expressly prohibited in the law. Although in North Dakota the courts have acknowledged that the legislature may have relaxed laws dealing with consensual sexual behavior, it has not gone so far as to decriminalize all sexual relations between consenting adults, such as BIGAMY, INCEST, and prostitution. And in Minnesota, the state supreme court declared in 2005 that for the purposes of a prostitution law making solicitation of sex for hire in a public place a crime, a moving vehicle on a public highway does not constitute a public place.

Prostitution laws often do not criminalize the search or payment for a prostitute's services. Where customers are prosecuted, their penalty is generally lighter than for the prostitutes. Sex workers are generally held in custody after being arrested, while male customers are released with a notice to appear later in court. Prostitutes typically are not eligible for release on bail or their own recognizance because of their lack of status in the community and because they may spread SEXUALLY TRANSMITTED DISEASES.

Alabama's constitution was recently amended to address prostitution in Jefferson County. The language used is gender neutral: "(d) No person shall solicit, compel, or coerce any person to have sexual intercourse or participate in any natural or unnatural sexual act, deviate sexual intercourse, or sexual contact for monetary consideration or other thing of value. (e) No person shall agree to engage in sexual intercourse, deviate sexual intercourse, or sexual contact with another or participate in the act for monetary consideration or other thing of value and give or accept monetary consideration or other thing of value in furtherance of the agreement."

Prostitution Law Challenges

Challenges to laws against prostitution have generally been unsuccessful. Grounds cited have included vagueness in the statutory language used, including allegations that the U.S. Constitution's due process clause is violated by a failure to give sufficient notice to individuals about the nature of the acts prohibited. Prostitution laws have also been attacked as an impermissible violation of PRIVACY. A right to solicit for prostitution has been alleged, based on the right of free speech contained in the FIRST AMENDMENT (1791).

In only some cases involving extreme vagueness, where "immoral acts" referred to in the law were not clearly defined, have prostitution statutes been struck down by the courts.

In states that have adopted constitutional EQUAL RIGHTS protections, prostitution laws have been challenged on the basis of their unequal or selective enforcement against women. In 1977 the supreme court of Massachusetts upheld such a law, noting that the record did not establish that male customers were not also prosecuted. Around the same time, Wisconsin's state supreme court ruled in 1974 that in order for a female prostitute to avoid prosecution on equal protection grounds, she must prove that the failure to prosecute male patrons was selective, persistent, discriminatory, and without justifiable prosecutorial discretion. Courts have also ruled that police departments are justified in using more male decoys to catch prostitutes than females to catch male customers, because they are focusing on those profiting from the transactions rather than the consumers. Even where prostitution statutes are gender neutral, selective enforcement is regularly upheld.

With respect to homosexual prostitution, laws that target same-sex solicitation have been struck down as an infringement of free expression protected by the First Amendment. For example, in *State v. Thompson* (2002), the Ohio supreme court found that a law prohibiting the solicitation of "homosexual or lesbian" activity was unconstitutional, whereas a law that prohibited *"all* offensive solicitations of sexual activity" would have passed muster.

Other than prohibitions against HUMAN TRAFFICKING, laws relating to consensual prostitution may be trapped in the American past. In an earlier era information about CONTRACEPTION was considered obscene, serving alcoholic beverages was constitutionally prohibited, and many forms of gambling were illegal. Now Las Vegas, Nevada, thrives on legalized gambling and the sale of liquor, and to some extent the state allows the historic vice of prostitution, as regulated by local government. Should prostitution at last be more widely recognized as an activity that is so rooted in human nature that it cannot be effectively

Prostitution has existed throughout recorded history in spite of social, moral, religious, and legal condemnation. When this prostitute was documented in Peoria, Illinois, by the Farm Security Administration in 1938, it was estimated that this all-American city had 140 sex workers. Except for a few counties in Nevada, the practice is illegal in the United States.

curbed by law? The current tenor of the times—witnessing something of a backlash against the extension of sexual, homosexual, and WOMEN'S RIGHTS—would indicate that the country is still not ready to accept legalized prostitution, other than in some parts of Nevada.

See also LEWD BEHAVIOR; STATE AND LOCAL GOVERNMENT.

PRURIENT INTEREST

ROTH V. UNITED STATES (1957) was the first case in which the U.S. Supreme Court tackled the extent to which the FIRST AMENDMENT (1791) to the U.S. Constitution protects OBSCENITY under the right of free speech and freedom of the press. Associate Justice William J. Brennan Jr.

concluded on behalf of the Court that obscene material was, by definition, not protected by the First Amendment. To be found obscene, questionable material must be "taken as a whole," he said, and must appeal to the "prurient interest" of "the average person, applying community standards."

In Latin, *prurio* means to itch. The word *prurient*, which is derived from it, means obsessive interest in improper matters, especially of a sexual nature. In footnote 20 of Justice Brennan's opinion in *Roth*, the Supreme Court referred to the definition of *prurient* in Webster's New International Dictionary (unabridged, second edition, 1949) as "Itching; longing; uneasy with desire or longing; of persons, having itching, morbid, or lascivious longings; of desire, curiosity, or propensity, lewd."

The definition of obscenity developed in *Roth* would be argued over and refined for many years to come. In another Supreme Court case, MILLER V. CALIFORNIA (1973), the phrase "prurient interest" (together with "patently offensive") was analyzed as part of an inquiry into the definition of the concept "community standards" set forth in the *Roth* decision. At issue were the exact locations to which the *Roth* definition of obscenity applied: nationwide or local, and if local what size should the community be? Material that might appeal to the prurient interest in Peoria, Illinois, might not in San Francisco. The *Miller* decision resolved the question by holding that both prurient interest and patent offensiveness could be measured by local rather than national standards. However, as later Supreme Court decisions would show, definitions of these terms would still not vary significantly from place to place, despite the ruling in *Miller*.

State lawmakers and courts know that they have to conform to Supreme Court pronouncements on matters involving protections under the U.S. Constitution that are made applicable to the states under the Fourteenth Amendment (1868). To a large extent, definitions in state laws and court decisions thus fairly closely track those in federal constitutional law. Most state laws thus have incorporated some version of the Supreme Court's notion of prurient interest. As one example, the South Carolina code, title 16, chapter 15, Offenses Against Morality and Decency, article 3, Obscenity, Material Harmful to Minors, Child Exploitation, and Child Prostitution, section 16-15-305 (C)(3), provides that "'prurient interest' means a shameful or morbid interest in nudity, sex, or excretion and is reflective of an arousal of lewd and lascivious desires and thoughts."

State courts have also grappled with the definition of prurient interest. *City of St. George v. Turner* (1993) involved bed sheets hung in a store on which customers painted graffiti, including a representation of a nude woman and female genitalia added by one budding artist; in its decision Utah's supreme court noted that although community standards provide the legal reference point for determining prurient interest, mere NUDITY or a simple reference to or discussion of sex does not, as a matter of law, appeal to the prurient interest. In *State v. Johnston* (1996), a North Carolina court explained that a definition of prurient interest in sex used during a trial for disseminating obscenity (it was called an unhealthy, abnormal, lascivious, shameful, or morbid sexual interest) could not have been misunderstood by the jury to include a normal interest in sex.

A federal appeals court held in *Polykoff v. Collins* (1987) that the Arizona supreme court did not over-broadly construe the definition of prurient interest despite a jury instruction that permitted conviction for obscenity if the items in question excited only normal sexual thoughts and desires, which are constitutionally protected. In *Commonwealth v. Rich* (1981), a Pennsylvania court held that the failure of a Philadelphia obscenity ordinance to define prurient interest did not render it unconstitutional.

Perhaps the laws and court cases serve only to confirm the dictum of U.S. Supreme Court Justice Potter Stewart in the case JACOBELLIS V. OHIO (1964). He declared that while he may not be able to define hardcore PORNOGRAPHY, "I know it when I see it." The definition of obscenity and pornography, except in the case of minors and CHILDREN, has all but been made superfluous in the modern era. What is now legally available to adults in bookstores, in motion pictures, on videos and disks, and on the INTERNET has raised the bar for proving that such material is obscene or pornographic and therefore beyond constitutional protection. But as has happened in the past, the pendulum may swing back at any time.

See also ADULT MATERIALS; CENSORSHIP; LEWD BEHAVIOR; SEXUALLY ORIENTED BUSINESSES.

r

RADIO

See Censorship; Entertainment Industry; Federal Communications Commission; Media.

RAPE

Rape is a violent sex act perpetrated by a stronger individual or one who has power over another. In a democratic society in which all citizens are presumed equal, forced sexual intercourse constitutes physical domination of one citizen by another sexually aggressive citizen against the victim's will. A 2003 National Crime Victimization Survey by the U.S. Department of Justice estimated that some two hundred thousand American women twelve years of age or older were victims of rape, attempted rape, or sexual assault; it is likely that more than half again as many cases go unreported. These rapes may have resulted in more than four thousand pregnancies. Probably one in six rape victims is under twelve years of age. Men and boys can also be rape victims. Same-sex rapes may occur in restricted settings such as prisons, military camps, same-sex schools, and churches. And, although rare, women can be guilty of rape, especially as an accomplice.

In the National Crime Victimization Survey, rape is defined as forced sexual intercourse, whether the force is physical or psychological. Threats, bribes, intimidation, or violence are types of force that may be used. As to the amount of force required to constitute rape, in *United States v. Bryant* (1969), a federal appeals court noted that the requirement of force would be satisfied "if the defendant applies any amount of force against another person in the absence of what a reasonable person would believe to be affirmative and freely-given permission to the act of sexual penetration."

Under common law, the definition of rape is unlawful carnal knowledge of a woman, which requires sexual penetration, without her consent. Federal law treats rape as a form of sexual abuse or aggravated sexual abuse, and most state laws include rape as a type of sexual assault or sexual battery on either gender. Varying degrees of rape may be charged, such as first-degree rape when serious physical injury has been inflicted. The modern trend is to view rape not primarily as a sex act but rather as a violent crime linked to feelings of rage or hatred by the assailant. A large majority of rapes are committed by persons known to the victims, but a rapist has less than a 10 percent chance of being arrested, prosecuted, and ultimately found guilty of the offense.

Men's reproductive urge has often been used to justify their aggressive behavior toward women. (Think of the stereotypical cartoon of the caveman, dressed in animal skins with a large club over his shoulder, dragging a similarly clad woman by her hair off to his cave.) Throughout history and in many parts of the

In the 1970s women on university campuses began campaigns to "take back the night" to reduce intimidation by rape. This poster by Katy Taylor was produced by New York Women Against Rape as part of the broader effort to promote laws that would allow women to feel and be more secure from sexual assault.

world today, rape has been and is still condoned or goes unpunished. It has sometimes been used as an instrument of war to destroy the morale of invaded populations, although it is a war crime under the Geneva Conventions of 1949. However, rape in America and most of the nations of the world is a serious, if often ambiguous, crime. From a 1680 court decision in England comes the famous legal warning: "rape . . . is an accusation easily to be made and hard to be proved, and harder to be defended by the party accused, tho never so innocent."

The traditional legal view of rape, as handed down through the common law in America, required physical penetration of the vagina by the male sex organ, accompanied by force or the threat of force beyond the actual act of penetration. Rape may also be accomplished by fraud or deceit or by using drugs or intoxicants to more easily subdue a victim. Traditionally, rape could be proven if it was carried out against the victim's will, as evidenced by her sustained physical resistance. Consent was conclusively presumed when the act was done by the husband. Under common law, a female under ten years of age was deemed incapable of granting her consent, thus giving rise to the offense of statutory rape.

Trials often favored the defendant. If an accusation was not made promptly, it might be deemed not genuine. Prior sexual conduct of the accuser could be used to impeach her credibility. Judges might instruct juries that because, as the English judge indicated, rape is easy to charge and hard to defend against, the victim's testimony should be scrutinized carefully.

Although laws against rape have changed, many potential difficulties remain in prosecuting offenders. Victims may feel ashamed or blame themselves for allowing it to happen. The trauma and social stigma associated with making a public charge of rape, especially against a relative or an acquaintance, can keep a victim from coming forward. Some people in the law enforcement and justice systems remain insensitive to or prejudiced against women who may try to file rape charges. The outcome of a trial may turn on just two witnesses: the victim and the alleged rapist. Besides having to contend with a daunting legal system to obtain justice, female rape victims often must deal with many other issues. They may contract AIDS-HIV or other SEXUALLY TRANSMITTED DISEASES, and they may become pregnant, for which emergency CONTRACEPTION is now sometimes available.

Federal Law

In its decision in *United States v. Morrison* (2000), a case involving the rape of a student by a varsity football player at Virginia Polytechnic Institute, the U.S. Supreme Court foreclosed any federal avenue for redress of rape and other SEX OFFENSES by private actions, as opposed to criminal action by state governments.

(Civil rights violations, however, have this remedy under the Fourteenth Amendment.) Citing its decision in *United States v. Lopez* (1995), which struck down a law making it a federal offense to possess a firearm in a zone around a school, the Court held that CONGRESS could not similarly rely on the Constitution's commerce clause to "regulate non-economic, violent criminal conduct based solely on that conduct's aggregate effect on interstate commerce." Attorneys general of thirty-eight states had supported VICTIMS' RIGHTS to sue, agreeing that local remedies for violence against women were inadequate and that national regulation was needed.

The VIOLENCE AGAINST WOMEN ACT (1994), under which the *Morrison* case was brought, addresses a wide array of gender-based violent and abusive sexual behavior, including stalking. Some of the provisions include mandatory restitution for sex crimes, programs for assistance and education to reduce sexual violence and abuse, protection for battered women and children, and increased penalties when victims are under sixteen years of age.

Federal statutory law covering sexual abuse, including rape, applies in federal jurisdictions such as federal prisons. To prove such a crime, it must be shown that a defendant knowingly caused another person to engage in a sexual act by using force or the threat of force or that he or she put the person in fear of death, serious bodily injury, or kidnapping; physical restraint qualifies as the use of force. A defendant may be convicted even if the victim is mentally incapable of understanding or physically unable to decline or communicate unwillingness to engage in the act. Aggravated sexual abuse requires, in addition to the sex act, a greater degree of threat or fear or actions that cause a person to become unconscious, including the administration of a drug or an intoxicant that impairs the person's ability to appraise or control his or her conduct. The traditional marital exemption in the case of rape by a husband or a wife has been abandoned. Punishment may include a fine and imprisonment for up to life, but the death penalty cannot be imposed for the rape of an adult.

State Law

The more modern state laws relating to rape generally contain gender-neutral terms and include anal and oral sex as well as vaginal penetration; some cover digital and mechanical methods of penetration as well. Some laws have broadened the evidence for finding coercion or restraint, and others have lessened the requirement that a victim offer continual active resistance. Additional changes include raising the age for statutory rape, which varies from state to state from twelve to eighteen years; reducing the emphasis on the defendant's state of mind in reading or misreading the victim's consent; lessening the importance of the promptness of the complaint; negating the need for corroboration of the victim's charges; and, by means of RAPE SHIELD LAWS, generally trying to exclude the victim's prior sexual conduct from evidence. To a large extent, judges no longer instruct jurors to give the victim's testimony special scrutiny.

Only a few state constitutions address rape or other SEX OFFENSES. The Hawaii and New Jersey constitutions provide a right of public access to information on people convicted of certain offenses. Nebraska's constitution denies bail in cases of "sexual offenses involving penetration by force or against the will of the victim." The South Carolina constitution sets the age of consent to sex at fourteen years.

What was traditionally defined as rape is now called SEXUAL ASSAULT or sexual battery, using gender-neutral language, although the basic elements of the crime remain the same. In West Virginia, for example, a person is guilty of sexual assault in the first degree when the person "engages in sexual intercourse or sexual intrusion with another person and, in so doing, inflicts serious bodily injury upon anyone or employs a deadly weapon in the commission of the act." Penetration, force, and a lack of consent on the part of the victim are key elements in proving the crime.

Penetration. The exact amount of penetration required to constitute rape is not always agreed on. In *State v. Albert* (1998), the majority opinion of

Connecticut's supreme court declared that penetration of the labia majora (outer lips of the vagina) constituted penetration, while the dissent argued that the vagina itself must be penetrated. Statutes in Maine and Vermont require only "direct physical contact between the genitals" and "contact" of the organs for penetration. Impotence is not necessarily a defense against a charge of rape. In *State v. Kidwell* (1976), an Arizona case, an impotent defendant was convicted of rape because of testimony that some slight penetration occurred. Emission by the male is not generally necessary, and proof of emission does not necessarily prove penetration.

Consent. Because crimes require both a physical act and an intent to commit the act, a general intent on the part of the perpetrator is all the proof that is required to show that a defendant voluntarily committed a rape and is sufficient for a conviction. But in interpreting the question of a woman's CONSENT, some courts have found relevance in the defendant's state of mind. In the California case *People v. Mayberry* (1975), the state supreme court ruled that because of the severe penalties that may result from conviction for rape, when testimony by the woman and the man regarding the question of consent differs markedly, the defendant's version, if reasonable, may be the basis for acquittal. A third line of cases requires a showing of recklessness regarding the consent rather than simply negligence on the defendant's part in "misreading" the lack of consent.

Force. The presence of force is a basic element of rape statutes. The majority require either force or a lack of consent, although some laws require both. The amount of force found necessary by the courts varies greatly. The two standards generally applied are that (1) the amount of force used is beyond that necessary for the act of intercourse, and (2) the amount of force necessary to commit the act of intercourse is sufficient to constitute rape. Where a victim is incapable of granting or withholding consent, the second standard is generally used. In the Illinois case *People v. Borak* (1973), the rape occurred during a gynecological examination and the victim was both surprised by and

unaware of the perpetrator's intentions. But where the consent of the victim is an issue, the first standard is more likely to be used.

Threats and Coercion. Actual force is not necessary, even under the old common law definition of rape; the threat of force is sufficient. It must be real, however, and the reaction to the threat must be reasonable. State cases indicate that a threat against a third party may be sufficient. According to the Model Penal Code (1962), compulsion "by threat of imminent death, serious bodily injury, extreme pain or kidnaping" constitute the required level of threat. Roughly half of state statutes include similar language.

Coercion is a more problematic basis for establishing rape. In a 1990 Montana case, a high school principal was acquitted of "intercourse without consent" after he coerced a student into having sex by threatening to keep her from graduating. Fraud may also pose a difficult problem for proving rape. In the case of a woman who mistakes a man for her husband and proceeds to have intercourse, such deception is even more difficult to analyze. Focusing on the necessary consent element, this type of fraud would probably sustain a rape conviction, as did the gynecological examination in the *Borak* case.

Drugs. Rape following the administration of DRUGS and intoxicants is mentioned in the laws of approximately one-third of the states; the Model Penal Code refers to cases in which a substance given to a woman without her consent significantly impairs "her power to appraise or control her conduct." The use of stimulants actually aggravates the crime of rape in some jurisdictions because it shows premeditation by the perpetrator. A state of unconsciousness is usually required, but a lesser degree of impairment (as with DATE RAPE drugs) is sufficient in a number of jurisdictions. Romantic seduction—as opposed to rape—may rely on alcohol or other inhibition reducers such as marijuana, so the question of how much is too much and who is to blame for the seduced party's state of mind is not always clear.

Statutory Rape. Although few states use the exact term *statutory rape*, these laws penalize sexual intercourse with a partner who is less than an age limit set by statute. The most frequent age is sixteen years, but in other states it ranges between twelve (Alabama), thirteen (Louisiana, New Jersey, New Mexico, Ohio, Pennsylvania, and Tennessee) and eighteen (California, Idaho, and Wisconsin) years. In addition to setting a minimum age below which a minor cannot consent to sexual intercourse under any circumstances, statutory rape laws may give an age at which an individual can legally consent (typically between sixteen and eighteen years), indicate an acceptable age difference between a defendant and a victim above the minimum age, and specify a minimum age for prosecution of a defendant.

In most states, illegal sexual relations with a child, especially between an adult male and an underage girl, are treated as a crime that, unlike rape, cannot be defended against by proving that the victim consented to the sex act. Even a mistake by the perpetrator as to the age of the victim may not be a defense. In addition to making the adult responsible for knowing the other person's correct age, this type of strict liability protects the victim and generally eliminates the requirement that a victim testify against a defendant. Some states, however, allow a defense based on a mistake as to the victim's age; others allow it for older but not younger victims. Colorado, for example, permits such a defense for minors of more than fifteen years of age.

Most statutory rape laws are gender neutral. However, in *Michael M. v. Superior Court of Sonoma County* (1981), the Supreme Court reviewed a California law under which a seventeen-year-old-male could be guilty of statutory rape but a fourteen-year-old female could not. Such a distinction in age was not unconstitutional, said the Court, because the state has a legitimate interest in protecting against unwanted PREGNANCY in underage females.

Marital Rape. Until 1975, when South Dakota abolished the spousal exception for rape, a married woman could not prove that she was raped by her husband because of the long-held notion that the consent given at the time of marriage was consent, without exception, to sexual relations with one's husband.

Today every state and the District of Columbia has changed its laws to also make spousal rape a crime. No state any longer grants a husband an exemption from a charge of marital rape solely on the basis of a legal marriage to the victim, but some states still consider it with other extenuating factors except where the couple are separated; other states exempt the husband only from prosecution for lower degrees of rape involving nonviolent acts. The New York court of appeals, in *People v. Mario* (1984), found a statutory distinction permitting rape in marriage to be obsolete and declared it unconstitutional on the grounds that "there is no rational basis for distinguishing between marital rape and nonmarital rape."

Various rationales have been asserted to defend the marital exemption for rape, such as protection of marital privacy from government intrusion and potential reconciliation between the spouses. But these justifications are overshadowed by rape's violent nature and the fact that once such a charge has been filed by one spouse against the other, reconciliation does not appear to be a viable option. As for the argument that rape within marriage is difficult to prove, the courts have found that it is probably no more difficult to prove than is rape outside marriage. Some allege that if only crimes that could not be falsely charged were on the books, only murder would be a crime.

Civil Suits. Under some state laws, a rape victim may bring a civil action against the perpetrator for damages, including for pain and suffering, mental anguish, humiliation, and loss of social standing. Punitive damages may also be awarded. The husband of a married victim may even have a separate and derivative cause of action.

Contacts

Rape Victim Advocates, 228 South Wabash Avenue, Suite 240, Chicago, IL 60604 (888-293-2080). www.rape victimadvocates.org.

National Sexual Assault Hotline (800-656-HOPE).

See also CHILD ABUSE; DOMESTIC VIOLENCE.

State Statutory Rape Age Limits[1]

State	Age of Consent	Minimum Age of Victim	Age Difference between Victim and Defendant[2]	Minimum Age of Defendant to Be Prosecuted
Alabama	16	12	2 years	16
Alaska	16	–	3 years	–
Arizona	18	15	2 years[3]	–
Arkansas	16	–	3 years if victim is < 14	20[4]
California	18	18	–	–
Colorado	17	–	4 years if victim is < 15; 10 years if < 17	–
Connecticut	16	–	2 years	–
Delaware	18	16	–	–
Florida	18	16	–	24[4]
Georgia	16	16	–	–
Hawaii	16	14	5 years	–
Idaho	18	18	–	–
Illinois	17	17	–	–
Indiana	16	14	–	18[4]
Iowa	16	14	4 years	–
Kansas	16	14	–	–
Kentucky	16	16	–	–
Louisiana	17	13	3 years if victim is < 15; 2 years if < 17	–
Maine	16	14	5 years	–
Maryland	16	–	4 years	–
Massachusetts	16	16	–	–
Michigan	16	16	–	–
Minnesota	16	–	3 years if victim is < 13; 2 years if < 16	–
Mississippi	16	–	2 years if victim is < 14; 3 years if < 16	–
Missouri	17	14	–	21[4]
Montana	16	16	–	–
Nebraska	16	16	–	19
Nevada	16	16	–	18
New Hampshire	16	16	–	–
New Jersey	16	13	4 years	–
New Mexico	16	13	4 years	18[4]
New York	17	17	–	–
North Carolina	16	–	4 years	12
North Dakota	18	15	–	18[4]
Ohio	16	13	–	18[4]

State	Age of Consent	Minimum Age of Victim	Age Difference between Victim and Defendant[2]	Minimum Age of Defendant to Be Prosecuted
Oklahoma	16	14	–	18[4]
Oregon	18	15	3 years	–
Pennsylvania	16	13	4 years	–
Rhode Island	16	14	–	18[4]
South Carolina	16	14	[5]	–
South Dakota	16	16	3 years	–
Tennessee	18	13	4 years	–
Texas	17	14	3 years	–
Utah	18	16	10 years	–
Vermont	16	16	–	16
Virginia	18	15	–	18[4]
Washington	16	–	2 years if victim is < 12; 3 years if < 14; and 4 years if < 16	–
West Virginia	16	–	4 years if victim is < 11	16 or 14[4]
Wisconsin	18	18	–	–
Wyoming	16	–	4 years	–

1. A number of exceptions and special cases are included under various state laws. This chart reflects basic age limits only.

2. If a victim is above the minimum age. This age differential is the maximum age difference between a victim and a defendant to permit evidence that the victim gave consent.

3. The defendant must be in high school and under 19 years of age.

4. The minimum age applies only if a victim is above a specified age.

5. Intercourse is illegal if the victim is 14–16 years of age and the defendant is older.

Source: The Lewin Group, report to the U.S. Department of Health and Human Services, 2004

RAPE SHIELD LAWS

During the sensational RAPE trial of the professional basketball star Kobe Bryant, stemming from an alleged incident in a Colorado hotel in 2003, attorneys for the defendant alleged that the nineteen-year-old victim had had sex with two other men the day before the incident in question and again fifteen hours after saying that she had been raped. They also argued in the case (*People v. Kobe Bryant*) that Colorado's rape shield law, which generally precludes the introduction of a rape victim's sexual history, should not be applied in this case because it hampered the defendant's main line of defense—that the sex act was consensual—and because the rape shield law denied the defendant his constitutional right to confront his accuser.

Despite attempts by the defense to have portions of the victim's "intensely personal, highly sensitive, and potentially embarrassing" medical history admitted during the trial, the presiding judge ruled that the state's rape shield law would be upheld and thus her prior sexual history would be excluded. The felony SEXUAL ASSAULT charge against the basketball player was dismissed in September 2004 because of the accuser's decision not to testify and to file a civil suit for damages instead. But advocates for rape victims, unhappy with the young woman's treatment, warned that the outcome could have a chilling effect on the reporting of rape by other victims.

Before the 1970s, evidence of a rape victim's sexual history was usually admissible in a trial. The rationale was that if the victim had often consented to having sex in the past, it was more likely that she had consented in the instant case. (CONSENT by the victim is often a defense to a charge of rape.) Sexual history was thought to be important in assessing a victim's credibility as a witness who had brought the charge of rape. Permitting the introduction of such evidence tended to discourage rape victims from coming forward for fear of being embarrassed or humiliated in court. As one British jurist noted long ago, however, even a prostitute can be a victim of rape.

Protection of Victims' Rights

A backlash against the U.S. Supreme Court's extension of rights in the 1960s to persons accused of crimes—such as requiring that suspects taken into custody be advised of constitutional rights established in *Miranda v. Arizona* (1966)—began a steady promotion of VICTIMS' RIGHTS laws in the states. Today nearly all states have statutory or constitutional provisions addressing the rights of crime victims.

In 1974 Michigan adopted the first law to shield rape victims from evidence of their sexual history. By the end of the 1980s, nearly all states and the District of Columbia had enacted some form of the law; only Arizona has no rape shield law. In any prosecution for rape, attempted rape, or conspiracy to commit rape, all state rape shield laws preclude the admission into evidence of an alleged rape victim's reputation or prior sexual conduct. Such laws, however, may not be applicable in pretrial hearings or conferences or in civil lawsuits, as opposed to criminal prosecutions.

State rape shield laws fall into roughly four categories based on the extent and type of exceptions to the law permitted:

(1) About half of the state laws contain legislated exceptions, such as admission of evidence of prior sexual relations between the accuser and the defendant; alternative sources of semen, PREGNANCY, or injury; a pattern of prior sexual conduct by the complainant; bias or motive to fabricate the accusation; a reasonable mistaken belief by the defendant as to the victim's consent; and prior false accusations of sexual assaults by the accuser.

(2) The rape shield laws of eleven states and the District of Columbia are modeled on federal law. In 1978 CONGRESS enacted rule 412 of the Federal Rules of Evidence, which provides that evidence offered to prove that a victim engaged in other sexual behavior or had any sexual predisposition is generally inadmissible in any civil or criminal proceeding involving alleged sexual misconduct. The state laws following this rule all provide that an exception may be made if a judge determines that the federal or state constitution requires it.

(3) Nine states have no legislated exceptions, but they give judges the discretion to grant them.

(4) Four states have split on when an exception can be granted: California and Delaware allow evidence to attack the credibility of the victim or complainant but not to prove her consent to sexual relations with the defendant. In Nevada and Washington, the exception is just the reverse.

Courts generally require that a rape victim be given notice if her sexual history will be the subject of inquiry so that she may object or at least set limits on the extent of the inquiry. However, a defendant may be able to persuade a judge before the trial that an exception to the rape shield law is applicable.

The U.S. Supreme Court, in *Michigan v. Lucas* (1991), addressed an exception to the Michigan rape shield law that permitted a defendant to introduce evidence of his own past sexual conduct with the victim if he gave timely written notification of his intent to do so. Michigan's court of appeals had determined that precluding the defendant's evidence was a violation of the Sixth Amendment (1791) to the U.S. Constitution, which protects an accused's right to confront his accuser and to compel witnesses on his behalf. Timely notice of the defendant's intent to offer such evidence was not given, however. The Supreme Court concluded that, in view of the defendant's failure to give timely notice as required by the rape shield law, the Sixth Amendment was not so rigid as to preclude a denial of the right to introduce evidence of his prior sexual conduct with the victim.

Challenges to Rape Shield Laws

Rape shield laws have been challenged on the grounds that they violate a defendant's constitutional right to due process and the right to confront one's accuser. The Supreme Court, in *Olden v. Kentucky* (1988), confirmed that the right of confrontation protected by the Sixth Amendment includes the reasonable right of cross-examination to impeach a complaining witness. Other arguments against these laws include the facts that since the 1970s, when the laws were being adopted, PREMARITAL SEX has become more common, sexual behavior is more openly discussed, and women are less intimidated in asserting their legal rights. Some argue that with all of the legal exceptions available and the lack of uniformity among state laws, rape shield laws are not just or effective in any case.

Courts have generally balanced the two competing interests here: (1) The state's interest in protecting a sexual assault or rape victim from harassment and potential humiliation at trial as well as the highly prejudicial effect that evidence of prior sexual behavior may have on a jury. (2) A defendant's right to a fair trial. They have concluded that the protection provided by a rape shield law outweighs the possible harm to the accused's defense. A trial court has discretion to allow evidence of the witness's prior sexual history, and exclusion of testimony about a victim's alleged promiscuity does not necessarily deny the defendant an effective cross-examination to impeach the witness.

Crimes relating to sexual behavior or that take place in a sexual context are often difficult for the law to deal with consistently. In addition, general rules of evidence established for other types of crime often seem to be counterproductive when the prohibited conduct relates to sexual behavior. The reason for rape shield laws—to encourage victims of rape to come forward and report crimes—is sound. It is only the application of such laws in a legal system that places a high value on protecting the rights of the accused that may make them of questionable value in arriving at the truth during a trial.

See also DATE RAPE.

RELIGION

Religious bodies in the United States have attempted to influence sexual behavior since the arrival of the Puritans in the seventeenth century. From this Christian sect came the word *puritanical* (something marked by stern morality). Secular laws relating to sexual behavior are still being influenced by religious ideas. For example, since the U.S. Supreme Court's decision in *Roe v. Wade* (1973), which recognized women's constitutional right to abortion, Christian conservatives have successfully lobbied CONGRESS and many states for laws limiting the decision's application. Strong support has also come from religious communities for state laws and constitutional amendments denying homosexuals the right to marry, and laws regarding WOMEN'S RIGHTS, REPRODUCTIVE RIGHTS, and CHILDREN have also been influenced by religious principles.

Yet, embodied in the establishment clause of the FIRST AMENDMENT (1791) to the U.S. Constitution, which is applicable to the states under the Fourteenth Amendment (1868), is the principle of separation of church and state: "Congress shall make no law respecting an establishment of religion, or prohibiting the free exercise thereof." This guarantee in the Bill of Rights, encompassing the first ten amendments to the Constitution, has been the subject of continual debate as to what it covers, from a religious group's belief in the right to have multiple spouses or to the constitutionality of the George W. Bush administration's faith-based funding initiatives and the promotion of religious tenets in publicly funded sex education programs.

Thomas Jefferson envisioned "a wall of separation" between church and state, but many Americans have come to view the nation as being "under God," a phrase that was added to the Pledge of Allegiance by an act of Congress in 1954, thereby indicating that such a wall is not always considered desirable. In Utah 73 percent of the population is Mormon, or members of the Church of Jesus Christ of Latter-day Saints, a fact that cannot help but influence politics and laws in that state. A basic dichotomy for all religious people in the United States lies in their desire for protection of their religious beliefs under the Constitution and other laws and, at the same time, their desire to use the power of the state to extend their beliefs to others, especially in matters relating to sexual behavior.

The First Amendment to the contrary, church and state have long been entwined in American society. Similar legal privilege has been given to the priest-penitent relationship as to the doctor-patient, husband-wife, and lawyer-client relationship. The MARRIAGE ceremony, in which two people are joined to legalize their sexual relations and any CHILDREN brought into the family, has traditionally been conducted by religious leaders, such as ministers, priests, and rabbis, even though couples can legally be married by any duly authorized civil authority. The liberalization of DIVORCE laws in the last half century has conflicted with various religious precepts, especially those of the Roman Catholic Church; although a couple married in the Church can legally obtain a divorce under the laws of their state, the divorce may not be recognized by the Church, and an ANNULMENT may have to be obtained from the Church before the rights and privileges of membership are restored.

A summary follows of some major areas in which religion and sexual behavior intersect with the law.

Sex Education

High rates of teen PREGNANCY, especially in the South and the West, led states and the federal government to pursue measures to reduce the incidence of unplanned births. The U.S. DEPARTMENT OF HEALTH AND HUMAN SERVICES administers SEX EDUCATION programs in schools that attempt to provide students with information directed at avoiding pregnancy before they can handle such responsibility and helping prevent the spread of SEXUALLY TRANSMITTED DISEASES, including AIDS-HIV.

Clashes between church and state have arisen over such government-funded programs. One federally sponsored, faith-based effort by an organization named Silver Ring Thing included quotes from the New Testament and exacted pledges of virginity and sexual ABSTINENCE until marriage. These programs avoid discussions of contraception and abortion. In August 2005 HHS suspended funding for Silver Ring Thing activities, and in the same year the AMERICAN CIVIL LIBERTIES UNION brought suit to stop funding for the religiously motivated aspects of the department's sex education program.

Contraception

The constitutional right of couples to use contraception has been upheld by the U.S. Supreme Court in two landmark cases, GRISWOLD V. CONNECTICUT (1965) and *Eisenstadt v. Baird* (1972). The law seems well settled in this area of sexual behavior. No one is forced to used contraceptives if their use contravenes a person's conscience or religious beliefs.

Yet the Catholic Church believes that nearly all forms of contraception are a sin and must be avoided. The only exceptions are abstinence and the "rhythm" method, whereby intercourse is restricted to periods during a woman's menstrual cycle when she is less likely to conceive. Although some Catholics ignore these teachings, the Church's instruction does lead devout believers to eschew contraceptives; its ban on the use of condoms as a part of its campaign against artificial birth control also makes it difficult to prevent the spread of sexually transmitted diseases. Most Protestant denominations do not consider birth control a sin, nor does Islam; it is also not forbidden in the Jewish faith, although the most conservative members of Judaism allow it only if it will prevent a pregnancy that may harm a woman.

Some religious groups seek to restrict birth control and FAMILY PLANNING through government regulation. They oppose the use of emergency contraceptives such as the "morning-after pill" (Plan B), which can stop conception after intercourse, and the "abortion pill" (RU-484 or Mifiprex), which interdicts the development of

THE PILL
IS A NO-NO

ITEM 81 © 1968 PANDORA PRODUCTIONS BOX 807 WAYZATA MN 55391

The Roman Catholic Church opposes abortion as well as the use of contraceptive pills and devices—a teaching documented in this 1968 poster featuring Pope Paul VI. Most other religions do not discourage contraception, which was legalized by the U.S. Supreme Court in 1965.

the embryo weeks after intercourse. Because the latter drug, approved by the Food and Drug Administration at the end of the administration of President Bill Clinton, acts on a fertilized embryo after conception, it is the subject of attack by those who, for religious or moral reasons, believe that human life begins at conception.

Abortion
The official position of the Catholic Church regarding having or performing an ABORTION is that, like artificial contraception, it is a sin. Again, this religious concern

is based on a belief in the sanctity of a human life from the time of conception. Both Catholics and some Protestant worshipers share this belief. Consequently pressure has been brought to bear on political leaders to have this view reflected in federal and state laws. In the 2004 elections, many religious leaders urged their congregants to vote against pro-choice candidates.

Members of conservative Protestant sects and Catholics have actively influenced Congress and state legislatures to pass laws restricting a woman's right to an abortion as declared by the Supreme Court in *Roe v. Wade*, a decision they hope to see overturned. Such restrictions in many cases have been upheld by the Court. For example, in PLANNED PARENTHOOD OF SOUTHEASTERN PENNSYLVANIA V. CASEY (1992), the Court refused to reject a state law requiring a twenty-four-hour waiting period and the CONSENT of a minor's parent before obtaining an abortion. The Court did turn aside a proposed restriction that married women notify their husbands, because it would treat them like children—dependent on their husbands for actions involving their own bodies.

A related national debate about the RIGHTS OF THE UNBORN is taking place over the morality of STEM-CELL RESEARCH AND CLONING, which may use excess human embryos created as a result of ASSISTED REPRODUCTIVE TECHNOLOGY. Arguments against the conduct of this research, underpinned by religious beliefs, assert that using embryonic stem cells results in the destruction of potentially viable human life. Opponents stressing a "culture of life" succeeded in 2001 in having President George W. Bush suspend future federal stem-cell research using new lines of cells. More than half of opponents of stem-cell research cite religious reasons for their beliefs.

Sexual Abuse
Recent disclosures have shown that some religious leaders have been personally involved in SEX OFFENSES. Since 1950 about five thousand Roman Catholic priests and deacons have been accused of sexually abusing more than twelve thousand children in the United States. Most of the abuse took place from the

mid-1960s to the mid-1980s, with cases reportedly declining since the early 1990s. Some priests have been brought to trial, and some have been found guilty. In other cases, Church authorities have agreed to monetary settlements to avoid public trials.

In addition to the crime of CHILD ABUSE itself, the Church hierarchy has been accused of covering up these offenses and often simply transferring pedophile priests to new locations instead of reporting the crimes and addressing the plight of the victims. Proposals made in 2006 to relax statutes of limitations for filing civil abuse suits in states such as Colorado and Maryland were met with lobbying efforts by the Church to defeat them. In 2003 California and Massachusetts enacted one-year reprieves in which victims could file suits despite the expiration of legal time limits.

The aftermath of these scandals has been costly, according to a 2006 annual report by the Church that put the amount spent on settlements so far at approximately $1.5 billion. Some eighty properties of the Catholic diocese of Tucson, Arizona, alone had to be sold to pay off $3.2 million in sex abuse claims. The Tucson diocese as well as those in Spokane, Washington, and Portland, Oregon, all declared bankruptcy. In Colorado a woman was awarded $1.2 million for having been molested by an Episcopal minister, although in *Moses v. Diocese of Colorado* (1993) the amount was reduced to $700,000. That a priest or another religious person in a position of authority would sexually molest children and that church authorities would act to cover up such crimes has to some extent reduced the public's historical trust of religious leaders as well as of institutions that are accorded privileges under the law with regard to taxes and confidentiality in priest-penitent communications.

Homosexuality

Some religions have recently taken official positions against HOMOSEXUALITY. Some leaders and members have condemned homosexuals' way of life, homosexuals' leadership roles in various churches, and the right of homosexuals to marry in the same way as heterosexuals or to attain an alternative form of officially recognized

relationship, such as a civil union or a domestic partnership. Some reasons for opposition to homosexual rights include the biblical proscription against SODOMY, possible dilution of the family structure as purportedly ordained by God, and a fear that approval of the "homosexual lifestyle" will encourage young people to adopt it or to be corrupted by it.

In 2003 the Offices of the Congregation for Doctrine of the Faith, then headed by Joseph Cardinal Ratzinger (now Pope Benedict XVI), issued a document entitled Considerations Regarding Proposals to Give Legal Recognition to Unions Between Homosexual Persons. "There are absolutely no grounds for considering homosexual unions to be in any way similar or even remotely analogous to God's plan for marriage and family," it states. Many religiously inspired groups have lobbied Congress and state legislatures in opposition to SAME-SEX MARRIAGE. In addition to putting grassroots political pressure on legislators to pass "defense of marriage" laws (legal prohibitions against the right of homosexual couples to marry and enjoy the many benefits that marriage provides under federal and state law), conservative Protestants and many Catholics have mounted successful campaigns in more than twenty states—including Alaska, Georgia, Kansas, and Ohio—to limit marriage by state constitutional amendment to "one man and one woman." Today only Massachusetts allows homosexual couples to marry, and only Vermont and Connecticut permit civil unions for them.

The matter of homosexual congregants and leaders has generally been handled within religious organizations themselves, with denominations from Episcopals to Conservative Jews wrestling with issues such as the ordination of bishops and rabbis. As the AIDS epidemic became a matter of public concern in the 1980s, conservative Christian leaders, including the Reverend Jerry Falwell, blamed homosexuals for bringing God's wrath in the form of the disease. To what extent these positions by religious leaders have influenced voters, lawmakers, government officials, and judges in dealing with homosexual issues can only be a matter of speculation.

Polygamy

All states have laws against marriage to more than one husband or wife at the same time; BIGAMY is the secular form of this offense. The religious form of multiple marriage, called POLYGAMY, was once a tenet of the Mormon Church in the United States. Polygamy was institutionalized in 1852, during the era when the West was being settled, but the Mormons were forced to renounce the practice so that Utah could become a state. Congress banned polygamy in 1862, although it was not until 1892 that Utah itself prohibited the practice, allowing it to enter the Union in 1896. Several other western states, including New Mexico and Oklahoma, have state constitutional provisions prohibiting polygamy. In two landmark cases, *Reynolds v. United States* (1879) and *Davis v. Beason* (1890), the U.S. Supreme Court upheld the constitutionality of federal laws banning polygamy and measures to enforce them in certain western territories before they became states.

Yet from time to time, sizable numbers of religious adherents or leaders of obscure sects are reported to be still engaging in polygamy. In addition, the Muslim Koran allows a man to have up to four wives—although this practice is illegal in the United States.

Censorship

There has always been a thin line between freedom of expression as guaranteed in the First Amendment and religious intolerance of perceived blasphemy. Evidence of this can be found in the self-censorship imposed in 2006 on MEDIA representations of the prophet Mohammad after Danish cartoons depicting him caused retaliatory riots by Muslims in several countries. But American religious adherents have often become actively involved in enforcing CENSORSHIP with respect to sexual matters, either by forcing self-censorship on various industries or influencing laws.

The Comstock Act (1873), for example, criminalized the mailing of OBSCENITY, which was then defined to include information on contraception. Christian moral activists sought to censor such material, because they thought that it led to promiscuity and PROSTITUTION. During the early days of the movie industry at the turn of the twentieth century, an organization of American Catholics called the National Legion of Decency threatened boycotts to pressure movie moguls into adopting a strict code of what could be shown in motion pictures. Protestant-led groups including the International Reform Bureau and the Women's Christian Temperance Union promoted even-stricter legislation to censor the film industry. To thwart these efforts, movie producers adopted a self-censorship code and brought in an elder of the Presbyterian Church to administer it. Known as the Hays Code (1930), it prohibited sexual innuendo, references to ADULTERY, vulgarity, obscenity, and provocative dress, among other indiscretions.

To a large extent, religions are guardians of culture. To paraphrase ALFRED KINSEY, the pioneering researcher on sexual behavior, whereas the law generally concerns itself with protecting persons and property, in regard to sexual behavior the law tends to be more concerned with protecting traditions. However, in a country that prides itself on religious freedom, it is an often difficult task for lawmakers and judges to treat those of different religious beliefs as equally as possible. In a democracy, a religious tenet can be translated into law by a majority of legislators or a majority of voters, but at that point such a law may become an imposition on minority rights. It is thus a continuing challenge for modern democracies to abide by majority rule while protecting minorities from discriminatory laws approved by a majority of the moment.

See also DEFENSE OF MARRIAGE ACT; FEDERAL MARRIAGE AMENDMENT.

REPRODUCTIVE RIGHTS

No fundamental right related to reproduction is expressly guaranteed in the language of the U.S. Constitution, but the term *reproductive rights* has been adopted by pro-choice proponents in the ongoing war over issues related to SEX EDUCATION, FAMILY PLANNING, CONTRACEPTION, and ABORTION. Those supporting freedom of choice when it comes to reproduction believe that women, as the bearers and primary caregivers of CHILDREN, should have a largely unfettered right to make decisions about their role in the reproductive process. Others, identified as pro-life, believe that society, through the law, should play a greater part in reproduction. To a lesser extent, both factions acknowledge men's role in making such decisions.

Under the Comstock Act (1873), named for the antivice crusader ANTHONY COMSTOCK, information about contraception was banned from the U.S. mail as OBSCENITY. From that time until after World War II, WOMEN'S RIGHTS under the U.S. Constitution were declared by the U.S. Supreme Court to be limited to the right to vote guaranteed by the Nineteenth Amendment (1920). It was not until the SEXUAL REVOLUTION of the 1960s and 1970s, spurred in part by the introduction of the birth control pill, that women began a systematic campaign to gain control of their own reproductive activities. Sex for pleasure, rather than just for procreation, had always been an option, but the sexual revolution, the Pill, and the relaxed morality of the second half of the twentieth century ushered in the era of women's reproductive rights.

Sex Education

Reproductive rights include the right of access to information about the process of reproduction, given that the first step toward becoming a responsible adult capable of procreating depends on unbiased and accurate information. But a battle currently rages at both the federal and state levels among citizens, lawmakers, and judges over what may and may not be proper to teach students in public schools about sexual behavior, contraceptives, PREGNANCY, and AIDS-HIV and other SEXUALLY TRANSMITTED DISEASES.

At the federal level, the U.S. DEPARTMENT OF HEALTH AND HUMAN SERVICES has initiated programs and provided funding as part of the faith-based initiative instituted by President George W. Bush shortly after taking office in 2001. This effort emphasizes ABSTINENCE until MARRIAGE as the best way to avoid disease and PREGNANCY. It also limits information about the use of condoms and abortion to prevent unwanted pregnancy.

Although most states authorize sex education programs in schools, they are locally administered and often bring controversy. Some states legally promote abstinence or prohibit teaching about abortion. Others mandate lessons on AIDS to prevent the spread of disease.

Family Planning

Sex education is an important element in family planning, the process by which individuals and couples can determine whether to have children, how to have them—for example, naturally, by ASSISTED REPRODUCTIVE TECHNOLOGY, or by adoption—how many children to have, and when to have them. As the science of reproductive technology progresses, additional options such as determining the sex of the child, eye and hair color, and even height and weight may become available, however morally repugnant to some people.

The law regarding family planning has evolved during the twentieth century, beginning with prohibitions against sex education, contraception, and contraceptive information. To avoid prosecution for violating postal laws prohibiting the mailing of obscenity, MARGARET SANGER, founder of the PLANNED PARENTHOOD FEDERATION OF AMERICA, had to flee the United States after she published information about contraception and family planning. Although family planning is no longer illegal, recent policy of the federal government, the MILITARY, and some states is to deny public funding for some family planning options, especially abortions.

Contraception

In *GRISWOLD V. CONNECTICUT* (1965), the Supreme Court made the use of contraception by married couples a right of PRIVACY protected by the Constitution. Then, in *Eisenstadt v. Baird* (1972), the Court extended this right to unmarried couples. Contraception is not generally subject to regulation by the government today. There are exceptions, however.

Approval by the Food and Drug Administration is required for the sale of drugs in the United States. The agency has withheld approval of over-the-counter sales of an emergency contraceptive called the "morning-after pill," which is available with a doctor's prescription. Plan B and a similar drug, Preven, prevent fertilization by blocking hormones and can be effective if taken after intercourse. Opponents of this type of contraceptive in particular contend that allowing it to be easily available to young, unmarried women will encourage promiscuity and increase the spread of sexual diseases.

Some persons oppose contraceptives of all types at all times, even for use by married couples. The Roman Catholic Church, for one, remains officially opposed to contraception by artificial means. Some pharmacists, including members of Pharmacists for Life International, refuse to fill contraceptive prescriptions. According to the reasoning of these pro-life supporters, a potential human comes into existence at conception—the moment a male sperm cell fertilizes a female egg cell—thereby triggering a government obligation to protect that nascent being.

Abortion

In its decision in *Roe v. Wade* (1973), the Supreme Court held that state laws banning and criminalizing abortion were an unconstitutional invasion of the right of a woman, in consultation with her physician, to control her own reproductive processes. The decision based a state's right to protect an unborn fetus on the three trimesters of pregnancy. It gave an expectant mother the most control to decide whether or not to have an abortion during the first three months, when the fetus is most dependent on her for survival; it gave the state the most control to limit abortion during the last three months, when a child is more likely to be able to live outside the womb. The Court has also permitted state restrictions on the basic right to abortion. In PLANNED PARENTHOOD OF SOUTHEASTERN PENNSYLVANIA v. CASEY (1992), the Court allowed a state-mandated twenty-four-hour waiting period for an abortion and parental notification for a minor seeking an abortion.

An alternative to surgical abortion became available in the United States in late 2000. RU-486, which may be taken up to forty-nine days after the beginning of a woman's last menstrual cycle to block a pregnancy from continuing, is known as the "abortion pill." It

gained FDA approval in late 2000. Within the next year, reports indicated that about one-third of women eligible to use RU-486 chose it over the more traditional surgical option.

In response to physically intimidating protests by abortion opponents, some states have enacted laws to punish attacks by antiabortionists. California defines such a crime as one "committed partly or wholly because the victim is a reproductive health services client, provider, or assistant, or a crime that is partly or wholly intended to intimidate the victim ... from becoming or remaining a reproductive health services client, provider, or assistant." Massachusetts has a similar law against protesting and distributing information in the vicinity of reproductive health-care facilities. In *Opinion of the Justices to the Senate* (2000), the Massachusetts supreme court declared that legislation creating a buffer zone around a health care facility does not violate the constitutional rights of freedom of speech or assembly. However, the U.S. Supreme Court, by an 8–0 decision in *Scheidler v. National Organization for Women* and *Operation Rescue v. National Organization for Women* (both 2006), affirmed that federal law, including the Racketeer Influenced and Corrupt Organizations Act (1970), could not be used to enjoin protesters from blockading abortion facilities, although injunctions obtained under these laws had reduced protestor violence at such sites.

Right to Procreate

The right to procreate is a peculiarly male right. It was first addressed by the Supreme Court in *Skinner v. Oklahoma* (1942), a case in which a state law that permitted forced STERILIZATION was struck down and procreation was declared a fundamental right. Several state courts have recently dealt with this right in the context of CHILD SUPPORT laws and "deadbeat dads." In 2005 the combined child support arrearage in the United States was more than $100 billion. The federal government and the states have taken steps to help single mothers collect child support payments awarded by a court, usually after the legal separation or DIVORCE of the child's parents.

A Wisconsin court took the unusual step of restricting a delinquent father's right to procreate as a condition of his probation. On appeal, in *State v. Oakley* (2001), the state's supreme court narrowly upheld the restriction, noting the crisis in the collection of child support; it also observed that, although the right to procreate is a fundamental right, probation is always accompanied by certain restrictions of rights. The court further noted the defendant's history of fathering children and not supporting them. A U.S. Supreme Court review of *Oakley* was denied in 2002.

Two years later, an Ohio court, relying on slightly different facts, came to a different conclusion. In *State v. Talty* (2004), the court declared that requiring the defendant to make "all reasonable efforts to avoid conceiving another child" during his five-year probationary period was overbroad; unlike the *Oakley* case, no provision had been made to lift the restriction if the probationer became current with his child support payments.

The right to procreate is allied with the right to marry, which was also declared a fundamental right by the Supreme Court in *Loving v. Virginia* (1967) and *Turner v. Safley* (1987). The Court in these two cases, respectively, struck down a state MISCEGENATION law that had made it a crime for a black person and a white person to marry and upheld the right of PRISONERS to marry, even if they may not be able to consummate the marriage during their period of incarceration.

Historically the cultural, social, political, religious, and legal framework in which women live has been almost entirely devised by males. Although women bear most of the responsibility for human procreation, for most of history they have had little input into the legal and political decision-making process. With the sexual revolution and the attainment of nearly EQUAL RIGHTS under the law, women have increasingly fought to retain control over their reproductive lives.

Contact: Center for Reproductive Rights, 120 Wall Street, New York, NY 10005 (917-637-3600). www.reproductiverights.org.

See also CALDERONE, MARY S.; ETHICS; SEXUALITY INFORMATION AND EDUCATION COUNCIL OF THE UNITED STATES.

REVERSE DISCRIMINATION

See DISCRIMINATION.

ROE v. WADE

See ABORTION; REPRODUCTIVE RIGHTS.

ROTH v. UNITED STATES

For advertising and selling a magazine containing erotic literature and pictures of people in the nude, Samuel Roth (1893–1974) was convicted of the crime of sending pornographic or obscene material through the mail. When the U.S. Supreme Court ruled 6–3 against his appeal in *Roth v. United States* (1957), its opinion written by Associate Justice William J. Brennan Jr. held that OBSCENITY was not protected by the FIRST AMENDMENT (1791) to the U.S. Constitution; therefore, according to the ruling, federal and state laws banning or otherwise regulating obscenity were not necessarily unconstitutional. Before *Roth* the Court had dealt with obscenity in an ad hoc manner and had avoided a direct confrontation with freedom of expression.

In *Ex parte Jackson* (1878), the Supreme Court agreed that CONGRESS could exclude objectionable materials from delivery through the U.S. mail. An act of Congress in 1873—promoted by the self-proclaimed defender of decency ANTHONY COMSTOCK—had made it a misdemeanor to mail any "obscene, lewd, or lascivious, or filthy book, pamphlet, picture, paper, letter, writing, print, or other publication of an indecent character." The Court found that "the object of Congress has not been to interfere with the freedom of the press, or with any other rights of the people; but to refuse its facilities for the distribution of matter deemed injurious to the public morals." At this time it was considered unquestionable that obscenity, regardless of the context, was outside the scope of constitutional protection.

In the first half of the twentieth century, the Court upheld criminal obscenity laws in several cases, including

Mug shots were taken of Samuel Roth when he was jailed in 1930 for publishing obscene material, beginning with long extracts from James Joyce's *Ulysses* (1914). Convicted several decades later of sending obscene materials through the U.S. mail, he served five more years in jail after the U.S. Supreme Court's precedent-setting 1957 case, *Roth v. United States.* The decision confirmed that obscenity was outside the protection of the First Amendment.

one involving the 1925 book *An American Tragedy,* written by the well-known American author Theodore Dreiser (1871–1945) (on which the 1961 movie *Splendor in the Grass* was based). After World War II, however, the Court began more closely examining the basis for the assumption that antiobscenity laws were constitutional. For example, in *Winter v. New York* (1948), the justices said: "We do not [agree] that the constitutional protection for a free press applies only to the exposition of ideas. The line between the informing and the entertaining is too elusive for the protection of that basic right." In *Stanley v. Georgia* (1969), the Court would go so far as to opine that the right

to impart and receive "information and ideas, regardless of their social worth . . . is fundamental to our free society."

In *Joseph Burstyn, Inc. v. Wilson* (1952), the Supreme Court reversed an earlier opinion to hold that motion pictures were protected by the First Amendment. In *Butler v. Michigan* (1957) it laid the groundwork for tackling head-on the issue of obscenity vis-à-vis the First Amendment's guarantee of freedom of expression. In doing so it discarded the practice of determining obscenity by judging the effect of selected portions of the offending material on the most impressionable juvenile—a test imported from an 1868 decision in the

English case *Regina v. Hicklin.* As the Court put it: "We have before us legislation not reasonably restricted to the evil with which it is said to deal. The incidence of this enactment is to reduce the adult population of Michigan to reading only what is fit for children."

The basic constitutional question addressed by the Supreme Court in *Roth v. United States* was whether a federal law criminalizing the mailing of "obscene, lewd, lascivious, or filthy" material violated the First Amendment guarantees of freedom of speech and the press. A case considered at the same time, *Alberts v. California,* addressed whether a state obscenity law violated First Amendment provisions "as they may be incorporated in the liberty protected from state action by the Due Process Clause of the Fourteenth Amendment." (Initially the Court had held that the Bill of Rights applied only against the federal government and could not be used to strike down state laws or actions. But gradually, case by case, the Court began to incorporate the rights in the Bill of Rights and make them applicable to the states. The First Amendment guarantee of freedom of speech was made applicable to the states by the Supreme Court in 1927 and the guarantee of freedom of the press in 1931.)

In considering the appeal of Samuel Roth's conviction, the Supreme Court began by citing its earlier decisions, including *Ex parte Jackson,* in which it had "always been assumed that obscenity is not protected by the freedoms of speech and press." Federal and state obscenity laws thus had been deemed constitutionally permissible. Other forms of speech such as perjury or price fixing had similarly been found by the Court to be outside the protection of the First Amendment.

But the reason for finding that the First Amendment did not cover obscenity was that obscenity was thought to be "utterly without redeeming social importance." However, if the First Amendment protects all ideas, even hateful and distasteful ones, a test of whether certain material is obscene must guarantee that no other protected ideas are conveyed with it. Sex and obscenity are not synonymous. The test

for obscenity, the Court held in *Roth,* is "whether to the average person, applying contemporary community standards, the dominant theme of the material taken as a whole appeals to the prurient interest."

In the developing history of sex and the Constitution, the *Roth* case confirmed that obscenity was beyond the protection of the First Amendment but established that the definition of obscenity must be narrowly tailored to prevent the CENSORSHIP of information and ideas that the amendment is intended to protect. The test as enunciated in *Roth* obviously left many elements undefined. But from 1957 to 1967, the Supreme Court issued opinions on thirteen major obscenity cases delineating the boundary between obscenity and the First Amendment's protections of free expression, and in MILLER V. CALIFORNIA (1973) the Court fleshed out the standards for determining obscenity.

As the justices said in *Roth:* "The fundamental freedoms of speech and press have contributed greatly to the development and well-being of our free society and are indispensable to its continued growth. Ceaseless vigilance is the watchword to prevent their erosion by Congress or the State." The bar today for protection of obscene material—whether in books, photographs, magazines, movies, live performances, art, or other forms of expression—is as low as it has ever been. Pornographic material available to anyone on the INTERNET, unless restricted by technical means, is basically unlimited except for some extremes such as sadistic or violent sex or sex involving CHILDREN. When the Supreme Court struck down the COMMUNICATIONS DECENCY ACT (1996), viewing its provisions attempting to impose censorship on the Internet as unconstitutionally broad, the definition of obscene material that can be prohibited or punished by the government became even narrower. It is doubtful that any further narrowing will take place in the near future.

See also ADULT MATERIALS; *A BOOK NAMED "JOHN CLELAND'S MEMOIRS OF A WOMAN OF PLEASURE" V. ATTORNEY GENERAL OF THE COMMONWEALTH OF MASSACHUSETTS*; NUDITY; PORNOGRAPHY; PRURIENT INTEREST.

S

SAME-SEX MARRIAGE

The clash of principles involved in the issue of homosexual or same-sex marriage is testing the fabric from which the U.S. Constitution is woven. On one side are the U.S. Supreme Court's decisions in *Romer v. Evans* (1996) and *Lawrence v. Texas* (2003), which held that homosexuals are as entitled as heterosexuals to equal protection of the law, and decisions such as *Zablocki v. Redhail* (1978) and *Turner v. Safley* (1987), which accorded the right to marry a high national priority—at least for heterosexuals.

On the other side are cases such as *Baehr v. Lewis* (1993), in which the supreme court of Hawaii declared that "we do not believe that a right to same-sex marriages is so rooted in the traditions and collective conscience of our people that failure to recognize it would violate the fundamental principles of liberty and justice that lie at the base of all our civil and political institutions." Although an appeal was filed, the case was made moot when the Hawaiian constitution was amended in 1998 to limit MARRIAGE to "opposite-sex couples." The U.S. Supreme Court has yet to tackle the issue head on.

Those who would deny the right to same-sex marriage often do so on religious and moral grounds, but little evidence exists of any "normal" form of marriage except as defined by various human societies throughout history. Culturally and historically, there have been many variations on the concept of marriage—a recognized relationship between adults that establishes certain rights and responsibilities, particularly with respect to CHILDREN and property. For example, anthropologists have come across societies that condone the marriage of a woman and several men and marriages in which a husband may "visit" but not live with his wife. The Koran provides that a man "may marry other women who seem good to you: two, three, or four of them." The Old Testament says: "And David knew that the Lord had established him as king over Israel.... In Jerusalem David took more wives and became the father of more sons and daughters." Many other examples can be found of marriages joining other than one man and one woman as husband and wife.

Even some same-sex partnerships, although not recognized under the law, have been culturally accepted to some degree. In the nineteenth century, some American women lived together in long-term monogamous relationships referred to as a "Boston marriage," and some women passed for much of their adult lives as men with wives. Several other countries—among them Belgium, Canada, Spain, and the Netherlands—have extended to gays and lesbians the same rights of married heterosexual couples.

Federal Law

The federal government has no direct responsibility under the U.S. Constitution for regulating marriage, but in 1996 CONGRESS enacted the DEFENSE OF MARRIAGE

Same-sex unions are seen by many Americans as a threat to the traditional institution of marriage. Attempts by some homosexual couples to make lasting commitments to one another and to receive the same benefits as heterosexual married couples have instead resulted in statutes and constitutional amendments defining marriage in such a way as to ban same-sex marriage or other unions.

Act. The law basically restricts federal benefits and privileges conferred by the status of marriage to those joined in the legal union of one man and one woman. The law's authority is said to rest on the full faith and credit clause in Article IV of the Constitution, which grants Congress authority to "by general Laws prescribe the Manner in which Acts, Records, and Proceedings shall be proved, and the Effect thereof."

The Supreme Court's decision in LAWRENCE V. TEXAS (2003), affirming the right of homosexual SODOMY in the privacy of one's own home, could form the basis for challenges to the constitutionality of the Defense of Marriage Act. However, Congress's power with respect to federal benefits not guaranteed by the Constitution is difficult to challenge in the courts. It has, for example, been able to routinely deny federal funding for ABORTION, although the Supreme Court ruled in *Roe v. Wade* (1973) that the procedure is legal under certain conditions.

State Law

Only one state, Massachusetts, has legalized same-sex marriage, and then only after it was ordered by a court to do so. In *Goodridge v. Department of Public Health* (2003), the denial of a marriage license to same-sex couples was held unconstitutional under the state constitution's equal protection provision. The Massachusetts constitution (which predates the U.S. Constitution by nine years), declared the commonwealth's highest court, "protects matters of personal liberty against government incursion as zealously, and often more so, than does the Federal Constitution." It added that "barring an individual from the protections, benefits, and obligations of civil marriage solely because that person would marry a person of the same sex violates the Massachusetts Constitution." In 2004 the U.S. Supreme Court declined to hear the state's appeal from *Goodridge* (and in 2006 the groundbreaking plaintiffs announced plans to divorce).

Although the Massachusetts same-sex marriage provisions were originally limited by the Republican governor to commonwealth residents, some municipalities openly defied the restriction and some

State Laws Prohibiting Same-Sex Marriage

State	Type of Law	Pending Change[1]	State	Type of Law	Pending Change[1]
Alabama	Constitution		Missouri	Constitution	
Alaska	Constitution	Legislation	Montana	Constitution	
Arizona	Statute	Ballot Initiative	Nebraska	Constitution	
Arkansas	Constitution		Nevada	Constitution	
California	Statute	Ballot Initiative and Legislation	New Hampshire	Statute	
			New Jersey	–	
Colorado	Statute	Ballot Initiative	New Mexico	–	
Connecticut	Permits Civil Unions		New York	–	
Delaware	Statute		North Carolina	Statute	
Florida	Statute	Ballot Initiative	North Dakota	Constitution	
Georgia	Constitution		Ohio	Constitution	
Hawaii	Constitution		Oklahoma	Constitution	
Idaho	Statute	Amendment	Oregon	Constitution	
Illinois	Statute	Ballot Initiative	Pennsylvania	Statute	Legislation
Indiana	Statute	Legislation	Rhode Island	–	
Iowa	Statute	Legislation	South Carolina	Statute	Amendment
Kansas	Constitution		South Dakota	Statute	Amendment
Kentucky	Constitution		Tennessee	Statute	Amendment
Louisiana	Constitution		Texas	Constitution	
Maine	Statute		Utah	Constitution	
Maryland	Statute		Vermont[2]	Statute	
Massachusetts	Permits Same-Sex Marriage	Legislation	Virginia	Statute	Amendment
			Washington	Statute	
Michigan	Constitution		West Virginia	Statute	
Minnesota	Statute	Legislation	Wisconsin	Statute	Amendment
Mississippi	Constitution		Wyoming	Statute	

1. Changes pending 2006.
2. Also permits civil unions pursuant to a court decision.

Source: The Heritage Foundation, April 2006

legislators proposed allowing nonresident homosexuals to marry. As of May 2005 it was estimated that six thousand of these marriages had been performed. In March 2006, however, the Massachusetts supreme court, in *Cote-Whitacre v. Department of Public Health,* barred same-sex marriage for out-of-state residents. The state legislature also took up a measure to amend the Massachusetts constitution to retract the commonwealth's historic recognition of all individuals' right to marry.

Nearly all states have either adopted constitutional amendments or passed statutory provisions banning same-sex marriage by defining marriage as being between one man and one woman; thirty-seven are the states' version of the Defense of Marriage Act. As of 2006 twenty states had adopted constitutional amendments along these lines; proposed amendments were to be on the ballots in six to eight other states, including Arizona, Colorado, Idaho, South Carolina, South Dakota, Tennessee,

Virginia, and Wisconsin. Eleven states, including California in addition to Massachusetts, have pending similar legislation or ballot initiatives; in 2005 the California legislature attempted to legalize same-sex marriage, but the law was vetoed by Governor Arnold Schwarzenegger. Only six states—Connecticut, Massachusetts, New Jersey, New Mexico, New York, and Rhode Island—and the District of Columbia have no explicit prohibition against same-sex marriage. However, in New Jersey, the state's superior court concluded, in *Lewis v. Harris* (2003), that same-sex couples had no right to marry, in part because of a public need to promote the traditional notion of the family and to remain in legal harmony with other states.

Civil Unions. A Vermont law fully effective in 2001 and another in Connecticut enacted in 2005 permit a form of same-sex marriage known as civil union (also legalized in Britain, Denmark, Finland, France, Germany, and Switzerland). In Vermont two persons of the same sex who are not related to each other and are not already in a civil union or a marriage, are at least eighteen years of age, and are competent to enter into a contract are eligible for civil union status. As with a request for a marriage license, a town clerk must issue a same-sex couple a license if they meet the requirements and pay a $20 fee. A civil union may be solemnized by the same officials who are empowered to legalize a marriage. Once entered into, the civil union provides all the rights and obligations of marriage. Spouses in a civil union are taxed in Vermont the same as married couples. Termination of a civil union is carried out by the same process used by married couples filing for dissolution of a marriage in family court; a six-month residency, as with a DIVORCE, is also required. By statute, Vermont has simultaneously affirmed its support of heterosexual marriage.

A number of states use language in their laws that precludes the possibility of civil unions or alternate forms of same-sex marriage. For example, the Oklahoma constitution states in article II, The Bill of Rights, section 35: "Marriage in this state shall consist only of the union of one man and one woman. Neither this Constitution nor any other provision of law shall be construed to require that marital status or the legal incidents thereof be conferred upon unmarried couples or groups."

Domestic Partnerships. Another form of committed same-sex relationship available in some states is called a domestic partnership or a life partnership. This arrangement permits payment of certain employee benefits, such as a partner's insurance coverage, that are provided to a spouse in a heterosexual marriage. Because these arrangements are not recognized under federal law, the benefits may be taxed as income. Many private employers also provide domestic partner benefits, as do state subdivisions such as municipalities, although they may be preempted by state laws.

A proposed law in Maryland would create a "certificate of life partnership" to be issued by the state department of health and mental hygiene to unmarried couples over eighteen years of age who are living together. The intent of the law is to provide dignity and equal rights to people in committed relationships. Opponents argue that the law is just a step toward homosexual marriage.

Divorce and Related Issues

Except in Massachusetts, where heterosexual and homosexual marriages are treated alike, homosexual relationships are similar to those of UNMARRIED CO-HABITANTS (couples living together out of wedlock). However, unlike the way courts began to enforce private agreements between unmarried heterosexual couples, as in the California "palimony" case *Marvin v. Marvin* (1976), courts have been reluctant to extend to same-sex couples the right to make private agreements governing potential future separation. In *Jones v. Daley* (1981), a California court would not enforce such an agreement between men living together. But later cases in California and other more tolerant states have moved toward treating opposite-sex and same-sex cohabitants equally in these matters.

Issues related to child custody and support in cases involving homosexual partners are generally treated on a par with heterosexual UNMARRIED PARENTS in more tolerant states. The Massachusetts supreme court, in *Bezio v. Patenaude* (1980), held that a woman's preference for a same-sex partner is not sufficient reason to deny a mother the custody of her child. The Wisconsin supreme court, in two cases in 1978—*Isaacson v. Isaacson* and *Schuster v. Schuster*—similarly upheld the right of lesbian mothers to retain custody of their CHILDREN even when the noncustodial fathers became able to support them.

How the issue of nontraditional versus traditional marriage will ultimately be resolved is beyond prediction. In 2006 the highest courts of New York and Georgia upheld the constitutionality of a state law and a state constitutional amendment, respectively, banning gay marriage; similar cases were moving through the courts in New Jersey, Washington, and several other states. While the states, acting as "laboratories of democracy," are approaching the problem from several angles, a movement has been under way to add a FEDERAL MARRIAGE AMENDMENT to the U.S. Constitution. Supported by President George W. Bush and other social conservatives, this would permanently (unless repealed) preclude the extension to nonheterosexual couples of the basic right of marriage. Arguments against such an amendment include the fact that the Constitution's purpose is to guarantee rights of citizens and limit government infringement—rather than to enshrine a denial of rights to certain citizens. The amendment has failed several times, including in 2006, to gain the votes required for passage by Congress.

See also ALIMONY; BISEXUALITY; CHILD SUPPORT; DISCRIMINATION; HOMOSEXUALITY; SPOUSAL RIGHTS AND DUTIES.

MARGARET SANGER

"When the history of our civilization is written," said the English historian and futurist H. G. Wells (1866–1946) in 1931, "it will be a biological history, and Margaret Sanger will be its heroine." Margaret Sanger was an American pioneer who paved the way for EQUAL RIGHTS and REPRODUCTIVE RIGHTS for women,

promoting the education of women about CONTRACEPTION, FAMILY PLANNING, and, more broadly, population control. In 1998 the feminist activist Gloria Steinem wrote about Sanger: "She taught us, first, to look at the world as if women mattered."

Margaret Higgins was born on September 14, 1879, in Corning, New York, the daughter of a devout Roman Catholic Irish American mother who died of tuberculosis after giving birth to eleven children. Her father was a free-thinker who made a meager living as a stonemason. Her mother's early death, which Margaret attributed to frequent childbirth and poverty, spurred her to find a better way of life for herself—and ultimately for other women.

Helped by two older sisters, Margaret went to college and later became a nurse in 1900. She studied to become a registered nurse but stopped in 1902, when she married an architect, William Sanger. Like her mother, she was prone to tuberculosis but bore three children before the family moved to New York City in 1911. Her living room, she said, "became a gathering place where liberals, anarchists, socialists and IWW's [members of the Industrial Workers of the World] could meet." Her socialist and labor activities, coupled with her emerging feminist politics and nursing background, led her to write a column, "What Every Girl Should Know," on female sexuality and hygiene for the *New York Call*.

In 1913 her column was banned because she discussed venereal disease, but the following year she began publishing her own radical feminist monthly named *The Woman Rebel*. In it she championed the right of a woman to be "absolute mistress of her own body." However, her discussion of birth control, a term coined in her publication, brought an indictment against her for violating postal laws, which prohibited sending obscene materials through the U.S. mail. She fled to Europe to avoid prosecution, but her estranged husband was jailed under the federal law initiated by the antivice crusader ANTHONY COMSTOCK; Sanger had been tricked into giving one of Comstock's operatives a copy of his wife's *Family Limitation* (1914), a pamphlet describing various methods of contraception.

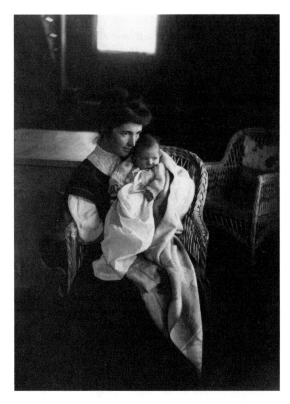

A pioneer in changing U.S. laws regarding birth control and family planning, Margaret Sanger was herself a mother whose five-year-old daughter died suddenly in 1915. In large measure because of her efforts, the U.S. Supreme Court in 1965 and 1972 struck down state laws banning the use of contraceptives by married and unmarried couples, respectively.

After several affairs, including with H. G. Wells and the English psychologist Havelock Ellis (1859–1939), who wrote a number of books on the psychology of sex, Margaret Sanger returned to New York in 1915 to stand trial. Although she was eager to use the publicity generated by her husband's trial to promote her cause, the charges against her were dropped; for one, the government did not want to prosecute her as a grieving mother after her five-year-old daughter Peggy died that year.

Having seen birth control clinics in Holland in 1914, Sanger decided to open her own medically supervised clinic in Brooklyn in 1916. It became the first of many PLANNED PARENTHOOD FEDERATION OF AMERICA

clinics. After her prompt arrest and conviction for the clinic's activities (it was open only nine days), for which she spent a month in prison, the state appellate court determined that doctors were permitted to prescribe birth control for women if medically necessary to treat a disease but could not give "promiscuous advice to patients irrespective of their condition." However, the opinion in *People v. Sanger* (1918) added that *disease* could be broadly defined to include "any alteration in the state of [the] body which caused or threatened pain or sickness," thus extending the ruling beyond venereal disease to cover PREGNANCY. The decision was considered a victory for the birth control movement on its road to end "compulsory motherhood."

In 1921 Sanger founded the American Birth Control League, and two years later she opened the Birth Control Clinical Research Bureau, later renamed the Margaret Sanger Research Bureau. The bureau kept patient records and statistics on the effectiveness of contraceptive methods. Sanger set up the National Committee on Federal Legislation in 1929 to lobby to give doctors the right to dispense contraceptives, but the Roman Catholic Church mounted an aggressive effort to derail her efforts. Her cause gained momentum when a federal court of appeals ruled in *United States v. One Package* (1936) that physicians were exempt from the ban on the importation of contraceptives, making their distribution by U.S. doctors for medical purposes also legal.

After World War II, Sanger focused on establishing an international birth control movement. In 1952, working with family planning advocates around the world, she helped create an organization named International Planned Parenthood, which would become part of a network of 125 affiliates managing some 866 health centers worldwide, the largest private international organization promoting family planning. She also worked to secure funding for development of the first effective birth control pill, a contraceptive that helped usher in the SEXUAL REVOLUTION in America, including the right to an ABORTION.

Margaret Sanger, although suffering from a weak heart, continued to travel and lecture on the subject to which she had devoted her life. She would live to see the U.S. Supreme Court uphold the right of married couples to use birth control in *Griswold v. Connecticut* (1965), but she died in Tucson, Arizona, the following year. Her work made an extraordinary impact on the rights of women and access to family planning the world over.

See also Feminism; Motherhood.

SEPARATION

See Divorce.

SEX CLUBS

See Sexually Oriented Businesses.

SEX EDUCATION

The battle over sex education in America has been waged since at least the late nineteenth century. In 1873 Congress passed the so-called Comstock Act, named after the antivice crusader Anthony Comstock, which in part forbade mailing information about contraception; the prohibition was based on a fear that the use of contraceptives would lead to immorality. This law, however, did not deter all efforts to make contraceptive information and devices available to those who wanted them. Subsequently the social purity and social hygiene movements arose to promote chastity and sexual abstinence as the best methods of preventing unwanted pregnancy and sexually transmitted diseases.

During the early twentieth century, advocates of education about sex and contraception supported reserving sexual activity for marriage. Until the 1960s premarital sex might involve only petting (caressing and fondling) but not actual sexual intercourse. The sexual revolution of the 1960s and 1970s changed such inhibitions. Women were freed from the fear of pregnancy by the advent of the birth control pill, and

premarital sexual intercourse became more socially acceptable. The new, less strict morality that ensued brought an urgency to the sex education movement.

In 1964 Mary S. Calderone helped establish the Sexuality Information and Education Council of the United States to support education about sexual behavior. Then, suddenly, with the legalization of contraception—as a result of the case *Griswold v. Connecticut* (1965)—state laws banning the use of contraception were declared unconstitutional. A new emphasis on freedom of information about sexuality and contraception replaced the old reticence on the subject. In that same year, Congress enacted Title III of the Elementary and Secondary Education Act, which contained funding for training teachers in human sexuality.

In 1971 the U.S. Committee on Population Growth recommended sex education and the provision of information on contraceptives for young people. Six years later a New York law that prohibited the distribution or sale of contraceptives to minors was struck down by the U.S. Supreme Court in *Carey v. Population Services International* (1977). This decision affirmed that the right to contraception was not just a matter for married couples or adults, but was a right of every individual under the Constitution's privacy protections. It also opened the door to an expanded role for sex education classes.

School-based Programs

Training for teachers in sex education was promoted in 1912 by the National Education Association despite controversy over what information about sexuality should be available to the public at large. It was 1940, however, before the U.S. Public Health Service began strongly advocating sex education in schools, calling it an "urgent need." By the 1950s programs sponsored by the American School Health Association and the American Medical Association were publishing materials for use in sex education classes in public schools.

All states now generally permit some type of sex education. The administration of these programs is a local matter, and many school boards have been split over the nature of their curriculum. Although courts have

State Sex Education Policies

State	Required by Law		Content, if Taught		Parental Role	
	Sex Education	STDs/HIV	Abstinence	Contraception	Consent Required	May Opt Out
Alabama		•	Stress	Cover		•
Alaska	•	•				
Arizona			Stress		•[1]	•[2]
Arkansas			Stress			
California		•	Cover	Cover		•
Colorado						•
Connecticut		•	Cover			•
Delaware	•	•	Cover	Cover		
Florida	•	•	Cover		•	
Georgia	•	•	Cover			•
Hawaii	•	•	Stress	Cover		•
Idaho						•
Illinois		•	Stress	Cover		•
Indiana		•	Stress			
Iowa	•	•				•
Kansas	•	•				•
Kentucky	•	•	Cover			
Louisiana			Stress			•
Maine	•	•	Stress	Cover		•
Maryland	•	•	Cover	Cover		•
Massachusetts						•
Michigan		•	Stress			•
Minnesota	•	•	Cover			•
Mississippi[3]			Stress			•
Missouri		•	Stress	Cover		•
Montana	•	•	Cover			•[2]
Nebraska						
Nevada	•	•			•	
New Hampshire		•	Cover			
New Jersey	•	•				•
New Mexico		•	Stress	Cover		
New York		•	Stress	Cover		•[2]
North Carolina	•	•	Stress			
North Dakota						
Ohio		•	Stress			•
Oklahoma		•	Stress	Cover		•
Oregon		•	Stress	Cover		•
Pennsylvania		•	Stress			•[2]
Rhode Island	•	•	Stress	Cover		•

State	Required by Law		Content, if Taught		Parental Role	
	Sex Education	STDs/HIV	Abstinence	Contraception	Consent Required	May Opt Out
South Carolina	•	•	Stress	Cover		•
South Dakota			Cover			
Tennessee	•	•	Stress			•
Texas			Stress			•
Utah	•	•	Stress		•	
Vermont	•	•	Cover	Cover		•
Virginia			Cover	Cover		•
Washington		•	Stress	Cover		•
West Virginia		•	Stress	Cover		•
Wisconsin		•				•
Wyoming						

1. Parental consent is required only for sex education, not STD/HIV education.
2. Opting out is permitted for STD education only.
3. Localities may override state requirements for sex eduation topics.

Source: Guttmacher Institute, 2006

upheld the legality of requiring students to attend sex education classes over their parents' objections, local school jurisdictions often accede to parents' requests.

Some states—including Delaware, North Carolina, and Rhode Island, as well as the District of Columbia—require sex and AIDS education in schools. Alabama, Michigan, and Pennsylvania are among nearly twenty states that mandate AIDS education only. Some states prohibit any reference to ABORTION as an option in the case of an unwanted pregnancy. For example, Louisiana law provides: "No program offering sex education instruction shall in any way counsel or advocate abortion." Connecticut, Michigan, and South Carolina also expressly restrict the discussion of abortion in sex education classes.

Many states mandate that ABSTINENCE (refraining from sexual activity with a partner) be emphasized as the best method of birth control and protection against disease. Although abstinence is undoubtedly a good way to avoid pregnancy and most sexually transmitted diseases, the evidence is that many young people do not refrain from all sexual contact with oth-

ers. For those who are not abstinent, information about other types of protection, such as condoms, is critical to stemming the tide of teenage pregnancies and the spread of disease. In 2004 Texas, which has the nation's highest teenage birth rate, declared that school sex education textbooks could discuss only abstinence despite surveys showing that about 90 percent of the state's citizens want both abstinence and contraception taught to TEENAGERS.

The main rationales usually given for educating young people about sex are to prevent pregnancy and mitigate the spread of disease. But in a survey conducted in 2004 by National Public Radio, the Kaiser Family Foundation, and the Kennedy School of Government at Harvard University about what parents feared most about their seventh- to twelfth-grade children having sexual intercourse, 36 percent of respondents said that it was "that they might have sexual intercourse before they are psychologically and emotionally ready." Twenty-nine percent were more concerned about sexually transmitted diseases, and 23 percent were more worried about the possibility of pregnancy.

The Battle of Ideas

The legal implications of sex education for adolescents in public schools go beyond conflicts between abstinence-only and contraception proponents. It is obvious that sex education in the schools is an important tool in combating the problems of teen pregnancy, AIDS-HIV infection, and other sexual diseases. Yet divisive social issues such as abortion, sexual morality, and the rights of homosexuals are flashpoints that can make the sex education curriculum a battleground for parents and educators.

In the more recent legal battles in the states, the main issue has been whether students are being given accurate instruction or information arising from nonscientific moral or religious tenets. In *Coleman v. Caddo Parish School Board* (1994), for instance, the Louisiana court of appeals had to deal with a challenge from parents who contended that the textbook being used in seventh- and eighth-grade classes violated state law, which prohibits the inclusion in sex education materials relating to "religious beliefs, practices in human sexuality, [and] subjective moral and ethical judgments of the instructor or other persons." Moral comments on sexual orientation and abortion were also contained in the book. A number of inaccurate statements in the textbook were held by the court to be improper under state law.

Although it may not infringe a person's right of privacy to have different points of view about sexual behavior presented in a classroom environment, to force or require a person to take a pledge in front of others not to engage in sexual activity until marriage—and if never married, presumably forever—may do so. Moreover, the nature of such pledges is not always spelled out. Does abstinence include any sexual activity other than vaginal intercourse, or does it exclude masturbation, passionate kissing, and romantic touching?

In 2005 irate parents of seven- to ten-year-old students in California, who had unwittingly given permission for their children to answer questions in school about the children's sexual behavior, lost a

Would you be more careful if it was you who got pregnant?

FOR BIRTH CONTROL HANDBOOK. WRITE N.E.F.P.; 791 TREMONT ST.; BOSTON, MASS. 02118

Pregnancy has far greater consequences for women than for men. By asking men to empathize with their female sexual partners, this poster used between 1965 and 1980 attempted to educate them about their responsibility for using contraception.

case in the U.S. Court of Appeals for the Ninth Circuit. The court held that the U.S. Constitution does not grant parents the right to interfere in the curricula of public schools. The political fallout from this decision, *Fields v. Palmdale School District*—which caused the U.S. House of Representatives to pass a resolution calling for a rehearing of the case—undoubtedly will continue to help make sex education issues a heated topic for some time.

See also FAMILY PLANNING; SANGER, MARGARET.

SEX OFFENDERS

According to *Sexual Behavior in the Human Male* (1948), the groundbreaking study by the sex researcher AL-FRED KINSEY, "It is ordinarily said that criminal law is designed to protect property and to protect persons.... The fact that there is a body of sex laws which is apart from the laws protecting persons is evidence of their distinct function, namely that of protecting custom." The different nature of laws regarding sexual behavior has often led to different punishment and treatment of sex offenders compared with penalties meted out to others who break the law. Like hate crimes, sex crimes, especially when they are violent and directed against CHILDREN, have been singled out for harsher treatment under federal and state laws.

Punishment of sex offenders has not been consistent historically. In his *Commentaries on the Laws of England* (1765–70), William Blackstone (1723–80) related that certain acts of lewdness and offenses against decency were punished with fines and imprisonment. He also noted that during the period of the English Commonwealth (1649–60) under Oliver Cromwell, "incest and wilful adultery were made capital crimes." After the restoration of the monarchy and a consequent liberalization of social mores, the courts took "no cognizance of the crime of adultery, otherwise than as a private injury."

Cultural factors have also played a role in determining the severity of punishment for SEX OFFENSES. For example, in the South after the Civil War (1861–65), the RAPE of a black woman generally went unpunished. But the rape of a white woman by a black man was considered a serious crime, as portrayed so dramatically in Harper Lee's book *To Kill a Mockingbird* (1960). In fact, it was generally presumed in the South that a white woman would never under any circumstances, except if threatened, CONSENT to have sexual relations with a black man. Today the possibility of prejudice remains in the prosecution, trial, conviction, and punishment of black men for all types of sex crimes.

During the late twentieth century, U.S. Supreme Court decisions began to extend rights to persons accused of crimes—for example, requiring in *Miranda v. Arizona* (1966) that suspects taken into custody be advised of their legal rights. Viewing these decisions as unnecessary accommodations to criminals, many citizens and state legislators began to focus instead on VICTIMS' RIGHTS. Following national news stories of particularly gruesome sex crimes involving children, laws governing sex offenses began increasing punishment and, most significant, adding restrictions on convicted sex offenders after they had served their time.

Types of Punishment

Before the end of the 1970s, sex offenders were sometimes called sexual psychopaths because their harmful behavior defied clear psychiatric explanation. Although perpetrators of sex crimes are still treated as a special type of criminal, the prosecution of sex offenses is subject to the same rights of the accused granted to other offenders, as well as the same exceptions. A rule of the Supreme Court devised in *Blockburger v. United States* (1932) disallows the defense of double jeopardy (being tried twice for the same crime) where a single act may constitute two crimes that require different types of proof, as in the case of rape and incest; RAPE requires proof that a person has had sexual relations by force, whereas INCEST requires proof that a person has had sexual relations with a relative in a category proscribed in a particular jurisdiction. Not all states follow the *Blockburger* rule, however, so they treat prosecution for either offense as giving rise to double jeopardy. Special exceptions are also made for some sex offense prosecutions, such as in Federal Rule of Evidence 413, which permits introduction of evidence of a defendant's prior sexual assaults in a prosecution for a similar crime.

Options for punishment for all types of crime include fines or incarceration in prison, or both. On occasion some type of personal performance may also be required, such as providing community service or attending classes designed to modify behavior. Increasingly, violent offenders are subject to civil confinement after serving their prison terms.

Criminal Punishment. Sex offenses generally carry stiff penalties, but leeway is often allowed to tailor the punishment to fit the seriousness of the particular offense and the circumstances of the crime. At the federal level, for crimes in territory under federal jurisdiction, the U.S. Code provides that an offender convicted of sexual abuse "shall be fined ... , imprisoned not more than 20 years, or both"; a person convicted of aggravated sexual abuse "shall be fined ... , imprisoned for any term of years or life, or both"; and someone convicted of sexual abuse of a minor (where the victim is between twelve and sixteen years of age and is at least four years younger than the offender) "shall be fined ... , imprisoned not more than 15 years, or both."

All states have laws detailing the degrees of various sex offenses and penalties for those offenses. In Nebraska, for one, SEXUAL ASSAULT in the first degree is a class II felony, which carries a maximum penalty of fifty years' imprisonment. In Idaho rape is "punishable by imprisonment in the state prison not less than one (1) year, and the imprisonment may be extended to life in the discretion of the District Judge, who shall pass sentence." Oregon specifies three degrees of the crime of sexual abuse: first degree, which is a class B felony and carries a maximum prison sentence of ten years; second degree, which is a class C felony and carries a maximum sentence of five years; and third degree, which is a class A misdemeanor and carries a maximum sentence of one year.

Additional Penalties. Nebraska's laws include a provision mandating that if a person is found guilty of sexual assault in the first degree a second time, the offender is to be sentenced to a minimum of twenty-five years in prison and "shall not be eligible for parole." A Nebraska constitutional amendment denies bail for anyone charged with treason, murder under certain circumstances, and "sexual offenses involving penetration by force or against the will of the victim." New Jersey law provides additional penalties for sex offenders, ranging from a maximum fine of $2,000 for conviction of a crime in the first degree to $500 for conviction of a crime in the fourth degree.

California, Illinois, and Minnesota are among states that have laws penalizing HATE CRIMES, which include offenses motivated by prejudice based on sex, GENDER, or sexual orientation. The laws differ in how they punish such crimes, with some making the hate crime a separate offense while others increase the degree of the underlying crime or enhance the sentences meted out for conviction of the underlying crime.

Civil Confinement. One way in which sex offenders may be punished over and above the penalty for the sex offense itself is by the use of civil commitment laws, which have generated some controversy. These laws permit a dangerous sex offender, after serving his sentence, to be indefinitely confined in a psychiatric institution or until a new determination is made that he is no longer dangerous to society. The government's ability to impose this additional form of punishment stems from its police power to act to protect the public health and safety and, on occasion, public morals. Critics claim that postprison civil confinement provides a false sense of public security, is extremely costly, and delays treatment of offenders that should begin at the time of their initial incarceration.

Nearly all states have statutes that permit the involuntary civil commitment of any mentally ill persons if they present a danger to themselves or others. As of 2004 about sixteen states—ranging from Arizona and California to Kansas, Minnesota, Wisconsin, to Virginia, South Carolina, and Florida—had civil commitment laws that specifically address sexually violent offenders; at least four others, including New York, were in the process of considering such laws. South Carolina's Sexually Violent Predator Act (1998) defines a sexually violent predator as a person who "(a) has been convicted of a sexually violent offense; and (b) suffers from a mental abnormality or personality disorder that makes the person likely to engage in acts of sexual violence if not confined in a secure facility for long-term control, care, and treatment." In 2002 the act prevailed in state court against a challenge under the state constitution's ban on ex post facto (after the fact) laws; the act was also found not to violate either the double jeopardy or the ex post facto clauses of the U.S.

Constitution. In *Kansas v. Hendricks* (1997), the Supreme Court ruled that the Kansas Sexually Violent Predator Act (1994) was not unconstitutional and that the state had only to establish that the individual in question was dangerous and could not control his actions because of a mental illness or an abnormality.

Sterilization. In some cases STERILIZATION of sex offenders is threatened. A law in the state of Washington imposes on a person found "guilty of carnal abuse of a female person under the age of ten years, or of rape" the added punishment of "an operation to be performed upon such person, for the prevention of procreation." California, Florida, and Texas are among a handful of states that allow the use of DRUGS or surgery to castrate repeat sex offenders. Efforts in Virginia to allow offenders to choose voluntary castration in return for freedom at the end of their sentence have not survived concerns that this solution could be deemed unconstitutional cruel and unusual punishment.

Restrictions after Release

MEGAN'S LAW—named after Megan Kanka, a seven-year-old victim of a twice-convicted sex offender and pedophile—was enacted by CONGRESS in 1996 to require all fifty states to set up a notification system to advise communities when a dangerous sex offender moves into their neighborhood. In 2004 Hawaii amended its constitution to declare, "The public has a right of access to registration information regarding persons convicted of certain offenses against children and persons convicted of certain sexual offenses." In *State v. Tadewaldt* (1996), a Montana case, a sentence of forty-five years for failure to register as a sex offender was affirmed, although a dissent noted that the length of the sentence should be considered cruel and unusual punishment.

The U.S. Supreme Court upheld the constitutionality of registration laws and their retroactive extension in *Smith v. Doe* (2003) and *Connecticut Department of Public Safety v. John Doe* (2003). Because these statutes are not intended as criminal punishment but instead concern a matter of public safety, said the Court, they do not violate the Constitution's prohibition in Article I, section 9, against ex post facto laws.

Postincarceration restrictions on sex offenders remain a legal and political issue in many states and municipalities. In April 2005 the mayor of Miami Beach proposed rewriting municipal laws to virtually prohibit registered sex offenders from moving into the city. Five months later, the mayor of Baltimore, Maryland, suggested that child sex offenders who were released from prison should be made to wear electronic ankle bracelets so that their whereabouts could be constantly monitored. An apparent act of vigilantism arose in April 2006, when several registered sex offenders were shot to death by a man who later killed himself; the only connection the police could find was that his victims were among some thirty-four former sex offenders that the killer had looked up on Maine's online sex offender registry.

The Federal Bureau of Investigation oversees the operation of a National Sex Offender Registry, whose Web site directs inquiries to state sex offender registry Web sites. The Office of Justice Programs in the U.S. Department of Justice jointly administers a project called the Center for Sex Offender Management with the National Institute of Corrections, State Justice Institute, and American Probation and Parole Association. The center's mission is to enhance public safety by preventing further victimization through better community management of sex offenders. Recent statistics show that some 375,000 sex offenders have been registered in the United States.

Contacts

National Sex Offender Registry, Crimes Against Children Unit, Federal Bureau of Investigation, U.S. Department of Justice, 935 Pennsylvania Avenue, NW, Washington, DC 20535-0001 (202-324-3000). www.fbi.gov/hq/cid/cac/registry.htm www.nsopr.gov.

Center for Sex Offender Management, c/o Center for Effective Public Policy, 8403 Colesville Road, Suite 720, Silver Spring, MD 20910 (301-589-9383). www.csom.org.

See also CHILD ABUSE; CRIMES AGAINST CHILDREN UNIT (FBI).

SEX OFFENSES

Sex offenses are acts that violate state or federal laws proscribing certain sexual behavior and that carry a risk of prosecution and punishment. They may be actions that are absolutely prohibited, such as child molestation, or that are appropriate under certain conditions and not others, such as intentional intimate touching. Behavior such as rape or sexual assault may be charged as a felony punishable by more than a year in jail. Lesser sex crimes, among them indecent exposure and public NUDITY, are generally charged as misdemeanors and carry less stringent penalties. In addition to imprisonment, sex offenses, like hate crimes, tend to carry a special public stigma; sentences may be enhanced because of the particular odiousness of a crime. SEX OFFENDERS may also be subjected to special treatment even after they have served their sentence: restrictions on where they can live and work, requirements under statutes such as MEGAN'S LAW to report where they are living, and in some extreme cases, civil commitment in an institution to keep them away from society.

Sex offenses differ from most other types of crime in that the same sexual behavior might be legal in a different context. Sexual intercourse between a husband and a wife is expected, for example, but with the evolution of WOMEN'S RIGHTS, the law now recognizes that in a MARRIAGE the woman has the right not to consent to intercourse; therefore, a husband can be convicted of raping his own wife. Consensual sexual relations between two parties who are not married are generally no longer a crime, but if the behavior involves an underage child and an adult or close relatives, the same act may constitute the crime of statutory rape or incest.

Historical Taboos

Even before the development of language, human society enforced the apparently universal incest taboo. Rulers in ancient Egypt and Peru violated it with impunity, however, to prove that their divinity placed them above such mortal constraints. With the advent of language, the proscription against certain sex acts was codified into law. The Ten Commandments declare, for example, "Thou shalt not commit adultery," and the Code of Hammurabi, who reigned in Babylon from 1792 to 1750 B.C.E., prescribed punishment for adultery.

In colonial America, RELIGION strongly influenced laws regarding sexual behavior (an effect that has continued in cycles to the present with respect to limitations on such practices as ABORTION and to laws banning SAME-SEX MARRIAGE). Fornication and adultery were prosecuted in the quarterly courts of the Massachusetts Bay Colony in the seventeenth century; as a result, incidents of premarital sex and out-of-wedlock births were apparently rare. In the next century, however, sex outside marriage—especially between white males and servants or slaves in the southern American colonies—became more prevalent.

While the nineteenth century ended under the reign of Victorian morality, the works of the Marquis de Sade (1740–1814), a Frenchman who was imprisoned for sexual offenses, and Baron Richard von Krafft-Ebing (1840–1902), a pioneer German psychiatrist and neurologist who published his *Psychopathia Sexualis* in 1886, began to loosen society's tight grip on sexual behavior. In the United States the Roaring Twenties connoted a movement toward sexual freedom, which was reflected to an extent by the ratification in 1920 of the Nineteenth Amendment to the U.S. Constitution, giving women the right to vote. By the end of the twentieth century, many laws formerly prohibiting certain sexual behavior—including adultery, fornication, the use of CONTRACEPTION, abortion, miscegenation, and sodomy—were no longer in force or at least were seldom prosecuted.

Today most sex offenses can be roughly divided into consensual and nonconsensual acts. Other behavior sometimes regarded as sex crimes, from indecent exposure to the use of obscene language in public, is committed alone but may affront or offend others. The following examples give representative sex offenses in each of these classes.

Consensual Offenses

CONSENT is an important element in distinguishing between acceptable and criminal sexual behavior and determining the nature of a sex offense. For example, incest and prostitution may be considered consensual crimes that generally lack the violent nature of nonconsensual sex offenses, such as sexual assault or CHILD ABUSE. Consensual sex offenses often include acts related to MARRIAGE, the family, and other personal relationships and involve actions ranging from fornication, adultery, and bigamy to custodial sexual misconduct.

Incest. The INCEST taboo remains in most human societies. Although the historical rationale for laws against sexual relations between relatives remains scientifically unproven—the belief that they can lead to genetically defective children—the act is still a serious crime in most jurisdictions. Under West Virginia law, to cite one instance, the penalty for incest is five to fifteen years in the penitentiary, plus a fine of up to $5,000, plus payment of any medical and related costs if a minor is involved; additional punishment is possible in the case of a parent or a custodian of a child to whom the offender owes a duty. The contemporary rationale for incest laws is that the practice can cause serious disharmony in a family and mental trauma to family members.

Bigamy. BIGAMY (having two spouses at the same time) is a serious crime in all states. The Model Penal Code developed in 1962 by the American Law Institute, an organization dedicated to clarifying and simplifying the laws, recommends that ordinary bigamy be treated as a misdemeanor. In contrast, the code calls for POLYGAMY—a religious practice of having multiple spouses, usually wives—to be treated as a felony. No states have adopted the ALI recommendations outright, but they indicate the stronger sense of social outrage at the concept of polygamy. Several western states, including Utah, have provisions in their constitutions denouncing the practice. Utah's laws include the crime of bigamy, which is a felony, and child bigamy, in which the instigator of the act is eighteen years of age or older and the other party is under that age. This offense, which includes bigamous cohabitation in addition to bigamous marriage, is punishable as a more serious offense than bigamy.

Sodomy. SODOMY has been legally defined in numerous ways, from anal intercourse to including nearly all forms of nonreproductive sex. In *Bowers v. Hardwick* (1986), the U.S. Supreme Court upheld a Georgia law against homosexual sodomy under the definition of "any sexual act involving the sex organs of one person and the mouth or anus of another"; the penalty was imprisonment for up to twenty years. But the Court overruled *Bowers* in LAWRENCE V. TEXAS (2003), concluding that homosexual sodomy in one's own home is protected by the PRIVACY rights inherent in the Bill of Rights (1791), as declared by the Supreme Court in *GRISWOLD V. CONNECTICUT* (1965). Under the *Lawrence* ruling, laws against sodomy between consenting adults in private are unconstitutional. In striking them down, the Court noted that such regulation touched "upon the most private human conduct, sexual behavior."

Adultery and Cohabitation. In roughly half of the states, ADULTERY and fornication are crimes that are still on the books but are typically not enforced. Courts had long denied that laws against adultery and fornication violated the constitutional right of privacy. However, following the *Lawrence v. Texas* decision, it is doubtful that the former rationale for upholding such laws in still tenable. Laws penalizing UNMARRIED CO-HABITANTS (two persons living together out of wedlock) remain in force in some jurisdictions although seldom enforced. In Virginia, for example, it is still a misdemeanor to have PREMARITAL SEX or commit adultery.

Miscegenation. Even after the Civil War (1861–65) and the abolition of slavery, laws in many southern states prohibited marriage between white and black persons. These MISCEGENATION laws were unanimously declared unconstitutional by the Supreme Court in *Loving v. Virginia* (1967), which held that the laws violated the equal protection clause of the Fourteenth Amendment (1868).

Prostitution. PROSTITUTION, what some consider a victimless crime, is outlawed in almost all federal and state jurisdictions, except for several counties in Nevada. Many state laws go into great detail criminalizing prostitution's various aspects, but at the enforcement level the application of the law tends to break down. Either there is little or no enforcement or the enforcement discriminates against prostitutes, leaving their clientele—without whom the business would not thrive—off the hook.

Nonconsensual Offenses

The language used in federal and state laws regulating nonconsensual sex offenses lacks uniformity. Terms such as *rape, sexual assault, sexual battery,* and *sexual abuse,* among others, are used to describe such crimes. In addition, the penalties vary depending on the jurisdiction and on the degree of the offense; for example, conviction for aggravated sexual assault carries the possibility of a greater sentence than for sexual assault alone. Some states have also adopted laws creating a special category of HATE CRIMES that may include violence against women and homosexuals; these statutes increase the penalty for crimes that are motivated by prejudice or by hatred of the victim.

Sexual Assault. SEXUAL ASSAULT is a broad term that encompasses other more specific physical sex acts, ranging from fondling to aggravated sexual assault. In law, an assault is the threat of force, while battery is the actual infliction of physical harm. To a large extent, this distinction has been dissolved, so that now sexual assault covers the full range of proscribed physical sexual behavior that constitutes crimes under federal and state jurisdictions. Sometimes included under this rubric are RAPE, sexual abuse, child molestation, incest, some forms of SEXUAL HARASSMENT, and lewd behavior, including INDECENT EXPOSURE. However, sexual behavior that constitutes sexual assault is typically viewed as involving some force or the threat of force and does not involve consensual sexual activity.

Rape. Although the crime of rape has a long history, in the modern era it has become less amenable to simple legal analysis. Rape is considered the act of having carnal knowledge of a woman by force and against her will, but there are many nuances in the specific facts of each crime. Where no consent was given, the force necessary to constitute the crime of rape has often been held by the courts to be the act of penetration itself. By using new DRUGS to commit so-called DATE RAPE, a perpetrator may avoid having to use any force to accomplish the sex act and renders the victim incapable of giving or withholding consent.

All states have laws making rape a serious crime, but they vary on how the offense is categorized. For example, the Ohio code, in title 29, Crimes–Procedure, chapter 2907, Sex Offenses, states under Rape: "No person shall engage in sexual conduct with another when the offender purposely compels the other person to submit by force or threat of force." The Illinois code, under article 11, Sex Offenses, does not mention rape but instead in the section Criminal Sexual Assault, under Criminal Offenses, describes "an act of sexual penetration by the use of force or threat of force."

Sexual Abuse. On the federal level, the Sexual Abuse Act (1986) replaced federal laws expressly citing rape with laws that encompass rape and other forms of sexual abuse. (Rape is still addressed in other sections of the U.S. Code, such as in programs to assist rape victims and state law enforcement agencies in dealing with rape cases. Under the federal sentencing guidelines, contained in Title 18, section 3559, rape is included in the list of serious violent felonies for sentencing purposes.)

The pertinent provisions of the U.S. Code relating to sex offenses are found in Title 18, sections 2241 through 2245, governing crimes prosecuted within the maritime and territorial jurisdiction of the United States, including federal prisons. The code addresses aggravated sexual abuse, sexual abuse, sexual abuse of a minor or ward, abusive sexual contact, and sexual abuse resulting in death. *Aggravated sexual abuse* is defined as "knowingly [causing] another person to engage in a sexual act—(1) by using force against that other person; or (2) by threatening or placing that other person in fear that any person will be subjected to death, serious bodily injury, or kidnapping." These sections also deal with crimes against children, including crossing a state line with the intent to engage in a sexual act with a person who has not attained the age of twelve years and sexual abuse of a minor or a ward, which includes those in official detention or under the custodial, supervisory, or disciplinary authority of the accused.

Female Genital Mutilation. Although female genital mutilation (female circumcision) is primarily a violent act against girls and women carried out in other countries, efforts have been made in the United States to criminalize such conduct here as well. Legislation entitled the Federal Prohibition of Female Genital Mutilation Act was introduced in both houses of Congress in 1995. Although the Senate passed its bill, no final action was taken on the measure. The U.S. Department of State has characterized the fear of female genital mutilation in other countries as persecution justifying a grant of asylum to potential victims.

Human Trafficking and Sex Tourism. Crimes associated with HUMAN TRAFFICKING have reached a global scale. The United States has joined with other nations to reduce this form of sexual slavery, which generally takes young girls from poor circumstances and transports them to more affluent countries for prostitution. Sex tourism is a related crime that involves providing prostitutes to individuals who travel ostensibly as tourists or on business; it likewise often involves the coerced services of underage females.

Sexual Exploitation

Sexual exploitation covers a large area of sex-related offenses, generally of a commercial nature, from prostitution to pornography. The term is increasingly used with respect to activities that may harm CHILDREN and sometimes specifically females. For example, the Mann Act (named for its sponsor, Representative James R. Mann of Illinois) in 1910 declared it a federal crime to transport women across state lines for immoral purposes. The act's reach was extended

by the Supreme Court in *Caminetti v. United States* (1917), making even private amorous trips across state lines illegal. The act, which begins at Title 18, section 2421, of the U.S. Code, falls under the supervision of the Child Molestation and Obscenity Section of the Criminal Division of the U.S. Department of Justice.

Under Title 18 of the U.S. Code, chapter 119 authorizes the Justice Department to use judicial orders to intercept wire and oral communications in cases involving the sexual exploitation of children. The language of chapter 110, section 2251, Sexual Exploitation of Children, states in part: "Any person who employs, uses, persuades, induces, entices, or coerces any minor to engage in . . . any sexually explicit conduct for the purpose of producing any visual depiction of such conduct, shall be punished."

States also promulgate laws against sexual exploitation, crimes that are often included in sections governing prostitution or obscenity and pornography. Behavior prohibited under these laws may include instances in which a perpetrator entices, uses, or coerces others, including children, to perform sex acts from which the perpetrator seeks to profit or gain some benefit. For example, in Illinois, under Criminal Offenses, article 11, Sex Offenses, the section headings include Indecent Solicitation of a Child; Indecent Solicitation of an Adult; Sexual Exploitation of a Child; Pandering; and Pimping. Here PANDERING includes compelling a person to be a prostitute, while pimping involves taking money from a prostitute without lawful consideration, "knowing it was earned in whole or in part from the practice of prostitution." Sexual exploitation of a child under the Illinois law includes engaging in sex acts in the presence of a child or exposing his or her sex organs for the purpose of arousal or gratification, enticing a child to remove his or her clothes for the purpose of sexual arousal or gratification of the person or the child, or both. Another section entitled Exploitation of a Child defines the crime to include compelling a "child or severely or profoundly mentally retarded person to become a prostitute." Using or forcing children to perform sex acts or participate in pornography is also a crime. In most cases, all of these crimes are felonies; if misdemeanors, they may become felonies after the first offense.

Single-Party Offenses

Criminalized sexual behavior also encompasses what many now consider to be victimless crimes. Such activities, from nude dancing to pornography, are gradually losing their social stigma and thus their criminal status. Some public sexual behavior that is committed alone and does no physical harm is nonetheless prohibited under state laws.

Lewd Behavior. LEWD BEHAVIOR may include lewd and lascivious cohabitation and even solicitation for sex or prostitution. In a confrontation between the freedom of expression found in the First Amendment (1791) to the U.S. Constitution and a city ordinance requiring erotic dancers to wear pasties and a G-string, the U.S. Supreme Court noted in *City of Erie v. Pap's A.M.* (2000) that for many years the city had concerns about the detrimental effect of "certain lewd, immoral activities" on the "public health, safety, and welfare"; the Court thus declared the ordinance constitutional.

Obscenity. A major distinction between crimes involving sexual behavior and most other crimes is the fact that not only is the physical behavior itself often proscribed, even representations of such behavior may be a crime under obscenity laws. There is no legal prohibition, for example, against representations in print or the movies of robbery or murder—a staple of many literary and film genres—but that is not the case with representations of sexual activity. This is true especially if such depictions can be accessed by minors or if they are so hard-core (extremely offensive) as to come within the U.S. Supreme Court's definition of obscenity propounded in cases such as *MILLER V. CALIFORNIA* (1973) and *Young v. American Mini Theatres, Inc.* (1976). PORNOGRAPHY includes representations of erotic or sexual behavior that may not be obscene as defined by laws and the courts; the difference depends on many factors, including the context, the standards of the audience, and whether it is viewed in private or offered to the public.

A typical state OBSCENITY law today reads like this one in Indiana: "A matter or performance is obscene . . . if: (1) the average person, applying contemporary community standards, finds that the dominant theme of the matter or performance, taken as a whole, appeals to the prurient interest in sex; (2) the matter or performance depicts or describes, in a patently offensive way, sexual conduct; and (3) the matter or performance, taken as a whole, lacks serious literary, artistic, political, or scientific value." The Indiana law also proscribes the production and distribution of obscene performances or materials, making either violation a class A misdemeanor or a class D felony if it involves "any person who is or appears to be under sixteen (16) years of age."

Personal Perversions. Other forms of sexual perversion are similarly prohibited under state law. These include necrophilia (the use of a dead body for sexual satisfaction); BESTIALITY (sexual relations with an animal); and possession of child pornography. Regarding the latter, in *Osborne v. Ohio* (1990), the U.S. Supreme Court held that such possession could be prohibited by law because of the government's interest in curbing exploitation of the children used in producing pornographic materials.

Related Offenses

Other crimes related to sexual activity can be identified. These include performing an abortion that is unlawful under state requirements, such as the need to provide a waiting period and to notify parents in the case of a minor; clandestinely viewing or taking pictures of someone in private, such as by a peeping Tom; harassing or discriminating against a person on the basis of sex or sexual orientation; and making obscene telephone calls. Sex offenses can involve related crimes, such as kidnapping, physical and mental injury, and negligently or intentionally infecting another person with AIDS-HIV or other SEXUALLY TRANSMITTED DISEASES. Another category of offense related to sexual behavior consists of crimes or civil wrongs committed in the course of performing medical procedures related to sexual matters, such as enhancement of breasts or sexual organs; prenatal care, childbirth, and postnatal care of patients; genetic or DNA testing; and transsexual therapy and surgery.

In addition to criminal prosecution of sex-related behavior, a civil remedy for wrongdoing under state tort law may be available to victims. Some states recognize the torts of "alienation of affection" (the deprivation of one spouse of the right to the aid, comfort, and society of the other) and "criminal conversation" (the seduction of another man's wife), which is analogous to the crime of adultery. In *Norton v. Macfarlane* (1991), the supreme court of Utah abolished criminal conversation, which was considered to be an actionable injury to the husband; the court reasoned that the offending act is a mutual one, but only one party is held liable. The decision let stand the tort of alienation of affection.

In regulating sexual behavior, the law attempts to find an acceptable balance in accordance with the Constitution and society's general level of acceptable morality at a given time. The harm that physical sexual behavior may cause, including mental harm, is real and can be scientifically and medically proven. Yet what one person may think is offensive or obscene, another may see as an example of personal freedom of expression. The "free love" morality advocated during the SEXUAL REVOLUTION stands at one end of a continuum and total government CENSORSHIP at the other.

As criminalized sex offenses are pared down, some people argue that all such acts except those that cause a direct injury to another—sexual assault or child molestation, for example—should be removed from our laws. The nature of some sex offenses, related as they are to the primal urge to procreate, makes them difficult to proscribe. If laws are perceived as arbitrary and unjust, they tend to be ignored and in time abandoned. As American social and moral attitudes change further, so undoubtedly will the laws regarding sexual behavior.

See also HOMOSEXUALITY; PRURIENT INTEREST; SEXUAL ENHANCEMENT; TELEPHONE SEX; VICTIMS' RIGHTS; VOYEURISM.

SEXISM

See DISCRIMINATION; EQUAL RIGHTS; WOMEN'S RIGHTS.

SEXUAL ABUSE

See CHILD ABUSE; DATE RAPE; DOMESTIC VIOLENCE; INCEST; RAPE; SEX OFFENSES; SEXUAL ASSAULT; SEXUAL HARASSMENT; VIOLENCE AGAINST WOMEN ACT.

SEXUAL ASSAULT

Forcing another person to have sexual relations or sexually injuring someone is generally a crime. Sexual assault is a subset of the more general category SEX OFFENSES and may refer to acts of RAPE, CHILD ABUSE, and INCEST, as well as SEXUAL HARASSMENT and INDECENT EXPOSURE. Indecent assault occurs when someone takes liberties short of sexual intercourse with another person against his or her will. An aggravated sexual assault is made with the intention of committing another crime such as rape, murder, or robbery and may increase the punishment for the underlying crime.

The legal definition of *assault* (from Old French and the Latin *assultus*, meaning to leap on or attack) is a threat to strike or to harm; *battery* is the legal term for actually causing the harm, but laws often blur the distinction. A sexual assault is defined under Arizona law as "intentionally or knowingly engaging in sexual intercourse or oral sexual contact with any person without consent of such person." In Florida sexual battery is characterized as "oral, anal, or vaginal penetration by, or union with, the sexual organ of another or ... [such] penetration of another by any other object; however, sexual battery does not include an act done for a bona fide medical purpose." Sexual assault laws are typically GENDER neutral, so either a male or a female may be charged with committing the crime against a female or a male. In addition to being a crime, assault in civil law is a tort for which private damages may be recovered.

According to the Rape, Abuse, and Incest National Network (800-656-HOPE), every two and one-half minutes somewhere in America someone is being sexually assaulted. In 2002 the U.S. Department of Justice identified 247,730 incidents of rape and sexual assault, of which 79,870 were sexual assaults. Sixty-seven percent of the assaults reported were made on juveniles under the age of eighteen years, and 34 percent of the victims were under twelve years. These Justice Department personal crime statistics are kept in four categories: forcible rape, forcible sodomy, sexual assault with an object, and forcible fondling.

Federal Law

Criminal statutes at the federal level relate to those areas of exclusive federal jurisdiction and occurrences in which states do not have exclusive jurisdiction, such as crimes that cross state lines and kidnapping. Sexual assault or its equivalent is referred to in several titles of the U.S. Code and elsewhere, examples of which are described below.

Under Title 18 of the U.S. Code, section 2242, Sexual Abuse, states: "Whoever, in the special maritime and territorial jurisdiction of the United States or in a Federal prison, knowingly—(1) causes another person to engage in a sexual act by threatening or placing that other person in fear ... or attempts to do so, shall be fined ... [and] imprisoned not more than 20 years, or both." Section 3559, Sentencing Classification of Offenses, provides: "(A) the term 'assault with intent to commit rape' means an offense that has as its elements engaging in physical contact with another person or using or brandishing a weapon against another person with intent to commit aggravated sexual abuse [including rape] or sexual abuse." Title 42, The Public Health and Welfare, chapter 46, notes that the crime of sexual assault emcompasses conduct that "includes both assaults committed by offenders who are strangers to the victim and assaults committed by offenders who are known or related by blood or marriage to the victim."

According to Federal Rule of Evidence 413, "In a criminal case in which the defendant is accused of an offense of sexual assault, evidence of the defendant's commission of another offense or offenses of sexual assault is admissible [at trial], and may be considered for its bearing on any matter to which it is relevant." The term *offense of sexual assault* includes "contact, without consent, between any part of the defendant's body or an object and the genitals or anus of another person," as well as "deriving sexual pleasure or gratification from the infliction of death, bodily injury, or physical pain on another person." Conspiring to commit the offense of sexual assault is also a crime. However, certain types of unwanted touching, such as of the knee or outer thigh, or sexually offensive conversation or telephone calls do not constitute behavior that would be admissible under the 413 rule.

Title 42, The Public Health and Welfare, chapter 46, authorizes grants by the attorney general of the United States "to increase the availability of legal assistance necessary to provide effective aid to victims of domestic violence, stalking, or sexual assault who are seeking relief in legal matters arising as a consequence of that abuse or violence, at minimal or no cost to the victims."

The U.S. Supreme Court has not had many opportunities to directly address sexual assault issues. *United States v. Lanier* (1997), involving a state judge found guilty of sexually assaulting five women, revolved around the issue of a perceived constitutional right "to be free from sexually motivated physical assaults and coerced sexual battery." The Court differed with a lower court's holding that a violation of this right depended on a factual situation that was "fundamentally similar" to Supreme Court precedents, saying that the only criterion was that the Court's precedent must give reasonable warning that the conduct in question violates constitutional rights.

But in *United States v. Morrison* (2000), the Supreme Court had a significant impact on sexual assaults against women. In its 5–4 decision, the Court struck down as unconstitutional a provision of the VIOLENCE AGAINST WOMEN ACT (1994) that permitted private lawsuits against anyone "who commits a crime of violence motivated by gender"; similar suits had been authorized by CONGRESS to enforce civil rights violations against minorities. Associate Justice David Souter, in his dissent, noted the irony of protecting the states from federal encroachment by vacating a law supported by the attorneys general of thirty-eight states, who cited the inadequacy of state resources to effectively handle the volume of sexual assault cases.

State Law

State constitutions do not for the most part directly address sexual assault. Hawaii's constitution, however, was amended in 2004 to give the legislature power to define certain sexual offenses, including sexual assault crimes, as well as to ensure the public's right to information on persons convicted of offenses against CHILDREN and certain types of sex offenses (as mandated by statutes modeled after MEGAN'S LAW).

All states have statutory criminal laws regarding sexual assault, if not always under the same terms. Iowa uses *sexual abuse* to mean sexual assault and defines it as a sex act between persons "done by force or against the will of the other." New York uses a number of terms related to sexual assault and sexual battery, including *forcible touching, sexual abuse, aggravated sexual abuse, persistent sexual abuse,* and *a course of sexual conduct against a child.*

South Carolina defines *sexual battery* as "sexual intercourse, cunnilingus, fellatio, anal intercourse, or any intrusion, however slight, of any part of a person's body or of any object into the genital or anal openings of another person's body, except when such intrusion is accomplished for medically recognized treatment or diagnostic purposes." The state also has a specific provision on spousal sexual battery, stating that when it is "accomplished through use of aggravated force" it can result in imprisonment of up to ten years. The law, however, requires that the "offending spouse's conduct must be reported to appropriate law enforcement authorities within thirty days."

In Florida the stepfather in an incest investigation was officially charged with familial sexual battery. Under Florida law, "A person 18 years of age or older who commits sexual battery upon, or in an attempt to commit sexual battery injures the sexual organs of, a person less than 12 years of age commits a capital felony." The same crime committed by a person under the age of eighteen years is eligible for life imprisonment.

Exactly which behavior constitutes sexual assault in its various forms has not always been easy to define. A Vermont court, in *State v. Murphy* (1970), opined that proof of specific intent is required in cases of assault with intent to murder, rape, or rob, but that no specific intent is required in the case of simple assault. In *State v. Warholic* (2004), a Connecticut court found that DNA from the victim and a smaller amount of male DNA on a sexual aid used in an attack constituted sufficient evidence to sustain a conviction for assault in the second degree. In the Pennsylvania case *Commonwealth v. Brown* (1992), an inmate who knew that he was HIV positive and could transmit the disease through bodily fluids was found guilty of simple assault for throwing fecal matter in a prison guard's face. But in *State v. Cabana* (1997), a New Jersey court ruled that offensive touching is not sufficiently serious to warrant criminal prosecution for simple assault when contact was incidental rather than stemming from an intent to assault the victim.

In *State v. Albert* (1998), Connecticut's appellate court held that digital penetration only between the folds of the labia majora without reaching into the vagina constitutes a finding of "vaginal sexual intercourse" that would support a conviction for first-degree sexual assault. The West Virginia supreme court, in *State v. Kearns* (2001), held that the prosecution's failure to disclose that the defendant had visited his estranged wife at her home a week before his alleged sexual assault and battery on her violated the defendant's right to due process, because the crux of the case was whether she had been forced to have sex against her will.

Special evidentiary exceptions are allowed in trials for sexual assault, including the introduction of evidence of prior similar sexual assaults. Some states recognize a "tender years" exception to the hearsay rule of evidence (typically barring information a person has been told but does not know personally) for children up to eleven years; the exception permits statements by a child or a developmentally challenged adult made to third parties that relate sexual or other types of abuse. Other exceptions include a "prompt outcry" made following an attack or a "fresh complaint" report made by a complainant at the earliest opportunity after an assault. Some states go further and admit the "first complaint" made even if it occurred at a time well after the alleged act. In *Commonwealth v. Montanez* (2003), a fifteen-year-old girl complained to a friend that her mother's live-in boyfriend had been sexually assaulting her since she was nine and one-half years old; a Massachusetts court found that the complaint, made only after the boyfriend moved out, was not admissible as a "fresh complaint" or a "tender years" exception but that it was admissible as evidence of her state of mind to explain why she delayed reporting the abuse.

Sexual assault—like DOMESTIC VIOLENCE, rape, and incest—often occurs in the context of the family or is committed by individuals who are known to the victim. Placing a person in fear and harming them in a sexual manner is treated as a serious crime. Such assaults may lead to harsh punishment as well as legal and social stigmas that accompany the perpetrator for life.

See also CONSENT; DATE RAPE; SEX OFFENDERS; TELEPHONE SEX.

SEXUAL DEVICES

See WILLIAMS V. MORGAN.

SEXUAL ENHANCEMENT

Cosmetic surgery procedures performed to better one's personal appearance or to enhance sexual attraction have increased in the United States from 7.4 million in 2000 to 9.2 million in 2004. A significant number of these operations involve some form of enhancement of the breasts (enlargement or reduction), sculpting of buttocks, or makeover of male or female genitals; breast augmentation procedures alone numbered 264,140 in the United States in 2004. In the case of transsexual conversions, restructuring of the sex organs takes place.

Because a number of these medical procedures are of recent origin, the law is undergoing some reevaluation as technology and treatment options expand. For the most part, governing laws are those that deal with the practice of medicine as well as psychological and physical therapy. Professional standards of practice apply to those responsible for providing such services in the medical fields of diagnostics, testing, surgery, and psychiatry. Except in egregious cases, doctors and other medical professionals are generally given wide latitude under the law.

A patient seeking to have any type of medical procedure, especially one involving surgery or other invasive procedure, will require a medical evaluation and preoperative care. Patients are evaluated for high risk and advised of measures that can be taken to deal with them. Informed CONSENT must be obtained from the patient before any treatment is begun. To cite one case, in *Bang v. Miller* (1958), a Minnesota court upheld a doctor's liability for failing to advise a patient that a prostate operation would result in STERILIZATION. Legal liability is also affected by professional ETHICS. In *Macy v. Blatchford* (2000), an Oregon court noted that although a physician may violate his ethical duty to maintain an objective state of mind by engaging in a sexual relationship with his patient, such a relationship does not of itself establish that a lack of objectivity resulted in the recommendation of additional surgery.

The increase in sexual enhancement surgery has led to a spurt of lawsuits for mistakes. The most recent high-profile legal problems relate to the use of silicone breast implants, which are alleged to cause medical problems. A single malpractice case can result in millions of dollars in liability; many states have set caps on the amount of recovery allowable to avoid stressing the medical system and producing large insurance losses. In class-action suits, the claims of a large number of similarly affected plaintiffs are aggregated for the purposes of trial—among them cases begun in the 1990s alleging harm from the silicone used in breast implants.

Breast Implants

Since Carol Doda, a popular topless dancer, had her breasts surgically enlarged in 1964, millions of women have undergone similar cosmetic surgery on their breasts without raising any legal problems. Concerns about breast implants began in the 1980s, however, when thousands of women claimed that the silicone implants leaked. Serious health problems tied by claimants to the implants include lupus, which affects the body's immune system and can result in infection, depression, kidney disease, and joint damage. As a result of the complaints and lawsuits based on recipients' illness, silicone breast implants were removed from the market in 1992; saline-filled implants were not affected. The Food and Drug Administration continued to allow silicone gel implants for mastectomy patients in medical experiments. In 2005 the FDA again recommended against allowing silicone breast implants back on the market.

The severity and extent of injuries linked to silicone breast implants were so great that federal legislation authorized the National Institutes of Health, an agency of the U.S. DEPARTMENT OF HEALTH AND HUMAN SERVICES, to "conduct or support research to examine the long-term health implications of silicone breast implants." In a 2001 letter supporting this move, the president of the NATIONAL ORGANIZATION FOR WOMEN, Kim Gandy, said that, in addition to health risks associated with breast implants, many women have suffered financial ruin as a result of debilitating health problems that prevented them from working. A National Academy of Sciences study in 1999 reported that although silicone implants could be responsible for localized problems such as hardening or scarring of breast tissue, evidence did not show that the implants caused major diseases such as lupus or rheumatoid arthritis.

One of the litigants was Charlotte Mahlum of Elko, Nevada, whose suit against the Dow Chemical Company alleged that one of her silicone implants had ruptured; about 10 percent of the gel could not be removed because it had become too embedded in her tissue. In 1995 she was awarded $4.1 million, but an additional $10 million in punitive damages set by the jury was struck down by the Nevada supreme court in 1998. To compensate tens of thousands of women claiming similar injury, a bankruptcy court in Michigan approved a $3.2 billion settlement in 1998 against the Dow Corning Company, the Dow Chemical subsidiary that actually made the implants. As a result, Dow Corning entered bankruptcy proceedings but emerged in 2004. Other companies that made the implants included Bristol-Myers Squibb and Bioplasty.

Genital Surgery

Today genital makeovers can be accomplished almost as easily as a house or wardrobe makeover. The *Wall Street Journal* noted in 2005 that one of the fastest growing medical operations is cosmetic vaginal surgery. Surgery has been performed on male sex organs for a long time to counteract erectile dysfunction (the inability to get or maintain an erection), to enlarge the penis, or to reattach a severed organ, as was done after Lorena Bobbitt cut off her husband's penis in 1993. Although there is a low risk of complications with such procedures, failure to properly perform the procedure may bring a lawsuit for damages to compensate for painful scarring or nerve damage.

Sex-Reassignment Surgery

In 1952 Christine Jorgensen, formerly George William Jorgensen Jr., became a celebrity as one of the first Americans to have sex-reassignment surgery, which was carried out in Denmark. In the ensuing half century, many people with GENDER dysphoria (gender-identity disorder) have been surgically transgendered, generally going from a male to a female. The reassignment surgery cannot actually create a transgender man who can reproduce or a woman capable of conceiving children.

The law has had difficulty dealing with the rights of transsexual or transgender persons. Dr. Rene Richards, a transsexual tennis professional, brought suit against the United States Tennis Association because she was denied the right after sex-reassignment surgery to play in the women's division. In *Richards v. United States Tennis Association* (1977), a New York court sided with Richards, at least to the point of ruling that a test used to weed out men masquerading as women was not applicable in this case, where there was no attempt to masquerade as anything other than what she had become through a laborious process of therapy and surgery. Karen Ulane, a former male who was a pilot for Eastern Airlines, was fired as a result of her sex-reassignment surgery. A federal court, in *Ulane v. Eastern Airlines* (1984), upheld the adverse personnel action, concluding that the term *sex* as used in Title VII of the Civil Rights Act of 1964, the federal antidiscrimination law, means only a person's sex at birth. It thus held that Title VII does not prohibit DISCRIMINATION against transsexuals; Ulane's appeal was denied by the U.S. Supreme Court in 1985.

Psychological Treatment

Sex therapy is treatment for various sexual difficulties, including impotence, frigidity, or painful intercourse. Most states regulate the practice of psychology; for example, Nevada requires psychologists to be licensed, and the law provides grounds for denying, suspending, or revoking such licenses. A few states such as Florida, however, actually regulate the practice of sex therapy. Florida law provides: "Only a person licensed [and] who meets the qualifications set ... may hold himself or herself out as a sex therapist." The qualifications "may refer to the sexual disorder and sexual dysfunction sections of the most current edition of the Diagnostic and Statistical Manual of the American Psychiatric Association or other relevant publications."

In many instances, sexual dysfunction or gender dysphoria may be treated with forms of psychotherapy or DRUGS. As a prelude to sex-reassignment surgery,

patients undergo therapy, including hormones and other drugs to bring their bodies into a state more like that of their new sexual configuration. In *Jane Doe v. Boeing Co.* (1993), the supreme court of Washington held that an employee with gender dysphoria undergoing a year-long procedure, dressing and acting like a woman preparatory to sex-reassignment surgery, could not dress other than as a male at work or use the women's restroom until after the surgery. But in *Doe v. Bell* (2003), a New York court noted, "Research has found that forcing youths with GID to dress in conflict with their [sexual] identity ... causes significant anxiety, psychological harm, and antisocial behavior." Therefore, the court reasoned, "Jane Doe" could be treated as an exception and allowed to dress as a girl in a foster-care facility for boys.

Contact: Society for Sex Therapy and Research, 409 12th Street, SW, Washington, DC 20090 (202-683-1644). www.sstarnet.org.

See also BIOETHICS; HOMOSEXUALITY; TRANSSEXUALISM.

SEXUAL EXPLOITATION

See CHILD ABUSE; CHILDREN; SEX OFFENSES.

SEXUAL HARASSMENT

Men and women, at least biologically, are not the same. The survival of the species is predicated on male-female attraction and sexual reproduction. Some forms of assertive sexual behavior that promote mating and reproduction are obviously acceptable, among them flirting, dating, and consensual sexual relations. But in settings such as the workplace and the classroom, how far is too far when it comes to sexual behavior? Sexual harassment includes unwanted and illegal sexual advances, crude comments, improper touching, demands for sex in return for favorable treatment, and other forms of threatening and discriminatory

State Laws Prohibiting Sexual Harassment in the Workplace

Alabama. Courts allow suits based on invasion of an employee's right to privacy.

Alaska. Laws cover employers with fifteen or more employees and require employers to post a notice prepared by the state's human rights commission.

California. Statute permits employers to be sued and requires that employers take action to ensure a workplace free of sexual harassment.

Colorado. Statute prohibits sexual harassment in the workplace.

Connecticut. Law requires anti-sexual-harassment training for employers with more than fifty employees and posting of an anti-sexual-harassment notice in the workplace by employers with two or more employees.

Delaware. Statute covers sexual harassment and requires posting of anti-sexual-harassment provisions and an explanation of how to file a complaint.

Hawaii. Statute covers sexual harassment and requires employers to affirmatively raise the issue, express disapproval, and take steps to prevent it.

Idaho. Statute covers sexual harassment.

Illinois. Statute covers sexual harassment.

Maine. Statute covers sexual harassment and requires employers to provide employees an annual notice that sexual harassment is illegal.

Massachusetts. Statutes cover employers with six or more employees, mandate annual written notice to employees, and require that steps be taken to prevent sexual harassment.

Minnesota. Statute demands that employers include a non-harassment policy in their conditions of employment and take timely and appropriate action if it occurs.

Missouri. Statute covers sexual harassment.

New Hampshire. Statute covers sexual harassment.

North Dakota. Statute covers sexual harassment and imposes responsibility on employers to be aware of any harassment and take timely and appropriate action.

Pennsylvania. Statute covers sexual harassment.

Rhode Island. Statute covers employers of fifty or more.

Vermont. Statute requires that employers adopt an anti-sexual-harassment policy.

Washington. The state's unfair labor practices law has been interpreted to include sexual harassment.

West Virginia. Statute covers sexual harassment.

Wisconsin. Statute covers sexual harassment.

Source: "Sexual Harassment in the Workplace," www.sexual harassmentpolicy.com. © 2005 Employers Publications LLC

behavior. The practice generally refers to adult or adolescent behavior and not to actions caused by or affecting CHILDREN, and it may also involve discrimination on the basis of sexual orientation or even by women against men. The goal of sexual harassment is to intimidate and otherwise attempt to make another person uncomfortable simply because of a difference that does no one any direct harm.

Social constraints, religious prohibitions, and laws against SEXUAL ASSAULT and RAPE have been used as countervailing forces to various types of harassment. Unfortunately these measures do not always work, even in a modern society that guarantees EQUAL RIGHTS for all citizens. In 2005, for example, a New Hampshire judge resigned his position after being suspended for groping five women at a conference on sexual assault and DOMESTIC VIOLENCE. A judicial conduct committee found that such acts "demeaned his judicial office and cast reasonable doubt in the eyes of the public on his continuing capacity to act in an impartial manner." The judge resigned after pleading no contest to simple assault, reduced from a charge of sexual assault.

The movement for equal rights and equal pay for women has led to the enactment of federal and state laws that prohibit DISCRIMINATION and harassment against women in the workplace and in educational settings, including in sports activities.

Federal Law

It has been difficult for federal courts to find a basis solely in the U.S. Constitution for protecting against sexual harassment in the workplace and educational institutions. While the equal protection clause of the Fourteenth Amendment (1868) and the due process clause of the Fifth Amendment (1791) were used by the Supreme Court in cases such as *Reed v. Reed* (1971) and *FRONTIERO V. RICHARDSON* (1973) to declare unconstitutional state and federal laws that discriminated on the basis of sex, discrimination in the private sector has not been as easy to protect against. The Equal Rights Amendment that CONGRESS sent to the states in 1972 was not ratified by the ten-year deadline, but many of the amendment's aims, including protection for women—and in some cases men—against sexual harassment, have been obtained through legislation and court interpretations of existing laws.

Workplace Harassment. Sexual harassment against employees and business associates has existed since women entered the workforce. Even before the failed Equal Rights Amendment was drafted, Congress acted to extend some protection against workplace harassment by passing Title VII of the Civil Rights Act of 1964. Under the act, sexual harassment is defined as follows:

Unwelcome sexual advances, requests for sexual favors, and other verbal or physical conduct of a sexual nature constitute sexual harassment when (1) submission to such conduct is made either explicitly or implicitly a term or condition of employment, (2) submission to or rejection of such conduct by an individual is used as the basis for employment decisions that affect such individual, or (3) such conduct has the purpose or effect of unreasonably interfering with an individual's work performance or creating an intimidating, hostile or offensive working environment.

The Equal Employment Opportunity Commission's compliance manual, quoting a federal appeals court decision in *Henson v. City of Dundee* (1982), ex-

plains that "the challenged conduct must be unwelcome, 'in the sense that the employee did not solicit or incite it, and in the sense that the employee regarded the conduct as undesirable or offensive.'"

In some early cases brought under Title VII, courts still had reservations about its intent. In a 1974 decision, a court held that discrimination against a woman that involved a sexual affair with her supervisor did not occur because of her sex, but because of an "inharmonious personal relationship with him." Another decision held shortly thereafter that sexual demands are not prohibited by Title VII because "the attraction of males to females and females to males is a natural sex phenomenon and it is probable that this attraction plays at least a subtle role in most personnel decisions." But these opinions are no longer valid.

Today two categories of sexual harassment are recognized under federal law: (1) the quid pro quo (something for something); and (2) the creation of a hostile environment. The former refers to situations in which someone who has authority over another solicits or demands sexual favors in return for giving favorable treatment or withholding adverse actions. The latter form encompasses prohibited behavior by coworkers or those in authority that threatens or offends because of the victim's sex.

By 1982 federal courts were holding that where a male supervisor solicits sex from a female employee, it "will therefore be a simple matter for the plaintiff to prove that, but for her sex, she would not have been subjected to sexual harassment." In 1986 the U.S. Supreme Court, in *Meritor Savings Bank v. Vinson*, held that Title VII protected individuals from discrimination in the workplace based on intimidation, ridicule, and harassment, including requests for sexual favors and unwelcome sexual advances. *Meritor* confirmed the Equal Employment Opportunity Commission's definitions of quid pro quo and "hostile environment" harassment.

The line between flirting, joking, and sexual harassment may at times be a fine one, but in many successful actions the behavior was egregious and clearly beyond any subtlety. In *Burns v. McGregor Electronic Industries, Inc.* (1992), a federal appeals court found that to a reasonable person the harassing conduct complained of was "sufficiently severe or pervasive to alter the conditions of employment and create an abusive work environment." The complaining female employee alleged that the owner of the company showed her "advertisements for pornographic films in *Penthouse* magazine, talked about sex, asked her to watch pornographic movies with him, ... made lewd gestures, such as ones imitating masturbation, ... continued to ask for dates and wanted to engage in oral sex so she would 'be able to perform [her] work better.'" The owner was quoted as saying: "I'm tired of your fooling around and always turning me down. You must not need your job very bad."

The two cases entitled *Jenson v. Eveleth Taconite Co.* (1991, 1993) marked an important step in the struggle for legal protection against sexual harassment in the workplace. Although several federal courts had dealt with the question of class-action suits for discrimination as early as 1988, *Jenson I* is acknowledged as the first case to find defendants liable to a class (a group of complainants similarly situated) for extensive sexual harassment. Being able to bring a class-action suit provides stronger clout than if many individuals had to fight the same battle alone. The *Jenson* cases lasted some fifteen years, during which the victims' numerous attempts to settle the matter were rebuffed by Eveleth's lawyers.

In *Jenson II*, a federal district court concluded that to establish a pattern of discrimination based on a claim of sexual harassment in a class-action suit, the plaintiffs must show that they belong to the protected group; they were subjected to unwelcome sexual harassment; the harassment was based on their sex; the treatment altered the terms, conditions, or privileges of employment for reasonable women; and the employer knew or should have known of the harassment and failed to take proper remedial action. In 1998, just before a new trial was to begin, fifteen women settled for a total of $3.5 million to end a complaint filed fourteen years earlier.

In 1998 the Supreme Court revisited sexual harassment in two important cases: BURLINGTON INDUSTRIES, INC. V. ELLERTH and *Faragher v. City of Boca Raton*. Twelve years earlier in *Meritor Savings Bank,* the Court's majority opinion had admitted that the "debate over the appropriate standard for employer liability has a rather abstract quality about it." Arguments arose over the extent to which an employer can be held liable for sexual harassment involving its employees, depending on notice of the acts, company policy, mechanisms for reporting internally, and so forth.

In *Burlington,* the Court dealt with a case of quid pro quo sexual harassment, while *Faragher* was based on the creation of a hostile work environment for women. In both cases, however, the violator was a supervisor. The Court declared that in such cases where the result is tangibly adverse to the victim, the employer is vicariously liable regardless of any defense that might be presented. This ruling draws on principles of agency law, under which an employer can be held responsible for an employee's actions.

The communications revolution has introduced a new form of sexual harassment: by e-mail. A number of well-known companies—including the Xerox Corporation, *New York Times,* and Dow Chemical Company—have terminated employees for inappropriate use of e-mail and the INTERNET. These firings resulted from employees' using e-mail to send sexually explicit messages and pornographic materials. In one court case, the many occasions on which a coworker exposed women to PORNOGRAPHY that he had downloaded onto their computers persuaded the court that the employer should have known about the harassment and was therefore liable for it.

Remedies for violations of sexual harassment laws vary widely. They may include injunctive relief requiring that an offender take or refrain from some action or ordering an employer to enforce antiharassment policies and restore a victim to a previous position. Monetary damages for lost wages or promotions may also be awarded. If a court finds that the harassment included the crime of sexual assault or sexual battery, punishment may include a fine and imprisonment.

Harassment Based on Sexual Orientation. Court rulings have also evolved with respect to sexual harassment based on sexual orientation. A federal court of appeals stated in *Dillion v. Frank* (1992) that alleged harassing actions toward the victim because of his assumed HOMOSEXUALITY, "although cruel, are not made illegal by Title VII." But in 1998 the Supreme Court, in *Oncale v. Sundowner Offshore Services, Inc.*, held that because "Title VII prohibits 'discriminat[ion] ... because of ... sex' in the 'terms' or 'conditions' of employment ... , this includes ... sexual harassment of any kind that meets the statutory requirements." The Court concluded that "sex discrimination consisting of same-sex sexual harassment is actionable under Title VII." In a later federal case, *Rene v. MGM Grand Hotel, Inc.* (2002), the victim was harassed by being "repeatedly grabbed in the crotch and poked in the anus, and ... singled out from his other male co-workers for this treatment." The court in this case commented that the victim "was treated differently—and disadvantageously—based on sex. This is precisely what Title VII forbids: 'discriminat[ion] ... because of ... sex.'"

Harassment in Education. Sexual harassment in educational settings may take several forms: by a teacher or another adult in authority over a student; by peers, or fellow students; and based on sexual orientation. Such behavior can be a violation of Title VII as well as of TITLE IX of the Education Amendments of 1972, which was enacted by Congress to address sexual discrimination in educational institutions that receive federal funding, including for sports programs. In *Franklin v. Gwinnett County Public Schools* (1992), the Supreme Court held that sexual harassment is included in "discrimination on the basis of sex" under Title IX. Federal courts have also recognized peer harassment of homosexuals as actionable under Title IX. Damages can include monetary awards from any school involved and in egregious cases may include punitive damages.

Various other avenues of redress have been recognized. In *Nabozny v. Podlesny* (1996), a federal appeals court found that continual assaults on a student because of his sexual orientation violated his right to equal protection under the Constitution. In a case of peer harassment, *Davis v. Monroe County Board of Education* (1999), the Supreme Court held that a federally funded school can be held liable under Title IX if school officials knew or reasonably should have known about the harassment and failed to remedy it. Another applicable federal law is Title 42, The Public Health and Welfare, chapter 21, Civil Rights, section 1983, of the U.S. Code. This section makes "[e]very person who, under color of any statute, ordinance, regulation, custom, or usage ... causes [anyone] to be subjected ... to the deprivation of any rights, privileges, or immunities secured by the Constitution and laws" liable for such acts.

State Law

State constitutional and statutory law regarding sexual harassment in the workplace and education varies widely. States such as New Hampshire, North Dakota, Pennsylvania, Rhode Island, West Virginia, and Wisconsin have statutes specifically prohibiting sexual harassment, whereas others include it in broader antidiscrimination laws. Connecticut, for one, requires sexual harassment training for employers of fifty or more persons but demands that employers of even two persons post a notice.

Workplace Harassment. The supreme court of California, in *Rojo v. Kliger* (1990), acknowledged a common law right to challenge a wrongful discharge from employment on the basis of sexual harassment; it ruled that a state civil rights act did not abrogate common law claims for discrimination in employment; that an employee did not have to exhaust administrative remedies under the civil rights law before seeking judicial relief; and that the state's public policy supported a lawsuit for wrongful termination by a private employer who violated that policy. Citing *Rojo*, a Maryland court, in *Watson v. Peoples Security Life Insurance Co.* (1991), found that under a state constitutional provision ensuring equality of the sexes, public policy supported a right of action against a private employer for sex-based discrimination, including sexual harassment.

A case in Vermont, *In re Towle* (1995), relied on the traditional legal principles of the "master and servant"; this term describes the relationship involved in a personal services contract between two parties. The court here concluded that having sex on the job, in this case nonconsensual, is an activity that employees should know is prohibited by employers. Employees thus are held to have implicit notice of the prohibited behavior, which in this instance resulted in termination of employment.

Harassment in Education. Minnesota has enacted a law that requires educational institutions to have written policies for sexual harassment outlining disciplinary action to be taken for violations; the state legislature has appropriated money to teach students from kindergarten to twelfth grade about preventing violence such as sexual harassment and sexual assault. Washington State has a law that requires post-secondary schools to develop and distribute policies and procedures for handling complaints of sexual harassment. South Dakota requires its board of higher education to develop rules and guidelines to eliminate GENDER discrimination against students, including sexual harassment.

In seeking relief for harassment by a teacher under state law, students or someone on their behalf can file a tort claim against the adult offender as well as school boards. Such claims often include allegations of a breach of fiduciary duty, intentional infliction of emotional distress, and negligent supervision. Another type of claim that can be brought in state courts is a common law tort claim against the offenders. These claims can be based on negligence, including the negligent infliction of emotional distress. In some cases, however, a school board may be accorded absolute sovereign immunity from liability for such claims under state law.

Harassment Based on Sexual Orientation. With respect to peer harassment of sexual minorities, state and local remedies may be more effective because of the reluctance of some federal courts to read into Title IX a clear protection against harassment on the basis of sexual orientation. Even in its decision under Title VII in *Oncale v. Sundowner Offshore Services*, the Supreme Court was reluctant to find that acts of harassment—men placing their penises on the victim's body and forcing a bar of soap up his rectum (which the Court would not even describe in the decision)—constituted an actionable sexual harassment claim by a homosexual man under the language of the act, that the harassing discrimination must be "because of . . . sex." Connecticut, Massachusetts, Minnesota, Vermont, and Wisconsin are among a number of states that have adopted laws extending protection to students who are harassed because of their actual or perceived homosexuality.

Contact: www.sexualharassmentsupport.org.

See also Bisexuality; Feminism; Sex Offenses; Transsexualism; Transvestism; Women's Rights.

SEXUAL MINORITIES

See Bisexuality; Discrimination; Homosexuality; Sexual Harassment; Transsexualism; Transvestism.

SEXUAL ORIENTATION

See Discrimination; Gender; Homosexuality; Sexual Harassment; Transsexualism; Transvestism.

SEXUAL REVOLUTION

The sexual revolution talked about today began in the early 1960s, around the time that the oral contraceptive known as the Pill became available. This revolution did not spring into existence full blown but came after a long period of social, political, and economic change in America and the rest of the Western world. Perhaps it was a matter of basic instincts catching up with the modern age. As Dr. David Reuben wrote in his immensely popular book *Everything You Always Wanted to Know About Sex—But Were Afraid to Ask* (1969):

"As a psychiatrist I am constantly impressed with one outstanding paradox presented to me constantly. In virtually every patient, I see a person living in the Space Age who has left his (or her) sexual organs in the Stone Age."

The sexual revolution was near its apogee when Reuben's book was published. It joined the company of other books such as *Sex and the Single Girl* (1962), by Helen Gurley Brown; *The Way to Become the Sensuous Woman* (1969), by Joan Garrity; and *Our Bodies, Ourselves*, first published as *Women and Their Bodies* in 1970 by the Boston Women's Health Collective. Other groundbreaking works about human sexuality preceding Reuben's book included *What Every Girl Should Know* (1920), by MARGARET SANGER; *Sexual Behavior in the Human Male* (1948) and *Sexual Behavior in the Human Female* (1953), both by ALFRED KINSEY; and *Human Sexual Response* (1966), by William H. Masters and Virginia E. Johnson. As society's sexual morality changed, many laws and interpretations of existing laws affecting sexual behavior would also change.

Rise of the Counterculture

America's sexual revolution had its roots in events that began in the first quarter of the twentieth century and lasted until the end of World War II in 1945. These included the decades-long struggle to enable women to vote and hold elective office, finally guaranteed by the Nineteenth Amendment (1920) to the U.S. Constitution; the Roaring Twenties, which ushered in economic excesses as well as flappers with reduced sexual inhibitions; and the national recognition of female celebrities, including the movie actress Mae West, singer Sophie Tucker, and exotic dancers Gypsy Rose Lee and Sally Rand. The Victorian era had been replaced with a newfound expression of feminine sexuality—exposed for many, if not all, to see.

World War II, which began in 1939, added to the impetus for women's liberation when many of them took jobs in the workforce that men had held before going off to war. A nascent national pride in women working in traditionally male jobs—like the icon Rosie the Riveter—liberalized their aspirations to be more than just stay-at-home moms. The civil rights movement in the 1960s, which was sparked by the U.S. Supreme Court's school-desegregation decision in *Brown v. Board of Education of Topeka* (1954), raised the consciousness of many women and supporters of WOMEN'S RIGHTS as they saw DISCRIMINATION against blacks being addressed by national and state lawmakers and courts.

The counterculture movement that grew out of the anti-Vietnam War protests in the 1960s and 1970s fed into the new desire for sexual rights and freedoms. "Free love" was proclaimed and communal living was revived as alternatives to the strict morality and model nuclear family of previous generations. Sex and DRUGS became the counterculture's linchpins, making hippies and the sexual revolution symbols of liberation for some and a threat to the American way of life for others. Throughout this era, laws regarding many aspects of sexual behavior—from MARRIAGE and DIVORCE to PORNOGRAPHY and promiscuity—were reshaped to accommodate the more diverse ways in which Americans viewed sex.

The Federal Response

Like the chicken and the egg, in some ways it is not possible to determine which came first: the sexual revolution or the law's response, especially the federal courts' interpretations of the law. For example, with respect to OBSCENITY, a federal judge in 1913 expressed doubt about the correctness of suppressing a work based on its ideas given guarantees of free speech in the FIRST AMENDMENT (1791). A year later, however, Margaret Sanger was indicted for writing "obscene" articles about CONTRACEPTION.

By the 1950s freedom of sexual expression was becoming a political concern. In 1955 a U.S. Senate subcommittee held a hearing on the relationship between pornography and juvenile delinquency. A year later, a poem by the Beat poet Allen Ginsberg (1926–97) was denounced as obscene, and the pelvic gyrations of an up-and-coming rock-and-roll singer, Elvis Presley (1935–77), were kept off-camera during a nationally televised show. Obscenity was becoming a hot item.

In *Roth v. United States* (1957), the Supreme Court finally tackled the problem of defining obscenity in order to draw a line between what is and what is not protected under the First Amendment. The Court has been consistent in declaring that obscene expressions or materials are not protected by the First Amendment. But what is "obscene?" The Court in *Roth* found basically that the context makes material obscene. Would the average person, applying contemporary community standards, as its test goes, find that the work or material, taken as a whole, appeals to the PRURIENT INTEREST, and is it utterly without any redeeming social importance?

In decisions in subsequent cases—such as *Jacobellis v. Ohio* (1964), *A Book Named "John Cleland's Memoirs of a Woman of Pleasure" v. Attorney General of Massachusetts* (1966), *Ginzburg v. United States* (1966), and *Miller v. California* (1973)—the Supreme Court refined its definition of obscenity. For the most part, as far as adults are concerned (the Supreme Court treats obscenity involving CHILDREN as a separate and essentially unprotected subject), obscenity could be equated with hard-core pornography for obscenity's sake alone.

The years 1972 and 1973 were pivotal ones in the sexual revolution. The Equal Rights Amendment, which would have implanted the equality of men and women in the Constitution, was passed by CONGRESS in 1972 and sent to the states for ratification. It would fail by a small margin in the ten years provided for ratification, but in its wake federal lawmakers and the courts began to expand women's rights. That same year, the FEDERAL COMMUNICATIONS COMMISSION approved community-access television channels on which some cities began allowing pornography to be shown. The following year the Public Broadcasting System aired a show entitled *Steambath*, in which, for the first time on broadcast television, a young actress, Valerie Perrine, exposed her breasts. The end of the military draft was announced at the same time, taking the impetus from the youth-led cultural revolution that had helped drive the sexual revolution.

Federal laws regarding actual—as opposed to representational—sexual behavior did not change much.

Sex crimes and public indecency remained on the books, and the courts did little to liberalize laws at the federal or state levels. Discrimination on the basis of sex, particularly against women in education and in the workplace, were an exception. Congress passed Title VII of the Civil Rights Act of 1964 and TITLE IX of the Education Amendments of 1972; the former prohibits sexual discrimination in the workplace, while the latter bars it in educational settings.

The rights to use contraceptives and to obtain an ABORTION, both of which were subjected to state prohibitions, were further exceptions. *Griswold v. Connecticut* (1965) and *Eisenstadt v. Baird* (1972) extended the constitutional right of PRIVACY to protect the use of contraception first by married couples and then by unmarried couples. Abortion, with some limitations, was also found by the Supreme Court in *Roe v. Wade* (1973) to be protected by the right of privacy—a still intensely controversial decision that some Supreme Court justices and political and religious leaders believe should be overruled.

As for the rights of sexual minorities, after decades of discriminating against homosexuals in the U.S. government, the Civil Service Commission revised its policies in 1975; and in 1998, by Executive Order 11478, President Bill Clinton added sexual orientation to the list of classifications, along with categories such as race and national origin, that were to be protected from discrimination in federal employment. Discrimination remains institutionalized in the MILITARY, however, under the "don't ask, don't tell" policy regulating the treatment of homosexuals in the armed services. In 2003, however, the Supreme Court in *Lawrence v. Texas* ruled that intimate homosexual behavior between consenting adults in private is protected by the right of privacy found in the Constitution.

Lawrence may represent the limit of the sexual revolution as far as the expansion of rights is concerned, at least for the foreseeable future. The pendulum of tolerance for rights related to sexual behavior seems to be heading backwards. If confirmation hearings on nominees to the Supreme Court in 2005 and 2006 are any bellwether, abortion rights are seriously under attack from conservative religious and political sectors. Efforts, many of them successful, to amend state constitutions to preclude homosexuals from marrying indicate that certain citizens oppose any further expansion of rights for homosexuals.

State Laboratories of Democracy

Despite the growing sexual revolution, the states generally lagged behind the federal government. Today Massachusetts is considered one of the more legally progressive states regarding sexual behavior, but in 1930 it banned Theodore Dreiser's *An American Tragedy* (1925) and D. H. Lawrence's *Lady Chatterley's Lover* (1928) as obscene books. New York City stopped public burnings of pornography in 1941 only when critics noted a parallel to Nazi book burning. Nonetheless, besting the federal government, several states—including California, Massachusetts, and Washington—added EQUAL RIGHTS language to their state constitutions in the 1970s, and most states adopted constitutional or statutory provisions prohibiting discrimination based on sex. As of 2005 only six states did not have some type of law against sexual discrimination.

Various other laws involving adult consensual sexual behavior were amended, reinterpreted by the courts, or relaxed at the enforcement level—for example, those relating to ADULTERY and fornication, UNMARRIED COHABITANTS, and PREMARITAL SEX. State obscenity and pornography laws were relaxed in accordance with Supreme Court decisions. DIVORCE laws generally mutated to feature no-fault options, with any reasonable private allocation of rights and obligations agreed to by the parties approved by the courts. Additional changes included a new willingness to incorporate SEX EDUCATION into the public school curriculum and to permit the operation of abortion clinics and more SEXUALLY ORIENTED BUSINESSES.

The new line in the legal sand has been drawn between the private rights of adult citizens to deal with their own sexual behavior without government interference and the public sphere, which is still highly regulated but not devoid of adult sexual activity, such as nude dancing, erotic bookstores, and adult movie theaters. Cable and satellite television, videos and DVDs, and the INTERNET have all opened up new avenues for adult sexual material.

There is probably no precise date when the sexual revolution will end, but the Supreme Court's decision in *Lawrence v. Texas* could represent the end of the line for the time being. A counterrevolution has already begun in the form of a return to the enforcement of religious morality through laws and government activities. Current federal government policies have been directed at limiting student sex education to instruction in ABSTINENCE until marriage, minutely restricting and perhaps withdrawing constitutional protection for abortion, and rejecting feminist goals such as equal rights for men and women and unfettered reproductive choice for women. The new wave of federal and state laws aimed at protecting marriage from homosexuals may be a manifestation of a deeper, more general concern by some citizens that the sexual revolution has gone too far.

See also ADULT MATERIALS; FEMINISM; HOMOSEXUALITY; LEWD BEHAVIOR; REPRODUCTIVE RIGHTS; SAME-SEX MARRIAGE; SEX OFFENSES.

SEXUAL SLAVERY

See HUMAN TRAFFICKING.

SEXUALITY INFORMATION AND EDUCATION COUNCIL OF THE UNITED STATES

Together with a lawyer, a sociologist, a family-life educator, a clergyman, and a public health educator, Dr. MARY S. CALDERONE founded the Sexuality Information and Education Council of the United States in 1964. SIECUS works to promote sound public policy and laws on issues related to sexuality and provides guidance on topics such as SEX EDUCATION, sexuality and RELIGION, sexuality and the MEDIA, sexually explicit materials, sexual orientation, GENDER equality, sexual exploitation, female genital mutilation, sexuality and aging, sexuality of persons with disabilities, masturbation, sexual health care, adolescent sexual health, adolescent contraceptive use, ABORTION, and AIDS-HIV. It also maintains the Mary S. Calderone Library, which includes more than five thousand volumes and a database exceeding twenty thousand citations to books, curricula, journal articles, and reports.

SIECUS, which was named the Sex Information and Education Council of the United States until 1998, takes an interdisciplinary approach to human sexual behavior. Recognizing individuals' different beliefs, values, knowledge, and behavioral traits, the organization draws on the science of anatomy and physiology and the biochemistry of the sexual response system to develop information about human sexuality. Its work looks at the context of traditional influences on sexuality, such as ethical and cultural concerns.

Sex and sexuality education are viewed by SIECUS as a lifelong process. Information can be inconsistent, conflicting, inaccurate, and incomplete given the various possible sources of information—parents, other family members, peers, partners, schools, religion, and the media. The organization thus promotes comprehensive, school-based sex education that is appropriate to a student's age, development level, and cultural background, along with training in human sexuality for teachers from prekindergarten through the twelfth grade. One of its media outreach programs underlines the inadequacies of ABSTINENCE-education programs.

SIECUS has taken clear positions on key issues. It promotes the civil rights of all people, regardless of sexual orientation. With respect to EQUAL RIGHTS, the organization contends that every woman, regardless of age or income, should have the right to a safe, legal, confidential abortion under dignified conditions and at a reasonable cost. As to religion, it supports church involvement in sex education, the sexual health of church members, and tolerance of

alternative forms of sexuality expressed by gays, lesbians, and bisexuals. The council promotes responsible and sensitive portrayals of sexuality in the media, without exploitation, gratuitous sexual violence, and dehumanizing sexual material. SIECUS believes that adults should have access to sexually explicit materials for personal use but that minors should be legally protected from all forms of sexual exploitation. It further promotes the idea that all sexual relationships should be consensual between partners who are developmentally, physically, and emotionally mature.

Other areas on which the council provides information include female genital mutilation, which it considers a violation of the human body and a threat to the physical and psychological well-being of women and girls; the sexuality of older persons; and the sexuality of persons with disabilities, including the provision of information for caregivers. In addition, SIECUS provides information on masturbation, sexual health care, and CONTRACEPTION for adolescents. It believes that AIDS-HIV requires strong government, private, and joint efforts to promote the prevention, treatment, and understanding of this major national and world health problem. SIECUS also joins with organizations to support technical assistance, training, and sex education in other countries.

Contact: Sexuality Information and Education Council of the United States, 130 West 42nd Street, Suite 350, New York, NY 10036-7802 (212-819-9770). www.siecus.org.

SEXUALLY ORIENTED BUSINESSES

The advertising maxim that "sex sells" is true in more ways than one. Throughout history sexual activity and sex-related services and products have been bartered and sold. In the United States today, the term *sexually oriented businesses,* however, generally refers to public commerce in so-called ADULT MATERIALS and services that are legal but subject to a certain amount of government regulation in addition to what other businesses receive. Sexually oriented businesses include adult bookstores, adult live entertainment activities such as nude dancing and sex clubs, adult movie theaters, and sales outlets for sexual devices and marital aids. PROSTITUTION, which is often considered a form of sexually oriented business, is illegal in all jurisdictions of the United States, except for some counties in Nevada.

Laws regarding adult businesses for the most part define such businesses, require special licenses, and restrict their operations, particularly with respect to their location in a community. According to the California code, for instance, the "legislative body of any county or city may regulate, pursuant to a content neutral ordinance, the time, place, and manner of operation of sexually oriented businesses, when the ordinance is designed to serve a substantial governmental interest, does not unreasonably limit alternative avenues of communication, and is based on narrow, objective, and definite standards"; lawmakers, adds the code, may consider "the harmful secondary effects that the business may have on the community and its proximity to churches, schools, residences, establishments dispensing alcohol, and other sexually oriented businesses."

Defining Adult Businesses

In a number of cases beginning with *ROTH V. UNITED STATES* (1957), the U.S. Supreme Court has worked at defining what is and what is not obscene. According to the Supreme Court, OBSCENITY has no protection under the FIRST AMENDMENT (1791) to the U.S. Constitution, but adult materials and adult businesses that are not obscene do have some constitutional protections. In *Young v. American Mini Theatres, Inc.* (1976), the Court made it clear that the First Amendment protects sexually explicit material and entertainment that is not obscene. The government has the right to impose reasonable restrictions on sexually oriented businesses to further legitimate goals, such as reducing the potential for crime or protecting public morals.

For the most part, regulation of adult-oriented businesses is a matter of state law. Texas, for one,

The U.S. Supreme Court has ruled that state and local governments can treat sexually oriented or adult businesses more strictly than other businesses through zoning and commercial regulation. Some approved restrictions include where such businesses can be located and the manner in which they are allowed to advertise.

defines sexually oriented businesses to mean "a sex parlor, nude studio, modeling studio, love parlor, adult bookstore, adult movie theater, adult video arcade, adult movie arcade, adult video store, adult motel, or other commercial enterprise the primary business of which is the offering of a service or the selling, renting, or exhibiting of devices or any other items intended to provide sexual stimulation or sexual gratification to the customer." Texas law also authorizes counties and municipalities to regulate such businesses. For purposes of the California law quoted above, a sexually oriented business is defined as "one whose primary purpose is the sale or display of matter that, because of its sexually explicit nature, may, pursuant to state law or local regulatory authority, be offered only to persons over the age of 18 years."

It remains for the courts to decide whether a particular business meets the criteria for such treatment. In *Wright v. County of Du Page* (2000), undercover police officers in Illinois testified that during their visits to a massage parlor, while completely nude, they were touched on the chest, back, and legs by female employees who wore nothing except a G-string and who rubbed their breasts against the officers; the court found that the establishment was an adult business for purposes of a zoning ordinance. In contrast, Delaware's supreme court, in *Richardson v. Wile* (1988), ruled that a video rental store that rents or sells X-rated videos is not per se (by itself) an adult entertainment establishment; the court noted that only those businesses that are likely to promote crimes of obscenity or prostitution required a license as a sexually oriented business.

Licensing Procedures

Because all businesses are required to have permits or licenses, many local governments have instituted special licenses for adult businesses. Depending on the moral climate in a particular locality, the administrative process for obtaining or maintaining such a license may be used effectively to force them to shut down altogether.

In several recent cases, the U.S. Supreme Court has addressed the procedures for granting and renewing licenses for adult businesses, including whether the licensing process acts as an impermissible prior restraint on freedom of expression. In *City News and Novelty, Inc. v. City of Waukesha* (2001), the Court—noting that the issue was moot because the company had since gone out of business—dismissed a petition by an adult business that had complained about the city council's rejection of its application for a license renewal. In *City of Littleton, Colorado v. Z. J. Gifts D-4, LLC* (2004), the Supreme Court returned to the problem of delays in granting licenses for adult businesses; here the issue was almost sidetracked by distinctions arising from previous cases between requirements that license applications be given a "prompt final judicial decision" or merely the "possibility of prompt judicial review."

The two earlier cases discussed were *Freedman v. Maryland* (1965) and *FW/PBS, Inc. v. Dallas* (1990). At issue in *Freedman* was whether the handling of administrative requests and judicial review had been expeditious and prompt, based on a system devised for prior CENSORSHIP of movies. The *FW/PBS* case involved strict government regulation of motels that rented rooms for periods of less than ten hours. In *Littleton v. Z. J. Gifts*, however, the Court glossed over possible distinctions regarding judicial review of a license rejection and found that Colorado's law "satisfies any 'prompt judicial determination' requirement." According to the Court, the ordinance requiring the licensing of adult businesses "considered on its face, is consistent with the First Amendment's demands" and "does not seek to *censor* material." Censorship, the prior restraint of free expression, was held by the Supreme Court in its landmark case *Near v. Minnesota* (1931) to infringe the First Amendment's freedom of the press, as made applicable to the states by the Fourteenth Amendment (1868).

The Maryland court of appeals, however, in *Pack Shack, Inc. v. Howard County* (2003), ruled that while a licensing scheme for adult entertainment businesses is not per se unconstitutional even if it acts as a prior restraint on speech, the disclosure requirements of the permit application at issue—which included the names and addresses of all persons with a financial interest in the business—failed to minimize the regulation's incidental burden on protected speech and was, therefore, unconstitutional.

Zoning and Other Restrictions

In the *Young* case cited earlier, the U.S. Supreme Court upheld a Detroit ZONING restriction on adult establishments, even though the materials and activities at issue were not legally obscene. A year before, in *Erznoznik v. City of Jacksonville* (1975), the Court had seemed to indicate that any expression deemed not legally obscene was entitled to absolute protection under the First Amendment. But in *Young* the Court's 5–4 decision determined that the regulation was constitutionally permissible because the films involved here were so sexually explicit that they were not entitled to absolute protection, the zoning ordinance in question did not totally restrict the material's availability, and the material would be considered very offensive by many people.

Later cases such as *Federal Communications Commission v. Pacifica Foundation* (1978) and *City of Renton v. Playtime Theatres, Inc.* (1986) continued this trend. The Supreme Court allowed restrictions on sexually oriented businesses based on a determination that highly objectionable materials, while not purveying obscenity as legally defined by the Court in cases beginning with *Roth,* could still be the subject of reasonable state control, especially if a law's intent was to protect neighborhoods, reduce crime, and preserve property values. In *Pacifica,* the Court approved FEDERAL COMMUNICATIONS COMMISSION sanctions for a broadcast that involved indecent but not obscene language; in *Renton,* the local government was allowed to disperse or concentrate adult theaters to mitigate any undesirable secondary effects they might cause.

In *City of Los Angeles v. Alameda Books, Inc.* (2002), the Supreme Court determined that an ordinance prohibiting two or more adult businesses in the same building could be constitutional. In reversing the lower federal court and remanding the matter to a federal appeals court, the Court noted that the ordinance in question was more akin to a land-use law rather than an attempt to suppress free speech or expression; thus, it required only "intermediate scrutiny" as in the *Renton* case, rather than "strict scrutiny," the latter reserved by the courts for statutes that on their face restrict free expression. The city's concern over a possible increase in crime because of a concentration of sexually oriented businesses was legitimate, the Court concluded.

In addition to special licensing requirements and limitations on location, other restrictions may be applicable to sexually oriented businesses. In *State v. Russo* (2000), for example, New Jersey's superior court upheld the constitutionality of a fifty-foot buffer zone around a sexually oriented business known as Hott 22, which had to include plantings to be approved by the municipal planning board. The court reasoned that the plantings would help screen the nude dancing establishment from minors and prevent blight in the neighborhood.

The freedom of expression guaranteed by the First Amendment in its free-speech and free-press provisions is aimed primarily at protecting the free exchange of political ideas and criticism of government actions and officials, all vital in a democracy. Protection for business communication is not as vital, giving the states and the federal government more leeway in regulating business activities that deal in forms of nonpolitical speech. Adult businesses are consequently subject to reasonable restrictions that further legitimate government goals, such as preventing crime and protecting average citizens and CHILDREN from offensive or objectionable materials.

See also ENTERTAINMENT INDUSTRY; MEDIA; NUDITY; STATE AND LOCAL GOVERNMENT.

SEXUALLY TRANSMITTED DISEASES

Evidence exists that the Akkadians, whose empire flourished in Mesopotamia between 2334 and 2230 B.C.E., were aware that venereal disease was acquired from having sexual relations. Today the United States has the highest rate of sexually transmitted disease (STD) of any industrialized nation: it is estimated that a quarter of all Americans—and half or more young people—will get some STD in their lifetime. The list of STDs is long, ranging in alphabetical order from AIDS-HIV to cervicitis, chancroid, chlamydia, gardnerella, gonorrhea, herpes, human papillomavirus (HPV or genital warts), nongonococcal urethritis (NGU), pelvic inflammatory disease (PID), pubic lice ("the crabs"), syphilis, trichomoniasis, vaginitis, and yeast infection.

Some of these diseases are more debilitating than others. For example, most women will not know if they have chlamydia unless they are tested for it. Yet some five thousand women die every year in the United States from HPV-related cancers. STDs can also result in infertility, and expectant mothers can transmit life-threatening diseases to their babies. Antibiotics have greatly reduced the scourge of once-deadly bacterial

STDs such as syphilis and gonorrhea, although the diseases are recurring especially among homosexuals. Viral STDs such as herpes and HPV are treatable but not curable; in 2006 the Centers for Disease Control and Prevention recommended that preteen girls receive a new anti-HPV vaccine to help prevent infection as well as cervical cancer.

Beginning with the early European settlers who had sexual relations with Native Americans, STD victims have often been doubly victimized by criticism for moral laxity. In the New World, according to *The History of New France* by Marc Lescarbot, published in three volumes between 1907 and 1914, "God has severely punished this vice by the pox." More recently some religious leaders in the United States have declared that AIDS-HIV is God's punishment for SODOMY committed by gay men. In 2005 a conservative U.S. senator from Oklahoma, Tom Coburn, who is also a physician, took to lecturing young members of his staff in the U.S. Capitol on the perils of sexually transmitted diseases, accompanied by a graphic slide presentation.

Education and Prevention

The U.S. Code contains a number of federal laws relating to STDs, including some that provide for state and federal cooperation in addressing the problem. For example, Title 42, The Public Health and Welfare, chapter 6A, subchapter III, Part A, section 283f, regarding requirements for conducting surveys of sexual behavior, lists as one of its goals the reduction in "the incidence of sexually transmitted diseases, the incidence of infection with [HIV], or the incidence of any other infectious disease." Section 247c authorizes the secretary of the U.S. DEPARTMENT OF HEALTH AND HUMAN SERVICES to "provide technical assistance to appropriate public and nonprofit private entities and to scientific institutions for their research in, and training and public health programs for, the prevention and control of sexually transmitted diseases."

In 2000 CONGRESS enacted a law that required the CDC and the Food and Drug Administration to inform the public about the effectiveness of condoms to protect against HPV and to determine if condom labels

You kept fit and defeated the Hun

Now— set a high standard
A CLEAN AMERICA !

STAMP OUT VENEREAL DISEASES—

Using war as an analogy for combating illness, this post–World War I poster sought to prevent the spread of venereal disease. However, like many other ills against which the government has waged wars—drugs, poverty, and terrorism, for example—sexually transmitted diseases such as AIDS have proved to be a tenacious adversary.

are medically accurate. A report by the director of the FDA's Office of Device Evaluation in 2004 noted that "latex condoms for men are a well-made medical device that laboratory studies have shown to provide an essentially impermeable barrier to particles the size of STD pathogens." Along with the CDC, the National Institute of Allergy and Infectious Diseases plays a key role in mobilizing and coordinating the nation's efforts to reduce and eradicate STDs.

Most states have laws addressing STD education and prevention. Oregon mandates that health education include information on responsible sexual behavior and hygienic practices to reduce the risk of infectious STDs, among other things. In Georgia the board of education is required to determine and prescribe minimum requirements and grade levels for SEX EDUCATION and AIDS prevention and to include instruction on how ABSTINENCE from sexual activity can prevent AIDS, STDs, and PREGNANCY. Tennessee law requires physicians or others treating persons infected with an STD to provide them with information about these diseases. Indiana specifies that applicants for a marriage license acknowledge in writing that they "have received information regarding dangerous communicable diseases that are sexually transmitted and a list of test sites for the virus that causes AIDS."

Testing and Treatment

In the U.S. Code, Title 42, section 247c, authorizes HHS to fund grant projects in the states to conduct activities such as "screening, . . . followup of diagnostic tests for, and diagnosed cases of, sexually transmitted diseases." The follow-up activities include "contact tracing of infectious cases of [STDs] and routine testing, including laboratory tests."

Most states have laws that expressly allow testing, treatment, and quarantine of individuals infected with STDs. Alabama, for example, permits a state or county health officer to petition a judge to compel testing, treatment, or quarantine where a person has been exposed to an STD. New York law authorizes a health officer to require a medical examination for STD infection and to determine the stage at which the infection is communicable; it also requires the physician performing the examination to report promptly to the health officer.

Prisoners. Florida, Oklahoma, South Dakota, and Virginia are among the approximately twenty states that authorize or require all PRISONERS to be examined and treated for STDs. To prevent the spread of disease, Vermont specifically mandates that, before probation or parole, medical treatment be given to a person convicted of PROSTITUTION who is infected with a venereal disease (from the Latin *Venus*, the goddess of love). West Virginia mandates testing and

treating of any person who has been convicted of SEX OFFENSES or sexual immorality.

Penalties. Most states make it a crime for a medical professional to fail to report positive STD tests to state or county health officials. State laws also often impose penalties for not cooperating with requirements regarding testing, treatment, or reporting on cases of STDs. Generally such penalties are misdemeanors, or lesser crimes, and carry a fine. California has an extensive list of possible related crimes, including violations by any person of any investigation, rules, or regulations pertaining to reporting or treating a person with STDs and failure of any physician, health officer, spouse, or other person to testify in the prosecution of that person; moreover, it is a misdemeanor for anyone to refuse to give information regarding STDs, to fail to comply with any proper control measure or examination for STDs, or to expose or infect others with STDs. Similarly, it is a misdemeanor in California for an infected person who knows that he or she is infected to marry or to have sexual intercourse.

Confidentiality. A handful of states—including Delaware, Montana, Nevada, and Washington—address confidentiality and access to records regarding testing and treatment for STDs. Kansas, for one, requires a woman's CONSENT to a test for syphilis within fourteen days of being diagnosed as pregnant, while Kentucky law declares that confidentiality is essential for the proper control and prevention of STDs. Montana law echoes the need for confidentiality and permits the release of information concerning a person infected or suspected of being infected with an STD only to authorized health department personnel or a physician who has written consent from the person whose file is requested or to a local health officer engaged in the eradication of STDs.

Minors. Most states have special requirements allowing minors to give their own consent for medical examinations for STDs. Connecticut, however, requires that a minor bear all of the costs of any services and that a report be made to state authorities on treatment of a minor under the age of twelve years for venereal disease. Montana permits a physician to notify the parent, guardian, or spouse of a minor being treated for a venereal disease when severe complications are present or anticipated or when major surgery or hospitalization is required.

TEENAGERS are among those most vulnerable to the risk of contracting STDs, given that up to two-thirds of new cases occur in those younger than twenty-five and in people with multiple sex partners. According to the Centers for Disease Control and Prevention, HIV, herpes, syphilis, gonorrhea, and genital warts can all be transmitted even through oral-genital contact, which many young people believe—erroneously—is a safe sexual practice. Because it is difficult for the law alone to protect individuals from risky sexual behavior, sex education at home and school helps fill this need.

See also CONTRACEPTION; HOMOSEXUALITY.

SINGLE-SEX EDUCATION

For most of human history, formal education was almost exclusively the privilege of males, if they could afford it. In 1792 the British feminist Mary Wollstonecraft (1759–97) wrote *A Vindication of the Rights of Woman*, demanding equal education opportunities for females. Early public education in America typically placed boys and girls in the same classroom in one-room schoolhouses, but until the second half of the twentieth century, the norm in institutions of higher learning was single-sex education.

In 2004 the federal government announced plans to relax long-standing restrictions to make it much easier to establish single-sex schools funded at taxpayer expense. Although the proposed change to U.S. Department of Education regulations was not made, by the beginning of the 2004–2005 school year thirty-five of the country's public elementary and secondary schools had been reestablished as single-sex educational institutions and some 119 others were providing single-sex classes within a coeducational setting; many such programs cater to minority communities.

Some parents and politicians believe that single-sex education has great potential benefits, but groups such as the American Association of University Women, AMERICAN CIVIL LIBERTIES UNION, National Association for the Advancement of Colored People, and NATIONAL ORGANIZATION FOR WOMEN disagree. The notion of "separate but equal" public schools appears to fly in the face of American constitutional law.

"Intermediate Scrutiny"

According to the Fourteenth Amendment (1868) to the U.S. Constitution, a state may not "deny to any person within its jurisdiction the equal protection of the laws." In the landmark case *Brown v. Board of Education of Topeka* (1954), the U.S. Supreme Court ended racial segregation in public schools, declaring that "in the field of public education the doctrine of 'separate but equal' has no place. Separate educational facilities are inherently unequal." The Equal Education Opportunities Act of 1974 states that "all children enrolled in public schools are entitled to equal educational opportunity without regard to race, color, sex, or national origin."

But federal cases involving GENDER segregation in public schools—DISCRIMINATION on the basis of sex—later avoided finding inequality as *Brown* would seem to have warranted. For example, in *Vorchheimer v. School District* (1976), affirmed by the U.S. Supreme Court in 1977, a federal court of appeals approved an all-male admissions policy at Philadelphia Central High School. The court noted that Philadelphia's public school system already had an all-girls high school and that both schools had a record of academic excellence.

In comparing racial and gender discrimination, federal courts have used a standard of "strict scrutiny" to review cases involving racial discrimination against a minority with a history of oppression by the majority; this standard means that the government bears a heavy burden to show that a discriminatory policy or law has a rational and legitimate purpose. In the case of discrimination against females, however, the standard of scrutiny, as established by the Supreme

Court in *Craig v. Boren* (1976), is only "intermediate," indicating that the government bears a lesser burden to prove that a discriminatory law or policy is necessary to accomplish a worthwhile objective.

Conflicting Views

Title IX of the Education Amendments of 1972 prohibits discrimination on the basis of sex in "any education program or activity receiving Federal financial assistance." Unlike the Fourteenth Amendment's equal protection clause, which applies to the states, this provision affects any public or private educational institution that receives federal money. Although the law does not expressly cover single-sex schools, in *Garrett v. Board of Education* (1991), a federal district court held that based on Title IX's legislative history, only single-sex schools in existence before the law's passage are exempt. New single-sex schools that wish to receive federal money could not be established.

In *Mississippi University for Women v. Hogan* (1982), a case not covered by Title IX provisions, the Supreme Court had ruled that under the equal protection clause and the intermediate standard of scrutiny the Court gives to sex discrimination allegations, single-sex schools must admit members of the opposite sex and no new single-sex schools can be created. The basis for the ruling in *Hogan* was that the single-sex institution failed to prove that admitting men to a historically all-female school was "substantially related" to achieving an "important governmental objective." Dissenting justices pointed out that the plaintiff Hogan had a choice of other coed nursing schools in the state, adding that the opinion, written by Associate Justice Sandra Day O'Connor—at the time the only woman on the Court—would in effect doom publicly supported women-only colleges, and it did. In *United States v. Virginia* (1996), the Court found itself compelled, without "exceedingly persuasive justification," to conclude likewise that all-male educational institutions that excluded women would be violating the Fourteenth Amendment's equal protection clause.

The confusion over whether or not single-sex schools are permissible—a federal district court in *Garrett*

saying yes, if grandfathered in, and the U.S. Supreme Court in *Hogan* and *Virginia* seemingly saying no—led Congress to intervene in 2001. The No Child Left Behind Act passed that year contains language permitting school districts to spend federal funds to promote single-sex opportunities as long as they are consistent with the law. It is left to the courts to interpret the law.

Evidence for the benefits of single-sex education is mixed: the National Association for Single Sex Public Education has produced data indicating that there are differences in how boys and girls learn, based on physical differences in the male and female brains. In contrast, the American Association of University Women indicated in a 1998 report that "there is no evidence that single-sex education in general 'works' or is 'better' than coeducation." Girls in particular might be seen as benefiting from a learning environment free of distractions caused by more agressive young males. Yet a current theory sees a crisis in boys' education, claiming that they are falling behind in academic achievement. However, a 2001 Ford Foundation report suggested that the academic success of both girls and boys is influenced more by other factors: small class size, strong curricula, and well-qualified teachers.

If a major purpose of education is to prepare a student for life in the adult world, then a coeducational environment is more reflective of a world in which both male and female students will ultimately live, work, and compete. "It is much harder for men to accept women as equal partners in their workplaces if they have never been required to compete with them in school," said Kim Gandy, president of the National Organization for Women, in 2004.

See also Equal Rights; Women's Rights.

SODOMY

Sodomy has traditionally been defined in the law as unnatural carnal copulation by humans with each other or with an animal (the latter more commonly known as bestiality). The word is derived from the biblical city of Sodom, which was reportedly destroyed by God along with Gomorrah because of the wickedness of its citizens. Some older statutes simply referred to sodomy as a "crime against nature" or the *crimen innominatum* (Latin for "nameless crime"). Early court cases tended to limit the definition to the sexual act of a male penetrating the anus of another male or to pederasty (sexual relations between a man and a boy).

Sometimes still characterized as a form of sexual perversion—behavior that does not conform to the "proper goal" of sexual activity—sodomy may include oral-genital contact, such as cunnilingus and fellatio. Problems arise in trying to define the proper goal of sexual activity. If the only goal is reproduction, then only heterosexual vaginal intercourse at appropriate times is not a perversion; but if pleasure is also a goal, then the definitions of sodomy and sexual perversion must be far more circumscribed.

Constitutional Law

The U.S. Supreme Court has dealt with the legality of sodomy, or at least adult consensual homosexual sodomy, in two important cases with very different outcomes: *Bowers v. Hardwick* (1986) and LAWRENCE V. TEXAS (2003). Challenges to state laws criminalizing sodomy and sexual perversion have been made typically on the grounds of vagueness. By way of background, courts require that for a statute to be constitutional under the U.S. Constitution's due process clause, it must give fair warning to individuals who contemplate engaging in activity that may be criminal and must provide adequate standards for enforcement agencies, trial courts, and reviewing courts. As the Supreme Court stated in *Lanzetta v. New Jersey* (1939), citing an earlier case, "the terms of a penal statute creating a new offense must be sufficiently explicit to inform those who are subject to it what conduct on their part will render them liable to its penalties ... [and] a statute which either forbids or requires the doing of an act in terms so vague that men of common intelligence must necessarily guess at its meaning and differ as to its application violates the first essential of due process of law."

But the Supreme Court, until the landmark *Lawrence* decision, tended to give lawmakers and lower courts the benefit of the doubt in cases involving sodomy statutes. In *Rose v. Locke* (1975), the justices reviewed a Tennessee law that used the phrase "crimes against nature." The Court found that such language adequately described the act of cunnilingus, for which the defendant had been prosecuted, and noted that it had twice before—in *State v. Crawford* (1972) and *Wainwright v. Stone* (1972)—upheld similar statutes. In the first case, the Court noted that a "crime-against-nature statute ... was derived from early English law and broadly embraced sodomy, bestiality, buggery, fellatio, and cunnilingus within its terms"; in the second case, a Florida statute "proscribing 'the abominable and detestable crime against nature' was not [found to be] unconstitutionally vague, despite the fact that the State Supreme Court had recently changed its mind about the statute's permissible scope" as to just exactly which behavior it encompassed.

At the time of the Supreme Court's 1986 decision in *Bowers*, the number of states that outlawed sodomy had shrunk from all fifty in 1961 to twenty-four and the District of Columbia. Under Georgia law, sodomy was a felony punishable by up to twenty years in prison and was defined as "any sexual act involving the sex organs of one person and the mouth or anus of another." The challenge to this law was based on the right of PRIVACY, which beginning with GRISWOLD V. CONNECTICUT (1965) had been found by the Supreme Court in the intent of a number of the provisions of the Bill of Rights (1791). However, in *Bowers* the Court, by a bare 5–4 majority, upheld the statute's constitutionality, noting that to claim that the right to engage in such conduct was guaranteed by the constitutional right of privacy or that it was "'deeply rooted in this Nation's history and tradition' or 'implicit in the concept of ordered liberty' is, at best, facetious." No one had actually been prosecuted under the Georgia law, because the district attorney had withdrawn the charge against the defendant. Hardwick nevertheless filed a civil suit in federal court attacking the statute's constitutionality.

A similar fact pattern brought the *Lawrence* case to the Supreme Court seventeen years later. The defendants, John Geddes Lawrence and Tryon Gardner, were found guilty under a Texas law making it a crime for two persons of the same sex to engage in intimate sexual activity. The Court overruled its decision in *Bowers*—striking down the Texas law for the very reasons that Associate Justice Byron R. White, who wrote the *Bowers* opinion, had declared to be facetious. As Justice Anthony M. Kennedy wrote for the 6–3 majority, "It is a promise of the Constitution that there is a realm of personal liberty which the government may not enter." Associate Justice Lewis F. Powell Jr. indicated that he would have voted against the majority in *Bowers* if the question of cruel and unusual punishment (up to twenty years' imprisonment) for a conviction under the Georgia sodomy law had been an issue.

Since *Lawrence*, questions over sodomy laws, at least as applied to the private acts of consenting adults, are now mostly moot. But just as *Bowers* was overturned, this issue could be revisited with a different membership on the Supreme Court.

Pederasty

Pederasty may refer specifically to anal intercourse between an adult and a child, but it also includes oral-genital contact and even bestiality. A legal definition of child sexual abuse requires sexual activity involving children and "abusive conditions," such as coercion or a large age gap between the participants as evidence of a lack of CONSENT. Child sexual abuse may include exhibitionism without contact with the child. Boys are often less likely to report sexual abuse because of the stigma attached and the fear of being called a homosexual.

Sex with CHILDREN, whether natural or unnatural, has long been and still is illegal in all states. The sodomizing of a child may be encompassed in laws against RAPE and forcible rape, INCEST, forms of sexual exploitation, and the molestation of children. Title 18 of the U.S. Code, subsection 2422(b), prohibits interstate coercion or enticement of a minor to engage in PROSTITUTION or other criminal sexual activity, and subsection 2241(c) prohibits the crossing of state lines with

the intent to engage in a criminal sexual act with a child under twelve years of age.

State laws address pederasty in various ways: Indiana's chapter on sex crimes defines child molestation as including "deviant sexual conduct"; South Carolina's code defines sexual conduct under Sexual Performance by Children to include "deviant sexual intercourse [and] bestiality"; and Washington State's code defines sexual intercourse in its law entitled Sexual Exploitation of Children as "including genital-genital, oral-genital, anal-genital, or oral-anal" sexual behavior and "penetration of the vagina or rectum by any object."

In the study of psychology, sodomy and pederasty come under the general rubric of paraphilia—sexual behavior that is often considered socially unacceptable. But as the law has evolved in the United States, sodomy defined as adult consensual sexual conduct not related to heterosexual vaginal intercourse, performed in private, is now protected by the right of privacy derived from the Bill of Rights. Pederasty (anal sexual molestation of children) has no constitutional protection.

See also CHILD ABUSE; DEVIANT BEHAVIOR; HOMOSEXUALITY; HUMAN TRAFFICKING; LEWD BEHAVIOR.

SPEECH, FREEDOM OF

See CENSORSHIP; ENTERTAINMENT INDUSTRY; FIRST AMENDMENT; MEDIA; NUDITY; OBSCENITY; PORNOGRAPHY.

SPOUSAL ABUSE

See DOMESTIC VIOLENCE.

SPOUSAL RIGHTS AND DUTIES

A spouse (from the Latin *sponsus*, meaning a betrothed or a bridegroom) is a husband or a wife, although in Massachusetts, where SAME-SEX MARRIAGE is legal, a homosexual partner in a MARRIAGE may also be considered a spouse. Under common law (the uncodified case law of England adopted by the states after independence in 1776), a husband and a wife were considered to be one person. A husband was required to support his wife—providing "necessaries" such as food, clothing, shelter, and medical care—and was responsible for her debts, both before and during their marriage, and for any torts committed by her; if she committed a felony in his presence, she was excused because of the presumption that she acted under compulsion. A wife was obligated to render services to her husband, including providing conjugal relations, companionship, affection, and the "exclusive right to her society." Neither one was considered competent to testify in court for or against the other, except in personal injury cases. Without the husband's CONSENT, a wife could not sue or be sued, enter into a contract, sell or give away property, make a will, or have control over her own earnings or other property.

State laws regarding spousal rights and duties have changed significantly since the establishment of the United States. During the second half of the nineteenth century, married women's property acts were enacted by the states to allow married women to sue and be sued in their own right and even to sue their husband in matters regarding property rights. Further impetus for change came in the twentieth century with the ratification of the Nineteenth Amendment (1920), which gave women the right to vote; World War II, during which many women filled in for men in the workplace; the SEXUAL REVOLUTION of the 1960s and 1970s; the WOMEN'S RIGHTS movement, reinvigorated around the same time; and the legalization of and improvements in methods of CONTRACEPTION and expansion of REPRODUCTIVE RIGHTS for women. In essence, the change has been from husbands having the lion's share of spousal rights and obligations to a relative equality of rights and obligations.

In addition to being governed by state laws, today spousal rights may be negotiated between the parties before marriage in PRENUPTIAL AGREEMENTS and in separation and DIVORCE settlements under court supervision, including the payment of ALIMONY. Terms of spousal and CHILD SUPPORT and child custody and visitation rights can all be determined by the parties as long as their decisions do not contravene public policy, are not significantly unfair to one party, and do not jeopardize the best interests of any CHILDREN.

It is doubtful that many married couples enter into marriage today without knowing that sexual relations are an expected part of the marital relationship, but many may lack a clear understanding of their spousal rights and duties in areas such as the following.

Family Names

The law has traditionally recognized a woman's right—not long ago, it was an obligation—to change her name upon marriage by assuming her husband's family name. When the husband was considered responsible for his wife's contractual and property interests, this requirement made legal sense. The use of the same family name by both spouses also simplified legitimization of their children, including entitlement to their father's support. Changing a woman's name also had strong social implications.

A woman no longer feels obligated to take her husband's name. Various arrangements among spouses have been devised, such as hyphenating both spouses' last names or, more rarely, jointly using one spouse's last name for a period of time and then subsequently changing their names to the other spouse's last name. In *Stuart v. Board of Supervisors of Elections* (1972), Maryland's court of appeals held that a woman does not have to change her name on a voter registration list after getting married.

As for children's names, courts have generally settled disputes between spouses on the basis of what is in a child's best interests. Other factors that may be taken into account include a child's name preference, whether a name change may cause disharmony in the family, and the parents' motive in proposing one name over another.

Benefits and Obligations of Marriage

In most jurisdictions, married couples have rights to:

- Maintenance and support from their partners

- A presumption of joint ownership of real estate as a tenancy in common and a right not to be held to a mortgage or an assignment of rights to creditors without the spouse's written permission

- Division of property according to state laws and court rulings

- Spousal benefits statutorily guaranteed to public employees, including health and life insurance and disability payments, as well as similar contractual benefits for private employees

- Equal treatment as married couples under state and local tax laws

- Family leave and public assistance benefits under state law

- Victims' and workers' compensation benefits as a family unit

- Remediation of spousal abuse

- Immunity from testifying against their partners, if they choose to invoke it

- Joint care and parenthood of children born to one of the spouses during the union

- Adoption of children jointly with their spouse or adoption of children brought to the union by the spouse

- Child custody in a divorce

- Involvement in involuntary hospitalization of a spouse, including the right to be notified and to initiate proceedings leading to a release

- Priority in appointment as guardian of an incapacitated spouse or priority to act for an incapacitated spouse in making health care decisions

- Priority in inheritance if a partner dies without a will and preference in being named legal executor of the estate

- Recovery for a spouse's wrongful death and the intentional infliction of emotional distress through harm to one's spouse

Source: Adapted from William N. Eskridge Jr. and Nan D. Hunter, *Sexuality, Gender, and the Law,* 2d ed. New York: Foundation Press, 2004.

Domicile

Domicile (legal place of residence) is an important concept that affects rights and duties such as how property is owned and transferred and where taxes are paid. Under common law, the right to determine a married couple's domicile belonged to the husband. It was not until 1971 that the *Second Restatement of Conflict of Laws,* a general treatise on the question of which state's law applies in certain situations, suggested that special circumstances might permit exceptions to the domicile-of-the-husband rule, such as a wife's living apart from her husband. Since then courts have also tended to liberalize the rule. For example, in *Samuel v. University of Pittsburgh* (1974), a federal court found that university residence rules requiring a wife to take the domicile of her husband were an unconstitutional denial of equal protection of the laws. The generally accepted rule now is that married women, like unmarried women and men, have the right to choose their own domicile.

Spousal Support

State courts have approached the question of spousal support during marriage from different points of view. The supreme court of Virginia, in *Shilling v. Bedford City Memorial Hospital* (1983), struck down a statute that imposed financial obligations only on the husband, calling it unconstitutional under the state constitution and the equal protection clause of the U.S. Constitution. In contrast, a Wisconsin's court, in *Marshfield Clinic v. Discher* (1982), upheld a statute that made husbands primarily responsible for their spouse's debts, noting that men generally earn more than women. The more modern trend is toward an equal sharing of financial obligations. A New Jersey court, in *Jersey Shore Medical Center v. Estate of Baum* (1980), held both spouses liable for the expenses incurred by one another, adding that a creditor should look first to the spouse who incurred a debt.

Health Care

Under common law, a spouse had a right to medical care as well as a duty to provide such care; failure to do so could incur criminal liability. Today courts generally hold a spouse to the duty of providing health care for the other spouse, unless the failure to provide it represents an action taken in good faith at the request of a competent spouse. In *People v. Robbins* (1981), a New York court absolved a husband of liability in the death of his wife, who had epilepsy and diabetes but believed that she had been healed after attending a religious meeting; he did not obtain medical attention for her conditions even though she discontinued prescribed medication.

Spouses also have the right under state laws to make medical decisions and terminate life support for one another if they become incompetent to make decisions for themselves. Many states have enacted natural death acts that allow mentally competent persons to specify in a living will whether they want to be kept alive by medical procedures when they become incompetent to make such determinations, but these laws generally give priority to spouses if a living will has not been made. As next of kin, spouses are additionally granted access to the remains of a deceased spouse.

Employment

In *BRADWELL V. ILLINOIS* (1873), the U.S. Supreme Court upheld the state's right to bar an otherwise qualified married woman from practicing law, declaring that the "paramount destiny and mission of woman are to fulfill the noble and benign offices of wife and mother. This is the law of the Creator." One of the most significant issues for the Court was that "a married woman is incapable, without her husband's consent, of making contracts which shall be binding on her or him." The Court underscored the "incapacities arising out of the married state" in that era. Since then, the legal bar to women's holding any jobs for which they are as qualified as men has been lifted but not removed entirely.

DISCRIMINATION in certain jobs is still permitted. Some rules against nepotism are aimed at preventing public officials and private employers from hiring unqualified spouses and encouraging favoritism in the workplace. With spouses working for the same employer, marital squabbles may spill over into the office. Conflicts may also arise in work scheduling and in the employer's interests—for example, where an elected official has

supervision over a spouse who is a government employee or where married lawyers might be unable to keep the interests of their clients confidential.

Some cases have challenged the rationale of such nepotism policies. Title VII of the Civil Rights Act of 1964, which prohibits employment discrimination based on race, color, religion, sex, or national origin, does not cover marital status. But in *Equal Employment Opportunity v. Rath Packing Co.* (1986), a federal court declared the company's no-spouse rule invalid after finding that the "business necessity" defense relied on by the company did not justify a policy that effectively discriminated against married women. In *Townshend v. Board of Education* (1990), however, a male teacher who was transferred out of his school when his wife became the principal challenged the school's policy of not employing spouses; he lost, because West Virginia's supreme court reasoned that the policy did not infringe on his right to marry—only on his right to be supervised by his wife.

Property

When a marriage is dissolved or either party dies, with or without a will, state laws govern rights to property, including property a person has brought into a marriage and property acquired during the marriage. Under common law, all property acquired during marriage was owned by the person who acquired it. Therefore, if the husband worked and the wife did not, all of his earnings belonged to him.

Arizona, California, Idaho, Louisiana, Nevada, New Mexico, Texas, Washington, and Wisconsin have community property laws that treat marriage as a partnership and marital property as owned equally; some of these states use an equitable (fair), rather than an equal, basis for determining spousal ownership rights. A majority of jurisdictions, whether originally based on common law or community property rights, now require equitable allocation of marital property, as provided by the Uniform Marital and Divorce Act (1970). This act requires that marital property acquired during marriage be fairly divided between spouses, taking into consideration each spouse's contribution, including a homemaker's services; the value of other property each spouse owns; the length of the marriage; and each spouse's economic situation, including the disposition of the family home. Such distributions are usually required only in the case of a divorce and only if there is no valid court-approved premarital or private divorce settlement on which to base the distribution.

Consortium

At common law, courts recognized a right to consortium by both spouses. In early American cases, *consortium* was defined as the right to services of a spouse and to his or her companionship and conjugal affection. In some personal injury cases against a third party, the spouse of the injured husband or wife may make a claim for compensation for the loss of consortium as a result of the negligence or intentional injury to the spouse. However, according to a Wisconsin appeals court decision in *Prill v. Hampton* (1990), an action for wrongful divorce cannot be brought against a third party who caused an injury to a spouse that leads to a divorce.

See also EQUAL RIGHTS.

STALKING

See DOMESTIC VIOLENCE; SEXUAL ASSAULT; VICTIMS' RIGHTS; VIOLENCE AGAINST WOMEN ACT; VOYEURISM.

STATE AND LOCAL GOVERNMENT

To a large extent, laws regarding sexual behavior are enacted, enforced, and interpreted by state and local officials. Provisions concerning sexual behavior are included both in statutes and in some state constitutions. Nearly twenty states, for example, have adopted constitutional language defining marriage to preclude same-sex marriage, and a handful of other states have pending amendments on the same subject that are due to be voted on. A similar number of state constitutions, twenty, contain prohibitions against sex discrimination.

The constitution of Hawaii, for one, provides that equal rights "shall not be denied or abridged by the State on account of sex"; guarantees equal protection of the laws and protection of civil rights against discrimination on the basis of sex; empowers the legislature "to reserve marriage to opposite-sex couples"; and grants the public access to information regarding persons convicted of certain sexual offenses. South Carolina's constitution contains a provision setting the maximum age for statutory rape at fourteen years.

At least in theory, state governments are similar in structure to the federal government in that they have three branches: legislative, executive (headed by a governor), and judicial. Laws are enacted by the legislature, signed by the governor, and interpreted and applied by the courts. State laws are collected in codes just as federal laws are published in the U.S. Code. Laws regarding sexual behavior are generally dispersed among various sections of state law, including those relating to criminal law, family law, health and welfare, labor, communications, and education.

Local governments are the creatures of state government. They have no independent sovereignty apart from the state's sovereignty, although some autonomy may be given to cities and municipalities through home rule provisions that insulate local government from state interference on a number of matters. Local laws or ordinances, as enactments of municipal legislative bodies are generally called, cover a range of sexual behavior and sex-related activities, from INDECENT EXPOSURE and PROSTITUTION to ZONING of SEXUALLY ORIENTED BUSINESSES.

Federalism

The U.S. Constitution, written in 1787 and ratified in 1789, creates a federal system of government with two levels of sovereignty: national and state. The national government has sovereign powers that are enumerated in the Constitution, and the states have the residual powers as recognized by the Tenth Amendment (1791) to the Constitution. The NINTH AMENDMENT (1791) also provides: "The enumeration in the Constitution, of certain rights, shall not be construed to deny or disparage others retained by the people."

The concept of federalism involves the interaction of federal jurisdiction with that of the states, a relationship that has been changing as a result of constitutional amendments and interpretations by the U.S. Supreme Court. The FIRST AMENDMENT (1791), for example, plays such an important role in the Constitution's protection of certain aspects of sexual behavior—the portrayal of sexual activity in literature and film, for one—but it originally applied only to the federal government. With the adoption of the Fourteenth Amendment (1868) and the Supreme Court's ruling in cases such as *Fiske v. Kansas* (1927) and *Near v. Minnesota* (1931), however, the protections were extended to the states by a process called the doctrine of incorporation. Since the *Fiske* decision, a number of other constitutional protections in the Bill of Rights have been similarly made applicable to the states. Based on this doctrine of incorporation, the Supreme Court was able to extend to the states the definition of OBSCENITY arrived at in *ROTH v. UNITED STATES* (1957) and a companion case, *Alberts v. California* (1957).

State Laws

Associate Justice Louis D. Brandeis, who served on the Supreme Court from 1916 to 1939, called the states "laboratories of democracy." By this he meant that state governments experiment with laws and programs that may influence other states and even the national government. Several significant issues related to sexual behavior—among them abortion restrictions, same-sex marriage, and stem-cell research—have recently been the subject of such state experimentation.

In addition to sex crimes, state laws govern issues such as ABORTION, CHILD SUPPORT and custody, DISCRIMINATION, DNA testing, DRUGS, EQUAL RIGHTS, FAMILY PLANNING, GENETICS, ILLEGITIMACY, juveniles, MARRIAGE, DIVORCE, MOTHERHOOD, PATERNITY, POLYGAMY, PREGNANCY, rights of PRISONERS, REPRODUCTIVE RIGHTS, SAME-SEX MARRIAGE, SEX EDUCATION, SEXUALLY TRANSMITTED DISEASES, STEM-CELL RESEARCH AND CLONING, STERILIZATION, RIGHTS OF THE UNBORN, VICTIMS' RIGHTS, and WOMEN'S RIGHTS.

Sexual Offenses. All states have similar criminal laws, although each state varies to some degree in the nature of the SEX OFFENSES covered, their nomenclature,

and the punishment specified. As a good example, the Illinois criminal code describes various offenses, such as ADULTERY; fornication; public indecency; indecent solicitation of a child (a person under the age of seventeen years) or of an adult; sexual exploitation of a child; custodial sexual misconduct; prohibition against SEX OFFENDERS in a school zone; approaching, contacting, residing with, or communicating with a child in certain places in which a child sex offender is prohibited; INCEST within families; BIGAMY; PROSTITUTION; solicitation of a sexual act; solicitation of a prostitute or a juvenile prostitute; PANDERING; keeping a place of prostitution or juvenile prostitution; patronizing a prostitute or a juvenile prostitute; pimping; exploitation of a child; obscenity; child pornography; tie-in sales of obscene publications to distributors; posting of identifying information on a pornographic INTERNET site; and child photography by a sex offender. Some states have laws against HATE CRIMES that enhance the potential punishment for various crimes if they are motivated by prejudice or hatred based on sex or sexual orientation.

Abortion. In *Roe v. Wade* (1973), the Supreme Court made abortions legal in the United States. Yet all states except Vermont have placed some restrictions on this federally guaranteed right, such as requiring a twenty-four-hour waiting period during which a woman is to be given information on alternatives to abortion as well as parental notification for minors, both of which were upheld by the Supreme Court in *PLANNED PARENTHOOD OF SOUTHEASTERN PENNSYLVANIA V. CASEY* (1992). South Dakota in 2006 passed what amounts to an antiabortion law that may test whether *Roe v. Wade* can be overruled now that the Court has two new members appointed by President George W. Bush. Some states, including California and New York, have passed laws protecting abortion clinics and workers from antiabortion protesters.

Same-Sex Marriage. This topic has also divided the nation into two camps, with Massachusetts equating same-sex marriage with heterosexual marriage and Connecticut and Vermont offering civil unions to same-sex couples as an equivalent of the traditional heterosexual marriage. Most other states have either a constitutional amendment or a law that bars same-sex marriages. Some state and municipal governments and private employers, however, have adopted limited domestic partnership rights for same-sex couples.

Stem-Cell Research. While the national government has in effect limited federally sponsored stem-cell research to a few existing lines (cells cultured and maintained in laboratories), several states have more aggressively promoted research using human stem cells. In 2004 the California Institute for Regenerative Medicine was established with the authority to raise $3 billion for embryonic stem-cell research and other biomedical studies. Ten other states have gotten into the race. Florida's public health laws include the statement that it "is the intent of the Legislature that Florida strive to become the nation's leader in biomedical research," which includes "coordinating voluntary donations to ensure an adequate supply of adult stems cells, placentas, or cord blood." New Jersey law addresses the use of embryonic stem-cell research, which is more controversial because of the moral implications raised by some people that such cells represent a form of human life that the government must protect.

Other Sexual Behavior. Many other areas of sexual behavior are treated differently in the states. Some states, for example, have laws regarding SEX EDUCATION that limit what can be taught regarding CONTRACEPTION and HOMOSEXUALITY, on the theory that honest and frank discussions can lead to encouragement of promiscuous or risky sexual behavior or condone or promote a homosexual lifestyle. About half of the states and the District of Columbia still have laws on the books criminalizing adultery, fornication, or unmarried cohabitation, although they are usually not enforced. In *LAWRENCE V. TEXAS* (2003), the Supreme Court determined that private sexual relations between consenting adults were out of bounds to state regulation. Unenforceable laws often remain unexpunged; for example, it was not until 1999 that the South Carolina constitution was amended to remove a prohibition against interracial marriage, even though the Supreme Court had struck down such laws in *Loving v. Virginia* (1967).

Laws regarding discrimination against sexual minorities also vary among the states, from no prohibition at all to prohibition based on sexual orientation as well as protection to the same extent as accorded discrimination on the basis of race or nationality.

Where state and federal authority may overlap, decisions of the U.S. Supreme Court are paramount over state court decisions because the U.S. Constitution is the supreme law of the land; all state and federal officers—legislators, executives, and members of the JUDICIARY included—are required to support the Constitution by oath or affirmation on taking office. Yet state courts sometimes review sexual behavior issues that influence national law. The Hawaiian supreme court's decision in *Baehr v. Lewin* (1993)—noting that a statute barring same-sex marriage would establish a sex-based classification that might not pass constitutional muster on equal-protection grounds—was a wake-up call for other states and the federal government that this issue could become a legal and political hot potato, which it did.

Local Laws

As enacted by municipal governments, applied by local courts, and enforced by local law enforcement agencies, local laws are even more diverse than state laws—as different as the populations of San Francisco and Salinas, Kansas. These ordinances deal principally with sex offenses such as public indecency, prostitution, and licensing and zoning of sexually oriented businesses, rather than with the even more controversial issues of abortion rights, RAPE, or same-sex marriage. Such issues, however, may arise in the narrow context of a city or a municipality.

Some municipal laws involving sexual behavior have made their way to the U.S. Supreme Court. In *City of Erie v. Pap's A.M.* (2000), for example, the Court upheld as constitutional an ordinance requiring a minimal covering for nude dancers. In *City of Los Angeles v. Alameda Books, Inc.* (2002), the Supreme Court agreed that a city could use its zoning power to attempt to decrease potential crime and urban blight resulting from adult businesses. In *City of Dallas v. Stanglin* (1989), the Court found that an ordinance creating a class of dance halls that restricted admission to TEENAGERS was not an unconstitutional infringement of the right of association under the First Amendment; the decision noted that such a restriction made exposure of teenagers to illegal drugs and promiscuous sex less likely.

State and local governments more closely reflect the various subgroups of American citizens. They are thus likelier to have more diverse views of how sexual behavior and the law should interface than does the federal government, which has to be more protective of a broad spectrum of minority interests. All these levels of government are a part of an ongoing experiment in constitutional democracy, which, for all its faults, provides for testing, change, and progress toward a freer, safer, and more prosperous society.

See also CONGRESS; LEWD BEHAVIOR; NUDITY; PRESIDENT; UNMARRIED COHABITANTS.

STATUTORY RAPE

See CHILDREN; CONSENT; RAPE; TEENAGERS.

STEM-CELL RESEARCH AND CLONING

Stem-cell research and cloning represent a brave new world of science and technology related to reproduction. Both have raised legal and ethical questions that are currently being debated in the United States. A stem cell is an undifferentiated cell that, unlike other body cells, can turn itself into one of several types of specialized cells. Such cells can be derived from adult tissue as well as umbilical cord blood and embryos. Compared to embryonic cells, however, the range of specialized cells that can be obtained from adult stem cells is limited.

This field of study with the potential to cure a number of human diseases began in the 1960s, when researchers found at least two types of stem cells in adult bone marrow and began using them in bone-marrow transplants to treat cancer. And then in 1997,

a team led by Ian Wilmut and Keith Campbell cloned a sheep named Dolly in Scotland by implanting the nucleus of an adult body cell into an egg cell from which the nucleus had been removed. A year later embryonic stem cells that could conceivably develop into two hundred cell types were isolated by researchers.

America is now in the throes of a fight for the nation's "soul" over these scientific and medical techniques, one that has pitted advocates such as a former first lady, Nancy Reagan, and the U.S. Senate Republican majority leader, Bill Frist, a doctor, against skeptics such as President George W. Bush and the President's Council on Bioethics. The debate hinges on whether it is ethical and should be legal to use embryonic stems cells, those derived from a developing human embryo in the earliest stage after fertilization, for medical research and treatment. According to the proponents of such research, at stake are possible cures for a number of painful and debilitating ailments such as Parkinson's disease, Alzheimer's, cancer, diabetes, and spinal-cord injuries. Opponents believe that every fertilized human egg cell is a potential person and that its use in research is tantamount to the murder of innocents. Some critics oppose the idea of paying women to donate their eggs for research. But a 2005 poll in a weekly Sunday newspaper found that only 29 percent of Americans were strongly or somewhat opposed to using stem cells for research; religious objections were cited by 57 percent of those opposed.

Stem-Cell Research

The U.S. Constitution and court decisions provide little guidance in the debate over stem-cell research. At issue is a woman's right to donate egg cells or unused fertilized eggs developed to conceive a child by ASSISTED REPRODUCTIVE TECHNOLOGY, cells that are then used for medical research and the treatment of people with injuries or disease. Does society, or a majority thereof, have the right to act on behalf of an undeveloped and unborn blastocyst (the first stages of embryonic development) to prohibit the use of such embryonic stem cells for experiments that may some day provide dramatic therapeutic cures for life-threatening

State Embyronic and Fetal Research Laws

State	Expressly Permits Fetal/Embryonic Research	Restricts Research on		Restricts Purchase/ Sale of Human Tissue for Research	Consent for Research Required
		Aborted Fetus/Embryo	Fetus/Embryo from Other Sources		
Alabama					
Alaska					
Arizona		•	•		
Arkansas		•	•	•	•
California	•	•		•	•
Colorado					
Connecticut	•			•	•
Delaware					
Florida		•			
Georgia					
Hawaii					
Idaho					
Illinois	•	•	•	•	•
Indiana	•	•	•	•	•
Iowa			•	•	
Kansas					
Kentucky				•	
Louisiana			•		
Maine			•	•	
Maryland	•		•	•	•
Massachusetts	•	•	•	•	•
Michigan		•	•		•
Minnesota			•	•	
Mississippi					
Missouri		•		•	
Montana		•			
Nebraska		•	•	•	
Nevada					
New Hampshire			•	•	
New Jersey	•				•
New Mexico			•	•	
New York					
North Carolina					
North Dakota		•	•	•	•
Ohio		•		•	
Oklahoma		•		•	
Oregon					
Pennsylvania		•		•	•

State	Expressly Permits Fetal/Embryonic Research	Restricts Research on		Restricts Purchase/Sale of Human Tissue for Research	Consent for Research Required
		Aborted Fetus/Embryo	Fetus/Embryo from Other Sources		
Rhode Island			•	•	•
South Carolina					
South Dakota	•		•	•	
Tennessee				•	•
Texas				•	
Utah			•	•	
Vermont					
Virginia			•	•	
Washington					
West Virginia					
Wisconsin					
Wyoming				•	

Source: National Conference of State Legislatures, 2006

diseases? Or should such research be encouraged with safeguards for the sanctity of life?

In 2001 the president announced that federal funds would be withheld from any research using stem cells except therapeutic stem-cell work involving existing lines of cells. Only twenty-two such lines existed at the time, and all of them had been contaminated with non-human molecules, making them subject to immunological attack; therefore, they were of limited research value. Other countries have taken a different tack. In the United Kingdom, which had three lines of embryonic stem cells, the production of new lines is legal and backed with government funding. The production of new lines is legal in Australia, Israel, Singapore, and Sweden and is also permitted under certain conditions in other nations. In the United States, a few institutions such as the University of California at San Francisco and Harvard University have independently undertaken stem-cell research. In 2006 CONGRESS overcame the president's opposition and voted to allow the National Institutes of Health to fund research on unused human embryos from fertility clinics, but the president vetoed the legislation.

Other rights that have been found in the U.S. Constitution may help guide decision making in this arena. The right of ABORTION was established by the U.S. Supreme Court on the evolving concept of the right of PRIVACY, which extends constitutional protection gleaned from several provisions of the Bill of Rights (1791) to personal acts relating to reproduction and intimate sexual relations. Just as the Constitution's FIRST AMENDMENT precludes the government from legislating against a Catholic for taking communion, the right of privacy encompassed in that amendment and others bars the government from telling a woman that she must carry a child to term and rear it after it is born. In cases such as *Roe v. Wade* (1973) and *PLANNED PARENTHOOD OF SOUTH-EASTERN PENNSYLVANIA V. CASEY* (1992), the Supreme Court undertook to balance a woman's right to an abortion against the interest of the state in protecting its citizens.

The Supreme Court's analysis of the right to die, in *Cruzan v. Director, Missouri Department of Health* (1990), may also be instructive for the other side of the debate. By upholding the state's right to require convincing evidence of an incompetent patient's desire to have medical life support removed, the Court set an important precedent and ruled that the state may "properly decline to make judgments about the 'quality' of a particular individual's life, and simply assert an unqualified interest in the preservation of human life to be weighed against the constitutionally protected interests of the individual." In view of the fact that an embryo's quality of life may be even worse than that of a terminally ill, comatose adult, the state may be able to assert an interest in preserving that life, or at least protecting against its extinction by use in medical research. This reasoning may be further supported if *Roe v. Wade* is overruled, as it could be with two new members, Chief Justice John G. Roberts Jr. and Associate Justice Samuel A. Alito Jr., recently appointed to the Court by a president who is an avowed antiabortionist.

In the wake of the federal government's restrictions on the use of embryonic stem cells, some states have enacted laws promoting such research. In 2004 California established the California Institute for Regenerative Medicine in part to make "grants and loans for stem-cell research." The governing law establishes "a right to conduct stem-cell research, which includes research involving adult stem cells, cord blood stem cells, pluripotent stem cells [unspecific cells that can develop into specific or differentiated cells such as liver cells or muscle cells], and/or progenitor cells.... Pluripotent stem cells may be derived from ... surplus products of in vitro fertilization [embryonic stem cells]." The California law also declares that no funds "shall be used for research involving human reproductive cloning."

New Jersey in 2004 approved an act concerning human stem-cell research that points to 128 million Americans who might be helped by this work. The act permits the use of embryonic stems cells for research and treatment but makes the cloning of a human a first-degree crime. Arizona and Pennsylvania have declared creation of new stem-cell lines from human embryos a felony. The Florida statutes, under title XLVI, Crimes, chapter 873, Sale of Anatomical Matter, section 873.05, state: "(1) No person shall knowingly advertise or offer to purchase or sell ... any human embryo for valuable consideration.... (3) A person who violates [this provision] is guilty of a felony of the second degree."

However, title XXIX, Public Health, section 381.855, Florida Center for Universal Research to Eradicate Disease, provides that the center, in addition to "sharing new techniques and new research findings," will coordinate "voluntary donations to ensure an adequate supply of adult stem cells."

Cloning

While debate rages over the ETHICS of stem-cell research, the consensus for banning the cloning of a human being seems broader, as indicated by the California and New Jersey laws cited above. The cloning process involves replacing the DNA in an egg cell with the DNA from an adult cell and causing the new egg (or zygote) to reproduce by dividing into more cells. This process creates a blastocyst (ball of cells), the inner cells of which are stem cells that can develop into differentiated cells of specific tissue, such as muscle or nerve cells. It is this form of cell reproduction from human eggs that raises major moral, ethical, and legal issues.

Whether the cloning is used for therapy to aid victims of injury or disease or for reproduction may be a determining factor in approval or disapproval of this process. Therapeutic cloning is used only to produce an embryo that never develops beyond a microscopic ball of cells in a laboratory, whereas reproductive cloning is intended to produce a whole organism, either human or animal. Congress has so far shown some ambivalence on the issue of banning human cloning outright. Since 2001 a proposed federal ban on all cloning, reproductive and therapeutic, has failed to win congressional approval, but it was reintroduced as the Human Cloning Prohibition Act of 2005. At present no federal law prevents private cloning of a human.

Only fifteen states have laws addressing human cloning, most of which ban it or funding for it. Arkansas, Indiana, Iowa, Michigan, North Dakota, and South Dakota prohibit human and therapeutic cloning. Rhode Island's law bans cloning for the purpose of initiating a PREGNANCY, but California and New Jersey specifically allow cloning for research purposes. Connecticut law makes it a crime to "knowingly (1) engage or assist, directly or indirectly, in the cloning of a human being,

(2) implant human embryos created by nuclear transfer into a uterus or a device similar to a uterus, or (3) facilitate human reproduction through clinical or other use of human embryos created by nuclear transfer"; the offense is punishable by a fine of up to $100,000, imprisonment for up to ten years, or both. Missouri law provides: "No state funds shall be used for research with respect to the cloning of a human person. For purposes of this section, the term 'cloning' means the replication of a human person by taking a cell with genetic material and cultivating such cell through the egg, embryo, fetal and newborn stages of development into a new human person."

Much like the debate that continues over the right to have an abortion, the controversy over stem-cell research and cloning hinges on who defines the RIGHTS OF THE UNBORN. If a cloned blastocyst can, under the proper circumstances—such as being successfully implanted into a woman's womb—develop into a human with all the rights and privileges accorded by law, should it be permissible to use and thus destroy that blastocyst for whatever salutary medical or scientific reasons? So far the jury of public opinion is divided on this question.

Gambling and PORNOGRAPHY were once criminalized because of concerns about their morality but are now thriving legalized businesses. As with those activities, the bottom line on stem-cell research and cloning may be how much benefit can be obtained by putting aside the moral issues. If enough people agree that the benefits, both medical to victims and economic to society, outweigh any moral concerns, this research may be promoted by the federal and state governments rather than prohibited or constrained by law.

See also BIOETHICS; GENETICS.

STERILIZATION

Sterilization is a procedure by which a person is rendered incapable of reproduction. A male may be castrated by having his testes removed, or he may have the vas deferens (the duct that transports semen from the testes) tied off or a section of it removed; this procedure, known as a vasectomy, is often irreversible. In women the ovaries, uterus, or uterine tubes may be removed. Removal of the ovaries—a rare procedure except in the case of diseased ovaries—is called an ovariectomy; removal of the uterus is called a hysterectomy; removal of the uterine tubes, now rarely done as a sterilization procedure, is called a salpingectomy. The simpler and now more common tying off, removal, or fusion by heat of the uterine tubes is called a tubal ligation.

Most states have laws regarding sterilization, which, like CONTRACEPTION and ABORTION, may be opposed on moral and religious grounds. For example, Kansas provides: "No person shall be required to perform or participate in medical procedures which result in sterilization of a person, and the refusal of any person to perform or participate in those medical procedures shall not be a basis for civil liability to any person." New Mexico law, in contrast, directs: "No hospital which permits any operation that results in sterilization to be performed therein or medical staff of such hospital shall require any person upon whom a sterilization operation is to be performed to meet any special qualifications which are not imposed on individuals seeking other types of operations in the hospital."

The Virginia code states that it is lawful for a licensed physician to perform "a vasectomy, salpingectomy, or other surgical sexual sterilization procedure on any person eighteen years of age or older, who has the capacity to give informed consent, when so requested in writing by such person." But the person requesting the procedure must be given a "full, reasonable, and comprehensible medical explanation as to the meaning and consequences of such an operation and as to alternative methods of contraception . . . by the physician." In *Pettengill v. United States* (1994), a federal district court held that this language did not mean that a physician's failure to obtain written CONSENT constituted negligence but that it may be a factor in determining the cause of the injury on which the case was based. The Virginia code also addresses cases of sterilization of persons incapable of giving informed consent and standards for court-ordered sterilizations.

The U.S. Supreme Court in *Buck v. Bell* (1927) upheld the Commonwealth of Virginia's right to sterilize inmates of state institutions who were determined to have a hereditary form of insanity or imbecility. At the time the eugenics movement, which promoted improvement of human hereditary characteristics through social intervention, was not yet tarnished by the Nazis' attempts to produce a master race. (Eugenics is the study of heredity patterns to improve the species by selective breeding.) After justifying the sterilization procedure performed without consent on Carrie Buck, one of three generations of feebleminded women, Associate Justice Oliver Wendell Holmes Jr. went on to posit that if "the public welfare may call upon the best citizens for their lives ... [why should it] not call upon those who already sap the strength of the State for these lesser sacrifices," such as sterilization. He then uttered the now-immortal words: "Three generations of imbeciles are enough."

Later Supreme Court cases, such as *Skinner v. Oklahoma* (1942) and *Eisenstadt v. Baird* (1972), have confirmed that procreation is one of a citizen's basic civil rights. In the *Skinner* case, the Court struck down a state law because it irrationally classified persons convicted of crimes according to who could and who could not be sterilized; the statute allowed exemptions for embezzlement and political crimes but not for larceny. As Associate Justice WILLIAM O. DOUGLAS wrote for the Court, there did not seem to be any rational reason for concluding that the propensity to commit larceny was inheritable, while a propensity to embezzle or commit a political crime was not. *Eisenstadt* extended to unmarried couples the right to use contraceptives that was granted to married couples in *GRISWOLD V. CONNECTICUT* (1965).

Sterilization now takes a back seat as a new era of eugenics dawns with the potential for using STEM-CELL RESEARCH AND CLONING to improve the human race. With a more humane emphasis on the rights of the individual and the need for consent to legitimize potentially irreversible medical procedures, the law regarding sterilization now tends to encompasses the general right of all citizens to make their own decision to reproduce or not reproduce. But as the debate continues over a woman's right to an abortion, the laws regarding the right to medical sterilization could again be reconsidered by legislatures and the courts.

In the fall of 2004, an Oklahoma doctor who was the Republican candidate for the U.S. Senate was suddenly reminded of a thirteen-year-old charge (in a dismissed lawsuit) that he had sterilized a woman without her knowledge. The candidate was put on the defensive when the woman again alleged that the doctor had told her several weeks after treating her for a life-threatening ectopic pregnancy, "By the way, I tied your tubes. But do not tell anyone, because I will get in trouble." (The candidate, Tom Coburn, was elected.)

See also BIOETHICS; ETHICS; REPRODUCTIVE RIGHTS.

SURGEON GENERAL OF THE UNITED STATES

In the summer of 2001 Dr. David Satcher, then the surgeon general of the United States, released a "call to action" unveiling science-based strategies that he said represented an effort to find common ground on which the nation could work to promote sexual health and responsible sexual behavior. Seven years earlier another surgeon general, M. Joycelyn Elders, was fired by President Bill Clinton for what some people believed was her support for educating CHILDREN about masturbation. Unrepentant, she later said: "Sexuality is part of creation, part of our common inheritance, and it reminds us that we are neither inherently better nor worse than our sisters and brothers. Far from evil, masturbation just may render heavenly contentment in those who dare." The president, with the advice and consent of the U.S. Senate, appoints the surgeon general for a four-year term. The seventeenth holder of this position, Vice Admiral Richard H. Carmona, was sworn into office on August 5, 2002.

The Office of the Surgeon General of the United States, which is part of the U.S. DEPARTMENT OF HEALTH

AND HUMAN SERVICES, traces its history to the end of the eighteenth century. In 1798 CONGRESS created the U.S. Marine Hospital Service, whose mission was to provide health care for sick and injured merchant seamen. The predecessor of today's U.S. Public Health Service, the office was reorganized in 1870 into a national hospital system under the supervision of a medical officer, the supervising surgeon, a title later changed to surgeon general of the United States.

ABORTION played a role in the position's vacancy from 1994 to 1998, as the president and the Senate could not agree on whether the next surgeon general would be a proabortion or an antiabortion advocate. One nominee withdrew after a Senate filibuster against his confirmation because the record indicated that he had performed abortions early in his medical career. Finally, in 1998 approval came for David Satcher, a nominee who had supported a federal ban on so-called partial-birth abortion.

The mission of the surgeon general's office includes responding to current and long-term health needs of the country, protecting and advancing the health of the nation by educating the public and advocating effective disease prevention, articulating scientifically based health-policy analysis, and advising the president and the secretary of health and human services on a wide range of health, medical, and health system issues. An important aspect of the office's responsibilities is domestic and international AIDS-HIV prevention efforts.

The office's role is principally advisory. Since 1964 it has issued some sixty reports on various aspects of health in America. A number of these address the health hazards of smoking, but some deal with matters related to sexual behavior: AIDS, child sexual abuse, sexual health, and responsible sexual behavior.

The surgeon general's call to action in 2001 cited some statistics on the nation's sex-related health problems: twelve million Americans infected each year with SEXUALLY TRANSMITTED DISEASES; nearly 900,000 living with HIV; unintended pregnancies accounting for almost half of all U.S. pregnancies; and some 104,000 children becoming victims of CHILD ABUSE every year. To counter these problems, the surgeon general proposed some strategies developed as part of a collaborative process. One was for education that would "recognize the special place that sexuality has in everyday life." A key component was ABSTINENCE in sexual behavior before marriage. Education programs, said the surgeon general, should "stress the value and benefits of remaining abstinent until involved in a committed, enduring, and mutually monogamous relationship." Other recommendations included to "assure awareness of optimal protection from sexually transmitted diseases and unintended pregnancy." The call to action noted "that there are no infallible methods of contraception aside from abstinence, and that condoms cannot protect against some forms of STDs." Additional suggested strategies called for strengthening families; more training in sexual health; improved access to health care, including the elimination of economic disparities in such care; and further scientific study of human sexual development and reproductive health covering the entire life span.

Other activities of the surgeon general's office include participation in health conferences and special health events and provision of information on health-related issues to CONGRESS. In 2005 the office sponsored a workshop entitled Making Prevention of Child Maltreatment a National Priority. On Thanksgiving 2005 the surgeon general declared the second annual National Family History Day to promote development of a family health history portrait for every American, to assist in screening for and treating inheritable diseases.

Contact: Office of the Surgeon General, 5600 Fishers Lane, Room 18-66, Rockville, MD 20857 (202-690-7694). www.surgeongeneral.gov.

SURROGATE MOTHERHOOD

See ASSISTED REPRODUCTIVE TECHNOLOGY.

t

TEENAGERS

Between the ages of twelve and twenty—the teenage years—young people change from being CHILDREN and become mentally, physically, and sexually mature adults. With respect to sexual behavior, teenagers during this period generally go from being a protected class under the law (statutory RAPE laws, for example, presume that girls below a certain age cannot knowingly CONSENT to sexual intercourse) to joining the class of adult citizens who are held responsible for their sexual behavior. A report in 2004 concluded that American teenagers, particularly boys, were delaying having sex. Yet 47 percent were found to have been sexually active in 2003, compared with 55 percent in 1995. In 2005 slightly more than half of young Americans between the ages of fifteen and nineteen years reportedly had engaged in oral sex.

The influential English jurist William Blackstone (1723–80), writing in his *Commentaries on the Laws of England* (1765–70) about "public wrongs," or crimes, distinguished minors "under twenty-five years old" as follows: *infantia* ("from birth till seven years of age"), *pueritia* ("from seven to fourteen"), and *pubertas* ("from fourteen upwards"). During the period from birth to ten and one-half years, children "were not punishable for any crime," he related. From ten and one-half to fourteen years, in contrast, a child could be punished "if found to be . . . capable of mischief [of telling right from wrong]; but with many mitigations, and not with the utmost rigor of the law." From fourteen years and above, punishment was the same as for an adult, including the death penalty.

Whether one today is called a teenager, a young adult, a youth, an adolescent, or a juvenile, this remains a unique period between childhood and adulthood in which a not-yet-adult person's sexual behavior seems to be particularly challenging for the law. Children are to be protected from OBSCENITY and CHILD ABUSE, so they are generally presumed to be victims. Yet they may also willingly participate in proscribed sexual behavior and at some point may change categories from presumed victims to proven abettors or offenders. Special laws and legal procedures thus deal with teenage victims and offenders—a long tradition in Anglo-American law.

Federal Law

The U.S. Constitution as drafted in 1787 had little to say about age limits, except to set minimums for holding some offices, such as those of congressional representative, senator, and president, all of whose age limits are higher than the teen years. However, the document does address teenagers in the Twenty-sixth Amendment (1971), which provides, "The right of citizens of the United States, who are eighteen years or older, to vote shall not be denied or abridged by the United States or by any State on account of age." The constitutional amendment came on the heels of a U.S. Supreme Court decision in *Oregon v. Mitchell* (1970); a year earlier an amendment to the Voting Rights Act of 1965 had extended voting rights to eighteen-year-olds, but this ruling limited the change to federal elections. The Twenty-sixth Amendment, which undoubtedly was influenced by the conscription of eighteen-year-olds for service in the divisive Vietnam War, made the age limit also applicable to the states. Previously voters had to be at least twenty-one years of age. By also lowering women's voting age to eighteen years, the amendment indirectly affected the only reference to sex in the Constitution: the Nineteenth Amendment (1920), granting women the right to vote.

The Supreme Court has had several occasions to address DISCRIMINATION involving teenagers. For example, in *CRAIG V. BOREN* (1976), the Court struck down an Oklahoma law that allowed females between eighteen and twenty years of age to purchase beer with a 3.2 percent alcohol content, whereas males had to wait until they reached the age of twenty-one. The theory behind the law was that males in the eighteen-to-twenty age group were far more likely to be arrested for driving under the influence of alcohol and for public drunkenness than females in the same age group.

As a general rule, the law assumes that adolescents, who may range from twelve to twenty-one years of age, do not have direct control over their own rights. In several cases, beginning with *Meyer v. Nebraska* (1923), the Supreme Court declared the principle that "the custody, care and nurture of the child reside first in the parents." In an opinion written for a plurality of the Court in *Troxel v. Granville* (2000), Associate Justice Sandra Day O'Connor declared that the "right of parents to the care, custody, and control of their children [is] perhaps the oldest of the fundamental liberty interests recognized by this Court."

The Juvenile Delinquency Act of 1948, as amended in 1974 and 1994, authorizes federal prosecution of misdemeanors by juveniles under the age of eighteen years within federal jurisdictions, such as national parks. Although most juvenile crimes are prosecuted under state law, the federal courts may hear several hundred delinquency cases a year. Federal courts also deal with appeals from state court decisions involving juveniles. In *Seling v. Young* (2001), the Supreme Court noted that a Washington law addressing sexually violent offenders applies to "prisoners, juveniles, persons found incompetent to stand trial, persons found guilty by reason of insanity, and persons ... convicted of a sexually violent offense."

State Law

To handle issues involving young people, many states have juvenile courts that deal with abuse and neglect; adoption; "status offenses" stemming from juvenile misconduct such as truancy, running away from home, and difficulties with parental discipline; and delinquency, or offenses that would be treated as misdemeanors or felonies if committed by adults. Some states have unified family court systems that address a broad range of domestic problems. But state laws vary on who is a minor or a juvenile and how they are treated under the law.

Many state age limits and requirements include or exclude some teenagers. California, for one, defines teenagers and young adults as "individuals between 13 and 24 years of age"; for purposes of the California Comprehensive Sexual Health and HIV/AIDS Prevention Act (2003), the state refers to "'age appropriate' ... topics, messages, and teaching methods suitable to particular ages or age groups of children and adolescents, based on developing cognitive, emotional, and behavioral capacity typical for the age or age group."

The areas in which teenage sexual behavior and the law intersect include intergenerational sex (sex between an adult and an adolescent). *Ephebophilia* (Greek for "adolescent love") is defined as the sexual attraction of an adult for an adolescent. Pederasty refers to a sexual relationship between an adult male and male adolescents. A "Lolita complex," derived from the 1955 book *Lolita* by Vladimir Nabokov (1899–1977), describes an adult male attraction to a female adolescent. Pedophilia is an attraction to prepubescent children.

Although parents may have rights to raise their offspring as they wish, subject to laws penalizing abuse and neglect, they cannot always control their children's sexual behavior. The same laws that apply to adults are often applied to adolescents, and the same legal concept of CONSENT may be relevant. About twenty states permit some form of consensual sexual activity as early as age fourteen; in a dozen states, the age is sixteen. Louisiana allows some consensual sexual activity by youngsters between thirteen and seventeen, so long as the male partner is not more than two years older than the other person. Such statutes are sometimes called "Romeo and Juliet laws" in reference to the young star-crossed lovers in Shakespeare's *Tragedy of Romeo and Juliet* (1594).

Statutory RAPE laws, however, make it a crime to have sexual intercourse with a partner who is less than the statutory age limit. In nearly all states, the crime may be committed by either a male or a female. Some states create categories of persons who commit offenses against adolescents. In Colorado, for example, anyone in a position of trust with respect to a victim may not have sexual contact with that person if he or she is under the age of eighteen years. Oregon makes it a crime to have sexual intercourse with a person under sixteen years of age who is a sibling, a child, or a spouse's child.

Unlike the *Craig* case cited above, the Supreme Court held in *Michael M. v. Superior Court of Sonoma County* (1981) that states can discriminate between males and females in the application of statutory rape laws. In this case, California had criminalized "sexual intercourse accomplished with a female not the wife of the perpetrator, where the female is under the age of 18 years." A seventeen-and-one-half-year-old male was prosecuted under the law for having intercourse with a sixteen-and-one-half-year-old female; he appealed his conviction, asserting that the law unfairly discriminated on the basis of GENDER. The Court concluded that the law was not unconstitutional under the equal protection clause of the U.S. Constitution, because the state's interest in preventing teenage PREGNANCY was legitimate and because the

consequences of sexual intercourse fall more heavily on the female, whom the statutory age was intended to protect.

In addition to teen pregnancy, other areas of sexual behavior that draw special concern or legal treatment include access to health care services, ABORTION, MARRIAGE (for those under the age of consent), SEXUALLY TRANSMITTED DISEASES such as AIDS-HIV, MOTHERHOOD, SEX EDUCATION, HOMOSEXUALITY, and discrimination on the basis of sex or sexual orientation. In such cases, however, the rights of minors can be protected only through the assistance of a parent or a guardian. On occasion, the rights of parents and an adolescent may be in opposition—for instance, in the case of a minor who seeks an abortion in a state that requires prior notice to parents.

The law is often more confusing when dealing with homosexual as opposed to heterosexual behavior. The benefits of a "Romeo and Juliet law" in Kansas, which treats sex between a male and a female teenager when they are more than fourteen years of age and not more than four years apart less severely than other forms of statutory rape, was denied to an eighteen-year-old male who had consensual sex with another male not quite fifteen years old. After an appeal supported by the Lesbian and Gay Rights Project of the AMERICAN CIVIL LIBERTIES UNION, the Kansas supreme court, in *State v. Limon* (2005), rejected the state's reliance on "traditional sexual mores." It noted that in LAWRENCE V. TEXAS (2003), the U.S. Supreme Court had declared consensual adult homosexual activity in private to be constitutionally protected and ordered that the defendant be recharged under the "Romeo and Juliet law," in accordance with the new ruling to treat gay and strait teens equally.

Society has a special duty to fashion laws that are flexible enough to deal with adolescents' individual problems, yet strict enough to deter the abusers and sexual predators who prey on young people's vulnerability and curiosity. The new era of the INTERNET, with its potential for cybersex, presents a challenging situation: here the freedom of information guaranteed by the Constitution to all adult citizens has made it difficult to completely protect young people from sexual predators and distributors of obscenity. Parents and the community are generally better able to deal with teenagers' sexual behavior than are elected legislators. But when they fail, the law must step in for the good of the young people and society.

See also CHILD ONLINE PROTECTION ACT; COMMUNICATIONS DECENCY ACT; INCEST; TELEPHONE SEX.

TELEPHONE SEX

Telephone sex is vicarious sexual behavior in which at least one of the parties is sexually stimulated by talking and listening to another person on the telephone. Although this activity may be pursued by mutual agreement, it is most often a service provided by one person for a fee. In addition to stimulating physical sexual activity, telephone sex may also serve as a means of sexual expression and release of sexual anxieties for individuals who wish to avoid personal physical contact or involvement with actual partners.

Commercial Telephone Sex

The key case in the area of commercial telephone sex is *Sable Communications of California, Inc. v. Federal Communications Commission* (1989). Sable Communications was engaged in transmitting sexually oriented prerecorded telephone messages, commonly known as dial-a-porn, to callers in and outside the Los Angeles metropolitan area. In its decision, the U.S. Supreme Court affirmed that while OBSCENITY is not covered by the freedom of expression protections of the FIRST AMENDMENT (1791) to the U.S. Constitution, language that is simply indecent is protected. The Court struck down as unconstitutional a provision in section 223(b) of the Communications Act of 1934 that banned indecent messages over the telephone, but it left intact a ban on obscene language.

In *Sable* the Supreme Court noted a theme that would carry through to later decisions regarding PORNOGRAPHY on the INTERNET: because the telephone, unlike television or radio, requires taking steps to access questionable material, CHILDREN are less likely to be exposed to adult-oriented material. In fact, commercial telephone-sex enterprises are able to screen recipients of such calls to determine their age, using identification numbers previously assigned or requiring a credit card. Not long after the *Sable* decision, however, many telephone-sex businesses moved offshore to bypass state restrictions on the use of 900 and 976 dialing prefixes, which are assigned to such businesses.

To avoid a charge of making an indecent telephone call to a person under eighteen years of age, California law provides that a caller may either require "the person receiving the obscene matter to use an authorized access or identification code … after taking reasonable measures to ascertain that the [recipient] was 18 years of age or older" or require "payment by credit card before transmission of the matter." A New Jersey statute regarding telephone companies states: "No telephone company the principal business of which is the provision of telephone service within this State shall provide a subscriber access to adult-oriented information-access telephone service originating in the State without written authorization from the subscriber.… '[A]dult-oriented information-access telephone service' means a class of telephone service where for a charge, in addition to the basic exchange charge, sexually explicit recorded messages are furnished." Washington is another state that has addressed this issue, although most states to date have not.

Obscene Phone Calls

Exhibitionism is a form of sexual behavior in which a person, almost always a male, attempts to obtain sexual satisfaction by shocking another person, almost always a female, using some type of antisocial behavior. Examples include exposing one's genitals or shocking or frightening a listener over the telephone. Sometimes the caller uses obscene language to scare or harass the person called.

Obscene or harassing telephone calls are prohibited under the Communications Act of 1934, as amended, and under state laws. For example, a Virginia law provides, "If any person shall use obscene, vulgar, profane, lewd, lascivious, or indecent language, or make any suggestion or proposal of an obscene nature, or threaten any illegal or immoral act with the intent to coerce, intimidate, or harass any person, over any telephone or citizens band radio, . . . he shall be guilty of a . . . misdemeanor."

In *Gilbreath v. State* (1995), a Florida court held that a criminal law prohibiting obscene or harassing telephone calls did not violate the First Amendment right of free speech as long as the statute is limited to calls made with the intent to harass, threaten, or abuse and directed to a location where the listener has a reasonable expectation of privacy. A court in Illinois held in *People v. Taylor* (2004) that a similar state law does not bar the use of vulgar or indecent language, except when the calls are made with an improper intent, such as harassment.

The big business that telephone sex represented at the time of the *Sable* case has been greatly eclipsed by the Internet. (According to a footnote in the opinion, the "dial-a-porn service in New York City alone received six to seven million calls a month for the six-month period ending in April 1985.") Now adults have easy access online to a wide range of sexually explicit visual and aural material. Yet, despite caller IDs and call blocking, obscene and sexually harassing telephone calls still constitute a significant problem for unlucky recipients, telephone service providers, and law enforcement.

See also FEDERAL COMMUNICATIONS COMMISSION; INDECENT EXPOSURE; LEWD BEHAVIOR.

TELEVISION

See CENSORSHIP; ENTERTAINMENT INDUSTRY; FEDERAL COMMUNICATIONS COMMISSION; MEDIA.

TITLE IX

The civil rights movement of the 1960s—aimed at ending DISCRIMINATION against black citizens—jump started a similar movement to achieve EQUAL RIGHTS for women. The Equal Pay Act (1963) of the Fair Labor Standards Act prohibited employers covered by the act from paying lower wages to one sex when the job requires "equal skill, effort, and responsibility, and [is] performed under similar working conditions." The following year Title VII of the Civil Rights Act of 1964 prohibited discrimination in the workplace "because of sex." In 1972 CONGRESS approved the Equal Rights Amendment (which was never ratified) and also passed Title IX of the Education Amendments to the Higher Education Act of 1965. The new education law was designed to keep federal funds from supporting sexually discriminatory practices in education programs and to protect citizens from such discriminatory practices.

Title IX declares: "No person in the United States shall, on the basis of sex, be excluded from participation in, be denied the benefits of, or be subjected to discrimination under any education program or activity receiving Federal financial assistance." A list of exceptions includes "educational institutions of religious organizations with contrary religious tenets," those "training individuals for military services or merchant marine," "social fraternities or sororities," and "voluntary youth service organizations."

Initially the U.S. Supreme Court broadly applied Title IX's provisions—for example, by finding an implied right to a private cause of action to enforce its provisions. But in 1984 the Court, in *Grove City College v. Bell*, began limiting the law's scope by declaring that only programs or activities that received direct federal financial assistance were covered. Congress then acted to subvert the Court's holding by passing the Civil Rights Restoration Act of 1987 over the veto of President Ronald Reagan, thus extending the law to cover any type of federal financial assistance, direct or indirect.

The standing of plaintiffs has also been broadened since the law was enacted. At first only applicants and students had standing to enforce it, but in 1982 the Court extended this right to employees of educational institutions. The defendants are generally those nonexempt educational institutions responsible for administering education programs and activities that receive federal funding, including school boards. According to cases such as *Flood v. Waiters* (1998), individuals cannot be held liable for violations of Title IX.

Claims involving SEXUAL HARASSMENT can be brought under Title IX as well as actions claiming unequal educational programming and unequal athletic opportunities; according to a Supreme Court decision in 1999, under certain conditions peer student harassment (for which a school could be held liable) may also be a violation of the law. Although Title VII of the Civil Rights Act of 1964, which prohibits discrimination on the basis of sex in the workplace, provides some guidance for interpreting Title IX, the two laws come at sex discrimination from different perspectives. The aim of the civil rights statute is to compensate victims, while the goal of the education law is to prevent federal funding of discrimination. Teachers, who are covered under both laws, tend to bring actions under Title VII. Moreover, although Title VII has a cap on the amount of damages payable and Title IX does not, the lower standards for establishing liability under Title VII make it the preferred law under which to file.

The primary agency responsible for enforcement of Title IX is the U.S. Department of Education's Office for Civil Rights. This office issues regulations and may administratively enforce its own interpretation of the law. The agency first investigates a complaint and then attempts to resolve the problem through informal means. If this fails, it may request that the U.S. Department of Justice file a formal complaint in federal court. As a last resort, the office may revoke the federal funding of any institution found to be in violation of the law.

In addition to termination of federal funding, Title IX may be enforced through private lawsuits. In *Cannon v. University of Chicago* (1979), the Supreme Court held that although Title IX lacks explicit language creating a private right of action, the law had been modeled on Title VI of the Civil Rights Act of 1964 (prohibiting discrimination on the basis of race, color, or national origin in federally assisted programs); therefore, the Court reasoned, Title IX, like Title VI, contained an implied right of private action. Citing *Cort v. Ash* (1975), the justices found that an implied right to use private suits was met if the plaintiff was a member of a special class that the law was intended to benefit; that there was evidence that lawmakers intended to allow for a private remedy; that such a remedy was consistent with the purpose of the law; and that there was no conflict between such a federal remedy and concerns of the states.

Remedies available for successful private lawsuits include injunctive and declaratory relief, equitable relief (including back pay and tuition), and compensatory and punitive damages. In *Franklin v. Gwinnett County Public Schools* (1992), the Supreme Court recognized the appropriateness of monetary damages in cases in which there was a finding of intentional discrimination. Punitive damages have been reserved for extreme violations of Title IX, although a federal district court held in 1997 that sovereign immunity precludes punitive damages against a municipal school district.

The protections of Title IX continue to be extended by the courts. For example, in *Jackson v. Birmingham Board of Education* (2005), the Supreme Court extended coverage to whistle blowers, in this case the coach of a girls' basketball team who was fired in retaliation for complaining that the boys' teams were given better equipment and practice facilities. In the majority opinion for the Court, Associate Justice Sandra Day O'Connor said: "Reporting incidents of discrimination is integral to Title IX enforcement and would be discouraged if retaliation against those who reported [violations] went unpunished."

Contact: Office for Civil Rights, U.S. Department of Education, 550 12th Street, SW, Washington, DC 20202-1100 (800-421-3481). www.ed.gov/about/offices/list/ocr.

TRAFFICKING

See HUMAN TRAFFICKING; PROSTITUTION.

TRANSGENDER PERSONS

See GENDER; TRANSSEXUALISM; TRANSVESTISM.

TRANSSEXUALISM

A transsexual is a person, generally a biological male, who considers himself to have been born with the wrong genitalia and thus the wrong sex. Transgender persons, as they are now commonly called, believe that their genetically determined sex, male or female, is incompatible with how they see themselves sexually. Acute psychological suffering may result from this dichotomy between one's sexual identity and one's sex organs. Today the condition is increasingly mitigated by sex-reassignment procedures, including behavioral, hormonal, legal, and even surgical steps to make an individual's sexuality comport with his or her perceived GENDER, as opposed to sex at birth. Transsexualism differs from TRANSVESTISM, whereby men in particular enjoy dressing as the opposite sex, and HOMOSEXUALITY, which involves sexual attraction to the same sex without serious gender issues. Transsexuals may engage in both heterosexual and homosexual relations, although they do not consider the latter contact as being homosexual given their gender dysphoria (discomfort with one's gender).

There is little historical evidence of transsexualism. The most convincing case has been made for the third-century-C.E. Roman emperor Elagabalus, who is reported to have acted as a woman, demanded to be honored as an empress, and sought medical help to physically change his genitalia to that of a woman. The condition was cited by ALFRED KINSEY in his 1948 report on male sexuality. Before Dr. John Money of Johns Hopkins University introduced sex-reassignment

Christine Jorgensen, formerly George William Jorgensen Jr., became world famous when she had transsexual surgery in 1952. The operation was performed in Denmark, where Jorgensen is shown leaving to return to the United States. Sex-change surgery has since helped many people who suffer from gender-identity disorder.

surgery to the United States in the late 1960s, it had been available mainly in European countries such as Denmark; while such surgery can go far to mimic the desired male or female anatomy, it cannot make the patient capable of reproduction.

Discrimination

DISCRIMINATION against transsexuals, while being addressed to some degree in laws and court decisions, is not being given the same attention as discrimination against women or racial and ethnic minorities. In *Farmer v. Brennan* (1994), a preoperative transsexual had been incarcerated in a federal prison system with other male prisoners. Alleging that prison officials were deliberately indifferent to his safety—constituting cruel and unusual punishment under the Eighth Amendment (1791) to the U.S. Constitution—he sued for damages for mistreatment and for an injunction against further confinement in a federal penitentiary. Although a lower court found that prison officials had not violated the prohibition against cruel and unusual punishment, the U.S. Supreme Court overruled the decision and remanded the case for reconsideration, thus acknowledging that transsexualism may be the basis of constitutional protection.

In *Long v. Nix* (1995), a federal district court held that placing a prisoner claiming to be transsexual in an inappropriate facility and denying the desired medical treatment without a hearing did not violate the prisoner's right to due process under the Fourteenth Amendment (1868). Then, in *Maggert v. Hanks* (1997), a federal appeals court found that a transsexual prisoner suffering from gender dysphoria was not a victim of cruel and unusual punishment when prison officials refused to provide costly treatment, estimated then at up to $100,000. Some federal courts, however, have upheld Medicaid coverage of transsexual surgery for indigent persons.

But courts have also ruled that employers are not required under Title VII of the Civil Rights Act of 1964—which prohibits workplace discrimination based on sex as well as race, color, religion, and national origin—to protect transsexuals from discrimination. In *Ulane v. Eastern Airlines, Inc.* (1984), a federal appeals court stated that "[w]hile we do not condone discrimination in any form, we are constrained to hold that Title VII does not protect transsexuals." In this case, a male airline pilot hired as Kenneth Ulane in 1968 was fired as Karen Frances Ulane in 1981 following a medical diagnosis that he was a transsexual undergoing sex-reassignment surgery. The court's decision was grounded in the traditional definition of sex, saying that if the term is "to mean more than biological male or biological female, the new definition must come from Congress." Because

Eastern Airlines discriminated against Ulane on the basis that she was a transsexual and not that she was a biological female, Title VII afforded no protection.

In *Ulane* the court discussed the problem of "an individual's sexual identity disorder or discontent with the sex into which they were born." A year later, a federal district court in *Doe v. U.S. Postal Service* (1985) heard the case of a man who had been denied a job after he informed his prospective employer that he was a transsexual. According to the court, he was entitled to a factual determination under the Rehabilitation Act of 1973 of whether he had been discriminated against because he was handicapped. The problem of distinguishing whether a transsexual is merely expressing a preference for having a different sexual identity or whether he or she is suffering from a condition that requires medical correction continues to muddy the waters in this area.

Some male transsexuals take hormones to emphasize the female aspects of their persona yet retain male genitalia. In *Goins v. West Group* (2001), such a transgender person had been granted a change in his birth certificate based on his "transidentified" status as a female and was hired by West Group. After he was transferred by the company to Minnesota, female colleagues complained to their supervisors about having to share restroom facilities with "her." Then the employer barred him from the women's restroom. The Minnesota supreme court ruled that the employer was not guilty of discrimination because restroom access was based on sex and not gender. The court left open the question of how access based on genitalia could be monitored, whether by some sort of regular inspection system or by a doctor's certification. Such a problem does not generally arise in public restrooms, only where the same people regularly use the same facilities.

Related Transgender Issues

In addition to outright discrimination, transsexuals also have a number of other legal hurdles to face. One reason is that many Americans still consider transsexualism to be voluntary, antisocial, and aberrant behavior.

The law has yet to act in a consistent and tolerant way toward them.

Name Change. Most states have refused to allow postoperative transsexuals to legally change the sex identification on their birth certificate. Having a masculine name legally changed to a feminine one is less problematic, however. In *In re Harris* (1997), a transsexual petitioned a Pennsylvania court for a name change from Brian to Lisa. On appeal the superior court granted the petition, ruling that the petitioner's desire for a name change to conform to a change of gender is generally sufficient to support the action; the court indicated that each petition must be evaluated on a case-by-case basis to determine whether "a legal name change would benefit both petitioner and the public at large and [comports] with good sense and fairness to all concerned." Some courts, citing possible fraud, have denied such changes unless the petitioner has undergone surgery, thereby pressuring transgender persons to undergo sex reassignment rather than rely on steps such as hormone therapy alone.

Marriage. Several problems may arise from MARRIAGE involving transsexuals. The Kansas supreme court ruled in *In re Estate of Gardiner* (2002) that state law permitted only marriage between a man and a woman, finding that a transsexual—even after surgically changing his genitalia—was still a male according to legislative intent. There are, however, two lines of thought on this question: (1) that sex at birth determines one's sex regardless of later changes or attempts to change, and (2) that sex at birth may be changed to comport with gender and be so recognized under the law. But a Kentucky court, in *Spina v. Spina* (2004), held that "once a male, always a male." It dismissed a female spouse's request to have her marriage annulled after her husband had his sex changed to female. Presumably the wife could obtain a legal DIVORCE under no-fault provisions or on grounds of irreconcilable differences.

Child Support and Custody. In re Karin T. v. Michael T. (1985) involved the mother of two children who sought CHILD SUPPORT from her "husband," a female who wore men's clothing and had changed her name from Marlene to Michael. A New York family court held that the "husband" qualified as a parent under state law, having "brought forth these offspring [by agreeing to the artificial insemination of her spouse] as if done biologically." As for child custody, the interests of the CHILDREN have to be taken into account; in many cases the parental rights of a transsexual may thus be terminated by a divorce or a separation and custody, and visitation rights may be denied.

See also ANNULMENT.

TRANSVESTISM

History, literature, and drama include many examples of men and women who dressed in the clothing of the opposite sex. Joan of Arc (1412–31) dressed as a man and led French troops into battle. The American author Mark Twain (1835–1910) clothed his character Tom Sawyer as a girl during some of his adventures. In the plays of William Shakespeare (1564–1616), all the female parts were played on stage by males.

Transvestism, or cross-dressing, is generally defined as the abnormal desire to dress in the clothing of the opposite sex. Sometimes referred to as transvestitism, the condition known as transvestic fetishism is defined in psychology as a sexual disorder marked by intense and recurrent sexual urges and fantasies involving cross-dressing. The condition is generally considered a male disorder, although some women wear men's clothing and attempt to pass as men in public. Transvestism may or may not be accompanied by a lack of comfort with one's own GENDER, and males who are female impersonators may or may not be transvestic fetishists.

Unless a fraud is perpetrated, cross-dressing is usually a victimless activity. However, in *P. v. P.* (1972), a New Jersey woman was granted a DIVORCE on the grounds of extreme cruelty because her husband turned out to be a transvestite. Some parents of elementary school students in Spurger, Texas, were apparently offended enough by a school tradition of having students reverse sexual roles and cross-dress on one day a year that in 2004 they ended the practice, which was then replaced with a day when all the students were to dress in camouflage clothing.

Criminalization

In the second half of the nineteenth century, a number of U.S. cities—including Chicago, St. Louis, and Oakland, California—adopted laws making it a crime to appear in public in the clothes of the opposite sex. Such an aberration was deemed to be the equivalent of other forms of LEWD BEHAVIOR, along with public NUDITY and exhibiting obscene pictures. In his book *Psychopathia Sexualis* (1886), the pioneering German psychiatrist Baron Richard von Krafft-Ebing (1840–1902) included behaviors such as cross-dressing in his catalogue of sexual pathologies, adding intellectual support for laws against cross-dressing that continued on the books in many places until the 1980s.

In *People v. Archibald* (1968), the supreme court of New York (not the state's highest court) affirmed the conviction of a cross-dressing man under a statute that prohibited a disguise "in a manner calculated to conceal his being identified." But ten years later, the Illinois supreme court overturned a conviction under a law that imposed a fine for appearing "in a public place … in a dress not belonging to his or her sex, with the intent to conceal his or her sex."

Federal and state courts soon began to further chip away at laws against cross-dressing on the grounds of their vagueness. As the chief justice of Ohio's supreme court observed in *City of Columbus v. Rogers* (1975), the problem with the language in the city ordinance, such as "a dress not belonging to his or her sex," is that in view of current fashions, "men

of common intelligence must necessarily guess at its meaning and differ as to its application," making it unconstitutional under the due process clause of the Fourteenth Amendment (1868) to the U.S. Constitution.

Discrimination

Transvestism can be associated with TRANSSEXUALISM, gender dysphoria (discomfort with one's gender), and gender-identity disorder. The supreme court of Washington State heard the case of a biological male who was dressing as a female and using the women's restroom as part of his psychological preparation for sex-reassignment surgery. In *Doe v. Boeing Company* (1993), the court held that gender dysphoria is not a handicap under the state's antidiscrimination laws and that Boeing did not discriminate against Doe by firing him for his refusal to conform to company directives on acceptable attire. However, the superior court of New Jersey, in *Enriquez v. West Jersey Health Systems* (2001), found that "gender dysphoria is a recognized mental or psychological disability … and qualifies as a handicap" under state law.

Like many aspects of sexual activity, the range of behavior related to cross-dressing is quite broad, and only some forms trigger legal implications. The difference between a man's dressing as a woman for a costume party, for example, and his dressing as a woman at work and using the women's restroom can be legally significant. When a person suffers from a specific psychological disorder that influences his or her behavior, the law generally should provide exceptions for what otherwise may be illegal behavior. When it comes to gender issues, the law is still catching up with modern science and changing mores.

See also HOMOSEXUALITY.

u

UNBORN, RIGHTS OF THE

Although the government has always asserted an interest in sexual behavior, the notion that unborn CHILDREN have rights is relatively new to U.S. law. It is a concept that developed as a counterpoint to the right to ABORTION established by the U.S. Supreme Court in *Roe v. Wade* (1973). Legal requirements for MARRIAGE are largely related to the state's interest in the support and rearing of children—a product of marriage—as well as in the protection of children's interests in the event of a DIVORCE. A child's nearly total dependence on her or his mother after conception and during its sequestration in the womb has traditionally limited the extent of government involvement during the gestation period.

An important aspect of governmental protection of fetuses is the determination of when an unborn child legally becomes a person. This conundrum has brought recent clashes between proponents of extending the right to life to an embryo at the moment of conception and those who assert that women have the right to control their own reproductive capabilities, at least before a fetus's viability, in the case of RAPE, and where an expectant mother's health or life is in danger. Some states, without scientific evidence to support them, have declared in legislation the precise time when a child's life begins in the womb. For example, the Missouri code was amended in 1988 to define this event: "The general assembly of this state finds that: (1) The life of each human being begins at conception; (2) Unborn children have protectable interests in life, health, and well-being; (3) The natural parents of unborn children have protectable interests in the life, health, and well-being of their unborn child." In outlawing abortion in 2006, a South Dakota law stated that the legislature concurred with conclusions "that life begins at the time of conception.... Moreover, the Legislature finds that the guarantee of due process of law under the Constitution of South Dakota applies equally to born and unborn human beings."

Mothers or Babies?

The debate over the nature and extent of the rights of unborn children—like some politicians' assertions in the 1970s that they spoke on behalf of a "silent majority" of citizens—is one that pits adult citizens who claim to speak for fetuses against similar adults who can speak for themselves. While clearly underpinned by religious beliefs, especially those of Roman Catholics and evangelical Christians, arguments for extending rights to the unborn are often couched in legal terms. To bolster the proposition that the U.S. Supreme Court has erred in denying citizenship to unborn children, some proponents cite the infamous Dred Scott case, *Scott v. Sandford* (1857), which denied citizenship rights to a black slave but was later overturned.

Those who argue instead for WOMEN'S RIGHTS and their REPRODUCTIVE RIGHTS rely on the right of PRIVACY gleaned from the Bill of Rights (1791), the first ten amendments to the U.S. Constitution, as enunciated by the Supreme Court in GRISWOLD V. CONNECTICUT (1965); later decisions, among them *Roe v. Wade* (1973), relied on this decision to find state laws banning abortion to be unconstitutional. The Court held in *Roe* that a woman, in consultation with her doctor in private, has a constitutionally protected right to decide whether or not to carry a fetus to term and that the state did not have a significant interest in protecting the life of a fetus in the early stages of its development.

It has been difficult to keep the debate over the rights of unborn children from impinging on the issue of abortion rights. However, a number of other clashes have arisen between the rights of the expectant mother and efforts to protect the rights of the child she is carrying.

Prenatal Substance Abuse

Many states have drug laws that make it a crime to deliver controlled substances to a minor, and these have sometimes been stretched to include a fetus. A Missouri statute, however, includes this language to avoid criminalizing a mother's personal actions during PREGNANCY: "Nothing in this section shall be interpreted as creating a cause of action against a woman for indirectly harming her unborn child by failing to properly care for herself or by failing to follow any particular program of prenatal care." A problem of enforcing laws that criminalize drug use during pregnancy is that if an expectant mother is convicted, she may be incarcerated in jail—not a healthy atmosphere for any child. In upholding a woman's conviction in South Carolina, the state supreme court ruled in *State v. McKnight* (2003) that a jury should decide the requisite criminal intent of a mother whose stillborn child had cocaine in her body. The U.S. Supreme Court refused to review the McKnight case in 2003, although it had held in *Ferguson v. City of Charleson* (2001) that nonconsensual urine tests of pregnant women for the presence of drugs were a violation of the Fourth Amendment (1791) to the U.S. Constitution.

In contrast, a Florida court in *Johnson v. State* (1992) overturned the conviction of a mother charged with delivery of a controlled substance (cocaine) to her child through the umbilical cord during birth; the court found that the law's legislative history did not indicate that the word *delivery* was meant to extend to the birth process. *In re Unborn Child of Starks* (2001) involved the mother of a six-month-old fetus who was arrested for manufacturing and possessing the drug methamphetamine; the Oklahoma supreme court refused to allow the state's department of human services to take custody of the fetus under the state's law regarding neglected children, noting that a fetus does not come under the statutory or judicial definition of a child. In Colorado the exclusion of a fetus from the definition of a child was similarly upheld in *Accord in the Interest of H.* (2003).

"Partial-Birth Abortion"

Thirty-one states and the federal government have passed laws restricting the rare procedure called "partial-birth abortion" by its opponents, although many of these statutes have been challenged in court and are not in force. Under state law this procedure is generally described as an abortion in which a doctor partially delivers a fetus vaginally, kills the fetus, and then completes the delivery. The Virginia code states: "Any person who knowingly performs partial birth infanticide and thereby kills a human infant is guilty of a . . . felony." The law, now enjoined, goes on to declare that "'partial birth infanticide' means any deliberate act that (i) is intended to kill a human infant who has been born alive, but who has not been completely extracted or expelled from its mother, and that (ii) does kill such infant, regardless of whether death occurs before or after extraction or expulsion from its mother has been completed."

Infanticide

Infanticide refers to the murder or killing of a child after birth. The act is thus distinguished from a legal abortion, a natural miscarriage, or fetal homicide (killing a child before it is born). The latter action is covered by rules regarding abortion and the intent of the person committing the act, whether the mother or another person.

State laws treat infanticide as any other murder or killing, including various degrees of culpability from involuntary manslaughter through premeditated first-degree murder. In the case of infanticide, special requirements may come into play. For example, in *State v. McGuire* (1997), the West Virginia supreme court noted that in "a prosecution for the homicide of a newly born infant, it is incumbent upon the State to prove that the infant was born alive [and] that the infant had an independent and separate existence from its mother."

Fetal Homicide

In 2004 CONGRESS enacted the Unborn Victims of Violence Act, partly in response to the highly publicized California trial for the death of Laci Peterson and her eight-month-old fetus; her husband, Scott Peterson, was found guilty of the first-degree murder of his wife and the second-degree murder of their child. The federal legislation makes it a separate offense to harm an unborn child while committing a violent federal crime against a pregnant women. At the signing President George W. Bush said: "With this action, we widen the circle of compassion and inclusion in our society, and we reaffirm the United States of America is building a culture of life." The term *culture of life* is often used by those who oppose abortion.

California, which has had a fetal-murder law since 1970, is one of more than thirty states that have statutes addressing violence and other harm to fetuses, and states such as West Virginia are proposing to enact such laws. Virginia's feticide law took effect on July 1, 2004, and shortly thereafter three persons were indicted under the statute. One case involved a charge of murdering an expectant mother and the unintended killing of her fetus in a fatal stabbing. The second case on similar charges involved a beating with a baseball bat.

In *Steven v. Rollen* (2003), the Missouri court of appeals affirmed a conviction for the murders of a pregnant woman and her seventeen-week-old fetus based on the state's felony-murder law, which applies if a "person" is killed while a defendant perpetrates a felony, in this case a robbery and a shooting. In doing so the court found a "significant distinction between a mother's right to terminate her pregnancy and the prosecution of a third party for murder of an unborn child without the consent of the mother."

Terminally Ill Expectant Mothers

Courts have generally held that a terminally ill pregnant woman has a right to decide her medical treatment, including procedures for giving birth. In *In re A. C.* (1990), for example, a court in the District of Columbia determined that as long as a terminally ill patient is mentally competent, her choice to have a cesarean birth that results in the death of the fetus must be honored. But where a pregnant woman refuses medical treatment—because of religious reasons, for instance—she may be forced to have the child delivered by cesarean section to save the life of a viable fetus.

See also DOMESTIC VIOLENCE; DRUGS; MOTHERHOOD; VIOLENCE AGAINST WOMEN ACT.

UNMARRIED COHABITANTS

Cohabitation occurs when a man and a woman—or less traditionally, persons of the same sex—live together in the same residence as if they were married. Early cases in U.S. law emphasized that such cohabitation must be continuous, rather than merely include visitations, and defined cohabitation as akin to ADULTERY, including acts of sexual intercourse. More recently, cohabitation has come to refer to a generally permanent relationship involving a heterosexual or homosexual couple who live together in the same household and assume to a large extent the same rights and duties as a typical married couple, including having sexual relations. The relationship may or may not involve the rearing of CHILDREN.

For much of American history, unmarried cohabitants were considered to be "living in sin." As late as 1978, a Wyoming court, in *Jelly v. Dabney*, found that the crime of "illicit cohabitation"—defined as the "dwelling or living together by a man and woman, not legally married to each other, in the manner of husband and wife, and indulgence in acts of sexual intercourse"—was punishable under a state prohibition of "lewdness." Few cases of this type were ever prosecuted, however. Unmarried couples could be granted, and in a handful of states are still granted, the rights of a common law marriage, in which a man and a woman, by agreement between themselves but without the benefit of a civil or a religious marriage ceremony, hold themselves out to be husband and wife. They have been accorded rights of married couples, including the right to file joint tax returns and to be considered spouses for insurance purposes.

In the past, people who were married but lived with a partner other than their spouse were sometimes viewed as committing the crime of BIGAMY. In *WILLIAMS v. NORTH CAROLINA* (1942, 1945), for example, a North Carolina couple who attempted to obtain divorces in Nevada from their respective spouses and then married each other in Nevada found themselves accused of bigamous cohabitation when North Carolina refused to recognize the Nevada divorces.

Modern Families

Since the *Jelly* case, U.S. law has moved rapidly away from criminalizing cohabitation by unmarried couples, which have become a sizable portion of the population. Between 1970 and 2002, U.S. Census figures show that the number of unmarried households rose from 10 to 16 percent of all 109 million households. The government is now gradually recognizing such arrangements as simply a way for two persons to live together without a formal MARRIAGE. This institutionalization of alternative families is changing the domestic legal landscape in America, both progressively and retrogressively.

Some legal analysts have noted that marriage's traditional privileged status in state law began eroding about the time of the "palimony" case of *Marvin v. Marvin* (1976). In this case, California's supreme court declared that "adults who voluntarily live together and engage in sexual relations are nonetheless as competent as any other persons to contract respecting their earnings and property rights" and that "a nonmarital partner may recover ... the reasonable value of household services rendered less the reasonable value of support received if he can show he has rendered [nonsexual] services with the expectation of monetary reward."

Since Lee Marvin's live-in partner, Michelle Marvin, was awarded a type of ALIMONY in the *Marvin* case, the legal nature of the family has become more privatized—that is, the rights and obligations are no longer set exclusively by state laws, and individuals are given more freedom to determine themselves many of the rights and duties of their particular form of family. State laws allowing no-fault DIVORCE have also helped erode some of the distinctions between married and unmarried cohabiting couples while making marriage less stable, as individuals can now decide for themselves when they wish to terminate a marriage relationship.

Although many states are adjusting their laws to accommodate new forms that do not fit into the mold of the traditional nuclear family—husband, wife, and children—many states and the federal government are acting to preserve the traditional family by denying homosexual couples the right to marry and by continuing to bar unmarried cohabitants from receiving benefits accorded marital partners.

Unmarried vs. Married Cohabitation

Now recognized as an essentially lawful arrangement, cohabitation by unmarried couples nonetheless does not provide many of the rights and privileges reserved legally for married couples.

Support. Cohabitation does not create any legal obligations on either party to provide financial and other types of support, which must instead be established by a written or an oral agreement. In the Georgia case *Holmes v. Holmes* (1998), a decedent's cohabiting partner, who admitted that she had lived with him without any promise of marriage or a contractual arrangement, was denied temporary support from his estate. But in New Jersey, in *Kozlowski v. Kozlowski* (1979), a court upheld support based on an unmarried cohabitant's contractual obligation. In the absence of an agrement, however, courts may deny alimony or an equitable distribution of unmarried cohabitants' property in the event of a separation.

Courts have generally held that language in a divorce settlement that terminates alimony if the spouse receiving support remarries does not cover the case where such a spouse cohabits without getting married. The supreme court of Alaska, in *Musgrove v. Musgrove* (1991), ruled that cohabitation alone would not terminate a former wife's maintenance payments. But the highest court in Alabama found that where a statute provided that periodic alimony would be terminated on proof of cohabitation, the ex-husband was not liable for support payments after the date his former wife began cohabitation.

Housing. Many states permit DISCRIMINATION in housing and ZONING against unmarried couples. In *City of Ladue v. Horn* (1986), for instance, a Missouri court of appeals found that a zoning ordinance that restricted residents to those related by blood, marriage, or adoption did not infringe on any fundamental rights or create a suspect classification for the purposes of discrimination and that the aim of the law—to prevent the erosion of traditional family life—was a valid one. In contrast, the New York court of appeals, in *Braschi v. Stahl Associates* (1989), held that gay partners may not be discriminated against under the rent-control laws of New York City. However, the next year, in *Levin v. Yeshiva* (1990), a New York court upheld a university's policy of offering housing only to spouses and dependent children of students.

Employment. Just as a married couple may face legal discrimination in employment because of rules against nepotism (employment of relatives), unmarried cohabitants may also face such discrimination.

In *Shahar v. Bowers* (1998), an attorney general of Georgia withdrew an offer of employment to a woman who planned to have a symbolic wedding ceremony with her lesbian partner; in balancing the attorney general's interest in hiring a person who would not reflect inappropriately on the office against the woman's constitutional right of association, a federal court of appeals found that his rights trumped hers.

Health and other employment benefits that have traditionally been extended to a married employee's spouse may be denied to an unmarried partner. State laws legally discriminate against extending benefits to unmarried partners because, as a California court explained in *Hinman v. Department of Personnel Administration* (1985), the state has a legitimate interest in promoting marriage. But a number of local governments and private employers are making heterosexual and homosexual unmarried partners eligible for some benefits by using the concept of domestic partnerships, which allow committed unmarried couples to be treated as spouses.

Inheritance. Most states still refuse to let unmarried partners inherit in the same way as spouses under intestacy laws (where the deceased does not leave a valid will). Some more progressive jurisdictions—among them, California, Hawaii, New Jersey, and Vermont— are making such inheritance possible through domestic partnership laws.

Torts. One spouse can bring a tort action for an injury or a wrong done to the other spouse. (A tort is an action that does not constitute a crime but for which the injured party can be compensated through court action.) State courts, however, are reluctant to extend this aspect of spousal rights to unmarried cohabitants. In *Graves v. Estabrook* (1994), however, a New Jersey court permitted recovery by a woman who had been in a long-term, well-established relationship with a man who was injured and died; she was engaged to be married to him and had witnessed the negligent act that caused the injury. But in *Elden v. Sheldon* (1988), a California court denied recovery by an unmarried cohabitant.

Contracts. The law has traditionally treated meretricious marriages (ones based solely on the provision of sexual favors) as against public policy because they are similar to PROSTITUTION; agreements between partners in such a marriage or between unmarried partners were generally held to be unenforceable. Today a minority of state courts continue to impose this rule against enforcing contracts between unmarried partners, although other, more enlightened state courts take the position that the contractual rights of unmarried and married partners should be treated similarly. As in the past, however, a contract will not be enforced if illicit sexual relations are a consideration or if the unmarried partners have not actually cohabited.

Children. Cohabitation has generally not been used to deny custody of children or visitation rights, as underscored by a California case, *In re Marriage of Wellman* (1980); here the court awarded a lesbian mother custody of her children after considering the custodial parent's "sexual proclivities upon the welfare of the [children] involved." Since the U.S. Supreme Court, in *Gomez v. Perez* (1973), struck down a Texas law that discriminated against illegitimate children in favor of children born to married parents, state laws and court decisions have generally become more balanced with respect to the rights of nonmarital children. An illegitimate child's right of inheritance from a biological father may, however, require a judicial determination of PATERNITY.

Although the U.S. Supreme Court has yet to decide the constitutionality of some retrogressive laws relating to untraditional couples, including those banning homosexuals from getting married, the Court's decision in LAWRENCE V. TEXAS (2003) was a watershed. In this case, laws against homosexual SODOMY between consenting adults in private were found to be unconstitutional. Such decisions reduce government's role in defining and controlling the private lives and sexual behavior of consenting adults. Yet with a more conservative Supreme Court, this trend toward the privatization of the family may be reconsidered.

See also CHILD SUPPORT; FEDERAL MARRIAGE AMENDMENT; HOMOSEXUALITY; ILLEGITIMACY; SAME-SEX MARRIAGE; SPOUSAL RIGHTS AND DUTIES; UNMARRIED PARENTS.

UNMARRIED PARENTS

Today many CHILDREN are born to or adopted and reared by unmarried parents. The percentage of births to unmarried persons rose from about 10 percent of all births in 1960 to nearly a third four decades later. Children have traditionally been considered by the law as a natural outcome of MARRIAGE, but there have always been occasions when the parents of a child were not married. Even before the erosion of the traditional nuclear family, children were sometimes born out of wedlock as a result of unmarried intercourse or RAPE or during a time when the parents' marriage was legally invalid for some reason. Now children can also be procreated by artificial means, such as in vitro fertilization, or by surrogacy, a process allowing an individual or a homosexual or heterosexual couple to become the parents of a child to whom another woman has given birth. In addition, a married person may become a de facto single parent when a separation occurs or when a spouse dies or is rendered incapable of parenting by disease or other disability; when spouses DIVORCE or obtain an ANNULMENT of their marriage, they may become de jure single or unwed parents.

Until recently U.S. law had focused on penalizing children born out of wedlock and, indirectly, their unmarried parents. Laws were directed at such parents specifically to encourage the rearing of children only in a married family setting. Now the stigma that the law and society had placed on unmarried parents and their children born out of wedlock has been mitigated to a large extent by court decisions and revised state laws. The paramount consideration has been redirected to what is best for the child regardless of the question of ILLEGITIMACY. A U.S. Supreme Court decision, in *Gomez v. Perez* (1973), for example, acknowledged that a state law cannot discriminate between marital and non-marital children in the matter of a statutory right of paternal child support.

Constitutional Law

Courts have generally declared that the rights, duties, and responsibilities of unwed single persons or couples, heterosexual and homosexual, with respect to their children are legally the same as those of married couples. Many of the following issues are applicable to married as well as unmarried parents.

Parental Rights. In two landmark cases, *Meyer v. Nebraska* (1923) and *Pierce v. Society of Sisters* (1925), the Supreme Court established the right of parents, within certain limitations, to rear their children without overweening government influence. In the first case, the Court struck down a state law that precluded teaching any language other than English to schoolchildren below the eighth grade; parents wanted a parochial teacher they had hired to teach their children German. In *Pierce* the Court invalidated a state law that precluded parents from sending their children between the ages of eight and sixteen years to parochial or private schools, holding that the law unreasonably infringed the parents' right to "direct the upbringing and education of children under their control."

Equal Protection. In *Levy v. Louisiana* (1968), the Supreme Court held for the first time that illegitimate children are persons within the meaning of the equal protection clause of the Fourteenth Amendment (1868) to the U.S. Constitution. In this case, the Court ruled that a nonmarital child could not be excluded by state law from recovering for the wrongful death of a parent. The justices continued to expand the rights of nonmarital children in *Gomez v. Perez* (1973), mentioned above, and in *Jimenez v. Weinberger* (1974), in which nonmarital children were found to be entitled to Social Security benefits.

Inheritance. James Kent declared in his *Commentaries on American Law* (1826), "A bastard being in the eye of the law *nullius filius* [the child of no one], . . . he . . . is incapable of inheriting as [an] heir, . . . nor can he have

heirs but of his own body." With respect to the right of inheritance today, in *Trimble v. Gordon* (1977), the Supreme Court found unconstitutional an Illinois law that did not allow nonmarital children to inherit from their fathers. A year later, however, the Court in *Lalli v. Lalli* permitted New York State to require proof of PATERNITY in the form of a court order in such cases. In a more recent case, *Nguyen v. Immigration and Naturalization Service* (2001), the Supreme Court found, at least as far as noncitizens are concerned, that having stricter statutory requirements for proof of paternity than for maternity in the case of unmarried parents does not constitute illegal sex DISCRIMINATION because of the difficulty involved in determining male parentage.

State Law

State laws now conform to the U.S. Supreme Court's rulings on the equality between illegitimate children and those born to married parents. Some states have gone beyond such decisions by requiring EQUAL RIGHTS for all their citizens in their constitutions or laws.

Child Support. State laws generally consider both parents of a child, whether married or not, to be responsible for his or her support. In a divorce or a legal separation, the rights and obligations of the parents will be determined in a court order. Otherwise both unmarried parents are required under most state laws to contribute to their children's support. Where there is a dispute, a court will determine how much each parent's contribution should be based on a number of factors, including the parent's gross or net income and, in some cases, the parent's potential earning ability in comparison with what he or she actually earns; the amount of the CHILD SUPPORT may be increased accordingly.

Children's Names. Under common law, illegitimate children were given no surname or family name at birth, but this changed as they began to be recognized as persons. In *Gubernat v. Deremer* (1995), a New Jersey court concluded that "in contested cases the surname of the custodial parent—the parent primarily charged with making custodial decisions in the child's best interest—shall be presumed to be consistent with that child's best interests." Such a presumption may be rebutted, however, to show that a different surname would better serve those interests.

Adoption. The majority of birth parents who give up a child for adoption are unmarried; more than 90 percent of these children are born to single parents, while the remainder are born to cohabiting parents. Unwed parents who wish to adopt a child can generally do so under state laws and adoption agency rules. States have different requirements for adoption; some states allow adoption even if a prospective parent is not a resident of the state in which the adoption will take place. No state law precludes unmarried adults from adopting, but Florida and Mississippi expressly prohibit adoption by homosexuals; Utah bars adoption by anyone cohabiting but not married; and Connecticut permits sexual orientation to be considered, despite a law against discrimination on this basis.

Inheritance. State laws differ widely on the question of inheritance by and from a nonmarital child. State courts traditionally have not allowed unmarried partners to inherit without a will or another legal agreement. But a few states have adopted laws that allow an unmarried partner to be treated like a spouse in a legal marriage. For example, Hawaii's domestic partnership law permits unmarried partners to be "reciprocal beneficiaries" in the case of death, and California's law extends most spousal rights to same-sex and unmarried heterosexual couples over sixty-two years of age. Most states allow a nonmarital child to inherit from an intestate mother, but they often have difficulty with cases involving unwed fathers.

In *Lowell v. Kowalski* (1980), a court in Massachusetts (which has an equal rights amendment to its state constitution) voided a state law requiring the parents of a natural child to be married before the illegitimate child could participate in an inheritance; to prevent fraud, it allowed some requirements to be placed on the right to inherit, such as proof that the decedent had acknowledged the child as his own. Louisiana has a state constitutional provision that prohibits discrimination on the basis of birth, a right that can also be used to invalidate statutes that treat nonmarital children unequally.

Wrongful Death. In line with the U.S. Supreme Court's extension of equal rights to nonmarital children, in *Guard v. State* (1997) Washington's state supreme court declared unconstitutional a statute that made the father of a nonmarital child ineligible to sue for the wrongful death of that child. An amendment to the state's constitution declares: "Equality of rights and responsibilities under the law shall not be denied or abridged on account of sex." Using this provision, an unmarried father was able to assert his rights over his child. The court found that the capacity to suffer the loss of a child was not unique to mothers.

See also ASSISTED REPRODUCTIVE TECHNOLOGY; MOTHERHOOD; PREGNANCY; UNMARRIED COHABITANTS.

U.S. DEPARTMENT OF HEALTH AND HUMAN SERVICES

The U.S. Department of Health and Human Services, a cabinet-level federal agency in the executive branch, develops policies and administers rules and regulations that relate to sexual behavior in various ways. Major functional areas of the department include CHILDREN and families, health care research and quality, disease control and prevention, safe food and DRUGS, and mental health services. A major aspect of its activities involves genetics as related to health, disease, therapy, and cloning.

HHS was created in 1953 as the Department of Health, Education and Welfare, but in 1979 most of the education programs were transferred to the newly created Department of Education. Before the twentieth century, most of the needs that the department addressed were handled by the states. In 1939, however, the Federal Security Agency was established to administer federal programs relating to Social Security, job placement, education, and public health. The nature of these federal programs had grown to such an extent by 1953 that a cabinet-level office was deemed necessary to oversee their administration.

The department's secretary is appointed by the PRESIDENT with the advice and consent of the U.S. Senate. The secretary advises the president on issues such as health, welfare, and income security plans, polices, and programs; directs the staff of the department; and promotes general public understanding of the department's goals and programs. The mission of HHS is to ensure public health and assist children and families. With field offices in ten major cities—including Atlanta, Dallas, Seattle, and Kansas City, Missouri—the department at some time touches the lives of nearly every American citizen with programs that range from prenatal care to services for the nation's elderly.

HHS provides information and services in the following areas related to sexual behavior: PREGNANCY, BREASTFEEDING, DOMESTIC VIOLENCE, SEXUALLY TRANSMITTED DISEASES (for example, gonorrhea, herpes, and syphilis), AIDS-HIV infection, and Rh blood-factor incompatibility. Included in the department are related agencies, such as the Administration for Children and Families, Centers for Disease Control and Prevention, Food and Drug Administration, and National Institutes of Health.

In the area of GENETICS, NIH oversees the National Human Genome Research Institute, which, along with private entrepreneurs, maps out the genetic code for many species, including humans. The Centers for Disease Control and Prevention has an office of Genomics and Disease Prevention. The SURGEON GENERAL OF THE UNITED STATES, an agency of the department's Public Health Service, directs a family-history initiative using genetic information; the agency also provides online resources for students and educators relating to genetics as well as genetic screening, counseling, and therapy services.

As the largest federal agency—its annual budget sometimes surpasses that of the Defense Department—HHS can influence how laws regarding sex-related matters are initiated, implemented, and changed. Through its substantial grant program, it determines priorities and means of implementation for activities ranging from sex education programs to research on sexually transmitted diseases and AIDS-HIV research, for example. The parent agency and its many subsidiaries help develop and carry out policies for the executive branch and propose legislation to CONGRESS on a wide range of health and citizen services related to sexual behavior.

One example of the impact of HHS on matters relating to sexual behavior is the agency's current distribution of substantial grants to faith-based organizations for SEX EDUCATION programs in the states. Although the executive branch announced at the beginning of 2005 that it would be doubling its efforts to promote ABSTINENCE-only sex education—requesting some $206 million for fiscal year 2006—several of these education programs have been criticized for violating the separation of church and state required by the FIRST AMENDMENT (1791) to the U.S. Constitution. In 2005 the AMERICAN CIVIL LIBERTIES UNION filed a lawsuit alleging the misuse of more than $1 million awarded by HHS for an abstinence-based program called the Silver Ring Thing, which included testimony about the value of accepting Jesus Christ and quoting from the Bible. Funding for the program was consequently terminated.

The department's Food and Drug Administration has also become embroiled in public battles over access to RU-486, known as the "abortion pill," and Plan B, called the "morning-after" CONTRACEPTION pill. In both instances the agency sought to delay approval of the drugs' use, despite medical evidence of their effectiveness and safety. During the administration of George W. Bush, people opposed to ABORTION and the wide availability of contraceptives to users of all ages found a sympathethic ear in policymakers at the Department of Health and Human Services.

Contact: U.S. Department of Health and Human Services, 200 Independence Avenue, SW, Washington, DC 20201 (202-619-0257). www.hhs.gov.

See also STEM-CELL RESEARCH AND CLONING.

V

VICTIMS' RIGHTS

The victims' rights movement began as a backlash against a number of U.S. Supreme Court decisions in the 1960s that seemed to favor criminals—among them *Miranda v. Arizona* (1966), which required law enforcement officials to advise suspects of their constitutional rights against self-incrimination and to representation by an attorney. Since then, the federal government has implemented laws to protect victims of crime and most states have enacted either constitutional or statutory measures addressing their rights. While these laws give victims certain general rights, such as to attend trials or to participate at sentencing, some are more specifically tailored to victims of SEX OFFENSES.

Victims' rights laws include, in RAPE cases, the use of RAPE SHIELD LAWS to exclude the introduction of a victim's prior sexual conduct during trial; in statutory rape cases (involving victims who are minors), a refusal to allow a defendant to allege that the victim had given her CONSENT; and in cases involving CHILDREN and other vulnerable victims such as mentally ill persons, allowing them to testify in court outside the view of the defendant. The federal government and some state governments also punish HATE CRIMES, either through specific hate crime laws or by enhancing the penalties for other crimes when such offenses are motivated by prejudice based on sex or sexual orientation, among other targets.

Federal Law

In 1990 CONGRESS enacted the Victims' Rights and Restitution Act, which set forth a bill of rights for all crime victims offering guidance to employees of the U.S. Department of Justice and other federal agencies engaged in the detection, investigation, and prosecution of crimes. "Victims of crime should be treated with compassion, respect and dignity throughout the criminal justice process," the act declares. A victim, it adds, "should have the right to be present at all proceedings related to the offense," except in the case of a witness whose testimony might be prejudiced unless she or he is at times excluded from the court. The act also specifies that victims should "have the right to information about the conviction, sentencing and imprisonment of the person who committed the crime against them."

With respect to sex offenses, in 1986 Congress passed the Child Abuse Victims' Rights Act, which gave children who were exploited a right to sue offenders for civil damages. The law, which is found in Title 18, section 2255, of the U.S. Code, authorizes a personal injury suit by a minor for actual damages and the cost of the suit, including reasonable attorneys' fees, and provides that a minor "shall be deemed to have sustained damages of no less than $50,000 in value." The action must be filed within six years after the right first accrues or three years after termination of any legal hindrance to bringing the suit, such as being underage.

VICTIM/WITNESS CERTIFICATION AND ELECTION CONCERNING INMATE STATUS

(This form is exempt from Freedom of Information Act release.)

PRIVACY ACT STATEMENT

AUTHORITY: 42 U.S.C. 10606 et sec., Victim's Rights and Restitution Act of 1990; 18 U.S.C. 1501 et sec., Victim and Witness Protection Act of 1982.

PRINCIPAL PURPOSES: To inform victims and witnesses of their post-trial rights; to determine whether the victim or witness of a crime elects to be notified of changes in the confinement status of a convicted criminal offender; and to record the election by the victim or witness of their desire to be notified about subsequent changes in inmate status.

ROUTINE USES: None.

DISCLOSURE: Voluntary; however, failure to provide identifying information will prevent the corrections facility from notifying victim or witness of changes in a criminal offender's status.

SECTION I - ADMINISTRATIVE INFORMATION

Installation _____ City _____ State _____ ZIP Code _____

Incident Number _____ Organizational Identifier (ORI) _____

SECTION II - CERTIFICATION OF NO VICTIM OR WITNESS
(Complete this section only if there are no victims or witnesses who are entitled to notification under the Victim's Rights and Restitution Act of 1990, and DoD Instruction 1030.2.)

As representative for the Government in the court-martial case of United States v. _____ ,
                                                                (Name of accused) (Last, first, middle initial)

_____ , convened by _____ ,
(Social Security Number)   *(Court-martial convening order number, date, and issuing command)*

I certify that this case does not involve a victim or witness entitled to receive information about the confinement status of the defendant as required by the Victim's Rights and Restitution Act of 1990 (Public Law 101-647; 104 Stat. 4820).

_____   _____
(Signature of person certifying)   *(Typed name (Last, first))*

_____   _____
(Date) (YYYYMMDD)   *(Grade and title)*

SECTION III - CERTIFICATION OF ADVICE TO VICTIM(S) AND WITNESS(ES)
(Complete this section when there are victims or witnesses entitled to notification.)

I certify that on this date I personally notified the victim(s) and witness(es) in the court-martial case of United States v.

_____ ,   _____ ,
(Name of accused) (Last, first, middle initial)   *(Social Security Number)*

convened by _____ ,
              (Court-martial convening order number, date, and issuing command)

whose sentence included confinement, of their right under the Victim's Rights and Restitution Act of 1990 (Public Law 101-647, 104 Stat. 4820), to receive information about the status of the inmate, to include length of sentence, anticipated earliest release date, likely place of confinement, the possibility of transfer, and the right to receive notification of a new place of confinement. I advised of the possibility of parole or clemency with an explanation of these terms. Additionally, I advised of the right to prior notification of the inmate's parole hearings, release from confinement, escape and death. I advised that to receive notification of the inmate's transfer, parole hearings, and release from confinement, the victim or witness must provide the information required in Section IV of this form. I advised all victims and witnesses that if they elect to terminate or reinitiate notifications, or if they change their address listed above, they must contact the Military Service Central Repository listed in Section V.

_____   _____
(Signature of person providing notification)   *(Typed name (Last, first))*

The Jacob Wetterling Crimes Against Children and Sexually Violent Offender Act (1994), found in the U.S. Code, Title 42, The Public Health and Welfare, section 14071, provides that a "determination of whether a person is a sexually violent predator . . . shall be made by a court after considering the recommendation of a board composed of experts in the behavior and treatment of sex offenders, victims' rights advocates, and representatives of law enforcement agencies." This law set the stage for MEGAN'S LAW (1996), which created a nationwide registration system for violent SEX OFFENDERS and gives victims and the general public the right to learn the whereabouts of certain perpetrators after their incarceration has ended.

In 2003 a resolution was introduced in Congress to amend the U.S. Constitution to add protection for the victims of violent crimes. The measure would underscore rights "to reasonable and timely notice of any public proceeding involving the crime and reasonably to be heard at public release, plea, sentencing, reprieve, and pardoning proceedings." The amendment is supported by the National Center for Victims of Crime, has bipartisan backing in Congress, and has been endorsed by President George W. Bush; as with even the most worthy of proposed constitutional amendments, however, it will have an uphill battle given a general inertia against amending the nation's supreme law.

State Law

The Idaho constitution contains a fairly typical victims' bill of rights in article 1, Declaration of Rights, section 22. Under this provision, victims are entitled

(1) To be treated with fairness, respect, dignity and privacy . . . , (2) To timely disposition of the case, (3) To prior notification of trial court, appellate and parole proceedings . . . , (4) To be present at all criminal justice proceedings, (5) To

---

The federal government and most states have laws that grant crime victims more access to the criminal process and input into such factors as sentencing. This federal form was developed to inform victims and witnesses of posttrial rights such as changes in an offender's status.

communicate with the prosecution, (6) To be heard, upon request, at all criminal justice proceedings considering a plea of guilty, sentencing, incarceration or release of the defendant, unless manifest injustice would result, (7) To restitution . . . , (8) To refuse . . . contact [with] or other request by the defendant . . . , unless such request is authorized by law, (9) To read presentence reports relating to the crime, [and] (10) To the same rights in juvenile proceedings, where the offense is a felony if committed by an adult.

Besides addressing victims in their constitutions and statutes, some states have enacted other relevant measures. For example, Nebraska criminal procedure (which in this case is similar to the 1990 federal victims act) provides that in sentencing a person for a sex offense that requires public registration as a sex offender, "[w]hen making its determination the court shall consider information contained in the presentence report and the recommendation of experts in the behavior and treatment of sex offenders, victims' rights advocates, and representatives of law enforcement agencies."

In some states, such as Idaho, a victim is allowed to contribute to the presentencing report that the judge reads before passing sentence. A number of states expressly permit rape victims to be present and speak at hearings on the offender's parole or the terms of release from prison. Connecticut has established an office of the victim advocate, "a person with knowledge of victims' rights and services" appointed by the governor. Nevada does not have a victims' bill of rights, but it does recognize a role for victims' rights advocacy organizations and requires in some cases that victims be given a form advising them of their rights.

In *State v. Alcaraz* (1999), a Nebraska court noted that a lower court's refusal to grant the defendant a separate trial rather than try him jointly with his codefendant was valid because it protected a SEXUAL ASSAULT victim from having to undergo the trauma of multiple trials. In *Payne v. Tennessee* (1991), the U.S. Supreme Court partly overruled earlier cases such as *Booth v. Maryland* (1987), in which it had concluded that the admission of a victim's impact statement (a recitation of how the victim or his or her immediate family had suffered because of the crime) violated the Eighth Amendment (1791) in a death penalty case. The Court's decision in *Payne* found that the Eighth Amendment does not on its face prohibit a jury in a capital sentencing proceeding from considering the evidence relating to the victim's personal characteristics and a murder's emotional impact on the victim's family. In this case a woman who had spurned the defendant's sexual advances was murdered along with her two-year-old daughter, and her three-year-old son was assaulted with the intent to murder.

The rise of victims' rights laws reflects the public's increased concern for meting out retribution to offenders and bringing closure to victims. Yet in the American legal system, victims' rights are balanced with the constitutional rights of those accused of crimes, who are by law presumed to be innocent. In cases involving violent and sexually offensive acts, the law has responded in a number of ways to invite input from victims and their representatives while it punishes criminals and seeks to deter future crimes.

Contact: National Center for Victims of Crime, 2000 M Street, NW, Suite 480, Washington, DC 20036 (202-467-8700). www.ncvc.org.

See also CRIMES AGAINST CHILDREN UNIT (FBI).

VIOLENCE AGAINST WOMEN ACT

To address the nationwide problem of forced sex and other violence against women—one that the states alone cannot cope with—the Violence Against Women Act (VAWA) was passed by CONGRESS and signed into law by President Bill Clinton on September 13, 1994. Based on studies showing that crimes disproportionately affecting women were being treated less seriously than comparable crimes against men, the act created certain federal programs and protections to address DOMESTIC VIOLENCE and SEXUAL ASSAULT; enhanced criminal penalties for certain violent crimes;

and provided VICTIMS' RIGHTS as well as assistance for battered immigrants and their CHILDREN. Administered by the U.S. Department of Justice and the U.S. DEPARTMENT OF HEALTH AND HUMAN SERVICES, the legislation has stressed community-coordinated responses and awarded funding to hire more prosecutors as well as improve domestic violence training for police officers, health and social services providers, and prosecutors.

Nine subtitles of the act, as reauthorized in 2000 and 2005, address specific issues and set up a variety of grant and training programs covering crimes and courts, services and outreach, children and youth, prevention, health, housing, economic security, immigrant issues, tribal programs and "communities of color," sexual assault services, and enhanced services for military victims. The OFFICE ON VIOLENCE AGAINST WOMEN was created in 1995 in the Justice Department to implement the act's programs.

The teeth of the 1994 act, contained in the original law's subtitle C (called the Gender Motivated Violence Act), created a federal civil remedy allowing private suits to redress gender-motivated violence. This provision, however, was found unconstitutional by the U.S. Supreme Court in *United States v. Morrison* (2000). The Court held in this case that the commerce clause of the U.S. Constitution did not grant Congress the authority to "regulate non-economic, violent criminal conduct based solely on the conduct's aggregate effect on interstate commerce." A majority of justices held that the act's federal remedy for violence against women by private offenders—as differentiated from action by the government—did not pass constitutional muster. It thus became unavailable to women victims of sexual or gender-based violence. The Court rejected the argument that just as Congress could use its powers under the commerce clause to provide a civil rights remedy for racial discrimination because of its impact on the economy, it could similarly use that power to remedy violence against women that prevents them from fully participating in the national economy. The decision did not affect federal prosecution of interstate crimes prohibited by the act.

Milestones in Combating Violence Against Women

753 B.C.E. The "rule of thumb" is devised to legally allow a husband to beat his wife with a rod no thicker than the base of his right thumb.

1500s. The English jurist Lord Hale pronounces that husbands cannot be guilty of marital rape.

1857. Massachusetts recognizes the spousal rape exemption but in 1871 declares wife beating illegal.

1911. Buffalo, N.Y., creates the first family court, removing domestic relations from the regular criminal justice system.

1960s. The feminist movement begins to draw attention to abuses of women and the need for shelters, counseling, and social and legal changes.

1967. Maine opens one of the first battered women's shelters in the United States.

1971. New York Radical Feminists, Chicago Women Against Rape, and others begin to speak out against rape.

1972. The first hotline for battered women begins.

1976. Pennsylvania becomes the first state to authorize protection orders for victims.

1976. The Domestic Violence Act allows a violent partner to be temporarily excluded from access to a civil injunction.

1977. Oregon enacts legislation mandating arrest in domestic violence cases.

1978. The National Coalition Against Domestic Violence is organized.

1979. The Office on Domestic Violence is established in the U.S. Department of Health and Human Services (but closed in 1981 by the Reagan Administration).

1981. The first annual Domestic Violence Awareness Week is celebrated.

1984. The Family Violence Prevention and Services Act authorizes federal funding for victims.

1984. Lenore Walker's book *The Battered Women's Syndrome* identifies the theory of "learned helplessness."

1985. In *Thurman v. Torrington,* a battered woman for the first time wins a judgment for police failure to protect her from a violent husband.

1987. The first nationwide hotline is established by the National Coalition Against Domestic Violence.

1988. The U.S. Surgeon General declares wife abuse the leading health hazard to women.

1988. The Victims of Crime Act is amended to require state compensation programs to assist domestic violence victims.

1993. The United Nations, followed by the Organization of American States, issues a Delcaration on the Elimination of Violence Against Women.

1994. O. J. Simpson is charged with murdering his wife and an acquaintance but is acquitted the next year; in 1997 he is found liable in a civil lawsuit and ordered to pay $33 million to the victims' families.

1994. Congress passes the Violence Against Women Act.

1996. 800-799-SAFE, the National Domestic Violence Hotline funded by the Violence Against Women Act, begins operation.

1997. President Bill Clinton signs a law that makes interstate stalking a federal offense.

2000. The Violence Against Women Act is strengthened to improve enforcement, extend legal aid to victims, and provide safe visitation for children.

2000. *United States v. Morrison* finds unconstitutional the act's allowance for private suits as a remedy for gender-motivated violence.

2005. The Violence Against Women Act (1994) is reauthorized to enhance arrests, enforcement of protection orders, and victims' assistance.

Sources: Adapted from SafeNetwork, for California Department of Health Services, 1999; and www.dvmillennium.org (Millennium: Ending Domestic Violence), 2006

Even before the *Morrison* decision was handed down, Congress had begun to strengthen VAWA's provisions. The new measures, which were signed into law on October 28, 2000, identified the related crimes of dating violence and stalking and provided for grants to law enforcement authorities to improve the enforcement of protection orders; legal aid to victims of domestic violence, stalking, or sexual assault; and education programs for victims of domestic violence and sexual assault. The law also provided for safe visitation for children whose parents are involved in domestic violence as well as protection for battered immigrant women, including access to legal representation.

Major provisions of the act still viable after *Morrison* include a provision that makes it a crime for a person to (1) travel across a state line "with the intent to injure, harass, or intimidate that person's spouse or intimate partner" and intentionally commit a crime of violence causing a bodily injury to the spouse or intimate partner; or (2) cause a spouse or an intimate partner to cross a state line by "force, coercion, duress, or fraud," resulting in the intentional commission of a crime of violence causing bodily injury to the spouse or intimate partner. Courts have held that the violent acts need not occur only during the travel. Another section bars a person from crossing a state line to violate a court protection order; it also imposes a penalty when one causes a spouse or an intimate partner to cross a state line and injures him or her in violation of a protection order.

VAWA amended the Immigration and Nationality Act (1952) to provide, among other things, that a battered immigrant spouse may self-petition for permanent resident status without having to apply through the abusive citizen or permanent resident spouse; it further attempts to remove the use of the immigration laws by abusers to control or abuse a domestic violence victim.

A revised Violence Against Women Act was passed in 2005 and signed into law in 2006. It includes enhanced programs and policies in the criminal justice system affecting adult and youth victims of domestic and dating violence, sexual assault, and stalking. The new law also addresses the needs of the disabled, Native Americans, immigrants, ethnic minorities, and women in rural communities. In addition, it aspires to enhance confidentiality protections for victims.

One of the programs created by the Violence Against Women Act is the National Domestic Violence Hotline (800-799-SAFE). Begun with a $1 million grant administered by the Department of Health and Human Services and supplemented with annual appropriations as well as private donations, the hotline is now run by the Texas Council on Family Violence in Austin, Texas.

Discretionary and STOP grants awarded by the federal government have helped state, tribal, and local governments and community agencies train personnel, establish specialized domestic violence and sexual assault units, hold perpetrators accountable, assist victims by supporting battered-women's shelters and RAPE crisis centers, provide outreach to homeless youth, and conduct education and training programs. Grants have also supported community partnerships among police, prosecutors, victim advocates, and others addressing violence against women. Since implementation of these programs and the violence hotline, one study has found that "victims are safer, better supported by their communities, and treated more uniformly and sensitively by first responders." Other studies have found an increase in domestic violence arrests as a result of support for specialized police units as well as a decrease in repeat behavior by offenders along with improved prosecution rates.

Contacts

Office on Violence Against Women, U.S. Department of Justice, 810 Seventh Street, NW, Washington, DC 20531 (202-307-6026). www.ojp.usdoj.gov/vawo.

National Domestic Violence Hotline (800-799-SAFE).

See also EQUAL RIGHTS; HUMAN TRAFFICKING; SEX OFFENDERS; WOMEN'S RIGHTS.

VIRGINIA, UNITED STATES v.

In 1996 the U.S. Supreme Court struck down the SINGLE-SEX EDUCATION policy of the Virginia Military Institute (VMI) in Lexington, Virginia. *United States v. Virginia* came after a long line of cases beginning with *Plessy v. Ferguson* (1896), in which the Supreme Court legalized DISCRIMINATION against blacks by giving its blessing to the "separate but equal" doctrine in public places. This policy lasted until the Court abandoned the legal fiction in its landmark decision *Brown v. Board of Education of Topeka* (1954), putting an end to such discrimination in public schools.

VMI was founded in 1839. At the time of the Supreme Court's decision in 1996, it was the sole remaining single-sex school in Virginia out of the state's fifteen institutions of higher learning. The only other all-male military college in the country was The Citadel in Charleston, South Carolina. Virginia had a history of thwarting coeducation: some sixteen years after the *Brown* ruling, the University of Virginia had to be ordered by a federal judge in 1970 to open its doors to women. Although the state had set up a parallel military-style education program for women at the Virginia Women's Institute for Leadership, that separate-but-not-so-equal school was no match for the educational opportunities at the prestigious VMI.

According to the Supreme Court's opinion, written by Associate Justice Ruth Bader Ginsburg: "VMI, beyond question, 'possesses to a far greater degree' than the VWIL program 'those qualities which are incapable of objective measurement but make for greatness in a ... school,' including 'position and influence of the alumni, standing in the community, traditions and prestige. Women seeking and fit for a VMI-quality education cannot be offered anything less, under the Commonwealth's obligation to afford them genuinely equal protection." In essence, the Court ruled that Virginia's categorical exclusion of women from the educational opportunities that VMI provides denied equal protection to women.

Chief Justice William H. Rehnquist wrote a concurring opinion, offering Virginia the option to provide a "separate but equal" facility to fulfill its obligation to women seeking a VMI-style education. Associate Justice Antonin Scalia—the lone dissenter in the 7–1 decision (Associate Justice Clarence Thomas did not participate because his son attended VMI)—asserted that the majority decision was effectively shutting down "an institution that has served the people of the Commonwealth of Virginia with pride and distinction for over a century and a half"; he contended that the Court was rejecting findings of 'gender-based developmental differences' supporting Virginia's restriction of the 'adversative' method [of education] to only a men's institution, and the finding that the all-male composition of [VMI] is essential to that institution's character."

Although Justice Scalia tried use the Court's decision to sound the death knell for VMI, for the first four years of the new millennium the school was named by *U.S. News and World Report* the "top liberal arts college in the U.S.," and the school's Web site (www.vmi.edu) features a picture of a woman athlete. The notion that traditions, bad ones as well as good ones, should trump the EQUAL RIGHTS of citizens was laid to rest, at least for the time being, in this landmark decision.

See also WOMEN'S RIGHTS.

VOYEURISM

As described by psychologists, voyeurism is a form of paraphilia—an activity through which sexual arousal is sought, using what are generally considered to be socially unacceptable means. In the case of voyeurism, such actions are characterized by the clandestine observation of others typically when they are undressing or engaged in sexual activity and may involve photographing or video recording the victims. The motives of voyeurs—generally young heterosexual males with unfulfilled sex lives—can range from carrying out a prank to having a compulsion or harboring an intent to harass and distress a victim,

Most people have a normal sense of curiosity about what others do behind closed doors. Voyeurism, however—as John Sloan captured in his print *Night Windows* (1910)—is an abnormal obsession with viewing others by invading their privacy. The artist depicts a man sitting on top of a building watching a woman in an apartment as she fixes her hair.

who is generally female. The risk of getting caught often adds excitement to acts of voyeurism.

At the federal level, voyeurism is rarely addressed directly in laws or court cases. However, in the definition of disabilities covered by the U.S. Code, voyeurism is expressly excluded under Title 42, The Public Health and Welfare, chapter 126, Equal Opportunity for Individuals with Disabilities, subchapter IV, Miscellaneous Provisions, along with HOMOSEXUALITY, BISEXUALITY, TRANSVESTISM, TRANSSEXUALISM, pedophilia, exhibitionism, GENDER-identity disorders, and other sexual behavior disorders.

Under Title 29, Labor, chapter 16, Vocational Rehabilitation and Other Rehabilitative Services, an exception from the category "individual with a disability" is also made for voyeurism and other sexual behavior disorders, in addition to compulsive gambling, kleptomania, pyromania, and disorders resulting from illegal use of DRUGS.

The U.S. Supreme Court has referred to voyeurism in the context of defining OBSCENITY. In *Ward v. Illinois* (1977), to support findings by the Illinois supreme court that a person had sold sadomasochistic materials in violation of the state obscenity statute, footnotes 3 and

4 of the Court's opinion cite "three voyeurism scenes, two of which involve watching lesbian love play" and "accounts of homosexual acts, masturbation, flagellation, oral-genital acts, rape, voyeurism, masochism and sadism."

Peeping Tom Laws

The so-called peeping Tom (named for the resident of Coventry, England, who was alleged to have been the only person to see the naked Lady Godiva on her ride) is often portrayed as an adolescent boy attempting to spy on the female object of his desire. Yet there is a more sinister form of voyeurism, one akin to stalking because of the emotional trauma that may be inflicted on a victim when she becomes aware of the act. Although some forms of entertainment—the movie *Psycho* (1960), for one—use voyeurism to evoke a mood in a character or the audience, voyeurism in real life may be considered trespassing and an invasion of PRIVACY with serious consequences.

All states have some type of law against voyeurism in its various forms. South Carolina law on eavesdropping, peeping, and voyeurism provides: "It is unlawful for a person to be . . . a peeping tom on or about the premises of another. . . . The term 'peeping tom,' as used in this section, is . . . a person who peeps through windows, doors, or other like places, . . . for the purpose of spying upon or invading the privacy of the persons spied upon and any other conduct of a similar nature that tends to invade the privacy of others."

Under the topic of disorderly conduct, Illinois bars anyone who knowingly enters "upon the property of another and for a lewd or unlawful purpose looks into a dwelling on the property through any window or other opening in it." Nebraska law provides that "[a]ny person, firm, or corporation that trespasses or intrudes upon any natural person in his or her place of solitude or seclusion, if the intrusion would be highly offensive to a reasonable person, shall be liable for invasion of privacy."

Not all peeping Toms want to evade detection. New Mexico law thus makes a misdemeanor of any

harassment that "consists of knowingly pursuing a pattern of conduct that is intended to annoy, seriously alarm or terrorize another person and that serves no useful purpose." Florida law directly targets visual surveillance of customers in a "merchant's dressing room, fitting room, changing room, or restroom when such room provides a reasonable expectation of privacy"; this offense is punishable as a first-degree misdemeanor.

Photographic and Electronic Voyeurism

The South Carolina statute mentioned previously also provides that "the term 'peeping tom' includes any person who employs the use of video or audio equipment for the purposes set forth in this [law]. . . . A person commits the crime of voyeurism if, for the purpose of arousing or gratifying sexual desire . . . , he or she knowingly views, photographs, audio records, video records, produces, or creates a digital electronic file, or films another person, without that person's knowledge and consent, while the person is in a place where he or she would have a reasonable expectation of privacy." The punishment for a first offense is a fine of up to $500 or imprisonment for not more than three years, or both. Florida, Hawaii, Idaho, and Texas are among other states that have similar provisions against voyeurism using video and other recording equipment.

Maryland's law regarding "visual surveillance with prurient interest" targets "any electronic device that can be used surreptitiously to observe an individual"; it defines a private place as a room in which a person can reasonably be expected to fully or partially disrobe or one in which she has an expectation of privacy, including offices, businesses, stores, recreational facilities, restaurants, taverns, hotels, motels or other lodgings, theaters or sports arenas, schools or other educational institutions, banks or other financial institutions, day care homes or other child custody facilities, or "another place of public use or accommodation."

In *State v. Burke* (2003), a court in New Jersey threw out a defendant's guilty plea to trespassing after he had used video equipment in his own home to record his guests taking showers and using the bathroom. The court held that acts of video voyeurism were not covered under a trespassing statute's peeping Tom provisions, because they require an intrusion by a perpetrator into the dwelling from a vantage point outside the house. The Georgia court of appeals, in *Kelly v. State* (1998), concluded that the fact that film used to record the invasion of privacy of a sixteen-year-old girl was undeveloped did not mean that the offense had not been completed.

Deciding that the state of Washington's voyeurism law did not cover invasions of privacy in public places, the state supreme court, in *State v. Glas* (2002), overturned a voyeurism conviction based on pictures of women in a shopping mall taken from the ground level in order to photograph underneath their skirts. Another Washington court, however, in *State v. Larson* (2003), found that a common dining room in a private nursing home was not a purely public place but an area in which residents and their families might have an expectation of privacy; therefore, a defendant's conviction for photographing a female resident's breasts underneath her blouse was upheld.

As the English poet W. H. Auden (1907–73) wrote, "Peeping Toms are never praised, like novelists or bird watchers,/For their keenness of observation."

See also LEWD BEHAVIOR; PRURIENT INTEREST; SEXUAL HARASSMENT.

W

WILLIAMS v. MORGAN

In *Williams v. Pryor* (1999), a U.S. district court rejected a challenge to an Alabama statute that banned the commercial distribution of sexual devices designed primarily for genital stimulation. While the court held that no constitutional right of sexual PRIVACY existed, it found that the statute lacked any rational basis. Thus, the plaintiffs were granted an injunction against enforcement of the law.

Two years later, the case came before the U.S. Court of Appeals for the Eleventh Circuit for review of the lower court's decision. The appellate court agreed that there was no constitutional right of sexual privacy, but it reversed the lower court. In protecting public morality, said the court, the law served the best interests of the state; therefore, it passed the "rational basis test." For laws that infringe on civil rights and WOMEN'S RIGHTS, courts use higher standards of scrutiny, termed "strict scrutiny" and "intermediate scrutiny," respectively. The level of scrutiny determines the amount of justification the government must show before imposing a burden on those rights. The "rational basis test" is the lowest level of judicial scrutiny.

This case might never have become significant, except that in 2003 the U.S. Supreme Court held in *LAWRENCE V. TEXAS* that a Texas law banning homosexual SODOMY was unconstitutional; the Court in that case cited the provisions of the Bill of Rights (1791), the first ten amendments to the U.S. Constitution, as the basis for the right of privacy the Court had first declared in it decision in *GRISWOLD V. CONNECTICUT* (1965). Asserting that the privacy of the marital bedroom was beyond the reach of government intrusion, *Griswold* struck down as unconstitutional a state law banning contraceptives.

The Alabama sexual devices case, after having been remanded to the district court, was appealed again to the federal appeals court in 2004, this time as *Williams v. Morgan* (the attorney general of Alabama, named as the respondent party, had changed). In upholding the law, the court noted that the statute at issue, entitled the Anti-Obscenity Enforcement Act, did not bar the use or possession of sexual devices, did not affect the distribution of related products such as ribbed condoms or virility drugs, and did not prohibit Alabama residents from bringing the devices from out of state. According to the court, the AMERICAN CIVIL LIBERTIES UNION, which was assisting the plaintiff in the case, was urging the court to take cognizance of a sexual right of privacy. But it pointed out that the U.S. Supreme Court had never before "recognized a free-standing 'right to sexual privacy.'"

The appeals court warned in conclusion that "[h]unting expeditions that seek trophy game in the fundamental-rights forest must heed the maxim 'look before you shoot.'" Then, quoting from the concurring opinion of U.S. Supreme Court Associate Justice Felix Frankfurter in *Dennis v. United States* (1951) that "[c]ourts are not representative bodies . . . designed to be a good reflex of a democratic society," the opinion concluded that if the majority of Alabama citizens want to allow the commercial distribution of sexual devices such as "vibrators, dildos, anal beads, and artificial vaginas," they can do so through the elected legislature.

A dissent referred to the recent *Lawrence* decision and noted that the majority opinion in *Williams* "refuses, however, to acknowledge *why* the Court in *Lawrence* held that criminal prohibitions on consensual sodomy are unconstitutional." This is because, said the jurist, our fundamental rights protect "individual choices 'concerning the intimacies of [a] physical relationship.'" He also asserted that there is little constitutional distinction between a ban on the sale of sex toys and a ban on their private use. "Alabama cannot be permitted to accomplish indirectly what it is not constitutionally permitted to do directly," he said.

Like the rush by some states to test the ABORTION decision *Roe v. Wade* (1973) once two new justices joined the U.S. Supreme Court in 2005 and 2006, the appeals court majority in *Williams* seems to have been trying to force a review of the *Lawrence* decision relating to sexual privacy. Both abortion rights and the rights of homosexuals apparently will continue to be the focus of legal challenges in the courts as well as in the legislative and executive branches of government.

See also CONTRACEPTION; SEXUALLY ORIENTED BUSINESSES.

WILLIAMS v. NORTH CAROLINA

For most of American history, the MARRIAGE relationship was viewed under the law as a contract among three parties: the wife, the husband, and the state. The government had and still has an interest in both marriage and DIVORCE—for example, with regard to the rearing and support of CHILDREN who are products of a marriage. The requirements and rules for marriage and divorce have thus been set by state laws. These laws, however, have not always been compatible, and the two cases of *Williams v. North Carolina* that came before the U.S. Supreme Court, first in 1942 and then

again in 1945, highlight the difficulties in reconciling marriage and divorce laws in the federal system of government created by the U.S. Constitution.

Until the late 1960s, state divorce laws did not provide for consensual or no-fault divorce. At least one of the spouses had to assert some grounds on which a court could dissolve the marriage. The spouse seeking a divorce typically had to prove that the other spouse had committed a marital offense, such as ADULTERY, and that he or she had not committed any such offense.

O. B. Williams was married to Carrie Wyke in North Carolina in 1916. Lillie Shaver was married to Thomas Hendrix in North Carolina in 1920. In 1940 O. B. Williams and Lillie Hendrix went to Las Vegas, Nevada, and on June 26 they filed for divorce from their respective spouses in that state. Their spouses did not appear in Nevada. On August 26 Williams was granted a divorce on the grounds of extreme cruelty, based on a Nevada court's finding that he was a "bona fide and continuous resident of . . . the State of Nevada, and had been such resident for more than six weeks immediately preceding" the divorce filing, as was required by Nevada law. Based on a similar finding, Hendrix was granted a divorce on October 4, 1940. She and Williams were married on the same day in Nevada, and they returned to North Carolina to live together as husband and wife. They were subsequently tried and convicted of "bigamous cohabitation" under the North Carolina code.

In its decision in *Haddock v. Haddock* (1906), the Supreme Court had treated a divorce proceeding as a suit against the status of the marriage itself, rather than as an action by one party against another. This type of suit—called *in rem* (Latin for "against the thing"), as differentiated from *in personam* (Latin for "against the person")—resulted in a situation in which a divorce could be obtained in the state where the parties were residing in good faith—and not just for the purpose of getting divorced—but the decree might not be recognized in another state with different rules. Thus, a person might be viewed as married in one state but not married in another.

The unsatisfactory outcome in *Haddock* did not square with the Supreme Court's earlier decision in *Atherton v. Atherton* (1901). In that case the Court had declared that "a husband without a wife, or a wife without a husband, is unknown to the law." Moreover, Article IV, section 1, of the U.S. Constitution requires: "Full Faith and Credit shall be given in each State to the public Acts, Records, and judicial Proceedings of every other State."

When the first *Williams* case arrived at the Supreme Court in 1942, the justices assumed that the six-week domicile in Nevada had been in good faith, even though it was obviously intended to take advantage of the state's more lenient divorce laws, and the Court required North Carolina to recognize the divorce proceedings as mandated by the Constitution.

But, like the proverbial bad penny that keeps coming back, the case returned to the Supreme Court in 1945. This time the Court, in an opinion delivered by Associate Justice Felix Frankfurter (who had written a concurring opinion in the first *Williams* case), held that North Carolina did not have to recognize the Nevada divorces and the marriage. In his concurrence in the first case, he had noted that the full faith and credit clause was applicable "when the judgment was rendered in accordance with settled procedural standards" and that "North Carolina did not base its disregard of the Nevada [divorce] decrees on the claim that they were a fraud and a sham."

In the second *Williams* case, however, North Carolina did contest the legitimacy of the six-week domicile requirement for a divorce in Nevada. The Court this time agreed that the laxity of the Nevada law regarding the short period of residency could be challenged by North Carolina. The Court further agreed with North Carolina that Nevada's residency period was unduly short and that the issue of the legitimate establishment of domicile in that state had not been challenged in an adversarial proceeding in Nevada (one in which a legitimate defense is presented as opposed to a proceeding in which the defense makes no appearance or no attempt to mount a legitimate challenge). These faults thus were found to constitute

grounds for North Carolina to refuse to recognize the divorces granted in Nevada.

Since the *Williams* cases, state laws have greatly liberalized the proceedings for obtaining a divorce. But as recently as 1975, in *Sosna v. Iowa*, the Supreme Court upheld a one-year residency period for couples moving to Iowa before a divorce could be granted. As Associate Justice William H. Rehnquist noted in that case, a state such as Iowa "may quite reasonably decide that it does not wish to become a divorce mill."

See also BIGAMY.

WOMEN'S RIGHTS

The Declaration of Independence announces "that all Men are created equal, that they are endowed by their Creator with certain unalienable Rights, that among these are Life, Liberty, and the pursuit of Happiness." There is no doubt that in the eyes of Thomas Jefferson, the document's drafter, and of the American colonists who voted to adopt the Declaration in 1776, the meaning of the word *Men* did not encompass women and slaves. Likewise, the preamble to the U.S. Constitution, drafted in 1787, begins with "We the People of the United States," but the phrase *the People* embraced neither women nor slaves.

This is not to say that when the Constitution went into effect in 1789, women did not have any inherent rights under the laws of the United States and the states of the union. For example, they were entitled to the rights of the accused set out in the Bill of Rights (1791), the Constitution's first ten amendments. Nevertheless, the justice system discriminated against women in many ways and barred them from juries or service as attorneys or judges.

Many of these legal disabilities persisted for well over a century, denying to women basic rights taken for granted today. In *Goesaert v. Cleary* (1948), a Michigan law barring women from certain jobs deemed unsavory, such as bartender, was upheld by the U.S. Supreme Court. Even in 1961, the Supreme Court, in

Hoyt v. Florida, upheld a state law that permitted the exclusion of women from juries. In *Williams v. McNair* (1971), a state law that permitted separate SINGLE-SEX EDUCATION for women was similarly upheld.

In addition to inequality between women and men, distinctions were made in the law between single and married women. Areas affected included married women's ability to enter into contracts and to own property in their own right. For roughly three-fourths of American history, married women were considered on a par with children—under the control of their husbands in most matters of any legal consequence. In *Riley v. New York Trust Co.* (1940), the Supreme Court approved a state law that required a married woman's domicile to be that of her husband; as late as 1966, in *United States v. Yazell,* the Court found constitutional a Texas law that denied married women the right to independently enter into contracts.

Even today, areas of legal DISCRIMINATION remain, such as with respect to selection for jobs, payment of wages, employment benefits, and service in the MILITARY. The denial of absolutely EQUAL RIGHTS—parity between women and men—stems in part from judgments in legislatures and the courts about what constitutes a rational basis for discriminating against women. The Supreme Court has also decided not to require "strict scrutiny" (the highest level) for laws that discriminate on the basis of sex, as it does for laws that discriminate on the basis of race or national origin. Men and women are biologically different, so the reasoning goes, and thus the legal system may have legitimate reasons for treating them differently.

The rights that American women now enjoy can generally be divided into two categories: rights they share with men and rights they hold separately because they are women. In the first category are all of the federal and state constitutional and statutory rights that either expressly or by interpretation apply to both sexes. In the second category are rights specifically extended to women, particularly in their capacity as mothers or potential mothers. Certain rights with respect to affirmative action to overcome past discrimination are shared to some extent by women with minorities that have historically suffered inequality along with women.

Shared Rights

The only express right based on sex in the U.S. Constitution is the Nineteenth Amendment (1920), which prohibits the denial of the right to vote on the basis of sex. Other language in the Constitution addressing equal protection of the laws and due process of law, however, has been used by the Supreme Court only since the late twentieth century to extend rights to women. For example, in *Reed v. Reed* (1971), the Court for the first time relied on the equal protection clause of the Fourteenth Amendment (1868) to find that a woman had an equal right to be considered qualified under state law for court appointment as the administrator of a decedent's estate. Even using a "rational basis test" for the law, rather than the higher-level strict scrutiny, to make the government prove its case for discrimination, the Court concluded that no rational reason existed for discriminating against women in such matters.

Another major evolutionary step came in the Supreme Court's decision in GRISWOLD V. CONNECTICUT (1965); here it discovered a right of PRIVACY protecting married couples' right to use CONTRACEPTION, which in *Eisenstadt v. Baird* (1972) was extended to unmarried couples. This right of privacy would play a significant role in the Court's decision in *Roe v. Wade* (1973), giving women the right to obtain an abortion.

Other extensions of rights at the federal level came through legislation. For example, the Equal Pay Act (1963) prohibits paying men and women differently for equal work and applies to nearly all employers. The aim of TITLE IX of the Education Amendments of 1972 is to ensure that discrimination against women does not prejudice them from having substantially the same educational opportunities as men; this law applies only to schools that receive federal funding and thus does not cover them all, even though it affects a majority of educational institutions.

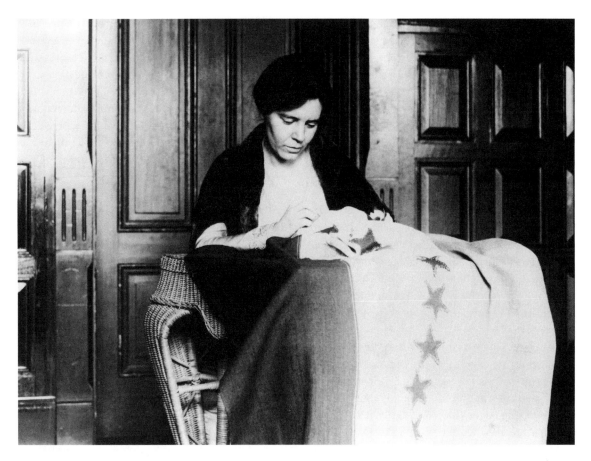

The only right of women expressly guaranteed by the U.S. Constitution is the right to vote, added in 1920. Alice Paul (1885–1977), a leading suffragist and women's rights advocate, sewed a star to a banner as each state ratified the Nineteenth Amendment. Here she tacks on the thirty-sixth star—the final one.

Title VII of the Civil Rights Act of 1964 prohibits employment discrimination on the basis of sex; because it applies only to employers with fifteen or more employees, not all discrimination was made illegal under the act. In this legislation, CONGRESS granted the federal courts power to order "such affirmative action as may be appropriate" to remedy cases of discrimination, including against women as well as racial minorities. The Supreme Court, in *Local 28 of the Sheet Metal Workers' International Association v. Equal Employment Opportunity Commission* (1986), affirmed that an appropriate remedy might include granting retroactive compensatory seniority to victims. An employer may

be required by a court to actively recruit women or minorities to correct an imbalance resulting from past discrimination. Private affirmative action by employers may encompass posting notices stating that they are an equal opportunity employer. Affirmative action, however, has its critics, who argue that legally sanctioned or mandated unequal treatment is not a fair way to make up for past discrimination because it results in reverse discrimination against innocent workers who are not female or members of a minority.

All but six states have amended their constitutions or passed laws to prohibit sex discrimination to some degree, and some state laws specifically declare a policy of equal rights. Hawaii, for example, provides that no person "shall be denied the equal protection of the laws, nor be denied the enjoyment of the person's civil rights or be discriminated against in the exercise thereof because of . . . sex"; it also provides that equal rights under the law "shall not be denied or abridged by the State on account of sex." Like Hawaii, several other states—including Delaware, Florida, and New York—have made the language in their constitutions gender neutral.

Women-Only Rights

Even after the Nineteenth Amendment finally granted women suffrage in 1920, the Supreme Court continued to limit constitutional guarantees of women's rights to this sole right to vote, and it technically remains the only specific grant of a constitutional right to women. All others are statutory or based on court interpretation.

Pregnancy. Congress declared in the Pregnancy Discrimination Act (1978) that discrimination by employers on the "basis of PREGNANCY, childbirth and related medical conditions" is equivalent to sex discrimination under Title VII of the Civil Rights Act and that pregnant women must be treated by employers the same as other employees disabled from work. The Supreme Court, in *Cleveland Board of Education v. LaFleur* (1974), had previously held that mandatory unpaid leave for pregnant school teachers was a violation of their right of privacy. In *Turner v. Department of Employment Security* (1975), the Court struck down Utah's denial of unemployment benefits to a woman in the last months of pregnancy and the first six weeks of motherhood, a denial that had been based on a presumption that she was unfit to work. The decision by the Utah state supreme court, from which the appeal was taken, found no discrimination, reasoning that if a man were pregnant the same rule would apply; this court noted that the plaintiff should "work for the repeal of the biological law of nature . . . [so] that man could also share in the thrill and glory of Motherhood."

Motherhood. One of the rights that now accrue to mothers is maternity leave. Employers of fifty or more persons are required to provide unpaid maternity leave and other types of family leave under the Family and Medical Leave Act (1993). Most states have various laws also extending unpaid maternity leave or other benefits to employees in the public and private sectors. Alabama, for example, allows qualifying public employees to purchase service credit in the public employees retirement system for up to one year while on maternity leave. Montana requires private employers to permit a reasonable leave of absence and use of sick leave immediately following the birth or adoption of a child. In Tennessee, public agencies and private employers of eight persons or more are required to offer female employees sixteen weeks of leave for the birth of a child.

Breastfeeding. No state law prohibits BREASTFEEDING in public, but as of 2006 forty-two states had enacted laws addressing this basic maternal function. These statutes range from specifically permitting breastfeeding in any public or private place to exempting breastfeeding from public indecency laws or encouraging breastfeeding education. California and nine other states have laws that govern the practice in the workplace. Tennessee requires employers to give a mother a daily unpaid break to express milk for an infant. Texas law encourages employment policies that allow work-site breastfeeding. Idaho, Nebraska, Oregon, and six other states exempt breastfeeding mothers from jury duty. Maine law uniquely directs courts in contested custody cases to take into consideration whether a child is under one year of age and being breastfed.

Child Custody. Because fathers traditionally had the legal obligation to support their CHILDREN, they were favored to obtain custody of any children in DIVORCE cases. By the 1920s, however, the "tender years" presumption resulted in courts' awarding mothers custody of young children. In another turnaround, by the 1960s fathers were challenging this trend on the grounds of sex discrimination—and winning. Soon courts began using the concept of "the best interests of the child" to make custody decisions. Today joint custody is typically awarded to both parents. Nonetheless, mothers gain more leverage in custody battles based on the needs of a young child and other factors that determine his or her best interests, such as the amount of time each parent can make available for parenting and any special needs for maternal attention by a particular child.

Abortion. A woman's right to have an ABORTION was declared by the Supreme Court in *Roe v. Wade,* but this ruling has since been subjected to numerous restrictions. The Court's decision to find unconstitutional a Texas law banning abortion was based on a woman's personal right of privacy; yet the Court also noted that as a fetus becomes progressively better able to survive on its own outside the womb, the state's interest in protecting the life of the child becomes more compelling. The result has been that states have placed more restrictions on the right of abortion in the second and third trimesters of pregnancy. Numerous states have also imposed a waiting period for women seeking an abortion and require parental notification in the case of minors. Another requirement allowed by the Supreme Court in PLANNED PARENTHOOD OF SOUTHEASTERN PENNSYLVANIA V. CASEY (1992) was that a woman must give her informed CONSENT before an abortion is performed, except in a medical emergency. A number of states have such a provision; in West Virginia, the requirement is part of the Women's Right to Know Act. Federal funding of abortions is banned, and many states have followed suit to deny public funding.

The movement for women's rights began around 1840 in the United States and grew from a general atmosphere of reform that included the promotion of temperance, the abolition of slavery, improved labor and prison conditions, and stricter laws against vice. The historic Seneca Falls Declaration of Sentiments and Resolutions, adopted by a convention held in 1848 in Seneca Falls, New York, declared among other things that "woman is man's equal—was intended to be so by the Creator, and the highest good of the race demands that she should be recognized as such." Leaders of the early stages of the women's rights movement in the United States included Lucretia Mott (1793–1880), Elizabeth Cady Stanton (1815–1902), Lucy Stone (1818–93), SUSAN B. ANTHONY (1820–1906), Dorothea Dix (1802–87), Margaret Fuller (1810–50), and Julia Ward Howe (1819–1910)—none of whom lived to see the adoption of the Nineteenth Amendment in 1920. The struggle for women's rights may have come a long way, but for many women it is still far from over.

See also BRADWELL V. ILLINOIS; CHILD SUPPORT; MOTHERHOOD; REPRODUCTIVE RIGHTS; SEXUAL HARASSMENT; SPOUSAL RIGHTS AND DUTIES; UNBORN, RIGHTS OF THE.

WRONGFUL BIRTH AND LIFE

See MOTHERHOOD.

Z

ZONING

The law attempts to regulate sexual behavior in a number of ways. For one, consenting adults may engage in sexual conduct in private, but such behavior may be proscribed if conducted without CONSENT, with CHILDREN, or in public. Governments may additionally restrict SEXUALLY ORIENTED BUSINESSES to certain designated sections of a community. Zoning, the means by which this kind of activity is controlled, is the division of a municipal corporation or other local jurisdiction into separate areas and the application of regulations for the use of property in the specified zones.

Local governments, which are subdivisions of the state in which they are located, make zoning decisions under the state's general police power. This power gives a jurisdiction the authority to provide for the public health, safety, welfare, and often public morals. To protect the community as a whole, governments may regulate private property or use eminent domain to take it for public use in return for just compensation to the owners, as required by the Fifth Amendment (1791) to the U.S. Constitution. The Fifth Amendment's so-called takings clause was front and center in a recent firestorm created by the U.S. Supreme Court's decision in *Kelo v. City of New London* (2005), which upheld the taking of private property simply to turn it over to private developers who could presumably make better economic use of it and thus provide a better tax base for the city.

In the wake of the Industrial Revolution and the rise of high-density cities, zoning became an important tool for local governments in the United States. Early in the twentieth century, the U.S. Supreme Court began to look at cases involving zoning decisions—including *Euclid v. Ambler Realty* (1926) and *Nectrow v. City of Cambridge* (1928)—in terms of whether local governments could show that they were using their police power to protect the public interest. The concept of the public interest expanded to the point that in 1974, the Court upheld a zoning ordinance of a small Long Island, New York, village in *Belle Terre v. Boraas* that restricted occupancy in single-family dwellings; the Court held that family needs such as a "quiet place where yards are wide, people few, and motor vehicles restricted" also deserve protection.

With respect to sexual behavior issues, however, the Supreme Court in *Erznoznik v. City of Jacksonville* (1975) concluded that a law banning the showing of films containing NUDITY at a drive-in theater visible from a public street was an unconstitutional infringement of the FIRST AMENDMENT (1791). The following year, the Court faced the issue of local governments' power to control sexually explicit material and OBSCENITY through zoning in *Young v. American Mini Theatres, Inc.* (1976). (That same year Time, Inc., offered Home Box Office subscribers R-rated movies via satellite and *Hustler* magazine printed nude photographs of Jacqueline Kennedy Onassis.) In *Young* the Court issued a landmark decision permitting the use of zoning to restrict the location of adult businesses selling sexually explicit films, magazines, and other items. The Court reasoned, in a 5–4 decision written by Associate Justice John Paul Stevens, that some content regulation was permissible under the U.S. Constitution. In this case the material was viewed as so sexually explicit that its protection under the First Amendment was marginal at best. The Court concluded that the zoning regulation was not so restrictive as to deny merchants access to the market for sexually explicit activities and that the material at issue could reasonably be considered extremely offensive to many people.

But the evolution of the Supreme Court's understanding of the line to be drawn between the Constitution's protection of free expression in sexually explicit materials, nude dancing, and other commercial sexual activity and the limit of the government's police power would be almost as tortuous as was its process of defining obscenity during this period.

In *Schad v. Mount Ephraim* (1981), the Supreme Court struck down a zoning ordinance that excluded all live entertainment, "whether a nude dance or some other form of live presentation," while allowing other commercial enterprises; the law was found to be too broad to pass muster under the First Amendment. Then, in *Renton v. Playtime Theatres, Inc.* (1986), the Court upheld zoning decisions that would either concentrate adult theaters, as the zoning did in *Renton,* or disperse them. Either solution was deemed acceptable to counteract secondary effects, such as a deleterious impact on the quality of urban life. The Court found that a city can rely on any reasonable evidence of harm in developing a protective zoning ordinance.

Another related case not directly involving zoning was *City of Erie v. Pap's A.M.* (2000), which contested an ordinance prohibiting expressive behavior such as nudity and erotic dancing. In this case the Supreme Court concluded, based on a line of cases dealing with the First Amendment's protection of expressive or symbolic speech, that where state or local laws attempt to regulate negative secondary effects of adult businesses and have only a minor or incidental effect on freedom of expression, they will not be declared unconstitutional. In *City of Los Angeles v. Alameda Books, Inc.* (2002), the Court, citing *Renton,* found that if a city "can decrease the crime and urban blight by exercising its zoning power, and at the same time leave the quantity and accessibility of speech substantially undiminished, there is no First Amendment objection, ... even if the measure is content based"—that is, if the ordinance is directed at certain types of expression, which in this case involved adult entertainment establishments.

Although the right to conduct a sexually oriented business is subject to restrictions, including zoning, many other types of business that present hazards to health, safety, and citizens' welfare have similarly been restricted throughout American history. The difference between a factory that pollutes the atmosphere of a nearby residential area and an adult business is that the restrictions on the latter must be balanced against protections of free speech and a free press to be constitutionally permissible.

See also ADULT MATERIALS; ENTERTAINMENT INDUSTRY; INDECENT EXPOSURE; STATE AND LOCAL GOVERNMENT.

SELECTED BIBLIOGRAPHY

In addition to a variety of published and online resources, including legal reference books and law review articles, the following publications were helpful references for statutory and case law information cited in this book:

American Bar Association. *Legal Guide for Women.* New York: Random House, 2004.

Barron, Jerome A., and C. Thomas Dienes. *Constitutional Law in a Nutshell.* St. Paul, Minn.: West Group, 1999.

Eskridge, William N., Jr., and Nan D. Hunter. *Sexuality, Gender, and the Law.* New York: Foundation Press, Thompson-West, 2004.

Friesen, Jennifer. *State Constitutional Law: Litigating Individual Rights, Claims, and Defenses.* 3d ed. Charlottesville, Va.: Lexis Publishing, 2000.

Ramsey, Sarah H., and Douglas E. Abrams. *Children and the Law in a Nutshell.* St. Paul, Minn.: Thompson-West, 2003.

Thomas, Claire Sherman. *Sex Discrimination in a Nutshell,* 2d ed. St. Paul, Minn.: West Group, 2001.

Weisberg, D. Kelly. *Family Law.* Emanuel Law Outlines Series. New York: Aspen, 2004.

ILLUSTRATION CREDITS

INDEX

*Encyclopedia entries are listed in
bold type. Page numbers in italics
refer to illustrations.*

A

Abduction of children, 84, 224–25
 See also Human trafficking
Abortion, 1–7
 "abortion pill," 5–6, 7, 82, 111,
  124, 280–81, 285, 362
 antiabortion plank of Republican
  Party, 259
 attempts to overrule, 259, 264
 bioethical concerns about, 38, 39
 constitutional basis for, 2, 155
 criminalization of, 306
 decline in, 1
 due process and, 2
 as a family planning option, 127
 fetal pain in, 3
 First Amendment and, 6
 funding of, 2, 7, 75, 127, 136, 223,
  290, 379
 NARAL Pro-Choice America and,
  223
 nonsurgical, 5–6, 7
 notification of husband before,
  2, 78, 245, 246
 NOW and, 225, 226
 parental consent for minors, 2,
  4–5, 78, 127, 245, 246, 266, 346
 "partial-birth," 2, 3, 4–5, 6, 343, 355

Planned Parenthood Federation
  and, 243, 244
 prisoners' right to, 261
 privacy and, 2, 264
 protests of, 6, 23, 138, 285
 public opinion on, 7
 religion and, 281
 restrictions on, 2–3, 29, 223,
  245–46, 281, 335
 right to, 2, 186, 285, 379
 SIECUS and, 321
 state laws on, 3–5, 7
 surgeon general and, 343
 trimester basis of, 2, 3, 186, 245,
  285
 undue burden on, 5, 245
 waiting periods, 2, 3
 See also Roe v. Wade; Unborn,
  rights of the
Abortion in the United States (1958),
 57
Abstinence, 8–9, 297, 298
 federal funding of programs, 362
 pledges of, 9, 298
 SIECUS and, 321
 Silver Ring Thing program, 21,
  280, 362
 surgeon general and, 343
Abuse. *See* Child abuse; Domestic
 violence
*Acanfora v. Board of Education of
 Montgomery County* (1974), 137

Accord in the Interest of H. (2003),
 355
Acquaintance rape. *See* Date rape
Adkins v. Children's Hospital (1923),
 92
Administration for Children and
 Families, 84, 161, 362
Adolescent Family Life Act (1981),
 8, 75
Adolescents. *See* Teenagers
Adoption
 American Fertility Association and,
  22
 by bisexuals, 41
 by homosexuals, 164
 incest and, 172
 unmarried parents and, 361
Adoption of C. C. (1997), 32
Adult, definition of, 9
Adult businesses. *See* Sexually
 oriented businesses
Adult materials, 9–11
 distribution of, 212
 First Amendment and, 9, 11
 for homosexuals, 152
 pornography in, 182, 249–50,
  251
 sadomasochistic, 370–71
 sexually oriented businesses and,
  321, 322
 See also Obscenity; Pornography;
  and specific media

Adult movie theaters. *See* Motion pictures

Adultery, 11–14
  artificial insemination and, 28
  cohabitation as, 356
  criminal conversation as, 307
  in Hays Code, 116, 117
  in history, 299, 302
  lack of enforcement for, 303
  as lewd behavior, 196
  in the military, 210
  religion and, 302
Advertisements
  for adult materials, 10, 152–53, 212–13
  for AIDS awareness, 17
  for contraception, *80*
Affirmative action, 96, 122, 376, 377
  See also Sex discrimination
Aggravated sexual assault, 17, 78, 85, 169, 205, 271, 273, 300, 304, 307, 308, 309
  See also Sexual assault
Aging, sex and, 321
AIDS Action Committee of Massachusetts v. Massachusetts Bay Transportation Authority (1994), 17
AIDS-HIV, 14–18
  American Civil Liberties Union and, 21
  American Medical Association and, 23
  bioethical concerns about, 38
  consent to release tests on, 78
  discrimination based on, 166
  First Amendment and, 17
  Human Immunodeficiency Virus (HIV), 14, 17
  Human Rights Campaign and, 168
  intentional infection with, 306
  privacy and, 265
  rape and, 272
  religion and, 282
  surgeon general and, 343
Air Force Academy, 209

Alabama
  age of consent to marry in, 77
  age of consent to sex in, 255
  AIDS education in, 297
  censorship in, 60
  divorce in, 112
  interracial fornication in, 215
  maternity leave in, 378
  paternity in, 241
  prison officials' conduct in, 262
  prostitution in, 267, 268
  sex education in, 166
  sexual devices in, 90, 373–74
  STDs in, 326
  unmarried cohabitants in, 358
Alaska
  breastfeeding in, 49
  equal rights in, 93
  genetic privacy in, 147
  necrophilia in, 90
  rape in, 77
  registration of sex offenders in, 205
  same-sex marriage in, 95
Albert, State v. (1998), 273, 309
Alberts v. California (1957), 182, 186, 288
Alcaraz, State v. (1999), 365
Alcohol
  date rape and, 86, 274
  domestic violence and, 105
  prenatal abuse of, 39, 253
  sex discrimination in sales of, 82–84
  sexual behavior and, 109
  teenagers and, 345
Alexander the Great, 41
Alfonso v. Fernandez (1993), 82, 187
Alienation of affection, 14, 307
Alimony, 18–19, 97
  effect of adultery on, 14
  modification of, 257
  "palimony," 19, 100, 188, 255, 292, 357
  prenuptial agreements and, 256, 257
  restoration of, 24
  unmarried cohabitants and, 358

Alito, Samuel A., Jr., 259, 340
Amber Alerts, 225
American Academy of Pediatrics, 61
American Association of University Women, 327, 328
American Bar Association, 123, 124
American Birth Control League, 294
American Civil Liberties Union, 19–21, *20*
  abstinence education and, 8, 362
  Child Online Protection Act and, 64
  cohabitation and, 14
  DNA sweep and, 101
  equal rights enforcement and, 120
  gay rights and, 190, 346
  Internet and, 71
  obscenity and, 53, 116, 249
  premarital sex and, 255
  sex education and, 280
  sexual privacy and, 373
  single-sex education and, 327
American Civil Liberties Union v. Ashcroft (2003), 64
  See also *Ashcroft v. American Civil Liberties Union*
American College of Obstetricians and Gynecologists, 81
American Federation of Government Employees, 262
American Fertility Association, 22
American Law Institute, 193, 303
American Library Association, 61
American Library Association, United States v. (2003), 11, 178–79
American Medical Association, 8, **22–24,** 124, 295
American Nurses Association, 124
American Pharmacists Association, 81, 124, 125
American Psychiatric Association, 312
American Samoa, human trafficking in, 169

American School Health Association, 295

An American Tragedy (Dreiser), 44, 287, 320

Americans with Disabilities Act (1990), 15, 42, 50, 150, 166

Amnesty International, 261

Anal beads, 374

Anal sex, 192, 196, 267
  bestiality and, 35
  child molestation and, 61, 67
  rape and, 273, 307, 309
  sodomy and, 17, 194, 303, 330
  See also *Lawrence v. Texas;*
    Sodomy

Annulment, 24–25, 100, 170, 280

Antenuptial agreements. *See*
  Prenuptial agreements

Anthony, Susan B., 1, **25–26**, 26, 133, 379

Anti-Drug Abuse Act (1988), 111

Apprendi v. New Jersey (2000), 160

Arbuckle, Roscoe, State of California v. (1922), 113–14

Archibald, People v. (1968), 353

Aristotle, 197, 240

Arizona
  AIDS-HIV education in, 17
  civil confinement in, 300
  community property in, 333
  covenant marriage in, 202
  equal rights in, 175
  polygamy in, 246
  prenuptial agreements in, 257
  prurient interest in, 270
  rape in, 77, 278
  same-sex marriage in, 291
  sex education in, 166
  sexual assault in, 307
  stem-cell research in, 340

Arizona v. Youngblood (1988), 147

Arkansas
  abortion in, 3
  adults-only bookstore section in, 11
  cloning in, 340
  surrogacy, homosexual, in, 164

Arp v. Workers' Compensation Appeals Board (1977), 122

ART. *See* Assisted reproductive technology

Art
  censorship of, 61
  nudity in, 229, 231, 265, 270

Art-film theaters, 60, 212
  See also Motion pictures

Artificial insemination, 27, 28, 29–30, 52
  See also Assisted reproductive technology

Artificial vaginas, 374

Ashcroft, John, 229

Ashcroft v. American Civil Liberties Union (2002), 10, 21, 60, 64, 118, 136, 178, 185, 204, 236, 250

Ashcroft v. Free Speech Coalition (2002), 69, 118, 137, 251

Assembly, freedom of
  abortion protests and, 6, 285
  First Amendment and, 134, 135, 138–39

Assisted reproductive technology, 27–32
  American Fertility Association and, 22
  bioethical concerns about, 39
  homosexuals and, 164
  parental rights in, 171
  Planned Parenthood Federation and, 243
  "test-tube" babies and, 51–52
  and unborn, rights of the, 22
  unused embryos from, 39, 337, 339, 340

Association, freedom of
  First Amendment and, 138–39, 228, 263–64
  homosexuals and, 138, 166–67, 358

Association for the Treatment of Sexual Abusers, 191

Asylum, for female genital mutilation victims, 305

Atherton v. Atherton (1901), 375

Attorney General v. Massachusetts Interscholastic Athletic Assn. (1979), 94

Attorney general, U.S., 156, 229, 249, 258, 308

Auden, W. H., 372

Augustus Caesar, 57

Ayotte v. Planned Parenthood of Northern New England (2006), 6–7

B

Baehr v. Lewin (1993), 188, 289, 336

Baehr v. Miike (1999), 87

Baker v. Carr (1962), 214

Ballard v. United States (1946), 141, 142

Baltimore, Maryland, tracking of sex offenders in, 301

Bang v. Miller (1958), 310

Banned materials. *See* Censorship; Obscenity; Pornography

Bantam Books, Inc. v. Sullivan (1963), 59

Barnes v. Costle (1977), 42

Barnes v. Glen Theatre, Inc. (1991), **33–34**, 115, 230–31

Barr, State v. (1970), 13

Bastards. *See* Illegitimacy; Unmarried parents

Battered-women's shelters, 368

Battered-women's syndrome, 106

Battery, 307, 308, 309, 315
  See also Sexual assault

Beecher, Henry Ward, 13

Behind the Green Door (1972), 212

Bell v. United States (1955), 267

Belle Terre v. Boraas (1974), 380

Belli, Melvin, 53

Bellotti v. Baird (1979), 67, 266

Bendich, Albert M., 53

Benedict XVI (pope), 282

Benefits
  for illegitimate children, 360

for unmarried cohabitants, 358
  See also Social Security; *and
    specific topics*
Bennett, Robert, 61
Best interests of the child, 31, 32,
  66, 164, 171, 217, 241, 242, 256,
  331, 361, 378, 379
Bestiality, 34–35, 89, 306, 328,
  330
Bezio v. Patenaude (1980), 293
Bias crimes. *See* Hate crimes
Bigamy, 35–37, 136, 199
  annulment and, 25
  "bigamous cohabitation," 357, 374
  as a misdemeanor, 303
  See also Polygamy
Bill of Rights (1791), 2
  American Civil Liberties Union
    and, *20*
  Douglas, William O., on, 107, 108
  right of privacy under, 185, 263–64
  See also First Amendment; Ninth
    Amendment; *and specific rights*
Bioethics, 37–40, 52, 125, 150
Bioplasty, 311
Birth control, coinage of term, 293
  See also Contraception; Family
    planning; Reproductive rights
Birth rate, 79, 297
Bisexuality, 41–43, 144
Bitty, United States v. (1908), 266
*Bivens v. Six Unknown Named
  Agents of the Federal Bureau of
  Narcotics* (1972), 96
Black, Hugo L.
  on contraceptive rights, 155
  dissent in *Ginzburg v. United
    States,* 213
  on First Amendment, 153
  on marriage, 198
  on press, freedom of, 182
Blackmun, Harry A., *184*
  on privacy, 228
Blackstone, William, 26, 77, 229,
  234, 299, 344
Blair v. Washington (1987), 94

Blakely v. Washington (2004), 160
Block, Herbert, 137
Blockberger v. United States (1932),
  299
Blogs, sexually explicit, 11, 179
Blunt, Matt, 261
BMG, 118
Board of Education v. Pico (1982),
  61
Bobbitt, Lorena, 234, 311
Boddie v. Connecticut (1971), 100,
  198
Bonadio, Commonwealth v. (1980),
  196
Bonynge, State v. (1990), 35
***A Book Named "John Cleland's
  Memoirs of a Woman of
  Pleasure" v. Attorney General of
  the Commonwealth of
  Massachusetts*** (1996), **43–45,** *44,*
  108, 152, 213, 236
Booker v. United States (2005), 160
Books, censorship of, 43–45, 53,
  58, 59, 60, 61, 211–12, 232,
  286–87
Bookstores, 11, 116, 239, 249, 322,
  324, 381
Booth v. Maryland (1987), 365–66
Borak, People v. (1973), 77, 90, 274
Bork, Robert H., 167, 227
"Boston marriage," 289
Bourdon's Case (1989), 124
*Boutilier v. Immigration and
  Naturalization Service* (1967), 189
Bowen v. Kendrick (1988), 8
Bowers v. Hardwick (1986)
  decision outlawing sodomy, 12, 33,
    195, 228, 303, 329
  overruled by *Lawrence v. Texas,*
    33, 186, 194, 303, 329, 330
Boy Scouts of America v. Dale
  (2000), 166
Bradley, Joseph P.
  on married women, 254
  on motherhood, 145, 221
  on right to practice law, 45

Bradwell, Myra, 45, 46, 47, 221
Bradwell v. Illinois (1873), **45–47,**
  91, 145, 221, 246, 254, 333
Bragdon v. Abbott (1998), 15–16
Branch Davidians, 248–49
Brandeis, Louis D.
  on right to be left alone, 194
  on states as laboratories of
    democracy, 335
  on women's labor regulation, 221
Brandenburg v. Ohio (1969), 248
Brandon v. County of Richardson
  (2001), 159
Braschi v. Stahl Associates (1989),
  358
Breast enhancement, 307, 310, 311
Breast implants, 310, 311
Breastfeeding, 47–51, 176, 378
Breedlove v. Suttles (1937), 92
Brennan, William J., Jr., 109
  on association, 138
  on contraceptive rights, 154
  on gender discrimination, 82, 92
  on marriage, freedom of
    association in, 199
  on obscenity, 44–45, 152, 181, 213,
    269, 286
  on sex discrimination, 50, 83, 142
Brewer, David J., 222
Breyer, Stephen J.
  on abortion, 246
  on abortion protests, 6
Bristol-Myers Squibb, 311
Broadcasting. *See* Federal
  Communications Commission;
  Entertainment industry; First
  Amendment; Media; Radio;
  Television
Brockdorff, United States v. (1997),
  62
Brockett v. Spokane Arcades, Inc.
  (1985), 236
Brooks, United States v. (2005), 210
Brown, Commonwealth v. (1992),
  309
Brown, Louise, 27, *51,* **51–52**

Brown v. Board of Education of Topeka (1954), 21, 83, 132, 153, 215, 318, 327, 369
Brownback, Samuel D., *131*
Bruce, Lenny, 43, **52–54**, *53*, 114, 141, 162
Bryant, Kobe, People v. (2003), 277
Bryant, United States v. (1969), 271
Brzonkala, Christy, 87
Buck v. Bell (1927), 342
Buckland, Richard, 183
Buckley, People v. (1971), 239
Buggery, 34, 329
See also Bestiality; Sodomy
Bureau of Alcohol, Tobacco, and Firearms, 249
Bureau of Prisons, 261
Burger, Warren E.
on adult materials, 10, 11
on equal rights, 119
on gender discrimination, 83
on obscenity, 212, 213
on sex discrimination, 142
Burgess, United States v. (1999), 180
Burke, State v. (2003), 371
Burlesque, 114, *114*, 212
Burlington Industries, Inc. v. Ellerth (1998), **54–55**, 315
Burlington Northern Santa Fe Corporation, 149
Burns v. McGregor Electronic Industries, Inc. (1992), 315
Burstyn v. Wilson (1952), 116
Bush, George H. W., 167
Bush, George W.
abortion and, 335, 362
bioethics commission of, 39, 259, 337
domestic violence and, 237
faith-based programs of, 279
family planning and, 128
Healthy Marriage Initiative and, 160
prison rape and, 262
same-sex marriage and, 165, 260, 293

sex education and, 284
stem-cell research and, 281, 337
and unborn, rights of the, 356
Butler v. Michigan (1957), 182, 287–88
Byrne v. Karalexis (1969), 108

C
Cabana, State v. (1997), 309
Cable television
blocking of, 60, 61
censorship of, 71, 162–63
exemption from federal regulation of, 115, 129, 204
Calderone, Mary S., *56*, **56–57**, 295, 320
Califano v. Goldfarb (1977), 84
California
abortion in, 3
abortion protests in, 285, 335
abstinence education in, 8
AIDS-HIV in, 16, 345
annulment in, 25
assisted reproductive technology in, 30
battered-women's syndrome in, 106
bioethics in, 40
breastfeeding in, 49, 378
castration in, 301
civil abuse suits in, 282
civil confinement in, 300
cloning in, 340
community property in, 333
date rape in, 87
domestic partnerships in, 19, 202, 358, 361
equal rights in, 94, 120–21, 122, 320
fertility treatment in, 125
fetal homicide in, 356
gender discrimination in, 144
hate crimes in, 157, 300
homosexual discrimination in, 166
insurance coverage for contraceptives in, 81

maternity leave in, 219
nudity in, 231
obscene language in, 236–37
obscenity in, 212–14, 288
paternity in, 241–42
pregnancy benefits in, 251–52
prescriptions in, 125
prisoners' rights in, 261
rape shield laws in, 278
same-sex marriage in, 292
sexual harassment in, 43
sexually oriented businesses in, 322
statutory rape in, 68, 346
STDs in, 326
stem-cell research in, 336, 340
surrogacy in, 32
teenagers, definition of, 345
telephone sex in, 347
California v. LaRue (1972), 230
California Institute for Regenerative Medicine, 336, 340
California Savings and Loan Association v. Guerra (1987), 219
Call blocking, 348
Caller ID, 348
Caminetti v. United States (1917), 305
"Camp followers," 210
Campbell, Keith, 337
Canada, parental leave in, 220
Cannon v. Cannon (2004), 120
Cannon v. University of Chicago (1979), 349
Carafano, Christianne, 71
Carey v. Population Services International (1977), 81, 295
Carlin, George, 136, 204
Carmona, Richard H., 342
Carnal Knowledge (1971), 59, 250
Carrier, People v. (1977), 35
Carter, Jimmy
draft registration of women and, 208
in *Playboy*, 41, 162

Castrated: My Eight Months in Prison (Ginzburg), 153
Castration, 301, 341
Catholic Charities of Sacramento, Inc. v. Superior Court of Sacramento County (2004), 81
CBS network, 203, 204
Censored (Seiler), 59
Censorship, 57–61
  of adult materials, 9–11, 212–14
  American Civil Liberties Union and, 21
  of cable television, 60, 61, 71, 115, 129, 162–63, 204
  of entertainment industry, 113–19, 203–4
  First Amendment and, 136–37
  of Internet, 63–65, 71, 118, 176–80
  of literature, 43–45, 53, 58, 211–12
  of media, 203–4
  of motion pictures, 58–60, 182, 212, 287
  of music, 115–16, 130
  of obscenity, 234–37, 288
  of pornography, 249–51
  religion and, 283
  self-censorship, 60–61, 64, 115, 116, 117, 118
  of sexually oriented businesses, 321–24, 380–81
  of video games, 118–19
  See also Obscenity; Pornography; *and specific media*
Center for Reproductive Rights, 286
Center for Sex Offender Management, 70, 301
Center for Work Life Law, 220
Centers for Disease Control and Prevention, 362
  AIDS-HIV and, 14, 16, 17
  assisted reproductive technology and, 27, 28,
  infertility and, 28
  STDs and, 9, 325, 327
Cesarean sections, 356
Chabas, Paul, 73

Chaplinsky v. New Hampshire (1942), 177, 235
Chapman, Nathaniel, 23
Chastity. *See* Abstinence
Chevron USA v. Echazabal (2002), 150
Chicago, domestic partnerships in, 202
Chicago Legal News, 46, 47
Child abuse, 61–63, 67–69
  by Catholic priests, 61, 62, 281–82
  domestic violence and, 104
  incest as, 174
  Kinsey, Alfred, on, 193
  pederasty as, 329, 330, 345
  by pedophiles, 191, 251, 282, 301, 330, 345, 370
  rate of, 84
  See also Child pornography; Children; Statutory rape
Child Abuse Prevention and Treatment Act (1974), 75
Child Abuse Victims' Rights Act (1986), 363
Child care, 220, 237
Child custody, 65, 97
  bisexuals and, 41
  fathers and, 378
  homosexuals and, 164, 292–93, 359
  mothers and, 217, 378–79
  prenuptial agreements and, 256
  "tender years" presumption in, 217, 309–10, 378
  transsexuals and, 352
  unmarried cohabitants and, 359
Child Online Protection Act (1998), 10, 11, 21, **63–65,** 71, 72, 75, 118, 178, 185, 204
Child pornography, 68–69, 250–51
  censorship of, 60
  child victims of, 67
  CyberTipline reports on, 225
  FBI and, 85
  Internet and, 179, 180. *See also* Internet

as lewd exhibition, 196
  nudity as element in, 232
  possession of, 69, 232, 250, 265, 306
  test for, 213
  video games and, 118
Child Pornography Prevention Act (1996), 118, 251
Child Pornography Tipline, 180
Child Protection Act (1984), 232
Child support, 65–66, 67
  assisted reproductive technology and, 28
  Cleveland, Grover, and, *258*
  collection of, 9, 285–86
  after divorce, 18, 65, 97
  for illegitimate children, 170, 360
  marriage, right to, and, 199
  mothers and, 217
  parental obligation for, 202
  paternity test for, 241
  prenuptial agreements and, 256
  transsexuals and, 352
  unmarried parents and, 360
  See also Alimony
Child Support Enforcement Amendments (1984), 66
Child Support Recovery Act (1992), 66, 84
Childbirth
  criminal responsibility for, 307
  discrimination based on, 378
  in Hays Code, 117
  shackling of prisoners during, 261
  See also Pregnancy
Children, 66–70
  abduction of, 84, 224–25
  access to adult materials, 9
  ban on having, 9
  best interests of, 31, 32, 66, 164, 171, 217, 241, 242, 256, 331, 361, 378, 379
  broadcast entertainment and, 115
  crimes against, 84–85, 205
  fetal homicide, 356
  human trafficking of, 168, 169

illegitimate, 170–72, 359–61

infanticide, 355–56

Internet access by, 63–65, 177–79, *178*, 180

names of, 30, 171, 331, 360–61

of polygamous marriage, 248

privacy rights of, 265

right to bear, 28

rights of, 67

schooling of, 67, 217, 360

sex of, determination of, 284

sexual exploitation of, 225, 305–6

STDs and, 326–27

television indecency and, 130

as victims, 62–63, 105

as witnesses, 62–63, 105, 309–10

wrongful death of, 361

See also Child abuse; Child custody; Child pornography; Child support; Internet; Paternity; Statutory rape; Teenagers; Unborn, rights of the

Children's Internet Protection Act (2000), 11, 178

Chlamydia, 324

Church and state, separation of, 8, 21, 135, 136, 248, 279, 362

Cialis, 111

Circumcision

female, 38, 305, 321

male, 38

The Citadel, 369

Citizenship of illegitimate children, 84, 171

City News and Novelty, Inc. v. City of Wauksha (2001), 323

Civic Awareness of America, Ltd. v. Richardson (1972), 128, 136

Civil confinement of sex offenders, 191–92, 299, 300–301

Civil Rights Act (1871), 157, 230

Civil Rights Act (1964), Title VII, 75, 92, 120, 221, 348

affirmative action under, 377

bisexuals under, 41–42

civil suits under, 349

employment discrimination under, 93

infertility treatments under, 29

marital status under, 333

maternity leave under, 219

pregnancy under, 50, 252, 378

sexual harassment under, 54, 145, 314

sexual minorities under, 165

sexual orientation under, 95

transsexuals under, 312, 351

Civil Rights Act (1991), 93

Civil Rights Restoration Act (1987), 348

Civil Service Commission, 165–66, 189, 319

Civil suits

for abuse by priests, 62, 282

children's right to sue, 363

for discrimination, 96, 315

for medical malpractice, 310–11

for rape, 275

for sexual assault, 307, 308–9, 315

under Title IX, 349

by unmarried cohabitants, 358

for violence against women, 366

See also Morrison, United States v.; Title IX

Civil unions, 292

alimony rights under, 19

in Connecticut and Vermont, 88, 130, 132, 164, 165, 189, 202, 282, 292

Defense of Marriage Act, effect on, 88

dissolution of, 100–101

inheritance under, 201

Civilization and Its Discontents (Freud), 240

Clark, Tom, on obscenity, 182

Clark, State v. (1982), 103

Clarke, Lige, *190*

Class-action suits

for discrimination, 315

for medical malpractice, 311

See also Civil suits

Clear Channel Communications, 204

Cleland, John, 43, 44

Cleveland, Grover, *258*, 260

Cleveland Board of Education v. LaFleur (1974), 251, 378

Clinton, Bill

bioethics commission of, 39

cloning and, 52

contraception and, 281

"don't ask, don't tell" policy of, 165, 259

family planning and, 128

genetic information discrimination and, 150

investigation and impeachment of, 76, 123, 141

sexual affairs of, 260

sexual orientation discrimination and, 41, 94, 95, 165, 168, 190, 319

surgeon general and, 342

Violence Against Women Act and, 366

women in combat and, 207

Clinton, Hillary, 123

Cloning, 340–41

ban on federal funding of, 52

bioethical concerns about, 38, 39, 40

Clothing

cross-dressing, 138, 146, 352, 353

of homosexuals, 70

nude dancers and, 33, 34, 115, *137*, 196, 230, 231, 265, 306, 323

nudity and, 228

of transsexuals, 146, 312

Coburn, Tom, 325, 342

Coeducation, 186, 327–28, 369

Cohabitation. *See* Unmarried cohabitants; Unmarried parents

Cohen v. California (1971), 136

Coitus interruptus, 79

Coleman v. Caddo Parish School Board (1994), 298

Colorado
  abortion in, 3
  adult business licensing in, 323
  adultery in, 12
  civil abuse suits in, 282
  genetic privacy in, 147
  hate crimes in, 165
  homosexual rights in, 167
  incest in, 173–74
  paternity in, 241
  prostitution in, 267
  rape in, 77
  same-sex marriage in, 291
  statutory rape in, 68, 346
  surrogacy in, 32
  and unborn, rights of the, 355
Columbus, City of v. Rogers (1975),
  353
Columbus, Ohio, cross-dressing in,
  353
Commentaries on American Law
  (Kent), 360
*Commentaries on the Laws of
  England* (Blackstone), 26, 77, 228,
  234, 299, 344
Commission on Obscenity and
  Pornography (1967, 1970), 10, 234
Commission on Pornography (1986),
  249
Commission on Safety and Abuse
  in America's Prisons, 260
Common law marriage, 132, 202, 357
Commonwealth v. See other party
Communications Act (1934), 129,
  347, 348
Communications Decency Act
  (1996), 10, 11, 21, 63, **71–72,** 75,
  118, 177–78, 179, 204, 288
Community property laws, 199, 257,
  333
Community service, for sex
  offenders, 299
Community standards for obscenity,
  234
  homosexual magazines and,
    235, 250

local versus national, 181–82
  in *Miller v. California,* 177, 249,
    270
  in *Roth v. United States,* 43, 58,
    288
  in three-part test, 45, 269, 319
  voyeurism and, 236
Computer dating services, 71
Comstock, Anthony, 45, 58, 72,
  72–73, 75, 80, 126, 154, 266,
  284, 286, 293
Comstock Act (1873), 45, 58, 72,
  75, 283, 284
Concealment, in marriage, 24
  See also Fraud
Condoms
  abstinence programs and, 284
  adolescents' use of, 9, 297
  availability in pharmacies, 81
  Catholic Church ban on, 280
  for contraception, 79
  for disease prevention, 18, 38, 325
  effectiveness of, 8, 343
  in the military, 210
  school distribution of, 81, 187
  for sexual enhancement, 373
"Conduct unbecoming an officer,"
  210
Confidentiality. *See* Privacy
Conflicts of interest. *See* Ethics
Congress, 73–76
  legislation by, 75–76, 258
  as reflection of majority will, 257
Conkling, Roscoe ("Fatty
  Arbuckle"), 113–14
Connecticut
  adoption by homosexuals in, 361
  civil unions in, 88, 130, 132, 164,
    165, 189, 202, 282, 292
  cloning in, 340
  contraceptive ban in, 80, 108,
    153–55. See also *Griswold v.
    Connecticut*
  infertility in, 29
  pregnant prisoners in, 261
  prostitution in, 267

same-sex marriage in, 292
  sex education in, 297
  sexual harassment in, 316
  sexual orientation harassment in,
    317
  STDs in, 326
  surrogacy in, 31–32
  victims' rights in, 365
*Connecticut Department of Public
  Safety v. John Doe* (2003), 205,
  301
Consent, 76–79
  for abortion by minors, 2, 4–5, 78,
    127, 245, 246, 266, 346
  for contraceptive use by minors,
    81–82
  genetic information and, 147
  in date rape, 87
  in determining a sex offense, 303
  husband's, for an abortion, 2, 78,
    245, 246
  in marriage, 24, 76–77, 198
  for medical testing, 78–79, 326
  in rape, 77–78, 271, 272, 273, 274,
    278
  to sex in marriage, 76–77
  to sexual relations, 79, 134
  to sterilization, 341–42
  by teenagers to sex, 346
Consortium, loss of, 199, 334
Consummation of marriage
  failure of, 25
  by prisoners, 260–61
Content-based regulation, 10, 163,
  381
  See also Censorship; Zoning
Contraception, 79–82
  in abstinence education, 8
  banned as obscene, 58, 73, 80,
    293
  bioethical concerns about, 38
  drugs for, 110–11
  emergency, 6, 19, 82, 111, 272,
    280, 284
  minors' rights to, 81–82
  parental consent for, 81–82

parental notification for, 81
the Pill, 79, 110, *281*, 317
Planned Parenthood Federation
    and, 243
privacy in, 153–55, 264
religion and, 280–81, 285, 294
right to use, 153–55, 284–85, 295
Sanger, Margaret, and, 293–95
See also Condoms; Family
    planning; *Griswold v.*
    Connecticut; Reproductive rights
Contracts
    by married women, 47, 197, 333,
        376
    nonmarital, 100
    prenuptial, 255–57
    surrogacy, 31
    by unmarried cohabitants, 359
Controlled Substances Act (1970),
    110
Copeland v. Commonwealth,
    (2000), 236
Cort v. Ash (1975), 349
Cosmetic surgery, 310–12
    for sex reassignment, 138, 311,
        350, 351
Cote-Whiteacre v. Department of
    Public Health (2006), 291
Cousins, marriage of, 172, 173, 198
Covenant marriage, 100, 202
Craig v. Boren (1976), **82–84**, 92,
    142, 328, 345
Crane, David B., 76
Crawford, State v. (1972), 329
Crawford v. Washington (2004), 105
Crick, Francis, 102
Crimes Against Children Unit
    (FBI), 67, **84–85**, 206
"Crimes against nature," 34, 35, 329
    See also Bestiality; Sodomy
Crimes of passion, 160
Criminal conversation, 307
Crisonino v. New York City Housing
    Authority (1997), 145
Cromwell, Oliver, 299
Cross-dressing, 138, 146, 352, 353

Cruzan v. Director, Missouri
    Department of Health (1990),
    339–40
CSI (television show), 182
Cummings v. Cummings (1920), 256
Cunnilingus, 196, 267, 309, 329
Curtis, Edward S., 217
Cybersex, 179–80, 346
CyberTipline, 180, 224–25

D
Dallas, City of v. Stranglin (1989),
    138, 336
Darrin v. Gould (1975), 94
Darrow, Clarence, 21
Darwin, Charles, 215
Date rape, **86–87**, 111–12, 274
    See also Rape
Daubert v. Merrell Dow (1993), 103
David (Michelangelo), 231
Davis v. Beason (1890), 135, 248
Davis v. Monroe County Board of
    Education (1999), 316
Davis, Nathan Smith, 23
Dawkins, Richard, 147
de Sade, Marquis, 302
"Deadbeat dads," 65, 285
    See also Child support
Death penalty, DNA evidence and,
    104
Declaration of Independence (1776),
    132, 227, 375
Deep Throat (1972), 116, 212
Defense Authorization Act (1992),
    207
Defense of Marriage Act (1996),
    75, **87–89,** 95, 130, 131, 161, 165,
    289–90, 291
    See also Federal Marriage
        Amendment; Same-sex marriage
Delaware
    bestiality in, 35
    gender-neutral language in, 144,
        378
    medical information privacy in, 79
    nude dancing in, 231

rape in, 77
rape shield laws in, 278
same-sex marriage in, 130
sexual orientation in, 95
STDs in, 326
Dennis v. United States (1951),
    373–74
Department of Social Services v.
    Father and Mother (1988), 215
DeSantis v. Pacific Telephone and
    Telegraph Co. (1979), 165
Detroit, sexually oriented business
    zoning in, 323
Deviant behavior, 89–90, 306, 329
    See also Bestiality; Sodomy;
        Voyeurism
Devine v. Devine (1981), 217
Dial-a-porn, 347, 348
Dickstein, Sidney, 153
Die, right to, 339–40
Dildos, 374
DiMaggio, Joe, 97
Disabled persons
    sex and, 321
    violence against women, 368
Disability
    exclusions for, 370
    pregnancy as, 378
Discrimination, 90–96
    against AIDS-HIV victims, 15–16,
        17
    alimony and, 19
    against bisexuals, 41–42
    in education, 91, 94, 348–49
    gender-based, 144–46
    on genetic information, 150
    infertility and, 29
    against married women, 197
    against mothers, 220
    in the private sector, 314
    reverse, 82–84, 92, 96, 122, 377
    against sex offenders, 299
    on sexual orientation, 94–96
    against teenagers, 345
    against transsexuals, 55, 144,
        145–46, 350, 351

against transvestites, 353

against unmarried cohabitants, 357–59

See also Employment discrimination; Homosexuals; Sex discrimination; Sexual harassment

Diseases, stem-cell research on, 337

See also AIDS-HIV; Sexually transmitted diseases

District of Columbia

bestiality in, 35

common law marriage in, 202

pregnant prisoners in, 261

prenuptial agreements in, 257

same-sex marriage in, 292

Divorce, 96–101

for adultery, 14

artificial insemination and, 28

attorney conflict of interest in, 124

drug abuse and, 112

embryos, disposition after, 31

fault-based, 100

incest and, 173

no-fault, 100, 357

nonrecognition of, 374–75

prisoners' right to, 261

rate, 96, 101, 160

same-sex relationships and, 101, 292–93

wrongful, 334

See also Alimony; Child custody; Child support; Prenuptial agreements

Dix, Dorothea, 379

DNA, 101–4, *101*

in cloning, 340

evidence, 102, 182–83

genetic information in, 146

paternity tests using, 104, 241

prisoners and, 102, 103, 261

relationship identification using, 103–4

testing, 38, 147, 150, 261, 265, 307

Doctrine of incorporation, 135, 235, 335

Doda, Carol, 311

Dodge, William E., 72

Doe v. Bell (2003), 312

Doe v. Boeing Company (1993), 353

Doe v. Bolton (1973), 109, 228

Doe v. Doe (1998), 32

Doe v. U.S. Postal Service (1985), 351

Dolly (sheep), 52, 337

Domestic partnerships, 202, 292

alimony rights in, 19

benefits in, 358

health care in, 95

inheritance in, 361

same-sex couples in, 164, 282, 336

Domestic violence, 104–7, 237–38, 367

See also Violence Against Women Act

Domicile

for divorce, 375

of a married couple, 25, 332

of married women, 376

Donahoe Higher Education Act (1991), 87

Donors, sperm. *See* Assisted reproductive technology

"Don't ask, don't tell" policy, 95, 165, 186, 209, 319

See also Military

Doran v. Salem Inn, Inc. (1975), 230, 231

Dost, United States v. (1986), 232

Double jeopardy, 191, 299

Douglas, William O., *107,* **107–9**

on adult materials, 10

on *A Book Named "John Cleland's Memoirs of a Woman of Pleasure,"* 235

on contraceptive rights, 154

on marital privacy, 199

dissent in *Miller v. California,* 213

on Ninth Amendment, 228

on nudity, 232

on obscenity, 45, 108, 235

on pornography, 250

on press, freedom of, 182

on privacy, 108, 263–64

on *Roth v. United States,* 108

on sterilization, 342

on women jurors, 141

Dow Chemical Company, 311, 315

Dow Corning Company, 311

Dred Scott case, 207, 215, 354

Dreiser, Theodore, 287, 320

Drugs, 109–12

bioethical concerns about, 38

in date rape, 78, 86, 87, 274

Food and Drug Administration approval of, 284–85

illegal use of, 111

prenatal abuse of, 63, 112, 253–54, 355

refusal to dispense, 124

for sexual dysfunction, 312

for sexual enhancement, 111–12

sexual response to, 318

See also Abortion; Contraception

Duress, in marriage, 24

E

Eastern Airlines, 55, 145–46, 312, 351

The Ed Sullivan Show, 116

Edison, Thomas, 58

Edison Manufacturing Company, 113

Education. *See* Abstinence; Sex discrimination; Sex education; Sexual harassment; Single-sex education; Title IX

Edwards, Robert, 51

Eisenhower, Dwight D., 111, 259

Eisenstadt v. Baird (1972), 28, 80, 109, 111, 127, 155, 186, 264, 280, 284, 342

Elagabalus, 350

Elden v. Sheldon (1988), 358

Elders, M. Joycelyn, 342

Eliot, T. S., 212

Elk Grove Unified School Dist. v. Newdow (2004), 65

Ellis, Havelock, 294
E-mail, 179, 315
  See also Internet
Embryos, disposition of, 31, 340
  See also Stem-cell research;
    Unborn, rights of the
Emergency contraception, 6, 19, 82,
  111, 272, 280, 284
Employee Income Security Act
  (1974), 28–29
Employment discrimination,
  91–96
  against AIDS-HIV victims, 15–16
  against bisexuals, 41–42
  on genetic information, 150
  against homosexuals, 94–95, 137,
    138, 164, 165–66, 168, 186, 188,
    189–90, 358
  against married women, 47, 333
  during pregnancy, 251–53, 378
  against transsexuals, 55, 144,
    145–46, 351
  against transvestites, 353
  in women's hours, 221–22
  See also *Bradwell v. Illinois*;
    Sex discrimination; Sexual
    harassment
Employment Non-Discrimination
  Act (1994), 167–68
"Enoch Arden statutes," 37
*Enriquez v. West Jersey Health
  Systems* (2001), 146, 187, 353
Entertainment industry, **113–19,**
  203–4
  zoning regulation of, 380–81
  See also Nude dancing; Sexually
    oriented businesses; *and specific
    topics*
Entertainment Software Ratings
  Board, 118
Ephebophilia, 345
Equal Education Opportunities Act
  (1974), 327
Equal Employment Opportunity
  Commission, 93, 120, 145, 253,
  314

*Equal Employment Opportunity
  Commission v. Rath Packing Co.*
  (1986), 333
*Equal Employment Opportunity
  Commission v. Sears, Roebuck
  and Co.* (1986), 93
Equal Pay Act (1963), 348, 376
Equal rights, **119–22,** 133
  indecent exposure and, 175
  in the military, 207–9
  state laws on, 120–22, 320,
    377–78
  voting rights of women, 92, 119,
    133, 184, 185, 214–15
  women's labor regulation, 221
  See also Bisexuals; Equal Rights
    Amendment; Homosexuals;
    Nineteenth Amendment;
    Sex discrimination; Single-sex
    education;Transsexualism;
    Transvestism; Women's rights
Equal Rights Amendment (1972),
  75, 83, 84, 119, 120, *121*, 133,
  142, 208, 225, 226, 314, 319,
  348
Equifax Services, Inc. v. Cohen
  (1980), 42–43
Erectile dysfunction, 111, 311, 312
Erie, City of v. Pap's A.M. (2000),
  34, 115, 137, *137*, 196, 230–31,
  265, 306, 336, 381
Eros, 152–53
Erznoznik v. City of Jacksonville
  (1975), 231, 323, 380
Esquire, 58
Essay on the Principle of Population
  (Malthus), 79
Estep v. United States (1946), 260
Ethics, 122–25
  of abortion providers, 2, 3, 5, 6, 7
  of government employees, 123
  of lawyers, 123–24
  of pharmacists, 38, 81, 122,
    124–25, 285
  of physicians, 23, 38, 90, 122,
    124–25, 310

Ethics in Government Act (1978),
  123
Euclid v. Ambler Realty (1926), 380
Eugenics movement, 342
Everson v. Board of Education
  (1947), 135
*Everything You Always Wanted to
  Know About Sex—But Were
  Afraid to Ask* (Reuben), 317–18
Evidence. *See* DNA; Trials
Ex parte Jackson (1878), 58, 286,
  288
Ex post facto laws, 191, 205,
  300–301
Exhibitionism, 347, 370
Expression, freedom of, 177
  adult materials and, 11
  conduct as, 136–38
  Douglas, William O., on, 108
  entertainment industry and, 113–19
  literature and, 45
  nude dancing as, 33, 34, 115, 230
  nudity as, 229–31
  obscenity and, 236, 287
  same-sex solicitation as, 268
  in schools, 70
  sexually oriented businesses and,
    10–11, 324
  "strict scrutiny" of discrimination
    and, 10
  zoning and, 10, 381
  See also Nude dancing; Nudity;
    Obscenity; Press; Speech
Extramarital sex. *See* Adultery;
    Fornication; Premarital sex;
    Unmarried cohabitants

F
Faith-based federal programs, 161,
  259, 279, 280, 284, 362
Falwell, Jerry, 140, 203, 282
Families
  changing form of, 28, 66, 198, 202,
    216, 240, 242, 249, 254, 318,
    357, 359
  names of, 331

prostitution and, 266

sexual battery in, 309

Family and Medical Leave Act (1993), 50, 217, 219, 253, 378

Family Building Act (2005), 28

Family court systems, 99, 187

Family leave, 50, 201, 217, 219, 253, 378

Family Limitation (Sanger), 126, 293

Family planning, 126–28

funding of, 127–28, 136, 284

Planned Parenthood Federation and, 243

right to, 284

Roosevelt, Theodore, on, 79, 259–60

Sanger, Margaret, and, 293–95

See also Contraception; Reproductive rights; Sanger, Margaret

Family Planning Services and Population Research Act (1970), 75, 128

Fanny Hill. See A Book Named "John Cleland's Memoirs of a Woman of Pleasure"

Faragher v. City of Boca Raton (1998), 55, 315

Farm Security Administration, 269

Farmer v. Brennan (1994), 350–51

Fathers. *See* Child custody; Child support; Illegitimacy; Paternity

Fatima's Serpentine Dance (1895), 59

Fay v. New York (1947), 92, 141

Federal Art Project, 50

Federal Bureau of Investigation

Branch Davidian raid by, 249

Crimes Against Children Unit, 67, 84–85, 206, 301

DNA analyses by, 103

Internet exploitation of children and, 180

missing children and, 224

National Sex Offender Registry, 206, 301

obscenity and, 116, 181

Federal Communications Act (1934), 75, 115

Federal Communications Commission, 75, 129–30

broadcast fines by, 129–30, 203–4

child pornography and, 68

obscene langauge and, 115, 129, 136, 204, 324

radio and television regulation by, 60, 115, 319

Federal Communications Commission v. Pacifica Foundation (1978), 129, 136, 204, 324

Federal Marriage Amendment (2002), 76, 88, **130–32**, 293

See also Same-sex marriage

Federal Prohibition of Female Genital Mutilation Act (1995), 305

Federal Trade Commission, 118, 179

Federalism, 334–35

Feldt, Gloria, 82

Fellatio, 196, 267, 309, 329

Female genital mutilation, 38, 305, 321

Female impersonators, 352

The Feminine Mystique (Friedan), 133

Feminism, 57, 79, **132–34,** 225, 250, 320

Ferguson v. City of Charleston (2001), 112, 253, 355

Fertility treatments. *See* Assisted reproductive technology; Infertility

Fertilization, 29, 81

Fetal homicide, 355, 356

Fetishism, 352

Field, Stephen J., 248

Fields v. Palmdale School District (2005), 298

Films. *See* Motion pictures

First Amendment (1791), **134–39**

American Civil Liberties Union and, 21

Douglas, William O., on, 108

See also Assembly; Association; Expression; Press; Religion; Speech

Fiske v. Kansas (1927), 335

Flagellation, 371

"Flashing," 229

Flood v. Waiters (1998), 349

Flores v. Flores (1979), 198

Florida

abortion in, 6

adoption by homosexuals in, 361

assisted reproductive technology in, 29

bioethics in, 40

castration in, 301

civil confinement in, 300

gender-neutral language in, 378

genetic privacy in, 147

hate crimes in, 159

marriage waiting period in, 198

pregnant prisoners in, 261

premarital sex in, 255

prenatal abuse in, 112

prisoners' rights in, 260

prostitution in, 267

sex therapy in, 312

sexual battery in, 307, 309

sodomy in, 329

STDs in, 326

stem-cell research in, 336, 340

surrogacy in, 31

voyeurism in, 371

Flynt, Larry, 139–41, *140,* 203

Flynt v. Ohio (1981), 139

Folsom, Frances, 258

Fondling, forcible, 308

Food and Drug Administration, 362

"abortion pill" and, 5–6, 7, 281

approval of drugs by, 110–11, 284, 285

breast implants and, 311

drugs in pregnancy and, 253

HPV and, 325

"morning-after pill" and, 23, 82, 111, 284–85, 362

Food, Drug, and Cosmetic Act
  (1938), 110
Forensic science, 147, 183
Fornication, 13–14, 196, 199, 215,
  254, 303
Fox network, 115
Frank, Barney, 163, 168
Frankfurter, Felix
  on courts, role of, 373–74
  on divorce, 375
  on obscenity, 203
*Franklin v. Gwinnett County Public
  Schools* (1992), 316, 349
Fraud
  in divorce, 375
  in DNA testing, 241
  in human trafficking, 169
  in inheritance, 361
  by a lawyer, 124
  in marriage, 24, 25, 36, 100,
    257
  by a partner, 368
  in paternity, 242
  in rape, 272, 274
  by transsexuals, 352
Frauds Exposed (Comstock), 73
Frazier, United States v. (1992),
  210
"Free love," 307, 318
Freedman v. Maryland (1965),
  59, 203
Freedom of Access to Clinic
  Entrances Act (1994), 6, 138
Freud, Sigmund, 172, 240
Friedan, Betty, 133, 134, 225
Frist, Bill, 15, 337
Frontiero v. Richardson (1973),
  83, 120, 122, **141–42**, 208
Fuck You! A Magazine of the Arts,
  116
The Fugs, 116
Full faith and credit clause, 88, 100,
  131, 290, 375
Full Faith and Credit for Child
  Support Orders Act (1994), 66
Fuller, Margaret, 379

Funding
  of abortion, 2, 7, 75, 127, 136, 223,
    290, 379
  for AIDS, 17, 18, 23
  of the arts, 60–61
  of domestic violence programs, 368
  of education, 348–49
  of family planning services,
    127–28, 136, 284
  of homosexuality, ban on
    promoting, 17, 166
  of legal services for crime victims,
    308
  of libraries, 11, 178–79
  presidential powers related to, 258,
    259
  of schools under Title IX, 376
  of sex education, 8, 295
  of stem-cell research, 40, 52, 281,
    339
  by U.S. Department of Health and
    Human Services, 362
  of violence against women
    programs, 237–38
FW/PBS, Inc. v. Dallas (1990), 239,
  323

G

Gaithright v. City of Portland
  (2006), 237
Gandy, Kim, 311, 328
Garcia, People v. (2000), 187
Garden of Eden (1955), 232
Garrett v. Board of Education (1991),
  328
*Gay Law Students Association v.
  Pacific Telephone and Telegraph
  Co.* (1979), 95, 138, 166, 188
Gay Men's Health Crisis v. Sullivan
  (1992), 17
Gay rights. *See* Homosexuality;
  Homosexuals
Gay Rights National Lobby, 167
*Gay Students Organization of the
  University of New Hampshire v.
  Bonner* (1974), 137

Geduldig v. Aiello (1974), 251
Gender, 143–46
  bioethics of change in, 38
  classification of, 43
  discrimination by, 144–45
  hate crimes based on, 157, 158–59
  identity, privacy of, 264
  versus sex, 352
  See also Bisexuals; Sex
    discrimination; Transsexuals
Gender-identity disorder, 146, 311,
  312, 350, 351, 352, 353, 370
Gender-Motivated Violence Act
  (1994). *See* Violence Against
  Women Act
Gender-neutral laws, 38, 68, 134,
  172, 268, 273, 275, 307, 378
Gender reassignment. *See* Sex
  reassignment
General Electric v. Gilbert (1976),
  50
Genetic exceptionalism, 147
Genetic information
  discrimination based on, 150–51
  insurance and, 147, 149
  privacy of, 147–49, 265
  property rights in, 151
  state laws on, 147, 148–49
  See also DNA; Paternity
Genetic Information
  Nondiscrimination Act (2005),
  150
Genetics, 146–52, 182
  founding of, 102
  homosexuality and, 167
  testing, crimes related to, 307
  U.S. Department of Health and
    Human Services and, 362
  See also DNA
Geneva Conventions, rape under,
  272
Genital surgery, 311
  See also Sex reassignment;
    Transsexuals
Georgetown University Law Center,
  221

Georgia
  abortion in, 109
  adultery in, 12
  AIDS crime in, 17
  common law marriage in, 202
  genetic privacy in, 147
  prostitution in, 267
  same-sex marriage in, 293
  STDs in, 326
  sodomy in, 303, 329, 330
  voyeurism in, 372
Gephard, Paul, 193
Gerber v. Hickman (2002), 261
Gibson, William, 176
Gilbreath v. State (1995), 348
Gillet-Netting v. Barnhart (2004), 29
Ginsberg, Allen, 53, 318
Ginsberg v. New York (1968), 118
Ginsburg, Ruth Bader
  on abortion, 246
  on single-sex education, 369
Ginzburg, Ralph, *152*
Ginzburg v. United States (1966),
  43, 44, **152–53,** 239, 240
Gitlow v. New York (1925), 230
Gittings, Barbara, *190*
Glas, State v. (2002), 372
GLBT persons, definition of, 41, 163,
  167
  See also Bisexuals; Homosexuality;
    Homosexuals; Transsexuals
*Globe Newspaper Co. v. Superior
  Court* (1982), 203
Goesaert v. Cleary (1948), 92, 375
Goines, David Lance, 15
Goins v. West Group (2001), 351
Goldberg, Arthur J., on
  contraception, 154
Gomez v. Perez (1973), 359, 360
Gonorrhea, 324, 325
Gonzaga University School of Law,
  47
Gonzales, Alberto, *229*
*Goodridge v. Department of Public
  Health* (2003), 161, 187, 290
Gore, Elizabeth "Tipper," 118

Government employees, ethics of,
  123
Graham v. Graham (1940), 256
Graves v. Estabrook (1994), 358
*Greenberg v. Miami Children's
  Hospital Research Institute, Inc.*
  (2003), 151
Gregg, United States v. (2000), 138
Griggs v. Duke Power Co. (1971),
  93
Griswold v. Connecticut (1965),
  153–55
  Douglas, William O., on, 107,
    108–9
  family planning and, 127
  legalization of contraceptive use
    in, 80, 111, 113, 280
  Ninth Amendment and, 227–28
  privacy right established in, 2, 135,
    186, 199, 284
  protection of intimate relationships
    in, 194
Grove City College v. Bell (1984),
  348
Grove Press v. Gerstein (1964),
  211, 212
Guard v. State (1997), 361
Gubernat v. Deremer (1995),
  360–61
Guccione, Bob, 139
Guttmacher Institute, 3, 82

H
Haddock v. Haddock (1906), 374
Hair (1967), 114, 230
Hamlet (Shakespeare), 172
Hannegan v. Esquire (1964), 58
Harlan, John Marshall, II
  on contraception, 127
  on labor regulation, 221
*Harper v. Virginia State Board of
  Elections* (1966), 214
Harris v. Forklift Systems, Inc.
  (1993), 54
Harris v. McRae (1980), 2, 75
Harvard University, 220, 339

Hate Crime Sentencing
  Enhancement Act (1994), 157, 167
Hate Crime Statistics Act (1990),
  156, 167
Hate crimes, 156–60, 363
  AIDS-HIV and, 17
  enhanced punishment for, 156–60,
    300, 304
  homosexuals and, 165
  Human Rights Campaign and, 168
  state laws on, 158–59
  transsexuals and, 145
Hawaii
  DNA collection in, 103
  domestic partnerships in, 19, 202,
    358, 361
  equal rights in, 122, 334, 378
  maternity leave in, 219
  prostitution in, 267
  rape in, 273
  same-sex marriage in, 87, 187, 188,
    289 336
  sex offender registration in, 301
  sexual assault in, 309
  voyeurism in, 371
Hays, William Harrison, 60, 116
Hays Code, 60, 116, 117, 283
Health information, privacy of.
  See AIDS-HIV; DNA; Genetics
**Healthy Marriage Initiative,
  160–61**
Hearsay evidence, child victims
  and, 62–63, 105, 309–10
Hefner, Christie, 163
Hefner, Hugh, 57, 141, **161–63,** *162*
Helms, Jesse, 16–17, 61, 166
Hendricks v. Hendricks (1998), 35
Henry VI, Part I (Shakespeare), 195
Henson v. City of Dundee (1982),
  314
Heredity, 146, 174
Hermaphrodites, 41, 144, 146
Heterosexuals, sexual identity of,
  144
*Hewitt v. State Accident Insurance
  Fund Corp.* (1982), 43

Hill, Anita, 234

Hill, State v. (2005), 112

Hillman v. Columbia County (1991), 16

Hinman v. Department of Personnel Administration (1985), 358

The History of New France (Lescarbot), 325

The Hite Report on Female Sexuality (Hite), 193

The Hite Report on Men and Male Sexuality (Hite), 193

HIV. *See* AIDS-HIV

Holm, State v. (2006), 37

Holman v. Indiana (2000), 42

Holmes, Oliver Wendell, Jr.

  on labor regulation, 221

  on speech, freedom of, 136

  on sterilization, 342

  on U.S. Constitution, 227

Holmes v. Holmes (1998), 358

Homophobia, 225

  See also Homosexuality; Homosexuals

Homosexuality, 163–67

  bioethical concerns about, 38

  effect on children, 70

  First Amendment and, 137–38

  genetic basis for, 147, 167

  religion and, 164, 282

  See also Homosexuals; Sexual orientation

Homosexuals

  abstinence and, 9

  adoption by, 165

  AIDS-HIV and, 15, 16–17, 166

  alimony and, 19

  assisted reproductive technology and, 30, 32, 165

  association, freedom of, 138, 166–67, 358

  child custody and, 165, 292–93, 359, 360

  crimes against, 156

  discrimination against, 94–95, 132, 137, 138, 164–67, 189–90

  domestic violence by, 104

  employment discrimination against, 94–95, 137, 138, 164, 165–66, 168, 186, 188, 189–90, 358

  families of, 242

  federal government and, 94, 165–66, 189–90

  hate crimes against, 165

  housing discrimination against, 358

  magazines and, 235, 250

  marriage alternatives for, 165–66

  maternity and family leave by, 219

  military and, 95, 165, 209–10, 259

  parental rights of, 171

  pornography and, 250

  privacy rights of, 263, 264, 265

  prostitution and, 268

  rights of, 164–65

  sex education and, 9, 95, 166, 298

  sexual harassment of, 316, 317

  sexual identity of, 144

  in social hierarchy, 133

  STDs and, 166, 325

  teenagers' consensual activity, 346

  as unmarried cohabitants, 356

  See also AIDS-HIV; Civil unions; Domestic partnerships; Same-sex marriage; Sodomy

Hopkins, State v. (2006), 112

Hostile work environment, 54, 55, 314, 315

  See also Sexual harassment

House of Representatives, 74

The Housewife's Handbook on Selective Promiscuity (Ginzburg), 152

Housing, of unmarried cohabitants, 358

Howe, Julia Ward, 379

Howl (Ginsberg), 53, 318

Hoyt v. Florida (1961), 376

Human Cloning Prohibition Act (2005), 40, 340

Human Genome Project, 146

Human papillomavirus (HPV), 9, 324, 325

Human Rights Campaign, 167–68

Human Sexual Response (Masters and Johnson), 152, 193, 318

Human sexuality, study of, 192

Human trafficking, 67, 84–85, **168–69**, 266–67, 305

Hurley v. Irish-American Gay Group of Boston (1995), 166

Hustler, 139, 140, 141, 203, 232, 380

Hustler Magazine, Inc. v. Falwell (1988), 140

Hyde, Henry J., 75

Hyde Amendment (1976), 2, 75

"Hypervariable Minisatellite Regions in Human DNA" (Jeffreys), 182

Hysterectomy, 341

I

I Am Curious Yellow, 108

Idaho

  abortion in, 3

  breastfeeding in, 378

  common law marriage in, 202

  community property in, 333

  estate administration in, 119

  juvenile sex offenders in, 70

  polygamy in, 246, 248

  rape in, 300

  same-sex marriage in, 291

  sex discrimination in, 83

  victims' rights in, 365

  voyeurism in, 371

  See also Reed v. Reed

Idaho v. Wright (1990), 62–63

Illegitimacy, 170–72

  assisted reproductive technology and, 28, 29

  fathers and, 361

  of homosexuals' children, 359, 360

  paternity and, 241

  from premarital sex, 254

  rate, 66

unmarried parents and, 359–61
See also Child custody; Child
support; Paternity
Illinois
AIDS-HIV in, 16
breastfeeding in, 49
child abuse in, 67
cross-dressing in, 353
DNA collection in, 103
equal rights in, 122
illegitimacy in, 170, 360
juvenile sex offenders in, 70
legal practice in, 45–47
legislators' code of conduct in, 123
pandering in, 239
pregnant prisoners in, 261
prescriptions in, 125
prostitution in, 267
rape in, 304
sex discrimination in, 45–47
sex offenses in, 335
sexual exploitation in, 305
voyeurism in, 371
Immigrants
AIDS-HIV and, 16
citizenship of illegitimate children
of, 84, 171
human trafficking of, 168
prostitution by, 266–67
as unmarried parents, 84, 171, 360
violence against women,
238, 366
Immigration and Nationality Act
(1952), 368
Impotence
as defense against rape, 274
drugs for, 111
sex therapy for, 312
surgery for, 311
In re A. C. (1990), 356
In re Adoption of Baby Girl L. J.
(1986), 31
In re Adoption of Charles B. (1990),
164
In re Baby M. (1988), 31
In re Berg (1998), 124

In re Estate of Gardiner (2002),
199, 352
In re Gault (1967), 70
In re Harris (1997), 352
In re John Z. (2003), 77, 187
In re Karin T. v. Michael T. (1985),
352
In re Marriage of Buzzanca (1998),
31
In re Marriage of Wellman (1980),
359
In re Martin (1993), 40
In re May 1991 Will County Grand
Jury (1992), 103
In re Piatt (1997), 124
In re T. W. (1997), 69
In re Towle (1995), 317
In re Unborn Child of Starks (2001),
355
In vitro fertilization, 22, 27, 30–31,
51
See also Assisted reproductive
technology
Incest, 68, 172–74, 198–99, 302,
303, 307
Incorporation, doctrine of, 135, 235,
335
Indecency complaints, in
broadcasts, 129–30
See also Federal Communications
Commission; Entertainment
industry; Media; Obscene
language
Indecent assault, 307
See also Sexual assault
Indecent exposure, 33–34, 175–76,
265, 336
See also Nudity
Indecent language, 347, 348
See also Federal Communications
Commission; Obscene language
Indiana
cloning in, 340
deviant behavior in, 90
equal rights in, 93, 122
nude dancing in, 33–34, 230

obscenity in, 306
pederasty in, 330
public indecency in, 33–34, 230
STDs in, 326
surrogacy in, 31
Infanticide, 355–56
Infertility, 28–29
American Fertility Association and,
22
bioethical concerns about, 38
early treatment for, 51
from STDs, 324
See also Assisted reproductive
technology
Infinity Broadcasting, 130
Inheritance
by illegitimate children, 170, 360,
361
in marriage, 199
by unmarried cohabitants, 358
Inside Deep Throat (2005), 116
Insurance
abortion coverage in, 3
AIDS-HIV coverage in, 16
for cohabitants, 357
contraceptive coverage in, 81, 110
for domestic partnerships, 164–65
genetic privacy and, 147, 149, 150,
265
for infertility treatments, 28–29
marital benefits, 201
pregnancy coverage in, 251–52
"Intermediate scrutiny" of sex
discrimination cases, 82, 83, 92,
120, 122, 145, 185, 324, 328, 373
International Abolitionist
Federation, 168
International Association of Chiefs
of Police, 123
International family planning
organizations, funding of, 128
International Labor Organization,
168, 266
International Planned Parenthood,
294
International Reform Bureau, 283

International Union, UAW v. Johnson Controls, Inc. (1991), 29, 252–53

Internet, 176–80
censorship of, 60, 63–65, 71, 118
children's access to, 68, 177–79, *178*
First Amendment issues, 176–79
indecency regulation of, 63–65, 71–72
political communication on, 204
teenagers, predators of, 346
Internet Crimes Against Children Task Force, 85
Interracial marriage, 36, 199, 215–16, 303, 336
Intersexuals, 41, 144, 146
See also Transsexuals
Invasion of privacy, 154, 228, 265, 266, 371, 372
See also Privacy; Voyeurism
Involuntary servitude. *See* Human trafficking
Iowa
cloning in, 340
divorce in, 375
incest in, 174
maternity leave in, 219
prenuptial agreements in, 257
same-sex divorce in, 100
sexual abuse in, 309
Isaacson v. Isaacson (1978), 293
Islam
contraception and, 280
plural marriage and, 283, 289
Israel v. Allen (1978), 173–74
It All Comes Out in the End, 108

J
Jackson, Janet, 115, 129, 233
Jackson, Michael, 61, 113, 114
Jackson v. Birmingham Board of Education (2005), 349
Jacob Wetterling Crimes Against Children and Sexually Violent Offender Act (1994), 205, 365

Jacobellis v. Ohio (1964), 43, 53, **181–82**, 212, 251
Jacobson v. Massachusetts (1905), 191
Jacobson v. United States (1992), 245
Jaffee v. Redmond (1996), 123
Jane Doe v. Boeing Co. (1993), 312
Jaycees, 90, 138, 199
Jean Doe v. Bell (2003), 146
Jefferson, Thomas
on equal rights, 375
on separation of church and state, 135, 248, 279
Jeffreys, Alec, 102, 104, **182–83**, *183*
Jeldness v. Pearce (1994), 261
Jelly v. Dabney (1978), 357
Jenkins v. Georgia (1974), 59, 250
Jennewein, Paul, *229*
Jenson v. Eveleth Taconite Co. (1991, 1993), 315
Jersey Shore Medical Center v. Estate of Baum (1980), 332
Jessup, Morris, 72
Jimenez v. Wienberger (1974), 360
Joan of Arc, 352
John Birch Society, 57
"John Cleland's Memoirs of a Woman of Pleasure." See *A Book Named "John Cleland's Memoirs of a Woman of Pleasure"*
Johnson, Lyndon, on affirmative action, 96
Johnson, Virginia E., 152, 193, 318
Johnson, State v. (1996), 270
Johnson v. Calvert (1993), 31
Johnson v. State (1992), 112, 253, 355
Jones v. Daley (1981), 292
Jorgensen, Christine, 311–12, *350*
Joseph Burstyn, Inc. v. Wilson (1952), 287
Journal of the American Medical Association, 23
Joyce, James, 58, 287

Judaism, contraception and, 280
Judges
ethics of, 122, 123
sexual offenses by, 308, 313
Judicial scrutiny, 185
See also "Intermediate scrutiny"; "Strict scrutiny"
Judiciary, 183–88
appointment of members, 185, 258–59, 264, 319–20
GLBT persons and, 168
strict versus expansive construction by, 226–27
Juries
sexual orientation of jurors, 187
women's service on, 91, 141–42, 375, 376
Justice for All Act (2004), 102
Juvenile courts, 345
See also Family court systems
Juvenile Delinquency Act (1948), 345
Juvenile offenders, 69–70, 345–46
See also Sex offenders

K
Kaiser, State v. (1983), 172, 174
Kameny, Franklin, 94, 164, **189–90**, *190*
Kameny v. Brucker (1961), 189
Kanka, Megan, 205, 206, 301
See also Megan's Law
Kansas
adultery in, 12
age of consent to marry in, 77
bestiality in, 35
civil confinement in, 191–92, 300
legal ethics in, 124
obscenity and minors in, 68
paternity in, 241
STDs in, 326
sterilization in, 341
teenage consensual activity in, 346
transsexual marriage in, 199
Kansas v. Hendricks (1997), **191–92**
Kass, Leon, 38

Kassama v. Magat (2002), 220

Kearns, State v. (2001), 309

Keeton v. Hustler Magazine, Inc. (1984), 139

Kelly v. State (1998), 372

Kelo v. City of New London (2005), 380

Kennedy, Anthony M.
on abortion restrictions, 245
on civil confinement, 191–92
on homosexual rights, 167
on sexual harassment, 55
on sodomy, 194, 195, 330
on television censorship, 163

Kennedy, John F.
on equal rights, 119
sexual affairs of, 260

Kenosha, City of v. Bruno (1973), 230

Kent, James, 360

Kentucky
abortion in, 3
adultery in, 12
breastfeeding in, 176
gender discrimination in, 144
medical information privacy in, 78
rape in, 77
STDs in, 326
surrogacy in, 31
voyeurism in, 265

Kidnapping
of children, 84, 224–25
for human trafficking, 168, 169
during sex offenses, 306, 308

Kidwell, State v. (1976), 274

Kil Soo Lee, United States v. (2003), 169

King, Martin Luther, Jr., 156

The King of Bigamists, 36

Kingsley Books, Inc. v. Brown (1957), 203

Kingsley Pictures Corp. v. Regents of the University of the State of New York (1959), 115

Kinsey, Alfred, 56, 79–80, **192–93**, 318
and abortion conference, 57

on bisexuality, 41
on sexual behavior and the law, 70, 283, 299

Kinsey Institute for Sex Research, 192, *193*

The Kiss, 113

Klinefelter's syndrome, 146

Knox, United States v. (2003), 232

Koresh, David, 248–49

Kovatch v. California Casualty Management Co. (1998), 43

Kozlowski v. Kozlowski (1979), 358

Krafft-Ebing, Baron Richard von, 302, 353

Krause, Erik Hans, *50*

Kroop, United States v. (1993), 210

Ku Klux Klan, 57

Ku Klux Klan Act (1871), 157

L

L.A.L. v. D.A.L. (1998), 30

Labine v. Vincent (1971), 170

Labor, regulation of women's hours, 221–22

Ladue, City of v. Horn (1986), 358

Lady Chatterley's Lover (Lawrence), 44, 320

Lalli v. Lalli (1978), 170, 360

Lamont v. Postmaster General (1965), 58

Lanier v. United States (1997), 308

Lanzetta v. New Jersey (1939), 329

Larry Flynt Publications, Inc., 139
See also Flynt, Larry

Larson, State v. (2003), 372

Latter-day Saints, Church of Jesus Christ of, 246, 280, 283

Law enforcement officials
AIDS and, 18
Amber Alerts and, 225
bisexuals and, 41
DNA and, 101, 103, 183
domestic violence and, 105, 106
drug entrapment and, 112
ethics of, 123, 188

hate crimes and, 156
Megan's Law and, 205
Internet and, 64, 85, 179, 180
rape and, 272, 304
telephone sex and, 348
victims' rights and, 363, 365
violence against women and, 368

Lawrence, D. H., 44, 320

Lawrence v. Texas (2003), **194–95**
Bowers v. Hardwick overruled by, 33, 186, 303
bigamy laws, effect on, 37
deviant behavior laws, effect on, 89, 90
fornication laws, effect on, 13
as limit of sexual revolution, 319, 320
Ninth Amendment and, 227–28
polygamy laws, effect on, 249
premarital sex, effect on, 255
privacy as basis for, 88, 139, 155
sodomy, decriminalization of, 35, 76, 94, 113, 161, 329, 330
teenage consensual activity, effect on, 346

Lawsuits. *See* Civil suits

Lawyers, ethics of, 122, 123

Leaves of Grass (Whitman), 58

Lebeck v. Lebeck (1994), 257

Lee, Gypsy Rose, 114, 318

Lehr v. Robertson (1983), 30

Lemon v. Kurtzman (1971), 8

Lesbians. *See* Homosexuality; Homosexuals; Same-sex marriage

Levin v. Yeshiva (1990), 358

Levitra, 111

Levy v. Louisiana (1968), 170, 241, 360

Lewd behavior, 195–96
breastfeeding and, 48, 49
cohabitation as, 357
as deviant activity, 89
as a victimless crime, 306

Lewinsky, Monica, 123, 141

Lewis v. Harris (2003), 292

Lewis v. State (2001), 122

Libel, 14, 58, 60, 140, 177, 203, 235
Liberta, People v. (1984), 78
Liberty, right of, 226–28, 264
Libraries, 11, 61, 178–79
Licensing of adult businesses, 323
  See also Sexually oriented
    businesses; Zoning
Lieberman, Joseph, 118
Lifchez v. Hartigan (1990), 28
Lifecodes Corporation, 102
Limbaugh, Rush, 134
Limehouse, United States v. (1932),
  215
Limon, State v. (2005), 346
Lincoln, Mary Todd, 47
Lister Institute, 102
Literature, censorship of, 43–45, 53,
  58, 211–12
Little v. Streater (1981), 104
*Littleton, Colorado, City of v. Z. J.
  Gifts D-4, LLC* (2004), 11, 239,
  323
Live shows, 114–15
  See also Nude dancing; Sexually
    oriented businesses
Livingston, Robert, 141
Local government, 334, 336–37,
  380
*Local 28 of the Sheet Metal
  Workers' International Asso-
  ciation v. Equal Employment
  Opportunity Commission*
  (1986), 377
Lochner v. New York (1905),
  150, 221
Lolita (Nabokov), 345
"Lolita complex," 345
London Society for the Suppression
  of Vice, 72
Long v. Nix (1995), 351
Lopez, United States v. (1995),
  87, 273
*Los Angeles, City of v. Alameda
  Books, Inc.* (2002), 10–11, 324,
  336, 381
"Louie, Louie," 116, 181

Louis XIV, 203
Louisiana
  community property in, 333
  covenant marriage in, 202
  DNA collection in, 101, 103, 265
  genetic privacy in, 147
  illegitimacy in, 361
  sex education in, 297, 298
  teenage consensual activity in, 346
The Lovers (Les Amants), 181
Loving v. Virginia (1967), 36, 113,
  199, 215, 303, 336
Lowell v. Kowalski (1980), 361
Luke Records, Inc. v. Navarro
  (1992), 115
Lychner, Pam, 205

M
Mack v. City of Detroit (2002), 95
MacKinnon, Catherine, 79, 133
Macy v. Blatchford (2000), 310
Madison, James
  and Bill of Rights, 135
  on censorship, 58
  on Ninth Amendment, 227
Magazines, 203
  bookstore sales of, 116
  censorship of, 58
  distribution of, 73, 152–53
  Larry Flynt's, 139–41
  homosexual, 152, 235, 250
  nudity in, 232
  pandering by, 239
Maggert v. Hanks (1997), 262, 351
Magic Mirror, 108
Maher v. Roe (1977), 2
Mahlum, Charlotte, 311
Mail
  censorship of, 58, 286
  contraceptives in, 72, 73, 75, 154,
    284
  homosexual magazines in, 152,
    235, 250
  obscene materials in, 45, 59,
    72–73, 75, 212–13, 235, 288,
    293

Maine
  abstinence education in, 8
  homosexual discrimination in, 166
  polygamy in, 248
  prenuptial agreements in, 257
  rape in, 274
  sex offender registration in, 301
Maloney, Carolyn B., 50
Malthus, Thomas, 79
Mann, James R., 168, 267, 305
Mann Act (1910), 75, 168, 267, 305
Manual Enterprises v. Day (1962),
  152, 235, 250
Maple Syrup disease, 174
Marbury v. Madison (1803), 184, 228
March for Women's Life, 226
Marcum v. McWhorter (2002), 12
Mario, People v. (1984), 275
Marital aids. *See* Sexual devices
Marital rape, 77, 78, 199, 272, 273,
  275, 302, 309
Marriage, 197–202
  certificate, *198*
  common law, 132, 202, 357
  confidentiality of communications
    in, 264
  consent in, 76
  consummation of, 25, 260–61
  of cousins, 172, 173, 198
  covenant, 100, 202
  domicile for, 25, 332, 376
  essential incidents of, 256
  Healthy Marriage Initiative,
    160–61
  immunity of spouses in, 199
  incest and, 173–74
  interracial, 36, 199, 215–16, 303,
    336
  meretricious, 266
  misrepresentation in, 24
  premarital sex and, 254
  prisoners' rights to, 30, 199,
    260–61, 286
  privacy in, 109, 127, 153–55, 199,
    264
  private ordering of, 97, 101

401

prohibitions against, 198–99
property in, 199, 256, 333–34
rate, 161, 197
recognition of, 374–75
religion and, 280, 289
right to, 199, 216, 263, 286, 289
sexual battery in, 309
sexual relations in, 12
spousal rights and duties in, 199,
    201–2, 330–34
state regulation of, 35–36, 198–99,
    200–201
tax penalty in, 201
of transsexuals, 199, 352
women's rights in, 331–34, 376
See also Alimony; Annulment;
    Bigamy; Divorce; Marital rape;
    Polygamy; Prenuptial
    agreements; Same-sex marriage
Married by America, 115
Marshall, John
  on constitutional construction, 228
  on judicial review, 184
Marshall, Thurgood, on equal rights,
  96
Marshfield Clinic v. Discher (1982),
  332
Martin, Clyde, 192, 193
Martin v. Ziherl (2005), 255
Martinez-Candejas, United States v.
  (2003), 169
Marvin, Lee, 19, 255 357
Marvin, Michelle, 19, 255, 357
Marvin v. Marvin (1976), 19, 100,
    188, 255, 292, 357
Maryland
  child pornography in, 179
  civil abuse suits in, 282
  domestic partnerships in, 292
  equal rights in, 120
  family planning in, 128
  indecent exposure in, 175
  voyeurism in, 371
Masochism, 371
Mason, George, and Bill of Rights,
  135

Massachusetts
  abortion protests in, 285
  adultery in, 12
  age of consent to marry in, 77
  AIDS awareness in, 17
  censorship in, 43–45
  civil abuse suits in, 282
  contraceptive ban in, 80
  date rape drugs in, 112
  DNA collection in, 101, 103
  domestic partnerships in, 95
  equal rights in, 94, 120, 320
  genetic privacy in, 150
  illegitimacy in, 361
  lascivious acts in, 90
  maternity leave in, 219–20
  obscenity in, 43–45
  polygamy in, 248
  privacy in, 265
  prostitution in, 268
  same-sex divorce in, 101
  same-sex marriage in, 130, 187,
    199, 290–91, 292
  sex offender notification in, 265
  sexual orientation harassment in,
    317
Massachusetts Bay Colony, 203,
  254, 302
Masters, William H., 152, 193, 318
Masterson, Chase, 71
Masturbation, 89, 130, 192, 196,
    236, 267, 298, 315, 321, 342,
    371
Maternity, genetic determination of,
  147
See also Motherhood
Maternity leave, 50, 218–20,
  251–53, 378
Mattachine Society, 190
Mayberry, People v. (1975), 274
McArdle Laboratory for Cancer
  Research, University of
  Wisconsin, 37
McCarthy, Joseph, 94, 189
McCorvey, Norma L. (Jane Roe),
  2, 7

McCourtney v. Imprimis
    Technology, Inc. (1991), 220
McGreevy, James, 163
McGuire, State v. (1997), 356
McIntyre v. Crouch (1989), 30
McKnight, State v. (2003), 112, 253,
  355
McLaughlin v. Florida (1964), 216
Media, 115, 203–4, 321
  See also specific media
Media Marketing Accountability Act
  (2001), 118
Medicaid, 2, 75, 111, 128, 223, 351
Medical procedures
  bioethical concerns about, 38
  criminal responsibility for, 307
  for sex reassignment, 138, 311,
    350, 351, 353
  for sexual enhancement, 310–12
Medicare, 111
Meese, Edwin, 249
Megan's Law (1996), 75, 205–6,
  237, 301, 302, 365
Mencken, H. L., 114
Mendel, Gregor, 102
Menninger Foundation, 191
Meritor Savings Bank v. Vinson
    (1986), 42, 54, 314, 315
Meyer v. Nebraska (1923), 67, 217,
  345, 360
Miami Beach, exclusion of sex
  offenders in, 301
Michael H. v. Gerald D. (1989),
  241–42
Michael M. v. Superior Court of
    Sonoma County (1981), 62, 68,
  275, 346
Michelangelo, 231
Michigan
  adultery in, 12
  AIDS education in, 297
  bestiality in, 35
  cloning in, 340
  equal rights in, 121
  indecent exposure in, 175
  premarital sex in, 255

rape shield laws in, 278

reverse discrimination in, 122

sex education in, 297

surrogacy in, 31

Michigan v. Lucas (1991), 278

Midwest Oilseeds, Inc. v. Limagrain Genetics Corp. (2002), 151

Mienhold v. U.S. Department of Defense (1994), 209

Mifeprex (RU-486), 5–6, 82, 111, 280–81

Military, 206–10

abortion in, 2

bisexuals in, 41

"don't ask, don't tell" policy, 95, 165, 186, 209, 319

homosexuals in, 95, 165, 186, 209–10, 259, 264–65

Human Rights Campaign and, 168

military academies, sex offenses at, 209, 210

prostitution and, 267

rape in, 271

sex discrimination in, 207–9

sex offenses in, 209, 210

STDs in, 210, *325*

unequal benefits in, 141–42, 208

Uniform Code of Military Justice, 2, 210

Miller, Arthur, *97*

Miller, Henry, 141, *211*, **211–12**

Miller, Samuel F., on sex discrimination, 45, 46

Miller v. California (1973), 59, 136, **212–14**

adult materials in, 10, 11

hard-core pornography, definition of, 153

local community standards in, 235–36

obscenity, definition of, 45, 113, 116, 139, 288

"prurient interest" in, 270

three-step obscenity test in, 177, 186, 249

Milton, John, 57

Minnesota

assisted reproductive technology in, 30

bestiality in, 35

civil confinement in, 300

expression, freedom of, 236

hate crimes in, 157

obscene telephone calls in, 237

paid maternity leave in, 219

sexual harassment in, 317

sexual orientation harassment in, 317

Minnesota Junior Chamber of Commerce, 90, 138, 199

Minor v. Happersett (1874), 92, 184, 185, **214–15**

Minors

abortion rights of, 2, 3, 6

definition of, 9–10, 64, 66

family planning rights of, 128

prohibited sexual conduct of, 35

See also Children; Teenagers

Minsky's Burlesque, New York City, *114*

Miranda v. Arizona (1966), 157, 206, 278, 299, 363

"*Miranda*" warnings, 206

Miscegenation, 36, 199, **215–16**, 303, 336

Mishkin v. New York (1966), 44, 152

Misrepresentation, in marriage, 24

Mississippi

adoption by homosexuals in, 361

age of consent to marry in, 77

infertility in, 29

premarital sex in, 255

Mississippi University for Women v. Hogan (1982), 328

Missouri

abortion in, 1, 2–3, 245

asssisted reproductive technology in, 30

child support in, 65

cloning in, 341

equal rights in, 94

prenatal care in, 355

prisoners' rights to abortion in, 261

and unborn, rights of the, 1, 354

unmarried cohabitants in, 358

women's right to vote in, 214–15

Model Code of Judicial Conduct (ABA), 124

Model Penal Code (1962), 36, 274, 303

Model Rules of Professional Conduct (ABA), 124

Mondale, Walter, 167

Monell v. New York City Department of Social Services (1978), 230

Money, John, 143, 350

Monroe, Marilyn, *97*, 161, 163

Montana

maternity leave in, 378

paternity in, 241

rape in, 77

sex offender registration in, 301

STDs in, 326, 327

Montanez, Commonwealth v. (2003), 310

Mooning, 175, 229

Moral Majority, 167

Morality, 122, 123. *See also* Ethics; Religion

Mormons, 246, 248, 280, 283

"Morning-after pill," 6, 23, 82, 111, 124, 126, 280, 284–85, 362

Morrison, United States v. (2000), 87, 105, 145, 157, 186, 272–73, 308, 366

Moses v. Diocese of Colorado (1993), 282

Motels, adult, 322, 323

Motherhood, 216–21, *217*

determination of, 241

discrimination against, 220

illegitimate children and, 171

maternity leave, 50, 218–20, 251–53, 378

responsibilities of, 217

rights of, 217

surrogacy, 27, 31–32, 216

unmarried parents and, 359–61
See also Assisted reproductive
technology; Children
Motion Picture Association of
America, 60, 116
Motion Picture Producers and
Distributors of America, 60, 116
Motion Picture Production Code,
117
See also Hays Code
Motion pictures, 116, 322, 323
censorship of, 58–60, 287
consenting adults and, 212
drive-in theaters, nudity at,
231–32, 323, 380
Hays Code for, 60, 116, 117, 283
National Legion of Decency and,
283
nudity in, 231–32
obscenity in, 181–82, 250
rating system for, 59, 61, 116, 212
regulation of, 115–16
sadomasochistic, 370–71
self-censorship of, 59, 60, 116, 117,
283
Mott, Lucretia, 379
Mrs. Warren's Profession (Shaw),
73
Muller v. Oregon (1908), **221–22**
Murphy, State v. (1970), 309
Musgrove v. Musgrove (1991), 358
Music, popular, 115–16, 130, 181
*Mutual Film Corp. v. Ohio Industrial
Commission* (1915), 116

N
Nabozny v. Podlesny (1996), 316
Naim v. Naim (1955), 215
Names
of children, 30, 171, 331, 360–61
of married women, 331
of transsexuals, 352
NARAL Pro-Choice America,
223–24
National Abortion Rights Action
League, 223

National Academy of Sciences,
176, 311
National Association for Single Sex
Public Education, 328
National Association for the
Advancement of Colored People,
327
*National Association for the
Advancement of Colored People
v. Alabama* (1958), 138, 227–28,
263
National Association of Theater
Owners, 116
**National Center for Missing and
Exploited Children,** 180, 224,
224–25
National Center for Victims of
Crime, 365
National Child Protection Act
(1993), 237
National Conference of State
Legislatures, 27, 147
National Conservative Political
Action Committee, 167
National Crime Victimization
Survey, 271
National Domestic Violence
Hotline, 238, 368
National Education Association,
295
*National Endowment for the Arts v.
Finley* (1998), 61
National Family History Day,
343
National Geographic, 261
National Human Genome Research
Institute, 362
National Institute of Allergy and
Infectious Diseases, 325
National Institutes of Health,
151, 311, 339, 362
National Institutes of Health
Revitalization Act (1993), 16
National Legion of Decency, 283
National Obscenity Enforcement
Unit, 249

National Organization for Women,
133, **225**, 311, 327, 328
National Science Foundation, 176
National Sex Offender Registry,
84, 205, 301
National Sexual Assault Hotline,
275
Native Americans
abortion and, 7, 223
nudity of, 228
STDs and, 325
violence against women, 107, 238,
366, 368
Naval Academy, 209–10
Near v. Minnesota (1931), 58, 136,
203, 236, 323, 335
Nebraska
abortion in, 3, 5
breastfeeding in, 378
hate crimes in, 159
indecent exposure in, 175
infertility in, 29
invasion of privacy in, 266
rape in, 273
sexual assault in, 300
surrogacy in, 31
victims' rights in, 365
voyeurism in, 371
Necrophilia, 89, 306
Nectrow v. City of Cambridge
(1928), 380
Nefertiti, 172
Nepotism, 333, 358
Nevada
annulment in, 25
community property in, 333
divorce in, 374–75
psychologists, licensing of,
312
prostitution in, 266, 304, 322
rape shield laws in, 278
STDs in, 326
surrogacy in, 31
victims' rights in, 365
New Hampshire
abortion in, 7

assisted reproductive technology in, 30

equal rights in, 42

legal ethics in, 124

sexual harassment in, 316

surrogacy in, 31, 164

New Jersey

cloning in, 340

domestic partnerships in, 19, 358

domestic violence in, 105

equal rights in, 93, 122

fornication in, 13

gender dysphoria in, 187

hate crimes in, 165

juvenile sex offenders in, 70

prenuptial agreements in, 257

prostitution in, 267

punishment of sex offenders in, 300

rape in, 273

same-sex marriage in, 292

stem-cell research in, 336, 340

surrogacy in, 31

telephone sex in, 347

New Jersey Citizens Against Paternity Fraud, 242

New Mexico

assisted reproductive technology in, 30

community property in, 257, 333

homosexual discrimination in, 166

polygamy in, 283, 246, 248

same-sex marriage in, 292

sterilization in, 341

voyeurism in, 371

New York

abortion protests in, 335

annulment in, 25

bigamy in, 36

child abuse in, 67

child pornography in, 250

contraceptives for minors in, 295

cross-dressing in, 353

date rape drugs in, 112

DNA collection in, 103

family planning in, 126, 294

gender-neutral language in, 378

homosexual discrimination in, 166

illegitimacy in, 170, 171, 360

married women's property in, 26

maternity leave in, 219

obscenity in, 152–53, 203

prostitution in, 267

same-sex marriage in, 292, 293

sexual abuse in, 309

STDs in, 326

women's rights in, 376

New York v. Ferber (1982), 68, 213, 232, 250

New York v. Heckler (1983), 128

New York City

Minsky's Burlesque, *114*

movie theaters in, *69*

unmarried cohabitants in, 358

New York Society for the Suppression of Vice, 72

New York Times, 315

New York Times Co. v. Sullivan (1964), 58, 140, 203

New York Women Against Rape, *272*

New Zealand, women's voting rights in, 27, 119, 214

Newspapers, censorship of, 203

See also *Near v. Minnesota*

Nexus (Miller), 212

Nguyen v. Immigration and Naturalization Service (2001), 84, 171, 360

Nichols, Jack, *190*

Nielsen/NetRatings, 177

Night Windows (Sloan), *370*

Nin, Anaïs, 212

Nineteenth Amendment (1920), 26, 27, 83, 97, 119, 133, 184, 185, 214, 254, 284, 302, 318, 331, 345, 376, 377, *377*, 378, 379

Ninth Amendment, 155, **226–27**, 334

Douglas, William O., on, 108, 109

nudity and, 229–30

right of privacy and, 135, 154, 263, 264

Nixon, Richard M., on family planning, 127, 259

No Child Left Behind Act (2001), 328

North Carolina

cohabitation in, 14

divorce in, 374–75

family planning in, 128

incest in, 173

insurance in, 110

juvenile sex offenders in, 70

premarital sex in, 255

prurient interest in, 270

North Dakota

abortion in, 3

cloning in, 340

obscene language in, 236–37

obscenity and minors in, 68

premarital sex in, 255

prostitution in, 267–68

sexual harassment in, 316

Norton v. MacFarlane (1991), 307

Norton v. Macy (1969), 94

Nude dancing, 229, 265, 322

as expression, freedom of, 33, 34, 115, 230

as lewd behavior, 196

screening around club, 324

zoning regulation of, 380

Nudism, 232–33, 265

The Nudist Jayne Mansfield, *162*

Nudity, 228–33

in child pornography, 118, 232, 250–51

at drive-in theater, 231, 232, 323, 380

in Hays Code, 117

indecent exposure and, 175

nudism, 232–33, 265

provocative excesses of, 115

public, 229–31, 265

representational, 231–32

See also Breastfeeding; Indecent exposure; Lewd behavior; Nude dancing

O

Oakley, State v. (2001), 286
O'Brien, United States v. (1968),
    33–34, 230
Obscene language, 43, 52–54, 136,
    235, 236–37, 302, 347, 348
Obscenity, 234–37
  adult materials and, 9–11
  children and, 68–69
  context of, 319
  definition of, 186, 270
  distribution of, 212–14, 240
  Douglas, William O., on, 45, 108,
    235
  Federal Communications
    Commission and, 129–30
  First Amendment and, 136–37,
    286–88
  Hays Code and, 60, 116, 117, 283
  mailing of, 58, 59, 72, 152, 235,
    286, 288, 293
  pandering with, 43, 44, 140,
    152–53, 239–40, 245
  press, freedom of, and, 203
  prisoners' right to adult materials,
    261
  prurient interest, appeal to, 269–70
  representations versus actual
    conduct, 113, 118, 181, 213–14,
    231–32, 249, 306
  scope of regulation of, 213
  sexual revolution and, 318–19
  state laws on, 236–37
  as a victimless crime, 306
  zoning regulation of, 380–81
  See also Entertainment industry;
    Internet; Literature; Motion
    pictures; Pornography; Prurient
    interest
O'Connor, Sandra Day
  on abortion, 7, 245
  on association, 138–39
  on discrimination, 90
  on parental rights, 345
  on prisoners' rights to marry, 199,
    260–61

  on sex discrimination, 349
  on sexual harassment, 54
  on single-sex education, 328
  on sodomy, 195
Oedipus complex, 172
Office of Child Support
    Enforcement, 241
Office of Family Planning, 127
Office of Juvenile Justice and
    Delinquency Prevention, 180
Office of National Drug Control
    Policy, 110, 111
Office of Population Affairs, 127
Office of Public Health and Science,
    127
**Office on Violence Against
    Women, 237–38**, 366
  See also Violence Against Women
    Act
Oh! Calcutta! (1969), 114, 176
Ohio
  assisted reproductive technology
    in, 29
  breastfeeding in, 49
  child custody in, 188
  child pornography in, 250
  infertility in, 29
  obscenity in, 181–82
  rape in, 304
  sex offender registration in, 265
  statutory rape in, 78
Oklahoma
  legal ethics in, 124
  polygamy in, 246, 283
  same-sex marriage in, 292
  sex discrimination in, 82–84,
    92
  STDs in, 326
  and unborn, rights of the, 355
Oklahoma City, lewd behavior in,
    195–96
Old Testament, and incest, 172
Olden v. Kentucky (1988), 279
Olmstead v. United States (1928),
    194
Olmstead v. Zimring (1999), 42

On the Origin of Species (Darwin),
    215
Onassis, Jacqueline Kennedy, 139,
    380
Oncale v. Sundowner Offshore
    Services, Inc. (1998), 55, 316,
    317
One Book Called "Ulysses," United
    States v. (1934), 58
One Package, United States v.
    (1936), 80, 126, 294
Operation Rescue v. National
    Organization for Women (2006),
    6, 285
Opinion of the Justices to the Senate
    (1996), 265
Opinion of the Justices to the Senate
    (2000), 285
Opinions of the Justices to the
    House of Representatives (1998),
    95
Oral sex
  bestiality and, 35
  with children, 61, 67
  Kinsey research on, 192
  as lewd behavior, 196
  pederasty and, 330
  rape and, 262, 273, 307
  in a sadomasochistic film, 371
  as sexual harassment, 315
  sodomy and, 329
  teenagers and, 244, 327
Orange Blossoms, 59
Oregon
  bestiality in, 90
  equal rights in, 43, 121
  family planning in, 128
  genetic privacy in, 147
  sexual abuse in, 300
  statutory rape in, 346
  STDs in, 325
  women's labor regulation in,
    221–22
Oregon v. Mitchell (1970), 345
Orr v. Orr (1979), 18
Orwell, George, 212

Osborne v. Ohio (1990), 69, 232, 250, 265, 306
Our Bodies Ourselves (Boston Women's Health Collective), 318
Out-of-wedlock children. *See* Illegitimacy
"Out speech," 138
Ovariectomy, 341
Overstreet v. State (2003), 103

P
P. v. P. (1972), 352
Pace v. Alabama (1883), 215, 216
Pack Shack, Inc. v. Howard County (2003), 323
Paine, Thomas, 133
"Palimony," 19, 100, 188, 255, 292, 357
Pam Lychner Sexual Offender Tracking and Identification Act (1996), 205
Pamela L. v. Frank S. (1983), 241
Pandering, 43, 44, 140, 152–53, **239–40**, 245
Paraphilia, 330, 369
Parental advisories
  for motion pictures, 59, 61, 68, 116
  for popular music, 118
  for television, 61
  for video games, 118–19
Parental consent
  for abortion, 2, 4–5, 78, 127, 245, 246, 266, 346
  for contraceptive use, 81–82
  for marriage, 77, 200–201
  for sex education, 81, 187, 296–97
Parental rights, 67
  in assisted reproductive technology, 171
  of mothers, 217
  of sperm donors, 30
  of unmarried parents, 360
Parents Music Resource Center, 118
Paris Adult Theatre I v. Slaton (1973), 10, 33, 45, 59, 108, 116, 186, 212, 235

"Partial-birth" abortion, 2, 3, 4–5, 6, 343, 355
Partial-Birth Abortion Ban Act (2003), 5
Pataki, George, 53
Paternity, 240–42
  assisted reproductive technology and, 29, 30
  DNA to establish, 104, 241
  genetic determination of, 147
  of illegitimate children, 170–72
Paul, Alice, *377*
Paul VI (pope), *281*
Payne v. Tennessee (1991), 365, 366
Pederasty, 329, 330, 345
Pedophilia, 191, 251, 282, 301, 330, 345, 370
Peek: Photographs from the Kinsey Institute, 193
Peeping Toms, 229, 265, 306, 371, 372
Penhollow v. Bd. of Commissioners for Cecil County (1997), 93
Pennoyer v. Neff (1877), 97, 99
Pennsylvania
  abortion restrictions in, 2, 243–45
  abstinence education in, 8
  AIDS education in, 297
  deviant behavior in, 90
  family planning in, 128
  gender discrimination in, 144
  indecent exposure in, 175
  sexual harassment in, 316
  stem-cell research in, 340
  trials involving children in, 105
Pennsylvania v. Richie (1987), 62, 67
Pensack v. City and County of Denver (1986), 11
Penthouse, 139, 162, 188, 232, 261, 315
People v. See other party
Peoria, Ill.
  prostitution in, *269*
  prurient interest in, 270

Peper v. Princeton Univ. Bd. of Trustees (1978), 93
Perrine, Valerie, 319
Perry v. Sindermann (1972), 8
Personal Responsibility, Work and Family Act (2005), 161
Perversions, 34–35, 89–90, 306
  See also Deviant behavior; *and specific types*
Peterson, Laci, 356
Peterson, Scott, 356
Pettengill v. United States (1994), 341
Pfizer Company, 111
Pharmacies, contraceptives in, 23, 81
  See also "Morning-after pill"; Pharmacists
Pharmacists
  bioethical concerns of, 38
  contraceptive prescriptions and, 81, 124–24, 285
  ethics of, 122, 124–25
Pharmacists for Life International, 81, 124, 285
Philadelphia
  prurient interest in, 270
  single-sex education in, 327
Photographs of children. *See* Child pornography
Physicians
  abortion and, 2, 3, 5, 6, 7
  assisted reproductive technology and, 29, 51
  bioethical concerns of, 38
  contraceptive importation by, 80, 126, 294
  ethics of, 23, 122, 124–25, 310
  improper sexual behavior of, 23, 90, 274, 310
  pregnancy counseling by, 126
  role in sexual behavior, 22
Pierce v. Society of Sisters (1925), 67, 217, 360
The Pill, 79, 110, *281*, 317
Pimping, 239, 267, 305, 335

Pinkus, Gregory, 110
Pitchfork, Colin, 183
Plan B (contraceptive), 23, 82, 111, 124, 280, 285, 362
Planned Parenthood v. American Coalition of Life Activists (2002), 6
Planned Parenthood Association of Utah v. Matheson (1983), 81
Planned Parenthood Federation of America, 243–45, *244*
  abortion and, 128, 244
  Calderone, Mary S., and, 57
  clinics of, 126, 127
  contraception and, 82
  founding by Margaret Sanger, 80, 284, 294
  funding of the Pill, 110
Planned Parenthood League of Connecticut, 153
Planned Parenthood of Houston and Southeast Texas v. Sanchez (2005), 128
Planned Parenthood of Southeastern Pennsylvania v. Casey (1992)**, 245–46**
  abortion restrictions in, 78, 127, 186, 243–44, 245–46, 264, 281, 285, 335
  liberty cited in, 195, 245
  notification of husband in, 2, 186, 245, 246, 281
  parental consent for minors in, 2, 78, 127, 245
  and undue burden on abortion, 245
  women's consent in, 379
Playboy, 57, 161–63, 232, 261
Playboy Enterprises, 177
Playboy Entertainment Group, 162–63
Playboy Entertainment Group, Inc., United States v. (2000), 10, 115, 163, 236, 250
Plessy v. Ferguson (1896), 83, 215, 369
Plexus (Miller), 212

Poe v. Ullman (1961), 127
Police. *See* Law enforcement officials
Polygamy, 135–36, 246–49, *247,* 283, 303
Polykoff v. Collins (1987), 270
Polyparenting, 216, 242
Pomeroy, Wardell, 192, 193
Pornography, 249–51
  adult, 249–50
  age limits for, 9–10
  children and, 68–69, 250–51
  e-mail, 315
  Eros and, 152–53
  Flynt, Larry, and, 139–41
  homosexual, 152, 235, 250
  in literature, 43–45, 53, 58, 211–12
  in motion pictures, 181–82, 212
  pandering with, 239
  prisoners and, 261
  privacy to possess and view, 250, 265
  soldiers and, 210
  See also Child pornography; Internet; *Miller v. California;* Motion pictures; Obscenity; *Roth v. United States*
Posner v. Posner (1970), 257
Postal laws. *See* Mail
Postnuptial agreements, 19. *See also* Prenuptial agreements
Potter, Van Rensselaer, 37
Potter v. Murray City (1985), 249
Pound, Ezra, 212
Powell, Lewis F., Jr.
  on sex discrimination, 142
  on sodomy, 330
Pregnancy, 251–54
  abstinence to avoid, 8
  bioethical concerns about, 39
  discrimination based on, 378
  drug use during, 253–54
  employment discrimination in, 251–53, 378
  from rape, 272, 275

  prenatal abuse and, 63, 112, 253, 355
  prenatal care and, 220, 253–54, 307
  prisoners' rights during, 261
  sex education to prevent, 295, 297
  terminal illness during, 356
  trimesters for abortion in, 2, 3, 186, 245, 285
  ultrasound in, 252
  wrongful, 220
Pregnancy Discrimination Act (1978), 50, 219, 252, 378
Premarital sex, 254–55, 295, 303
Prenatal abuse, 63, 112, 253, 355
Prenatal care, 220, 253–54, 307
Prenuptial agreements, 19, **255–57**
President, 257–60
President's Council on Bioethics, 27, 37, 38, 39–40, 52, 337
President's Drug Policy Council, 110
Presley, Elvis, 116, 318
Press, freedom of, 136–38, 203–4
  censorship and, 57
  Flynt, Larry, and, 139–41
  Ginzburg, Ralph, and, 152–53
  obscenity and, 234, 235, 286, 288
  prior restraint of publication, 58, 136, 203, 236
  zoning and, 381
  See also Internet; First Amendment; Media; Obscenity; Speech
Preven, 82, 111, 285
Prill v. Hampton (1990), 334
Prince v. Massachusetts (1944), 67
Prior restraint of publication, 58, 136, 203, 236
Prison Rape Elimination Act (2003), 262
Prisoners, 260–63
  American Civil Liberties Union and, 21
  cross-dressing by, 138

DNA testing of, 102, 103
juveniles, 262
marriage rights of, 30, 199,
   260–61, 286
pornography and, 261
pregnant women, 261
procreation by artificial
   insemination, 28, 30
protection from assault, 262–63
rape of, 273
rights of, 260–61
sexual minorities, 262–63
STDs and, 326
transsexuals, 350–51
Privacy, 153–55, 185, 186, 195,
   263–66, 376
abortion and, 2, 264
adultery and, 12–13, 14
AIDS-HIV and, 16
alimony and, 19
contraception and, 80, 263, 264
DNA testing and, 101, 103
Douglas, William O., on, 108–9
fornication and, 12–13, 14
genetic information and, 147–49
homosexuals and, 264
invasion of, 154, 228, 265, 266,
   371, 372
marriage and, 109, 127, 153–55,
   199, 264
nudity and, 265
obscenity and, 265
polygamy and, 249
prostitution and, 268
reproductive rights and, 354
same-sex marriage and, 88
sex offenders and, 265
sexual, right to, 264, 373–74
sodomy and, 194–95, 329
STDs and, 326
stem-cell research and, 339
victims and, 265
voyeurism and, 265
zone of, 154
Procreation, right of, 28, 30, 79,
   228, 263, 285–86, 342

Prohibition, 1, 9
Property rights
in divorce, 98–99, 100
in genetic material, 151
in marriage, 199, 256, 257, 333–34
of married women, 26, 331
in prenuptial agreements, 255–57
of unmarried cohabitants, 358
Prostitution, 266–69, *269*
drugs and, 112
by homosexuals, 268
human trafficking as, 168
legalization of, 169
locals laws on, 336
in the military, 210
by minors, 62, 67, 267
pandering for, 239
selective enforcement of, 268
STDs and, 326
as a victimless crime, 303–4
PROTECT Act (2003), 169
Protection of Children from Sexual
   Exploitation Act (1977), 232
Protection orders, 106, 368
Prurient interest, 269–70
adult materials and, 10
Carnal Knowledge (1971) and, 59
in Child Online Protection Act, 64
Federal Communications
   Commission and, 129
homosexual magazines and, 250
test in *Miller v. California,* 177,
   186, 213, 249
test in *Roth v. United States,* 43,
   45, 58, 136, 235, 288, 319
voyeurism and, 371
Psychiatrists, ethics of, 122
Psycho (1960), 371
Psychologists, licensing of, 312
Psychopathia Sexualis (Krafft-Ebing),
   302, 353
Psychotherapists, confidentiality
   and, 123
Public Broadcasting System, 319
Public Health Service, 295, 343,
   362

Public Health Service Act (1970),
   Title X, 127, 128
Public indecency. *See* Indecent
   exposure; Nudity
Public Utilities Commission v.
   Pollack (1952), 108
Publication, prior restraint of, 58,
   136, 203, 236
   See also Censorship; Press
Punishment of sex offenses,
   299–301
civil confinement after, 191–92,
   299, 300–301
for hate crimes, 156–60, 300, 304
for human trafficking, 169
prejudice in, 299
registration after, 70, 84, 205, 265,
   301, 302, 365
reporting of STDs, crimes related
   to, 326
   See also Hate crimes; *and specific*
   offenses
Puritans, 279
   See also Massachusetts Bay Colony
Purity movement, 72–73

Q
Quid pro quo sexual harassment,
   54, 55, 314, 315
   See also Sexual harassment

R
Racketeer Influenced and Corrupt
   Organizations Act (RICO) (1970),
   6, 23, 285
Radio
censorship of, 60, 61
obscene language on, 115, 129–30,
   136, 204, 324
regulation of, 115, 129–30, 203–4,
   319
satellite, 130
Rand, Sally, 318
Rape, 86, **271–75,** *272*
Bryant, Kobe, trial for, 277–78
child abuse as, 61, 307

consent in, 77–78, 278
crisis centers, 368
date rape, 86–87, 111–12, 274
definition of, 304
DNA testing for, 102
emergency contraception after,
    6, 19, 82, 272
federal jurisdiction over, 78,
    272–73
forcible, 187, 272, 274
in Hays Code, 117
HIV testing after, 16
human trafficking and, 169
in incest, 174
marital, 77, 78, 199, 272, 273, 275,
    302, 309
in prisons, 262–63, 273
rate, 86, 271, 308
same-sex, 271
state laws on, 273–75, 276–77
victims of, 86, 272, 365
See also Rape shield laws;
    Statutory rape
Rape shield laws, 273, **277–79**, 363
Rape, Abuse, and Incest National
    Network, 308
Rappe, Virginia, 113
Rating systems
  for motion pictures, 59, 61, 116, 212
  for popular music, 118
  for video games, 118
"Rational basis test" for
    discrimination, 82, 83, 145, 185,
    373, 376
RCA, 118
Reagan, Nancy, 337
Reagan, Ronald
  on family planning, 128
  on Title IX, 348
Recording Industry Association of
    America, 118
The Red Badge of Courage (Crane),
    58
Redeeming value
  of adult materials, 10, 213
  of child nudity, 232

of *Howl* (Ginsberg), 53, 318
of indecent exposure, 175
of literature, 43, 45, 236
of nudity in public performances,
    230
of obscene language, 235
obscenity as lacking, 288
proof of negative value, 236
of representations of nudity,
    231
test in *Miller v. California*, 250
test in *Roth v. United States*,
    43, 136, 319
See also Obscenity
Reed v. Reed (1971), 46, 83, 119,
    142, 145, 186, 376
Rees v. State (1995), 17
*Regents of the University of
    California v. Bakke* (1978), 96
Regina v. Hicklin (1868), 235, 288
Registration of sex offenders, 70, 84,
    205, 265, 301, 302, 365
Rehabilitation Act (1973), 15, 351
Rehnquist, William H.
  on divorce, 375
  on judicial scrutiny, 83
  on nudity, 33–34, 233
  on *Roe v. Wade*, 246
  on single-sex education, 369
Release from Sexual Tension
    (Calderone), 57
Religion, 279–83
  abortion and, 1, 6, 281
  abstinence education and, 8
  adultery and, 302
  AIDS-HIV and, 166
  annulment and, 24
  bigamy and, 36
  bioethical concerns of, 38
  contraception and, 79, 81, 82,
    280–81, 285, 294
  divorce and, 101
  First Amendment and, 135–36
  homosexuality and, 164, 282
  incest and, 172
  marriage and, 197, 198, 289

obscene language and, 236–37
polygamy and, 246, 248, 283
pregnancy and, 254, 356
sex education and, 21, 321, 362
sexual abuse scandal and, 61, 62,
    280–81
sodomy and, 194
STDs and, 325
stem-cell research and, 281
and unborn, rights of the, 354
Rene v. MGM Grand Hotel, Inc.
    (2002), 316
*Reno v. American Civil Liberties
    Union* (1997), 10, 21, 60, 63, 71,
    118, 130, 136, 177–78, 204, 236,
    250
*Renton, City of v. Playtime Theatres,
    Inc.* (1986), 324, 381
Reproductive rights, 21, 136,
    283–86
  See also Abortion; Contraception;
    Family planning
Restell, Madame, 73, *80*
Retroactive laws, 191, 205, 300–301
Reuben, David, 317–18
Reverse discrimination, 82–84, 92,
    96, 122, 377
  See also Affirmative action;
    Discrimination; Sex
    discrimination
Reynolds v. United States (1879),
    36, 136, 248
Rhode Island
  abortion in, 3
  genetic privacy in, 150
  pregnant prisoners in, 261
  same-sex marriage in, 292
  sexual harassment in, 316
Rhodes v. McAfee (1970), 174
"Rhythm" method, 126, 280
Rich, Commonwealth v. (1981),
    270
*Richards v. United States Tennis
    Association* (1977), 144, 312
Richardson v. Ramirez (1974), 248
Richardson v. Wile (1988), 323

Richmond Newspapers, Inc. v. Virginia (1980), 203
Right to Breastfeed Act (1999), 50
Riley v. New York Trust Co. (1940), 376
Rivera v. Minnich (1981), 104
Robbins, People v. (1981), 333
Roberts, John G., Jr., 223, 259, 340
Roberts v. United States Jaycees (1984), 90, 138, 199
Robertson v. Reinhart (2003), 19
Rochester, City of v. Carlson (1972), 239
Rock, John, 110
Roe v. Connecticut (1976), 217
Roe v. Wade (1973), 2
  attempts to overturn, 7, 244, 245, 246, 319
  Blackmun, Harry A., author of, *184*
  cited in *Lawrence v. Texas*, 195
  companion case to, 109
  NARAL Pro-Choice America and, 223
  privacy as basis for, 2, 127, 155, 264, 285
  religious efforts to restrict, 6, 279, 281
  restrictions on, 2–5, 127, 185, 186
  trimesters in, 2, 3, 186, 245, 285
  See also Abortion; *Planned Parenthood of Southeastern Pennsylvania v. Casey;* Reproductive rights
Rojo v. Kliger (1990), 316
Roman Catholic Church
  abortion and, 1, 6
  annulment and, 24
  contraception and, 6, 81, 82, 280, 281, 285
  divorce and, 280
  incest and, 174
  marriage and, 197
  popes, 240, *281*, 282
  "rhythm" method and, 126, 280
  same-sex marriage and, 282
  Sanger, Margaret, and, 294

sexual abuse scandal in, 61, 62, 281–82
and unborn, rights of the, 354
Romeo and Juliet (Shakespeare), 346
"Romeo and Juliet laws," 78, 255, 346
Romer v. Evans (1996), 167, 289
Roosevelt, Franklin D., 107, 260
Roosevelt, Theodore
  and Anthony, Susan B., 25
  on family planning, 79, 259–60
Rose v. Locke (1975), 329
Rosey Crucifixion (Miller), 212
Rostker v. Goldberg (1981), 84, 208
Rotary Club of Duarte v. Rotary International (1986), 122
Roth, Samuel, *287*
***Roth v. United States*, 286–88**
  community standards test in, 43, 58, 64, 139, 181, 182, 288
  deviation from, 152
  Douglas, William O., dissent in, 108
  Howl (Ginsberg), and, 53
  obscenity, delineation in, 116, 136, 212, 234, 288
  prurient interest test in, 43, 58, 64, 235, 288
  redeeming value test in, 45, 58, 213, 230, 288
  works judged as a whole in, 44, 58, 186, 288
  See also Obscenity; Pornography
Roussel Uclaf, 111
RU-486, 82, 111, 124, 280–81, 285, 362
Rubin, Gayle, 133
Russo, State v. (2000), 324
Rutledge, Wiley B., on children's rights, 67

S
Sable Communications of California, Inc. v. Federal Communications Commission (1989), 60, 347, 348
Sadism, 371

Sadomasochism, 192, 236, 370
Saks v. Franklin Covey Co. (2003), 29
Salome, 228
Salpingectomy, 341
Same-sex marriage, 289–93, *290*
  ACLU suit in Washington State, 19
  Defense of Marriage Act and, 87–89
  dissolution of, 101, 292–93
  efforts to prevent, 320
  federal laws on, 87–89, 289–90, 293
  Federal Marriage Amendment and, 130–32
  Healthy Marriage Initiative and, 161
  homosexual discrimination and, 95, 357
  in Massachusetts, 130, 187, 199, 290–91, 292
  religion and, 282
  right to, 164
  state laws on, 199, 291, 335–36
Samuel v. University of Pittsburgh (1974), 332
Sandburg, Carl, 56
Sanger, Margaret, 57, 73, 80, 126, 243, 284, **293–95,** *294,* 318
Sanger, People v. (1918), 126, 294
Satcher, David, 342
Satellite radio, 130
Satellite television, 129, 204
Sawatzky v. City of Oklahoma (1995), 196
Scalia, Antonin
  on bigamy, 37
  on ethics codes, 123
  on expression, freedom of, 34
  on pandering, 239
  on *Roe v. Wade*, 246
  on single-sex education, 369
  on sodomy, 195
The Scarlet Letter (Hawthorne), 12
Schad v. Borough of Mount Ephraim (1981), 34, 381

Scheidler v. National Organization for Women (2006), 6, 23, 226, 285

Schenck v. United States (1919), 136

School Board of Nassau County v. Arline (1987), 15

Schooling of children, 67, 217, 360
   See also Abstinence; Sex education

Schuster v. Schuster (1978), 293

Schwarzenegger, Arnold, 130, 141, 292

Schwenk v. Hartford, 262–63

Scopes, John, 2

Scott v. Sandford (1857), 207, 215, 354

Scroggins v. State (1990), 17

Sedition Act (1798), 57

Seiler, Conrad, 59

Self-censorship, 60–61
   AIDS and, 17
   by broadcasters, 115, 116
   on Internet, 64
   in motion pictures, 59, 60, 116, 117, 283
   in popular music, 118
   religion and, 283
   in video games, 118

Seling v. Young (2001), 345

Senate, 74

Seneca Falls Declaration of Sentiments and Resolutions, 26, 133, 379

Sentencing. *See* Punishment

"Separate but equal" doctrine, 83, 215, 327, 369

Separation, spousal, 96–97
   See also Divorce

Separation of church and state, 8, 21, 135, 136, 248, 279, 362

September Morn (Chabas), 73

Sex (West), 114

Sex and Humor (Kinsey Institute), 193

Sex and the Single Girl (Brown), 318

Sex clubs, 322
   See also Sexually oriented businesses

Sex discrimination, 91–94, 119–22
   in association, 90, 138, 199
   in breastfeeding, 47–51
   in child custody, 378–79
   classification by sex, 141–42
   in education, 91, 94, 348–49, 376
   in employment, 91, 92, 93, 375, 376, 377, 378
   in estate administration, 376
   gender discrimination, compared to, 42, 144–45
   in labor law, 221–22
   legal practice and, 45–47
   in military, 141–42, 207–9
   against married women, 47, 333
   paternity and, 360
   in pregnancy, 251–53, 378
   against prostitutes, 268
   in sale of beer, 82–84, 92
   in single-sex education, 327–28, 369
   See also Civil Rights Act (1964), Title VII; Equal rights; Title IX; Women's rights

Sex education, 295–98, *298*
   abstinence focus of, 8–9, 296–97, 298
   AIDS-HIV in, 16–17
   Calderone, Mary S., and, 56–57
   contraception in, 81–82
   funding of, 8, 295, 362
   homosexuality in, 95, 166
   parental consent for, 81, 187, 296–97
   Planned Parenthood Federation and, 243
   religion and, 280
   right to, 284
   SIECUS and, 321
   Silver Ring Thing program, 21, 280, 362
   state policies on, 296–97

STDs in, 295, 325–26
   See also Family planning

Sex offenders, 299–301
   children as, 69–70
   civil confinement of, 191–92, 299, 300–301
   punishment of, 299–301
   registration of, 70, 84, 205, 265, 301, 302, 365
   victims' rights and, 363–66
   See also Hate crimes; *and specific offenses*

Sex offenses, 302–7
   consensual, 303–4
   federal laws on, 304–5
   in the military, 210
   nonconsensual, 304–5
   punishment of, 299–301
   state laws on, 335
   See also specific offenses

Sex reassignment, 138, 307, 311–12, 350, 351, 353

Sex research, by Alfred Kinsey, 192–93

Sex therapy, 312

Sex tourism, 169, 225, 259, 305

Sex workers. *See* Prostitution

Sexism, 86, 222, 225
   See also Sex discrimination

Sexology, 193

Sexual abuse, definition of, 304

Sexual assault, 307–10
   definition of, 304
   in the military, 209
   with an object, 308, 309
   in prisons, 262–63
   rate, 271
   See also Child abuse; Date rape; Domestic violence; Incest; Rape; Sex offenses; Violence Against Women Act; *and other specific offenses*

Sexual battery, 307, 308, 309

Sexual behavior, representations of, versus actual conduct, 113, 118, 181, 213–14, 231–32, 249, 306

Sexual Behavior in the Human Female (Kinsey), 41, 192, 193, *193*, 318
Sexual Behavior in the Human Male (Kinsey), 41, 192, 193, 299, 318
Sexual devices, 90, 322, 373–74
Sexual enhancement, 310–12
  criminal responsibility for, 307
  drugs for, 111
  sex reassignment, 138, 311, 350, 351, 353
Sexual exploitation, definition of, 305
  See also Child abuse; Children
Sexual harassment, 312–17
  of bisexuals, 42
  of children, 70
  in education, 316, 317, 349
  in e-mail, 315
  in employment, 188, 313,314–15, 316, 317
  hostile work environment, creation of, 54, 55, 314, 315
  of married couples, 42
  in the military, 209
  obscene telephone calls as, 237
  quid pro quo, 54, 55, 314, 315
  same-sex, 55
  by sexual orientation, 43, 306, 313, 316, 317
  telephone sex as, 347–48
  See also Voyeurism
Sexual identity. *See* Gender; Gender-identity disorder
Sexual minorities. *See* Bisexuals; Homosexuality; Homosexuals; Transsexualism; Transsexuals; Transvestism
Sexual orientation
  of children, 70
  discrimination based on, 42, 94–96, 138, 144, 145–46, 190
  employment discrimination based on, 165, 168
  in federal employment, 41, 94, 165, 168, 190, 319

  harassment based on, 43, 306, 313, 316, 317
  hate crimes based on, 156, 157, 158–59
  of jurors, 187
  in the military, 95, 209–10
  privacy about, 264
  See also Bisexuals; Homosexuals; Transsexuals; Transvestism
Sexual perversions, 34–35, 89–90, 306
  See also Deviant behavior; *and specific types*
Sexual reproduction, 102, 146, 240, 340
Sexual revolution, 43, 197, 307, 317–20
Sexual slavery. *See* Human trafficking
Sexuality, definition of, 56, 144
Sexuality Information and Educational Council of the United States (SIECUS), 56, 181, 295, **320–21**
Sexually oriented businesses, 321–24, 322
  local laws on, 322, 336
  pandering by, 239–40
  regulation of, 60, 323–24
  zoning of, 380–81
  See also specific types
Sexually transmitted diseases, 324–27, 325
  abstinence to prevent, 8, 9
  adultery and, 12
  AIDS-HIV, 14–18
  contraceptives to prevent, 81
  human papillomavirus (HPV), 9, 324, 325
  infertility caused by, 28
  intentional infection with, 306
  marriage requirements and, 198
  in the military, 210
  Planned Parenthood Federation and, 243
  privacy and, 78, 265

  prostitution and, 268
  from rape, 272
  reporting of, 326
  sex education to prevent, 295, 297
  See also AIDS-HIV
Sexus (Miller), 212
Shahar v. Bowers (1998), 165, 358
Shakespeare, William, 172, 195, 239, 352
Sharp v. Lansing (2001), 122
Shaw, George Bernard, 73, 212
Shea, United States v. (1997), 103
Shepard, Matthew, 156
Sheppard-Towner Maternity and Infancy Act (1921), 75
Shilling v. Bedford City Memorial Hospital (1983), 332
Siegelbaum, United States v. (2005), 160
Silver Ring Thing program, 21, 280, 362
Single-sex education, 186, 327–28
  for men, 369
  for women, 376
Skinner v. Oklahoma (1942), 263, 342
Slander, 14, 60, 140, 177, 235
Slaughterhouse cases, 46, 47
Sloan, John, 370
Smith, Joseph, 246
Smith v. Doe (2003), 205, 301
Social purity movement, 72–73
Social Security, 131, 170, 202, 361
Social Security Act (1935), 128
Society for the Suppression of Vice, 266
Sodom and Gomorrah, 194, 329
Sodomy, 328–30
  bestiality and, 34–35
  Bowers v. Hardwick, criminalization under, 12, 33, 195, 228, 303, 329
  consent to, 76, 79
  decriminalization of, 33, 186, 194, 303, 329, 330
  as deviant behavior, 90

forcible, 308

HIV test after, 16

in incest, 174

Lawrence v. Texas, affirming right
to engage in, 194–95

in the military, 209

religion and, 194, 282

solicitation for, 196

Solicitation of sex

of a child, 305, 335

on Internet, 180

as lewd behavior, 306

same-sex, 196, 268

See also Prostitution

Sosna v. Iowa (1975), 100, 375

Soulia, People v. (1999), 174

Souter, David H.

on abortion restrictions, 245

on civil recovery for women
victims, 309

on nude dancing, 34

on sexual harassment, 55

South Carolina

civil confinement in, 300

genetic privacy in, 149

miscegenation in, 336

obscene language in, 236–37

pederasty in, 330

prenatal abuse in, 112

prurient interest in, 270

punishment of sex offenders in,
300

rape in, 273

same-sex marriage in, 291

sex education in, 297

sexual battery in, 309

statutory rape in, 334

voyeurism in, 371

South Dakota

abortion in, 7, 335

cloning in, 340

marital rape in, 275

prison officials' conduct in,
262

same-sex marriage in, 291

sexual harassment in, 317

STDs in, 326

and unborn, rights of the, 354

Southeastern Productions v. Conrad
(1975), 230

Southern, Edwin, 183

Spallanzani, Lazzaro, 29

Spam, sexually explicit, 179

Sparta, bisexuality in, 41

Speaks v. State (1968), 112

Spears, Britney, 25

Speech, freedom of

abortion protests and, 6, 23, 138,
285

AIDS-HIV and, 17

American Civil Liberties Union
and, 21

content-based, 10, 163, 381

entertainment industry and,
113–19

First Amendment and, 136–38

Flynt, Larry, and 139–41

gender issues and, 137

government benefits and, 8

Internet and, 176–79

mailing of obscenity and, 288

motion pictures and, 59

obscene language and, 52–54

obscenity and, 234, 235

prostitution and, 268

radio and television and, 60

telephone sex and, 60, 347–48

zoning and, 380–81

See also Expression; Internet;
Obscenity; Pornography; Press;
and specific media

Sperm donors, 30

See also Assisted reproductive
technology

Spina v. Spina (2004), 352

Spirit of Justice, 229

Spousal immunity, 199

Spousal rape. *See* Marital rape

Spousal rights and duties, 264,
330–34, 357–59

See also Marriage

St. Augustine, 79

St. George, City of v. Turner (1993),
270

St. Louis, prostitution in, 266

Stalking

Internet, 71

obscene telephone calls as, 237

victims of, 308

Violence Against Women Act and,
368

Stanley v. Georgia (1969), 69, 212,
250, 265, 287

Stanton, Elizabeth Cady, 26, 133,
379

Starr, Kenneth W., 123

State and local government, 187,
196, **334–37**

See also specific topics

State v. See other party

Statutory rape, 68, 274–75, 346

age of consent for, 78, 273, 275,
344

child offenders, 69

consent as defense to, 363

state laws on, 66, 276–77

Steambath, 319

Steffan v. Perry (1994), 95

Steichen, Edward, 56

Steinem, Gloria, 162, 293

Stem-cell research, 337–41

bioethical concerns about, 39, 337

embryos, use of, 31, 340

funding of, 40, 52, 281, 339, 340

religion and, 281

state laws on, 336, 338–39, 340

See also Cloning

Stenberg v. Carhart (2000), 3, 5

Stephenson, Sarah Hackett, 23

Steptoe, Patrick, 51

Sterility, 28

See also Assisted reproductive
technology

Sterilization, 341–42

infertility and, 29

of sex offenders, 263, 301, 342

wrongful pregnancy and, 220

Stern, Howard, 115, 129–30, 204

Stevens, John Paul
  on bioethics, 40
  on Internet regulation, 71
  on judicial scrutiny, 83
  on sex discrimination, 50
  on zoning of sexually oriented
    businesses, 381
Stevens v. Rollen (2003), 356
Stewart, Potter
  on contraceptive rights, 155
  on pornography, 181, 182, 234,
    251, 270
  on sex discrimination, 142
Stone, Lucy, 379
STOP grants, 237, 368
Stoumen v. Reilly (1951), 138
Stowe, Harriet Beecher, 13
Stowell, Commonwealth v. (1983), 12
Stratton v. Wilson (1916), 256
Streaking, 229
Strict construction of the U.S.
  Constitution, 155
"Strict scrutiny" of discrimination,
  10, 185, 188, 324, 327, 373, 376
Striptease shows, 114–15
  See also Nude dancing
*Stuart v. Board of Supervisors of
  Elections* (1972), 331
Studds, Gerry E., 76, 168
Suffrage. *See* Voting rights
Summit, Roland C., 62
**Surgeon General of the United
  States**, 47, **342–43**, 362
Surrogacy, 27, 31–32
  homosexuals and, 164
  motherhood and, 216
  See also Illegitimacy
Sutton v. United Airlines (1999), 150
Syphilis, 324, 325, 326

T
Tadewaldt, State v. (1996), 301
Tailhook Association sex scandal,
  209
"Take Back the Night" poster, 272
Talty, State v. (2004), 9, 286

Tariff Act (1842), 58
Tax laws, 75, 201
Tay-Sachs disease, 174
Taylor, People v. (2004), 348
Teachers
  harassment by, 316, 317
  pregnant, 251
  sex discrimination against, 349
Technorati, 179
Teen Sex: What About the Kids?, 130
Teenagers, 344–47
  abstinence education for, 8–9
  admission to dance halls, 337
  age of consent to marriage, 198,
    200–201
  birth rate of, 297
  consent to sex, 346
  contraception and, 81–82
  discrimination against, 345
  homosexual activity by, 346
  Internet access by, 63–65, 177–79,
    180
  premarital sex by, 255
  sex education and, 297
  sex rate of, 344
  STDs and, 324, 325, 326–27
  video games and, 118
  See also Children; Internet;
    Statutory rape
Telephone Indecency Act (1988), 60
Telephone sex, 60, 237, 306 308,
  347–48
Television, 203–4
  cable and satellite, 129, 204
  censorship of, 60, 61, 162–63
  indecency on, 129, 130
  pornography on, 319, 320
  regulation of, 115, 203–4
Television Communications Act
  (1996), 163
Temporary restraining orders
  (TROs), 106, 368
"Tender years" presumption in child
  custody, 217, 309–10, 378
Tennessee
  breastfeeding in, 378

maternity leave in, 378
same-sex marriage in, 291
sodomy in, 329
STDs in, 326
Tennyson, Alfred Lord, 37
"Test-tube" babies, 27, 30–31,
  51, *51*
  See also Assisted reproductive
    technology
Texas
  abortion in, 2
  breastfeeding in, 378
  castration in, 301
  community property in, 333
  cross-dressing in, 352–53
  DNA collection in, 103, 265
  equal rights in, 94
  family planning in, 128
  hate crimes in, 160
  infertility in, 29
  prenuptial agreements in, 257
  prisoners' rights in, 261
  sex education in, 17, 166
  sexually oriented businesses in,
    322
  sodomy in, 194–95, 264, 330
  teen birth rate in, 297
  voyeurism in, 371
  women's rights in, 376
Texas Council on Family Violence,
  368
Theater, nudity in the, 230, 265
  See also Entertainment industry;
    Motion pictures; Nude dancing;
    Nudity; Sexually oriented
    businesses
31 Photographs, United States v.
  (1957), 192
Thomas, Clarence, 234
  on civil confinement, 191
  on *Roe v. Wade*, 246
  on sodomy, 195
Thomas S. v. Robin (1994), 30
Thomasson v. Perry (1996), 186,
  209, 265
Thompson, State v. (2002), 268

Thoreson v. Penthouse International, Ltd. (1992), 188

Tilton, Elizabeth, *13*

Times Film Corp. v. City of Chicago (1961), 59

Tinker v. Des Moines Independent Community School District (1969), 70

Title VII. *See* Civil Rights Act (1964)

Title IX, Education Amendments (1972), 75, 92, 120, **348–49**, 376

female prisoners' rights and, 261

sexual assault and, 87

sexual harassment and, 316, 317

single-sex schools and, 328

Tompras, State ex rel. v. Board of Election Commissioners (2004), 94

Topless dancing, 230

See also Nude dancing; Nudity

Touching, improper, 309, 312

Toward a Feminist Theory of the State (MacKinnon), 79

Townshend v. Board of Education (1990), 333

Trammel v. United States (1980), 264

Transgender persons. *See* Transsexualism; Transsexuals

Transportation of minors across state lines, 35, 62, 67, 105, 168–69, 305, 308, 330, 368

See also Human trafficking

Transsexualism, 133–34, 138, 146, **350–52**

Transsexuals

crimes against, 156, 159

discrimination against, 55, 144, 145–46, 351

in hate crime laws, 145

marriage rights of, 199

prisoners' rights, 262–63

sex reassignment for, 138, 307, 311–12, 350, 351, 353

sexual identity of, 144

Transvestic fetishism, 352

Transvestism, 138, 146, **352–53**

Trespassing, 371

Trials

child victims and, 62–63, 105, 203

children's rights in, 70

DNA evidence in, 102–3

hearsay evidence in, 62–63, 105, 309–10

media coverage of, 203

military, 210

rape victims and, 272, 273, 275, 277–78

sexual assault, 309–10

victims and, 363

Trimble v. Gordon (1977), 170, 360

Tripp v. Hinckley (2002), 171

Troilus and Cressida (Shakespeare), 239

Tropic of Cancer (Miller), 211, 212

Tropic of Capricorn (Miller), 211

Troxel v. Granville (2000), 345

Truman, Harry S., and military integration, 207

Tuan Ahn Nguyen v. Immigration and Naturalization Service (2001), 84, 171, 360

Tubal ligation, 341

See also Sterilization

Tucker, Sophie, 318

Tucson, City of v. Wolfe (1996), 175

Turner v. Department of Employment Security (1975), 378

Turner v. Safley (1987), 30, 199, 260, 289

Twelfth Night (Shakespeare), 239

Twenty-sixth Amendment, 344–45

Twisted Sister, 118

2 Live Crew, 115, 118, 245

U

Ulane v. Eastern Airlines, Inc. (1984), 55, 146, 312, 351

Ulysses (Joyce), 58, 287

Unborn, rights of the, 354–56

abortion and, 1, 2, 245, 355

bioethical concerns about, 39

cloning and, 341

contraception and, 81

embryos, disposition of, 31, 340

fetal homicide and, 355, 356

Missouri law on, 1

prenatal abuse and, 253–54, 355

religion and, 281, 354

Utah law on, 3, 354

wrongful death and, 220

See also Abortion; Stem-cell research

Unborn Victims of Violence Act (2004), 356

Underwood v. Archer Management Services, Inc. (1994), 41

Unethical behavior. *See* Ethics

Uniform Code of Military Justice, 2, 210

Uniform Marital and Divorce Act (1970), 333

Uniform Marital Property Act (1983), 256

Uniform Parentage Act (1973), 30, 31, 241

Uniform Parentage Act (2002), 104

Uniform Premarital Agreement Act (1983), 257

Uniform Status of Children of Assisted Conception Act (1988), 31

United Nations, 168, 266

United States Tennis Association, 312

United States v. See other party

United Steelworkers v. Weber (1979), 96

University of California, Berkeley, AIDS awareness at, *15*

University of California, Hastings, 220

University of California, San Francisco, 339

University of Virginia, 369

University of Wisconsin, 37

Unmarried cohabitants, 356–59

children of, 359

contraceptive use by, 80
dissolution of relationships,
    100–101
inheritance by, 358
lack of the imprimatur of marriage,
    216
as lewd behavior, 195
premarital sex by, 255
rate of, 197
See also Civil unions; Domestic
    partnerships; Same-sex marriage
Unmarried parents, 359–61
assisted reproductive technology
    and, 29–30
birth rate of, 66
children of, 170, 359
single mothers as, 216
See also Illegitimacy
Urbaniak, Estate of v. Newton
    (1991), 16, 265
U.S. Commission on Obscenity and
    Pornography, 10, 234
U.S. Committee on Population
    Growth, 295
U.S. Constitution
executive branch under, 257–59
full faith and credit clause, 88,
    100, 131, 290, 375
incorporation, doctrine of, 135,
    235, 335
judicial branch under, 183–85
legislative branch under, 73
presidential powers under,
    257–59
strict versus expansive
    construction, 226–27
See also Bill of Rights; Congress;
    First Amendment; Judiciary;
    Nineteenth Amendment; Ninth
    Amendment; President; *and
    specific topics*
U.S. Department of Defense, Task
    Force on Sexual Harassment and
    Violence at Military Service
    Academies, 209
See also Military

U.S. Department of Education,
    327, 349
**U.S. Department of Health and
    Human Services, 361–62**
abstinence education and, 8
AIDS-HIV and, 16, 17
child abuse and, 84
family planning and, 127
Healthy Marriage Initiative and, 161
President's Council on Bioethics
    and, 39
sex education and, 21
STDs and, 325
violence against women and, 366
See also Centers for Disease
    Control and Prevention; Food
    and Drug Administration;
    National Institutes of Health;
    Public Health Service; Surgeon
    General of the United States
U.S. Department of Justice
enforcement of federal laws by,
    120, 258
Internet exploitation of children
    and, 180
obscenity enforcement by, 249
rape statistics by, 86, 271
sex offenders and, 70, 301
victims' rights and, 363
violence against women and,
    237, 366
U.S. Department of State, 305
U.S. House of Representatives, 74
U. S. mail
censorship of, 58, 286
contraceptives in, 72, 73, 75, 154,
    284
homosexual magazines in, 152,
    235, 250
obscene materials in, 45, 59,
    72–73, 75, 212–13, 235, 288,
    293
U.S. Postal Service, fundraising
    stamp by, *106*
U.S. Senate, 74
U.S. Sentencing Commission, 157

U.S. Supreme Court, 184
    See also specific decisions
USA PATRIOT Act (2001), 21
Utah
abortion in, 3
adoption by unmarried parents in,
    361
bigamy in, 36, 37
child support in, 65
criminal conversation in, 307
homosexual adoption in, 164
polygamy in, 246–48, 283, 303
pregnancy in, 378
prurient interest in, 270
religion in, 280
sex education in, 166
statutory rape in, 78
surrogacy in, 31
and unborn, rights of the, 3, 354

V
Valenti, Jack, 116
Vance v. Universal Amusements Co.
    (1980), 59
Vasectomy, 341
Vasquez v. Hawthorne (2001), 201
Vela, People v. (1985), 77
Vermont
abortion in, 335
civil unions in, 88, 100–101, 130,
    132, 164, 165, 199, 202, 201,
    292
domestic partnerships in, 358
domestic violence in, 105
genetic privacy in, 150
sexual orientation harassment in,
    317
STDs in, 326
Viacom, 115
Viagra, 111
Vibrators, 374
Victimless crimes, 306, 352
    See also Nude dancing;
    Pornography; Prostitution
Victims of Trafficking and Violence
    Protection Act (2000), 169, 237

Victims' rights, 363–66

AIDS-HIV infection, 17–18

for children, 67–69

civil confinement to protect,
191–92, 299, 300–301

civil recovery, 62, 275, 282,
308–9, 366

DNA testing, 102

domestic violence and, 104–6

emergency contraception and,
6, 19, 82, 111, 272, 280, 284

law enforcement and, 123

legal expenses, 308

privacy and, 265

punishment to protect, 299

after rape, 272, 273, 275

rape shield laws, 277–79

sex offender registration, 70, 84,
205–6, 265, 301, 302, 365

testimony at trial, 62–63

in Violence Against Women Act,
366, 368

See also Civil suits; Law
enforcement officials; *Morrison,
United States v.*

Victims' Rights and Restitution Act
(1990), 363

Video games, 118

Video voyeurism, 371–72

Videos, adult, 10, 113, 140, 141, 193,
249, 270, 320, 322, 323

*A Vindication of the Rights of
Woman* (Wollstonecraft), 92, 133,
327

Violence Against Women Act
(1994), 75, 87, 104, 123, 145, 157,
186, 237, 273, **366–68**

Violent Crime Control and Law
Enforcement Act (1994), 205

Virginia

adultery in, 303, 355

castration in, 301

civil confinement in, 300

domestic partner insurance in,
164–65

fetal homicide in, 356

fornication in, 13–14

gender discrimination in, 144

lewd behavior in, 195–96

miscegenation in, 215–16

nudism in, 233

obscenity in, 236

paternity in, 241

premarital sex in, 255, 303

same-sex marriage in, 292

STDs in, 326

sterilization in, 341–42

surrogacy in, 31

telephone sex in, 348

Virginia, United States v. (1996),
120, 186, 328, **369**

Virginia Military Institute, 120, 186,
369

Virginia Polytechnic Institute, 87, 272

Virginity, and annulment, 24

*Viriyhiranpaiboon v. Department
of State Police* (2001), 149

Vorchheimer v. School District
(1976), 327

Voting rights, women's, 25–26, 92,
119, 184, 185, 214–15

See also Nineteenth Amendment

Voting Rights Act (1965), 345

Voyeurism, 236, 265, **369–72**, 370

W

Wainwright v. Stone (1972), 329

Waite, Morrison R.

on legal practice by women, 46

on women's right to vote, 214

Walker, Lenore, 106

"Wall of separation between church
and state," 248, 279

See also Separation of church and
state

Wallace v. Pyro Mining (1990), 50

Ward v. Illinois (1977), 370–71

Warholic, State v. (2004), 309

Warren, Earl

on contraceptive rights, 154

on miscegenation, 216

on obscenity, 182

Washington

breastfeeding in, 49

community property in, 333

DNA collection in, 103, 265

equal rights in, 94, 320

illegitimacy in, 361

incest in, 172

obscenity in, 236

paid maternity leave in, 219

pederasty in, 330

pregnant prisoners in, 261

rape in, 77

same-sex marriage in, 19

sex offenders in, 345

sexual harassment in, 317

STDs in, 326

surrogacy for homosexuals in, 164

telephone sex in, 347

voyeurism in, 372

Washington v. Glucksberg (1997), 40

Watson, James, 102

*Watson v. Peoples Security Life
Insurance Co.* (1991), 316

*The Way to Become the Sensuous
Woman* (Garrity), 318

*Webster v. Reproductive Health
Services* (1989), 2–3, 81

Wechsler, Herbert, 193

Weiner, Anthony, 28

Welfare Reform Act (1996), 8

The Well of Loneliness (Hall), 58

Wells, H. G., 293, 294

Wellstone, Paul, 169

West, Mae, 114, 318

West Coast Hotel v. Parrish (1937),
150, 154, 221

West Virginia

abortion restrictions in, 379

equal rights in, 122

fetal homicide in, 356

incest in, 172, 303

infertility in, 29

premarital sex in, 255

rape in, 273

sexual harassment in, 316

STDs in, 326

Wetterling, Jacob, 205, 365
Whaley v. Whaley (1978), 188
What Every Girl Should Know (Sanger), 318
White, Bryon R.
  on nude dancing, 34
  on *Roe v. Wade*, 246
  on sexual exploitation of children, 250
  on sodomy, 330
White Slave Act (Mann Act) (1910), 75, 168, 267, 305
White slavery, 168
  See also Human trafficking; Prostitution
White v. Illinois (1992), 63
Wilkins, Maurice, 102
Williams, Roger, 228
Williams, State v. (2000), 265
Williams v. McNair (1971), 376
Williams v. Morgan (2004), **373–74**
Williams v. North Carolina (1942, 1945), 100, 357, **374–75**
Williams v. Pryor (1999), 373
Wilmut, Ian, 337
Wilson, E. O., 147
Wilson, Edmund, 212
Wilson, Heather A., 207
Winter v. New York (1948), 287
Wisconsin
  AIDS-HIV in, 16
  child support in, 285–86
  civil confinement in, 300
  community property in, 333
  equal rights in, 122
  genetic privacy in, 147
  pregnant prisoners in, 261
  prostitution in, 267, 268
  rape in, 77
  same-sex marriage in, 292

  sexual harassment in, 316
  sexual orientation harassment in, 317
Wisconsin v. Mitchell (1993), 159
Without a Trace, 204
Wollstonecraft, Mary, 92, 133, 327
The Woman Rebel (Sanger), 73, 293
Women Prisoners of District of Columbia Department of Corrections v. District of Columbia (1995), 261
Women's Armed Services Act (1948), 208
Women's Christian Temperance Union, 283
Women's rights, 375–79
  American Civil Liberties Union and, 21
  Anthony, Susan B., and, 25–26
  Bradwell, Myra, and, 45–47, 91, 145, 221, 246, 254, 333
  married women, 47, 331–34, 376
  in the military, 141–42, 207–9
  NOW and, 225–26
  property rights, 26, 331
  voting, 25–26, 92, 119, 184, 185, 214–15
  See also Abortion; Contraception; Equal rights; Nineteenth Amendment; Property rights; Reproductive rights; Sex discrimination; Spousal rights and duties
Women's Rights Convention, Seneca Falls, N.Y. (1848), 26, 133, 379
Work and Family Bill of Rights (2006), 221
World Health Organization, 266
World's Columbian Exposition, 73

Wright v. County of Du Page (2000), 322–23
Wrongful birth, 220
Wrongful death, 361
Wrongful life, 220
Wrongful pregnancy, 220
Wyoming
  pregnant prisoners in, 261
  prostitution in, 267
  women's voting rights in, 27

X
Xerox Corporation, 315

Y
Yarish v. Nelson (1972), 260
Yazell, United States v. (1966), 376
Young, Brigham, 246, 247
Young Men's Christian Association, 72
Young v. American Mini Theatres, Inc. (1976), 59–60, 116, 322, 323, 380–81
Youth, Pornography, and the Internet (National Academy of Sciences), 176

Z
Zablocki v. Redhail (1978), 199, 289
Zimmer, Dick, 205
Zoning, 380–81
  of adult bookstores, 239, 381
  of adult businesses, 10–11, 380–81
  of adult theaters, 381
  discrimination against unmarried cohabitants, 358
Zoophilia, 34
  See also Bestiality
Zule v. State, 17
Zygote intrafallopian transfer, 32